D0301690

THE RELIGIOUS THOUGHT OF CHU HSI

THE RELIGIOUS THOUGHT OF CHU HSI

JULIA CHING

OXFORD
UNIVERSITY PRESS

2000

UNIVERSITY PRESS

Oxford   New York
Athens   Auckland   Bangkok   Bogotá   Buenos Aires   Calcutta
Cape Town   Chennai   Dar es Salaam   Delhi   Florence   Hong Kong   Istanbul
Karachi   Kuala Lumpur   Madrid   Melbourne   Mexico City   Mumbai
Nairobi   Paris   São Paulo   Singapore   Taipei   Tokyo   Toronto   Warsaw

and associated companies in
Berlin   Ibadan

Published by Oxford University Press, Inc.
198 Madison Avenue, New York, New York 10016

Oxford is a registered trademark of Oxford University Press.

Library of Congress Cataloging-in-Publication Data
Ching, Julia.
The religious thought of Chu Hsi / Julia Ching.
    p.   cm.
Includes bibliographical references and index.
ISBN 0-19-509189-2
1. Chu, Hsi, 1130–1200—Views on religion.   I. Title.
B128.C54C465   2000
181'.112—dc21   99-19667

9 8 7 6 5 4 3 2 1

Printed in the United States of America
on acid-free paper

For my brothers, Tony and Frank

Preface

The scholar Ch'ien Mu, an authority on Chu Hsi and now deceased, told me around 1970 that he liked the philosophy of Wang Yang-ming better in his youth and that of Chu Hsi better as he grew old. I think he said so to many people, as I heard it repeated in Japan by Okada Takehiko. At that time, when I first met Ch'ien and afterward Okada, I was in my midthirties and finishing my study of Wang Yang-ming. I wantd very much to discover a short-cut to learning and wisdom. I am now past sixty and beginning to appreciate Ch'ien's remark. Although Yang-ming remains my hero, I have gained a lot of respect for Chu Hsi.

In fact, I have been interested in Chu Hsi for over two decades, having first presented a paper on him (later published) at Columbia University's University Seminar on Oriental Thought and Religion (1973). I realized even before then that I would not really understand Wang without also tackling Chu. I also discovered that, despite all their differences, they shared a similar spiritual vision, as well as a love of wisdom. Chu has left behind mountains of publications, quite appropriate for a man of such huge intellectual curiosity and boundless energy, but a legacy of thought not easy for a beginner to understand quickly. I have therefore taken some time to study him. I have chosen mainly to focus on his religious thinking, concentrating on the issues that Chu himself dealt with, including the Great Ultimate, the spirits, religious rituals, and his philosophy of human nature and personal cultivation. I cannot, of course, ignore his disputes with Lu Chiu-yüan nor his involvement with, as well as departures from, Buddhist and Taoist ideas. In order, however, to focus my attention better on the central questions, I have refrained from discussing in detail his life, his scholarship, and his political ideas, except when the point at issue demands some reference.

In discussing Chu's religious thought, I have to deal with philosophical, as well as religious and historical, data. I follow mainly the method of textual exegesis, within a broad historical-cultural framework. And I have sought not just to repeat or translate what the texts say but to offer a religio-philosophical interpretation in order to shed light on them. I have read widely Chu's own writings and *Classified Conversations*, focusing on what contains religious interest. I have also learned much from the writings of some of his predecessors and contemporaries and from many secondary materials published in Chinese and Japanese, as well as in English, French, and German. However, Chu himself wrote so much, and the field of Chu Hsi studies is so wide, that I cannot say I have read every line he wrote or every word on the subject.

I have avoided the excessive use of such terms as "monist" or "dualist" to describe Chu's philosophy. While the $li^a/ch'i^a$ metaphysical structure suggests a kind of dualism, his emphasis on the Great Ultimate as Li^a, and on Li^a being one with many manifestations, places him beyond strict dualism. I think that the best word to describe his system of thought is *architectonic*, since it contains many parts that are held together by certain main concepts. And I have desisted from portraying Chu as a theist or atheist. These terms have less importance in Chinese thought, although the quest for an ultimate or absolute remains the strong motivation for his religio-philosophical pursuit.

I have tried to approach my subject with sympathetic understanding, as recommended by the German thinker Schleiermacher's hermeneutics. He saw his role as making intelligible what others have said in speech and text and thus bringing truth to light. I am speaking here not only of entering into Chu Hsi's cultural context but also of seeking to grasp his meaning by reliving the development of his own religio-philosophical consciousness, to the extent that this is possible. I should mention that an idea of another German philosopher, Heidegger—the idea of truth as unveiling (Greek, *aletheia*)—is also helpful.

Chu himself speaks of intellectual discovery as uncovering a secret treasure, as in the case of understanding the *Doctrine of the Mean*. Its central teaching is not any prosaic middle point between two extremes but rather the discovery of one's own spiritual *middle*, the profound center of one's existence. It is this concept of the "middle" that Chu describes as the intellectual legacy passed down from the ancient sages, in a transmission that has been labeled (unfortunately) "orthodox" but that has certain characteristics of a *secret* being passed on, the secret about the discovery of ultimate reality, the Tao. Possibly, the very subtle and religio-spiritual nature of the subject matter renders it difficult to comprehend, not only for us, but even for Chu himself. After all, the quest includes a mystical dimension. The word "mysticism" has a Greek origin in *muein*, signifying closed eyes or lips, that is, silence, as associated with initiation rites, and therefore suggests a certain degree of mystery and secrecy. The Greek word *mustikos* was taken over by Christians to refer to the spiritual meaning of the Scriptures. In this respect, the term is quite applicable to the study of classical texts, as carried out by neo-Confucian scholars like Chu Hsi. Today, the word "mysticism" can refer to the quest for, and the experience associated with, spiritual meaning in the whole of life and the universe.

I should mention that I have used the word "Tao" to indicate what is considered the ultimate goal of understanding and striving in all the schools: Confucianism, Taoism, and Buddhism. Its specific meaning has to be decided by the context, which will disclose the affinities. For the Confucians, the Tao always retains a moral character. For the Taoists, concern about this ontological Tao has led them to cosmological horizons. For the Ch'an Buddhists, it is always interior and experiential.

There are many books on Chu Hsi. Several are written by the late Wing-tsit Chan, from whom I have learned much. I am not just repeating old information or interpretation in this book. Rather, I have labored to present, among other things, an account of the *Diagram of the Great Ultimate* that is based on a variety of sources, including the less known. I therefore have to interpret it in greater detail, and in a manner in which it has not yet been done in English. I have sought as well to be balanced and complete in discussing Chu's views on spirits and ghosts and in presenting an interpretation of the evolution of his thinking on the theory of equilibrium (*chung*[a]) and harmony (*ho*) of the *Doctrine of the Mean*. In my concluding chapters, I have offered critical voices, some authentic, others only ideological or even political, and I point out some problems of limitations on Chu Hsi's part, as well as of understanding on my own part. The final chapter deals with questions concerning his continuing relevance in our globalized society and to those urgent issues that press on us day by day. I have also included an outline of Chu's life and works (appendix A) and a more detailed examination of certain controversies surrounding the *Diagram of the Great Ultimate* (appendix B).

As I wrote this book, I could not help recalling the support and instruction I received from teachers, friends, colleagues, and students during all these years in a career that has spanned countries and continents. In Australia in 1971, Liu Ts'un-yan first introduced me to the riches of Taoist religion and afterward continued to help me understand Chu's involvement with Taoism. Kristofer Schipper, during our exchanges in Paris in 1992, encouraged me to continue to pursue these interests; at the same time, the École Pratique des Hautes Études was the place where my seminars on Chu Hsi on Buddhism and Taoism provoked instructive discussions that proved so helpful in the writing of these chapters, and I wish to thank Léon Vandermeersch for his kind invitation. The International Conference on Chu Hsi organised by Wing-tsit Chan in 1982, as well as other conferences on or related to Chu Hsi in North America, often under the leadership of William Theodore de Bary, and in Taiwan and mainland China, also offered stimulating exchanges on many topics regarding Chu, including some that I eventually incorporated into this book. Even earlier, a conference on Whitehead and Chinese philosophy around 1977, organized by John Cobb and leading to articles published in the *Journal of Chinese Philosophy* in 1979, offered an occasion for me to ponder Chu Hsi and Whitehead on the subject of God, a reflection that I include here, with some modifications, as appendix C.

I am especially grateful to the Chiang Ching-kuo Foundation and the Social Science and Humanities Council of Canada for providing me with research grants that enabled me to finish this project. I am fortunate also that a circle exists— indeed, not only in North America but also in Hong Kong, Taiwan, Japan, and China—whose common interest in Chu Hsi has proved a great stimulus. I was privileged to have met in Hong Kong early in my career the philosophers Tang Chün-I and Mou Tsung-san, and I later had the honor of meeting Fung Yu-lan (Feng Youlan) in China, and again in the United States, in the company of his daughter, Feng Zhongpu. These meetings and the exchanges made me feel that Chu's thought is still alive and meaningful. And I have tried to incorporate, to the extent possible, their views, both positive and negative, on various aspects of Chu Hsi's religious thought.

Many individuals have assisted me, either with inspiration and criticism or with finding bibliographical sources. I wish very much to thank David Dilworth for reading the draft manuscript during term time and for his stimulating and challenging questions, comments, and criticisms. Thanks are also due to colleagues all over the world: to Whalen Lai for his enlightening comments on the Great Ultimate and Buddhism; to Hoyt Tillman for his enriching historical horizons; to Richard Lynn and Frank Myers for software support; to Dan Overmyer for bibliographical pointers; to Yü Ying-shih for good scholarly advice; to Joshua Fogel at an earlier time for bibliographical materials in Chinese; to Robert Gimello, Joseph Adler, Alan Chang, and colleagues at the National University of Singapore for helpful comments and criticisms; to Seiko Goto for help with procuring bibliographical materials in Japanese. I wish also to thank several younger, talented persons for timely help: Kwok-yiu Wong for technical and bibliographical assistance; Ian Bell for careful reading of the manuscript; Joyce Tan and others for library research. I owe a constant debt to my spouse, Will Oxtoby, for always supporting my efforts with his careful scrutiny. I also thank the staff at Oxford University Press. As a full list would be too long, I thank everyone else, one and all.

It remains for me to explain that I decided to use Wade-Giles for transliteration, because I prefer the name of my philosopher spelled Chu Hsi rather than Zhu Xi. After all, Z. X. are not my preferred initials for him. I am also unhappy with the rendering of the long *e* sound with *i* in the Wade-Giles transliteration system and so try to use *yi* instead whenever that sound occurs. I provide the pinyin equivalent for all important historical names and use it as well for names of contemporary scholars and figures in mainland China. For twentieth-century Chinese figures outside the mainland, I have transliterated their names in the manner they themselves did. In transliterating technical terms, I am using superscripts to distinguish between homophones. Unless otherwise indicated, the translations into English are done by myself.

I am offering an explanation of key terms as appendix D, where I include especially those technical philosophical terms that come in pairs, as coordinates or opposites. Except for the Five Classics, I use italics for the titles of classical and philosophical texts. In the bibliography, I use Wade-Giles as well for the transliteration of all titles of books and articles from Chinese. I also offer a glossary of Sino-Japanese names and terms, which should further clarify transliterations.

Over the long period of studying Chu Hsi, my thoughts have evolved and developed. I take responsibility for any and all inadequacies or limitations, and look forward to learning further from my readers.

Toronto, Ontario   J. C.
March 2000

Contents

THE RELIGIOUS THOUGHT OF CHU HSI

The World of Thought in Chu Hsi's Time

Against the wind, [my door] can still shut itself;
On days with nothing happening, it's usually closed.
Closing and opening follow what's natural:[1]
Present here are *Ch'ien* [Heaven] and *K'un*[a] [Earth].

Chou Tun-yi[2]

Introduction

In opening a book, we place ourselves at a gateway. In Chinese, an introduction to any subject is usually called "entering the gate," or "entering the door" (*ju-men*). The gate leads symbolically to wisdom and sageliness. The two parent trigrams, *Ch'ien* ☰ and *K'un*[a] ☷, with their undivided *yang* and divided *yin* lines, usually represent the mysteries that are beyond the door. For Chou Tun-yi (Zhou Dunyi, 1017–73), the mysteries are with him in his own room, with the opening and closing of the door. Chou Tun-yi sees the door as sometimes closed and sometimes open. Favoring the natural, he does not insist that wisdom is to be found with the opening of the door but claims that it is there *in the* opening and closing. Here, of course, one may add that "opening and closing" can also serve as a metaphor for breathing and, by extension, to being at one with the universe.

The teachings of Chou Tun-yi, especially on the Great Ultimate, have much to do with Chu Hsi, also styled Hui-an (Zhu Xi, 1130–1200), who was born about sixty years after Chou's death. An open book permits us to enter into a subject matter. In our case, the subject of interest is Chu Hsi's religious thought or, if we wish, his religious "wisdom." We shall have to find this in the legacy of his writings: a very rich legacy indeed. As with Chou's description, we shall encounter a door that is sometimes open and sometimes closed or, perhaps, more often half-closed. This is due to the ambiguity of certain words and texts and the distance of time that separates us from them. But, to the best of my ability, I shall seek to open this door, in order to open the library containing Chu's thought. At times, however, the door will open only halfway, and I shall have to read between the lines and interpret according to the context.

To feel at home in Chu Hsi's thought, we first need to explore the world of thought in which Chu Hsi found himself and developed his own thinking.[3] Chou Tun-yi and other intellectuals of the eleventh century lived in the period called the Northern Sung (960–1127), when the dynasty had its capital in Kai-feng, and the country was united. Chu lived in twelfth-century China during the Southern Sung period (1127–1279), with its capital at Ling-an (present-day Hangchou) and with the north in enemy Jürchen hands. It was a time of political division, economic growth, and intellectual evolution, a period when China was continually besieged by aliens originally from beyond the Great Wall. The country turned inward, an isolationist move accompanied by philosophical and religious speculations that reinforced the prevalent moods, turning away from so-called escapist Buddhist influences and returning to selected Confucian sources for spiritual inspiration.[4] Eventually, a philosophical architectonic developed with its own religiosity, one that became identified with the name of Chu Hsi.

Chu Hsi stemmed from a family originally hailing from modern Anhui, in a prefecture called Hui-chou. But he was born farther south in Yu-hsi, Fukien, where his father, Chu Sung (Zhu Song, 1097–1143), was serving as a district sheriff. A scholar with strong philosophical interests, Chu Sung died prematurely, entrusting his thirteen-year-old son's education to friends. But this was no ordinary teenager. A precocious youth, Chu Hsi received his *chin-shih* degree at age eighteen. Yet his destiny was not to include climbing high on the official ladder of success. He served for some time as a magistrate in Fukien, spending most of his life in that region, usually in semiretirement. His philosophical and scholarly output was huge, as commentary after commentary appeared on several of the classics, the Four Books (*Great Learning, Doctrine of the Mean, Analects, Book of Mencius*), and a host of other works. He attracted many disciples and corresponded widely with other thinkers and scholars of the time. His school, called Min-hsüeh after Fukien,[5] became the dominant school of thought after his death.

Chu reacted with patriotic concern to the country's division while the north was ruled by the alien Jürchens. By building on the foundations laid down by his philosophical predecessors, often reediting and publishing their writings, he contributed to the intellectual life of his times and later. He gave his own responses to the challenges posed by Buddhism and Taoism. He also built a system characterized by a concern for cosmology and metaphysics and a focus on questions of human nature and the emotions, as well as on personal cultivation.

In the past, it was often assumed that Chu Hsi was a rationalist philosopher, with little to offer in the line of religious thinking. This tended to be the interpretation of certain Jesuit missionaries, who resented the development of the philosophy of *hsing*[a] and *li*[a], of nature and principle, that displaced what was to them a more agreeable universe of earlier religious beliefs in the Lord-on-High and Heaven. About seventy-five years ago, the Jesuit sinologist Stanislas Le Gall called Chu a materialist: "beau diseur autant que philosophe détestable, cet homme est parvenu à imposer, depuis plus de sept siècles, à la masse de ses compatriotes, une explication toute matérialiste des anciens livres."[6]

About four decades ago, a group of influential Chinese thinkers taking refuge in Hong Kong and Taiwan from Communism issued a "Manifesto for the

Reappraisal of Sinology and Reconstruction of Chinese Culture" (1958). Under Carsun Chang's (Chang Chün-mai, 1886–1969) leadership, Hsü Fu-kuan (1903–80), Mou Tsung-san (1909–95) and Tang Chün-i (1907–78) represented the harmony between the Way of Heaven (*T'ien-tao*) and the way of humans (*jen-tao*) as the central Confucian legacy, criticized the earlier Jesuits for their misunderstanding of such, and challenged Western sinologists to pay closer attention to this core spirituality.[7] Several signatories of this document developed their own philosophical systems by reinterpreting this legacy in the light of certain Western philosophies, and these became, posthumously, the content of contemporary Chinese philosophy.

More recently, two lines of thought have curiously converged. I refer on the one hand to the increasingly more focused study in the West of philosophers who are often called neo-Confucian, including Chu Hsi, revealing structures of thought that included undeniably spiritual and even religious dimensions.[8] I refer on the other hand to the earlier, ideologically critical studies of Chu Hsi and others by mainland Chinese scholars inspired by Marxism-Leninism and by the thought of Mao Zedong, who pointed out the religiosity present in these thinkers in order to *discredit* their thought.[9] Up to now, we have had no systematic presentation of Chu's religious thought, and so I have made it my task to offer one.

To better understand Chu Hsi's religious thought, I offer in this introduction a rather lengthy exposition on the background thinking on cosmology both earlier than, and as presented in the *Diagram of the Great Ultimate* (*T'ai-chi t'u*) of Chou Tun-yi. This includes speculations derived from the appendices to the Book of Changes and from the *yin-yang* and Five Phases theories, as well as Buddhist and Taoist ideas and practices. In fact, an understanding of Buddhism and Taoism as intellectual and spiritual legacies inherited and transformed by Chu Hsi is helpful for our understanding of both Chou's and Chu's religious, as well as philosophical, *Sitz im Leben.*

I shall then examine the various meanings of the terms *li*[a] and *ch'i*[a], the twin concepts that figure so much in Chu's metaphysical system. He owes these to Ch'eng Yi (Cheng Yi, 1033–1108), a serious man and a systematic thinker, who outlived his more gentle and outgoing elder brother, Ch'eng Hao (Cheng Hao, 1032–85) and made an important impact on the philosophical landscape. However, I shall not and cannot delve deeper here into many questions and issues that have direct reference to Chu Hsi. Instead, I seek in the Preface and this chapter only to map out a little of what the rest of the book will do. It will be seen that Chu Hsi's religious thought has Chinese roots going back to the texts we call the Confucian Four Books, as well as to the appendices to the Book of Changes, with certain influences from Buddhism and Taoism.[10]

The Cosmological Concerns

When is a theory cosmological, and when is it cosmogonic? Going back to Greek etymology, "cosmology" comes from combining *kosmos* (world) and *logos* (word). It usually refers to metaphysical theories about the origins of the universe. "Cosmogony," on the other hand, comes from *kosmos* and *genesis*, with the latter word referring to the origin of the universe. It has come to represent myth and symbol more than philosophy, especially creation myths. In the Chinese case, these two dimensions are usually present together. I shall refer to cosmology whenever the discussion is carried on in philosophical terms, with the help of symbols and diagrams. And I shall refer to cosmogony whenever the description comes with images and diagrams representing cosmic origins in mythical terms and without a philosophical explanation.

The very basic microcosm/macrocosm thinking is present on every level of mythmaking and philosophizing. Like the ancient Greeks, the Chinese regarded the human being as a mirror image of the universe, each constructed according to the same proportions and sympathetically attuned to the other with a kind of cosmic resonance. The human being is singled out as the "mind and heart" of the universe, giving it greater consciousness and direction, but never as apart from or opposed to it. Rather, the two depend on each other, as a child does on the parent. The union between the two is conceived as a conscious and animate continuum, as a sharing of life and experience that makes for order and harmony. This is due, not to chance, but to some kind of rational design, which is open to more direct or mystical communion. It is therefore from this vantage point of the "oneness of the heavenly and the human" (*t'ien-jen ho-yi*) that we shall continue our exploration of the many influences on Chu Hsi's religious thought.

The Book of Changes and Cosmological Speculations

Traditional Chinese philosophy developed very much as an exegetical process, with a steady stream of commentaries written on classical texts. It combines an appeal to the authority of the classics and their allegedly sagely authors, as well as an exposition of one's own thinking, presented somewhat as a European medieval philosopher commented on the sacred Scriptures while giving allegorical interpretations, or as a contemporary constitutional lawyer might bend the text to get certain desired answers, more relevant to our own times and his or her specific needs.

The Chinese title for the Book of Changes is *I-ching*, or *Yi-ching*. The word *ching*[b] refers to the warp of a fabric and, by extension, to a classic, while the word *i*, or *yi*[a], has a range of meanings, including "ease" and "change" or "flux." "Flux" here refers to cosmic changes in the natural universe as well as psychic changes in the mind, according to the macrocosm/microcosm correspondence that is basic to Chinese thinking. The Book of Changes is more than a divination text. It contains long sections of philosophical discussion, especially in its accretions called the Ten Wings, or appendices, attributed to Confucius. These accretions attracted the attention of Sung dynasty philosophers and led to the classic's being considered, among other things, a cosmological treatise.

With its hexagrams, judgments, images, and commentaries, the Book of Changes remains one of the most highly symbolic works of the world's wisdom literature. It has suffered much from the undeserved opprobrium of simpleminded rationalists and still awaits adequate deciphering and meaningful interpretation. The efforts of Carl Jung and Richard Wilhelm have pointed out a good direction by bringing to the fore the book's importance as a mirror of the human psyche and its perception of the world of its own consciousness.[11] This was always the scholarly Chinese understanding of the text, as we find in Chu and his predecessors and in many commentaries on the classic. But much remains to be done in order that its full richness might be made available to all, since the classic also deals with changes in the external universe.

Today, it is accepted that this classic owes its original inspiration to mathematical intuitions, with the divided *yin* and *yang* lines of the hexagrams referring to the foundations of binary arithmetic, given that numerals used to serve also as symbols for philosophical and religious speculations, often in an esoteric context. For centuries, the Book of Changes has been *the* book of wisdom par excellence. Chu is known to have written at least two works on this classic: *Inquiry into the Original Meaning of the Book of Changes* (Yi-hsüeh pen-yi) and *Introduction to the Book of Changes* (Yi-hsüeh ch'i-meng). He was particularly preoccupied with the concept of the Great Ultimate itself, as the embodiment of all truth and wisdom.[12]

The Yin-yang *and Five Phases Theories*

The origins of the *yin-yang* and Five Phases theories remain relatively unknown. How did such complex and seemingly arbitrary systems of interpretation of the universe and of human life arise? Were such terms as *yin* and *yang*, "water," "fire," "wood," "metal," and "earth" themselves symbols, and of what realities? How would knowing their symbolic significance affect our understanding of the *Diagram of the Great Ultimate?*

The theories arose in antiquity—*before* Confucius, who lived in the sixth century B.C.E.—at a time when religion was more important than philosophy, and the correlation between the natural and the human was always assumed. Generally speaking, it was understood that out of one primordial *ch'i*[a] have come the two complementary cosmic "energies" or principles—*yin* and *yang*—whose alternation and interaction have led to the evolution of all things. This is confirmed in the Great Commentary to the Book of Changes: "the alternation of *yin* and *yang* makes up the Tao."[13] Together, the *yin-yang* and Five Phases theories are important heuristic categories that give conceptual order to the traditional Chinese worldview. Joseph Needham speaks for many when he describes *yin* and *yang* as "an ancient hypostatisation of the two sexes . . . which appeared [in science] as negative and positive electricity, which in our own age have proved to constitute, in such forms as protons and electrons, the components of all material particles."[14]

The fundamental presupposition in *yin-yang* philosophy is that the human universe not only is a mirror of the natural universe but also is affected by events occurring in the natural universe, which it in turn affects. It is a logical development of the concept of the "sympathy of the whole"—a belief that Ernst Cassirer regards as fundamental to all magic ritual. This presupposition explains the age-old Chinese interest in astronomy (as well as astrology). Offi-

cials were appointed to scrutinize the heavens for the discovery of signs and por-
tents having a bearing on social life and order.

It is no accident that the words *yin* and *yang* should refer literally to shade
and sunlight and, by extension, to the moon and the sun. It is also no accident
that the names of the Five Phases are also those of the five "planets" best known
to early Chinese astronomers. Indeed, if we delve into the study of early Chinese
lunar and solar myths, we can infer that the *yin-yang* philosophy had its roots
in a religious tradition dominated by lunar myths and, in the course of time, also
incorporated into itself certain solar myths, as well as sacred symbols like Heaven
and Earth.[15] Later, elaborate theories of correspondence based on the interaction of *yin* and *yang* and the Five Phases would appear as a kind of allegorical
interpretation of early religions.

Wu-hsing (with *hsing*[b] signifying movement) is sometimes translated as Five
Elements, Five Agents, Five Forces, or Five Phases. They are all these, possibly
starting as material "elements" and moving on to serve as "agents" and then as
"phases" or paradigms of change for specific modes of being. They refer to
Water, Fire, Wood, Metal, and Earth, as enumerated in the chapter on the Great
Plan in the Book of History.[16] The list differs from the Greek and Indian four elements of earth, air, fire, and water. The Chinese list does not include air, or *ch'i*[a],
which is considered all-pervading and therefore too important to be in this group.
But it does include wood with otherwise inorganic elements, perhaps to represent better an animate and organic universe. The Five are perceived to function
in a correlative system that is based on the correspondence between the human
being and nature, microcosm and macrocosm. They denote relationships among
phenomena, including the ancient relational mode of "mutual conquest," according to which water conquers fire, fire conquers wood, wood conquers metal,
metal conquers earth, and earth, in turn, conquers water in an eternal cycle.
Other modes followed, an opposing one of "mutual generation," with wood engendering fire, fire leading to earth, earth producing metal, metal dissolving into
liquid or water, and water, in turn, nourishing wood.[17]

The Five are also correlated with other systems, such as the five planets in
the universe, the five viscera in the human organism, the five colors, and even
with classifications of what are not just five entities, such as the four directions
(plus the center), the four seasons, the Eight Trigrams, and so on, sometimes
rather mechanically and artificially.[18] When the Five are correlated with groups
of four, earth, which occupies the middle, is often left alone.

Lü's Spring and Autumn Annals (*Lü-shih ch'un-ch'iu*), allegedly third century
B.C.E., echoes the correlations:

> Heaven, Earth, and the myriad things are like the body of one human
> being, and this is called the Great Unity (*Ta-t'ung*). The multitude of ears,
> eyes, noses, and mouths and the multitudes of the five grains and cold and
> heat: these are called the multiplicity of differences that leads to a myriad
> things. Heaven makes all things flourish; the sage contemplates them, in
> order to observe his own kind, and explain how Heaven and earth were
> shaped, how thunder and lightning are produced, how *yin* and *yang* cause
> things to be, how people and animals are made peaceful and secure.[19]

The situation became more complex with the merger of the separate theories of *yin-yang* and Five Phases. The Book of Changes is based on *yin-yang* thought. The hexagrams of this book are often made to correspond with various systems, including astronomical and calendrical units, sometimes quite uncomfortably. With the emergence of the Han thinker Tung Chung-shu (Dong Zhongshu, c. 179–104 B.C.E.), *yin-yang* and Five Phases thinking became integrated into mainstream philosophical orthodoxy, and that means Confucianism. Tung has left behind the following piece outlining a preestablished harmony of the human being as a microcosm of Heaven and Earth:

> Heaven is characterized by the power to engender and extend things; Earth is characterized by the power to transform, and human beings are characterized by moral principles. . . . The human being has 360 joints, which match the number of Heaven [i.e., of days in the year]. With bones and flesh, the human body matches the Earth's thickness. The eyes and ears, with their sense of vision and hearing, resemble the sun and moon. The orifices and veins resemble rivers and valleys. The heart's feelings of sorrow, joy, pleasure, and anger are like Heaven's spiritual feelings. . . . The human being alone stands erect, looks straight forward, and assumes a correct posture. S/he is distinct from other creatures and forms a trinity with Heaven and Earth.[20]

Chu Hsi and his intellectual predecessors were accustomed to this way of thinking and revived the study of the Book of Changes for their understanding of themselves as human beings, the universe around them, and whatever higher power there may be. Indeed, they also made ready use of correlations to explain their own ideas of human nature and morality, including very fine points regarding the emotions and how these are made manifest.

The Spiritual and Ethical Concerns:
Focus on the Four Books

The governments of T'ang (618–907) and of early Sung China each attempted to restore the Confucian orthodoxy after periods of intellectual dominance by Taoism and Buddhism. A new edition of the Five Classics was published, together with the best available commentaries. But these could not attract the best minds, drawn to philosophical and religious issues by Taoism and Buddhism.[21] It took a long line of scholars and thinkers to fashion a new, smaller, classic corpus without discarding the Five Classics and their appendages. The thinker and stylist Han Yü (768–824) preached a return to the original sources of inspiration, especially to the *Book of Mencius*, a record of conversations of the fourth-century-B.C.E. sage. His friend Li Ao (fl. 798) brought into prominence the two treatises the *Great Learning* and the *Doctrine of the Mean* for their treatment of issues concerning human nature and emotions.[22] And of course, no one can forget the record of the master's own conversations, the *Analects* of Confucius.

Chu Hsi is known especially for having elevated the Four Books to near-canonical status. He wrote and edited commentaries to them that were eventually incorporated into the civil service examination curriculum. This is well known. What is less known is the role of the Five Classics in his thinking. Besides the Book of Changes, which received the most attention during the Sung dynasty, the Five Classics include the Book of History, the Book of Poetry, the Spring and Autumn Annals, and the ritual texts.[23]

Chu Hsi published the *Collected Commentaries on the Four Books* (*Ssu-shu chi-chu*), which included some of his and Ch'eng Yi's comments, as a single book. It acquired near-canonical status when it was made the core of the civil service examination syllabus in 1313.[24]

Chu Hsi himself wrote many commentaries, long and short, on the Four Books. These included the *Essential Meaning of "Analects" and "Mencius"* (*Yü-Meng yao-yi*) (1172); the annotated editions of the *Analects* and the *Book of Mencius* (*Lun-Meng chi-chu*) and *Questions and Answers on the "Analects" and "Mencius"* (*Huo-wen*) (1177); the annotated editions of the *Great Learning* (*Ta-hsüeh chang-chü*) and of the *Doctrine of the Mean* (*Chung-yung chang-chü*), together with his prefaces (1189). These Collected Commentaries on the Four Books, including the last two mentioned texts and the *Lun-Meng chi-chu*, were published in one volume in 1190.[25]

The Four Books, especially certain chapters and sections from the *Book of Mencius*, call attention to discussions on human nature: whether it is basically good and, if so, the whole question of human perfectibility, as well as how to cultivate such goodness. This focus is complemented in the *Great Learning* and the *Doctrine of the Mean*. Chu Hsi emphasizes the former's intellectual, moral, and political agenda for the pursuit of sagehood and the latter's teachings on a state of consciousness of emotional equilibrium and harmony that has mystical dimensions. Chu refers to the *Analects* and *Mencius* for guiding ideas, looks for support from the *Great Learning* for his emphasis on intellectual pursuit in the quest for sagehood, and relies on the more difficult and interior treatise, *Doctrine of the Mean*, for his central doctrine of emotional equilibrium and harmony. Together with the appendices to the Book of Changes, these Four Books serve as his principal, scriptural texts.

The Religious Concerns: Taoism and Buddhism

The Sung period witnessed a gradual revival of the Buddhist religion as a whole. The two big branches that prospered during that time were Ch'an and Pure Land. Both were more pragmatically oriented, products of an eclecticism between the Buddhist religion and native Chinese culture, and attracted larger followings. Of these two, Pure Land Buddhism drew its believers from among the general population, while Ch'an Buddhism, which had absorbed earlier philosophies coming from Yogācāra, T'ien-t'ai, and Hua-yen Buddhism, as well as from Taoist philosophy, was the favorite of scholars and intellectuals.

The eleventh-century philosophers Chang Tsai (Zhang Zai, 1020–77), Ch'eng Hao, and his brother Ch'eng Yi, and the later Chu Hsi, all regarded Buddhism as heterodox teachings. All of them were at one time students of Buddhism, especially of Ch'an, and were influenced by the religion. In their philosophical writings, they tend to speak of Buddhism and Taoism together. This is true of Chu Hsi's writings also. Like many of the others, he was interested in both Buddhism and Taoism in his youth, before turning seriously to the philosophy of principle (li[a]) and nature (hsing[a]). Buddhism—and Taoism—could give people what the Confucian teachings could not: an answer to the great questions about life and the universe and, in particular, the meaning of life itself.

Mahāyāna Buddhism holds as fundamental truth the dialectical presence of nirvāna in samsāra, the basis for its philosophy of nonduality. Since Buddhism rejects a substantial self, the idea emerges of a nonabiding nirvāna. This is what Hui-neng supposedly heard from the Diamond Sutra, occasioning his enlightenment: that one should produce an independent, or nonabiding, mind.[26] It points to the fleeting presence of an absolute, what is called mind or Buddha-nature.

Where Ch'an Buddhists refer to Buddha-nature or the metaphorical "original countenance" before one's birth, Taoist philosophical texts offer dialectical discussions of being (yu) and nothingness (wu[a]). While these maintain that the Tao itself is unnamable, and so more wu than yu, they argue for a primal ch'i[a], a substrative reality from which all things came. Although this ch'i[a] is not a purely materialist category, it is not accepted by Buddhists, who are committed idealists. However, as with the Confucians, both Taoists and Chinese Buddhists refer to the trigrams and hexagrams in the Book of Changes to find support for their respective teachings.

The Buddhist-Taoist heritage left behind a rich vocabulary, part of which was taken over by Chu Hsi and his predecessors and successors. I refer to the use of terms like "Tao," appropriated as the Confucian Way, which, together with t'i or pen-t'i (original substance, pure being), T'ai-chi (the Great Ultimate), and wu[a] (nothingness), all refer as well to ultimate reality. In some contexts, this can also be said of li[a], a term we shall discuss in more detail. The terms t'i and yung come from the neo-Taoist philosopher Wang Pi (Wang Bi, 226–49) in his commentary on Lao-tzu, chapter 4: "The Tao is empty, yet use (yung) will not drain it."[27] In Wang's commentary, the term t'i (literally, the "body"; by extension, "substance") is introduced to refer to the Tao-in-itself, in opposition to yung (literally, "use" or "function"). In this context, what is expressed is a double paradox, that of inexhaustible "use" and that of the Tao being empty yet full, since otherwise there is no sense to inexhaustibility.[28] Sometimes translated as "substance" and "function," t'i and yung are a pair of coordinate concepts referring to reality and its manifestation, or the latent and the manifest. These also acquired later Buddhist overtones with reference to the Two Truths theory, as in the work of the monk Seng Chao (d. 414), who speaks of truth and delusion (or what we might call the higher and lower truths or ultimate and mundane truths) as t'i and yung and as somehow identical.[29] These coordinate terms were frequently invoked by

Chu Hsi and his school. Underlying such usage is a metaphysics that distinguishes between the inner and the outer. The inner is assumed to be good and perfect. Being hidden and latent, it cannot always make itself manifest. This depends on the outer. Frequently, the inner, or latent, is called *t'i*, and the outer, or manifest, is called *yung*. Often *t'i* refers to a deeper reality in a still mode, whereas *yung* refers to its active manifestation. Truth is therefore discovered after a process of unveiling. Self-perfection is seen as an effort at interior liberation for the sake of exterior manifestation—of making known what one already possesses: the seeds of perfection.

Buddhism in Sung Times: The Ch'an Heritage

Chinese Ch'an, especially as represented by the popular southern school of Hui-neng (638–713) in the T'ang dynasty, is known for its preference for freedom of expression and respect of the natural, both of which entail some disrespect for the sutras and the traditions of the past. Such attitudes helped to unleash a certain creative genius in discussions of spirituality and mysticism, as well as in art and culture. Ch'an Buddhism calls itself:

> A special tradition outside the scriptures
> Not depending on the written word,
> Pointing directly to the human mind,
> Seeing into one's nature and becoming a Buddha.[30]

Calling itself "a special tradition" provoked so-called mainline Buddhists to oppose the Ch'an movement. The near-exclusive focus on mystical enlightenment (Chinese, *wu*[c]; Japanese, *satori*) also gives Ch'an an aura of mystery, enhanced by stories of secret transmissions of the *dharma* and the like.

Nevertheless, Ch'an Buddhism was able to spark a spiritual renaissance by urging people to make serious efforts to cultivate the mind by meditating, and by seeking to awaken the absolute or Buddha-nature within. In the ninth century, there was also a movement to reconcile the Ch'an of meditational practice and that of textual scholars, led by Tsung-mi (Zongmi, 780–841), a patriarch of both Ch'an and Hua-yen.[31]

An important and pivotal figure for the much later Sung Confucian movement, Tsung-mi offers a comprehensive framework to reconcile the metaphysical differences between many Ch'an sublineages, as well as between these and Confucianism and Buddhism. He believes in the Buddhist teaching of the four great *kalpas* as cyclical cosmic ages and defends this teaching against his critics. He raises questions about the prevalent Confucian-Taoist beliefs in the primordial *ch'i*[a] as the origin of Heaven and Earth and the myriad things. He points out that there is no reason why the *ch'i*[a], without intelligence, could produce intelligent beings. Should it be able to do so, then there is no reason why the same *ch'i*[a] does not give intelligence to grass and plants. Moreover, there is also no reason why rocks do not engender grass; and grass, humans. His preference is for a doctrine of *karma*, although he perceives problems in the inadequate explanations of this doctrine by certain Buddhist lineages.[32]

Basically, Tsung-mi acknowledges Confucianism and Taoism as also possessing a part of the truth. He is even ready to give a role to the primordial ch'i[a] in engendering material substance, provided it is also agreed that there is one true and spiritual mind (chen-yi ling-hsin) that gives rise both to the ch'i[a] itself and to the human mind as such. For him, after all, body and mind together make up the human being.[33]

Tsung-mi also discusses a recurring theme introduced by Buddhism into Chinese religious thought as early as the fifth century: that of sudden (tun) or gradual (chien) enlightenment. The sudden, or subitist, school advocates cultivation followed by a sudden awakening rather than a gradual or step-by-step awakening. This view was allegedly espoused by the seventh-century monk Hui-neng, whom Tsung-mi revered, but the lineage did not thrive for long after Hui-neng. With time, the earlier, speculative genius subsided, lending force to a focus on practical matters of spirituality. During the Sung dynasty, the Lin-chi and the Ts'ao-tung lineages both prospered, and their rival teachings on how enlightenment might be acquired attracted much attention.

At the time of Chu Hsi, Ch'an Buddhism was enjoying a late bloom, before its final decline during the post-Sung period. But the great days of intellectual discussion were over. Instead, what occupied attention was the question of meditation techniques. Differences between Ts'ao-tung and Lin-chi Buddhism, both derived from Ch'an, are sometimes represented by the words mo-chao and k'an-hua-t'ou. Mo-chao, or "silent illumination," underlines the importance of meditation as a spiritual exercise, and the Ts'ao-tung Buddhists were eager to point out that it did not refer to inactivity or passivity. Rather, silence is considered to be the primal stillness of the ultimate ground of the enlightened mind, which is naturally radiant and "shining." According to them, silent meditation and the quiet deeds of ordinary living are preferable to constant dwelling upon kung-an, riddles that they believed to be irrational and pointless. The Ts'ao-tung monk Hung-chih Cheng-chüeh (Hongzhi Chengjue, 1091–1157) compares quiet meditation to the effort of "the bird hatching the egg" and the inner light to "a ray penetrating past and present." He was not entirely opposed to kung-an, since he even composed some himself, but he saw quiet meditation as waiting for enlightenment rather than as a deus ex machina to force enlightenment.[34]

By posing an insoluble problem to reason and the intellect, the kung-an is supposed to lead to the dissolution of the boundary between the conscious and the unconscious in the human psyche and bring about a sudden experience, described metaphorically as the blossoming of a lotus or the emergence of the sun from behind clouds. K'an-hua-t'ou (literally, "contemplating a riddle") refers to the practice of meditating on a kung-an. In this respect, the advice of the Lin-chi master Ta-hui Tsung-kao (Dahui Zonggao, 1089–1163) is to keep the spiritual consciousness alive and alert, whether in sitting, moving, or reposing. He refers to a famous kung-an regarding whether the dog has Buddha-nature. The philosophical premise, of course, is that Buddha-nature is present in all sentient beings. The expected answer is therefore yes. However, when asked this question, the famous monk Chao-chou responded, "No." In Chinese the English word "no" is *wu*[a] (nothing, nothingness), pronounced *mu* in Japanese. But *wu*[a], or nothingness, is also a term that refers to ultimate truth in Buddhism. Chao-chou's reply is therefore richly suggestive.[35]

The Lin-chi criticized the Ts'ao-tung for teaching a passive mind; the Ts'ao-tung responded that if silent passivity is seen as belonging to the mind at its deepest core (*t'i*), active illumination remains its manifestation or function (*yung*).[36]

Ch'an's Yogācāra and Hua-yen philosophical heritage, which will be discussed later, contributed to metaphysical thinking with heuristic and linguistic tools. Ch'an's focus on truth and delusion stimulated interest in cosmic origins and the meaning of transcendence and immanence. Its emphasis was always on going beyond duality, and its names for ultimate truth included Buddha-nature, or the absolute mind. The disputes it sustained on questions like spiritual cultivation and enlightenment offered as well a focus of thought and debate to the Sung thinkers, including Chu Hsi, his predecessors, contemporaries, and successors. Its preference for dialogues rather than texts offered a model of discourse for these same thinkers. Its iconoclastic and anti-intellectual cynicism, however, was repudiated by many thinkers of the like of Chu Hsi, who were conscientious about their own calling as followers of the sages bent on perfecting themselves as well as helping others. Last, the very challenge it posed to the survival of the Confucian tradition called forth a whole movement of return to the original inspirations of Confucian spirituality. Ch'an's weakness actually gave Chu Hsi and others an opportunity to revive and transform Confucian thought. This would define, for the following eight centuries (for better and for worse), what has been regarded as the core meaning of Chinese philosophy.

Taoism in Sung Times:
Inner Alchemy and the World of Diagrams

By Sung times, Taoist philosophy was no longer dominant, although it had influenced Ch'an Buddhism with ideas and language and also with the symbolic thinking of the Book of Changes. Taoist religion, however, enjoyed a revival. The quest for longevity and immortality is a complex subject, demonstrating a passionate love of life and a dynamic desire to transcend finite boundaries. The usual supposition is that the quest is for physical immortality. But this is a simplistic view. The religious Taoist practitioner recognizes various levels and degrees of immortality. Physical immortality itself may refer either to the indefinite prolongation of biological life, to keeping the human organism in good health, or to keeping a dead body from corruption. There is also spiritual immortality; the wise man rises above material considerations and nourishes within himself a New Self, a new "spirit-body," which eventually achieves freedom by emancipation from the old "matter-body." The exercises for achieving such self-transcendence belong either to the quest for the outer elixir or to "inner alchemy," including yoga-like practices of meditation, aimed at mystical enlightenment, a symbol of spiritual immortality.[37]

The Taoist yogi is instructed in the importance of a morally upright life and advised to abstain from solid foods, especially prior to his meditative exercises.

They usually involve rhythmic breathing and the directing of energy, or *ch'i*[a], from the head through the body, accompanied by a kind of interior vision, by which the mind draws inner light from the outer universe to contemplate the human organism inside for the sake of promoting health and spiritual well-being. In this way, these "inner energy" exercises differ from those of Ch'an meditation, which involve the purifying or emptying of the inner self. Such Taoist exercises are thought to bring the practitioner in touch with the cosmic *ch'i*[a] or energy, and to preserve health, cure sickness, and even lead to the formation of a mysterious embryo within the body, a new, incorrupt self, to emerge as a butterfly from a cocoon.

The quest for the inner alchemy has another meaning. Taoists also use their techniques for exploring the human body to unlock the secrets of the universe outside, based on the familiar complementarity of microcosm/macrocosm. Their belief is that a precise knowledge of the human organism will give them a key to precise information about the galaxies above and the earth below. This provides a link between an interest in inner alchemy and that in astronomy, and even in cosmology.[38] It is understandable that the *Diagram of the Great Ultimate* appears to have many Taoist precedents that served multiple purposes.

Together with Buddhist thought, Taoist philosophy helped to focus Chu Hsi on questions of cosmology and philosophical psychology, supplying him with ideas and concepts, as well as a technical vocabulary, that inspired his metaphysical formulations. Chu practiced certain forms of Taoist yoga aimed at preserving health. He showed as well a great curiosity regarding Taoist religious texts.

The Great Ultimate: The World and Human Nature

To understand Chu Hsi's cosmology, it is necessary to go back to Chou Tun-yi's *Diagram of the Great Ultimate*. Chinese thinkers can draw on a long tradition of diagrams, going back to mythical times and to such pictures as the River Chart (*Ho-t'u*) and the Lo Writing (*Lo-shu*) (fig. 1). The River Chart was allegedly borne out of the Yellow River on the back of a dragon-horse and contained the Eight Trigrams or the data from which the trigrams were constructed. It was dated to the time of the mythical culture hero Fu-hsi, the "Animal Tamer" himself. The Lo Writing supposedly emerged on the back of a tortoise during the time when the legendary King Yü was controlling the floods. The Chart and the Writing are mentioned in such texts as *Analects* (9:8) and the Great Commentary to the Book of Changes—the best known of the Ten Wings.[39] In Sung times, the River Chart and the Lo Writing were represented by a magic square and a cruciform arrangement of numerical values, expressing the idea of the harmony that pervades the universe.[40]

A frequently alleged source for Chou Tun-yi's *Diagram* was what the Taoist hermit Ch'en T'uan (c. 906–89) passed to Mu Hsiu (979–1032).[41] It is named the *Wu-chi t'u* (literally, the *Diagram of the Limitless*, or *Infinite*, see fig. 2). This diagram represents the various stages of Taoist alchemy, possibly both inner and outer alchemy, the latter associated with the art of metallurgy, which permits

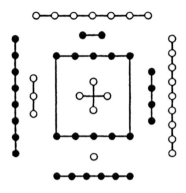

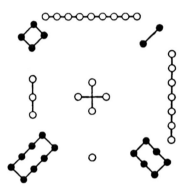

Figure 1. The River Chart (*Ho-t'u*) (*top*) and the Lo Writing (*Lo-shu*)

the human being to enter into nature itself to discover its hidden metallic essences for the purpose of purifying and transmuting them:

> What nature made in the beginning, we can likewise make, by returning to the procedure that she followed. What she is perhaps still making, by the help of the centuries, in her subterranean solitudes, we can cause her to finish in a single instant, by aiding her and surrounding her with better circumstances. As we make bread, so we can make metals.[42]

More probably, this diagram was used to help the task of inner alchemy. To do so, the Taoist diagram was read from the bottom upward; in this direction it reveals the secrets of working *in opposition to* nature in order to discover its mystery and to bring about some form of longevity and freedom. The Taoist practitioner regards his enterprise as one of theft: he is determined to "steal" the mystery from Heaven and Earth, just as he regards "Heaven and Earth as the thieves

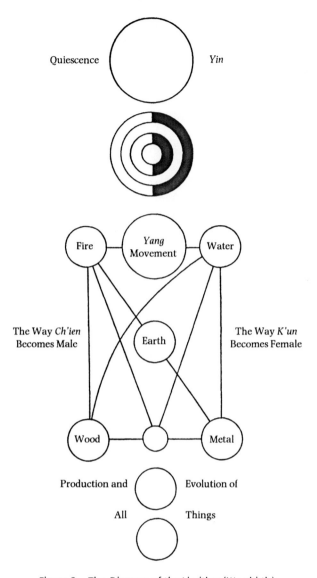

Figure 2.   The *Diagram of the Limitless (Wu-chi t'u)*

of the myriad things; the myriad things as the thieves of human beings; human beings as the thieves of the myriad things." The reasoning here is based on the mutual despoiling between nature and humans, as well as between humans and other creatures.[43]

We know little about Chou Tun-yi, who is the author of two short treatises and is usually identified as the teacher of the brothers Ch'eng Hao and Ch'eng Yi. They studied with him for about one year during their midteens and recall his Buddhist proclivities.[44] Whether Chou acquired knowledge of the *Diagram of the Great Ultimate* from any Taoist circle has been contested time and again. An extant poem by Chou, written apparently around age forty-four, says:

> Now beginning to contemplate the elixir's formula,
> I believe Ch'en T'uan had the mystery
> Of *yin-yang*'s creative transformations.[45]

This seems to establish a Taoist influence through Ch'en T'uan on Chou Tun-yi's explanations of *yin* and *yang*. But it does not confirm the transmission to Chou of a Taoist diagram that became his *Diagram*.[46]

It is well known that Taoists, as hermits, did not leave accurate records. We are not even sure of the dates of some of the transmitters mentioned, and there are huge time gaps between a few of these individuals. Thus, the Taoist transmission is difficult to substantiate even if many sources indicate such. On the other hand, it is difficult to dismiss too quickly all the arguments stemming from Taoist sources, given other known Taoist influences on Chou Tun-yi.

And what of the question of a Buddhist origin for Chou's *Diagram?* This is also associated with Tsung-mi, long before Taoists like Ch'en T'uan and Mu Hsiu came along. His *Diagram of Ālaya-vijñāna* (storehouse consciousness) purports to distinguish between truth and delusion (see fig. 3). The term *ālaya-vijñāna*, goes back to Yogācāra Buddhism and refers to the mind—not mind as it is experienced but as the one reality beyond all differentiation (Sanskrit, *citta*). All things are explained as this type of mind or consciousness, with ultimate reality understood as the fundamental storehouse consciousness, also called *tathatā* (suchness), Buddha-nature, and so on. However, through the acceptance of the two levels of truth, the ultimate and the relative, the *ālaya-vijñāna* is also spoken of in its state of process or differentiation as the *tathāgata-garbha*, or "storehouse of the Absolute," in which all reality and difference are embraced.[47] The above explanation allows us to see parallels between the *ālaya* consciousness and the Great Ultimate, both as beyond change and as in the process of change. Apparently, Buddhists regarded Chou as a disciple of a monk called Shou-ya, about whom very little is known.[48]

But if Chou got his *Diagram* or parts of it from the Buddhists or from Ch'en T'uan or his circle, he obviously changed the explanations and made his own mark on the diagram that bears his name. Whereas Taoists always read their diagrams from the bottom up, he gave his a different reading, from the top down, and with an independent explanatory text. By so doing, he changed the very character and significance of the *Diagram*, which became public and famous especially with Chu Hsi's teachings. Besides, where Taoists always understood all things as having come from a primal *ch'i*[a], with which they would associate the Great Ultimate, Chou's *Diagram*, according to Chu's interpretation, explains the Great Ultimate in terms of *li*[a], which transformed the whole interpretation.

The Buddhist diagram is really part of a huge chart that demonstrates the relations between the various Ch'an schools according to their doctrinal differences.[49] It includes a very early use of the circle enclosing the *Li*[b] and *K'an*

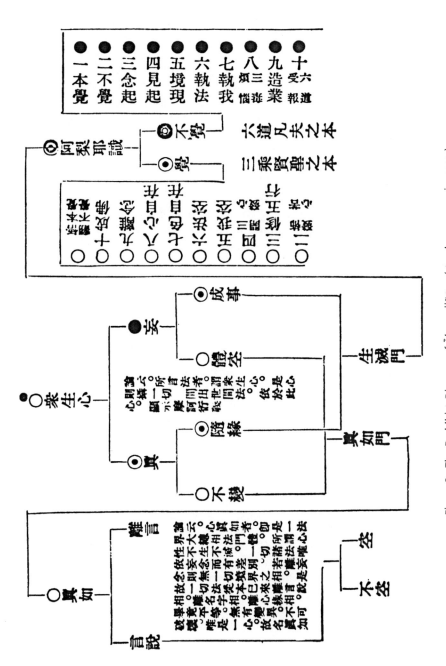

Figure 3. The Buddhist *Diagram of Ālaya-vijñāna* (storehouse consciousness)

trigrams ◐, a predecessor to the Taoist use as well as to Chou Tun-yi's. But if Chou was influenced by this chart, the influence could have been both direct and indirect, that is, also as mediated through the Taoists. Chou's *Diagram* is much more similar to the Taoist diagram than to the Buddhist diagram. Although the theory of two truths seems present in ideas articulated by Chou in his *Diagram*, the burden of his message is different. I would say that even with Taoist or Buddhist influence on the *Diagram* as *diagram*, Chou's personal mark comes through in his interpretation. In the final instance, Chou's work of independent thinking and transformation of ideas from Taoist and Buddhist sources was continued by Chu Hsi, who contributed his own interpretation to this philosophy of cosmic symbols.

Chou Tun-yi's *Diagram*

Chou's *Diagram* is less a commentary on any textual component from the Book of Changes and more of an exposition that takes certain ideas from this book as starting point and reference. As mentioned, it is intended to be read from top to bottom, following the course of nature rather than going against it (see fig. 4).

We find in his *Diagram* a series of circles set vertically that may be divided into three groups: two large circles at the top, another two at the bottom, and, in between, a group of five small circles joined by lines. The group of small circles is attached to a larger circle and adjoined underneath to a tiny circle.

Part 1 includes, as mentioned, two large circles. As we know the *Diagram* today, the top one is blank and is accompanied by the statement "*Wu-chi erh T'ai-chi.*" The one underneath has interlocking, semicircular areas of light and darkness, with the words *yin* (quiescence) and *yang* (movement) on the two sides. The light and dark areas spell out two trigrams from the Book of Changes, *Li*[b] ☲ and *K'an* ☵, when we take the light and dark areas to represent *yang* and *yin* lines.

Part 2 comprises the network of five small circles, identified by the words "water," "fire," "metal," "wood," and, in the center, "earth."

Part 3 includes two large circles, the first of which is flanked by two statements referring to two other trigrams from the Book of Changes: on the left, "the Way *Ch'ien* becomes male"; and on the right, "the Way *K'un*[a] becomes female." At the very bottom, underneath the final large circle, is the statement "Production and Transformation of the Myriad Things."

A quick first reading of Chou's *Diagram* yields certain key words such as "Great Ultimate" (*T'ai-chi*), the "Limitless" or "Immeasurable" (*Wu-chi*), "quiescence" and "activity" (*yin/yang*), the names of the Five Phases, and "male" and "female" (*Ch'ien* and *K'un*[a]), as well as "emergence (or "production") of the myriad things." These words are quite different in meaning and reference from those of Ch'en T'uan's diagram.

Chou's *Explanation of the Diagram of the Great Ultimate* is impressive for the simplicity of the diction, in which every substantive word has a technical meaning, and for the rhythm of the sentences, most of which have only four words

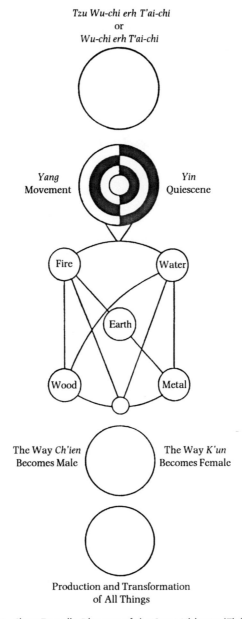

Tzu Wu-chi erh T'ai-chi
or
Wu-chi erh T'ai-chi

Yang
Movement

Yin
Quiescene

Fire

Water

Earth

Wood

Metal

The Way *Ch'ien*
Becomes Male

The Way *K'un*
Becomes Female

Production and Transformation
of All Things

Figure 4. Chou Tun-yi's *Diagram of the Great Ultimate* (*T'ai-chi t'u*)

each and are arranged in a parallel order, as with a prose poem. The text has discernible divisions, each of which carries forward a circular movement within the entire *Explanation* itself. I shall offer below a translation that should transmit something of the flow of ideas as well as the rhythm of words and sentences.

Let us now turn to the first phrase of the *Diagram's Explanation*, the beginning to which the whole process returns: *Wu-chi erh T'ai-chi*. There is controversy surrounding the first phrase, regarding not only the meaning but the words. Another version of the first phrase contains seven words: *Tzu Wu-chi erh wei T'ai-chi* (from the *Wu-chi* to becoming the *T'ai-chi*).[50] Why are there two versions of this phrase? Which came from Chou Tun-yi and which did not? Chu insisted on the five-word version, which appears in his edition of Chou's writings, even though he knew of the other version and its acceptance in some circles in his own lifetime. As this is a complex subject, I shall give fuller treatment of this controversy in appendix B.

I rely here also on the careful work of the Japanese scholar Imai Usaburō, who gives the evidence in detail.[51] He points out that many Japanese scholars in the past have considered the longer wording as authentic, after having carefully examined Chinese texts on the question. I am opting here tentatively for the seven-word phrase as coming from Chou, rather than Chu's five-word version, which became standard. I do so partly because I shall, in any case, consider the five-word phrase in the context of Chu Hsi's philosophy. It therefore appears reasonable to tentatively accept the seven-word phrase as coming from Chou Tun-yi.

Several versions of Chou's *Diagram* were in circulation in Chu's time. On the basis of scholarly evidence, Imai affirms that the version transmitted by Chu was the correct one. (But his other conclusion is that the longer version of the first phrase explaining the *Diagram*—rejected by Chu—gives the original wording.)[52] I shall now proceed to offer the presumed *general* meanings of Chou Tun-yi:[53]

> From the *Wu-chi* to becoming the *T'ai-chi* (*Tzu Wu-chi erh-wei T'ai-chi*).

If these are the right words, we see here a causal connection between the *Wu-chi* and the *T'ai-chi*, as well as the admission of nonduality. From the indeterminate *Wu-chi* emerges the Great Ultimate, a complex symbol enclosing the modes of *yin* and *yang*, the two *ch'i*[a].

> Great Ultimate moving, produces *yang*;
> Moving to an ultimate (*chi*[a]) and becoming still,
> [Great Ultimate] in stillness produces *yin*.
> Still to an ultimate, once more moving,
> Motion and rest alternating,
> Each as root of the other,
> Separating into *yin* and *yang*,
> Two Modes are thereby established.

So we find stillness and motion, rest and productivity. On this level, there is no denying that the two modes of *ch'i*[a] as *yin* and *yang* have emerged.

> *Yang* changing, *yin* uniting,
> [Great Ultimate] produces Water, Fire, Wood, Metal, Earth;
> Five *ch'i*[a] spreading in harmony,
> Four Seasons will run their course.

It is a return to traditional philosophy, and we are in the world of change and flux, as the Five Phases come into play. Why two become five is not explained, although the five small circles are connected by lines to the two large circles above. As represented in the *Diagram*, the set of five reconciles both the mutual-conquest and mutual-generation options, through various lines joining them to one another in a whole network. Following Chu Hsi's interpretation, we generally go from top to bottom and from right (the *yin* side) to left (the *yang* side). Reading diagonally first along one axis, then going up, only to go down again diagonally along another axis, we get the mutual-generation sequence, as Water engenders Wood, Wood nourished Fire, Fire leads to Earth, Earth produces Metal, Metal dissolves into Water, the starting point. For the mutual-conquest sequence, it is harder. We do have Water conquering Fire and Metal conquering Wood; but we have to go from left to right to get Fire overcoming Metal, with Earth intervening, and Earth overcoming Water, with Metal intervening.[54] The bottom small circle draws down the four corners and points to the two last circles, standing for Heaven and Earth and the myriad things.[55]

> Five Phases make up *yin-yang*.
> *Yin-yang* make up Great Ultimate,
> *T'ai-chi* is rooted in *Wu-chi*.

The wording of the last line here in Chinese is also subject to dispute. In Chu Hsi's version, it says, *T'ai-chi pen Wu-chi yeh*. But some claim that it should have been *T'ai-chi pen yü Wu-chi yeh*. The additional word, *yü*[a], is significant. A kind of preposition, it asserts that the Great Ultimate "came from" the *Wu-chi* as its root, rather than that it is rooted in the *Wu-chi*. Again, there is a causal connection rather than a dialectical identification of the *Wu-chi* and *T'ai-chi*.[56]

After completing a circular movement and returning to the *Wu-chi*, the text dwells for a while on the Five Phases and *yin* and *yang*, in order to move on to the appearance of the "myriad things":

> Five Phases are produced,
> Each with its own nature.
> Reality of *Wu-chi*,
> Essences of Two (*yin-yang*) and Five [Phases],
> In wonderful union integrating.

And then comes the explanation accompanying the two large blank circles at the bottom. The first one represents the two primal trigrams, *Ch'ien* (Heaven) and *K'un*[a] (Earth); the second one represents the production of the myriad things:

> The Way *Ch'ien* becomes male,
> The Way *K'un*[a] becomes female.
> The two Energies interact,
> [They] produce the myriad things.
> The myriad things produce and evolve, in unending transformation.

It appears that the words *wan-wu* (myriad things) are a novelty introduced by Chou Tun-yi, since they do not appear on any other similar diagram. This is an-

other hermeneutical device to strengthen the logic of the *Diagram*, with everything coming from the Great Ultimate, which itself comes from the *Wu-chi*. This
is also another way of making sure that transcendence is always balanced by
immanence.

To move now to another level. Clearly, in the *Diagram* and its *Explanation*,
Chou Tun-yi moves from the universe to the human being. He presents the
human being as the crown of the universe, as microcosm *of* the macrocosm.
He interprets human greatness—in the sage—as *fulfillment* of a Great Plan
which goes beyond the human being, a plan involving *yin* and *yang* and the
Five Phases. Evidently, the *Diagram* and its *Explanation* are highly symbolic
and require further elucidation.

> Alone the human being receives the highest excellence and is most spiritual;
> Shape is produced;
> Spirit develops knowledge;
> The five natures are moved, good and evil are separated;
> A myriad affairs emerge.

The "five natures" correlate with the Five Phases and are to be understood in
terms of the human being's innate ability to perform virtues. Mencius defends
the original goodness of human nature by appealing to the universal presence
of commiseration, shame, reverence, and discernment between good and evil as
the beginnings of the four virtues of humanity: benevolence, rightness, propriety, and wisdom.[57] This, however, accounts only for four virtues. Custom includes also faithfulness, which with the other four makes up the "five constant
virtues." Chou's list overlaps somewhat with Mencius's, without being exactly
the same, as we shall see later when he speaks of the sage.

In English, the word "virtue" tends to have a moral connotation, so that one
may be surprised to find wisdom among the virtues. In Chinese thought, wisdom is not merely an intellectual quality. In a society where all knowledge is
oriented to moral action, it refers also to moral knowledge. And since the human
mind is the source of *both* intellectual and moral dispositions, such knowledge
or its accumulation is also considered a virtue.[58]

The myriad human affairs are made parallel to the myriad creatures of the
universe. And this section comes to a close only with a eulogy of the sage, who
is Human Ultimate, image of the Great Ultimate itself:

> The sage settles all with the Mean, Rectitude,
> Benevolence, Rightness, while centering on Stillness;
> And establishes the Human Ultimate.

It is interesting that Chou chooses stillness (*ching*[a]) as one of the five virtues of
the sage, indeed, the central virtue, showing Chu's contemplative disposition and
possible influence from Buddhism and Taoism. The eulogy alludes to the words
of the Great Commentary to the Book of Changes. It ends with praise for the Book
of Changes itself:

So the sage unites his virtue with Heaven and Earth;
He unites his brilliance with the sun and moon;
He unites his order with the four seasons;
He unites his fortune and misfortune with ghosts and spirits.
The gentleman cultivates this and is fortunate;
The mediocre person transgresses this and is unfortunate.

Here, Chou proposes the sage as the human par excellence, a human ultimate and paradigm, who normalizes affairs with his "five virtues," and who participates in the cosmic process itself, assisting somehow in the return to the Great Ultimate.[59]

The *Diagram* and *Explanation* offer a certain worldview and view of life coming from one who has long sought for such with the help of the Book of Changes. An "unpacking" of the meaning of the *Diagram* and *Explanation* should help us with our own understanding of the world and of life, while also serving as a model of interpretation for those seeking to "unpack" the Book of Changes itself.

Another influence on Chu's cosmology comes from one of Chou's contemporaries, Shao Yung (Shao Yong, 1011–77), whom Chu never found completely acceptable.[60] The concept of *T'ai-chi* is also present in his philosophy. But his contemplation of nature is expressed more abstractly in terms of numbers. His interpretations of the Great Ultimate are much more abstract, involving an elaborate numerology.

Shao's diagram, coming from acknowledged Taoist origins, provoked in Chu less interest than Chou's (see fig. 5).[61] Shao reordered the sequence of the hexagrams, starting from the primordial divided (*yin*) and undivided (*yang*) lines, and moving to complexes of two, of three, of four, of five, and finally of six lines making up hexagrams. He arranged the hexagrams one after the other in a square of eight times eight. His diagram is known as the *Diagram of What Antedates Heaven (Hsien-t'ien-t'u)*. This title itself indicates a symbolic reference to a kind of preestablished harmony. In any case, his sequence makes manifest the mathematical foundations of the Book of Changes, which had been forgotten for centuries. It eventually caught the attention of the seventeenth-century German philosopher Leibniz, who got it from Jesuit missionaries and discovered in it his own dyadic, or binary, number system hidden in the order of the hexagrams when the *yin* − − and *yang* — lines are assigned numerical values of 0 and 1, but moving in an order inverted to his own (see fig. 5). Quite obviously, Shao's attempt to encompass all knowledge and truth in symbolic form mirrored the efforts of Leibniz, himself also a versatile genius.[62]

The philosopher Chang Tsai, a native of Ch'ang-an (Shensi), was Chou's contemporary, an uncle of the Ch'eng brothers, and another influence on Chu Hsi. He too shows an interest in cosmology that was not taken up by his nephews. Chang usually prefers to use the term Great Harmony (*T'ai-ho*). In this context, the Great Harmony, identified with the Tao, is another name for the Great Ultimate. But he describes it only in terms of *ch'i*[a], even of "wandering *ch'i*[a]." When this *ch'i*[a] is undispersed and invisible, it is called the Great Void (*T'ai-hsü*).[63] Thus,

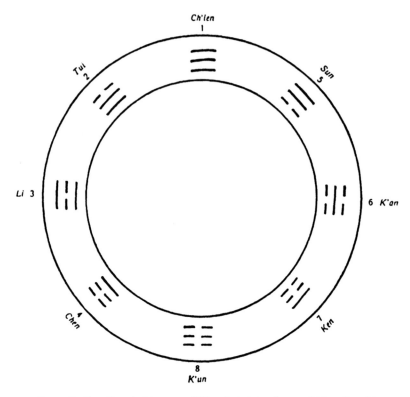

Figure 5. Shao Yung's *Diagram of What Antedates Heaven (Hsien-t'ien-t'u)*

the Great Void bears a likeness to the *Wu-chi*, just as the Great Harmony resembles the Great Ultimate. It would therefore appear that all these terms could refer to *yüan-ch'i* (primeval matter-energy) or, if we wish, a kind of prime matter or energy, whether in a dispersed or wandering, or an undispersed and invisible, form. Chu did not take to Chang's cosmology as such but found his "Western Inscription" a great inspiration. It is an expression of nature mysticism from a thinker often considered a materialist:

> Heaven is my father and earth is my mother, and I, a small child, find myself placed intimately between them.
>   What fills the universe I regard as my body; what directs the universe I regard as my nature.
>   All people are my brothers and sisters; all things are my companions.[64]

The Metaphysics of *Li*[a] and *Ch'i*[a]

The second generation of philosophers following Chou, Shao, and Chang did not share their elders' interest in cosmology. I refer here to the Ch'eng brothers, whose main contributions were to the metaphysics of *li*[a] and *ch'i*[a], so important in Chu's own system. In fact, this metaphysics makes up the basic structure of Chu's thought system, defining all other ideas. Chu Hsi's *Classified Conversations* devotes the first two chapters to this subject, under which the *T'ai-chi*, or Great Ultimate, is also discussed (ch. 1). In order to understand the Ch'eng-Chu metaphysics, I shall retrace certain technical terms to earlier times and older texts.

Of the two terms *li*[a] and *ch'i*[a], the word *li*[a] is harder to comprehend. It is mentioned in only a few ancient texts, and where it is mentioned, it usually has little importance. The *Shuo-wen* explains it in terms of patterns in jade.[65] The term is found outside the Confucian canon, appearing several times in *Mo-tzu*, where it usually refers to principle or reason.[66] It also occurs in *Kuan-tzu*, considered a Taoist text: "Names (*ming*) derive from reality (*shih*); reality derives from pattern (*li*[a]); *li*[a] derives from the properties (*te*) of things; properties derive from harmony (*ho*); and harmony derives from congruity (*tang*)."[67]

Turning to Confucian texts, the term is used in *Mencius* to refer to the harmonious cooperation of an orchestra, which becomes a metaphor for Confucius's achievements.[68] In *Hsün-tzu*, the term appears frequently. There, the *li*[a] of a particular thing is its configuration, its specific form, and every *li*[a] is subsumed in the great Tao, which is without specificity and so present in all things.[69]

In the "Record on Music" of the Book of Rites, a text dated to the third century B.C.E., the term occurs frequently, usually as the verb "to order," although there are also nouns referring to moral principles, and one can even find the expression "heavenly principle" (*t'ien-li*) so much favored by Chu Hsi.[70] In the *Doctrine of the Mean*, *li*[a] occurs once and refers to order and pattern. Interestingly, this same expression is also found in the Taoist text *Chuang-tzu*, again relating to music. In a conversation attributed to the mythical Yellow Emperor, we hear a discourse on heavenly music including the following: "Perfect music must respond to human needs, accord with heavenly principle (*t'ien-li*), proceed by the Five Powers (*Wu-te*, another name for the Five Phases), and blend with spontaneity."[71]

The appendices to the Book of Changes also mention *li*[a] when speaking of "simple and easy," a theme to be taken up by Lu Chiu-yüan (Lu Jiuyuan, 1139–93), which I shall discuss in chapter 7. Presumably, in this context, *li*[a] is especially discerned in the process and sequence of change. And this discovery is reflected by Ch'eng Yi and Chu Hsi.[72]

For Chuang-tzu, the heavenly *li*[a] is not much different from the heavenly Tao. The neo-Taoist philosophers prefer to speak of *ming-li*, combining the term *li*[a] with "name" and referring to a kind of language philosophy. But the third-century neo-Taoist Hsi K'ang (Xi Kang) introduced a different note when he spoke of *miao-li*, "wondrous *li*[a]," as "something cut off from ordinary discourse" and so apprehended only in mystical experience.

Later, the Buddhists appropriated the term, identifying it with *prajñā* and making it an ineffable and supramundane absolute. Its meaning varies somewhat depending on the school, whether Chinese Mādhyamika, Yogācāra, T'ien-t'ai, or Hua-yen. The best-known usage, and the most influential, is in Hua-yen Buddhism with its distinction between the two realms of *li*[a] (the noumenal) and *shih* (the phenomenal). The monk Tsung-mi discussed this in his commentary on the *Avatamsaka Sutra*, and for him, *li*[a] embraces all power and virtue.[73]

In Sung times, Chou Tun-yi uses the term to refer mainly to pattern and order, once in the context of rites and music, identifying rites (*li*[c]) with *li*[a].[74] Others, like Shao Yung and Chang Tsai, give it more the meaning of "principle," in terms of what makes up all things.[75] The Ch'eng brothers continue this trend, even identifying the *Li*[a] of one thing with the *Li*[a] of all things.[76] With Chu Hsi, the meaning of this philosophical term is completed: it is the principle that makes all things what they are, with their being and goodness, as well as the principle that makes the universe what it is, with its being and goodness. Chu speaks often of the one *Li*[a] between Heaven and Earth that has multiple manifestations.[77]

Summing up the history of the term *li*[a], it appears to have moved, with neo-Taoist philosophy and Buddhist metaphysics, from an immanent reference to a transcendent one. It would take Chu Hsi to keep the dimension of transcendence while regaining that of immanence.

The much older and more fundamental concept of *ch'i*[a] also has a depth of meaning that is not easily recovered. It is often translated as "breath," "energy," "ether," or "material force." It is not found in the Book of Changes but is present in many ancient texts, including the *Book of Mencius, Chuang-tzu, Kuan-tzu, Hsün-tzu, Lieh-tzu,* and *Huai-nan-tzu,* and often with a cosmological reference. Indeed, the word can be traced back all the way to the writings from the oracle bones of the Shang dynasty.[78]

The *Kuan-tzu,* a text dating to the fourth century B.C.E., alludes to some form of Chinese yoga for cultivating a very pure form of *ch'i*[a], understood as the essence of the stars above and the life of grain below:

> In all things the most spiritual,
> Having it is to live.
> Below, it generates the five grains,
> Above, it becomes the constellated stars.
> Flowing between Heaven and Earth,
> Call it ghost (*kuei*) and spirit (*shen*).
> When stored within the breast,
> Call that the sage.[79]

The *Huai-nan-tzu* is an early text going back to the second century B.C.E. that shows cosmological interests. It is mainly Taoist in inspiration while syncretistic in orientation and was compiled around the time when the Book of Changes was receiving its cosmological accretions. Its chief concept is the pervasive *ch'i*[a] in the universe, that which gives rise to all things, endowing them with life and energy.[80] We are speaking here of a substrative reality underlying the world as it appears to our consciousness:[81] a reality that not only is matter or material force but also has been sometimes described as psychophysical, as the Chinese do not separate mind and matter.

Needham asserts that *ch'i*[a] is found in every ancient text even indirectly concerned with nature. He sees in it an analogue of the Greek *pneuma* and says that "it could be a gas or a vapour, but also an influence as subtle as those which "aetherial waves" or "radioactive emanations" have implied for modern minds."[82] Ho Peng-yoke, Needham's collaborator, suggests: "To the early Chinese naturalists, this term seemed to bear some resemblance to what we now call 'matter-energy,' corresponding in a way to the *pneuma* of the ancient Greeks and the *prana* of the ancient Hindus."[83]

When appearing in Chinese Buddhist texts, *ch'i*[a] usually indicates a Taoist reference, as in the monk Tsung-mi when he distinguishes between Confucianism, Taoism, and Buddhism and states his preference for the *ālaya-vijñāna* or simply the *ālaya* (storehouse consciousness or eighth consciousness) over the original *ch'i*[a]. The *ālaya* is regarded as the most basic of eight kinds of consciousness, from which evolve the apparent external phenomena that in turn act upon it in a never-ending cycle. It is at the same time a storehouse of the "seeds" that cause defilement and those seeds themselves. Yet like the other seven kinds of consciousness, it is capable of being transformed into wisdom, after being purified of defilement.[84]

Ch'eng Yi distinguished between *li*[a] (principle, being, goodness), which belongs to the realm "above shapes" (*hsing-erh-shang*), and *ch'i*[a] (matter-energy), which belongs to the realm "within shapes" (*hsing-erh-hsia*), establishing thereby a structure for philosophical thinking that Chu Hsi accepted.[85] According to Chu Hsi, all things are made of both *li*[a] and *ch'i*[a]. He insists on the inseparability of these two coordinates: "there is no *ch'i*[a] without *li*[a] or *li*[a] without *ch'i*[a] under Heaven."[86] "Under Heaven" is a metaphorical expression for "the universe." Chu gives logical, though not temporal, priority to *li*[a] over *ch'i*[a]: "*Li*[a] comes first and then comes *ch'i*[a]." "First there is Heavenly principle (*T'ien-li*), then there is *ch'i*[a]." "*Li*[a] is one but its manifestation is myriad. When Heaven and Earth and the myriad things are spoken of together, there is only one *Li*[a]. When it comes to human beings, each has a particular *li*[a]."[87] But when asked which one *comes first* in the temporal order, he replies: "*Li*[a] never separates from *ch'i*[a]. But *li*[a] belongs to the realm above shapes, and *ch'i*[a] to the realm within shapes. When speaking of [this distinction], one is prior to the other."[88]

The terms *li*[a] and *ch'i*[a] sometimes bring to mind Aristotle's "form" and "matter," which together constitute all things. However, for Chu Hsi, *li*[a] is not merely a metaphysical concept; it has moral reference as well, which makes it difficult to comprehend when applied to nonhuman creatures.[89] Besides, the terms "form" and "matter" cannot accurately or adequately translate *li*[a] and *ch'i*[a], since in Aristotle, form is active and matter passive. In Chu Hsi, it is rather *li*[a] that is passive, and *ch'i*[a] that is active. Chinese philosophy is dynamic, just as its *ch'i*[a] is dynamic. While European philosophy, following Aristotle, tends to find reality in substance, Chinese philosophy, including Chu Hsi, tends to find reality in relation, in becoming. While the principle of identity in the West asserts that a thing cannot be and not be at the same time, Chinese philosophers always find things becoming something else, skipping, as it were, from the stage of formal logic to the stage of dialectical, Hegelian logic.[90] Chu sometimes seems quite ambiguous when speaking of Heaven or the heavenly principle. When asked, however, whether there is anything that transcends the universe, he answers in the affirmative: there is *li*[a] or *T'ai-chi*. "With this *li*[a] come this Heaven and Earth. Without this li^a there would be no Heaven and Earth or humans or things. . . . With this li^a comes this $ch'i^a$."[91] The problem is: He gives several meanings to the term "Heaven." We shall explore this issue in chapter 3. Here, it suffices to note that "Heaven and Earth" is an expression referring to the universe.

The history of Chinese philosophy after Chu Hsi may be described as a debate between those who wish to give more importance to li^a and those who wish to give more emphasis to $ch'i^a$.[92] Chu Hsi gives logical priority to li^a, but others, such as Lu Chiu-yüan and the later Wang Yang-ming (1472–1529), disputed this claim and, in doing so, either promoted a more positivistic view of human nature or infused a new meaning into the word $ch'i^a$ itself. The philosophers of $ch'i^a$ generally favored a nondualistic explanation of the cosmos and of human nature, giving an interpretation of $ch'i^a$ as matter or energy in a sense close to the Bergsonian *élan vital*. I refer to that current of consciousness in matter, likened sometimes to steam by Henri Bergson, that gives rise to living bodies, carrying life toward ever higher complexities and reaching its climax of freedom and achievement in the human being.

Speaking generally, the protagonists of li^a presume a preestablished pattern of harmony in the universe and in human nature, with the one Li^a and its myriad manifestations resembling, in some ways, a Leibnizian network of monads with God as supreme Monad through which and through whom all the others communicate. This harmony is to be recaptured and maintained by a proper balance of reason and the emotions, of moral striving sustained by intellectual pursuit. The protagonists of $ch'i^a$, on the other hand, are inclined to minimize the opposition between reason and the emotions. Without necessarily being always materialists, they tend to exalt the mind and heart over human nature and to absorb intellectual pursuit into moral and spiritual striving or vice versa.

Conclusion

I have presented discussions on the appendices to the Book of Changes and *yin-yang* and Five Phases theories to make possible an understanding of Chu Hsi's thought within the context of early Chinese cosmological and metaphysical discussions. I acknowledge that these discussions are fragmentary. They are nevertheless important, since they all presume a correlation and harmony between the macrocosm and the microcosm that is basic to mainstream Chinese thought, as reflected also in Chu Hsi and his immediate intellectual predecessors. I have also referred to the Taoism and Buddhism of his day to show the stimulus each contributed to the development of Chu's thought. There are important differences between the two currents of Buddhist thought and early Chinese thought. Even in Mahāyāna Ch'an Buddhism, one discerns a struggle to affirm the reality of the exterior universe, which is taken for granted by the mainstream Chinese philosophies, by Taoism, and by Chu Hsi.

From Chou Tun-yi, Chu Hsi derived an understanding of the world of things and of humans. This world is seen as the spontaneous reproduction of the interaction between the Five Phases and the principles of *yin* and *yang*, which, in turn, come from the Great Ultimate (*T'ai-chi*), a notion traced to the Book of Changes and referring to that which holds the universe together. Chou also describes the Great Ultimate as the *Wu-chi*, thereby giving rise to later debates about the concept's intended meaning. But his effort is generally directed toward the construction of a worldview that explains the countless phenomena of existence as having come from an original source, pure and undifferentiated, the totality of reality. In this way, he affirms the idea that reality is both "one" and "many," an idea that is basic to Chu Hsi's philosophical synthesis.

I wish to conclude this chapter with a poem, or *gatha*, that Chou Tun-yi allegedly received from a Buddhist monk. I believe it points out the goal of Chou's quest, as well as that of Chu Hsi himself:

> Before Heaven and Earth were, something already was.
> Shapeless and alone,
> It can be master of the myriad forms,
> And not wither with the four seasons.[93]

The Great Ultimate (*T'ai-chi*)

Standing high, one pillar of Heaven:
Mightily guarding the east.
Why speak only of the great *Ch'ien* and *K'un*[a],
And forget the work of grounding the Ultimate?

Chu Hsi[1]

Introduction: Cosmology in the Context of the Book of Changes

According to both himself and his biographer, Chu Hsi was interested in questions of cosmology from his early childhood. At age three, when his father pointed skyward to tell him, "This is heaven," he is reported to have asked, "What is above heaven?" And at age four or five, Chu asked, "What is heaven-in-itself (*t'ien-t'i*), and what lies beyond its peripheries?"[2] At age seven, while other children were playing in the sand, he sat by himself and drew in it the Eight Trigrams, the cosmological symbols of the Book of Changes.[3]

These naive and charming stories about Chu's early interest in the universe help us understand why, in his mature years, he included cosmology in his system and founded his philosophy on the concept of the Great Ultimate, as he learned it from Chou Tun-yi.[4] Chou was a relatively private and obscure man, with very few publications, whereas the Ch'eng brothers, his reputed disciples, became much better known. But Chou's idea of the Great Ultimate is barely reflected in them. It took Chu Hsi to promote this idea as part of the Confucian Tao and, in doing so, to promote Chou as an important link in the chain in the so-called line of orthodox transmission (*tao-t'ung*) that Chu himself established.

Nevertheless, it appears that Chu Hsi first heard of Chou Tun-yi's *Diagram of the Great Ultimate* at age thirty-seven. He responded positively to the idea of the Great Ultimate, wrote his own explanations for the *Diagram*, and prepared the *Chin-ssu lu* (1175) with help from his lifelong friend Lü Tsu-ch'ien (Lü Zuqian, 1137–81), placing Chou and his philosophy of the Great Ultimate at the beginning of the anthology.[5]

The concept of the Great Ultimate comes to us from the Great Commentary to the Book of Changes, which dates to the Han dynasty (206 B.C.E.–220 C.E.).

Unlike Ch'eng Yi, Chu explicitly acknowledged that the Book of Changes began as a divination text that took on philosophical accretions. The very term *T'ai-chi* is derived from the Great Commentary, one of the so-called Ten Wings of the Book of Changes. The thrust of the terms own symbolism and the explanatory text itself bear a strong resemblance to the orientation of the Book of Changes as a whole, and especially to the Great Commentary.[6]

The concept of the Great Ultimate (*T'ai-chi*) marks the climax of Chu's philosophical system. I am referring here to Chu's reinterpretation and transformation of Chou Tun-yi's concept, as given in Chou's *Diagram of the Great Ultimate* and its *Explanation*. He begins with it in both the *Chin-ssu lu* and in his recorded conversations. The concept became famous especially with his own contributions, which transformed its meaning by relating it to *li*[a] and *ch'i*[a].[7]

Great Ultimate: A History of the Concept

The first component of the term *T'ai-chi* signifies the great, the supreme, while the second refers to the utmost and ultimate. Indeed, the word *chi*[a] (ultimate) has long been used to designate "pole," whether a ridgepole or the Pole Star. Recalling Chu's poem with which we began this chapter, I wish to add another designation: the cosmic pillar joining Earth (*K'un*[a]) with Heaven (*Ch'ien*), of which the mountain to which the poem refers is a metaphor. The two great trigrams *Ch'ien* and *K'un* represent *yang* and *yin* as well as the beginning of all things. How the term *T'ai-chi* is used in the Great Commentary to the Book of Changes is indicative of its meaning in philosophy. Both there and in Chou Tun-yi's *Diagram*, it refers to the First Principle of the universe, which, by extension, is also the First Principle of human nature.

The primary concerns, as well as the language itself, of the *Diagram of the Great Ultimate*, are obviously metaphysical. What is proposed is an interpretation of the cosmos, of its origin, its cyclical process of movement and of return, in terms of the interaction of the Five Phases of change and transformation. With this comes an understanding of the human being as the perfect image of the cosmos— the human being whose shape and spirit correspond to *yin* and *yang*, whose "five principles of nature" correspond to the five cosmic phases, and whose concern for good and evil gives rise to the "myriad affairs" in the same way as the male and female in the universe give rise to the "myriad things."

The *Diagram of the Great Ultimate* has usually been interpreted in the context of neo-Confucian cosmology and metaphysics, as synthesized by Chu Hsi himself. But we can better appreciate Chu's contributions by looking into the many levels of meaning emerging from a broader context, including the antecedents and parallels to the *Diagram*.

From the Book of Changes and Lao-tzu

To the Book of Changes we owe not only the concept of *T'ai-chi* but also the symbols for the two primary trigrams, *Ch'ien* (Heaven) and *K'un*[a] (Earth), the "parents" of all the others. Words like *yin-yang* and the names of the Five Phases quickly bring to mind certain age-old concepts which have also gone into the making of this classic.

In the changes is the Great Ultimate.
This produces the Two Forces.
The Two Forces produce the Four Images (*hsiang*).
The Four Images produce the Eight Trigrams (*kua*).
The Eight Trigrams determine fortune and misfortune.
Fortune and misfortune give rise to the great activities.[8]

There is no mention here of any *Wu-chi*. We find only the *T'ai-chi*. The Two are interpreted as *yin* and *yang*, the Four as the images formed by doubling the *yin* and *yang* lines in four formations, corresponding to the four seasons, and the Eight are the family of trigrams from which the Sixty-four Hexagrams are derived. But in the midst of all this flux, the Great Ultimate is discovered as the generative force of flux itself.

We also find another dimension of thinking, namely, numbers (*shu*). Obviously, numbers are used here to suggest a need for intuitive awareness of the process of differentiation flowing from nondifferentiation, showing how the diversities of the modes of existence all emanate from the unity of the Ultimate.[9] But here, numerical values are assigned to the *linear* symbols, *yin* or *yang*, which make up the trigrams and hexagrams, themselves representations of a cosmic process mirrored in the human psyche. In another passage, of which this one is an echo, we find a similar use of numbers as symbols, with no explicit reference to trigrams and hexagrams, although with mention of *yin* and *yang* as mode changes. I refer here to *Lao-tzu*:

The Way begets One; One begets Two; Two begets Three; Three begets the Myriad Creatures.
The Myriad Creatures carry on their backs the *yin* and embrace in their arms the *yang* and are the blending of the generative forces of the Two.[10]

If we see the Way and One as representative of the *Wu-chi* and *T'ai-chi*, respectively, then the Two possibly refer to *yin* and *yang* and the Three to Heaven, Earth and human beings, who, in turn, beget the Myriad Creatures. The cosmic concern and the metaphysical language of both texts bear a strong resemblance to Chou Tun-yi's original words, as discussed in the last chapter. The difference with the first text is the Four Images and the Eight Trigrams, in which place Chou has substituted the Five Phases.

Interpretive difficulties arise because Chou's *Diagram* speaks not merely of a *T'ai-chi* but also of a *Wu-chi*. These difficulties are increased by Chu Hsi's language of *Wu-chi erh T'ai-chi*. Let us now turn briefly to the *Lao-tzu*, from which the term *Wu-chi* stems:

Know the male
But keep to the role of the female
And be a ravine to the empire. . . .
Then the constant virtue will not desert you

And you will again return to being a babe. . . .
Then the constant virtue will not be wanting
And you will return to the Infinite (*Wu-chi*).[11]

The message of *Wu-chi* here is of the reversal of the Tao. According to *Chuang-tzu*, and as cited by Chu Hsi, the term *Wu-chi* refers to the Infinite or Limitless.[12] It appears to refer to the Tao, the first principle that goes beyond all duality, including that of *yin* and *yang*.

In seeking to expound Chou's work by referring to the Book of Changes and *Lao-tzu*, I am myself proceeding in a circular manner, explaining one symbolic text in terms of two others. This kind of textual exegesis and hermeneutics cannot be avoided in discussing Chinese philosophy, on account of the highly metaphysical orientation of the language itself and the symbolic thrust of so many interlocked texts and allusions. This is also characteristic of the Chinese inclination to understand the human being in terms of the universe, and the universe in terms of the human being. To the Chinese philosopher, whether Taoist or neo-Confucian, each stands for the other, is a symbol for the other.

If we turn to Han dynasty apocryphal texts on the Book of Changes, we find another term, *T'ai-yi*, literally, the "Great Change," which refers to "nothingness." According to one text:

As the *T'ai-yi* begins to manifest itself,
The *T'ai-chi* comes to completion.
As the *T'ai-chi* comes to completion,
Ch'ien and *K'un*[a] operate.[13]

The *T'ai-yi*[a] is understood as the beginning before the emergence of *ch'i*[a], the formless and shapeless before the emergence of form and shape.[14] Besides, we find here the idea of the *T'ai-yi*[a] producing or engendering the *T'ai-chi*, an idea not found earlier. The second-century exegete Cheng Hsüan (Cheng Xuan) adds: "*T'ai-yi*[a] is nothingness; *T'ai-chi* is somethingness [i.e., being]. *T'ai-yi*[a] goes from nothingness to being. It is so called because the sage knows that it has *li*[a] but is without shape."[15] As with Taoist philosophy, the *T'ai-chi*, or Great Ultimate, represents here the manifestation of *T'ai-yi*[a] in the fullness of *ch'i*[a].[16]

We may also associate with this symbol of nothingness the beginning of all things—a beginning that was before all beginnings, sometimes termed "chaos." The myth of such chaos personified could be the forerunner to Lao-tzu's assertion that being comes from nothingness.[17] But there is another *T'ai-yi*[b] (Great One), written with a different word, that also occurs in the *Apocryphal Book of Changes*, possibly in relation to the River Chart.[18] It is also found in the *Huai-nan-tzu*: "Pervading Heaven and Earth, in chaotic simplicity, with nothing made or created, is the *T'ai-yi*[b] [Great One]. All come from this Oneness, but each becomes differentiated."[19] Kao Yu, the commentator to *Huai-nan-tzu*, associates this concept of the Great One to the supreme god of Han dynasty religion, also called the Great One: "The *T'ai-yi*[b] is the primal spirit, in charge of the myriad things."[20]

From Myth and Religion

Indeed, there is strong reason to associate the Great Ultimate also with the myth of the Pole Star, residence of the God *T'ai-yi*[b] (Great One), which sounds like the *T'ai-chi*. It is originally a name of the supreme deity in the time of the Warring States (403–221 B.C.E.) and later the principal god of the five gods worshiped in Han times (206 B.C.E.–220 C.E.), after an evolution which bears the mark of the influence of the Five Phases theory. The Pole Star is a symbol of transcendence and constancy. For the early observers of the heavenly bodies, it appears as a ruler of the circumpolar stars and a symbol of imperial authority on earth.[21] We read in *Analects* 2:1: "He who exercises government by means of his virtue may be compared to the star of the north, which keeps to its own place, and yet all the [other] stars turn toward it." Besides, *T'ai-yi*[b], followed by the later five gods of Han dynasty religion,[22] offers two parts of the tripartite scheme that Chou's *Diagram* contains: the One *T'ai-chi*, the Two *yin-yang* modes, and the Five Phases.

The myth became incorporated into Taoist religious beliefs; for the Taoist follower, the term "Great One" continued to signify the highest of the gods, as well as one of the many gods. The myth also became transformed in philosophical reflection with the discussion of the Great Ultimate as first principle and fullness of being, that beyond which the mind can conceive of nothing (*Wu-chi*).

Another early symbol of the Great Ultimate, which probably antedated Chou's *Diagram*, is a circle divided into two sections of light and darkness by a curved line in the middle. The dark section contains a spot of light, and the light section contains a spot of darkness ☯. The symbolism of *yin* and *yang*, of the presence of one in the other, is obvious.[23] In Chou's *Diagram*, this symbolism is expressed in a different way, by interlocking sections of light and darkness that make up— quite unaccidentally—the two trigrams of *K'an* and *Li*[b]. *Li*[b] and *K'an*, the Abysmal and the Clinging, are the son and daughter of the "parent" trigrams, *Ch'ien* and *K'un*[a], that is, Heaven and Earth. They represent the *ch'i*[a] of fire and of water. To have *K'an* and *Li*[b] present at this stage serves to introduce the Great Ultimate as present in the two modes of *yin* and *yang*, representing also the moon and the sun, and by extension, the dimension of time.[24] As will be mentioned in the following chapter, Chu also believes, with the earlier Taoist philosophers and the commentators on the Book of Changes, that the sediments of the *ch'i*[a] of water made up Earth, and the purest *ch'i*[a] of fire made up the luminaries, which, together with the rotating *ch'i*[a], make up Heaven. This gives the two trigrams another, more cosmological connection to the *Diagram*, while adding to it the concept of temporality.[25]

The *Diagram* itself finishes with the trigrams Heaven (*Ch'ien*) and Earth (*K'un*[a]) and the myriad things. The explicit mention of Heaven and Earth, between which the myriad things all find themselves, points to spatiality. Temporality and spatiality together are, for the Chinese, the universe. After all, *yü-chou*, a Chinese term for the cosmos, refers literally to time and space. To quote here Lu Chiu-yüan:

> Spatiality refers to the four directions plus above and below (*yü*).
> Temporality refers to what's past and what will yet come (*chou*).[26]

Since, as already mentioned, the trigrams *Li*[a] and *K'an* represent temporality, the four trigrams together include both time and space in the representation of the cosmos in the *Diagram*.

To this, however, Chu Hsi responds:

> This Great Ultimate is a huge thing. The "four directions plus above and below make up *yü*. What's past and what will yet come make up *chou*." But there's nothing quite as big as *yü*. When the four directions are pushed to the Limitless (*Wu-chi*), when the above and below are pushed to the Limitless (*Wu-chi*), how much bigger [our universe becomes!] Nothing [also] is as extended as *chou*, from past to present, back and forth without cease. We should understand this in our own minds. . . . Lu Chiu-yüan often speaks of [*yü-chou*]. But he only mentions it. He has no use for the beats and rhythm in it. [He] keeps it quite vacuous and empty.[27]

For Chu, Lu's mention of the cosmos is quite without meaning, since he has no cosmology to back it up. So he mocks it as a cosmos without musical resonance. This is remarkable because Chu is to interpret the Great Ultimate with the term *li*[a], an ancient term, which in *Mencius* (5B:1.6) described the harmonious cooperation of an orchestra.[28]

A Transformation of the Concept

The discussions of possible Taoist and Buddhist sources for Chou's *Diagram* could serve as a distraction from Chou's real contributions. Chou intended the *Diagram* for cosmological explanations. In this context, the more visible influences are the ones from Yin-yang and Five Phases theories, which came down from ancient China and became incorporated into the Book of Changes, even if Chu Hsi transformed the meaning he inherited from antiquity. It would appear from Chou's philosophical language that he was personally less influenced by Taoist religion than by Taoist philosophy, with his emphasis on *wu* (nothingness) and *ching*[a] (stillness or tranquillity). Chu Hsi himself received the *Diagram* as an illustration of cosmology and interpreted it as such. And this is the way it has come down to us. The *Diagram* also goes beyond Buddhist influence in its dialectical inclusion of both *Wu-chi* and *T'ai-chi*, according to Chu Hsi's interpretation. A clear effort to move away from the Buddhist preference for nonduality, as manifested in Tsung-mi's chart, this interpretation naturally led to Lu Chiu-yüan's criticism of Taoist influence on Chu and Chu's retort of Buddhist influence on Lu.

T'ai-chi as Chu Hsi's Secret Teaching

The *Diagram of the Great Ultimate* consumed very much of Chu Hsi's attention. If the correspondence it generated and the exchanges in his *Classified Conversations* are not counted, Chu contributed five essays or commentaries on this subject.[29] However, when we look into the evolution of the concept in Chu's teach-

ings, we discover something astonishing: that it had remained a secret teaching for over two decades.

Apparently, Chu heard of Chou's *Diagram* from his friend Chang Shih (Zhang Shi, 1133–80), a disciple of Hu Hung (Hu Hong, 1106–61). Hu Hung was the son of Hu An-kuo (Hu Anguo, 1074–1138), in turn the disciple of Hsieh Liang-tso (Xie Liangzuo, 1050–c. 1120), who studied with the Ch'eng brothers, especially with Ch'eng Hao. Hu Hung, Hu An-Kuo, and Chang belonged to the Hunan school. Chu and Chang exchanged ideas throughout their lives on a range of topics. Even though Chu became better known than Chang, Chang's influence on Chu was very strong. In 1167, Chu visited Chang and spent about two months with him in Hunan. Chang wrote a farewell poem that concluded with these two lines: "With sublime [minds], we contemplate the Great Ultimate: / No full ox lies beneath our eyes." The ox is an allusion to Chuang-tzu's chapter "Nurturing Life," where he recounts the story of the cook Ting, who carved the ox he cooked with such dexterity because his mind was on the Tao. The cook explained that when he first did this job, he could only see the ox itself. After three years he no longer saw the entire ox and could perform the task by spirit without looking with his eyes.[30] So Chang alludes to this story to explain that he and Chu had also reached that stage of spiritual contemplation beyond physical observation.

Chu's poem, quoted below, marked the occasion. He begins it by mentioning ice and charcoal, two opposing commodities, which represent his confused state of mind when he visited Chang:

> Once, carrying with me ice and charcoal,
> I learned from you about *K'un*[a] and *Ch'ien*,
> And, for the first time, the mysteries of *T'ai-chi*.
> Its message is hard to put into words. . . .
> The myriad transformations flow from this,
> The thousand sages share the same source.[31]

Six years later (1173), Chu completed his own explanations to the *Diagram of the Great Ultimate* as well as to Chou's Penetrating the Book of Changes (*T'ung-shu*). He regarded the Great Ultimate and Chang Tsai's "Western Inscription" (Hsi-ming) as the two most important teachings since Mencius. When asked why he wrote the *Explanations* on a teaching absent in Ch'eng Yi, he answered:

At that time the book was not known and [the teaching] could remain hidden. Today, it is widely known. If it is not well explained, later scholars will just have doubts and problems. Under these circumstances, I have no choice but to explain [*the Diagram of the Great Ultimate*].[32]

But he hesitated to teach it more widely, expecting controversy, presumably because of the alleged Taoist influence it contains. It was only fifteen years later, in 1188, that he openly taught the Great Ultimate together with his explanations of the "Western Inscription." As he explains it:

I dared not show people my two *Explanations* on the Great Ultimate and the "Western Inscription" when I first wrote them. Recently, I've often heard scholars pointing out problems with these two [original] works—sometimes because they have not understood the meaning of the texts, but they still made baseless attacks. I regretted this occurrence in private and decided to make public my *Explanations* in order to teach them to students and permit wider dissemination.[33]

He was then fifty-eight years old. He had meditated on the Great Ultimate for twenty-one years.

Chu maintains that Chou's Great Ultimate represents what Confucius and Mencius taught. This is hard to support, as extant texts from the circles around these two sages contain no mention of the term *T'ai-chi*. It rarely occurs in the writings of the two Ch'engs, as Chang Shih pointed out. Chu replied that he thought the Ch'engs were unable to accept this particular teaching from Chou.[34]

The Ch'eng brothers' relative lack of interest in questions of cosmology only highlights Chu's own curiosity and originality, even as a philosophical synthesizer. But Ch'eng Yi's second preface to his *Yi-chuan* does contain this reference:

Dispersed in things, the myriad transformations emerge. United in the Tao, there is no duality. That is why [the Great Commentary to the Book of Changes says:] In the Changes is the Great Ultimate, which engenders the two modes. The Great Ultmate is the Tao; the two modes are *yin* and *yang*. *Yin* and *yang* belong to the one Tao. The *T'ai-chi* is also the *Wu-chi*. The myriad things are engendered, with their backs to *yin* and embracing *yang*. They all have the Great Ultimate; they all have the two modes.[35]

Apparently, Chu's own disciples doubted the Confucian character of Chou's Great Ultimate. When they asked him why Ch'eng Yi did not give it as a teaching received from Chou, Chu said: "Because there were those who couldn't take it." When further asked why Confucius had not taught it, Chu stubbornly appealed to the argument from silence: "How do you *know* Confucius didn't?"[36]

Why was it regarded as unacceptable at the time? The controversies we have touched upon can suggest a few reasons. I might add that cosmological discussions were rare in the Confucian tradition, which preferred usually to deal with the here and now, without pushing too hard on the frontiers of speculation. Indeed, discourses on Heaven were regarded as somewhat beyond reason, because beyond the readily knowable, and therefore the domain of the Taoists, whether approached philosophically or otherwise.

In Chu's time, more than a century after Chou's death, the *Diagram of the Great Ultimate* was not being taught by other thinkers. It had been relegated to the realm of the esoteric and unthinkable, even of the heretical. It therefore took courage on Chu's part to revive and transform its teaching and make of it a vital part of his system, which eventually became mainstream.

That he himself was preoccupied with it all his life is borne out by the evidence that he was still thinking of and teaching the *Diagram of the Great Ultimate*—and the "Western Inscription"—at night in his home several days before his own death. There is no question that it was an important and integral part of his teachings. Chu's biographer, Wang Mao-hung (1668–1741), says: "Chu revered the two texts his entire life, and even [during his final days] earnestly instructed his disciples on them, showing in a profound and manifest manner the importance of going back to the cosmic origins."[37]

It is nevertheless interesting that the Great Ultimate and Chu Hsi's explanations of the *Doctrine of the Mean* were considered somehow "secret" teachings. Possibly, the many controversies surrounding the teaching of *Wu-chi erh T'ai-chi* give us a clue as to why Chu Hsi was for so long reluctant to talk about it, to bring it out of obscurity and darkness into light.[38] Both the *Diagram of the Great Ultimate* and the doctrine of emotional equilibrium and harmony require a meditative discipline. The Great Ultimate cannot just be *reasoned*. It has to be understood in contemplation. Equilibrium and harmony both refer to states of meditative consciousness. Such a consciousness is aimed at penetrating a cosmic mystery, through the mind and heart's descent into the depths of its own being, which is where it meets the mind and heart of the universe. Perhaps, I should say, this is where it discovers itself to *be* the mind and heart of the universe, in a mystical consciousness that unites the self and the universe.

Nevertheless, Chu Hsi uses metaphysical language in an effort to explain the Great Ultimate philosophically. He relies on Ch'eng Yi and Chang Tsai for his metaphysical structure of *li*[a] and *ch'i*[a]. But concerning the Great Ultimate, he also has to choose between the two concepts: does the Great Ultimate consist more of *ch'i*[a], the primal energy of the Taoists, or is it constituted more by *li*[a], the principle of being and goodness? Eventually, his answer would be: the Great Ultimate is more *li*[a] than *ch'i*[a], but it is also *li*[a] *in ch'i*[a].

The Great Ultimate: *Li*[a] or *Ch'i*[a]?

Regarded as a cosmological treatise, the Book of Changes cannot answer all the questions that it raises. It is better understood when examined in the larger context of early Chinese philosophy, which gives us some basic concepts of nature and the cosmos.

I have discussed *li*[a] and *ch'i*[a] in the preceding chapter. Suffice it to say that these became the most important concepts in Chu Hsi's philosophical system. In the case of *li*[a], it took over some of the earlier meanings, as order or system and as pattern, but acquired metaphysical connotations, so that *li*[a] signifies the intrinsic nature of things, or "why things are what they are." It also took on a normative dimension, of "what ought to be."[39]

As for *ch'i*[a], in the light of our earlier discussion of the *Apocryphal Book of Changes*, I shall quote here from the *Lieh-tzu*, a somewhat later text that is allegedly based on an earlier, pre-second-century-B.C.E. one:

> The Great Beginning was the start of *ch'i*[a]. . . . *Ch'i*[a], shape, and stuff were all there but not separate. That is why we say they were indeterminate. . . .

The myriad things were [then] indeterminate, and not separate one from the others. If you [were to] look, you wouldn't see them; if you [were to] listen, you wouldn't hear them; if you [were to] follow, you wouldn't touch them. That is why we say *yi*.[40]

In the beginning, there was *ch'i*[a]. From the Chinese viewpoint, human beings and the myriad creatures that make up the universe are all different configurations of *ch'i*[a]. They share in the same life-energy and in the spirit that constitutes it. This was the way philosophers interpreted cosmic and human beginnings before the time of Chou and Chu.

Indeed, Chu offers his own understanding of the emergence of the primal human pair:

> In the beginning of Heaven and Earth, how did the human race take its start? Naturally it happened with the formation of *ch'i*[a], giving rise to two humans. After that came so many myriad things. That is why [the *Diagram*] mentions the Way of *Ch'ien* making the male, and the Way of *K'un*[a] making the female. Only after that does it talk about the transformation of the myriad things. Had there not been the original pair of two humans, how would we have today so many people?[41]

Ch'i[a] obviously remained an important concept in the time of Chu Hsi and his predecessors. It is associated with both Taoist and Confucian thinking, although its origins are more Taoist, as already mentioned in chapter 1. From the philosophers Chang Tsai and Ch'eng Yi, Chu himself learned to reflect deeply with the help of *ch'i*[a] and its coordinate *li*[a]. Indeed, these two concepts—and we should place *li*[a] before *ch'i*[a] for logical, as well as ontological, considerations—are the warp and woof of the philosophical fabric that makes up Chu's system, into which he also introduced the Great Ultimate. But *ch'i*[a] appears in the explanatory text of Chou's *Diagram* only once: in the words the "five *ch'i*[a]," that is, the *ch'i*[a] of the Five Phases.

If *li*[a], a metaphysical concept introduced by Hua-yen Buddhism, serves as an organizing principle, imposing a form on *ch'i*[a], the latter remains the individuating principle. We are what we are because of the kind of *ch'i* we are endowed with. Nevertheless, Chu's great contribution is the logical and ontological priority he gives to *li*[a] over *ch'i*[a] in his philosophy, which marks it as essentially different from Taoist philosophy. On the other hand, following Ch'eng Yi, he demonstrates as well his difference from Hua-yen Buddhism by his acceptance of the substrative reality *ch'i*[a] into his system in place of the phenomenal *shih*, which, together with *li*[a], gives structure to Hua-yen philosophy.

Chu Hsi makes a few comments on Chang Tsai's cosmology, especially regarding how the *ch'i*[a] of *yin* and *yang*, which Chang calls "wandering *ch'i*[a]," gives rise to human beings and the myriad things.[42] He also thinks Chang's Great Void (*T'ai-hsü*) originally referred to the *Wu-chi* but eventually only referred to *Wu*[a].[43] He otherwise refrains from making lengthy quotations and remarks. Chu does not find in Chang's Great Harmony (*T'ai-ho*) and Great Void the same creative tensions that he discerns in Chou's Great Ultimate. Even more, he does not favor Chang's declared preference for *ch'i*ᵃ, regarded more as matter than spirit, as constituting both the Great Harmony and the Great Void:

> Question: When Chang Tsai says the Great Void is *ch'i*ᵃ, what is he saying?
> Answer: He is also saying *li*ᵃ. But he is not clear about it.
> Question: What of the Great Harmony?
> Answer: It also refers to *ch'i*ᵃ.[44]

The problem with Chang's cosmology is his tendency to reduce everything to *ch'i*ᵃ, thus making any distinction between the Great Void and the Great Harmony superfluous and giving the impression of teaching materialism. Chu knows this and so pronounces: "Generally what [Chang] said then had many mistakes."[45]

All the same, Chu shows much attachment to the "Western Inscription." While admitting that Chang is referring to *ch'i*ᵃ when Chang says, "What fills the universe I regard as my body; what directs the universe I regard as my nature,"[46] Chu still maintains repeatedly (although without ground) that Chang's whole teaching in the "Western Inscription" may be summed up by the sentence "*Li*ᵃ is one but with many manifestations."[47] And he tries to associate the teaching of the "Western Inscription" with the Great Ultimate:

> *Wu-chi erh T'ai-chi!* This does not say there is something glittering somewhere. It only says there used to be nothing except for this *li*ᵃ, and with this *li*ᵃ comes this *ch'i*ᵃ [and so on. . . .] The "Western Inscription" corroborates all of this.[48]

The Two Faces of the One Symbol

For Chu Hsi, the topmost circle in Chou's *Diagram* represents *Wu-chi erh T'ai-chi*. In contrast to the second circle, which is a configuration of black and white bands, it is quite empty; its very emptiness signifies the transcendence of the concept represented. Only with the second circle do we move to the concept of change, with the alternation of light and darkness. This does not mean that each of these circles represents a different reality. After all, Chu also admits that the Great Ultimate is present within change itself. He wishes at the same time to safeguard its transcendence of change and its immanence in change.

But then, to prevent the *T'ai-chi* from becoming only a thing among many, Chu insists on its being also *Wu-chi*. I shall elaborate on this when I discuss his disputes with Lu Chiu-yüan in chapter 7. From Chu Hsi's own explanation of the Great Ultimate in terms of the *Wu-chi*, we perceive that the term represents a concept that is actually beyond conceptualization and that can be described only with words which suggest the infinity transcending all space and shape. A possible image is the sky, which appears infinite, and which, under the name Heaven, is an apt symbol for the concept of the Great Ultimate.

Chu asserts that the *Wu-chi* refers to the Limitless: that beyond which one can go no further. In English, we might use the words "infinite" or "immeasurable."

Chou Tun-yi's contribution is thus in making clear that the Great Ultimate transcends being and nothingness, shape and form, space and time.[49] And while Chu affirms that Lao-tzu teaches being as coming from nothingness, he insists that Chou does not. According to him, the term *Wu-chi* refers, not to nothingness, but rather to that which transcends both being and nothingness. He explains this by reference to Chou's mystical insight:

> For Master Chou has seen the Tao-in-itself and knows it to be beyond ordinary conceptions. Heedless of others' criticisms and of his own advantage or disadvantage, he bravely came forward, uttering the truth that no one has dared to express. Henceforth scholars could clearly perceive the wonder of the Great Ultimate, which belongs neither to being nor to nothingness, neither to space nor to form. If one would only see this, one would know that this venerable man has really received the secret which has not been transmitted since the time of the thousand sages.[50]

"Uttering the truth that no one has dared to express"—this hints at why Chu himself hesitated for over two decades before making public his teaching of the Great Ultimate. It was a concept from outside the Confucian tradition, and it was best understood through mystical experience, which is private and subjective. The apparent truth it points to is very public: about the universe and our relationship to it. But there is also a more esoteric message: that of transcendence. For *T'ai-chi* is also *Wu-chi*. And the negative language, together with the transcendence it represents, was not easily acceptable to a philosophical world dominated by disciples of the two Ch'engs. Besides, the term "Tao-in-itself" (*Tao-t'i*) is more Taoist than Confucian, and Chu knew it. I am thinking of both classical Taoist philosophy and neo-Taoist philosophy, the latter of which has influenced generations of religious Taoists as well in their practice of yoga and meditation for the sake of union with the Tao.

For Chu Hsi, the Great Ultimate subsists of itself and does not depend on the action or effect of others. It is supreme and capable of generating other things.[51] Chu also says that the Great Ultimate was present "before the beginning of Heaven and Earth."[52] Presumably, the reference to Heaven made in relation to Earth is as nature rather than a supreme power. But this statement also confirms the status of the Great Ultimate as that which was prior to the natural universe and which was somehow the cause of the alternation of motion and rest or stillness in *yang* and *yin* which gave birth to all things. Here, it is interesting that Chu generally refrains from much discussion of the *Wu-chi* except in the context of the *T'ai-chi*.

For Lu Chiu-yüan, Chu's description of the Great Ultimate as a secret teaching was unacceptable. "Who says the [teaching of the] Great Ultimate was ever hidden from people?" he replied to Chu's letter. "[Did you] use words that show your study of Ch'an Buddhism? To keep a teaching private to oneself as a secret and then, while holding on to this secret, to present [other] often lengthy textual expositions only permits what is hidden to leak out."[53]

From the Great Ultimate to Li[a]

Does the Great Ultimate belong to the realm of *li*[a] or of *ch'i*[a]? Chou Tun-yi never answered this question clearly, but Chu was quite sure of his own answer: "*Wu-chi erh T'ai-chi*. This is shapeless but full of *li*[a]. Master Chou is afraid that people will look for another Great Ultimate outside the Great Ultimate, and so calls it *Wu-chi*."[54]

The word *li*[a] does not appear in Chou's explanatory text. However, there is a short chapter in Chou's *Penetrating the Book of Changes* which bears the title "Hsing, Li, Ming," that is, "Nature, Principle, and Destiny." In it, Chou says:

> The Two *ch'i*[a] and the Five Phases interact and produce the myriad things. The Five [tend toward] differentiation; the Two [tend toward a single] reality. Their duality is rooted in unity. The Myriad constitute the One; the One divides into the Myriad. Myriad and One are equally correct; Small and Great both have their own norm.[55]

Obviously, Chou is speaking here of the cosmic process, of *yin* and *yang* as two modes of change for the Five Phases, and of the basic unity in the multiplicity. Fung Yu-lan points out the designation here of *yin* and *yang* as energy or ether (*ch'i*[a]), a name given in the *Diagram*'s *Explanation* to the Five Phases themselves. Chou appears to assign both Two and Five to the same realm of becoming, while pointing out that where the Five Phases perform a function of differentiation, the Two Energies of *yin* and *yang* serve to bring multiplicity back to unity in the circular process in which becoming flows from being and always returns to being. But he never refers to the One as either *li*[a] or *ch'i*[a]. Fung believes this indicates that Chou had *li*[a] in mind when he discussed *T'ai-chi*.[56] This is hard to substantiate, since the *li*[a] and *ch'i*[a] coordinates came into use after him, especially with Ch'eng Yi, who made them the backbone of his structure. Even if Fung is correct, it still took Chu to make explicit what is implicit in Chou's work. Chu's definitive contribution is in interpreting Chou's Great Ultimate with the help of the concept of *li*[a], those "principles" that constitute all things, a viewpoint that he inherited from Ch'eng Yi. *Li*[a] may be defined as organizing and normative principles. In Chu Hsi's words: "The Great Ultimate is simply the excellent and supremely good normative principle (*tao-li*). . . . What Master Chou calls the Great Ultimate is the exemplary virtue (*piao-te*) for all that is good and perfect in Heaven and Earth, in men and things."[57]

As a principle of plenitude, the most perfect *Li*[a], or the Great Ultimate, is also for Chu a primal, ontological archetype, indeterminate and therefore belonging to the realm above shapes, the realm of Tao. In this sense, it is more like Plotinus's One, a being beyond beings, rather than a being among beings, the *li*[a] with a small letter, which is limited and determinate. It is also the highest good. That is why Fung Yu-lan compares it to Plato's Form of the Good and to Aristotle's God.[58] This is of course to be understood in the context of the outer manifestation or function (*yung*) more than in that of the inner reality or substance (*t'i*). In Chu's philosophy, the Great Ultimate serves the function of the Form of the Good in Platonism, or that of God in Aristotelianism.

On another level, that of becoming, Chu also sees the Great Ultimate as being present in the *ch'i*ᵃ of *yin* and *yang*. With the Great Ultimate, we are already in transition to the realm of change, the realm of *ch'i*ᵃ, the dynamic energy behind movement and change. After all, "the *T'ai-chi* moves and engenders *yang*. When its motion reaches an Ultimate, there is stillness. In stillness it engenders *yin*."⁵⁹ Chu is, of course, merely repeating Chou's words. But he sees the Great Ultimate also as *ch'i*ᵃ, indeed, dispersing into five kinds of *ch'i*ᵃ—the Five Phases— and then distributing into the myriad things. However, generally speaking, he associates it more with *li*ᵃ. We might explain the differences by distinguishing between the two faces of the Great Ultimate, a principle both of being (*li*ᵃ) and of becoming (*ch'i*ᵃ).

Why did Chu interpret the Great Ultimate more in terms of *li*ᵃ than of *ch'i*ᵃ? I would venture that he wished to rise above any purely materialist interpretation of what he regarded as First Principle of all beings and goodness. In so doing, he also kept a distance from its alleged Taoist origins. But in assigning the Great Ultimate more to the realm above shapes, that of the invisible and transcendent *li*ᵃ, a passive principle, albeit the principle of all goodness and being, Chu made his own contribution. He differentiated the Great Ultimate from what we shall discuss in the next chapter: the ghosts and spirits (*kuei-shen*), who belong more to the realm of *ch'i*ᵃ.

Chu repeatedly insists that the Great Ultimate is full of *li*ᵃ, that which constitutes the myriad things, that which also determines good and evil.⁶⁰ It is prior to things and yet also after the creation of things; it is outside *yin* and *yang* and yet operates in the midst of *yin* and *yang*; it penetrates all things, is absent nowhere, and yet originally was without sound, smell, shadow, or echo. The following explanations may possibly deflect certain criticisms about some of the contradictions: "What is called *T'ai-chi* is only the *li*ᵃ of the two *ch'i*ᵃ [of *yin* and *yang*] and the Five Phases. It's not that there is another entity called *T'ai-chi*. In terms of *li*ᵃ, one cannot say it's there; in terms of things, one cannot say it is not there."⁶¹ "*T'ai-chi* is present in *yin* and *yang* as *yin* and *yang*, and in the Five Phases as Five Phases. It is only one and the same *li*ᵃ. Because it is the Ultimate [*li*ᵃ], it is called the Great Ultimate."⁶²

The Great Ultimate as *Li*ᵃ is Chu Hsi's comprehensive philosophical principle, that which determines the whole of his philosophical design, that in which he grounds the development of his entire thought. This may surprise us when we recall how Chu heard of this concept only in his late thirties. However, he had been drifting philosophically for a long time, apparently all during his twenties and well into his thirties. Grasping the concept of the Great Ultimate, Chu would take giant steps in constructing his philosophical system.

The Great Ultimate, or *T'ai-chi*, is *li*ᵃ but present in *ch'i*ᵃ. If described only as *li*ᵃ, it remains on the abstract level. When described as the *li*ᵃ of *ch'i*ᵃ, it takes on a certain existence in the process of change and transformation. To maintain some kind of transcendence for *T'ai-chi*, Chu uses the metaphor of a horse to describe the relationship between the Great Ultimate and change as *T'ai-chi* "riding on the incipiency (*chi*ᵇ) of motion and a stillness." In other words, it does not depend on *ch'i*ᵃ while being involved in *ch'i*ᵃ.⁶³

Chu Hsi also appears to say that Chou's Great Ultimate is the *totality* of being—of all the principles (*li*ª) of the myriad things brought together into a single whole. In other words, he repeats that *Li*ª is one but its manifestations are many:

> There is only one *li*ª that permeates all things. It is like a grain of millet, growing to become a seedling, which produces a flower. The flower bears seeds that become millet again. . . . One ear of millet will bear one hundred grains and yet each grain is integral to itself. . . . Every thing has its *li*ª, but all *li*ª are one and the same.[64]

Chu alludes frequently to a Buddhist metaphor when explaining how *li*ª is one but its manifestations are many:

> Just as the moon is in heaven:
> It is only one,
> Yet it is reflected in rivers and lakes;
> It can be seen everywhere;
> It should not be called divided.[65]

He says also that the Great Ultimate is present in all things: "Every human being has a Great Ultimate; every thing has a Great Ultimate. What Master Chou called *T'ai-chi* is the paradigm of ten thousand virtues for Heaven and Earth, human beings and things."[66] When asked whether he was referring to the Great Ultimate here as *li*ª or as *ch'i*ª, he answered, "As *li*ª."[67]

A question that arises concerns whether the Great Ultimate is simply the totality of all the individual *li*ª in all things, or whether it is *also* the great *Li*ª, that is, the *Li*ª of the universe, as somehow transcendent of the individual *li*ª.[68]

Fung Yu-lan answers that it is both. He reminds us that Chu Hsi has said: "Originally there is only one Great Ultimate. Each of the myriad things partakes of it, and yet each holds the Great Ultimate in entirety."[69] Fung refers to the Buddhist *tathāgata-garbha* (storehouse of the absolute) idea, which maintains that each and every thing is the *tathāgata-garbha* in its entirety while possessing within itself the natures of all other things.[70] This means that there is a difference between the *tathāgata-garbha* or Great Ultimate per se and the natures or principles of all things.

The important difference is that if the Great Ultimate is only the totality of all the principles of things, it would not transcend these things. To ensure such transcendence, Chu Hsi insisted that the Great Ultimate is also the *Wu-chi*. And in doing so, he showed that his Great Ultimate is very much like the philosophical and religious Absolute in other traditions. As an example, I quote the fifteenth-century German philosopher of paradox, Nicholas of Cusa, a bishop and cardinal and an ecumenist who strove for the reunion of the Eastern and Western churches. For him, the universe is a likeness of the Absolute, also called God:

> God, by reason of his immensity, is neither in the sun nor the moon, yet in an absolute way he is. So the universe is neither in the sun nor in the moon, yet in a restricted fashion it is. . . . [In] the universe identity consists in

diversity as unity consists in plurality. . . . The universe, then, is not the sun nor the moon, yet it is in the sun in the sun and the moon in the moon; on the other hand, God is not the sun in the sun nor the moon in the moon but He is without plurality and diversity what the sun and moon are.[71]

Also: "God is in all things in such a way that all things are in him."[72] Interestingly, Nicholas of Cusa recounts how his whole system came to him with a sudden illumination received during a return voyage from Greece.[73] So he, too, has seen the Tao-in-itself, although he calls it by another name.

A Cyclical Process

I suggested earlier that the Great Ultimate also refers to a cyclical, cosmic process. This touches on the question of the Great Ultimate as first principle. The Great Ultimate may be considered the first principle if we are speaking logically but not if we are speaking temporally.

In the *Classified Conversations*, Chu is asked this question and answers:

Question: Is [the process] beginning with the movement of *yang* and ending with the engendering of human beings and things a simultaneous event, or is it divided into orderly phases?
Answer: We cannot speak of temporal sequence for the Tao, but there is need of order. . . . There must have been a universe before the Great Ultimate, just as we have daylight today following yesterday's dark night. . . . In the beginning things were dim and dark, with brightness emerging gradually. That's why there is order, but everything is already there.
Question: If we go back to before the Great Ultimate in this way, shouldn't we do so for what follows?
Answer: Of course.[74]

The answer is quite ambiguous in relation to temporal sequence but clear in affirming cyclical change. Here, the Great Ultimate represents cosmic change, not from nothing to something, but from darkness to light, again and again. It is a reflection of the reversion of the Tao in the *Lao-tzu*. The trouble is in relating this answer to the Great Ultimate as the first principle. Is the Great Ultimate one or many, if we can speak metaphorically of "before" and "after"? I presume that the same idea of *li*[a] being one with many manifestations should explain this paradox.

What this also suggests is a possibly infinite universe. In mature life, Chu applies Shao Yung's cosmic chronology to the understanding of Chou's concept, mentioning cyclical "generations" of 129,600 years. "But then, before those 129,600 years, there was another big change, and so on and so forth."[75] When asked if the universe can ever be destroyed, he answers no, except that when human beings become thoroughly depraved, there will be a cosmic catastrophe, followed by further regeneration.[76]

With the revolution in high technology and the development of those skills that carry the seeds of destruction for humankind, perhaps our looming crisis today may help us accept Chu's suggestions on how to understand cosmic order and change.[77] On the other hand, Chu has not chosen to say much about the ceaseless, cyclical change initiated by the Great Ultimate. He generally seems satisfied with the top-to-bottom reading of the *Diagram*, with its presumed suggestion of one life span at a time and its focus on one universe: our present one.

An Examination of the *Wu-chi*

It is possible to better understand Chu's conception of the Great Ultimate by examining a controversy between him and the Lu brothers. The Chu/Lu controversy over the Great Ultimate can be examined in the exchange of correspondence between Chu Hsi and the Lu brothers in 1188–89.[78] The questions discussed include textual and ideological problems—Confucianism versus Taoism—as well as serious philosophical issues.

First is the etymological-lexical problem. In ordinary parlance, the word *chi*[a], with a wood radical, refers to the ridgepole of a roof, the highest horizontal timber of a house. As this is frequently equidistant from all four sides, Lu Chiu-yüan asserts it to have two connotations: the first being an "extreme" or ultimate; and the second, an extended meaning of the "middle"—the Mean, even the Mean of emotions, which he contends is the meaning in ancient texts. When signifying the ultimate, it requires no further help from another term, such as the *Wu-chi*. But without resorting to the *via negationis*, he prefers to understand the Great Ultimate in terms of the Mean—the cosmic principle in terms of psychic equilibrium—as he claims Chou Tun-yi himself has done in *Penetrating the Book of Changes*.[79]

Indeed, for Lu, to say *Wu-chi* would be tantamount to saying there is no "middle," which he cannot accept. Chu Hsi, on his part, sees *chi*[a] in the context of the Book of Changes as meaning "pole" or "ultimate," with a normative connotation, as in *huang-chi* (imperial ultimate) or *min-chi* (people's ultimate). In the case of the expression *Wu-chi*, he insists that it refers to that which is formless, shapeless, and spaceless, and therefore invisible, inaudible, and beyond all sense knowledge.

Chu agrees that the word *chi*[a] in *T'ai-chi* literally refers to the ridgepole of a roof but emphasizes the fact that it has *many* meanings and refers philosophically to the "Ultimate," the utmost in perfection. He insists that its primary importance is in representing the cosmic first principle, but that certain thinkers take it to stand for the Mean or middle precisely because it has so many meanings.[80]

Chu prefers to argue on metaphysical grounds. He says to Lu Chiu-shao: "Without mention of *Wu-chi*, *T'ai-chi* becomes only a thing [among other things] and cannot be the root of myriad transformations. Without mention of *T'ai-chi*, *Wu-chi* becomes empty and cannot be the root of the myriad transformations."[81] He sees *Wu-chi* and *T'ai-chi* as two sides of the same reality, the ultimate reality that is also the ontological ground of change and transformation. Then, answering Lu Chiu-shao's criticism that *Wu-chi* is an empty concept, Chu asks him: "I don't know if what you call *T'ai-chi* is a visible or an invisible thing. If it is invisible but full of *Li*ᵃ, then clearly *Wu-chi* is invisible while *T'ai-chi* is full of *li*ᵃ. Why should one speak of it as empty?"[82]

The Lu brothers argue that since the term *Wu-chi* is not found even in those passages of the *T'ung-shu* where Chou Tun-yi discusses the problem of the One and Many, of *yin-yang* and the Five Phases, there is ground for questioning whether he even intended to incorporate it in his *Diagram* and *Explanation*. The fact that it is there could be an interpolation or represent an earlier, less mature view which Chou later repudiated.[83]

In a long reply to Lu Chiu-yüan, Chu has this to say about the textual problems surrounding the Book of Changes:

> According to what I see, Fu-hsi created the [trigrams of the Book of] Changes, going from line to line; King Wen explained [the lines] of the Changes, going from [the hexagram] *Ch'ien* on, all without mentioning *T'ai-chi*. But Confucius mentioned it. Confucius praised the [Book of Changes], moving from *T'ai-chi* to other concepts, without mentioning *Wu-chi*. But Chou Tun-yi mentioned it. After all, the earlier and later sages all follow the same line and develop one another's thinking.[84]

He seems to be arguing from the coherence of the concept, invoking the sages who allegedly contributed to its evolution. Here, of course, the mention of Fu-hsi and the much-venerated King Wen, father of King Wu of Chou, follows the tradition about the formation of the Book of Changes, and the reference to Confucius is to him as the alleged author or compiler of the Ten Wings, or appendices, which offer much more philosophical content to the Book of Changes.

Chu also emphasizes that giving two names does not make two things, that the *T'ai-chi* is also called the Tao: "Master Chou calls it *Wu-chi* because [the *T'ai-chi*] has no shape and occupies no space. . . . Should you now criticize this, you are also saying that the *T'ai-chi* has a shape and occupies space."[85]

Lu Chiu-yüan does not accept the argument, asserting that Confucius never used the term *Wu-chi*, which is quite unnecessary for understanding *T'ai-chi* as the Tao.[86] He also objects to the term *Wu-chi* because it stems from the Taoist, rather than Confucian, tradition. He points out how *Lao-tzu*, chapter I, refers to Nothingness (*wu*) or the Nameless as the Beginning of Heaven and Earth, and to Being (*yu*) or the Named as Mother of the myriad things, and later identifies the two. He criticizes the inherent ambiguity of this doctrine, which would seem to make nothingness the source of being.[87]

The argument is more than merely textual or ideological. The Lu brothers fear that naming the Great Ultimate as the *Wu-chi* is equivalent to negating the ground of Confucian ethics, which is rooted in the metaphysical first principle. As Lu Chiu-yüan puts it: "This principle (*li*ᵃ) is what the universe originally possessed. How can one say it is not there (*wu*)? Should one consider it as nonexistent, then the ruler will not be a ruler, the minister not a minister, the father not a father, the son not a son."[88]

The Lu brothers are not against the idea of the Great Ultimate. They just interpret it differently. For them, the Great Ultimate is the cosmic paradigm, that upon which the sage, as human paradigm, models his own life and behavior, ensuring within himself the harmony of the emotions that is a mirror of the harmony of the cosmos and, by so doing, ensuring also social harmony for the human universe. This is the teaching of the *Doctrine of the Mean*, one of the Four Books so revered by the Confucian tradition.

Chu Hsi, on his part, attempts first and foremost to safeguard the transcendence of the Great Ultimate. "If we don't mention *Wu-chi*, then the *T'ai-chi* becomes like one [of many] things and not the root and ground of the myriad transformations. If we don't mention *T'ai-chi*, then the *Wu-chi* becomes empty and [also] cannot be the root and ground of the myriad transformations."[89]

The controversy over the *Wu-chi erh T'ai-chi* concerns more than the paradox inherent in the statement itself. Such also reminds us of Lao-tzu's philosophy with its apparent ethical indifference, and it refers also to the cult of immortality that surrounded the usage of the term *T'ai-chi* and of the diagram bearing its name. Chu Hsi, however, claims ignorance regarding the antecedents of the *Diagram*. He bases his defense of the usage of the term on philosophical grounds only: "Lao-tzu speaks of being and nothingness as two things. Master Chou speaks of being and nothingness as one. They are as different as the south is from the north."[90]

One may discern in this position an eagerness to assimilate into his intellectual synthesis and world outlook certain ideas and insights which issue out of both philosophical and religious Taoism. Chu Hsi had an avid curiosity. His ambition was to encompass all knowledge, to find a place for all knowledge in his own system. For this he recommended "investigation of things"—to discovering their principles, their "Great Ultimates." Only after this is done does he await enlightenment, *the* Ultimate beyond all Ultimates. For him, the first principle (Great Ultimate) is therefore at the same time beginning, end, and exemplar of all things. Chu Hsi could accept no limit to his horizons. His principle is to include everything and therefore to exclude nothing (*Wu-chi*).

A possible reason for Chu's preference for balancing the *Wu-chi* and the *T'ai-chi* in a creative tension rather than opting for the *T'ai-chi* as coming from the *Wu-chi* could well be his preference for the priority of *li*[a] over *ch'i*[a]. Given the Taoist propensity for seeing in the primal *ch'i*[a] the beginning of all things, Chu would be reluctant to say that the *T'ai-chi*, which is more *li*[a] than *ch'i*[a], came from the *Wu-chi*, which Taoists would interpret in terms of *ch'i*[a]. In maintaining the tension between *Wu-chi* and *T'ai-chi*, Chu is far from choosing a dualistic interpretation of the origin of the universe. Rather, he is opting for the primacy of *li*[a]. After all, the *Wu-chi* and the *T'ai-chi* are only two faces of the same dialectical unity.[91]

Certainly, the differences between Chu and Lu extend to the whole range of their philosophical views, including their interpretations of the microcosm/macrocosm relationship. Chu Hsi makes certain distinctions between the metaphysical realm (above shapes) and the physical realm (within shapes). For him, the Great Ultimate belongs to the former realm, and the two modes of *yin* and *yang* belong to the latter, even if the former is also said to be immanent in the latter. For Lu, however, the two realms are almost identical, the macrocosm being immanent in the microcosm.[92]

Let me recall that Chu published his *Explanations to the Diagram of the Great Ultimate* in 1188. It appears that his correspondence with the Lu brothers was being widely circulated then among scholars, and that therefore he could wait no longer to publish his long-held views on this subject to a wider audience. From Chou Tun-yi's extant works, Chu "received the secret which has not been transmitted since the time of the thousand sages." He was finally ready to share the secret. His teachings on the Great Ultimate were to become open and public.

Conclusion

Was Chu overambitious? Does the Great Ultimate, in his interpretation, remain unassimilated in his system of li^a and $ch'i^a$? This is the opinion of some scholars. Yamanoi Yū argues that Chu never uses the term *T'ai-chi* in explaining the Four Books, the most important and defining corpus of texts for the Confucian tradition.[93] This is quite true. But the Four Books contain hardly any cosmological references, and I respect Chu for not imposing such a category from outside the corpus to explain the meaning of the texts. I believe, though, that Chu has offered the beginning of a solution by calling the Great Ultimate the li^a of the $ch'i^a$ of *yin* and *yang*, the agents of change and transformation. I would like to rest the case here, pointing to Chu's efforts to create a philosophical architectonic, with the Great Ultimate at its top. Whether the entire edifice possesses sufficient coherence is another question.

As already shown, Chu's interest in cosmogony is manifest in his poetry. He refers, for example, to the K'un-lun Shan, a vast mountain range in western China considered by Taoists as a divine abode, and a symbol also of both the sky and the human head. In his poem, Chu appears to use it to represent primarily the sky, that image of the Great Ultimate, and offers his philosophical beliefs in these words:

> K'un-lun is huge and peerless,
> The edges go deep and wide.
> *Yin* and *yang* do not stop interacting,
> Winter and summer replace each other.
> [Fu] Hsi, the ancient and divine emperor
> With wondrous wisdom looked once up and down.
> No need for horses and charts,
> Human words have made it clear.
> One principle (Li^a) penetrates all
> Radiantly, and not with vague images.
> Honor to the Venerable Wu-chi [i.e., Chou Tun-yi]
> Who made this clear to me.[94]

K'un-lun Shan, the abode of the gods, appears to stand for the Great Ultimate, attributed to the mythical culture hero Fu-hsi, inventor of the trigrams for the Book of Changes. It is interesting that Chu disclaims here the need for "horses and charts," a reference to the legend of the River Chart, in which the trigrams appeared on the back of a dragon-horse emerging from the Yellow River. He opts rather for philosophical understanding modeled on sagely wisdom, declaring that "one principle penetrates all," and therefore reinterpreting Chou's diagram with the help of Ch'eng Yi's metaphysics.

The philosophy of the Great Ultimate offers a metaphysical interpretation of the cosmos, including its origin and its cyclical process of movement and of return to rest, in terms of the interaction of the cosmic force of *yin* and *yang* with the Five Phases (Fire, Water, Wood, Metal, and Earth). The Great Ultimate is the Tao of the universe, less its cause than its source, its ontological exemplar. But it is also source as ontological beginning, since Chu speaks of the Great Ultimate as what transcends time and space, as opposed to that which lies within time and space. For that reason, the Great Ultimate is also called the *Wu-chi*, that beyond which the mind can go no farther. And it is the untranslatable, the Nameless, that of which the mind can make no determinate concept. A dialectical language is used here, a language not only difficult to translate but also open to diverse interpretations. One way of understanding is to take the statement *Wu-chi erh T'ai-chi* as a Ch'an Buddhist riddle, a *kung-an* or *koan*, that is meant to provoke us to go beyond discursive thinking into the realm of the intuitive and the mystical. This does not render the concept Buddhist. It just involves borrowing a Buddhist technique to propel the mind to go beyond words and concepts, names and their translations.

By analogy, we might say the Great Ultimate is like God or necessary being in Thomas Aquinas's system, that which *subsists*, in and of itself, without depending on others, while all others *exist*, in and of the Great Ultimate. But the analogy is imperfect, as the Great Ultimate is, on another level, immanent as well as transcendent. It is above all things and yet present in all things. It is above motion and rest and yet involved in a cyclical cosmic process. The dialectic goes on.

To speak of the Great Ultimate in itself is to remain on the level of the One. But the One can only be understood when opposed to others, to the Two, and to the Many, in a dialectic that is as truly Chinese as the macrocosm/microcosm outlook. And so, if the Great One, the Ultimate, through the symbol of the Pole Star, ruler of its own constellation, represents Being, then the sun (*yang*) and the moon (*yin*) represent becoming, that which comes about with alternation of activity and quiescence, with relativity. The mythical, religious, and philosophical meanings of our symbols are themselves convergent; they lead us from the basic intuition of the "sympathy of the whole" to an enriched understanding of how the human being and the universe can discover themselves in each other, and all things in themselves.[95] The study of the symbolism of the Great Ultimate is itself also indicative of the wealth of thought and knowledge one can derive from the formidable Book of Changes itself, so often maligned and misunderstood and yet a veritable mirror of both the cosmic and the psychic universe. By his incorporation of Chou's cosmology into the synthesis of his philosophy, Chu Hsi was consciously attempting to integrate the entire cosmological legacy of the Chinese tradition as he knew it, in a form in which it could be transmitted to later generations.

The Great Ultimate is at the same time above change and within change and creativity. The Great Ultimate is present also in the Five Phases, in the changes they effect, and in the final "fruit" that their collaboration and interaction bring about. For the Chinese philosophers—for Chou Tun-yi, Chu Hsi, and the Lu brothers—the One is actually also many, since *li*ª is one but manifest in many, while the many is also One, as its manifestations. Being is the principle of becoming, and becoming is also transmuted into being. The richness and profundity of the Chinese macrocosm/microcosm outlook allows comparisons with Western philosophers known for their dialectical logic and synthetic genius. Nicholas of Cusa is one such philosopher, whose *coincidentia oppositorum* goes back to Neo-platonist philosophy and to the medieval mystical thinker Meister Eckhart; and there was A. N. Whitehead, of whom more will be said.

The *coincidentia oppositorum* is actually the secret of Chinese philosophy, the explanation for its unique development, the symbol of its aspirations. In this light, the universe is indeed a circle, the center of which is everywhere and the circumference nowhere. To understand the Great Ultimate is also to understand the ultimate mystery in the universe—the cosmic as well as the human. When one possesses such knowledge, one is seen to rise, indeed, to the status of the sage.

THREE

Spiritual Beings (*Kuei-shen*)

Spring colors in the West Garden beckoning,
I rushed up there in straw sandals.
A thousand blossoms and ten thousand buds in red and purple:
Who knows the creative mind of Heaven and Earth?

Chu Hsi[1]

Introduction

The attractions of nature drew Chu to reflections on the creative mind of Heaven and Earth and, associated with this, to questions about spiritual beings. In this context, I shall deal with Chu's views on the existence of a supreme being and of beings like ghosts and spirits. I shall also explain Chu's interpretation of the natural universe—of Heaven and Earth and how they came to be. While Chu treats the subject of ghosts and spirits before that of a supreme deity, I shall proceed from discussion of Heaven to ghosts and spirits, in order to give more systematic order to the chapter. My discussion of Heaven in this chapter should be read while keeping in mind my discussion of the Great Ultimate in chapter 2.

I may note here that Chu does not appear to have struggled as much over the concept of spiritual beings as he struggled over more human subjects such as *jen*[a] or human consciousness and the unmanifest (*wei-fa*) and manifest (*yi-fa*) states relating to the emotions. Most of what he has to say about spirits comes from the *Classified Conversations*. While the subject is an important part of his teachings, it does not occupy the principal place, which is given to the Great Ultimate.[2]

Interestingly, his answers show an influence from Ch'eng Yi, his acknowledged philosophical predecessor, while differing from Ch'eng's own and, indeed, going beyond Ch'eng.[3] Driven by a great intellectual curiosity, Chu demonstrated his desire to understand the origin and structure of the universe. Here, his tendency is to use the theory of *yin* and *yang* and the Five Phases, as well as explanations deriving from the theory of numbers, to present his own philosophy of nature and then to go on to elucidate the big religious questions concerning a supreme deity and other spiritual beings with the theoretical legacy he received from Chang Tsai and Ch'eng Yi.[4]

On Heaven

In discussing the spiritual world according to Chu, I shall begin with Heaven, a concept he inherits from the remote past and reinterprets to give it new, philosophical content. "Heaven" (*T'ien*) is a term that has many meanings, in both English and Chinese, including the physical and natural and the spiritual and supernatural. Chu Hsi is keenly aware of this ambiguity. He acknowledges that the word sometimes refers—physically—to the "azure sky," that is, to the firmament above or nature in general; sometimes it refers—religiously—to a ruler (*chu-tsai*) above, a godlike-figure; and sometimes it refers—philosophically—just to principle (*li*ª), that is, a source of moral values also present in the human mind or heart as conscience.[5]

The third sense mentioned above is what Chu inherits from the Ch'eng brothers, who exalt heavenly principle, or *T'ien-li*, but emphasize the continuum between the human and the heavenly. Hsü Fu-kuan refers to their flat or horizontal intellectual universe which has humanized Mencius's Heaven, removing from it the more transcendent dimensions which came from the religion of antiquity. As a consequence, their world has only one level, that of the here and now. In his opinion, Chu Hsi's emphasis on the Great Ultimate marks his difference from this purely humanistic viewpoint, giving Chu's universe a more vertical dimension pointing as well to the hereafter.[6] Hsü's views are generally corroborated by Tang Chün-i, who also emphasizes the difference between the Ch'eng brothers' philosophies and those of their predecessors Chou, Shao, and Chang when it comes to a transcendent Heaven as present in the predecessors.[7]

I shall follow Chu's three senses of the term "Heaven," moving from the physical to the religious and then the philosophical.[8] Our discussion will deal with medieval Chinese worldviews underlying issues in the philosophy of nature that intersect with those in the philosophy of religion.

Heaven as Nature

Chu Hsi discusses Heaven sometimes as physical nature and sometimes as deity, but never quite in an entirely desacralized context. His vision of the cosmos, like that of many scholars of his time, is that of a vast open space, with celestial bodies floating in it at rare intervals. For him, the term "Heaven" can represent the cosmos, including therefore earth itself: "Heaven adheres to Earth's form through *ch'i*ª, and Earth attaches itself to Heaven's *ch'i*ª. Heaven comprehends Earth; Earth is one of the things within Heaven."[9] In discussions with disciples, Chu mentions with approval Ts'ai Yüan-ting's (Cai Yuanding, 1135–98) idea that the Sun and Moon are within Heaven, while Heaven is within the emptiness of the Great Void (*t'ai-hsü*), a term favored by Chang Tsai.[10]

In Chu's view, Heaven includes the immediate atmosphere of Earth as well as the blue firmament. Here, we have to accept that he spoke as a man of his times, with limited knowledge and information about the physical universe. For him, the universe is geocentric: Earth is situated at the center, surrounded by water, while its periphery touches Heaven, both above and below. Heaven rotates rapidly around Earth, which it covers as an egg encloses its yolk. And it is by this rotation, indeed, that Earth maintains its stability of position without falling.[11] Chu also made detailed calculations of the movements of the Sun, Moon, and stars, supporting the theory of seven intercalary months in nineteen years.[12]

Let us remember that the vast or infinite spatial context, contrary to the Ptolemaic-Aristotelian universe of solid concentric crystalline spheres, was regarded as more liquid than solid. Ironically, as Joseph Needham points out, the Jesuit missionaries, forbidden to spread to China the new idea of a heliocentric universe on account of the controversy over Galileo in Church circles, opposed the theory of liquid heavens and sought to replace it with the old Greek idea of the heavens as immutable and solid, an idea that would soon become obsolete in Europe itself.[13]

Traditional Chinese astronomy focused its attention on the Pole Star and the circumpolar stars as the basis for macrocosm/microcosm thinking. Just as the immutable Pole Star was surrounded by other stars that revolved around it, so too the emperor on Earth was the center for his court ministers (*Analects* 2:1). Chinese astronomy developed a system of equatorial divisions defined by points (*hsiu*) at which hour circles transected the equator. The *hsiu* are therefore segments of the celestial sphere that may be compared to segments of an orange.[14]

Chu devotes many discussions to Heaven or to "Heaven and Earth" (*T'ien-ti*), especially in the context of the natural universe.[15] He sees the emergence of the universe as a movement from chaos to order, from the undifferentiation of *ch'i*[a] to differentiation between *yin* and *yang* modes: "In the original chaos before Heaven and Earth were separated, I think there were only water and fire. What was sediment in the water became Earth. Today, when we rise high and look at the mountains, they all seem to present wavelike shapes."[16] As I said in Chapter 2, according to the ancient Taoist and eclectic texts, in the beginning there was only *ch'i*[a]. So Chu is speaking specifically of the *ch'i*[a] of water and fire rather than of water and fire themselves. The sediments of the *ch'i*[a] of water made up Earth, and the purest *ch'i*[a] of fire made up the luminaries: the Sun, Moon, and stars that, together with the rotating *ch'i*[a], make up Heaven.[17] We note here water and fire, the two symbols for the trigrams *K'an* and *Li*[b], and their presumed roles in the cosmogonic process.

The mention of water and fire is interesting, among other reasons because Chu was so enamored of Chou's *Diagram of the Great Ultimate*, a symbolic cosmogonic representation. As mentioned in chapter 1, it includes the representation of *yin* and *yang* in a circle enclosing two semicircles with areas of light and shade, which also stand for unbroken (*yang*) and broken (*yin*) lines of the Book of Changes' trigrams. The designated *yang* symbol is the trigram for fire, *li*[b], and the *yin* symbol is the trigram for water, *k'an*. Here too, water and fire appear early in the cosmic process of becoming. They appear as symbols, not as material elements, as in the Five Phases.

In a poem, Chu expresses his philosophical sentiments in these words:

> I watch the changes of *yin* and *yang*,
> Rising and falling within the Eight Cords.[18]

Gazing back, [I see] no beginning.
Looking forward, how can [I detect] an end?
The highest principle is here present,
Always the same, now and in the myriad generations.
Who said that Chaos (*Hun-tun*) has died:
A fool's talk to shock the deaf and blind![19]

For Chu, the sun has the strongest light, whereas the Moon only reflects the light from the Sun. Stars, however, are separated into those with their own light, "regular stars" (*ching-hsing*), and those without such, the irregular ones that we call planets. "The irregular stars are *yang* inside *yin*; the regular stars are *yin* inside *yang*." Presumably, this is so because the planets are bright objects formed of the *yin-ch'i*, while the real stars are the cohesion (i.e., *yin* of the *yang-ch'i*).[20]

Chu correlates his reflections on Heaven as physical nature with the Five Phases, which make up the middle part of Chou's *Diagram*. According to Chu, the interaction of the *ch'i*[a] of *yin* and *yang* gives rise to the Five Phases, which therefore belong to the same *ch'i*[a] in the universe:[21] "The best in the *ch'i*[a] goes to make spirits (*shen*[a]). [The Five Phases of] Metal, Wood, Water, Fire, and Earth are not spirits. Spirits are responsible for the emergence of these Five."[22] Here I have used the plural for the word "spirit," which in Chinese may be understood as either singular or plural. I find it interesting that Chu, in the course of explaining how the cosmos came to be, should offer his opinion on how *shen*[a], usually regarded as spirits, came to be, from the quasi-material *ch'i*[a], as well as how *shen*[a] gave rise to the Five Elements or Phases, considered as matter or "stuff" (*chih*[a]), made of *ch'i*[a].[23]

Obviously, Chu had Shao Yung and Chang Tsai in mind when he discussed these questions, because he praised each for their contributions.[24] In keeping with his own teachings on the investigation of things and extension of knowledge, Chu demonstrates his keen observation of natural phenomena and his layman's interest in astronomy, astronomical instruments, and calendrical calculations, as well as his philosopher's penchant for trying to offer theoretical explanations.[25]

Heaven as Lord and Master (Chu-tsai)

Such empirical reflections led Chu to wonder about the existence of a greater power. When asked whether Heaven has a "ruler" or "master," he would often give cryptic replies: "[Heaven] naturally rotates like this without cease. But it is not quite right here to say that there is [a ruler]. . . . Neither can one say there is no ruler whatsoever."[26] To make sense of what he says here, let us remember that Chu explains the word "Heaven" (*T'ien*) in the classics in different ways, according to the contexts. He comments upon the anthropomorphic Lord-on-High (*Shang-ti*) of the classics by saying that while it is incorrect to say that there is "a man in the heavens" who is lord and ruler of the world, the judge of sin and evil, it is equally wrong to say that "there is no such ruler." But even this lord should be understood in terms of *Li*[a]. This means that *Li*[a] serves as a kind of ruler in Heaven.[27]

This is where Heaven differs from ghosts and spirits. Heaven is regarded as belonging to the realm of *li*[a]; ghosts and spirits, more to that of *ch'i*[a]. Commenting on *Analects* 3:13, "He who offends Heaven has no one to pray to," Chu says, "Heaven is *li*[a]. It is supreme and peerless."[28]

Are there then two Heavens: one made of *ch'i*[a], and adhering to Earth, as a yolk does to the egg, and the other belonging only to the realm of *li*[a], a pure form without dynamic, material content or energy and superior to everything else, as is the Great Ultimate?

Chu does not answer such a question directly. There are terms that Chu Hsi used following Chang Tsai's lead.[29] They are *t'ien-hsin* (heavenly mind) and *t'ien-ti chih hsin* (the mind of Heaven and Earth).[30] He frequently used the latter to refer to the creative and life-giving power of Heaven and Earth or nature at large. He used the former several times analogously to refer to the ruler's mind. He also used it in Chang's sense to indicate Heaven's greatness: "Heaven is so great that there is nothing outside. It embraces all things. When [my mind] overlooks any of the principles of things, then it is not all-inclusive and not like Heaven's mind."[31] He seems to be speaking of a higher intelligence and intentionality and offers what might seem an argument from design about the existence of God:

> Should [Heaven and Earth] have no *hsin*[a], then cows would give birth to sheep, and the peach tree would produce pears. But [Heaven and Earth] . . . have been able to maintain self-determination [in these things]. . . . The *hsin*[a] is the locus of [Heaven and Earth as] ruler. That is why we say Heaven and Earth take the production of things as their *hsin*[a].[32]

When asked if this *hsin*[a] of Heaven and Earth is spiritually intelligent (*ling*), he answers: "We cannot say that the mind of Heaven and Earth is not spiritually intelligent. But it does not have to think and reason as do human beings."[33]

Referring directly to the ancient belief in a supreme deity, the Lord-on-High, he says: "As the word 'human' (*jen*[b]) resembles the word 'Heaven' (*T'ien*), the word *hsin*[a] resembles the word 'Lord' (*ti*)."[34] It would appear that he is trying to avoid anthropomorphism while admitting a creator—a power and intention in Heaven that directs the creative forces of the universe. But this is difficult to accomplish. When asked also if this *hsin*[a] is the "ruler" (*chu-tsai*), he responds: "Truly, the mind is the ruler. But what we call *chu-tsai* is nothing but *li*[a]."[35]

He falls back on a nonanthropomorphic, somewhat pantheistic explanation of Heaven as ruler and master, if we recall that *li*[a] as *T'ai-chi* serves also as the supreme One. But while it is clear that the word for "human" resembles that for Heaven (*T'ien*), a graph often interpreted as a man with a big head, Chu does not quite explain how the word for "mind" resembles that for the "lord." Nothing in their known etymologies suggests that. Besides, the association of mind with *li*[a] is also unusual, as Chu usually regards mind to be the locus of *ch'i*[a]. This is a subject that will come up in chapter 5, on human nature. We are left here only with an ambiguity about the Heaven above Heaven-and-Earth. Is it pure *li*[a] or is it *li*[a] and *ch'i*[a]? To put it differently, is Heaven above Heaven-and-Earth, this Heaven which has a mind of its own? And when "mind" is used with reference to Heaven, is it only used as a metaphor, or does it signify an intelligent Heaven?

These questions are made more difficult because Chu also declares that the human being is "the mind-and-heart of Heaven and Earth." In one context, he is referring to fortunes and misfortunes, calamities and perversities, as results of human passions or desires.[36] He appears to be once more identifying the transcendent with the immanent, while emphasizing human freedom to shape destiny.

Heaven, the Heavenly Principle (T'ien-li), and the Heavenly Mind (T'ien-hsin)

As already mentioned in chapter 1, the term *T'ien-li* is found in the chapter on music in the Book of Rites, where it refers to human nature in itself and is contrasted with material desires,[37] and in *Huai-nan-tzu*, where it refers to the pure nature (*hsing*[a]) received from Heaven.[38] It was frequently used by the Sung philosophers, especially the Ch'eng brothers, who obviously preferred to speak of *T'ien-li* rather than of *T'ai-chi*. Indeed, Chu quotes Ch'eng Hao as saying: "Although I have learned certain things from teachers, I have discovered myself the meaning of the two words *T'ien-li* through personal reflection and experience."[39] For Ch'eng Hao, *T'ien-li* refers to a natural, spontaneously creative force present in humans as well as in Heaven. For Ch'eng Yi, it assumes as well a normative value, especially as opposed to human passions (*jen-yü*). It took Chu Hsi to identify this with Chou's Great Ultimate.[40]

Chu sometimes uses the word "Heaven" to refer to the Great Ultimate. While commenting on Chou Tun-yi's *Diagram of the Great Ultimate*, he has this to say, quoting first a sentence from the Book of Poetry that emphasizes the transcendence of Heaven: "The operations of high Heaven have neither sound nor smell.[41] Yet [Heaven] is really the axis of creation and the origin of all things."[42]

But he also identifies Heaven dialectically with the human being, balancing transcendence with immanence. Here, he is regarding Heaven as a moral force present within the self. When asked about offering incense to Heaven, he replies that since Heaven is within the self, there is no such need. He appears to partly slip to another level, of Heaven as physical nature, or at least uses this as a metaphor, when he continues: "Our body is operating with Heaven, like a fish in water, with a whole belly full of water."[43]

Chu often invokes Heaven in his discussions of the metaphysical *li*[a]. For him, the highest *Li*[a] is the *T'ien-li*, the "principle of heaven." "There is only one great *Li*[a] in the universe." "Heaven acquires it and becomes Heaven; earth acquires it and becomes earth."[44]

Chu discusses this, not only in the context of his cosmology or philosophy of nature, but also within the framework of his doctrine of cultivation, with its dialectic between the moral mind (*tao-hsin*) and the human mind (*jen-hsin*), relating the former to the heavenly principle and the latter to human passions.[45]

So this Heaven, or rather, the *Li*[a] of Heaven, represents a higher force or power than the azure sky, higher even than the simple *li*[a] itself, if that is possible. It is the "moral mind," the sublime moral law, or, if we wish, the Natural Law when this is understood as a moral dictate.[46] Human beings are subject to this Heaven, from which they receive their li^a. "Nature ($hsing^a$) is the li^a that human beings receive from Heaven."[47] Elsewhere, Chu says: "Where there's heavenly principle, there are also human passions. To adhere to this heavenly principle, one needs to have a point of repose. If this repose is not quite right, human passions will emerge."[48]

Not that human passions are necessarily opposed to the heavenly principle. Chu even asserts that these are found one in the other, thus keeping something of Ch'eng Hao's understanding of *T'ien-li*. According to Chu, "At birth, all is heavenly principle. Human passions emerge later."[49] He appears here to be affirming the innocence of human nature at birth, deferring the arrival of passions to a later time.

However, between the two a battle line is soon drawn. "In the human mind, when heavenly principle is preserved, human passions will suffer defeat, and when human passions win, heavenly principle will be destroyed."[50]

And heavenly principle, for all its vulnerability, is understood as goodness. As Chu also asserts, the heavenly principle, the principle of the highest good, is another name for the Great Ultimate. "The Great Ultimate is only the principle of Heaven and earth and all things. There is a Great Ultimate in Heaven and earth and there is a Great Ultimate in each of the myriad things."[51]

It helps us to better understand Chu's Great Ultimate when we hear him say: "The heavenly principle comes first, and $ch'i^a$ follows. $Ch'i^a$ accumulates to become physical stuff ($chih^a$), and nature ($hsing^a$) emerges."[52]

The problem is: is the Great Ultimate—and Heaven qua heavenly principle, for that matter—pure Li^a? If so, how can the Great Ultimate, as a passive principle, albeit of Heaven, give rise to its own $ch'i^a$ and to interactions between the $ch'i^a$ of *yin* and *yang* and so start the entire cosmic process going? Is not the Great Ultimate, qua heavenly principle, only a formal or exemplary cause?

It would appear that Chu prefers generally to speak of *T'ien-li* in a supreme and ultimate sense but uses *T'ien-hsin* whenever he wishes to underscore the all-embracing and dynamic creativity of Heaven. Whenever the word "mind" is used rather than "principle," there is more of a sense of dynamism and consciousness. Presumably, *T'ien-hsin* is a manifestation of the more passive *T'ien-li* and represents that aspect of Heaven that directs cosmic growth and transformation. To the extent that it is $hsin^a$, it is full of $ch'i^a$. But the relative obscurity of this term seems to suggest that it has less importance than *T'ien-li*. Perhaps I may suggest that heavenly principle, or *T'ien-li*, is a philosophical term representing Heaven qua Heaven, referring therefore to the great Li^a-in-itself that is manifest in $ch'i^a$ as Heaven's mind, or *T'ien-hsin*.

Ghosts and Spirits

The question of a supreme deity cannot be discussed in isolation from the broader question of the existence of ghosts and spirits. In Chinese antiquity, both Confucians and Taoists articulated certain beliefs and attitudes regarding the afterlife. Speaking generally, Confucian thinkers did not show too much concern about death, which was regarded as beyond human control, while Taoist philosophers considered it to be part of a natural process of becoming and change, which need not evoke sadness or mourning.[53]

The belief in spiritual beings is associated with these attitudes. Confucius and his followers inherited from antiquity a classical corpus of rituals presupposing belief in a spiritual universe including a supreme Lord-on-High or Heaven (T'ien), a multitude of spirits or deities governing the world of nature, and ancestral spirits, the spirits of the deceased. Many of the rituals were funerary ones; others involved sacrificial offerings, which, by Chu Hsi's time, were usually liquors and cooked food. These rituals were observed by the entire people, from the Son of Heaven down, depending, of course, on the particular ritual itself, as commoners were forbidden to honor directly the supreme Heaven.

Do Ghosts and Spirits Exist?

Two important words in the Chinese religious vocabulary are shen[a] and kuei. Usually spoken together as kuei-shen, they refer to phenomena considered mysterious and often associated with ghosts and spirits. Shen[a] refers literally to spirits and deities, the spiritual, or the mysterious, and kuei to ghosts, the spirits of the deceased, or the ghostly.

Like other philosophers of his time and earlier, Chu Hsi was not comfortable with the popular belief in ghosts and spirits. His esteemed predecessors Ch'eng Hao and Ch'eng Yi appeared to have been disbelievers. When asked where he stood, Ch'eng Hao showed his discomfort: "Should I say they don't exist, then why did the ancients say what they did? Should I say they exist, you might ask me how to find them."[54] Elsewhere Ch'eng Yi explained more fully:

> The ancients who spoke of ghosts and spirits did so on account of sacrifices. . . . And they did not mention any words they heard [from these], or talk about what shapes and forms they saw. . . . I heard that those who enjoyed discussing ghosts and spirits had never seen or heard any. . . . Even if they actually heard or saw something, they need not be believed. It could be a case of mental illness or visual illusion.[55]

When a disciple asked about a natural fear of such ghosts and spirits, even when he did not believe in their existence, Ch'eng Yi answered: "You need to have your ch'i[a] calmed; then you will naturally not be disturbed."[56]

Chu's own beliefs are built on Confucian foundations. He recognized that the classics presuppose the existence of ghosts and spirits and even regulate rituals of offerings to some of them, rituals that were still followed in his own time. He struggled with the passage in the Analects (3:12) regarding sacrifice, that one should make offerings as though the spirit were present, but acknowledged that there could be no sincerity if there was no faith.

Quoting the *Analects*, "Before I can serve people, how can I serve ghosts? Before I know life, how can I know death?" (11:11), as well as "Respect the ghosts and spirits, but keep a distance from them" (6:20), Chu considers it more important to seek an understanding of those things that are "urgent and immediate," and when such understanding becomes penetrating, the truth about ghosts and spirits will also come to light.[57] In other words, it is more important to know more about life and to serve the living. For "ghosts and spirits belong to the second order of things. They are without shapes or shadows and most difficult to understand."[58]

When asked whether they exist, he answers: "How can I give a quick answer? . . . Let us comprehend what is comprehensible. What we cannot comprehend, we'll set aside and await the time when we understand thoroughly what we do every day in our lives. That is when the *li*[a] of ghosts and spirits will also become clear."[59]

He shows some contradiction when he attributes to the ancient sages the belief in ghosts and spirits but admits that their existence is difficult to explain: "With regard to ghosts and spirits, sages and worthies have clearly pronounced their opinions. All we need is to read carefully the ritual texts."[60] The ritual texts demonstrate generally a preoccupation with mourning and funerary rites, which presuppose a belief in the survival in some form of the spirits of the deceased.

The Book of Rites also includes prescriptions for sacrificial rituals to many deities. These include the spirits of Heaven and Earth; of the seasons; of the Sun, the Moon, and the stars; of the four directions; of mountains, forests, rivers, and valleys; of clouds, winds, and rain. "Strange phenomena are all called spirits (*shen*[a])," the Book of Rites says, and "deceased humans are called ghosts (*kuei*)."[61] The Institutes of Chou list the three classes of spirits. The heavenly deities include the spirits of the mythical Five Emperors and the spirit in charge of human destinies. The earthly deities include the spirits of the altars of grain and Earth, of the oceans, and of the five domestic sacrifices. The spirits of deceased humans include the spirits of the ancient sages and of culture heroes who taught people agriculture and the like.[62] I consider this a rather comprehensive list of deities and spirits, especially deities associated with nature and natural phenomena. Traditionally, spirits are divided into three categories: the heavenly deities, involving the creative transformations of *yin* and *yang*; the spirits of deceased humans, called ghosts; and the spirits to whom sacrifices are offered, especially ancestral spirits.[63]

When Chu Hsi speaks of ghosts and spirits, he usually mentions supreme Heaven itself in a special and unique category, while calling everything else "ghosts and spirits." He also gives special attention to ancestral spirits. Indeed, ghosts and spirits, together with the upper and lower souls, make up the core of Chinese religious thinking. Following Confucian customs, the universe is divided into the world of the living, which is bright, and the world of the deceased, which is dark. These two worlds, however, interact through prescribed sacrificial rituals.[64]

Chu articulates his hesitation to affirm such beliefs: "Where ghosts and spirits are concerned, even sages found it hard to explain the principles [governing them]. One should not say there is really something; yet one should not say there isn't really something."[65] Apparently, he is not sure himself as to what and how much to believe. But then, when referring to the Ch'eng brothers' manifest disbelief in ghosts and spirits, he says: "The two Ch'engs did not initially deny the existence of ghosts and spirits, only that of what our world today calls ghosts and spirits."[66] It would therefore appear that he himself believed in certain ghosts and spirits, as recorded in the ritual texts, but not in all ghosts and spirits venerated in his own day.

The Upper and Lower Souls (Hun-p'o)

The Confucian teaching on the upper (*hun*) and lower (*p'o*) souls is intimately connected to that on ghosts and spirits. In the *Annals of Tso*, a Confucian text, we find these words from Tzu-ch'an:

> When a human being is first born, we see what is called the animal soul (*p'o*). After this is produced comes the spirit (*hun*). Through the concentrated use of many things, the upper and lower souls grow stronger and more energetic, eventually developing spiritual intelligence.[67]

To this, the commentator Tu Yü adds that the lower soul belongs to the *ch'i*[a] of the body or form, and the upper to the *ch'i*[a] of the spirit.[68]

In the Book of Rites, Confucius answers a disciple's question on ghosts and spirits by explaining the human souls: "*Ch'i*[a] refers to what is strong in spirits. *P'o* refers to what is strong in ghosts. Combining ghosts and spirits [in sacrifices] is the most sublime teaching."[69] The text continues: "All living things must die. In death, they return to the Earth and are called ghosts. . . . Their *ch'i*[a] rises up in brightness . . . and become spirits."[70] The commentator Cheng Hsüan adds that the upper soul is responsible for breathing, the lower for sensations like seeing and hearing.[71]

Chu Hsi speaks of the lower and upper souls as belonging, respectively, to the body and to the spirit. According to him, the body precedes the spirit, which emerges with the development of consciousness. The upper soul is made of *yang-ch'i*; the lower, of *yin-ch'i*. Following Ch'eng Yi, he says that the upper soul is invisible but active, while the lower soul has a shape like crystal, tends to be passive, and makes our sensations possible. With age, our sensations suffer because our lower soul weakens.[72]

Chu also discusses the dispersal of *ch'i*[a] in terms of the two souls. As explained in the Book of Rites, at death the upper soul rises to Heaven, while the lower soul descends into the Earth.[73] Chu stresses that *hun* and *p'o* are nothing but two aspects of the functions of man's *ch'i*[a] and, as such, are correlated with *yang* and *yin* and with *shen*[a] and *kuei*: "When dead they are called *hun* and *p'o*; when alive, they are called *ching*[c] [meanings include "essence" and "semen"] and *ch'i*[a]; when shared with Heaven and Earth, they are called *kuei* and *shen*[a]."[74] He explains in greater detail what happens at death: "When a human being is about to die, there is hot *ch'i*[a] that rises up [from the body]. This is what people mean by the upper soul rising. The lower body turns cold, which is what people mean by the lower soul descending."[75]

And so, the two souls live together in interdependence for a life span and then part company. The upper soul is supposed to rise up to Heaven but sometimes remains near the Earth as a ghost, as will be discussed later in this chapter. The separate existence after death, whether of spirits of sages and holy men or of ghosts seeking appeasement for violent deaths, indicates a belief in the survival of the spirit after the death of the body.

This belief is nevertheless vague and ambiguous. There is no clarification of how long the spirit continues to exist. Instead, Chu speaks of the dissipation of *ch'i*[a] after death, leading us to wonder what kind of survival could follow. To quote Chu again: "What is called spirits (*ching-shen*), upper and lower souls (*hun-p'o*), endowed with knowledge and consciousness, is all the doing of *ch'i*[a]. That is why they exist when *ch'i*[a] is accumulated and don't exist when this is dissipated."[76]

A Philosophical Rationalization

While sometimes repeating Ch'eng Yi's description that ghosts and spirits are manifestations of the creative and transformative processes of the universe,[77] Chu basically follows Chang Tsai, who says: "Ghosts and spirits are the natural manifestations of the two *ch'i*[a] [of *yin* and *yang*]."[78] As such, they belong to the realm within shapes, or the physical realm, rather than to the metaphysical realm, which is beyond shapes and forms.[79] "[They are] like that which is spiritual and intelligent inside this *ch'i*[a]."[80]

Chu alludes to the Book of Changes by agreeing that *shen*[a] represents what is difficult to understand. He offers a rationalistic, demythologizing explanation of the workings of *ch'i*[a] in so-called ghosts and spirits: "Spirit (*shen*[a]) means to stretch (*shen*[b] [a homophone]); ghost (*kuei*) means to contract (*ch'ü*). When winds, rainstorms, thunder, and lightning are first manifest, we have *shen*[a]; when [they] cease. . . , we have *kuei*."[81] He is referring to the stretching and contracting of *ch'i*[a]. He also correlates ghosts and spirits with the two modes of *ch'i*[a] when he says: "*Kuei-shen* are nothing but the growth and diminution of *yin* and *yang*."[82] Here, he is continuing Chang Tsai's position, as well as the Han scholar Wang Ch'ung's naturalistic thinking reflected in the *Balanced Inquiries*.[83]

Chu adds that ghosts and spirits seem to be the "spiritual intelligence present in this *ch'i*[a]." On that account, they belong, with *ch'i*[a], to the realm within shapes, with spirits regarded as manifesting the "best" and "most brilliant" of *ch'i*[a]. As such, the spirits reside in the mind-and-heart, which is also the locus of *ch'i*[a].[84]

Chu also explains ghosts and spirits according to the hermeneutical concept of the latent and the manifest. Often the latent is understood to be reality, or *t'i*, sometimes called *pen-t'i* (translated as "original substance"), while the manifest is its function (*yung*). In this light, *kuei-shen* are not only related to *ch'i*[a]. According to Chu, *shen*[a] manifests *li*[a] even though it is contingent on *ch'i*[a]. "To perceive *shen*[a] only in terms of *ch'i*[a] is a mistake."[85] Nevertheless, as the invisible partner of *ch'i*[a], *li*[a] may be called the latent reality or original substance (*pen-t'i*) of the universe while spirits are its creative and visible manifestations (*hua-kung*). This may be difficult for the reader to accept. Here, the focus is not on spirits' being visible but on their manifestations' being so.

Basically, Chu Hsi's philosophy renders ghosts and spirits into natural phenomena, based on *yin-yang* theories. However, in popular belief, natural phenomena themselves continued to be regarded as manifestations of the deities. For example, thunder and lightning were thought to be the workings of the "thunder god" (*lei-shen*).[86] Chu speaks of the Sun, Moon, and stars, constituted by the "purer" *ch'i*[a], as *shen*[a],[87] and of natural forces, like rain, wind, dew, thunder, day, and night, as "manifestations" of the *good* "ghosts and spirits." In other words, he sees certain natural phenomena as manifestations of *ch'i*[a], and others, like lightning and thunder, as merely manifesting the friction of *ch'i*[a].[88]

Chu distinguishes three different senses in the concept *kuei-shen*. The first sense refers to normal and regular phenomena, manifestations of the correct and upright *kuei-shen*. The second sense refers to the phenomena that are difficult to understand, for which incorrect and evil *kuei-shen* are responsible. When we read his words, we find that both senses have to do with natural phenomena: "The sudden blooming of flowers . . . and the sudden occurrence of thunder, wind, or rain . . . are all *shen*[a]. People notice them often enough and see nothing strange. But the sudden ghost whistles and ghost fires . . . are regarded as strange."[89]

In a third sense, *kuei-shen* are objects of sacrificial offerings and can be reached by human prayers. Here he includes the *shen*[a] of Heaven and Earth, of the astral bodies, of mountains and rivers, of cold and heat, of the state and of each household.[90] In doing so, he appears to be accepting popular beliefs in ghosts and spirits.

Chu also makes distinctions between *shen*[a] and *kuei*, correlating them with the *yang* and *yin* modes of *ch'i*[a]. For him, ghosts refer to what is spiritually effective of the *yin* energy, and spirits refer to what is spiritually effective of the *yang* energy.[91]

What are the manifestations of the "incorrect" *ch'i*[a]? Why do certain deceased persons appear in ghost forms, and others not? Chu speaks of *ch'i*[a] dispersing at the death of a human being except in those cases where, because of violence or abnormality of death, *ch'i*[a] remains and even causes the appearance of ghosts. Such undispersed *ch'i*[a] of the deceased is responsible for the appearance of ghosts. Other cases may involve persons who in life cultivated their *ch'i*[a] so well that it disperses only with difficulty, sometimes leading to unusual phenomena such as dark skies, strong winds, and thunder at the moment of death.[92] But this does not happen to sages, who are content to die. "Who has ever seen Yao and Shun as ghosts?" Chu asks.[93]

Chu appears to accept the presence of both "orthodox" ghosts and spirits, those to whom offerings are made according to government regulations, and "heterodox" ghosts and spirits, venerated in *yin-ssu* (illegal temples) and representing "incorrect" *ch'i*[a]. The efficaciousness of heterodox ghosts and spirits is attributed more to the faith of those assembled than to the power of the ghosts and spirits themselves. And he asserts that these illegal temples should be eliminated.[94]

Philosophically, Chu seeks to integrate the human with the natural, attributing all transformations to the two modes of *ch'i*[a] and calling their manifestations ghosts and spirits. Practically, however, he remains open to the possibility of supernatural or preternatural presences and phenomena, to which he can offer no rational answer.

On Communing with the Spirits

The *Doctrine of the Mean* (ch. 16) puts these words about ghosts and spirits into Confucius's mouth:

> How abundantly the ghosts and spirits display their powers! We look for them and don't see them; we listen for them and don't hear them. Yet they produce all things without fail. They make all under Heaven fast and purify themselves and put on their best clothes to offer sacrifices. And then, like water overflowing, they seem to be hovering overhead, on the left and on the right.[95]

It also praises sacrificial rituals in the following words:

> [King Wu and the duke of Chou] occupied the places of their forefathers, practiced their rituals, performed their music, revered those whom they honored, loved those whom they favored, and served the dead as if they were alive. . . . The sacrifices to Heaven and Earth had as their purpose to serve the Lord-on-High; the rituals of the ancestral temple had as their purpose to make offerings to ancestral spirits.[96]

On Ancestral Spirits

Chu Hsi attempts to rationalize the belief in ghosts and spirits without discrediting it completely. His intention is to reconcile his philosophical assumptions with the great sacrificial traditions that have come down from the past, presumably from the ancient sages. After all, he realizes better than some of those who preceded him the importance of keeping those established rituals that presuppose a belief in ghosts and spirits. To make this intelligible, he remarks that our *li*[a] and *ch'i*[a] put us in communion with the *li*[a] and *ch'i*[a] of all things. Referring to his hermeneutic for the words *kuei* and *shen*[a], Chu explains: "In sacrificial rituals, ghosts and spirits are made to descend, because the *ch'i*[a] that contracted can also expand and stretch."[97]

According to him, the human mind and heart commune with *kuei-shen*[a] on account of the *ch'i*[a] in the heart, which, when moved, touches the *ch'i*[a] of the spirits and ghosts. This occurs especially through ritual action, including divination.[98] Chu explains that the emperor, whose responsibility is to care for everything between Heaven and Earth, must keep his mind in touch with Heaven and Earth. And those who, like himself, practice the way of the sages can also keep in touch, through *ch'i*[a], with the mind of the sages.[99]

Speaking especially of the ancestral cult, which presumes that communion with ancestral spirits is possible, Chu says that descendants share with their ancestors the same *ch'i*[a], and although the ancestors' *ch'i*[a] is dispersed, it can be recalled by descendants when offerings are made to ancestors—with reverence and sincerity:

> Although with death, [the *ch'i*[a]] dissipates, it still may not completely dissipate. That is why sacrifices may have a way of affecting [the deceased] and getting them to come down. It is not known if the *ch'i*[a] of the earliest ancestors are still around, but as those who make offerings are descendants who have the same *ch'i*[a], there is reason for them to make contact. Still, what is dissipated cannot regather.[100]

Until very recently in the twentieth century, perhaps in some places still today, ancestral spirits were remembered through certain family rituals, including a ritual dinner banquet on anniversary dates. When asked how one might expect ancestral spirits to partake of such a sacrificial meal, when the ritual impersonator, usually a descendant of a younger generation, has eaten it first, Chu answers:

> Descendants inherit the same *ch'i*[a] from their ancestors. When this *ch'i*[a] is responsive, all conversation and eating and drinking will be as if the ancestors are present [at the ritual meal]. This will console the filial sons and grandsons and not leave things abstract and beyond their imagination. This shows that the ancients' use of impersonators for the dead had a deep meaning and fulfilled the expectations of sincerity.[101]

The remote ancestors lived so long ago that it must have been difficult even for people of Chu's time to think of their *ch'i* as not having dispersed. This is a problem for Chu, to teach both the dispersal of *ch'i* after death and its regathering, especially in the case of ancestral veneration.[102] The reference to an impersonator regards an ancient custom no longer carried out in Chu's time, which will be further discussed in chapter 4.

Chu continues by referring to what was happening in his own day: "Today, when people offer sacrifices with sincerity, their ancestors will also descend."[103] The contradictions inherent in Chu's exposition are obvious. Chu never explains how contact can be made if the dissipated *ch'i*[a] cannot regather. The moral seems to be that it is better to make offerings just in case contact can be made.

Although asserting that heredity confers the same *ch'i*[a], Chu still maintains that there is only one *ch'i*[a] for everyone, so it is possible to commune ritually— always with reverence and sincerity—with the spirits of those not related by blood, "because all come from the same source. . . . This is true even of Heaven and Earth, of mountains and rivers, and of ghosts and spirits."[104]

Is he speaking of a universal *ch'i*[a] for all, and particular ways of participating in it that permit heredity to make certain claims? It is not clear. But the emphasis on reverence and sincerity is important, as these arise from the minds and hearts of those assembled in ritual.[105]

On Spirit Possession and Other Phenomena

Take the case of shamans, who belonged to a respectable class in antiquity, but whose social positions had fallen low by Chu's time. He approved of the inclusion in the Institutes of Chou of an official palace position for a female shaman (wu) in charge of "religious" affairs (wu-chu chih[b] shih), including prayers and incantations.[106] Where Ch'eng Yi showed a deep distrust of shamans and spirit possession,[107] Chu was much more open. He said of the phenomenon of spirit possession known to him from occurrences in his own days: "Nowadays many ghosts and spirits take over the bodies of living persons and speak through them. . . . Among today's shamans, there are those who can make spirits descend too."[108]

In his commentary on the Nine Songs, Chu speaks of shamans being possessed by spirits or deities (shen[a]). Chu mentions the term ling (spiritual intelligence) in speaking of the phenomenon of possession and calls the shaman ling-tzu, which is to say, a child of the deity. He speaks of the shamanic experience as follows: "This describes the deity descending into the body of the shaman. . . . In antiquity, the shaman induces the descent of the deity; the deity descends and possesses the shaman. . . . So the body remains the shaman's, while the mind and heart are the deity's."[109]

Chu observes that the shamanic phenomenon is often associated with musical performance, presumably during a kind of séance as the music moves from a rhythmic beating of the drum to a cacophony of notes. As the music becomes discordant, the deity takes over the shaman's body in an experience that delights the deity.[110]

We may note some contradictions here with Chu's avowed philosophical allegiances, not only on account of the nonrational character of spirit possession but also because of the known Confucian preference for harmony in music rather than discord. And yet, it is discordant music that induces the deity's descent, with the resultant sensation of pleasure on the part of the possessing spirit.

Chu was ready to accept other people's testimony on ghosts and spirits. But he was unable to distinguish folklore evidence such as giants' footprints from belief in the existence of ghosts and spirits.[111] He appeared to respect such phenomena as spirit-writing, which refers to purported written answers from spirits, in particular from the Purple Maiden Goddess, who is supposed to be in charge of spirit writing, while repeating that he "didn't know what to make of it."[112]

In this light, we can understand his acceptance of such legendary materials as the River Chart (allegedly carried out of the river by a dragon-horse at the time of the mythical Fu-hsi) and the Lo Writing (allegedly borne up by a sacred turtle from the River Lo and offered to the legendary Yü, the Flood Controller).[113] As Chu himself puts it:

Heaven and Earth cannot speak and rely on the sage to write books for them. Should Heaven and Earth possess the gift of speech, they would then express themselves better. The River Chart and the Lo Writing are [examples of] what Heaven and Earth have themselves designed.[114]

Ts'ai Yüan-ting was very influential in Chu's attitudes toward these diagrams associated with the Book of Changes. Ts'ai helped Chu with the *Introduction to the Book of Changes*, possibly writing portions of it. Chu discussed with Ts'ai many of his own works in preparation, including those on the Four Books, the Book of Poetry, and the Book of Changes.[115] A scholar's scholar, Ts'ai was well versed in a whole range of subjects, including music, astronomy, mathematics, and geography, as well as rituals and the art of war. Chu allegedly made the remark, "People find it hard to read easy books; Ts'ai Yüan-ting finds it easy to read hard books."[116]

At the head of his other work on the Book of Changes, the *Original Meaning of the Book of Changes*, (*Chou-yi pen-yi*), Chu Hsi appended nine diagrams, including the legendary River Chart and the Lo Writing.[117] The locus classicus for the River Chart is the Book of History, "Ku-ming," and that for the Lo Writing is allegedly "Hung-fan," at least according to an explanation predating Chu. The appendices to the Book of Changes make reference to both these diagrams as corroborating the teachings of the Book of Changes itself.[118]

The River Chart and the Lo Writing are simple diagrams. When both are compared with the more complex numbers and emblems of the Book of Changes, it is found that the emblems in the former are round, and those in the latter are square. According to the River Chart, "The heavenly numbers are the odd ones of *yang*; the earthly numbers are the even ones of *yin*."[119]

In Sung times, several versions of the River Chart and Lo Writing attracted the attention of the public, including Chu Hsi. He gives his own exposition of each in terms of numbers and numerology, making up veritable "magic squares," in the second case yielding horizontally, vertically, and diagonally the sum of 15. Chu Hsi discusses them in mathematical terms also in his conversations with Ts'ai, in his other correspondence, and in his essay on these diagrams.[120]

Conclusion

As we have seen, where spiritual beings are concerned, Chu Hsi explicitly denies the existence of an anthropomorphic deity as supreme being. His acceptance of Heaven as a higher power points not only to a horizon of transcendence but also to a possibility that this transcendence does not necessarily exclude a creative power with spiritual intelligence.

Chu Hsi composed a fairly long rhymed piece, which he wrote out and placed on his wall for a constant reminder. It begins with these lines:

> Straightening my clothes and hat,
> Keeping my glance respectful,
> Abiding deep in my mind,
> Facing [with reverence] the Lord-on-High.[121]

The first two lines refer to correct comportment, but the following two lines bring to the fore a profound religious sentiment that Chu calls *ching*[d] and I translate as "reverence." Reverence involves the presence of another, a greater-than-me, whether that be the moral nature within or the Lord-on-High, the supreme deity.

But is the supreme deity what Chu means by the Lord-on-High? Yes, if by that term we refer to *li*[a]. But here lies an ambiguity in Chu's thought: it is equally wrong to believe in a supreme, anthropomorphic deity and not to believe in an all-powerful deity. His difficulty appears to be with anthropomorphism rather than with theism. His "Lord" is a god of philosophy, a philosophy of *li*[a] or principle, and yet, at the same time, it is not without the consciousness called spiritual intelligence, which would endow it with what we may call personal characteristics. We can attribute this to his effort to reconcile a rationalistic philosophy— demonstrating what may be termed pantheistic Buddhist influences—with a theistic tradition transmitted from China's antiquity and from the Confucian classics.

The Japanese scholar Yamanoi Yū points out the transcendent nature of Heaven as "creator and organizer of the universe" and its derivation from the ancient Confucian classics, which retained a powerful influence on Chu's philosophy.[122] There was, besides, the powerful tradition, alive in Chu's own day, of offering ritual sacrifices to various deities of different ranks and to ancestral spirits. When it comes to this established order that came down from antiquity, Chu was no social revolutionary. We shall deal with this subject in the next chapter.

Chu prefers to interpret, whenever possible, in metaphysical terms, even where he acknowledges the possibility of other modes of understanding. We have seen this preference in his rendering of the meaning of *kuei-shen*, admitting the presence of "ghosts and spirits" while seeking to understand them in terms of a philosophy of *li*[a] and *ch'i*[a] and even reinterpreting the terms to allow for a scientific understanding of natural phenomena.

The discussions concerning the nature of *T'ien-li*, and whether it can also be understood as representing a *personal* creator, were already heated in the late sixteenth century when the Jesuit missionary Matteo Ricci wrote his *True Meaning of the Lord of Heaven* (*T'ien-chu shih-yi*) largely to dispute the philosophical interpretations of the Sung and Ming thinkers which were obscuring the personal or anthropomorphic character of the earlier concept of a Lord-on-High. One question is whether *li*[a] has "spiritual intelligence" (*ling-chüeh*). If that is so, then *li*[a] may be regarded as possessing a personal character.[123] This is where my earlier indications of an argument from design may give cause for reflection. And we should not forget here the Great Ultimate, also called the heavenly principle. The cosmic process to which it gives rise is a cyclical one, of eternal return and regeneration. Yet it would seem that for Chu Hsi, all this happens, not out of chance, but by eternal design.

Chu leaves behind unresolved questions, among them the survival of spirits after death, in his attempts to combine a philosophy of *li*[a] and *ch'i*[a] with an acceptance of religious beliefs and practices of venerable antiquity. His theory of ghosts and spirits and upper and lower souls is consistent with his basically rationalist philosophy and with his metaphysics of *li*[a] and *ch'i*[a]. On this account, Mou Tsung-san says that Chu slips unconsciously into a horizontal system in his discussions of the Great Ultimate and Heaven.[124] But I find that Chu is unable to be a complete rationalist because of his desire to accommodate ancient beliefs in the Lord-on-High or Heaven, which he obviously respects and to which he gives serious reflective attention. Besides, he never forgets the great ritual practices prescribed in the classical texts, as we shall see in the following chapter.

This is also where Chu Hsi shows himself to be a greater thinker than his predecessors, especially the Ch'eng brothers, from whom he derived his *li*[a]/*ch'i*[a] system. He was not afraid to attempt what they did not, to seek to understand philosophically the great questions that we call religious. If the answers sometimes elude him, we cannot deny that his attempts help to cast light on them and contribute to a partial understanding of them, so that those who come after him can at least understand better the complexities involved. Beneath an apparent occasional arbitrariness in his use of language, such as *kuei* and *shen*[a], Chu shows a philosophical creativity, locating all questions and their answers within his own semantic system.

I started this chapter with a poem from Chu Hsi exclaiming how the beauty of nature reveals the creative powers of Heaven and Earth. I conclude now with two lines from another of Chu's poems, expressing regret for verbosity and disclosing another side of Chu Hsi, a more mystical side:

> The Tao is learned in silence through wordless transmission,
> How wrong for me to have made many empty talks on Heaven![125]

Heaven, like the Tao, is perhaps better understood in silence. But we ordinary mortals would be all the poorer without Chu Hsi's words.

Rituals (*Li^c*)

Wandering at ease in the realm of ritual rules,
Losing myself in the house of humanity and rightness.
I do have the desire for this,
But not the strength to carry it out.
Wearing the maxims of former masters,
Carrying the torch for ancient martyrs—
Only by private and daily practice,
May I fulfill these counsels.

Chu Hsi[1]

Introduction

A conversation between the elderly Chu and a friend explains his lifelong and personal interest in rituals:

Since age fourteen,[2] I've been without a father. I finished mourning for him at age sixteen. We followed at that time the sacrificial rites as we knew them at home. Ritual texts were not available, but what we did was rather proper, as my now-deceased mother was very devoted to sacrificial matters. When I reached seventeen or eighteen, I started to study and compile various family rituals, so that we became better prepared.[3]

Chu has always been admired for the breadth of his scholarship. He contributed to the study of classics, especially by his work on the Book of Changes, which he regarded mainly as a divination text, and on the Book of Poetry, which includes love songs that he admitted had been given arbitrary political explanations by commentators. Chu also gave much attention to the study and annotation of the classical ritual texts.[4]

When we study all that Chu has left behind of his thoughts on ritual, we find that he approached the subject both as a scholar doing historical research on classical texts and commentaries and as an aspiring practical reformer wishing to offer a new ritual system for his own age. Presumably, he had his personal concerns, as revealed by what he said about the early loss of his father.[5]

Here, it is understood that the English word "ritual" is translating the Chinese term li^c primarily in its connotation of ritual practices and only secondarily including the meaning of moral propriety or correctness. Our attention will be focused more on ritual as religious practice, very much a part as well of philosophical discussions of li^a, or principle, with the understanding that ritual practice was considered a means of self-cultivation and of maintaining and promoting social harmony. That is why the term li^c also represents a Confucian virtue associated with such practice, as is reflected in the *Analects*. However, in Chu Hsi's case, there is little discussion of propriety and much of rituals. Presumably, he felt that propriety was adequately discussed in the context of the five constant virtues, including humanity, rightness, wisdom, and faithfulness, and did not require much exclusive attention.

A Scholar of Ritual

In Chinese antiquity, the ritual system, as described in the extant classics, was written for the instruction of the court and various degrees of nobility and officeholders. Ritual practice was thus the prerogative of the aristocracy. Consequently, the Book of Rites declares that "rituals do not reach down to the commoners."[6] In later times, various dynasties promulgated their own ritual instructions, such as the *K'ai-yüan li* of the T'ang dynasty and the early Sung *K'ai-pao t'ung-li*, which closely followed the T'ang model.[7]

Such prescriptions and proscriptions were not always observed, but their existence created intellectual and moral ambiguities in the interpretation and practice of rituals. Also, they did not cover mourning, funerary, and memorial rites, so important in a society where filial piety was the primary virtue, and remembrance of the deceased ancestors was required. This vacuum was increasingly filled by Buddhist and Taoist services, which were not so status-related. In this context, we can better understand Chu's efforts to reinterpret the ritual texts and promote ritual reforms.

Chu defines ritual as "the rubrics of the heavenly principle (*T'ien-li*) teaching people [moral] norms." They are not themselves pure principles (li^a), which are "empty" or abstract, but are intended for practical application.[8] Rituals, therefore, are dynamic expressions of the principle of Heaven, which may also be called natural law. This helps us appreciate the depth of attachment Chu shows to the ritual tradition, both as a scholar and as a follower of ritual.

In this regard, Chu preferred Ssu-ma Kuang's (1019–86) work on family ritual, *Family Precepts (Chia-fan)*, to the Ch'eng brothers' opinions on the subject, showing his impartiality in things scholarly.[9]

Chu presumes that there once existed a large corpus of ritual texts, which were lost with the burning of books under the notorious Ch'in emperor (213 B.C.E.). He urges the study of the extant texts restored by Han scholars—not separately but in conjunction with one another.[10]

Three classical texts on ritual have long been revered by tradition: the Book of Rites (Li-chi) deals with political and ritual institutions and rules of social interaction but includes important philosophical chapters; the Ceremonials (Yi-li) deals more with questions of rubrics and etiquette; the Institutes of Chou (Chou-li) focuses on alleged political institutions of the Chou period (1111–249 B.C.E.).

We find Chu's attitude toward ritual and the ritual texts in many of his other works. He believed that all three classical texts originally belonged to the same corpus.[11] He recommended that the Ceremonials be regarded as the main text, that the Book of Rites be studied with it, and that the Institutes of Chou serve as a reference for the other two texts.[12] And he believed that the dynastic institutes should also be studied. These positions issue from his fundamental convictions regarding the intended meaning of the classic ritual texts themselves and the historical and practical importance of dynastic ritual institutions.

Chu accepted the Institutes of Chou as giving a generally correct description of the institutions attributed to the duke of Chou and did not regard it (as did Hu Hung) as a forgery made up by Liu Hsin for the usurper Wang Mang (r. 9–23 C.E.). But he did not see the text as coming from the duke's own hand:

> The Institutes of Chou and the Ceremonials can be entirely believed; the Book of Rites is [mixed]; parts of it can be believed, parts of it cannot. The institutions described in the Institutes of Chou were established by the duke of Chou, but the language is someone else's.[13]

Chu also says that even the duke of Chou might not have put everything in the Institutes of Chou into application, since the text lists too many official positions. The situation might have been like that of the T'ang dynasty's Six Institutes (Liu-tien), an extant text that was not really followed even during T'ang times. He adds (one may assume, with a smile): "Take the proscription [of the Institutes of Chou] against catching shrimps and prawns. Would it not be cruel to establish an official position just to make sure *that* was followed?"[14]

In the case of the Ceremonials, Chu proposes that it was not written down by the ancients as an entire book. Rather, the accumulation of customs has preceded the writing of the text, and one should distinguish between what is constant and what is changing in ritual.[15]

To support the claim that the Ceremonials constituted the core of the classic, and the Book of Rites served as its explanation or commentary, Chu mentions how the Ceremonials discusses rituals dealing with capping, weddings, archery, and banquets, while the Book of Rites follows up with an exposition of their meaning. But he also recognizes the mixed character of the contents of the Book of Rites, which includes not only what he calls "later materials" (from the Warring States period, 403–221 B.C.E., or later, rather than from Confucius or earlier), such as the lengthy "Diverse Rituals" (Ch'ü-li), but also writings that do not directly deal with ritual, such as the Great Learning (Ta-hsüeh) and the Doctrine of the Mean (Chung-yung), two texts to which he gave special attention.[16] Generally, he accepts the Book of Rites as a pre-Han text, and, citing internal evidence, proposes that the T'an-kung chapters came from the disciples of Confucius's disciple Tzu-yu, since they show such respect for Tzu-yu himself.[17]

In making these textual judgments, Chu Hsi stood in opposition to his predecessor the famous Sung reformer Wang An-shih (1021–86), who preferred the Book of Rites to the Ceremonials and even abrogated the study of the latter, while also exalting the Institutes of Chou. Chu says:

> Since . . . Wang An-shih changed the old system of rituals, giving up the Ceremonials, he left behind only the Book of Rites [in the curriculum], thereby abandoning the classic for its commentary, deserting the roots for the branches. The abuses have been great.[18]

Wang An-shih left behind his own work on The Institutes of Chou, under the name *The New Meaning of the "Institutes of Chou"* (*Chou-kuan hsin-yi*), which, together with his commentaries on the Books of History and Poetry, made up a new official syllabus for the Imperial University (T'ai-hsueh) when he was prime minister.

If classical texts did not come entirely from the sages but assumed form under various hands, what is one to say about the authority of the texts themselves? Could the words be changed once the texts had become established? To this question, Chu's response was: "Changing the words in the classical texts risks provoking scholars to a mind of irreverence. . . . But [in cases where the text would not make sense without changes], why desist from changing?"[19]

Presumably, he would not allow anybody to tamper with the classics but considered *himself* an exception. He added another paragraph to the *Doctrine of the Mean*, originally a chapter from the Book of Rites, in order to explain the passage "The extension of learning lies in the investigation of things."[20] In giving expression to his ambitions of reforming the ritual system, he discloses his own self-consciousness as a sage:

> The ancient rites are difficult to put into practice today. I have said that [we need] a great sage to arise in these later ages to overhaul them completely and wake people up to the fact that one need not follow every complicated detail that the ancients laid down. [What is important] is following the general intention of the ancients.[21]

Thus, in the *Comprehensive Explanations*, we find that passages from the classic *Dictionary of Ancient Terms* (*Erh-ya*) regarding relatives are inserted to make up for what the Ceremonials (*Yi-li*) itself lacked. Other texts are also used to make up for what is lacking on state rituals and school rituals.[22]

The Compendium on Ceremonials

Two other persons were involved in Chu Hsi's major work on ritual: his friend Lü Tsu-ch'ien, with whom he frequently discussed questions of philosophy and classical learning, and his disciple and son-in-law Huang Kan (Huang Gan, 1152–1221), a good scholar of little means who would eventually compile Chu's biography and complete one of his works on ritual.[23] Lü came from an illustrious family which had served the Sung dynasty well. He was a *chin-shih* of 1163 and was successively a professor at the National University and a compiler in the Bureau of National History. Both a Confucian thinker and a historian, he is known as the founder of one of the three principal schools of Southern Sung thought—the other two being associated with Chu and Lu Chiu-yüan. While Chu's school later became known as the school of *li*[a] (principle) and Lu's that of *hsin*[a] (mind), Lü Tsu-ch'ien's, based in eastern Chekiang, was concerned with reconciling the divergences between Chu and Lu. It also placed greater emphasis on socioeconomic questions and on the priority of political commitment.[24] Lü had some interest in questions of the mind and human nature but focused more on historical and institutional issues. His premature death was bitterly mourned.

We have correspondence from Chu to Lü (1175–81). Among other things, Chu outlined for Lü a plan that closely followed the order of chapters in the Ceremonials itself and that he apparently intended to follow in his own proposed work.[25] We also have Chu's letters to Huang Kan, in which he instructs the younger scholar in mourning and funeral rites.[26]

Chu wrote about the Book of Poetry and the Book of Changes before working on ritual. When asked about the ritual texts, he said on one occasion:

[These] need to be divided into categories, such as cappings, weddings, funerals, and sacrifices, together with other miscellaneous ceremonials. . . . One should investigate similarities and differences and make judgments regarding their propriety. Unfortunately, my strength is no longer sufficient, and I must leave it to someone else to do.[27]

In 1194, Chu submitted a petition for the use of books from the Imperial Library and requested stipends for the living expenses of more than ten students to serve as scribes, as well as for help with defraying the cost of paper and candles. This was in order to accomplish the study on classical ritual texts.

Your minister is living in retirement and studying the theories [of rituals] with several other scholars. We wish to use the Ceremonials as the classic, incorporating what the Book of Rites and other classical, historical, and miscellaneous texts concerning rituals say under this basic classic, with complete and systematic listing of commentaries and the teachings of the scholars.[28]

Such a petition resembles very much what in our own times would be an application for a research grant submitted by a senior scholar. In Chu Hsi's case, it was not successful.[29] This explains some of the difficulties Chu encountered in his research efforts and possibly why the work would eventually be left incomplete. Indeed, it appears to have been an uphill battle all along. Chu would outlive several of his friends and collaborators, only to find himself sick and unable to finish his project. At age sixty-nine, he wrote to a friend:

I cannot help treasuring my remaining days on earth, especially as the work to compile a [collected] commentary on the rituals is beginning to take form but cannot be finished in a rush. Should I have more than a year to live and be able to complete the task, I shall be able to die in peace.[30]

Until twenty-two days before his death, Chu Hsi was still working on his *Comprehensive Explanation*. His ambition was to focus on the Ceremonials, gathering together the explanations found in the two versions of the Book of Rites, by Tai the Younger and Tai the Elder, using the Institutes of Chou as a reference book, and putting together as well the commentaries of the Han and T'ang periods and the ritual texts and decrees of his own day to further elucidate the history of the development of ritual.[31]

Chu never completed this great work on ritual, although his extant writings on the subject exercised an important influence. His disciple Huang Kan completed the revision of the section on funeral rites, adding a supplement (twenty-nine chapters) to the *Comprehensive Explanation*, but even Huang died before finishing the work.[32] After that, another disciple, Yang Fu, continued with revisions of previously planned sections on sacrificial rites (chs. 16–29). Thus, together with what Chu Hsi has left behind, the final work has a combined length of sixty-six chapters.[33]

While not from the same hand, this extant publication includes much of what Chu originally planned for the entire work and remains a formidable contribution to the field of ritual studies.[34] The sage Confucius was always regarded as an expert in ritual. Following his example, Chu steeped himself in the study of the same subject and became a model for other scholars' emulation. After Chu's time, a work on ritual compiled by Chiang Yung (eighty-five chapters) sought to emulate Chu's plan.

Chu Hsi was mainly a private scholar. During his lifetime, he lacked the necessary official patronage to complete his research on ritual and to put into effect his own ideas of ritual reform. It is therefore interesting to observe the influence exerted by the publication of his posthumous works. In particular, the *Comprehensive Explanation* has become an important scholarly contribution to the field of ritual studies. And the *Chia-li*, or *Family Rituals*, which will be discussed next, has had a wide practical influence in the traditional societies dominated by Confucian culture.

The Family Rituals *and the Textual Controversy*

The work commonly called Chu Hsi's *Family Rituals* (*Chia-li*) comes down to us from the Sung dynasty in two editions: a shorter and a longer one. The shorter one comprises five chapters and a supplement (one chapter), and the longer one has ten chapters and incorporates Yan Fu's annotations as well as those of the later Lui Kai-sun. The longer edition includes a section on ordinary rites, another on the capping ceremony, five on funeral rites, and two on sacrificial rites.[35]

In its shorter edition, the *Family Rituals* diverges from the longer version. It has exercised a great influence. Of the four rites included, initiations, weddings, and funerals make up the three rites of passage, while the fourth deals with the veneration of ancestors. They are called family rituals because they were performed at home, with the head of the family serving as mediator between the living and the dead. They fulfilled the needs of the general populace, who found the dynastic state of little relevance to their own lives.

In this work, basically a liturgical text, Chu Hsi is concerned with many ritual details, regarding the setting up of an ancestral altar and ways of serving the spirits; the capping of young boys between ages fifteen and twenty and the hair-pinning of young girls at age fifteen or when engaged, usually according to ancient prescriptions; and the many stages that lead to marriage, such as betrothal, exchange of gifts, and the like. The details include methods for making ritual vestments, complete with illustrations.[36] The longest chapter (the fourth) deals with mourning and funeral rites; the final chapter describes different types of sacrifices to ancestors, whether at home or at the grave site. The work as a whole supports the practice of venerating the ancestors, since all the rituals are basically directed to that goal. After all, the duties of adulthood, and of marriage itself, are all oriented to serving ancestral spirits.

The controversy over Chu Hsi's works on ritual concerns especially the authenticity of *Family Rituals*. The case deserves some scrutiny. It has been said that the text itself was first completed in 1170, only to be immediately stolen but recovered and published posthumously. This loss and recovery have been adduced as reasons for discrepancies between what is said in this text and in *Yi-li ching-chuan*.[37]

We have some documentary support for Chu's authorship. I refer to a preface to this work, written by Chu himself, and included in his *Collected Writings*.[38] There is also mention of *Family Rituals* in Chu's official biography by Huang Kan[39] and in a Chronological Biography, compiled not long after his death, which even gives the date of its completion (1170), when Chu was in mourning for his mother's death.[40]

On the other hand, the seventeenth-century scholar Wang Mou-hung, an authority on Chu Hsi, has published several works voicing his doubts regarding the authenticity of *Family Rituals*. These are based upon the lack of mention in Chu's own writings in general and the possible confusion of the sections on family rituals within *Yi-li ching-chuan* with the independent treatise attributed to him. Besides, he quotes Chu Hsi as giving sickness and old age as reasons for not being able to compile his planned work on family rituals, which was to be based on Ssu-ma Kuang's work but with references to other works on the subject.[41] This statement directly contradicts any assertion that the book had been completed twenty years earlier.

Huang Kan's words in Chu's biography should be scrutinized. He said: "[Chu Hsi] . . . worked at compiling a book on ritual, working assiduously, but was unable to complete what he did. As for *Family Rituals*, they have been much put into practice by the world. But this had witnessed many changes afterward, and [he] never had time to make a complete revision."[42] Huang was obviously referring to the independent treatise bearing Chu Hsi's name as compiler. Could he also be hinting that the treatise as known to the world was not solely the work of Chu Hsi?

The Japanese scholar Uno Seiichi appears ready to hold that the attribution of *Family Rituals* to Chu Hsi is spurious.[43] On the other hand, Ch'ien Mu argues, with help from Ch'iu Chün, that this is not the case.[44]

It has also been pointed out that divergences between *Family Rituals* and the family rituals portion of *Yi-li ching-chuan* can be explained. While the latter work represents Chu's classical scholarship, his inquiry into ancient rituals, the former work was intended for practical application, representing his reformist tendencies in the changes and adaptations he made.

Without having settled all lingering doubts regarding the authorship of the famous treatise on family ritual, let us turn to the subject of Chu Hsi as a reformer of ritual.

A Reformer of Ritual

Chu Hsi explains that ritual constituted an important area of scholarly specialization in antiquity. Scholars transmitted knowledge and information from generation to generation regarding everything from rituals at court and at the royal ancestral temples to the customary practices of commoners in villages and city neighborhoods. However, such careful scholarly attention had been interrupted, knowledge about ancient ritual was no longer current, and many things in the classical texts could no longer be understood.[45]

This does not mean that Chu Hsi wanted to restore ancient institutions, or even keep the rites of antiquity without change. In fact, Chu Hsi was ready and eager to change the forms of ancient rituals, just as eager as he was to reinterpret the ancient message of Confucianism for people in his own day. And he was not the first scholar to do so. Others, such as Ou-yang Hsiu (1007–72) and Ch'eng Yi, also wrote on family rites.[46]

Chu told his students at the White Deer Cave Academy of his plans to reform ritual, apparently at a time before he was ready to compile his major compendium:

> It is not enough for scholars to be versed broadly in the literature of the six arts of the ancient kings, to recite it aloud with knowledge of its words, to explain its meaning. . . .
>   Ritual (*li*[c]) must be put into practice. What is recited and explained must be followed by action.[47]

On Divination and Geomancy

The *Doctrine of the Mean* affirms the practice of divination in the following words:

> The way of perfect sincerity is to have foreknowledge. Lucky omens always accompany the flourishing of a country or a family; unlucky omens come with its pending decease. These are visible through milfoils and turtles and in the movements of the four limbs.[48]

In our own day, Chinese methods and theories of divination and geomancy have begun to fascinate the West as well as the East. The Book of Changes is consulted by many in the West, who look to it for answers in critical moments. Carl Jung speaks of such consultation as a kind of spiritual dialogue with an ancient book that is somehow regarded as an oracle. Such consultation requires self-knowledge for thoughtful and reflective people:

> The ancient Chinese mind contemplates the cosmos in a way comparable to that of the modern physicist, who cannot deny that his model of the world is a decidedly psychophysical structure. The microphysical event includes the observer just as much as the reality underlying the *I Ching* comprises subjective, i.e., psychic conditions in the totality of the momentary situation.[49]

Jung speaks of the element of chance involved in consulting this oracle as a principle of "synchronicity," which takes the coincidence of events in space and time as meaning more than mere chance but rather as an interdependence of events among themselves as well as with the psychic states of the observers.[50]

Without defining the term specifically in this context, the philosopher Ch'eng Yi uses *li*[a] (principle) in the sense of rational method, as well as mental disposition, to explain the efficacy of divination. In this sense, he confirms Jung's much later interpretation:

> Although milfoils and tortoise [shells] are not sentient beings, the reason why they are used in divination, and why divination yields results of fortune or misfortune, is certainly on account of this *li*[a]. Because they have this *li*[a], [the oracles] are asked certain questions and give certain responses. Should one approach [divination] with a selfish mind and the wrong hexagrams, one will not get the correct responses.[51]

In his only published work, a commentary on the Book of Changes, Ch'eng Yi limited himself to the Ten Wings, which are philosophical accretions to that text. He believed that all principles are to be found in these commentaries, so that one need study nothing else to understand the classic. He was basically following Wang Pi's approach, although his interpretation was Confucian rather than Taoist. And he personally repudiated all practice of divination.[52]

Chu clearly departs from his philosophical predecessor in this regard. While understanding the repugnance of some scholars who were uncomfortable with the nonrational character of divination, Chu says:

> [This classic] was originally meant for divination. The sage [Confucius] gave it words to explain to people, and so uttered many ideas about it. Today, when we study the Book of Changes, we need not be cautious and wait for something to happen first to resort to divination. Even in ordinary daily living, we can savor it to see how what it has to say to us bears an impact on the situation in which we find ourselves.[53]

Since Chu believes in the possibility of the living communicating with the spirits of the deceased, he does not dismiss divination practices out of hand. Where Ch'eng emphasizes manipulation of methods, as well as self-knowledge, in divination, Chu sees the human being as listening with great reverence to communications from the ghosts and spirits:

> In reading every hexagram and line, one should have an empty mind as for divination, in order to get what the words are pointing at, and decide on fortune and misfortune. . . . This is useful [for everyone and everything], from the princes and nobles down to the common people, for cultivating the self and governing the country.[54]

The difference between Chu and Ch'eng Yi regarding divination stems from their fundamentally different attitudes toward the existence of a world beyond, the transcendent. Chu Hsi's philosophy permits in some way a belief in ghosts and spirits that Ch'eng Yi's does not.[55] Here too, Chu differs from Lü Tsu-ch'ien, who regards divination as a reflection of one's own mind, and therefore an unnecessary practice for decision making.[56]

For Chu Hsi, divination is part of self-cultivation, since it promotes self-examination and the nurturing of one's innate moral mind. Only perfect sincerity without any little bit of selfishness, says Chu Hsi in commenting on the words of the *Doctrine of the Mean*, can enable the perception of the kind of "incipiency" (*chi*) that we would understand as the subtle signs of future events.[57] He usually expects the scholar to consult the Book of Changes rather than patronize professional practitioners. In part to help others in this direction, Chu wrote his two books on the Book of Changes: the *Original Meaning* (*Chou-yi pen-yi*) (1177) and the *Introduction* (*Yi-hsüeh ch'i-meng*) (1186). Chu's opinion, since then confirmed by other scholars, is that the core text with its trigrams and hexagrams began as a divination manual, using notions of fortune and misfortune for didactic purposes.[58] This is a clear divergence from the earlier ontological and moral approaches to the classic by Wang Pi and others. In the *Original Meaning* he includes a section that gives instruction on how the text may be used, with the help of milfoil stalks, for divination purposes.[59] In both works, he combines the mathematical and numerological interpretations of Shao Yung and the metaphysical interpretations of Ch'eng Yi. His own interpretation is thus a kind of synthesis that has since been regarded as orthodox.

Geomancy, or *feng-shui*, especially regarding the selection of graves for deceased parents and ancestors, is related to divination. It is interesting that Chu also diverges here from Chang Tsai and Ch'eng Yi on its merits. Whereas these two considered geomancy irrational, especially when controlled by so-called *yin-yang* masters, Chu defended such practices on the selection of graves, followed them himself, especially in burying family members, and praised Ts'ai Yüanting's expertise on the subject. Ts'ai apparently came from a family of diviners and geomancers. His views on these subjects are said to have influenced Chu greatly.[60]

Chu's memorial to the throne (1194) outlined his views on geomancy over the issue of where to bury Emperor Hsiao-tsung:

> Your minister has heard that burying means hiding. It is the way of hiding the physical remains of ancestors . . . which should be done with a heart of cautious seriousness and sincere reverence. The goal is peace and security in the long run, so that if the body is whole, the spirit of the deceased will find peace, descendants will flourish, and the sacrificial ritual will not be interrupted. . . . That is why the ancients always turned to divining with stalks to make their decisions in choosing a burial site. . . . Should the choice not be correct, the ground will not offer good fortune, and there will be water and hidden springs. ants, and underground winds that are destructive of the inside, leading to lack of peace for the body and spirit and the risk of death and misfortune to descendants.[61]

By resorting to this utilitarian argument, Chu is parting company with other scholars like Ssu-ma Kuang and Ch'eng Yi, who disliked the selfish motivation of securing prosperity for oneself by ensuring proper *feng-shui* for deceased parents.[62]

To choose proper grave sites, divination is necessary. Chu admits that divining with stalks was no longer practiced because the skill had been lost but asserts that other methods exist to help choose sites. He eventually concludes that several auspicious sites be found before a final decision is made.[63] He also recommends that the dead be buried with their heads to the north, according to the Book of Rites, and that they be placed with their backs to the *yin* and so profit from the *yang* forces of sunshine. He disagrees with certain geomancers' theories that he finds faulty but upholds the practice of geomancy itself:[64]

> The practice of geomancy is like that of acupuncture and the use of moxa. There is a fixed point that cannot be off by a hair. If a physician cauterizes the way censors are now choosing grave sites, then the whole body would be injured when one point is attacked.[65]

It is recorded that on at least two occasions, Chu himself participated in divination, undertaken on his behalf by his disciples. The first occasion (1195) was after he had prepared a memorial to the throne criticizing certain policies involving the powerful Han T'o-chou (1151–1234). This was at a time when his own teachings were being savagely attacked by Han's supporters.[66] Chu himself refers to the first occasion:

> I've been thinking of retiring but couldn't decide. . . . A few days ago, I divined with the help of the Book of Changes and got the bottom line of the hexagram *Tun*. Since this has been revealed, they [my enemies] cannot do much [if I retire]. What is the use of running away from [my destiny]?[67]

It allegedly resulted in his decision to burn the draft memorial and retire completely from public life, assuming the name of the hexagram, *Tun* (escape), and calling himself Tun-weng (Retired Old Man).[68]

The second occasion, two years later (1197), was during a time of great stress, when he was being persecuted officially for his "false learning," and when his disciple Ts'ai Yüan-ting had been banished, as a scapegoat for Chu:

> After his meal, he went downstairs, walked west a bit and sat down in the middle [of the room] as for meditation. . . . [A disciple] divined and got the [sixty-second hexagram] *Hsiao-kuo* [slight excess]. [The explanation says,] "the prince shoots his arrow and takes the bird in the cave." [The interpretation] was that the master was not personally in danger but Ts'ai would be hurt. The master was then sound asleep but woke up on hearing his disciples talking.[69]

It appears actually that on each occasion, Chu did not take the initiative but accepted the result. Ts'ai died the following year in exile, and Chu himself succumbed two years later.[70]

On Mourning and Funeral Rites

Since Chu believed in adapting ancient rituals to the new conditions of his own times, he wanted to simplify mourning and funeral rites. Among other things, he criticized the custom of wearing ancient mourning garments for such rituals. In vivid and even playful language, surprising on account of the subject under discussion, he says:

> [These ritual prescriptions] make people weary. What we should have is something vital, like having a live snake to play with. Otherwise [one] can only play with a dead snake. . . . Should we fulfill everything prescribed in the [ancient] mourning rites, we would be unable to cry and show emotions of sadness. . . . After all, when one is sad and confused, how can one have a mind to follow the complicated details of ancient ritual . . . ? By only following the rites customary today, we are not doing wrong but rather are permitting feelings of sadness to express themselves.[71]

An ancient rite performed after the death of a family member is called the "Summoning of the Soul." It was usually carried out by members of the family, who went to various parts of the house, including the rooftop, with the deceased's clothing, to wail and to beg the soul to return to the body.[72]

The anthology *Songs of Ch'u* (*Ch'u Tz'u*, also known as *Songs of the South*) has a section entitled "Summoning the Soul," which offers in poetic language a dramatic plea that in turn begs and coaxes the soul to return to the body, arguing the inhospitableness of the other regions as reasons for coming home:

> O soul, come back! In the east you cannot abide:
> There are giants a thousand storeys tall,
> Who seek only for souls to catch,
> And ten suns that come out together,
> Melting metal, dissolving stones. . . .

O soul, come back! In the south you cannot stay:
People there tattoo their faces and blacken their teeth.
They sacrifice human flesh
And pound their bones to paste . . .

O soul, come back! The west holds many perils:
The moving sands stretch on for a hundred leagues . . . ,
And you will drift there forever,
With nowhere to go in that vastness . . .

O soul, come back! In the north you cannot stay:
The layered ice rises high there,
and the snowflakes fly
for a hundred leagues and more. . . .

O soul, come back! Climb not up to Heaven above,
Where tigers and leopards guard the gates. . . .

O soul, come back! Go not down to the Land of Darkness,
Where the earth-god lies, nine-coiled, with dreadful horns. . . .

O soul, come back! Return to your old abode.[73]

The geographical survey is rather accurate for the times, when the country saw itself with the sea to the east, perhaps sometimes plagued by tidal waves, and with deserts to the west, cold Siberia to the north, and uncivilized aborigines in the south.

According to Chu, this section expresses the emotions of Sung Yü, disciple to the exiled poet Ch'ü Yüan. Commenting on the passage, Chu Hsi says of the alleged author:

Sung Yü laments Ch'ü Yüan's undeserved exile and fears that his upper and lower souls may depart and not return. So following the customs of the country, he relies on the command of the Lord- [on-High] and uses a shaman's words to summon it. From the point of view of ritual, it is rather vulgar. But it is a prayerful expression of great love, recording the surviving intention of the ancients.[74]

Chu Hsi also regards favorably another ancient custom, that of having an impersonator (shih) represent ancestors at sacrifices. This was apparently done in Shang and Chou times, when a family mourning the loss of an older person would choose a younger person, usually a grandchild, to serve as his or her impersonator during the rituals, when this younger person would receive offerings in place of the deceased. The custom is mentioned in ritual texts such as the Book of Rites.[75]

When asked about the intention of this ancient ritual practice, Chu answered:

The ancients used impersonators in all sacrificial rituals. This happened not just in family rituals but also in rituals offered to nondomestic spirits. I don't know what happened at sacrifices for Heaven and Earth, but dare say that they would have been the only exception.[76]

The ritual exegete Tu Yu (735–812) described this as a primitive custom that had not been changed by the time of the sages but was no longer done in Tu's own time. Tu was not dismissive about the impersonator's role, as he pointed out the prevalence of like customs among ethnic groups living near the majority Han Chinese population.[77] Chu adds some hearsay information that the custom still remained among certain aboriginal tribes within and on the peripheries of China. They would select a handsome man to be an impersonator of ghosts and spirits and would feast him and venerate him during the rituals, sometimes for days.[78]

Chu also mentions having heard from a man from Ch'ung-an (Fukien) of a village where a head of a family was selected every year in rotation from about forty families to serve as *chung-wang* (royal mediator) and to receive sacrifices and prayers. When a new selection took place at year's end, the elders of the village prepared wine and music for the festivities. During the entire year, the man chosen had to live in fear and reverence, complying with the expectations of the villagers. Should floods and droughts take place, this man would be blamed. According to Chu Hsi, such activities appear to preserve the intentions of the ancients, as recorded in the classical texts. Thus he adds, "It would seem that the ancients' custom of having impersonators had its own deep meaning and should not be dismissed as merely a primitive custom."[79]

In these instances, we see Chu as a kind of social anthropologist, deeply interested in local and regional customs. Not only is his great intellectual curiosity evident, but his impartial judgment, his respect for human customs, including those with religious significance, and his ability to correlate the past with the present are demonstrated.

Chu personally made prayers and offerings to ancestral spirits and ritually reported certain of his actions to the sages.[80] In these cases, he reasons that the descendants' live *ch'i*[a] has the power to summon back the ancestors' dispersed *ch'i*[a].[81]

Referring concretely to the corrupting effects of the presence in graves of organic materials (such as food), which attracted ants and other insects, Chu insists that it is more important to protect the bodies of the deceased from corruption. Thus the ancient customs of having neither nails nor paint nor stain on the coffins are not to be observed.[82]

Chu Hsi was not ready to accept Buddhist customs of cremating the dead, which he regarded as opposed to Confucian teachings of filial piety and the expectation that the body be returned intact to the ancestors. Well aware that many preferred the funeral rites of Buddhism and Taoism, Chu says that the presence of Buddhist monks and Taoist priests could be tolerated, but cremation of the parents' remains could not be tolerated. He adds that the son should oppose the father's wish even when the latter desired such for the mother, as cremation was considered demeaning to the parents' bodies.[83]

The desire to make rituals relevant is expressed in Chu's preface to *Family Rituals*. Distinguishing between rank and order as well as feelings of love and respect, which represent the foundation (*pen*) of ritual, and capping, wedding, funeral, and sacrificial ceremonies, which are rather expressions of decorum (*wen*), Chu asserts that what was known at his time of the rituals of antiquity concerning houses and palaces, utensils and clothing, and general social demeanor was no longer relevant. His own purpose was to discover from his reading of ancient and modern texts that which was constant and to make of it a book representing an independent opinion.[84]

On Civic Rituals

As a magistrate, Chu Hsi performed various public rituals that were accompanied by food offerings to local deities and that were performed to request rain or good weather or to thank the deities for granting such requests. When asked whether offerings made to the spirits of the mountains and rivers and of Heaven and Earth are only expressions of human sincerity that do not signify any communion with higher powers, he replied:

> Should we say no one comes to enjoy the offerings, then why such solemnity during sacrificial ritual, and feelings of awe, reverence, and service to higher powers? Should we say there really is someone coming amid the clouds and with carriages and a great retinue, then it sounds quite ridiculous.[85]

Again, he voices the inherent contradictions without entirely resolving them. These rituals were all part and parcel of what we may call medieval Chinese *civil religion*. However, Chu did not favor graven images and objected to making one of Confucius in the White Deer Cave Academy, preferring to use a wooden tablet in rituals honoring the sage.[86] With Ou-yang Hsiu, he rejoiced that the local prefectures still celebrated sacrifices to the gods of the earth and grain, of wind and rain and thunder, because, he reasoned, without these celebrations all ancient rituals would be lost.[87]

The Question of Illegal Temples

From Chu Hsi's description, we learn of popular devotion to various deities, usually historical figures honored after their deaths by those who desired their protection. Such popular devotion was sometimes expressed through animal sacrifices—rather than food offerings—and met with official disapproval.

It appears that "illegal temples" were illegally established temples where such sacrificial rituals took place, and also where monks or nuns assembled. As magistrate of Chang-chou (Fukien) (1190), Chu issued instructions counseling certain nuns to return to society. It appears that these were living in illegally established monasteries, and that in at least one case, a nun had been accused of fornication. Chu's arguments against such a way of life were essentially drawn from Confucian morality:

> It has been said that conjugal life belongs to human morality, and that the relationship between husband and wife, as the most important of the three relationships, should not be abandoned. . . . Buddhist and demonic per-

verse teachings . . . have confused people's minds, leading grown men and women to give up marriage and abandon family life for what is called the cultivation of the way, in vain hope for reward in the next life. If the whole world should follow such, there would be no human being left after only one hundred years.[88]

Looking back from today, such action would be deemed against religious freedom as well as women's liberation. But in the context of his times, the state had control over temples and temple life. As a magistrate, Chu was merely enforcing the state's laws on such matters, while putting into practice also his own personal beliefs about morality. It may be pointed out that the word *mo* (demonic) is sometimes used to designate Manichaeism, which had some support in Fukien. In this case, the nuns were probably Buddhist, or considered themselves Buddhists, even if there had been Manichaean influences.[89]

Chu also held himself aloof from certain practices that he considered as superstitious. When he was at Hsin-an, near his native place, he knew of a temple called Wu-t'ung-miao that was supposed to offer efficacy in divination practices. Many scholars frequented the place and encouraged Chu to make a visit. He steadfastly refused. Once, when he had indigestion and a snake appeared, he was told that it was on account of his not having visited the temple. He replied that his stomach upset was due more to food and should not be falsely attributed to the temple. To show his resolve, Chu said that should the temple have real power, it could cause him to die and be buried at once close to his ancestral graves nearby, which would not have been a great misfortune.[90]

Chu's Practice of Ritual

In his personal life, Chu was a correct man. He was an early riser and careful to a fault about his clothes and posture and about the rules of hospitality. However, he was not above enjoying himself, sometimes even indulging himself a bit when it came to drinking with friends and disciples. In fact, although he was very serious about self-cultivation, he also preferred to "find the truth naturally and with spontaneity."[91]

As a householder, Chu took part in various domestic rituals and made prayers and offerings to ancestral spirits as well as to those of deceased relatives and friends, for many of whom he left behind memorial essays. As a teacher of disciples, he led his disciples in ritual practice, beginning the day with an incense offering and paying respect to Confucius's image. There is every reason to assume that he did everything with great sincerity.[92]

Chu was concerned about the place of ritual in public life. When he held official positions, Chu was assiduous in his ritual practice. First as assistant magistrate in T'ung-an (1153–57) and later as prefect of Nan-k'ang (1179–81) and of Chang-chou (1190), he performed sacrifices to Confucius and made special addresses on those occasions. He also prayed for rain during a drought and for sunshine when the rainfall was excessive.[93]

Chu also took certain public positions regarding rituals and politics. During the Sung dynasty, several difficult ritual cases arose involving the proper placement of ancestral tablets at imperial ancestral sacrifices, and these provoked some scholarly attention, both at the time and later.[94] During Chu's own lifetime, many scholars, including himself, were upset when Emperor Kuang-tsung asserted that ill health prevented him from officiating at his deceased father's (Emperor Hsiao-tsung) funeral.[95] Chu begged permission to resign from his official post in Hunan, saying that without a proper example at the top, a mere scholar like himself could not maintain the loyalty of the people.[96] He also prepared a memorial to the throne emphasizing the duties of filial piety. But he did not have to submit it, because the incident led to the early accession to the throne of Kuang-tsung's son, Ning-tsung, who assumed the ritual duties at his grandfather's funeral.[97] Later, Chu submitted his own proposals regarding the positions of the tablets of deceased imperial ancestors at sacrifices offered to them, but his opinions were not followed.[98]

Chu Hsi expressed his regret that rituals no longer were a priority for government, and that ritual experts could hardly be found in the country:

> In ancient times, rituals were a specialist's field and were always kept up as such. For that reason scholars taught and transmitted what they knew, observed them, and practiced them all their lives. . . . From the ancestral temples and the palace halls above to the scholars and villagers below, ritual regulations were very clearly articulated. It was still so during Han and T'ang times. But now, there is not a single expert.[99]

Music and Ritual

In traditional China, ritual was always associated with music. Both Confucius and Chu Hsi approved of this combination. And of course, both ritual and music were intended for didactic ends. Chu refers to Ch'eng Yi when he says:

> Ritual is only order; music is only harmony. These two words contain so much meaning. There is nothing under Heaven that is without ritual and music. Should you place two chairs here, when one is not correctly placed there is no order, and . . . with disorder comes lack of harmony. Even with thieves and robbers, there is ritual and music. For there has to be someone in charge, and others who obey. . . . Otherwise, they cannot stay together for one single day.[100]

Elsewhere, when responding to a disciple about this unity of ritual and music, Chu said: "Ritual focuses on reverence (ching[d]). With reverence comes harmony. This is where ritual and music are one in essence (t'i). . . . Reverence and harmony both come from the mind and heart (hsin[a])." When asked if both come also from principle (li[a]), he replied: "You may say so, but it is better [literally, "more intimate" (ch'in-ch'ieh)] to say the heart."[101]

While believing in a unity of ritual and music, Chu realizes that there are those, following the Book of Rites, who place music before ritual, and others, like Chou Tun-yi, who place ritual before music. He emphasizes that "the sincerity of ritual is the foundation of music, and the foundation of music is the sincerity of ritual."[102] Apparently, he sees both as an expression of the natural, of T'ien-li. Still, he tends to sympathize with Chou's idea that sincerity should govern ritual as harmony should govern music, and that order should somehow precede harmony.[103]

In other words, for Chu, ritual and music are distinct only in function. An admirer of ancient music, and a believer in its pedagogical value, he said of it in his discussion of the six arts:

> In the educational pedagogy of the ancients, rituals, music, archery, charioteering, writing, and arithmetic must all be included without exception. Among these [arts], music was taught with particular diligence. . . . On account of the rhythm of music, those who learn it can neither rush it nor slow it down. With time, [music] can transform one's emotions and nature.[104]

Of course, not all music can contribute to the proper cultivation of human emotions and human nature. Chu is aware of this and recommends music with slower tempo and lower notes, as found in antiquity, when harmony of the emotions was given a high priority. Referring to emotions that music brings, he says, "Sadness and hate came in [later] as desirable."[105] It is a reminder of Chou Tun-yi's words: "Music was used in antiquity to calm the mind, and in our own days to enhance the passions."[106] Chu also approves of Chou's explanation: "Ritual is li[a] (principle), while music is harmony. With principle governing yin and yang comes harmony."[107]

For the follower of Confucius, music has metaphysical meaning. According to the chapter on music in the Book of Rites, music echoes the oneness and harmony of all things in the universe. But Chu did not believe it possible to recover and restore the music of antiquity and was satisfied with purifying the music of his own day, to ensure that it would help to cultivate peace of mind.[108]

Apparently, Chu learned in his youth to play the ancient lute (ch'in[b]), considered to be Confucius's instrument of choice. In later life, he even composed some songs for it, teaching these orally to others. Once, for example, when a disciple visited with a lute, Chu had this to remember:

> As the night advanced, the moon was bright, the wind and dew grew bitterly cold. [He] plucked the strings and played songs that sounded sad and strong. After that I playfully composed the chao-yin . . . [and the fan chao-yin] . . . , and taught it to him by word of mouth.[109]

Where music is concerned, he moved from practice to theory: from playing the lute to studying the scales, and then to discussing the philosophy of music. The year before his death, Chu wrote a treatise on the music of the lute (1199).

Ts'ai Yüan-ting published some works of his own, including the *A New Study of Musical Notations* (*Lü-lü hsin-shu*), for which Chu wrote a preface. Chu planned to write a larger work with the collaboration of Ts'ai. But this was to be another one of his unfulfilled wishes.

Conclusion

Although Chu Hsi has recently attracted quite some attention in English-language scholarly circles, not enough attention has been given to his contributions to ritual. Yet it was in great part Chu's need to accommodate ritual practices that pushed him to look for answers to bigger questions regarding the existence of the deities and spirits honored by rituals. Besides, Chu's ideas on ritual have become an important legacy in East Asian culture, not only in China and Japan but especially in Korea, where premodern life was governed by Chu Hsi's work on family rituals.

Chu Hsi's ideas on ritual, as well as his own exemplification of those ideas in life and in public office, are instructive not only for the specialist of Chinese intellectual and religious history but also for others interested in ritual. We see, on the one hand, Chu the scholar and exegete, ever intent upon discovering the intended meaning of the ancient texts. Here his contributions include his belief that the Ceremonials was the core classic and that the Book of Rites was an elaboration of the Ceremonials, as well as his acceptance of the Institutes of Chou as a genuine classical text. We find, on the other hand, Chu Hsi as a man of action, a reformer at heart, with the desire to establish a revised ritual system for his own time, a desire that did not see fulfillment. We also discover Chu Hsi as a man of the people, interested in the people's beliefs and practices, including divination, geomancy, and shamanism, giving these his approval whenever he can find reason for doing so.

Placing Chu Hsi in a wider perspective of ritual history, we can suggest a few comparisons with developments in other traditions. Chu's attention to the classical texts, his search for precedents in ritual practice, is not unlike the attention of the jurist, especially in those traditions where ritual and law converge. I am thinking of the Talmudic tradition, where the discussion would be more concerned with the worship of God and the observance of the Sabbath than with the ancestral cult. I am also thinking of the Islamic tradition, where law is equally central and demanding in the believer's daily life. And then there is canon law and its interpretation within the Roman Catholic Church. While law is generally not as important for Christianity as it is for the other religions of Semitic origin, it remains very important for the Catholic clergy and for members of the monastic orders. In this broader light, and examined from the vantage point of our own time, Chu Hsi appears as a moderate reformer, desirous of making the Confucian ritual tradition relevant by adjusting it to the needs of his time.

Human Nature (*Jen-hsing*) and the Ethics of Perfectibility

A pond of half a *mou*, like a bright mirror:
Heaven's light and clouds' shadows glistening on it.
And whence comes this clear transparence?
Its source, the living water.

Chu Hsi[1]

Introduction

What is the human being, and wherein lies his or her worth? This question has been asked—by humans—probably as long as humans have existed. Human beings have always been fascinated with themselves, with their limitations as well as their potentiality for greatness. They have been fascinated with this question also because it can never be fully answered. And yet, one must keep on asking and, in so doing, reveal one's humanity—that which differentiates the human from the rest of nature.

The human being's continuity and discontinuity with the rest of nature—herein lies the *Problematik*. Humans belong, without doubt, to the animal order, but they are not exclusively of that order. This appears, at least, to be the conclusion of common sense—witness our domination of the universe. In what concerns ethics, the prerational schools take their points of departure from an emotional or volitional base, as seen in Hume's principles of morals or Nietzsche's will to power. The postrationalists prefer escape, seeking peace of mind in a spiritual life that may be deemed unworldly, as with the Greek Skeptics or the Chinese Taoists. But those who have not despaired of reason assert its adequacy in regulating passions, as do Plato and Aristotle, the Stoics, and all Confucian schools. While this places Aristotle close to the Confucian camp, he sees humans as rational animals, and rationality is the distinguishing characteristic that has dominated the Western understanding.

For the follower of Confucius and Mencius, the characteristic is rather the human being's moral nature: that there is potentiality for moral self-transcendence and perfection. This has been hailed as the great Chinese discovery: the autonomy of human morality. And yet, humans seem capable also of behavior that has been termed—somewhat inappropriately—beastly; the recent history

91

of genocides offers a telling example. To use the language of religious mythology, human nature seems to possess both angelic and demonic proclivities, leaving us to wonder even more what is the meaning of the human. The human being is a product of nature and yet the creator of culture. He or she moves freely between the two realms; the interpretation and emulation of the one has led to the creation and embellishment of the other. But the human being has no other interpreter of himself or herself but the self. And such interpretation varies over a range of possibilities, depending, usually, upon the emphasis given to one or the other of the two realms which a human being straddles.[2]

In the Chinese Confucian tradition, the tendency has been to emphasize the human being as an autonomous moral subject and his or her perfectibility. The context in which this has been done, from Mencius on, and especially by the neo-Confucian thinkers, has shown a development from a simple, practical moral philosophy to a moral metaphysics, to use Kantian terms, grounded in the belief in the innate goodness of moral feelings and open to almost an infinitude of possibilities of human greatness.[3] To that extent, the Confucian tradition has been one-sided, because it has not considered the darker, and sometimes demonic, side of human nature as have other Chinese philosophical traditions.

A Theory of Human Nature

The human being's place in the natural universe can be better understood through a contemplation of the Chinese word hsing[a], a character compounded of two words, "mind" (or "heart") and "life." It refers primarily to human nature, that which we receive with life. But it also refers to the natures of other creatures. All things, indeed, have been endowed by Heaven with hsing[a], that which makes them what they are. In a treatise on Ch'eng Hao's Discourse on Nature, Chu Hsi quotes him as saying that this comes inborn. And while the nature of a being is regarded as originally good, it cannot be separated from physical form, which comes with matter-energy (ch'i[a]) and is, depending on its quality, prone to both good and evil:[4] "To use the purity and impurity of water as a metaphor, the water's purity represents the goodness of nature. . . . Its impurity represents the extreme partiality of physical endowment."[5]

Chu Hsi's philosophy is all the more representative of the Chinese humanist tradition because it is a conscious synthesis of previous philosophies. It comprises the naturalist legacy of the Taoists and Buddhists, according to the interpretation of his predecessor Chou Tun-yi, and the psychist and culturalist legacy of the Confucians themselves, modified by an undercurrent of Buddhist influences and articulated by the brothers Ch'eng Hao and Ch'eng Yi and their uncle Chang Tsai.

Chu's high esteem of Chou Tun-yi is demonstrated by his description of Chou as sa-luo, an expression that is difficult to translate. It refers to being natural and spontaneous and to freedom from selfishness. In this sense, Chou's personality is likened to a gentle breeze and a bright moon, pleasing metaphors taken from nature itself.[6] And so, the neo-Confucian ideal of the sage, coming to us from

Chu Hsi and others, discloses a strong influence from philosophical Taoism, with its emphasis on oneness with the Tao, although the principal influence remains the Confucian texts.

Chu Hsi recalls: "When I was in my early teens, I read how Mencius said sages are not different from us. I was happy beyond words, thinking that it is easy to become a sage. Only now have I realized how difficult this is."[7] And so he embarked on a personal journey, which started with reading the Confucian Four Books and the Five Classics. That did not prevent his involvements with Buddhism and Taoism for over ten years, until about age thirty. A kind of conversion followed, as Chu chose to return to Confucian texts as well as Confucian self-cultivation. He would still take some time to settle down philosophically. The theories that he developed afterward about human nature and the emotions, and about self-cultivation, reflect his personal endeavors, his groping for the right way to sagehood, as well as his classical and textual studies.

Not only is the task of sagehood difficult, but so too is the work on theories regarding human nature that take for granted human perfectibility. Chu's philosophy developed in interaction with that of others, both those who preceded him and those who were his contemporaries. His theory of human nature, and of goodness and evil in this nature, depends much on Chang Tsai and Ch'eng Yi. His doctrine of equilibrium and harmony, as well as his theory of jen[a], emerged out of discussions with his friends from Hunan, especially Chang Shih (Zhang Shi, 1133–80). And, like his explanations of many other subjects, they come from reflections on, as well as differences with, what Ch'eng Yi had to say. The consequence of such interaction, both dialogue and dialectic, is the development of Confucian moral metaphysics, grounding Chu's ethics as well as his doctrine of self-cultivation in a metaphysic of moral feelings or emotions.

Chu Hsi's teachings on human nature and ethics have come down especially in short treatises, in his correspondence, and in the *Classified Conversations*. They have developed alongside his teachings on self-cultivation, so that it is difficult to separate one from the other.[8] Before he begins to praise human excellence as the crown of the universe, Chu takes care first to establish the roots of humanity in the cosmos and to analyze the human existential in terms of good and evil. For Chu Hsi, as for the mainstream of Chinese philosophy, the human being and the cosmos are paradigms for each other. Thus, evil loses its significance in the affirmation of human perfectibility, as expressed through the doctrine of sagehood. It is, of course, premature here to judge him for what may appear as naïveté, as insensitivity to the whole of human existence, or as inability to confront the entire human situation. It is more important first to discover his own meaning and import.

It is my intention to offer here an exposition of Chu Hsi's theory of human nature, by moving, with him, from the natural environment, the cosmos, to the human being and human nature, and then, from human nature to the cultural and social environment, before returning once more to the cosmos. This is essentially the method of Chu Hsi himself. And this method offers us its own hermeneutic, as is already reflected in chapter 2, on the Great Ultimate. By following this, I hope to make clear the macrocosm/microcosm outlook that is so basic to Chu's thinking and to present his theory of the human as one that mediates between two extremes: that of an absolute continuum of nature, as found in the various modes of materialism, including the Marxist one, which is now dominant in China, and that of an idealist exaltation of humanity above nature. This second position is found in the Platonic heritage and, even more, in various Gnostic varieties of Christianity, which neglect the natural as inherent in the human and result in the philosophical alienation of human beings from themselves.[9]

The World as Macrocosm

From Chou Tun-yi, Chu Hsi derives the belief that the human being participates in the excellence of the *T'ai-chi*, possessing a moral nature of *li*[a] that comes to him through the cosmic transformations. In other words, human nature is both moral and ontocosmological. Contact with external things provided the occasion for evil, as deflection from the good rather than a positive presence. The perfect man, the sage, is completely sincere (*ch'eng*). His mind-and-heart is like clear water, which reflects like a bright mirror, quiet when passive, upright when active or moved by emotions.

For Chu Hsi, as for other representatives of the mainstream of Chinese philosophy, the world, the natural universe, is not only the environment in which human beings find themselves. It is also a reflection, the image of the human, as the human also is image of the universe, each depending on the other for its completion and fulfillment. And the universe is above all the ontological model for human nature and existence, for the world and the human are seen as essentially related, incomprehensible except in terms of this relatedness.

A terse expression of the world regarded as our ontological paradigm is given in Chu Hsi's philosophy of the Great Ultimate, the topic of chapter 2. The philosopher appears to be especially exhilarated with the cycle of life and renewal. He finds it in the universe. He also declares to have discovered it in our moral life. Virtue is creative; it produces and multiplies itself and, in so doing, renders complete the harmony between the human and the universe. So what is being exalted is our moral nature, with its power of self-perfection, through an imitation of the world of nature, seen in the excellence of its creative processes. The presupposition is always the *goodness* of both human nature and the nature of the universe, as well as the correlation between the two—a correlation that is both ontological and moral.

The Human as Microcosm

Cosmological and metaphysical speculations are integral to many attempts at understanding human nature. The Great Ultimate—the One—is also the Great Paradigm, the Cosmic Paradigm, that in which the Human Ultimate—the One Man—the Human Paradigm, finds his own exemplar. For Chu Hsi as well as Chou Tun-yi, the Great Ultimate serves as the symbol of the human, the exemplar for the human. It is the principle of highest excellence, comprehending within itself the plenitude of both being and becoming. Of the myriad things that are produced, the human being is singled out for special attention as the crown of the universe, receiving his own excellence from the Great Ultimate and reflecting back upon it. Let us quote now from Chu Hsi:

> I use many words; actually, all is said in the one [term] of the Great Ultimate. For the Great Ultimate resembles human nature. Its motion and rest, *yang* and *yin*, correspond to the motion and rest of the human mind (*hsin*ᵃ). The Five Phases of Metal, Wood, Water, Fire, and Earth correspond to the five constant virtues of humanity, rightness, propriety, wisdom, and faithfulness; the production and transformation of the myriad things corresponds to the [emergence of the] myriad affairs.[10]

Chu Hsi has also offered an interesting analogy between the *Diagram of the Great Ultimate* and the human organism.

> Speaking of the human body, the breath we inhale and exhale is [the *ch'i*ᵃ] of *yin* and *yang*; the limbs and flesh and blood resemble the Five Phases. Its nature is *li*ᵃ; its *ch'i*ᵃ is like the seasonal changes of spring, summer, autumn, winter; its stuff (*wu*) is metal, wood, water, fire, and earth. Its *li*ᵃ is humanity, rightness, propriety, wisdom, and faithfulness.[11]

The Japanese scholar Yamanoi Yū points out certain inconsistencies in Chu's philosophy of the Great Ultimate and asserts that it is not an important part of his system. I agree with his first assertion that apparent inconsistencies may be found, but not with the second. I find that Chu's incorporation of the Great Ultimate into his theory of human nature and self-cultivation seems quite thorough, and that the Great Ultimate as a concept helps our understanding of the rest of Chu's philosophy.[12]

Ontological Differences between Humans and Others

A question that arises concerns the metaphysical difference between humans and other creatures. Are the *li*ᵃ and *ch'i*ᵃ alike in all? If so, this suggests a continuum of beings without a sharp distinction between humans and nonhumans, including the a inorganic universe. In some contexts, Chu emphasizes that "*li*ᵃ is the same in all things, while *ch'i*ᵃ is not."[13] Yet he acknowledges the human being as the most intelligent creature on Earth, possessing a "nature of five constant virtues." Next to us, birds and beasts are dull but sentient, whereas flourishing and withered plants have no consciousness but are not without the *li*ᵃ that makes them what they are.[14] Chu points out instances, however, where animals show moral sense, such as tigers and wolves demonstrating the bond of affection between parents and children, and ants and bees demonstrating the bond of loyalty between rulers and subjects.[15]

Nevertheless, he asserts elsewhere that there are differences in both the *li*ᵃ and *ch'i*ᵃ that constitute humans and other creatures:[16] "The endowments of humans and things differ in shape and ch'i[a]. That is why the mind may be brighter or duller, and the nature may be more complete or less complete."[17]

There is evidence that Chu sees a hierarchy of beings, moving from humans to the other sentient beings, to the organic world of plants, and then to the inorganic rocks and sand:

> What we call jen[a] is the most important of the four virtues of the nature (hsing). . . . Only human nature is the most spiritual and can have all these four virtues, manifest as the four beginnings. [But] things [i.e., animals] have partial and inadequate [endowments of] a ch'i[a], with duller and obscure minds, so they cannot have everything . . . , although we cannot say they have no natures. And the li[a] in those living things that have no sensations . . . also follow their shapes and ch'i[a] . . . , but we still cannot say they have no natures.[18]

Tang Chün-i explains that earlier in his life, Chu tended to follow Ch'eng Yi in saying that li[a] is similar in all and ch'i[a] is what differentiates. Later, Chu spoke of differences in the quality of ch'i[a] as well as in the degree of completeness of li[a].[19] In that case, ch'i[a] remains the individuating factor between humans and nonhumans, as well as among humans, especially when we take into account Chu's explanations for the rise of evil in human nature, which will be discussed later in this chapter.

Mind versus Nature

In the philosophy of Chu Hsi, nature, or essence (hsing[a]), is usually identified with the "principles" (li[a]) that constitute human beings and other creatures, making them what they are and giving them their inherent being and goodness. Still, principles alone cannot make nature, or essence, manifest. It requires the assistance of ch'i[a], the dynamic, material component, which gives shape and individuation to all things. Where li[a] carries with it strong Buddhist metaphysical associations, ch'i[a] is an older, native Chinese concept.[20]

And then there is hsin[a], a word usually translated as "mind" and sometimes as "mind-and-heart." In Mencius, it refers to the center of being that is the self-reflective source of all our conscious and moral activities: the heart as the origin of the good emotions as well as the mind as source of moral principles. In the Great Learning and the Doctrine of the Mean, the moral mind is what is prominent. In Buddhist, especially Ch'an, texts, it signifies being, reality, even ultimate reality. So its meaning extends far beyond the English word "mind." It may be better rendered by the Latin mens as the apex of the soul, its innermost sanctuary, or by the French coeur, in the sense assigned it by Blaise Pascal. It is the meeting point of the intellect and the will.[21]

Just as nature (hsing[a]) is full of principle (li[a]), the mind (hsin[a]) is full of ch'i[a]. For "nature is li[a]. It is called nature in relation to mind, and called li[a] in relation to things."[22] "Nature is like T'ai-chi. The mind is like yin and yang. T'ai-chi resides in yin and yang and cannot leave them. Yet T'ai-chi is still T'ai-chi, and

yin and *yang* are still *yin* and *yang*. That is the same with nature and mind."[23]
According to Chu, human nature transcends mind while being inseparable from
it, the way *li*[a] transcends *ch'i*[a] without being separate from it. But where nature
is passive, mind is dynamic. Mind is what the *Great Learning* calls "bright virtue," the "empty, unobscured intelligence, comprising all principles and responding to all affairs."[24] Chu even uses the word *shen-ming* ("god," or "spirit") to
describe the role of *hsin*[a] in the human being.[25] After all, it is the mind that is
in charge of the person, of his nature and his emotions. The mind is that with
which we govern the body. It is one, not two; subject, not object; and controls
the external world rather than being controlled by it. Human nature is like a
repository for principles, which are always good, but only the mind can act
upon them. For this reason, the mind is essential in the investigation of
principles:[26]

> The *li*[a] in human mind is called nature. Nature is like the mind's field. What
> fills its otherwise empty space is *li*[a]. The mind is the house of the spirit, the
> ruler of the body. Nature comprises all these principles about the Way,
> which are received from Heaven and present in the mind. When manifest
> in cognition, perceptions, thoughts, and anxieties, we have emotions. That
> is why we say the mind controls nature and emotions.[27]

It is interesting that emotions are regarded as what the mind manifests, including on the cognitive level. According to Chu, *jen*[a] belongs to human nature,
while compassion is an emotion, manifest in the mind.[28] In this sense, he likes
to repeat Chang Tsai's insight that "the mind is in control of the nature and the
emotions."[29] He remarks that this is an innovation not found in *Mencius* or in
the work of the Ch'eng brothers, who have not been able to see nature and the
emotions together and equally. For Chu, emotions are active and dynamic, and
the mind rules over them like a general over a hundred thousand troops. "Speaking generally, mind and nature seem to be one and yet are two; [they seem to
be] two and yet are one."[30]

Although Chu insists on the priority of *li*[a] over *ch'i*[a], and therefore of nature
over mind, he remains fascinated by the human mind for its dynamism and hidden mysteries. He expresses this over and over again in poetry:

> The mind's mysteries cannot be measured;
> They enter and exit, riding the power of *ch'i*[a].
>
> . . . .
>
> Divine light shines from the nine extremes;
> Deep thought grasps the myriad nuances.[31]

This is another example of Chu's fascination with discovery, with the quest to
unravel the mystery that so challenges him, that can also challenge us. And the
light is not far away. It is shining from the highest reaches of Heaven, the nine
extremes. In a comparable metaphor, the poem at the beginning of the chapter
tells us that water (mind) is always clear because it is continually being nurtured
by its living source.

*Li*ᵃ: Immanent and Transcendent

I have already spent some time discussing the Great Ultimate (*T'ai-chi*) in a cosmic context. We know that according to Chu Hsi, it is also present within us. "Every human being has a *T'ai-chi*. Every thing has *T'ai-chi*."[32] Chu completes Chou's legacy by integrating it with Ch'eng Yi's a concept of *li*ᵃ. Thus the transcendent, the absolute, is also immanent not only in the totality of the universe but also in every individual human being—indeed, in every individual thing. Yet humans and other creatures differ according to what each has received of *ch'i*ᵃ. "The physical constitution of dogs and horses being what it is, [dogs and horses] know only how to do certain things."[33]

How can there be one Great Ultimate that is also present in the myriad things? The answer: "This is like having only one moon in the sky but when its light is scattered over rivers and lakes, it can be seen everywhere."[34] Here we have once more the idea that there is only one principle with many manifestations, an idea that marks another contribution from Chu Hsi. But this immanence appears to remain latent in most people. It has to be made manifest, to become actualized, by self-cultivation.

Chu recognizes Chou's *T'ai-chi* as the source and fullness of all being and perfection. He calls it *T'ien-li* (heavenly principle), using a term found in Ch'eng Hao and Ch'eng Yi. "The Great Ultimate is just the principle of Heaven and Earth and the myriad things."[35] "The Great Ultimate is the virtuous examplar of Heaven and Earth, humans and things, and a myriad of goodness."[36]

A problem arises, however, when one tries to describe the relationship between the Great Ultimate, which is immanent in human nature, and the *li*ᵃ, which constitutes human nature. Are they one and the same, especially since the *li*ᵃ is frequently described as having come from Heaven, indeed, as the "heavenly principle" (*T'ien-li*)? Speaking from the texts, there is much ambiguity in this area. The language Chu Hsi uses may lead us to think that the Great Ultimate in human nature *is* also the *li*ᵃ constituting human nature. Chu seems to say as much. But Fung Yu-lan is of the opinion that they are different, that whereas the *li*ᵃ constituting human nature is usually manifest, through *ch'i*ᵃ, the Great Ultimate requires personal cultivation and liberation in order to become manifest.[37] I think it may be useful to see the immanent Great Ultimate as the *fullness* of *li*ᵃ in human beings, a fullness which is usually not manifest except in the persons of the sages. In other words, the identity between the Great Ultimate and *li*ᵃ in the nature of sages is not true of ordinary humans. It can, however, be made so by a process of cultivation. Therefore, its manifestation is also in terms of degrees, depending on the person's nearness to sagehood. If we prefer, we may talk in terms of the divine spark within, found in everyone, which can enlighten and take over when permitted.

Physical Endowment and the Problem of Evil

Chu Hsi is heir to a tradition, the Confucian tradition as transmitted and interpreted by Mencius and others. In this tradition, a key doctrine concerns universal human perfectibility—that every person can become a sage like the ancients Yao and Shun. This is an optimistic teaching, which claims to see the unity of humankind in the universally accessible goal of sagehood. This teaching is grounded in the belief that human nature is originally good and can be made perfect by personal cultivation. Indeed, in the metaphysics of Chou and Chu, the human being represents the summit of the universe, participating in the excellence of the Great Ultimate and possessing the nature which has come to him through the interaction of *yin* and *yang* and the Five Phases. Human nature is originally good, or "sincere" (*ch'eng*). Whence, then, comes evil, that ugly fact of human life and experience?[38]

Chu is well aware of this problem, which Chou generally neglected. Chu attempts a metaphysical answer, drawing upon the philosophies of both Chang Tsai and the Ch'eng brothers. I refer here once more to the philosophical distinction between *li*[a] and *ch'i*[a].

As already mentioned, for the Ch'engs as well as Chu Hsi, *li*[a] and *ch'i*[a] are the two coordinate principles which constitute all things. In the case of Chang Tsai, little mention is made of *li*[a], but much more of *ch'i*[a]. Chang distinguishes between the two dimensions of human nature: the heavenly nature, which is good, and the physical nature, which individuates and limits it and makes it capable of evil. An individual's nature depends on the quality of the *ch'i*[a] with which it is endowed, what is called "capacity" (*ts'ai*). This gives recognition to a certain dualism in human nature.[39] As an explanation for the problem of evil in human nature, it received the enthusiastic approval of Chu Hsi: "The theory of the endowment of *ch'i*[a] began with Chang Tsai and the two Ch'engs and has contributed much to the school of the sages and will be a great help to future scholars."[40]

Indeed, this distinction between heavenly and physical nature marks an important step forward in Chinese philosophical anthropology. It also rendered obsolete the earlier distinction made by Mencius and his followers between human nature as it is at birth and as it is later, which was problematic because it is practically impossible to judge the goodness or evil of an infant's nature. The oft-quoted parable of a man's spontaneous reaction at the sight of a child falling into a well[41] can only be an example of the natural reaction of a *cultured* human being, and not of raw human nature.

Accepting Chang Tsai's contribution, Ch'eng Yi explains the effect of *ch'i*[a] on human nature with the introduction of a new term, that of "capacity" (*ts'ai*): "Nature (*hsing*[a]) comes from Heaven; capacity (*ts'ai*) comes from *ch'i*[a]. When the *ch'i*[a] is pure, so is the capacity; when the *ch'i*[a] is impure, so too is the capacity. Capacity may be good or evil; nature is always good."[42] Thus *li*[a], though wholly good in itself, loses its perfection with actualization through *ch'i*[a], owing to the limitations imposed by the latter. This is true of physical things as well as of human nature. The language used to describe such a limitation is that of impediments to the "manifestation" of *li*[a]. Physical endowments vary in humans; persons who receive the *ch'i*[a] in its purity and transparency are endowed with a natural ease for sageliness, whereas those who receive it in its impurity and opacity experience a stronger attraction for evil. In spite of varying physical endowments, all human beings can become perfect, with greater or lesser ease, since all possess *li*ᵃ as well as *ch'i*ᵃ.

Starting from Ch'eng Yi's theory of "capacity," Chu goes on to explain the role of emotions in human nature and particularly in the rise of evil. He also brings in here the importance of a the mind-and-heart (*hsin*ᵃ), the unifying principle of nature and the emotions:

> Nature is the *li*ᵃ of the mind; emotions are the movement of the mind; capacity is that by which emotions act in a certain manner. Emotions and capacity are very close to each other. But emotions are consequent to their encounter with [external] things.[43]

Quoting Chang Tsai:

> "The mind is that which controls nature and the emotions." It is based on nature but operates through emotions. . . .
>   The mind may be good or evil; nature is always good.[44]

Inequality of Endowments

In following the teachings of Chang Tsai and the Ch'eng brothers, Chu made his own contribution by clarifying the relationship between human nature and emotions and by clearly accepting the mind as the unifying agent between the two and as the determining agent for good and evil actions. And he has done more. He has also discussed the question of consciousness. This question concerns the *locus* of man's spiritual and intellectual activity. Does consciousness pertain to *li*ᵃ or to *ch'i*ᵃ, to nature or to the mind?

Chu Hsi answers clearly that the mind is the locus of consciousness (*chih-chüeh*). According to him, the locus of intelligence (*ling-ch'u*) is the mind alone and not nature, because nature is pure *li*ᵃ, and *li*ᵃ, although the principle of perfection, is a passive principle. It is only through union with *ch'i*ᵃ that consciousness can appear.[45] Thus, consciousness pertains to the concrete world, the world over which the mind exercises control. But it is not explained how intelligence and consciousness are related.

Here we touch upon another problem: that of inequality in human endowments notwithstanding original goodness and universal perfectibility. Chu Hsi explains this in terms of the differences in physical endowments of *ch'i*ᵃ. He agrees with Han Yü (768–824) that there are different grades in human nature and praises Ch'eng Yi and Chang Tsai for their philosophical explanation of such differences. He admits, with them, that some men have a purer endowment of *ch'i*ᵃ than others:

> Human nature is always good, yet some men are good from their births on, and others are evil from their births on. This is due to differences in physical endowment. . . . The goal of education is to transform physical endowment. But such transformation is very difficult.[46]

Chu Hsi has not articulated a theory of human freedom, as such. But the theme of freedom runs through the entire spectrum of Confucian thought. Without freedom, there can be no self-determination, no self-transcendence, not only in the ethical sphere but also in the social and political spheres.

Chu incorporates as well the teachings of his philosophical predecessor Chang Tsai concerning *ch'i*ᵃ. According to this view, emotions (*ch'ing*), which are manifestations of *ch'i*ᵃ, become occasions for evil whenever they show excesses. As a method of self-perfection, and for control of emotions, Chu proposes the cultivation of (1) a disposition of reverence (*ching*ᵈ) through quiet-sitting (*ching-tso*), a form of meditation and self-examination, accompanying correct behavior, and (2) the investigation of things through assiduous study. He claims that this dual formula of reverence and study can contribute toward the state of psychic harmony (*ho*) characterizing the due proportion of emotions described in the *Doctrine of the Mean*.

Emotions

According to Ronald de Sousa, "What is morally interesting about human life is played out in the domain of the emotions. When we focus on their connection with sins, the capacity of the emotions will be deplored. When we focus on virtues, it will be celebrated."[47] Let us examine the discussions of emotions given in the classical Chinese texts, as well as in Chu Hsi's commentaries on this subject. I refer here to Mencius's teachings of the beginnings of virtue in human nature; the discussion of the four emotions—pleasure, anger, sorrow, and joy—in the *Doctrine of the Mean* and of the state prior and posterior to the rise of these emotions; and the seven emotions enumerated in the chapter on the evolution of rites in the Book of Rites, which adds three—love, hatred, desire—to the *Doctrine of the Mean*'s four and changes joy, an emotion so close to pleasure, to fear.[48] These are the pivotal texts that Chu Hsi accepts and incorporates into his own theory of human nature and his doctrines of sagehood and self-cultivation.

The most important text is the *Doctrine of the Mean*: It begins with certain definitions of nature (*hsing*ᵃ), of the Way (Tao), and of instruction (*chiao*). It sets these definitions in a cosmic context: "What Heaven has conferred is called nature; exercising this nature is called the Way; cultivating the Way is called instruction. The Way is that which may not be left for an instant. . . . Therefore, the gentleman is watchful over himself when he is alone." And then, immediately following the above preface comes this passage about the emotions: "Before the rise (*wei-fa*) of joy, anger, sorrow, and pleasure, [the mind-and-heart] may be said to be in the state of equilibrium (*chung*). When they have arisen and reached due proportion, there is what may be called the state of harmony (*ho*)."[49] The description is of two states of consciousness, before and after the rise of emotions. They are sometimes called the unmanifest and manifest states of the mind-and-heart. I have translated *chung* as "equilibrium". In Chinese, it is the same word as "middle," "the Mean."

Chu says that, as *li*[a], the Great Ultimate is also nature (*hsing*[a]) in human beings and, with the two modes of motion and rest, produces the five constant virtues. He even calls the Great Ultimate the *li*[a] of emotions, both before these become manifest and after: "Before they turn manifest (*wei-fa*), pleasure, anger, sorrow, and joy constitute the unmanifest [mind]. They too have a Great Ultimate. When manifested (*yi-fa*), they also have a Great Ultimate."[50] For Chu Hsi, nature is not directly tangible, since it belongs to the order without shapes. It can be reached only through the manifest emotions (*yi-fa*). For that reason, emotions are very important. Indeed, in Chu's metaphysical structure, emotions rank with nature and mind, with mind as the controlling agent of the other two:

> Nature is not possible to describe. If we say nature is good, it is only be-cause we see the four beginnings of compassion, modesty, and so on, and [through these] we find nature to be good. It is like seeing the clarity of moving water and knowing then that the source is pure.[51]

Emotions as Good

On first hearing, the four beginnings of virtue may sound like a list of moral principles. But on reading *Mencius*, there is no doubt that these have to do with moral feelings or emotions. For this reason, Mencius uses the word *hsin*[a] to mean a *sensitive* mind or heart—in this case, much more heart than mind:

> Mencius said: "No man is devoid of a heart sensitive to the sufferings of others. . . . The heart (*hsin*[a]) of compassion is the germ of humanity (*jen*[a]); the heart of shame, of dutifulness or rightness (*yi*); the heart of courtesy and modesty, of propriety (*li*[a]) or the observance of rites; the heart of right and wrong, of wisdom (*chih*[c]). The human being has these four germs [be-ginnings] just as he has four limbs."

The "four beginnings of virtue—[compassion, shame, modesty, and the discern-ment between right and wrong] are not welded on to me from the outside; they are in me originally."[52] The word *hsin*[a] is the same word Chu uses in his refer-ences to that which controls human nature and emotions. But the Mencian context in which this word occurs is a broader, almost "naturalistic" one when compared to the neo-Confucian context in which Ch'eng Yi, Chang Tsai, and Chu Hsi make use of the same word, which, by their time, has acquired certain metaphysical connotations from Buddhist philosophy. However, for both Mencius and Chu Hsi, the human mind or heart is the seat of emotions as well as of intel-ligence and volition.

The word *hsin*[a] refers here to certain sentiments of the heart: for example, that which impels a person to forget his own interests and rush to the rescue of a drowning child. And we may especially wonder at the inclusion of a sense of right and wrong among these basic sentiments, these "emotions" of the heart. In Kantian terms, Mencius offers an empirical ground for morality: that of moral feeling, based on human nature and its spontaneous, even instinctive choice of the good in moments of crisis calling for altruism. Upon this foundation of moral feeling, he has built his entire doctrine of human perfectibility, of the possibility of attaining the highest ideals of sagehood and virtue. Chu Hsi has accepted this foundation without question. He has, indeed, used it as a starting point in the elaboration of his own views on human nature and the emotions. To quote him here:

> Where mind-and-heart, nature and emotions, are concerned, Mencius and Chang Tsai have given the best explanations. [Mencius says], "the heart of compassion is the beginning of humanity."[53] Now humanity is nature (hsing[a]), and compassion is emotion (ch'ing), which arises necessarily from the mind-and-heart (hsin[a]). [Chang Tsai has said:] "The mind unifies nature and the emotions."[54] As to nature, it is just principle (li[a]) . . . and not a physical thing. . . . That is why it is entirely good.[55]

In commenting upon Mencius, Chu Hsi continued to develop the teachings of his immediate predecessors, especially Chang Tsai and the Ch'eng brothers. He has done so without violating the intentions of Mencius. But he has also gone beyond Mencius, for he has made his own contribution as well, clarifying the relationship between nature and the emotions, while accepting mind (hsin[a]) as the unifying agent between the two—indeed, as the determining agent for good and evil actions: "The mind . . . embraces all principles and can know all things and affairs. . . . When we do our best by the mind, it will naturally become bright and [reflect all things,] so that every thing and affair will conform to the correct principles."[56]

The philosophical tradition coming from Mencius, with its emphasis on human perfectibility, based on the doctrine of man's orginal goodness, offers an important foundation for the positive evaluation of human emotions. The doctrine of the original goodness of human nature is grounded in the doctrine of the morality and goodness of certain human emotions. Chu affirms that his ethics, which owes so much to Mencius's teaching of the four beginnings of virtue, is based on moral feeling. For him, the four beginnings are moral feelings that direct us to the good.

> Nature is the principle (li[a]) of the mind; the mind is the ruler of the body. The four beginnings of virtue are emotions; they are the visible manifestations of the mind. The four originate in the mind, but that which makes them what they are comes from the li[a] of human nature.[57]

The *Book of Mencius* is not the only important Confucian text discussing the role of emotions. The *Doctrine of the Mean* enumerates four emotions and distinguishes between the state of consciousness prevailing before the rise of these emotions and that prevailing afterward. I shall now turn to a deeper examination of this second text.

Emotions as Ambivalent

In the Confucian tradition, different opinions had been voiced regarding the goodness and evil of original human nature, with the fourth-century-B.C.E. Mencius opting for good and the third-century-B.C.E. Hsün-tzu opting for evil (with the understanding that education can change human nature for the better). In such discussions, emotions are often made to bear the responsibility for good or evil.

The *Doctrine of the Mean* concludes on a note of harmony and equilibrium: "This equilibrium is the great root of all under Heaven; this harmony is the universal Way of all under Heaven. Let the states of equilibrium and harmony prevail, and a happy order will reign throughout Heaven and Earth, and the myriad things will all be nourished."[58] This interesting statement makes the reader feel that the cosmos also palpitates with emotions, and that he or she can make a difference in modifying these cosmic emotions. The praise is of equilibrium, or the "Mean," the state of consciousness which prevails *before* the rise of emotions, as well as of harmony, the state of consciousness which prevails when emotions are maintained in proper balance. The obvious warning is to guard against excessive emotions. This is something we all recognize: that emotions in excess, whether anger, pleasure, or sorrow, can be highly destructive (even an excess of joy can be disruptive). In other words, emotions have the power to do good as well as evil. They possess a great power of motivation for good, as well as a volatile quality, a power of disruption, even of destruction. For this reason, they should be kept under control.

A problem is that, in asserting human goodness, Mencius appears not to have permitted any possibility for evil to arise. It took Ch'eng Yi to refine this teaching by pointing out the varying physical endowments in human nature. All this is not to deny human goodness, but to explain the rise of evil in the case of an excessive manifestation of emotions.

The problem of the emotions and their relationship to human nature as well as to mind or heart is a difficult one. Chu Hsi clearly acknowledges that the four beginnings belong to the order of emotions, but he makes a distinction between the four and the seven by saying that "the four beginnings manifest *li*[a] and the seven emotions manifest *ch'i*[a]." The word *fa* ("manifest" or "issue forth") is ambiguous, so that the same statement might be translated as "the four beginnings issue from *li*[a], and the seven emotions issue from *ch'i*[a]." Such a statement puts greater distance between the four and the seven and, indeed, between *li*[a] and *ch'i*[a]. But Chu continues by saying that he sees a real similarity between the emotions and the virtues.[59]

But why make any distinction between the four and the seven, if they are all emotions? Are the four superior to the seven, or is the distinction between them purely arbitrary and textual? These questions saw little discussion in China but very much in Korea—lasting several centuries. Some thinkers insisted on a greater separation between the four and the seven, while others saw more of a continuum.[60]

The Ethics of Self-Transcendence

Organically part and parcel of his philosophical system, Chu Hsi's ethics is difficult to represent in isolation from the whole. Besides, the Chinese approach to
ethics is quite different from the many schools we find in today's West, which
tend to focus on ethical theories, dwelling often on analyses of words like "be"
and "ought," "right" and "good," with the aim of making cognitive distinctions
without direct bearing on the good and moral life. In this regard, the growing
importance of applied ethics is making an impact, even if this subfield tends as
well to carve out preferred specific domains of ethical action rather than to discuss the moral person.[61]

Self-transcendence goes beyond self-fulfillment, and thus Chu Hsi's philosophy differs from Aristotle's because the latter emphasizes the fulfillment of one's
nature. Neither is Chu Hsi's philosophy exactly the same as Plato's, with Plato's
preference for envisaging the human form as somehow imprisoned in the flesh.
Nevertheless, Chu's philosophy does bear similarities to *both* Aristotle's and
Plato's. For Chu Hsi, the goal of human existence *is* self-fulfillment, but the definition of self-fulfillment *is also* self-transcendence, that is, transcending one's
selfish desires and becoming a sage.

The preferred concern of Confucian ethics is the pursuit of the highest good,
as articulated in the text Chu loved, the *Great Learning*. The language is therefore of self-transcendence in the moral and spiritual sense. The goal is to become
a sage, after the examples of Confucius and Mencius, as well as others who were
their moral examplars. The preoccupation is therefore not with what is or is not
moral but with *how* to achieve sagehood, granted the presupposition that all have
the innate goodness and potential to become sages.

The problem of evil is all the more important on account of the problem of
self-transcendence. Recognition of moral evil and human fallibility is prerequisite to any desire and resolution to transcend oneself. Human nature is both the
given and the *yet to become*—that which we can shape, within the limitations of
our historical situation.

However, to affirm that the human being possesses naturally a desire to become better, and that this desire is possible of fulfillment, is not enough. One still
has to show the *way* by which such fulfillment is to be realized. Without practice, there is no assurance that theory can be tested, and without testing, theory
remains empty—a powerless wish or, rather, a wish capable of destroying the
person through frustration but incapable of its own fulfillment.

Many questions have been raised in this regard. For example, are sages born or
made? If they are born, are they not superhuman? Would they have emotions—
the occasion for evil? If they are made (self-made), why are they so few? Why did
they exist only in the remote or historical antiquity? Generations of Chinese thinkers have grappled with these questions, to which Chu Hsi also fell heir.

Confucius himself says that some sages are born and others are made—sometimes, after great difficulties. He speaks of some men who are born with wisdom,
and others who must acquire it.[62] Chu Hsi appears generally to accept this an-

swer. The fact, however, that he acknowledges very few historical figures—and all in the remote past—as sages implies that he did not think that many sages were "born" sagely. Indeed, it may be argued that what some may be endowed with at birth is a greater capacity and ease, and that no one is outside the existential law of striving for perfection.

And so Chu tempers his optimism regarding human nature with a touch of realism regarding the existential differences between human beings, as well as the difficulties of changing the given physical endowment. Nevertheless, perfection is always within grasp, and with it, the acquisition of perfect virtue, *jen*[a].

A Doctrine of *Jen*[a63]

The Chinese word *jen*[a] has been interpreted variously by those who claim to know its etymology. The most common explanation is that the human radical next to the two horizontal strokes represents a virtue practiced in interaction with others. Another is that the two strokes represent the ancient symbol for "upper," bringing to mind an upper, or superior, man and the virtue that is enjoined upon such a person. A third explanation is that it resembles a man carrying a heavy burden, hence signifying "bearing and enduring."[64]

In discussing Chu's doctrine of *Jen*[a], I shall use the capitalized term to distinguish it from the lowercased *jen*[a], which is one of the constant virtues, in which case jen[a] resembles kindness, although Chu himself tends to use the term to speak of the universal virtue. Indeed, Chu has left behind his own definition of *Jen*[a] as the "principle of love and the character of the mind." *Jen*[a] is the principle of love precisely because, as a universal virtue, it encompasses other virtues: *yi, li*[a] *chih*[c], and *hsin*[a].[65] Indeed, it is the source from which other virtues flow: "Of the five constant virtues [humanity (*jen*[a]), rightness (*yi*), propriety (*li*[a]), wisdom (*chih*[c]), and faithfulness (*hsin*[b])], *jen*[a] is the most fundamental. . . . The pursuit of *jen*[a] through reverence is the key to learning."[66]

The five constant virtues govern the five moral relationships. *Jen*[a] governs the parent-child relationship, *yi* the ruler-subject, *li*[a] the husband-wife, *chih*[c] the elder and younger siblings, and *hsin*[b] that between friends. The list of five is an accumulated one, showing the influence of Mencius, who taught the importance of rightness (or justice), adding it not only to *jen*[a] but also to Confucius's other preference, propriety (or right conduct), *li*[c]. It is interesting to have wisdom included as one of the constant virtues, since wisdom is understood sometimes in a cognitive sense, as universal knowledge, and sometimes as a penetrating understanding of truth itself, which would make it the other side of *jen*[a] as universal, practical virtue. And then there is *hsin*[b], the conformity of the person to his or her words, that is, truth or faithfulness.

To say that *Jen*[a] is a character of the mind is to stay on the abstract level. That is why Chu also asserts that *Jen*[a] is the principle of love, moving his discussion to a more practical and experiential level.

Chu Hsi developed his definitive teaching on *Jen*[a] after he had finalized his doctrine on emotional equilibrium and harmony (*chung-ho*), which is discussed in the next chapter, on personal cultivation. He spent several years on the latter question, but he was reflecting at the same time on the question of *Jen*[a], which took even further pondering. He was then in his forties, and both teachings should be considered important reflections of his mature thinking. And this thinking goes far beyond that of Confucius and Mencius, even if these sages provided him with a starting point for his speculations. Chu would represent *Jen*[a] as a creative power, present in the cosmos as well as in human hearts and minds. He was actually offering reflections on a subject that was increasingly receiving a cosmic and, one might add, a mystical dimension.

Jen[a] *and Love* (Ai)

If *Jen*[a] is the "principle of love," is it also love (*ai*) itself? This was certainly the belief of Han Yü, who defined *Jen*[a] as universal love (*po-ai*).[67] Ch'eng Yi has asserted:

> Because Mencius said that "the feeling of commiseration is *jen*[a]," later scholars have regarded love (*ai*) as *jen*[a]. But love is emotion (*ch'ing*), and *jen*[a] is nature (*hsing*[a]). It is therefore a mistake to say that *jen*[a] is love. Han Yü erred in saying universal love is *jen*[a]. The man of *jen*[a] loves universally, but one may not therefore confuse *jen*[a] with universal love.[68]

This assertion started many discussions that continued with Chu and his disciples. Chu distinguished between love and desire or passion (*yü*[b]), because love does not include any desire to possess. Lao Ssu-kuang expresses this point well:

> Love itself is a faculty of the mind and heart and cannot be called evil. Desire indicates a motivation coming from selfishness and is therefore evil. In other words, an emotion that abides by *li*[a] is not a desire, but an emotion that does not abide by *li*[a] is desire.[69]

It would appear that the Chinese word here for love (*ai*) is understood less in terms of the Greek *eros* and more in terms of *agapē*. While Chu respects Ch'eng Yi, he agrees more with Han Yü that *Jen*[a] also includes love, and he regards Ch'eng as having erred in differentiating between *Jen*[a] and love. For him, *Jen*[a] is the source of love, even if the concept "love" as an emotion cannot exhaust the meaning of *Jen*[a]. Here he differs as well from his friend Chang Shih, who followed Hu Hung's teachings, centered on human nature and the mind as two aspects of the same reality, the *li*[a].[70] Chang had earlier influenced Chu by shifting Chu's focus from the unmanifest mind (*wei-fa*) to the manifest (*yi-fa*), from pure contemplation for its own sake to more action. Chu was on close terms with Chang, with whom he exchanged numerous letters, which disclose how he was moving to his own viewpoints on such issues as the mind, unmanifest and manifest, the nature of *Jen*[a], and the practice of meditation or quiet-sitting. Eventually, he would influence Chang himself on some of these issues.[71]

Naturally we should not label love as Jen[a]. Neither should we separate love from Jen[a]. For the substance of Jen[a] is the principle of love. That there is unity between self and all things is the reason for loving all things. But the principle of love does not exist for, and is not premised on, the theory of the unity of all things. . . . Jen[a] is the principle of love and the way of life.[72]

To say that Jen[a] is the principle of love is also to exalt an emotion, love. As one of the seven emotions, love cannot exhaust the meaning of Jen[a], which is a source or principle of this love. In taking Han Yü's side against Ch'eng Yi on this point, Chu demonstrates his high regard for human emotions when they are properly manifest, and this in turn demonstrates his high regard for much of human life and culture, which emotions often rule or inspire.

Jen[a] as Character of Mind

Chu starts his "Treatise on Jen" with a cosmic perspective, on the generative power of Jen[a]: "Heaven and earth take the production of things as their mind and heart. The generation or production of humans and things partakes of this mind of Heaven and Earth, [which becomes] their minds. Therefore, to speak of the character of the mind . . . is to speak of Jen[a]."[73] He is saying that the mind of Heaven and Earth generates things, and in receiving life, human beings all participate in this mind, which is manifest in Jen[a]. As usual, he does not argue that this is so, except by mentioning certain passages from the Book of Changes. He also describes Jen[a] as "the source of all morality and the root of all moral action."[74] Here he likens it to Ch'eng Yi's metaphor of Jen[a] as a seed of grain, which contains life and the ability to grow. When human beings regard the productive mind of Heaven and earth as their own, they also possess Jen[a], for Jen[a] has the potential to grow.[75] And because of the presence of the universal Jen[a], the particular virtues of jen[a], yi, li[c], and chih are able to activate themselves and become the feelings of commiseration, shame and dislike, respect and reverence, right and wrong, described in Mencius as the four beginnings of virtue, and proceed to motivate all morality and moral action.[76]

In the final analysis, Chu's position is not very different from Ch'eng Yi's or Chang Shih's.[77] To clarify this, I shall briefly explain Chang's position.

Jen[a] as Consciousness

In interpreting Confucian morality, Jen[a] is always pointed out as *the* virtue par excellence, the source and foundation of all other virtues. And this universal virtue of the classical age takes on life-giving qualities in later times with the philosophers Chou Tun-yi and Chang Tsai, attaining even cosmic proportions with the Ch'eng brothers: "A medical treatise describes the paralysis of the hands and feet as absence of jen[a]. This is a very good description. The person of Jen[a] is one with Heaven and Earth and all things."[78] This analogy is usually attributed to Ch'eng Hao. From him came the teaching that *Jen*[a] refers to consciousness, a teaching that became the trademark for the Hunan school and its followers. Chu discussed this subject in a voluminous correspondence with Chang Shih, who, among other things, found it difficult to accept *Jen*[a] as the principle of love.[79] Chu and Chang each wrote a treatise on *Jen*[a] and exchanged it with the other for comments and criticisms.[80] When we compare the two men's final works, we find a remarkable similarity in their outlooks.

Chu likes certain teachings of Han Yü but thinks that he does not distinguish properly between nature and emotions. Chang Shih is also somewhat critical of Han. Chang speaks of *Jen*[a] as being present in stillness and, together with the other virtues, serving as the origin of Heaven and Earth and all things. Chu criticizes Chang and his Hunan school for representing *Jen*[a] as the mind's consciousness (*chüeh*). He says they are merely following in the footsteps of Hsieh Liangtso and Ch'eng Hao, for whom such consciousness tends to be restricted to sense perceptions:[81] "It is permitted to say that the humane person's mind has consciousness, but not that this mind's consciousness is *Jen*[a]. For the consciousness of the humane person's mind refers to *Jen*[a] embracing the functions of the four [beginnings of virtue]."[82]

Chu finds that the followers of the Hunan school share a tendency to use the mind to pursue the mind, presumably in meditation, which he opposes for its subjectivity and circularity; he is also opposed to the rigidity with which they pursue their goal in their self-cultivation. Citing the *Analects*, "The humane (*jen*[a]) person delights in the mountains; the wise person delights in the waters," Chu responds that delighting in nature and finding repose and relaxation are permitted to those who practice self-cultivation and pursue *Jen*[a].[83] He wants to render more humane and less ascetic the work of self-cultivation.

It would appear that Chu was nevertheless influenced by the Hunan school, since it is a short distance between being conscious of the oneness of the self and the universe, which was Ch'eng Hao's contribution, and being conscious of *Jen*[a] as a cosmic power of production. What Chu objected to was *reducing Jen*[a] to consciousness itself, and especially to sense perceptions as consciousness. He wished rather to safeguard a more transcendent dimension of *Jen*[a], which Ch'eng Hao actually helped to develop.

In this respect, Chu even persuaded Chang Shih to join in his critique of certain passages in Hu Hung, published by Chu as *Misgivings about Hu Hung's "Understanding Words"* (*Hu-tzu chih-yen yi-yi*). Chu insisted that the *Great Learning* be followed in self-cultivation.[84]

There is a question about Chang Shih's "Treatise on *Jen*," which was completed after Chu's own. Mention has already been made of Chang's moving closer to Chu's views. The surprise is that several of Chu's pupils, including Ch'en Ch'un, thought that Chang's treatise came from Chu's hands.[85] Since Chu Hsi personally compiled Chang Shih's writings, could he have exercised his privilege as editor to the extent of rewriting his friend's treatise? This has been asserted, and because of Chu's aggressive editing practices, exercised even on classical texts like the *Great Learning*, as well as on other texts, such as Hu Hung's *Understanding Words*, I have my suspicions, as does Liu Shu-hsien.[86]

Humanity (Jen[a]) and Sincerity (Ch'eng)

Chu's treatment of the closely linked virtues of Jen[a] and ch'eng represents the apex of his teachings on self-cultivation. Jen[a] is the supreme ethical goal, but to realize it actively is to become ch'eng.[87]

The doctrine of sincerity (ch'eng) comes especially from the Doctrine of the Mean. In the text's brief chapters 21–26, we find an exposition of ch'eng that raises the virtue of sincerity to an ontological level.

The term ch'eng is made up of two parts: a component meaning a word (yen) and a component meaning "accomplishment" (ch'eng). In the Shuo-wen, it is explained as truthfulness.[88] When words agree with what the mind regards as real, we have the virtuous quality represented by the English word "sincerity." But the Chinese word has a more profound meaning. The Doctrine of the Mean explains it as "self-completion" and associates it also with brightness, clarity, or intelligence: "When intelligence comes from sincerity, it is called nature (hsing[a]). When sincerity comes from intelligence, it is called instruction. With sincerity comes intelligence; with intelligence comes sincerity."[89] Obviously, ch'eng is not only one of the moral virtues here. It is regarded in relation to the intelligence that may be termed ming (brilliance), a Chinese word that is associated with insight, including mystical insight, and is explained by Chu as "reflecting everything": "The virtue of the sage is with his nature; it is the way of Heaven. He first understands the good and then makes it real. The learning of the worthy comes from instruction; it is the way of man. With sincerity there is nothing that is not understood."[90]

The Doctrine of the Mean says that only the world's most sincere persons can fulfill their own natures and the natures of others and of things and then "participate in the transforming and nurturing powers of Heaven and Earth and form a trinity with these" (ch. 22). And "only the most sincere under Heaven can transform" (ch. 23).

> The most sincere has the ability to know things in advance. When a country or family is about to flourish, there will be good signs; when it is about to perish, there will be bad omens. Such are seen through [divination] by milfoils and tortoises and felt in the four limbs [of the sincere person]. . . . That is why the most sincere person is like a spirit.[91]

It would appear that the word ch'eng refers to a personality who, through a profound understanding of the good, reflected in behavior and action, has become one with the universe and its powers of knowledge and is endowed with the intelligence of the spirits. "That is why the gentleman regards achieving sincerity as a most precious goal."[92] And "that is why the greatest sincerity is ceaseless,"[93] or as Chu explains, "without any falsehood or pretension, it is naturally [practiced] without cease."[94] Presumably, the most sincere is always sincere, for sincerity represents the most perfect realization of virtue, rendering the person a mediator between Heaven and Earth.[95]

Conclusion

I began this study with a question on what the human being is and wherein lies human worth. I spoke of a double identity, related both to nature and to culture. My assumption throughout has been that humanity is a universal. And I have presented Chu Hsi's theory of human nature as one attempt at formulating a rational explanation of the internal dynamics of such a universal. For him, as for the entire Confucian tradition, the human being as moral subject has an almost infinite possibility of self-fulfillment in sagehood.

In quoting the *Doctrine of the Mean* on emotions, we find the correspondence made between the two ideal states of consciousness (before and after the rise of emotions) and cosmic harmony and prosperity. The microcosm/macrocosm parallel is clear. But it leaves one wondering what the two states of consciousness are really about, which state is preferred (the *wei-fa* or the *yi-fa*, and why psychic equilibrium and harmony should affect cosmic equilibrium and harmony. The problem with the classical and other texts that we have is that they speak of the prior or unmanifest state (*wei-fa*) and the posterior or manifest state (*yi-fa*) without ever really explaining the structural differences between them. They also speak of the correspondence between emotional equilibrium and harmony and cosmic harmony without explaining why this should be so. What the texts point to is a unitary experience between the human and the cosmic in which the subject-object dichotomy is transcended. But what the deeper meaning of this transcendence is and how it is to be achieved are problems that Chu Hsi wrestled with for years. In the next chapter, I offer a few tentative answers to some of the questions that have arisen and also discuss his gradual evolution of a theory on this subject, which he calls the theory of equilibrium and harmony (*chung-ho shuo*).

Personal Cultivation (*Hsiu-sheng*)

Against the north windows, reclining with the sage-kings of yore,
Having known so long the joy of reading books.
The joys of reading are endless joys:
I play the lute as a warm wind blows.

Chu Hsi[1]

Introduction[2]

The affirmation that human nature is perfectible, that the human being naturally possesses a desire to transcend the narrow goals of self-survival and self-
satisfaction, implies that this desire is somehow possible of fulfillment. But how?
A *way* by which such fulfillment is to be realized must be shown. Without speci-
fying a way, there is no assurance that the theory can be tested, and without
testing, the theory remains empty—a powerless wish or, rather, a wish capable
of destroying the person through frustration and incapable of its own fulfillment.

As a young man, Chu Hsi was fired with the greatest ambition for a human
being: that of finding wisdom. For this, he read widely, seeking answers to the
mystery of life not only from the Confucian classics but also from Buddhist and
Taoist texts. He learned a lot and, as already mentioned, acquired his *chin-shih*
degree at the tender age of eighteen. But he did not feel he was headed in the right
direction. Therefore, at age twenty-three (1153), Chu sought out Li T'ung's (Li
Tong, 1093–1163) company and, from 1160 on, regarded Li as his teacher. Li
was himself a disciple of Lo Ts'ung-yen (Lo Congyan, 1072–1135), who was in
turn a disciple of Yang Shih (Yang Shi, 1053–1135), and through Yang, Li could
trace back his intellectual lineage to Ch'eng Yi. This does not mean that Li agreed
completely with Ch'eng Yi; in fact, Chu became more influenced by Ch'eng in
his later years through his own reading and reflections. But Li was the person
who oriented Chu to Confucian studies and away from his youthful infatuation
with Buddhism and Taoism.

As we examine further and at closer range Chu Hsi's practical doctrines, we
discover evidence against accepting a widespread, conventional image of him
as a model of rigid moral propriety and a dispenser of prescriptions and proscriptions regarding the correctness of human relationships. True, Chu Hsi does

speak of the three bonds and the five relationships—the warp and woof of Confucian social morality.[3] He was himself a model of correct living, by his own account watchful over the least movements of his mind and heart. But he does not devote his principal attention to questions pertaining to duties and obligations, virtues and vices. He appears rather to have set his mind on higher things.[4]

It is my belief that Chu Hsi's doctrine of personal cultivation belongs to the realm of practical moral philosophy while also going beyond it to embrace a spiritual and ascetic doctrine with mystical implications. It is also firmly grounded in the more speculative parts of his philosophy, namely, in his metaphysics of human nature, especially in his view of the human being as the microcosm of the universe, participating in the cosmic process and assisting in the perfection of the universe through efforts of self-perfection. I believe that within a generally well-balanced thought structure, problems of internal consistency are of a lesser order than problems of external consistency with the entire Confucian tradition. However, the latter have received much more attention and scrutiny from those whose chief concern is doctrinal orthodoxy.[5]

In earlier chapters, I discussed the place of the Great Ultimate in Chu Hsi's thought. In this chapter, I shall assert that Chu's philosophy is at the same time theoretical and practical. In fact, it is often difficult to separate the practical from the theoretical. To the extent that I can, I am moving now from a review of Chu's teachings on human nature, human emotions, and the human mind-and-heart (hsin[a]) to the problems of "preserving the mind and nurturing nature" (ts'un-hsin yang-hsing), that is, to his practical teachings on personal cultivation. I wish to see the exact place given to meditation, or quiet-sitting, examine his teachings on practicing reverence and extending knowledge, and evaluate the importance of the pursuit of knowledge in his whole formula of self-cultivation, before making some concluding observations.

Heavenly Principles versus Human Desires

When we turn from Chu Hsi's cosmology and metaphysics of human nature to his practical moral philosophy, we find a certain continuity of both language and thought. In both his ethics and his doctrine of cultivation, Chu Hsi continues to speak of the Great Ultimate and of li[a] (principle) and ch'i[a] (matter, energy). He does not abandon one realm, that of speculative thought, in order to enter another, that of moral action and spiritual cultivation. He integrates the two in a philosophy which is, on every level, both theoretical and practical.

Relying always upon the metaphysical distinction between li[a] and ch'i[a], Chu speaks of a certain opposition between heavenly principle (T'ien-li) and human desires (jen-yü). The work of cultivation lies in giving complete manifestation to the one and in controlling the other. The sage is the person who is able to rid himself of the impediments imposed by ch'i[a] through human desires or passions and so make manifest his heavenly principle, which seems to be another name for the Great Ultimate within.[6]

With Chu's construction of a new philosophical synthesis comes the definitive acceptance of a certain formulation of the new Confucian message, a terse formula supposedly containing the essentials of the doctrine of the sages. This is taken not from the Four Books but from the Book of History, considered to be one of the earlier classics. It is taken from a chapter allegedly transmitted to posterity in the old pre-Ch'in script—"Counsels of Great Yü"—even though the authenticity of this chapter is subject to doubt, and Chu himself acknowledges the problem. Complete in sixteen Chinese characters, this cryptic formula may be translated:

> The human mind (*jen-hsin*) is prone to error,
> But the moral mind (*tao-hsin*) is subtle (*wei*).
> Remain discerning and single-minded;
> Keep steadfastly to the Mean [or Equilibrium; i.e., *chung*ᵃ].[7]

As mentioned in the last chapter, the "Mean" refers to the state of emotional equilibrium allegedly present before the rise of emotions. In this formula, which served as a kind of credal statement for neo-Confucian followers, the Mean is understood as what permits us to discover the moral mind and is possibly the *locus* of the moral mind.

In his preface to the annotated edition of the *Doctrine of the Mean*, Chu refers to this formula as the eternal message of the ancient sages, associating the *tao-hsin* with *T'ien-li* and the *jen-hsin* with *jen-yü* (human desires) and emphasizing the need for the one to dominate the other. According to him, this is to be done by adherence to the Mean. For him, the Confucian Way (Tao) may be described as this psychic equilibrium, a state of mind-and-heart that reflects original human goodness in the *wei-fa* and enables the seeker to pursue and acquire sagehood. Indeed, this formula became central to his system of "orthodox transmission" of the Confucian truth, which he considered lost since Mencius and only rediscovered by Ch'ou Tun-yi and the Ch'eng brothers. He regarded himself as an heir in this intellectual lineage, with the mission of passing to later generations this important message.[8]

In this chapter, I shall discuss Chu's theories on psychic equilibrium and harmony as states of consciousness of the human mind-and-heart. They are basic for our understanding of his evolving teachings on spiritual cultivation, culminating in his doctrine of reverence, which he received from Ch'eng Yi. This doctrine presumes a dichotomy between heavenly principles and human desires and the need to cultivate the former and curtail the latter.

Such a moral struggle was unappealing, and its emphasis antagonized some people. Even Chu himself acknowledged that he originally found the task daunting:

> The treasured mirror frightened me years ago:
> Buried [under dust], it yielded no clues.
> The dust is now gone, and brightness has returned.
> The treasured mirror can once more reflect [light].[9]

Truth is here regarded as being uncovered, even unveiled, with removal of the dust; the metaphor for truth is the light that is reflected and the mirror that reflects it: the *treasured* mirror.

Why should the mirror have frightened him? I believe that the mirror represents his inner self, which used to frighten him with the weight of its dust. What, then, is represented by the dust? Presumably, it is *jen-yü*, literally, "human desires," which are given an ambivalent connotation:

> The mind is like water; nature is like the tranquillity of still water; emotions are like the flow of [moving] water, and human desires are the waves. Just as there are good and bad waves, so too there are good desires . . . and bad passions that rush out like wild and violent waves. . . . When Mencius said that emotions can help people to do good, he meant that the correct emotions flowing from our nature are originally all good.[10]

Chu does not condemn human desires in themselves. He condemns wild and violent passions—the "bad waves"—and devotes much of his philosophy to a theory of moral and spiritual cultivation by which such passions can be controlled and the goodness of the heavenly principle (*T'ien-li*) can be recovered.

All the same, the caution against emotional excess and the exhortation to maintain constant control and balance spell out a certain distrust of human nature itself, which makes self-conquest an imperative in moral striving. In themselves, some emotions may be good, others neutral, while excessive and violent emotions are definitely dangerous. Besides, the power of emotions is such that they require constant checking. "Therefore, the gentleman is watchful over himself when he is alone (*shen-tu*)."[11] Such vigilance in solitude lies at the core of Chu Hsi's teachings on self-cultivation. As an optimist regarding human nature, he believes that sagehood may be attained; as a realist who is aware of the need for control, he has formulated a theory of personal cultivation that puts us on guard against our own excesses and facilitates the cultivation of the beginnings of goodness in our nature. Throughout this process of formulation, we notice that his theory of self-cultivation is also *his own* way of improving himself, of cleansing his spiritual mirror, of recovering its original purity.

A Doctrine of Psychic Equilibrium (*Chung*[a]) and Harmony (*Ho*)[12]

As we know, the teaching of psychic equilibrium and harmony is found in the *Doctrine of the Mean*, one of Chu's favorite texts. He says of it:

> This book begins by speaking of the one *Li*[a] and then spreads out to discuss the myriad things, only to conclude again with the one *Li*[a]. When one opens [the text] out, [the *Li*[a]] fills the universe.[13] When one rolls [the text] up, [the *Li*[a]] hides itself in secrecy. The meaning to be savored is limitless.

[This doctrine] is full of real learning. The good reader will make discoveries by meditating on it and retain something for use throughout life without ever exhausting its wealth.[14]

He is speaking of what he personally finds precious in the text. The note of secrecy is interesting, as he is suggesting that the language is coded or, at least, that it hides as much as it reveals. The basic meaning of what I translate as "meditating" is "playing" (wan-suo), that is, playing over and over with the words, as one does in chewing and savoring a delicacy.

With this, we return to the subject discussed in the previous chapter: of wei-fa and yi-fa in human consciousness and what the terms really mean. After all, when is the human being ever free from the rise of emotions? Perhaps, one might answer, as an infant or a young child. An infant cannot yet express himself or herself, but a young child can. Chu Hsi decided that the young child (ch'ih-tzu) enjoying peace of mind may have emotional harmony, the yi-fa state, but not the wei-fa state, since, in spite of a certain innocence, he or she is not always free of emotions.[15] The problem is, according to Chu, that one cannot find the moment prior to the unmanifest wei-fa, and neither can one change what follows the manifest yi-fa.[16]

I find the teaching on equilibrium and harmony (chung-ho shuo) the heart of Chu Hsi's philosophy, whereas the Great Ultimate is the comprehensive source or principle. Speaking dialectically, one may identify one with the other. More often, one sees a microcosm/macrocosm correlation between an ideal, human state of consciousness and a cosmic Ultimate. Both are difficult to comprehend, but the obscurity this time is due more to the kind of experience the teaching presupposes or expects, an experience that is beyond ordinary consciousness. For believers in the Mencian teaching of original human goodness, the pristine state of wei-fa is more highly valued than the posterior state, or yi-fa. But what is this kind of consciousness? Is it recoverable, or is it only a hypothetical ideal?

From the text of the Doctrine of the Mean, we know that the wei-fa is free of emotions. We may also surmise that it is free as well of concepts and images. I am referring here to a state of consciousness that we may term pure experience, or pure consciousness, when the mind-and-heart is content to be fully present to, and focused on, itself, in a supranormal state. It is a consciousness that goes beyond all particular activities of the mind-and-heart and can only be inadequately described. It is an experience that goes beyond being conscious of what is occurring, to simply being conscious. It is a state of consciousness of ultimate reality, or of the supreme Tao. It points to an out-of-the-ordinary, that is, mystical, experience.[17]

I am intentionally not making any distinction here between so-called introvertive and extrovertive mysticism, as does W. T. Stace. Following the Doctrine of the Mean, Chinese philosophers like Chu Hsi take for granted that the experience we call mystical gives us the truth about the universe. Besides, the microcosm/macrocosm correspondence is so embedded in the Chinese consciousness that the Confucian and Taoist traditions do not differentiate between introvertive and extrovertive mysticism. For the Confucian, meditation is about reaching the transformed state of *wei-fa* or *yi-fa*, and then participating as well in the cosmic transformation. For the Taoist, meditation usually begins and ends with visualizing light in the cosmos, while the practice is of the inner elixir. Each time, it is the whole that is experienced, according to the language of expression following the experience and to the extent that the experience can be examined.

I am not saying that Chu was himself a mystic. But I am saying that he belongs to a tradition that takes for granted the noetic quality of such an experience, a quality that practitioners do not limit to the subjective alone. This does not mean that I am denying mystical states that do not include a kind of cosmic consciousness. I am saying that for purposes of our discussion, such cosmic consciousness frequently accompanies a mystical consciousness occurring deep in the self.

As to how this occurs, we may get some help from more modern writings. In his book *The Varieties of Religious Experience*, William James describes instances of mystical experience that bring with them a cosmic consciousness. He quotes a Canadian psychiatrist and mystic who says that this consciousness is "a consciousness of the cosmos, that is, of the life and order of the universe. Along with the consciousness of the cosmos there occurs an intellectual enlightenment which alone would place the individual on a new plane of existence."[18] The psychiatrist and mystic says of his own mystical experience that "I saw that the universe is not composed of dead matter, but is, on the contrary, a living Presence; I become conscious in myself . . . that I possessed eternal life then. . . . I had attained to a point of view from which I saw that it must be true.[19]

We are speaking of a state of cosmic consciousness with a strong noetic quality. We have not yet distinguished between *wei-fa* and *yi-fa*. The text from the *Doctrine of the Mean* concludes by associating with both a kind of cosmic flourishing. While the language of *wei-fa* suggests something hypothetical, and that of *yi-fa* something that can be actual, the search for *wei-fa* by so many suggests that it was considered achievable, if only with difficulty. What is implied is a kind of cyclical movement: the return to one's original nature, the recapture of the springs of one's being, and, for the Confucian moralist, allowing this to permeate one's daily living.

It has been said, for example, that Chu's teacher Li T'ung practiced meditation with assiduity in order to experience something of the state of consciousness prior to the rise of emotions.[20] In Li's own words: "In the past, when I studied with Lo Ts'ung-yen, we used to sit in meditation facing each other all day. . . . He told me to contemplate in stillness the so-called state of equilibrium before the rise of [emotions] (*wei-fa*)."[21]

The Old Doctrine

Chu Hsi followed in Li's footsteps for some years, seeking to capture the *wei-fa* state in his meditations. He found it difficult, as the mind represented a constant flow of consciousness while life and the world constituted a succession of things and events. But after Li's death (1163), he gradually moved away from Li's influence. In 1166, Chu tentatively formulated his own theory on equilibrium and harmony, which he would call the "old doctrine" after it was superseded by another doctrine. Chu arrived at his old doctrine after many exchanges with Chang Shih, by correspondence and in person.

In 1167, he visited Chang Shih in T'an-chou and discussed with him a range of things, including Chou's *Diagram of the Great Ultimate*, the diverse interpretations of *jen*[a], and the meaning of equilibrium and harmony, that is, of *wei-fa* and *yi-fa*. After a prolonged visit of two months, their discussion of harmony and equilibrium continued by correspondence. Chang preferred *yi-fa* to *wei-fa* and did not regard meditation so highly; Chang also asserted that one should seek contemplation or stillness in action. Chu struggled with this for a long time because of his attachment to his teacher Li T'ung.

He gives an account of it as follows:

Earlier in life, I learned from Li T'ung the [teaching of the] *Doctrine of the Mean*, while seeking for the meaning of the unmanifest mind (*wei-fa*). But the Master died before I got it. . . . Hearing that Chang Shih inherited the teaching of Hu Hung, I went to ask him about this. He told me what he knew, but I was still not awakened. After my return home, I thought long and hard, forgetting food and sleep. One day I sighed and told myself: "From the cradle to the grave, through talk and silence, action and stillness, we usually [experience] the manifest (*yi-fa*) state of consciousness. Only the *wei-fa* state is not yet manifest." After that I no longer had doubts, believing that the meaning of the *Doctrine of the Mean* is there [i.e., in the manifest state].[22]

Chu was struggling over a spiritual problem about the unmanifest mind (*wei-fa*). A concern with this usually represents as well a concern with the importance of stillness or contemplation in one's life. But the language with which he described the struggle appears intellectualist: he "thought long and hard" and came to a decision that the manifest state (*yi-fa*) is more important. This signaled a new-found belief that the *wei-fa* is present in the *yi-fa* and, therefore, that it is not as necessary to practice prolonged meditation. Metaphysically, it also entailed the association of *wei-fa* with human nature, and *yi-fa* with mind-and-heart.

In four letters addressed to Chang Shih, all written in 1166–67 before Chu's visit to Chang, Chu reports his intellectual evolution and his reactions to their exchanges. These may be considered sources for what Chu would call his "Old Doctrine on Equilibrium and Harmony."[23] He refers to the *wei-fa* as the eternal life force (*sheng-sheng pu-yi chih chi*) responding without cease to the flow of events in life. In itself, it is still and unmanifest, as a "wholeness" (*hun-jan ch'üan-t'i*). In its manifestation, it interacts with a perpetual flux of events and things. Moral effort lies in cultivating the shoots of moral consciousness put forth by the *wei-fa*.[24] Generally, Chu assigns the *wei-fa* to human nature (*hsing*[a]) and the *yi-fa* to mind (*hsin*[a]), although he acknowledges that this distinction is a very fine one: "In a flash of thought there is this *t'i* (reality) and *yung* (function). The manifest (*yi-fa*) is just gone and the unmanifest (*wei-fa*) is coming forth. There is no break between the two."[25]

The New Doctrine

With Chang's endorsement of his thinking, Chu was basically at peace for a few years. But new doubts emerged during conversations with Ts'ai Yüan-ting in 1169. Chu decided to reread Ch'eng Yi's words on the subject. This would lead him to a repudiation of Chang's teacher Hu Hung and to a new doctrine on equilibrium and harmony, centered on the practice of reverence and study. This was a corollary to his belief that the two states of *wei-fa* and *yi-fa* belong to the same reality, the mind, rather than to nature and the mind, respectively. The manner in which he reached his new doctrine was as sudden as his earlier resolution of the same problem:

> Taking up once more Ch'eng Yi's book [after conversing with Ts'ai] and reading it slowly with a humble mind and a calm disposition, [I found that] my problems all dissolved after a few lines. After that I knew the original state of human nature and the emotions . . . is so straight and clear. My earlier readings were not thorough enough, giving rise to unnecessary problems, so that my pains only led to misunderstanding.[26]

Once again, he had a flash of insight, but after extensive reading rather than quiet meditation. He decided not to exalt *yi-fa* over *wei-fa* but to regard the two as belonging to the same reality. This marked a definitive departure from Li T'ung's and Chou Tun-yi's emphasis on stillness and *wei-fa*, and even from Chang Shih. It also gave more balance to his teachings of self-cultivation.[27] He was then thirty-nine years old and would continue to develop this theory throughout his life.

It is interesting that Chu Hsi should assert that *wei-fa* and *yi-fa* manifest the same reality. This idea accords with his interpretation of *Wu-chi* being also *T'ai-chi*. It is a clear instance of his preference for accepting both transcendence and immanence in a dialectical manner. It also shows the inner coherence of his thinking, as developed in his philosophical system, which embraces cosmology, human nature, and a doctrine of self-cultivation.

From 1170 on, Chu concentrated on Ch'eng Yi's exhortation to abide in reverence and extend knowledge, a formula that offers more balance between action and contemplation. Meditation is not an end in itself but a means to an end, to achieve an attitude of reverence (*ching*[d]). Although an interior disposition, maintained in and out of meditation, reverence is principally applied to a life of activity. True, Chu continues to place priority on knowledge as a guide to action—knowledge of the principles of things, that is, intellectual knowledge. In this context, he defines reverence as basically a scholar's intellectual and moral disposition, which is quite different from the kind of stillness or tranquillity that a contemplative like Chou Tun-yi emphasized. Increasingly, Chu would speak of reverence more in terms of self-conquest and intellectual pursuit.[28] This later, definitive doctrine of emotional equilibrium and harmony reflected his personal, intellectual, and spiritual shifts especially during his twenties and thirties.[29]

In his annotated edition of the *Doctrine of the Mean*, which he was to publish with his commentaries on the *Great Learning*, the *Analects*, and *Mencius* over twenty years later, Chu would explain:

As Heaven and Earth are one body (*t'i*) with us, when my mind-and-heart is correct, the mind-and-heart of Heaven and Earth is also correct. . . . There is the reality itself (*t'i*) and there is its manifestation or function (*yung*). Although there are differences in the [two modes of] action and stillness, the reality is first established before the manifestation comes. In actuality they are not two different things. [30]

He is going beyond *wei-fa* and *yi-fa*, and even beyond action and stillness. But what does all this really mean? We get our clues from his practical teaching on reverence. I refer here to a teaching regarding a disposition of reverence, directed at one's own innate moral nature, and opposed to "human desires." In this new light, Chu continues to teach the usefulness of quiet-sitting, or meditation, but only for contemplating the mind-and-heart rather than for achieving any mystical breakthrough. [31]

Shortly thereafter, Chu also enunciated his doctrine of *Jen*[a], which has been discussed in the previous chapter. It, too, demonstrates his differences with Hu Hung and Hsieh Liang-tso, who were closer in spirit to Ch'eng Hao and interpreted *jen*[a] in terms of perceptions or consciousness. [32]

Practicing Meditation

The Confucian term for meditation is quiet-sitting (*ching-tso*). It suggests strong Taoist and Buddhist influences, calling to mind Chuang Tzu's "sitting and forgetting" (*tso-wang*) and the Buddhist practice of *dhyāna* (meditation), from which the names Ch'an and Zen are derived. [33] Chu Hsi practiced Taoist and Buddhist meditation for many years. His biography reveals his fondness for conversations with Buddhist monks when he was still preparing for civil examinations. In his writings, we can find an essay on using breath control as a form of Taoist meditation. [34] Chou Tun-yi and the Ch'eng brothers all practiced quiet-sitting, but Chu Hsi would make a special effort to show the distinctiveness of Confucian quiet-sitting and its difference from Taoist and Buddhist meditation.

For the Buddhist, meditation is an exercise by which the mind concentrates upon itself to the exclusion of all distracting thoughts and for the sake of attaining unity and harmony with one's innermost self. For the Taoist, the same usually applies, frequently with an additional motive of preserving health and prolonging life. For the Confucian, unity and harmony are sought for, together with the knowledge of the *moral* self, of one's own strengths and weaknesses, with the goals of achieving self-improvement, of becoming more perfect in the practice of virtues and the elimination of vices and therefore in the fulfillment of one's responsibilities to the family as well as to society at large:

Quiet-sitting is not to enter *samādhi* as with Ch'an Buddhist meditation, stopping one's thought processes. Rather, one needs only to contemplate the mind-and-heart, not permitting it to run riot, and rest one's thinking. In this way the mind will be calm and without distractions and naturally concentrated. [35]

Chu Hsi gives an important role to quiet-sitting in his method of self-cultivation. He regards meditation as a means toward an end, that of moral perfection of the self, rather than as an end in itself. For Chu himself, quiet-sitting makes possible a fuller manifestation of the heavenly principle within. Meditation, therefore, is a time when the person gathers the self together inwardly, calms the emotions, examines the conscience, and fills the mind-and-heart with principles of right action so that a disposition of reverence may permeate his entire life. However, Chu disapproves of what seems to be self-absorption. For him, quiet-sitting is directed to duty and common sense, which are always more important than the search for quietude:

> Although we speak of focusing on tranquillity, we are not about to abandon things and affairs to find it. As human beings, we also need to serve our rulers and parents, relate to friends and spouses, govern servants and subordinates. We cannot leave everything in order to do quiet-sitting behind closed doors, refusing to attend to things and affairs.[36]

It is interesting that Chu Hsi has been taken to task, especially by the scholar Yen Yüan (Yan Yuan, 1635–1704), for exaggerating the importance of quiet-sitting, even for recommending the practice of spending half a day in quiet-sitting, and half a day reading books.[37] Actually, this reference comes up only once in Chu's recorded conversations, in a specific context with a single disciple, even if it made a deep impression on some later thinkers.[38] I am referring to the advice he gave a disciple who was bidding him farewell:

> In the course of a day it is best to reduce idle talk to but a sentence or two, and to meet only with one or two idle guests. If one is always in noise and turmoil, how can he study well . . . ? When there's a day free of [business] affairs, without one having to earn his living, then [it is good] to spend half of it doing quiet-sitting and half of it reading. After a year or two of such, there will surely be [visible] progress.[39]

In this piece of personal advice, I find important the balance of meditation with study. On another occasion, Chu has guarded against excessive emphasis on quietude. He is reported to have said: "Today, scholars sometimes say that they should spend half a day daily in the practice of quiet-sitting. I find it a mistake."[40]

Was Chu Hsi principally a "quietist," a contemplative absorbed in his inner life, to the neglect of his outer activities? His earlier love of meditation lends reasonableness to this kind of thinking, although his later development was in a somewhat different direction. Compared to other scholars, Chu did not live a very active life. In the long span of seventy years, he spent relatively little time in public service, usually considered a necessary priority for any disciple of Confucius.[41] In spite of this, in mature life Chu tended to limit meditation only to keeping focused, while spending a lot of time reading books and writing commentaries. When we consider the near-feverish pace with which he worked as a scholar, we can hardly call him a quietist.

Was Chu Hsi then too much of an activist, a man who unites his knowledge with his action, who looks for truth, or at least confirmation of truth, in action?

Of knowledge and action, Chu has said that they are necessary to each other as the eye is to the foot in walking: "In the case of temporal sequence, knowledge comes before action; in the case of importance, action is more important than knowledge."[42] It would therefore appear that he advocated balance, placing moral priority on action while never resting in his search for knowledge.

I should point out that the emphasis on stillness or tranquillity was an older teaching of Chu's that he developed before he was thirty-nine. After that, he moved more and more to a balanced formula of reverence and study. He first talked of stillness but later preferred reverence because it can be practiced in both activity and tranquillity.

Expressing his ideas through metaphors, Chu first discussed self-cultivation in terms of cleaning or polishing a mirror, as I have mentioned earlier. The human mind is originally pure, capable of reflecting all things. Personal cultivation requires the practice of "keeping still" (ching[a]), which permits one to restore and maintain the original purity of the mirror by removing from mind all selfish desires. When this is accomplished, the mind will function as a clear mirror, quiet and still when passive, straight and upright when active, that is, when stirred up by emotions. In other words, it is capable of uniting action with contemplation and stillness.[43]

The allusion to the mirror metaphor calls to mind the two famous gathas of the Ch'an monks Shen-hsiu and Hui-neng during a succession struggle to the patriarchate. Each compared the mind to the mirror, the former regarding it as reflecting all things, and the latter challenging the very foundations of the mind's existence.[44]

Chu also spoke of the mind in the image of water containing a pearl. Cultivation is compared to removing the pearl from impure water:

Human nature is originally clear, but it is like a precious pearl immersed in impure water, where its luster cannot be seen. After being removed from the water, [the precious pearl] becomes lustrous of itself as before. If one would realize that human desires are what obscures [one's nature, one should be able] to find illumination.[45]

How, specifically, is the task of polishing the mirror or of rescuing the pearl to be carried out? Chu Hsi moved from an emphasis on stillness to propose eventually the double effort of maintaining an attitude of reverence toward one's own inner nature and its capacity for goodness and of pursuing "the investigation of things and the extension of knowledge," a doctrine identified especially with Ch'eng Yi. In other words, he envisaged a certain moral and spiritual attentiveness over oneself which is accompanied and strengthened by the acquisition of knowledge, both about oneself and about the world.[46]

I wish now to explain further Chu's mature and practical ideas of self-cultivation. I refer here to the spiritual cultivation which nourishes the attitude of reverence and makes possible its extension into one's external life.

A Disposition of Reverence

The Ch'eng brothers both believed in the ideal of a scholar-contemplative, and Ch'eng Yi is especially known for his love of meditation, or quiet-sitting. In his turn, Chu Hsi also practiced meditation—some would say, too much. However, Chu did not believe in stillness or tranquillity as a principal practical and spiritual focus. He chose rather to make central in his teachings of personal cultivation the concept of reverence, which Ch'eng Yi had emphasized. This is, in his mind, an attitude that unifies the inner and the outer in human lives.[47] And he corrects Chou Tun-yi by saying: "Chou emphasizes quietude and tranquillity. But the word ching[a] should only be interpreted as reverence (ching[d])."[48]

The word ching[d] figures prominently in Chu Hsi's doctrine of cultivation. The fact that scholars have translated the term differently (reverence, seriousness, composure) shows the difficulty of explaining its Chinese usage in general and Chu's intended meaning in particular. The usage of the word can be traced to various Confucian classics, including the Book of History, where the ancient sage kings are frequently described as being "reverentially obedient" to the Lord-on-High or Heaven, while their descendants are exhorted to imitate such reverence. The term occurs less frequently in the Four Books. With Confucius, it is used more with regard to oneself than to a higher being: "In retirement, to be sedately gracious; in doing things, to be reverently attentive; in contact with others, to be very sincere."[49] The Book of Changes continues in the same vein when it says: "the gentleman practices reverence to maintain inner rectitude and rightness to ensure exterior correctness."[50] It is a sentence that Ch'eng Yi and Chu Hsi frequently invoked.[51]

The first text counsels "reverence" in action, whereas the second text refers to a more interior vigilance. There is even a connotation of "fear and trembling," of awe in the presence of a greater power. This is what the Japanese scholar Satō Hitoshi singles out for comment: the component of fear in this reverence.[52]

For both Ch'eng Yi and Chu Hsi, "reverence" points to the process by which the original unity of the mind is preserved and made manifest in one's activity. Chu speaks of abiding in reverence (chü-ching), defining it in terms of single-mindedness and freedom from distraction (chu-yi wu-shih) and comparing it to the Buddhist practice of mindful alertness (hsing-hsing). He also associates it specifically with the teaching of "vigilance in solitude" of the Doctrine of the Mean. And he is careful to admonish his disciples to guard against a "dead" reverence that merely keeps the mind alert without also attending to moral practice. Following in Ch'eng Yi's footsteps, Chu Hsi continues to give the meaning of the word a dimension that transforms it from the earlier, occasional usage in Confucian thought to a doctrine of personal and spiritual cultivation:

Reverence does not mean one has to sit stiffly in solitude, the ears hearing nothing, the eyes seeing nothing, and the mind thinking of nothing. . . . It means rather keeping a sense of caution and vigilance and not daring to become permissive [with oneself].[53]

Chu does not forget Mencius's teaching. He agrees that reverence also means "preserving the mind" (ts'un-hsin) without allowing it to become dissipated: "When our mind-and-heart is 'outside,' it should be drawn inward; when it is 'inside,' it should be pushed outward. This is the meaning of the *Book of Mencius*.[54]

However, he expresses a preference for *Analects* 13:19, explaining that such a discipline of vigilance over the mind is helpful when the mind already understands all the principles (*li*[a]). On the other hand, "what use is there in merely keeping watch over an empty mind?"[55] Elsewhere, he clearly says that reverence refers to keeping the principles of Heaven and getting rid of human desires. The word *ch'ü*, "to rid oneself of," is strong indeed, indicating revulsion for human desires. In any case, reverence is part and parcel of his philosophy of *li*[a] and *ch'i*[a], pointing to the constant need of growing in virtue and keeping the human desires at least under control.

As Ch'eng Yi says, "Cultivation (*han-yang*) requires the practice of reverence."[56] The term *han-yang* includes the meaning of "nurturing." The aspirant to sagehood needs to nurture the seeds of goodness in his mind-and-heart, and reverence refers to this process of nurturing as well as to the goal of harmony of the emotions—an abiding state of mind characteristic of the sage.

The *doctrine* of reverence, nevertheless, is a Ch'eng-Chu innovation and, as such, not found in the early texts. It became the central teaching in Chu Hsi's philosophy of self-cultivation and the leading idea with which he explains the *Doctrine of the Mean*. However, it is close to the Buddhist teaching of mindfulness, as Chu's critics also pointed out.

A Chinese term for practicing reverence in self-cultivation often used by Chu Hsi is *shou-lien* (literally, "collecting together"). It also has the practical meaning of "gathering" a harvest, but its usage in neo-Confucian writings made it a technical term. Its closest parallel in English is the term "recollection." The English word "recollection" is usually understood in terms of "remembrance." It is, however, a technical term in spirituality referring to the "collecting" or "gathering" of one's interior faculties, keeping them silent and "recollected" in an atmosphere of peace and calm, in preparation for formal prayer or in an effort to prolong the effects of such prayer.

In a work on Christian spirituality, Canon Jacques Leclerq says:

> The word recollection has no meaning for many worldly people. . . . Yet recollection is the chief disposition required for the interior life. It is not itself interior life but it is so much a condition for it and prepares us for it to such an extent that it almost necessarily develops it. . . . It is simply the calm which is born into the soul through solitude and silence. . . . Man has need of it to find himself as well as to find God.[57]

Chu Hsi also talks about the need for scholars to "always keep recollected (*shou-lien*) without allowing oneself to become dispersed."[58] But if the immediate goal of keeping reverent and recollected is similar to that of Christian recollection, the ultimate end is not necessarily the same. In the Chinese context, there is no specific reference to *finding God*, even if one may argue for similarity in the quest for the absolute.

Reverence and Self-Conquest

"To master oneself and return to propriety is *jen*[a]."[59] It would appear that self-mastery, or self-discipline, is required as a prerequisite for the practice of *jen*[a]. And with *jen*[a] comes *yi* (rightness), a virtue governing our external behavior, which keeps *jen*[a] from becoming too subjective, a mere private emotion.[60]

The term *k'o-chi* comes from *Analects* 12:1, where Confucius explains the meaning of *jen*[a] to his favorite disciple, Yen Hui, in terms of *k'o-chi fu-li*: to subdue one's self and recover the virtue of propriety. To quote the *Analects* on the *specific* duties of self-conquest: "Look not at what is contrary to propriety; listen not to what is contrary to propriety; seek not what is contrary to propriety; make no movement which is contrary to propriety." Seen in this light, self-conquest is the negative side of the positive effort of seeking self-perfection, and a necessary corollary in any doctrine of personal cultivation based on a realistic evaluation of human nature.

Chu Hsi derived his dual formula of reverence and extension of knowledge from Ch'eng Yi. He also made his own contribution, by emphasizing self-conquest (*k'o-chi*) as an integral part of cultivation. Whereas Ch'eng Yi makes occasional mention of *k'o-chi*, Chu Hsi integrates it in his system, speaking of it much more, as in connection with reverence and the extension of knowledge in this vivid parable:

> To use the example of a house: reverence represents the watchman who keeps guard at the door, self-conquest refers to resisting thieves, and the extension of knowledge refers to the investigation of things and affairs pertaining to one's own house as well as what comes from outside.[61]

Elsewhere, Chu Hsi compares self-conquest to irrigating the fields and to keeping the room clean and the mirror shining.[62] For Chu Hsi, the goal of self-conquest is to nurture the heavenly principle by overcoming human desires not only at the moment of the awakening of selfish desires but also through the practice of caution before the rise of emotions. Chu Hsi became increasingly emphatic about the need for thoroughness in the work of self-conquest, using such language as "uprooting" weeds and "killing" thieves or rebels.[63]

Chu recognizes that self-conquest, instead of adding another dimension to his doctrine of personal cultivation, merely assists the task of reverence. It is a lifelong task, never to be interrupted, but becomes easier as one goes on and as selfish desires recede.

The recovery of propriety is nothing other than the achieving of perfect virtue, *Jen*[a]. Chu acknowledges that the "highest" degree of reverence eliminates the need for self-conquest, but he takes care to add that such an achievement may only be assumed to have been attained by sages, whereas ordinary persons must continually attend to self-conquest.[64]

The task of self-conquest issues clearly from the belief in the opposition of heavenly principles and human desires. Many of Chu's critics objected to the dichotomy. It certainly contributed to a stereotyped image of the master as a joyless ascetic, constantly exhorting others to correct their vices. Chu was aware of this image of himself. To a friend, he addressed these lines of a poem:

> The task of conquering self lies in daily living:
> I know you haven't heard it for a while.
> I write this as a friend, if a bit presumptuous,
> No, this isn't a book on Correcting Vices.[65]

A Life of Rightness

If the doctrine of reverence addresses the inner disposition necessary in the quest for a good life, the teachings of rightness cover the person's exterior moral behavior. The Chinese word for "rightness" (yi) is sometimes translated as "justice." The *Shuo-wen* explains it as the dignity of the self.[66] Presumably, the righteous person lives according to his or her conscience with a sense of dignity and integrity.

Interestingly, Chu has not left behind as much on the subject of rightness as he has on that of reverence. Presumably, he regards moral action to be well served by the Confucian tradition and considers reverence to be an attitude of the mind that would of itself overflow into one's external, public life.

Humanity and rightness are sometimes discussed together, as two principal virtues. Chu speaks of humanity (Jen[a]) as substance (t'i) and of rightness as function (yung). "By being broad and universal, Jen[a] serves as substance; by responding harmoniously to external affairs, yi serves as function. When humanity is established and rightness is working, our human nature is stabilized."[67]

In explaining humanity, rightness, propriety, and wisdom as four virtues, Chu comments that the first two are "soft" virtues whereas the second two are "hard" virtues. "Humanity has the meaning of compassionate love, while rightness has that of firmness and determination."[68] "Humanity is its own substance. Propriety refers to its rubrics, while rightness refers to the judgment and control humanity exercises, and wisdom attends to the discernment of humanity."[69]

This reflects Chu's attention to the whole without neglecting its parts. Together with propriety and wisdom, rightness serves to promote perfect virtue, Jen[a]. However, to the extent that rightness concerns one's external behavior, referring largely to the realm of "application" or "earnest practice" (li-hsing), Chu Hsi largely relegates its exercise to a place following reverence and intellectual inquiry. And this is why the Lu brothers, intent more on the practice of virtues, were displeased with Chu's doctrine of self-cultivation.

Intellectual Pursuit: Extending Knowledge

Chu Hsi frequently refers to Ch'eng Yi's dictum that "self-cultivation requires reverence; the pursuit of learning depends on the extension of knowledge."[70] We now come to the extension of knowledge (*chih-chih*), which, for Chu, is insepa-rable from the "investigation of things" (*ko-wu*).

In his commentary on the text of the *Great Learning*, Chu offers an expansion of the meaning of this sentence: "The investigation of things consists in the ex-tension of knowledge":

> If we wish to extend our knowledge to the utmost, we must investigate the principles of all things with which we come into contact. For the human mind or spirit is ordained to knowledge, and the things of the world all contain principles. So long as principles are not exhausted, knowledge is not yet complete.[71]

We have not quite moved from moral self-cultivation to a purely intellectual pursuit of knowledge. For Chu Hsi, knowledge refers primarily to moral knowl-edge—the knowledge of the good—as discovered in life itself, through the prac-tice of reverence as already described, and in Confucian classical texts, particu-larly the Four Books, through careful and reflective study. Chu gives a place of honor to intellectual pursuit while teaching an all-comprehensive theory of knowledge based on his philosophy of principle—that all things are made of *li*[a] and *ch'i*[a] and that the human mind is ordained to seek and possess the *li*[a] of things.

Where practice is concerned, Chu Hsi says that the student is to move from the known to the unknown, proceeding from the knowledge he already possesses of the principles of things and continuing his investigation until the task is fin-ished. This happens as a sudden breakthrough, a penetrating experience, at the end of a long and arduous process of search and exertion:

> After exerting himself in this way for a long time, he will suddenly find him-self possessed of a wide and far-reaching penetration. The qualities of all things, both internal and external, subtle and coarse, will all then be ap-prehended, and the mind, in its entire substance (*t'i*) and in its relation to things (*yung*), will become completely manifest. This is called the investi-gation of things; this is called the perfection of knowledge.[72]

Thus, if the mind is ordained to know the truth of principles, truth itself also modifies the mind, making it manifest and radiant (*ming*). Here we observe a circular motion, from the mind to *things* and then back to the mind—but not just from the mind to the mind. For Chu Hsi regards the mind as embracing all principles, and all principles as being complete in this mind. If a person cannot "preserve" his mind (*ts'un-hsin*), neither will he be able to investigate principles to the utmost. We see here the interdependence of the doctrine of reverence and the need of concentration with the teaching of the extension of knowledge and the investigation of principles. Together, they make up Chu's complete formula for self-cultivation, a formula he learned from Ch'eng Yi and carefully elaborated, making it a necessary part of his entire system.

Chu relates this pursuit of principles to the doctrine of self-cultivation found in the *Book of Mencius*. He identifies the task of extending knowledge and investigating things to "developing the mind to the utmost, knowing one's nature and knowing Heaven,"[73] a doctrine of introvertive, philosophical mysticism which he seeks to explain in terms of his own metaphysics of mind and nature, the principles of things, and the principle of Heaven. And he sees a certain sequential order in which this self-cultivation is to be organized, with the extension of knowledge as the first step in the long search for sagehood, preceding the work of "making the intention sincere, rectifying the mind, and cultivating the person" of the *Great Learning*. Thus, he envisages perfect virtue (*Jen*[a]) as the crowning achievement of a long life of investigating principles and extending knowledge, the fruition of a life of diligent scholarship and careful moral cultivation.

Book Learning

In Chinese, there is a difference between studying (*hsüeh*) and book learning (*tu-shu*). The former is a more general term, which, in a philosophical context like ours, refers as well to learning to become a sage, that is, a spiritual quest. The latter refers to studying from books, a much more specific task. In his *Classified Conversations*, Chu discusses both concepts, incorporating book learning into studying.[74]

I have no problem with Chu's teaching of extension of knowledge as an effort of self-cultivation, since, as already mentioned, I regard his understanding of knowledge as primarily moral *in intention*. But knowledge is also primarily intellectual *in operation*. It is placed prior to action, *moral* action, which has to be based on principles painstakingly acquired from the extension of knowledge.

"In learning one cannot afford not to learn from books. . . . As [knowledge] increases inch by inch, the effort will eventually bring fruition. Not only do principles become clear but the mind becomes settled."[75] The increase of knowledge *inch by inch* emphasizes that systematic efforts to study intensely are of great benefit to a comprehensive and intuitive understanding of principles. However, the scale is not necessarily in favor of the quantitative aspect of learning. Chu Hsi's hermeneutics aims at experiential understanding, carefully prepared for after ridding the mind of preconceptions concerning the text. "Reading has as its goal to contemplate the meaning of sages and worthies, and through this knowledge to contemplate further the meaning of nature."[76] He offers advice regarding how one is to "read books," using strong metaphors to emphasize the importance of a careful and thorough reading of the texts, likening reading to "catching a thief," to a "fierce general doing battle," and to a "tough magistrate" prosecuting criminal cases:[77] "One should read over and over, understanding every word and paragraph, and looking up various explanations and commentaries . . . until the meaning has become one with the mind."[78]

And, lest we regard this as drudgery, I shall quote from a poem, "The Pleasures of Study during the Four Seasons," attributed to Chu Hsi:

> Time slips by: don't let young light grow old:
> The only good thing in life is to read.

And the joys of reading—what are they?
The window view is green and the grass is not cut.[79]

The joys of reading assume a certain close familiarity with the texts, in a personal experience that permits meaningful appropriation and transformation of character. In this sense, reading brings one into communion with the mind-and-heart of the sages, which is also the mind-and-heart of the universe:

The joys of reading are the joys of being yourself,
I rise to enjoy the bright moon high up on a frosty night.
. . . .
The joys of reading—where may these be found?
In a few plum blossoms, where [I see] the heart of Heaven and Earth.[80]

Perhaps, in the conventional portrait of Chu the scholar, looking serious and proper, we may find a faint smile, one that crossed his face when he was reading.

An Elitist System?

There may be a problem in Chu's making intellectual pursuit a cornerstone of moral striving: it necessarily makes intellectuals of sages. This is perfectly acceptable in a system like Plato's or Aristotle's, which sees the complete person's life as demonstrating a balanced range of intellectual and moral virtues, but it implies the inaccessibility of sagehood to all those who are deprived of the possibilities of intellectual development. It also subordinates wisdom to learning and information. Mencius asserts that every person can become a sage, and Chu Hsi accepts this assertion. How can sagehood be universally accessible in practice if everyone must first *study* the principles of morality as these are laid down in the Confucian texts? In Chu's own times, much of the population was illiterate, deprived of the opportunity of receiving a formal education and book learning. How many of them can be considered potential sages? Is not Chu Hsi the scholar speaking to other scholars about a goal of scholarship rather than the goal of life itself? Surely, when Mencius said that every person can become a sage, he was not merely referring to scholars.

Remember, however, that Chu considers intellectual pursuit as *secondary* to the cultivation of reverence. "Book learning is a matter of secondary importance," he repeats several times in his *Classified Conversations*.[81] He sees book learning as playing primarily the role of *assisting* the task of stabilizing the mind, giving it strength to oppose selfish desires. Still, book learning is regarded as very important to the task of investigating the principles of everything that makes up our world, and that, in turn, is very important to self-cultivation. As Chu mentions in a memorial to the throne: "Nothing is more urgent than a study of principles, and [this] necessarily involves book learning."[82]

Chu does not deny the universal accessibility of sagehood. Rather, Chu sees himself as a scholar and a teacher of scholars, a guardian of the Confucian tradition of scholarship. Of course, Mencius's teaching of the universal possibility of sagehood has relativized the importance of *particular* traditions, whether these be Confucian, Taoist, or Buddhist. Chu was surely aware of this fact. In mature life, however, he made a definite choice for himself, consciously becoming a follower of the Confucian school and committing himself also to the task of redefining and upholding the Confucian mission. In this context, he sees the need to make clear distinctions. For him, a Confucian (*ju*) is not simply any well-meaning person who respects the moral law governing human relationships. He must also possess a penetrating understanding of the principles of this moral law. In other words, he must be more than a scholar (*ju*); he must also be committed to following the Confucian way. In this light, we may also understand how the Confucian school became transformed in the Sung dynasty into the School of the Way (*Tao-hsüeh*).

We reach here a very controversial aspect of Chu's teachings, disputed especially by his contemporary and rival thinker Lu Chiu-yüan, as well as by Lu's spiritual heir of three centuries later, Wang Yang-ming (1472–1529). They preferred to teach the practice of virtues in action while making of intellectual pursuit a useful but not necessary component of cultivation. And between the two of them they developed a metaphysics of the universe and of human nature that is consonant with their doctrine of cultivation, a doctrine that effectively identifies the mind and human nature.[83]

Conclusion

Toward the latter part of his life, at age sixty-one, Chu published an essay in which he further integrated Chou Tun-yi's ideas on the Great Ultimate with the moral life:

> The exalted words of Master Chou on the marvels of *Wu-chi erh T'ai-chi* are inseparable from our daily living. His profound explorations into the transformations of *yin, yang,* and the Five Phases are inseparable from humanity, rightness, propriety, wisdom, firmness and suppleness, good and evil. . . . What is called the Great Ultimate is nothing but the common name of the principles of Heaven, Earth, and the myriad things.[84]

Some would say that this tends to erase the difference between the transcendent and the immanent.[85] I see it as an increased effort to locate the transcendent in the immanent, the *wei-fa* in the *yi-fa*, thus raising the latter to a higher level. Seen from this perspective, the Great Ultimate is dialectically present in our daily consciousness, in our *yi-fa*. Chu Hsi tempers his optimism regarding human nature with his realism about human nature. He acknowledges both the accessibility of sagehood and the difficulty of achieving it. He offers a dual formula for personal cultivation, knowing well that it cannot serve all, especially the uneducated. But he does not say that they are deprived from achieving the ultimate goal. He seems to think that some are called only to a life of practical morality, which is admirable in itself. However, his constant admonition to those others fortunate enough to be his students—whether in his own day or much later, through his writings—is to strive to achieve an even greater goal, through the cultivation of the heavenly principles within, while fighting against all the difficulties that threaten from without.

There is a perceivable problem with Chu Hsi's negative view of human desires (*jen-yü*). The very term points out the ambiguity. If so-called selfish desires are *human*, why are they so decried? Depending on contexts, one might argue that Chu is against excesses of human desires. But Chu's teaching of self-cultivation, with its exhortation to fight human desires and to conquer one's baser instincts, leaves behind a less-than-confident estimation of human perfectibility.

Perhaps, Chu's analysis of evil in human nature is a solid contribution to a tradition that shows excessive optimism regarding human nature. But the bifurcation of heavenly principles and human desires also discloses a basic malaise with the human condition which has made many people unhappy, especially when his doctrines became orthodox. It makes the goal of sagehood more remote, while human existence becomes the battlefield for struggle against one's own innate tendencies toward self-preservation and self-fulfillment. Perhaps, too, Chu could have placed a greater emphasis on self-transcendence and less on self-conquest.

I should not neglect the question of sudden illumination, especially when Chu himself alludes to it by remarking on a sudden breakthrough after arduous study. Such an intellectual breakthrough may occur intuitively, as a sudden flash of the mind grasping a certain truth. It may not be a mystical experience, if by this we refer to pure experience, that which goes beyond subject-object distinctions to the whole of reality. But we have no reason to think he rejects the mystical experience in itself. He just perceives the attainment of wisdom and sagehood as a task requiring much effort and struggle—a lifetime of cultivation, including possibly the accumulation of encyclopedic knowledge, to *prepare* the person for such an experience. This is why his contemporary and rival Lu Chiu-yüan finds him misguided. For Lu Chiu-yüan and others, Chu Hsi's doctrine of self-cultivation has its limitations. I shall address this subject in the following chapter.

A mirror to polish, a pearl to be rescued from impure water, so that each should shine—such are the metaphors Chu Hsi delights in using, metaphors coming from Taoist and Buddhist sources, to represent the task of personal cultivation as he sees it: an arduous task, but not without its reward. The person who strives to cultivate himself or herself may not necessarily become a sage. But we may hope he or she will become a more humane person, having first discovered transcendence in immanence, the constant in the transient, and meaning in every moment of time.

Philosophical Disputes with Lu Chiu-yüan

The universe is my *hsin*[a], and my *hsin*[a] is the universe.
Sages arise in the eastern seas; they have the same *hsin*[a], the
same *li*[a].
Sages arise in the western seas; they have the same *hsin*[a], the
same *li*[a].

Lu Chiu-yüan[1]

Introduction[2]

So far, I have situated the development of some of Chu Hsi's ideas in the context of discussions and debates with others, whether with a friend, like Chang Shih, or with a disciple, like Ts'ai Yüan-ting. But I have preferred to treat Chu's thinking thematically rather than concentrate on the discussions and debates. In this chapter, however, I shall dwell on the philosophical discussions and disputes that Chu Hsi and Lu Chiu-yüan entered into on a variety of subjects and occasions. I do so because I believe Lu to be Chu's only philosophical equal, and also a powerful rival, among their contemporaries. An exposition of their exchanges will highlight a whole range of issues on which they professed agreement or disagreement.[3]

I shall begin with the Goose Lake Monastery Debates, which marked their first meeting. While the more important part of those disputes were conducted via the exchange of poems, there were also discussions regarding the order of the Nine Hexagrams. I have incorporated into chapter 2 the Chu-Lu disputes on "Wu-chi erh T'ai-chi," which will not be repeated here. I shall conclude with Lu's lecture at the White Deer Cave Academy on "Rightness versus Profit," sometimes regarded as a sign of personal and philosophical reconciliation between the two thinkers.[4]

Intellectual Inquiry or Honoring Moral Nature: The Goose Lake Monastery Debates (Part 1)

The Goose Lake Monastery Debates between Chu Hsi and Lu Chiu-yüan marked an important event in the history of Chinese thought, chiefly because they disclosed the differences between two of the greatest representatives of the movement of thought known in the West as neo-Confucianism. The differences that manifested themselves during this debate had repercussions for many centuries, particularly in Ming times (1368–1644), with the emergence of Wang Yangming, a self-proclaimed heir of Lu Chiu-yüan. The impact of these differences would make itself felt even outside China, particularly in Japan and Korea.

In this study, I offer a historical reconstruction of the events, an exegetical analysis of the problems discussed, an interpretation placing these problems in a wider perspective. I hope to show how this event, which occurred in China eight hundred years ago, was not a hair-splitting affair with little consequence for us today but concerned a problem that is both universal and contemporary: the conflict between learning and wisdom, formulated, in Chinese terms, as that between intellectual inquiry (*tao-wen-hsüeh*) and honoring moral nature (*tsun-te-hsing*).

The question of a conflict between honoring moral nature and intellectual inquiry comes from the *Doctrine of the Mean* (ch. 27): "The gentleman honors his moral nature and follows 'study and inquiry.'" It is interesting that reference is to both, especially to "honoring" nature, giving the impression of great reverence for one's moral, human nature. Certainly, this points to Mencius's teaching of human nature as originally good and to the person possessing all he or she needs inside in order to lead a virtuous life.

Chu Hsi and Lu Chiu-yüan agree on the importance of "honoring moral nature." But they disagree on the emphasis to be given to "study and inquiry." While both are moral philosophers committed to the Confucian values, it is usually said that Lu focuses on the former, whereas Chu emphasizes the latter, in their respective teachings on self-cultivation. Chu himself says as much: "What Lu Chiu-yüan talks about pertains exclusively to 'honoring moral nature,' whereas I emphasize in my daily discourse 'study and inquiry.'"[5] Of course, this is to be understood in a general sense, since Lu usually abstains from speaking about human nature (*hsing*[a]), preferring to focus on the mind (*hsin*[a]).

Before beginning, I wish to mention how the English word "debate" can be used only in a modified sense to suit the Chinese context. This word usually connotes formal and public presentations, in an organized and systematic fashion, of certain arguments for and against a given proposition. In this Chinese context, however, the term represents scholarly discussions highlighting certain differences between two men on the subject of the Confucian quest for sagehood. The discussions revealed basic differences between the two men's thinking.

A Historical Reconstruction

For some time, Chu's good friend Lü Tsu-ch'ien, who also knew Lu Chiu-yüan, had hoped to bring about a meeting between Chu and Lu to give them the opportunity to discuss their differences. This meeting was arranged after a visit which Lu paid him in Chu of Chekiang in the summer of 1174.

The following summer, in 1175, Lü went to visit Chu Hsi in Fukien and stayed with him long enough to prepare the compilation of *Reflections on Things at*

Hand (*Chin-ssu-lu*).[6] After that, they went together to meet Lu and others at Goose Lake that same summer, probably in June. The Lu brothers probably went by boat from Chin-hsi of Kiangsi,[7] finishing the rest of the journey by sedan-chair.

According to Lu Chiu-ling (1132–80), the disputes lasted three days; according to Chu's *Chronological Biography*, their stay was about a week; and according to Lü's account it went on for about ten days.[8] Perhaps, formal discussions took only a few days, and the rest of time was spent in a more pleasant way, visiting the surrounding country. But this is mere conjecture.

As for the place, the Goose Lake Monastery was situated fifteen *li*[d] north of the Yen-shan Prefecture, in the eastern part of today's Kiangsi. The name *ō-hu* comes from a lake that had disappeared before Chu's time.[9] A Ch'an Buddhist monastery had existed on the mountain's peak in the mid-eighth century, during the T'ang dynasty. Later, in the tenth century, another was built to replace it, probably lower down the slope.[10] After the location was made famous by the Chu-Lu disputes, a Confucian academy was constructed (1250) next to the site of the monastery, at the request of a local official. At the Wen-tsung Academy named for Lu, sacrifices were offered there to the four masters who took part in the disputes: Chu Hsi, Lü Tsu-ch'ien, Lu Chiu-yüan, and his elder brother, Lu Chiu-ling. Destroyed during the Mongol invasions, it was rebuilt in Ming and Ch'ing times (1644–1911) and once more restored in our own days.[11]

The chief figures in the disputes were Chu Hsi and Lu Chiu-yüan. Chu was forty-five years old and already a well-known scholar and philosopher. He had acquired his *chin-shih* degree in 1148, twenty-seven years earlier. He had official experience as assistant magistrate (1153–56) in T'ung-an, of Fukien. After that, he remained in Fukien, the province of his birth, doing mostly scholarly work. He had addressed an important memorial to the throne (1162) and had had three interviews with Emperor Hsiao-tsung (1163). But he had not received an important position in the government and had resigned himself to a life of semiretirement.[12] In that situation, he devoted himself to writing and publishing. Until that year, 1175, his completed writings included the compilation of the *Surviving Works* of the Ch'eng brothers, commentaries on the *Analects* and *Mencius*, and commentaries on the two works of Chou Tun-yi: *T'ai-chi t'u-shuo* and *T'ung-shu*.[13]

Before he met the Lu brothers, Chu Hsi had struggled with the theory of emotional equilibrium and harmony (*chung-ho shuo*) of the *Doctrine of the Mean*. He had reflected hard and changed his position twice before formulating, at age forty, a final doctrine on the subject (see Chapter 5 and 6). He had also written a commentary on Chou Tun-yi's *Diagram of the Great Ultimate* but had not yet published it (see chapter 2).

Lu Chiu-yüan was the youngest of six brothers, of whom at least two others shared his philosophical interests: Lu Chiu-shao, the fourth in order of birth, who later in life (together with Chiu-yüan) began a dispute with Chu Hsi concerning *Wu-chi* and *T'ai-chi*, and Lu Chiu-ling (Lu Jiuling), the fifth, who was also present at the Goose Lake Monastery.[14]

Lu Chiu-yüan was Chu's junior by nine years. A self-taught man, Lu came from a Chin-hsi family that owned a herbal store. He was then thirty-six years old, having received his *chin-shih* as a mature man, at age thirty-three. The late date of his degree probably had an effect on his views about intellectual pursuits. He had published nothing and written very little—a few examination essays, letters, and poems. But he already had a reputation for scholarship and wisdom. An essay he wrote on a subject chosen from the Book of Changes had impressed his examiner, Lü Tsu-ch'ien (1172). Lü spoke of it to another examiner, chief counselor Chao Ju-yü (d. 1196), who was equally impressed.[15]

In spite of the age difference, the two men had both reached maturity in their philosophical development. But the dispute shows that Lu did not understand Chu's new theory of emotional equilibrium and harmony and went too far when he attacked Chu for being "fragmented" in his learning.[16]

The organizer of this first meeting between Chu and Lu, who until that summer had known each of them by name only, was the elder scholar Lü Tsu-ch'ien, a scholar and gentleman blessed with an irenic disposition. Although only two years older than Lu Chiu-yüan, he could be considered Lu's "teacher" because he judged Lu's examination. In assisting Chu's compilation of the anthology *Chin-ssu lu*, Lü was also leaving behind an important contribution to the understanding of the Sung dynasty philosophical legacy.[17] Also at the meeting were at least three other men: Liu Tzu-ch'eng; Chao Ching-ming, prefect of Lin-ch'uan of Kiangsi; and Chao Ching-chao. The latter two were fellow countrymen of the Lu brothers.[18]

The meeting was intended to give Chu and Lu the occasion to discuss the whole gamut of their philosophical differences. As it happened, the events of the first day marked the whole atmosphere of the talks. Of those present, Lü Tsu-ch'ien sought to help Chu and Lu find common ground, and Lu Chiu-ling also actively participated in the discussions. But the Chaos and Liu had largely passive roles as observers and listeners.

Although the subjects of the disputes were not clearly formulated, the discussions and disagreements that occurred show that the central focus was on the problem of how to teach disciples regarding sagehood and its attainment. Certain lines from the *Great Commentary to the Book of Changes* were especially relevant in this context, bringing to the fore the conflict between learning and wisdom. Chu Hsi appeared mainly as a learned man, interested in sagehood but regarding it as the fruit of wide learning as well as personal cultivation. Lu Chiu-yüan preferred to emphasize the inner development of the original mind, before advising wide learning, since he saw wisdom as coextensive with the whole of one's life and with the development of a virtuous character. For him, wisdom was the unity of personal insights into both life and the classics but, as such, quite independent of learning itself.

The Poems Exchanged

It appears that the Lu brothers were not in entire agreement among themselves before the meeting. They discussed their individual differences on their journey, resolving them to a certain extent, with Lu Chiu-ling acquiescing to Lu Chiu-yüan's views.[19] Each wrote a poem as a summary of his own personal outlook.

Both of these expressed preference for wisdom, but Lu Chiu-yüan's was clearer, focusing more on the problem and meaning of sagehood itself, as well as the alleged "simplicity and ease" of its quest.

After reaching their destination, the Lu brothers met Lü Tsu-ch'ien, Chu Hsi, and the rest of the company. Lü Tsu-ch'ien asked Lu Chiu-ling about his recent insights in study. Lu then recited the first four lines of his poem:

> The babe-in-arms knows love, and growing up learns respect.
> Ancient sages pass on this mind.[20]
> With a base, one can build a house.
> Without space, no hill will mount up.[21]

This is an expression of belief in the inborn ability to practice virtue, an ability that serves as starting point for the quest of sagehood.

Chu Hsi then remarked to Lü Tsu-ch'ien that Lu Chiu-ling had already gone over to Lu Chiu-yüan's side. But all continued to listen to the rest of the poem, which says:

> Fondness for commentaries brings and thistles,
> Concern for fine points causes the ground to sink.
> Value friendship and mutual counsel:
> Know that great joy is ours today.[22]

This contains a rebuke directed to Chu Hsi, well known for his love of reading, his prolific writing of textual commentaries, and, thus, his interest in the detailed meaning of words and sentences. But the poem ends on a friendly note.

After the whole poem had been recited, Chu Hsi held a discussion with Lu Chiu-ling, presumably about the content of the poem. But it is not known precisely what was said. Then, Lu Chiu-yüan also ventured to read his own poem:

> Graveyards evoke sorrow; ancestral shrines, respect.
> 'Tis our unpolished mind through all ages.
> Tiny drops make up a mighty ocean,
> Small rocks pile up as Mounts T'ai and Hua.[23]
> Easy (yi^a) and simple ($chien$) effort ($kung-fu$) brings lasting greatness.[24]
> Fragmented work stays drifting and aimless.
> To know how to mount from the lower to the higher,
> Find out truth and falsehood this very day.[25]

It is said that Chu Hsi turned pale after hearing the first six lines and was very unhappy when Lu had reached the end. So all present decided to rest for the day.

The Metaphysical Differences

Why did these verses so provoke Chu Hsi? I shall not dwell on the personality differences between Chu Hsi and Lu Chiu-yüan, except to say that Chu recognized Lu's brilliance of mind and quickness but found him abrupt, too self-assured, and very eager to voice his own opinions in the presence of an older and established scholar, without listening much to the other party.[26]

Chu prefers to speak of *li*[a] (principle, being, goodness), which he also calls *hsing*[a] (nature) in humans and things. For him, mind (*hsin*[a]) refers more to consciousness, to the active side of human beings, which, on account of its very dynamism, is capable of evil, whereas *hsing*[a], the passive principle, is full of goodness. This interpretation of human nature and of the possibility of evil is consonant with his basic interpretation of reality itself. For while the one *Li*[a] represents what is basically real in a latent form, dualist tendencies come to the fore in a manifest form, expressed in the opposition of *li*[a] to *ch'i*[a], the individuating, physical principle, which limits the potentiality for goodness.

The Lu brothers go beyond such duality to speak of "mind" (*hsin*[a]) as that which is constant through all ages. For Lu Chiu-yüan, *hsin*[a], the mind, is one with *li*[a], the principle of goodness, which is present in humans as nature (*hsing*[a]), and so constitutes a single undifferentiated continuum with the whole of reality, without tension, without conflict. His basic philosophical principle is a reflexive one, going from the mind back to the mind. As Lu Chiu-yüan puts it:

> The universe is my mind (*hsin*[a]), and my mind is the universe.
> Sages appeared tens of thousands of generations ago:
> They shared this mind; they shared this principle (*li*[a]).
> Sages will appear tens of thousands of generations to come:
> They will share this mind; they will share this principle.
> Sages appear over the four seas:
> They share this mind; they share this principle.[27]

Chu Hsi also sees the spiritual legacy of the ancient sages as lying in "mind"—the moral mind (*tao-hsin*). He sees it in contrast to the "human mind" (*jen-hsin*), which is full of a *ch'i*[a], and is subject to errors. To him, they represent two different realms, that of virtue, or heavenly principles, and that of human emotions or passions.

Lu, on the other hand, identifies the human mind with the moral mind, the potential with the actual. On this account, he expressed a reservation regarding the second line in Lu Chiu-ling's poem: "Ancient sages pass on this mind," for which he substituted, in his own poem, the line: "'Tis our unpolished mind through all ages." He wishes to emphasize the oneness of the mind, the seed of sagehood present in all, and that ultimate reality with which the sage becomes one.

The third and fourth lines of Lu Chiu-yüan's poem generally echo those corresponding lines in Lu Chiu-ling's, emphasizing the need of having a base or foundation, on which is to be built the whole edifice of sagehood. But Lu Chiu-yüan brings in a note of "smallness": it is the small that leads to the great, the endurable. The imagery, however, of the base for construction, of drops of water or stones and rocks accumulating, suggests that sagehood is also "acquired," demanding time and perseverance, even if the growth of water into ocean and stones into mountain is natural rather than forced. The seed is there, but it requires cultivation, or rather, it could somehow cultivate itself, as the end is already present in the beginning, and the work itself is one with both beginning and end. For this reason, Lu speaks also of the task of sagehood as being "easy and simple," consisting of *one* effort always, rather than multiple steps, such as those involved in textual exegesis.

The Practical Differences: Easy and Simple?

The Chinese words *yi*[a] and *chien* ("easy" and "simple") are not so easily or simply translatable into English. The word *yi*[a] (ease) carries also connotations of unity and singleness, as well as other meanings, such as the opposite of "difficulty." The word *chien*, too, besides signifying that which is "easily" comprehensible, refers to singleness and unity, the integration of parts in the whole or, rather, the absence of discernible parts. Together, therefore, the two words represent a movement away from multiplicity, toward the oneness of all things.

In his poem, Lu opposes the "easy and simple" to Chu's fragmented efforts. This is usually taken to mean that Lu prefers a direct, integrated approach, both to the study of the classics and to the quest for sagehood, which, for him, is after all the final goal, that to which all other activities should be made subject. But what is this easy and simple approach? Is it really easy and simple, or subtle and elusive? Is it *only* an approach, or does it refer also to the meaning of wisdom, the secret of ultimate reality?

In the Great Commentary to the Book of Changes, where the words "easy and simple" (*yi-chien*) come from, they are used to describe the knowledge and action of the creative and receptive principles of the universe, Heaven (*Ch'ien*) and Earth (*K'un*[a]):

"The Creative knows through the easy; / The Receptive can do things through the simple."[28] What is being described is therefore the natural and harmonious interaction and mutual responsiveness between the two principles, to which all things owe their being. The words "easy" and "simple" connote spontaneity, immediacy, unity, as opposed to systematic learning, complex methodology, multiplicity. The later lines from this same section put these words into the context of sageliness:

> What is easy, is easy to know;
> What is simple, is easy to follow.
> He who is easy to know attains fealty.
> He who is easy to follow attains work.
> He who possesses attachment can endure for long;
> He who possesses works can become great.
> To endure is the disposition of the worthy man;
> Greatness is the field of action of the worthy man.[29]

The quest for sagehood is thus compared to the spontaneous and harmonious exchange by which Heaven and Earth produce all things. The human quest is modeled upon a metaphysical process. It appears to be the spontaneous and natural destiny of man to seek sagehood. And the goal seems assured to him who endures and perseveres.

The last two lines of this section from the Book of Changes unite the cognitive aspect of the search for wisdom with the existential perfection which this brings:

> By means of the easy and simple we grasp and principles (li^a) of the whole world.
> When the principles of the whole world are grasped, therein lies perfection.[30]

It is therefore against this perspective of the ease and simplicity of the quest for wisdom and sagehood, which are identified with the understanding of all things through their being and goodness, that we are to understand the concluding lines of Lu's poem.

The quest, actually, is far from "easy." A strong resolve is required to enter into it and to continue therein. It is less a work to be done than a state of mind and being, in which one remains only by dint of constant self-renewal, of vigilance over oneself, of caution and apprehension. It is an existential quest in which one's whole being is engaged, not just one's intellectual activities or social, ethical behavior. It is a case of readiness to lose all for the sake of gaining all, of losing oneself in the discovery of a new self, a true self. It is a quest in which the goal will always remain elusive, in which success can hardly be measured in quantitative terms. It can hardly ever become a "popular" quest, so that, for all the simplicity and ease with which Lu Chiu-yüan describes sagehood, sages—real ones—will not thereby become more abundant.

In the context of Lu Chiu-yüan's poem, however, do these words refer merely to the quest of the Confucian Tao or wisdom or also to the meaning of wisdom itself? To answer this question, we may consider Lu Chiu-yüan's additional argument, which the others present stopped him from developing. After finishing his poem, he had remarked: "Before the time of the sages Yao and Shun, what book was there to read?"[31]

Yao and Shun were the greatest sages, ancestors of all sages. It is their "mind" which the Confucian and neo-Confucian followers of the School of Sages are supposed to interpret and transmit. And yet, these ancient sages lived in a time when no books were written about sagehood. They did not have to engage in intellectual inquiry to become sages. They merely lived virtuously and, by so doing, found wisdom.

Lu Chiu-yüan identifies wisdom with virtue, not with any particular virtue but with that universal virtue which informs the whole of a sage's life: jen^a. In a letter, he explains this same truth. Quoting Mencius, who says that the Way (Tao) refers to jen^a (perfect virtue), Lu identifies this jen^a with $hsin^a$ (the mind) and li^a (being, goodness).[32] It is that which we already have and yet look for, that which we find when we are awakened to its presence within ourselves (fa-$ming$ pen-$hsin$).[33] In practical terms, it is the virtue with which we love our parents, respect our brothers, and have compassion for the child falling into the well, and so on. It has come to us from Heaven. With it, one knows how to do good without having to learn, and one also has the power to put this knowledge into action. On account of it, one can say: "All things are present within me. When I turn back to reflect upon myself in sincerity, I have a great joy."[34]

But if Lu's reference to Yao and Shun emphasizes the moral and existential aspect of the quest for sagehood, it also points to what lies beyond the quest itself—the meaning of sagehood. If this is expressed in terms of the sages' mind—the *original* mind of the earliest sages—what is implied is not merely that the fullness of insights can be interpreted and transmitted, if only by inspiration, but also that the notion of sagehood represents. the metaphysical reality of union with the Tao, the ultimate reality.

The story is told of how Lu's best-known disciple, Yang Chien (1140–1226), discovered for himself the meaning of the original mind. Lu had simply stated that the original mind refers to the four beginnings of virtue: compassion (humanity), shame (rightness), acquiescence (propriety), and discernment between right and wrong (wisdom). This had not satisfied Yang Chien. But Lu reminded him of how during a court session Yang had been able to determine the innocent and the guilty, and that this discernment came from the original mind. Hearing this, Yang suddenly awoke to the meaning of the words, saying, "I suddenly realized how this mind [of mine] has no beginning and no end, and penetrates all things."[35]

In view of this statement, it appears that the original mind is more than the power to discern between right and wrong. It is rather that from which this power proceeds: our innermost being, which is one with all that is true and good. The ethical and the metaphysical are not two separate spheres but rather two dimensions of the same reality.

In all this, it may be assumed that Lu Chiu-yüan was influenced by Buddhist teachings. Not that he read many Buddhist texts. He admitted to having read such sutras as *Śūraṅgama*, *Yüan-chüeh*, and *Vimalakīrti*, as did Chu Hsi.[36] But his insistence on the oneness of reality and on the role of spiritual enlightenment in the quest for wisdom manifests strong Ch'an Buddhist overtones. With all this, however, Lu Chiu-yüan was not a Buddhist. He considered himself a Confucian and was committed to the Confucian ideal of social responsibility, as shown in his performance of official duties in a series of minor posts. His criticisms of Buddhism were less severe than those of Chu Hsi, but even the latter regarded him as a fellow Confucian while regretting the extent of Buddhist influence on his thought. Lu Chiu-yüan, on his side, was to criticize Chu Hsi for showing Taoist influences, especially in maintaining that *T'ai-chi*, the Great Ultimate, was at the same time *Wu-chi*, the Limitless.[37] This was an example of the ideological differences between the two thinkers. Neither lived in an intellectual vacuum, and their willingness to learn from non-Confucian sources demonstrates their openness and is one of the reasons for the richness and depth of their thinking. But Chu frequently remarked on Lu's showing Buddhist influences, and Lu naturally retorted with comments about Chu's own Taoist influences.

Although Chu did not give an instant answer to Lu's question about what books could be found before the time of Yao and Shun, he would write years later:

In remote antiquity, before the written word came to be, students had nothing to read. Those above average intelligence were expected to achieve perfection by themselves without studying. But after sages and worthy men have left behind writings, the Tao is well recorded in the classics. Even a sage like Confucius cannot refrain from studying these.[38]

The Nine Hexagrams: The Goose Lake Monastery Disputes (Part 2)

The discussions at the Goose Lake Monastery[39] also touched upon a section of the Book of Changes that is usually referred to as the Nine Hexagrams (*chiu-kua*). These are also given in the Great Commentary, supposedly offering a manner of living in times of difficulties and anxieties. They deal therefore with character formation or the practice of virtue.[40]

The Nine Hexagrams are explained three times. Generally speaking, the first paragraph attempts to relate each to character cultivation, the second seeks to point out the special characteristics of each, and the third describes the fruits which come from them. As Richard Wilhelm explains, the movement is from within outward. "What is wrought in the depths of the heart becomes outwardly visible in its effects."[41]

I shall cite the paragraphs here:

> *Treading* shows the basis of character.
> *Modesty* shows the handle of character.
> *Recovery*, the stem of character.
> *Perseverance* brings about firmness of character.
> *Decrease* is about cultivation of character.
> *Increase* is about the fullness of character.
> *Oppression* is the test of character.
> *The Well* is the field of character
> *The Gentle* is the exercise of character.
>
> *Treading* is harmonious and attains its goal.
> *Modesty* gives honor and shines forth.
> *Recovery* is small, yet different from external things.
> *Perseverance* shows manifold experiences without satiety.
> *Decrease* shows first what is difficult and then what is easy.
> *Increase* shows the growth of fullness without artifices.
> *Oppression* leads to perplexity and thereby to success.
> *The Well* abides in its place, yet has influence on other things.
> *The Gentle* enables one to weigh things and remain hidden.
>
> *Treading* brings about harmonious conduct.
> *Modesty* serves to regulate the mores.
> *Recovery* leads to self-knowledge.
> *Perseverance* brings about unity of character.
> *Decrease* keeps harm away.
> *Increase* furthers what is useful.

Oppression teaches one to lessen one's rancor.
The Well brings about discrimination as to what is right.
The Gentle enables one to take special circumstances into account.[42]

Chu Hsi regards the Book of Changes as having originally been written for divination purposes and explains it as such.[43] He judges the appendices to have been added much later and to contain moral and metaphysical meaning. But he says of the section on the Nine Hexagrams that these have been selected for special discussion because they help us to live under difficult circumstances: "In discussing how to live with difficulty and anxiety, the sage discovered by chance these Nine hexagrams. . . . [But it doesn't mean that] outside these Nine Hexagrams, there is no help for dealing with difficulties and anxieties."[44] According to him, there is no special reason why the Hexagrams thus selected should be placed in the order in which they are found. Nor does the number nine itself have any particular significance.[45]

However, at Goose Lake, Lu Chiu-yüan gave his views on the order of these hexagrams, and especially the position of the third listed, *Fu* (Recovery), which follows *Lü* (Treading) and *Ch'ien* (Modesty). Taking his cue from the linear formations given, Lu says that the hexagram *Lü* is formed of Heaven above Marsh below, to teach man to regard Heaven and Earth as that from which he has received his body and to live—tread—according to his principles. In so doing, man will encounter successes and failures, which show the possession or lack of modesty. With modesty, one keeps his spiritual energy (*ching-shen*) recollected inside and thus recovers (*Fu*) his original mind.

Lu adds that the hexagram Recovery is followed by those of Perseverance (*Heng*), Decrease (*Sun*[a]), Increase (*Yi*[b]), and Oppression (*K'un*[b]) because with the recovery of one's mind, there is yet need of perseverance and of diminution of selfishness to accompany the growth of the heavenly principle. In this way, dangers and difficulties, including oppression, will not be able to move the mind. And then, one will have real insights into the Way.[46] We are not told how Lu explained the Well (*Ching*[e]) and the Gentle (*Sun*[b]) in relation to the rest. But apparently, his general exposition impressed Chu Hsi and Lü Tsu-ch'ien.

These somewhat forced interpretations of the Nine Hexagrams illustrate Lu Chiu-yüan's approach to the classics. As he had said: "The Six Classics are my footnotes, and I am the footnote to the Six Classics."[47] For him, to acquire wisdom, or the Tao, is to *become* wise oneself, to become one with the Tao, by cultivating what one already has of the Tao, which is inborn and yet capable of growth. Study of the classics may help to achieve this goal, as one finds that personal insights are confirmed by the words of the classics. It acts also as proof of the validity of the spiritual message of the classics. A circular process is thus involved: I find in the classics what I already have and know, which proves to me that the classics are useful and have their place in the quest for wisdom.

In the case of his interpretation of the Nine Hexagrams, the central insight concerned the Recovery of the original mind. The original mind refers to our inborn ability to know and do good or, rather, one's being-born-good, the state of goodness which is one's by nature, which becomes obscured in the course of one's life, but which may still be repossessed. In seeking this recovery, there are difficulties and dangers. But one thing alone is necessary: to hold on, not to give up. In other words, the aspiring sage is always doing the same thing—he is always striving to repossess himself in the depths of his own being, a being born good and born of goodness.

And since this *is* the Book of Changes, a text that interacts in a special manner with the reader, reflecting his mind, we may say that Lu's subjective interpretation of the Nine Hexagrams has validity especially for himself. After all, Lu Chiu-yüan considers the mind, *hsin*[a], as possessing the power to determine and perfect itself, at the same time a subject and an object, an immanent principle that is open to goodness, to the transcendent. It is the heart of human reality and of *all* reality, which he regards as receiving meaning from human consciousness and human understanding.

The conflict between learning and wisdom was actually a recurrent feature in the history of Chinese thought. And we have here also the difference between a more objective approach to the Book of Changes, based on historical and textual concerns, and a more subjective one, based on pure intuition and psychic resonance. In a sense, the Goose Lake Monastery Debates were more than a temporal event. They gave expression to an inner tension lying at the heart of the Confucian quest that concerns reason and intuition or, better still, intuitive reasoning and almost pure intuition. For all the intuitive subtleties and textual complications, this tension has been creative and fruitful and is responsible for much of the richness and fecundity of the whole Confucian legacy.

Three years after the Goose Lake Monastery meeting, the Lu brothers lost their mother and wrote to Chu for advice regarding funeral rituals. Chu gave his opinions, after which Lu Chiu-ling, the more conciliatory brother, traveled to visit Chu in Yüan-shan, at another Buddhist monastery (1178). They were together for three days and expressed different ideas about study and cultivation, although the atmosphere was much friendlier.[48] Chu happily addressed a poem to Lu Chiu-ling, in which the first half expresses personal sentiments of separation and reunion, as well as reminiscence of the Goose Lake experience:

> Your virtue and its influence I have always admired:
> After three years of separation, all the more so.
> I walk casually out of the cold valley, cane in hand,
> To meet you once more, crossing the distant mountain by sedan.

The latter half focuses on the exchange of ideas which takes place in dialogues and discussions—and presumably, disputes. The poem concludes with an allusion to wisdom, which lies beyond the reach of learning and, indeed, of time itself:

> The more closely we discuss our old pursuits,
> The deeper becomes our new knowledge.
> Yet, reaching a point of no words,
> We forget there is past and present in this life.

Rightness versus Profit: A Lecture

At the Goose Lake Monastery, Chu and Lu Chiu-yüan met for the first time, even though they had known each other from their writings as well as from mutual friends. At Yüan-shan, Chiu-ling gave a letter from Chiu-yüan to Chu Hsi in which Chiu-yüan distinguished Confucians from Buddhists by "rightness and profit," words taken from the *Analects*. Unfortunately, two years later, Chiu-ling died (1180).

Between 1175 and 1181 (between Chu Hsi and Lu Chiu-yüan's first and last meetings) and also afterward, the two exchanged letters frequently to discuss various subjects. Wing-tsit Chan says that over forty letters were exchanged, often several a year.[49] Often, they had disagreements. In spring 1181, Lu Chiu-yüan visited Chu Hsi at Chu's White Deer Cave Academy in Nan-k'ang, where Chu was serving as prefect. He was accompanied by six disciples and requested Chu to write a tomb inscription for the deceased Lu Chiu-ling. Chu received them with warm hospitality, invited Lu to a pleasant boat ride together, and consented to Lu's request. Chu also invited his guest to give a lecture to the students gathered there. Lu selected the well-known passage from *Analects* 4:16 "The gentleman understands rightness; the small man understands profit."[50]

In his lecture, Lu emphasized the importance of discerning one's resolve (*chih*e). Because we are influenced by what we learn, he says, the distinction between rightness and profit depends on our resolve to seek one or the other. As success at the examination hall often depends on the student's skills and the examiner's preferences, it should not mark the distinction between the gentleman and the small man, in spite of what the world might think. Otherwise, he cautions, one runs the risk of studying the sages' words but going against them in action. Besides, after the initial success, one would be tempted to consider the emoluments of officialdom as a standard of achievement rather than devoting oneself to serving the people. In conclusion, Lu encourages all present to resolve to seek rightness while preparing for examinations and to look forward to serving the country and the people as gentlemen and without selfishness:

> [The master] has renovated this place as a lecture hall. The founder's intentions are earnest. Everyone who comes here should not move from their resolution [to pursue rightness]. Toward this end, let us encourage one another to persevere and not go against our resolves.[51]

It is recorded that Lu moved his audience to tears, while Chu Hsi himself felt so hot that he could not stop fanning himself. In order to commemorate the event, Chu asked Lu for a written copy of the lecture and had it engraved in stone.[52]

Lu's lecture marked a point of agreement and personal reconciliation between the two men, even if the private conversations showed disagreements. It was also their final meeting. Afterward, Chu commented in private:

> Lu really likes to argue. Ch'eng Yi had said: "Only with deep understanding comes devoted preference."[53] Lu, however, insists on preference before

understanding. But I think that where rightness or profit is concerned, more people understand first and then make their choice of preference. If one knows nothing, how can there be a preference?[54]

Other Disputes

There were also human factors that disturbed their relationship. For example, shortly after Lu Chiu-ling's visit, Chu Hsi accepted a disciple, Ts'ao Chien, who had first studied with Lu Chiu-yüan and in whom Chu saw much promise, perhaps, eventually, as the person most competent to carry on his own teachings. On Ts'ao's premature death, Chu wrote an epitaph (1183) which recorded Ts'ao's intellectual conversion from Lu's school to his own. This account displeased Lu and his disciples.[55]

Around the same time, Chu was describing Lu's teachings in these words:

In the context of the shallow and partial intellectual discussions of recent years, Lu's teachings stand out as different, but they were undeniably derived from Ch'an Buddhism. . . . [Attempts] to hide [their lineage] and cover up . . . in order to deceive will not succeed, except to deceive oneself and to go down into the realm of insincerity.[56]

Five years later, the debates by correspondence started on the subject of the "Great Ultimate and yet the *Wu-chi*," revealing the deep and irreconcilable differences between the two men (see chapter 2).

Learning or Wisdom?

Generally, Chu continued to criticize Lu for not placing enough emphasis on intellectual inquiry and book learning, as well as for being influenced by Ch'an Buddhism. Lu, in return, criticized Chu for excessive indulgence in book learning.[57]

A great scholar and a bibliophile, Chu was unable to stop himself from reading, especially whenever he got hold of a new book. From time to time, he would regret his own enslavement to books, as he said in a poem:

> At the river's source, new colors red and green,
> Evening rain and morning calm appeal even more.
> Burying my head in books: how long will this be?
> Better give up and look for spring![58]

The reading of this poem prompted Lu to declare: "Chu Hsi is now enlightened. What a happy occurrence!"[59] But Chu was actually unable or unwilling to liberate himself from his addiction to reading.

Following Lu Chiu-shao, Chiu-yüan debated with Chu by correspondence in 1188 over the meaning of *Wu-chi erh T'ai-chi*. I shall not dwell on these debates except to say that Lu insisted this teaching did not come from the sages. I have already talked about these differences of opinion at some length in chapter 2. Suffice it to say here that their correspondence, which Lu disseminated widely among friends and disciples, probably led Chu to the publication of his works on the Great Ultimate.[60]

When Lu Chiu-yüan died in 1193, Chu led his disciples to mourn him in a temple as a friend and then said, after a long pause: "It is regrettable that Kao-tzu has passed away."[61] The reference is to Mencius's contemporary and rival Kao-tzu. In *Mencius* 6A, we find some exchanges between the two men. They were on opposite sides of such issues as human nature—whether it is originally good or neutral—and on humanity and rightness, with Kao-tzu asserting that while the virtue of humanity is internal to us, that of rightness is external.[62]

In comparing Lu to Kao-tzu, Chu was referring to Lu's praise of Kao-tzu: "I once heard Lu discuss Kao-tzu's sayings. Generally, he praised Kao-tzu's teachings as lofty, . . . because his own views resembled Kao-tzu's."[63] He was considering himself as Mencius, and Lu as Kao-tzu, a kind of heretic figure who did not believe that human nature was originally good. He also attributed Lu's alleged lack of understanding to his neglect of book learning.[64]

Elsewhere Chu said:

> In discussing Buddhism [with someone] . . . , Lu said: "Buddhists basically agree with us Confucians. What is different regards [such issues] as rightness versus profit and public versus private." But this statement is wrong. Otherwise, we Confucians would share the same truth with Buddhists. Should that be so, how could there be a difference when it comes to rightness or profit? The difference lies at the very source of things. We Confucians believe in the reality of the myriad principles; Buddhists hold that they are all empty. . . .
> . . . Lu only regards what he sees in his own mind as internal. What others say is not at all internal . . . but rather external, just as rightness is . . . for Kao-tzu.[65]

The question regarding rightness's being internal or external is important, because, following the recorded conversation with Kao-tzu, the *Book of Mencius* quotes the master as going on to formulate his teaching on the four beginnings of virtue to support his belief that human nature is originally good: "The mind of compassion pertains to humanity, the mind of shame to rightness, the mind of respect to observance of rites, the mind of right and wrong to wisdom."[66] The philosophical belief that the four beginnings are internal is for Mencius an important support to his theory of human perfectibility. No wonder Chu Hsi was displeased to hear Lu Chiu-yüan diverge from this teaching. This was probably more on account of his own preference for this particular doctrine than to any sanctimonious respect for texts. After all, Chu was not himself a stickler for the words of ancient texts and, as we know, was perfectly ready to emend the text of the *Great Learning* to prove his own points.

Is it correct or even fair to characterize Chu Hsi as intent on learning while Lu Chiu-yüan looked for wisdom? The contemporary philosopher Tang Chün-i has proposed that the differences between Chu and Lu should be understood not simply as between honoring moral nature and emphasizing intellectual pursuit but rather between the *efforts of cultivation* each preferred in honoring moral nature. Chu concentrated on dissolving the selfish desires or passions that come with physical endowment in order to make manifest heavenly principle. Lu preferred to teach others to awaken the mind's unity with *li*[a]. There is, of course, the deeper issue dividing them, their views on *hsin*[a] and *li*[a].[67] I shall address the more practical difference before moving to the more speculative question. What is affirmed is that the two men shared the same spiritual quest while following different methods to achieve a similar goal because of differences in philosophical presuppositions.

The Ch'an theme of gradual or sudden awakening finds renewed attention in differences between Chu and Lu. In my view, Ch'eng Yi and Chu Hsi both recognized the universal capacity for sagehood and wisdom but saw its acquisition as a task that required tremendous effort, usually the fruit of a sudden, inner enlightenment that followed the accumulation of encyclopedic knowledge and the permeation of the spirit of reverence and stillness throughout daily living. But Chu's emphasis was very much on step-by-step accumulation of knowledge: "There isn't something like understanding all principles through understanding one principle. One needs to accumulate [knowledge] gradually. . . . In learning, there is the principle of gradual (*chien*) [cultivation], not that of hurriedness."[68]

Lu as Prophet of Pure Insight

Lu Chiu-yüan disagreed with the assumption underlying this approach. For him, human nature is in itself an entirely adequate instrument for its own perfection. It is not only the tranquil locale where enlightenment occurs. It is identical with the dynamic *hsin*[a], which Lu regarded to be somehow one with ultimate reality (Tao). Whoever seeks enlightenment should therefore grapple with this *hsin*[a], this Tao, without allowing himself to be distracted by other affairs and pursuits. It is reported that one evening, while on a walk in the moonlight, Lu sighed and said to a disciple, "Chu Hsi is great like Mount T'ai [in his scholarship]. It's too bad that he has not learned to see the Tao and is wasting energy."[69] This is an enlightened man's comment about an unenlightened man.

The emphasis on inner enlightenment may give the impression that Lu's internalization of the whole pursuit of wisdom tends to the inner pull of self-cultivation in silence and contemplation at the expense of social involvement. Chu's balanced method of both extension of knowledge and reverence would seem more outer-oriented, since it takes the person out of himself, to the investigation of truth in the classical texts and in the natural universe. In fact, however, Chu's attention is focused on *hsing*[a] (nature), which he regards as containing all principles (*li*[a]) in potency, and which awaits the effort of being cleared from the obscurity cast upon it by human desires. It is a more passive principle, which must be acted upon through the work of *hsin*[a], the mind-and-heart, which controls both nature and the emotions. For this reason, Chu places emphasis on quiet-sitting as a technique which assists in the restoration of the human being's pristine goodness. And his principal doctrine in cultivation is that of reverence, inherited from Ch'eng Yi, which he recommends for uniting the interior life with the exterior.

Lu's vantage point is quite different. There is no sense, he maintains, in pursuing the intellectual path when one does not understand honoring moral nature.[70] His teaching of cultivation is grounded in the *Analects*, and his basic principle, *hsin*[a], a source of dynamic action, comes from Mencius. Lu loved repeating from *Mencius* "First build up the nobler part of your nature,"[71] and "That by which humans differs from the brutes is small. The common man loses this feature; the gentlemen retains it."[72] While Lu is not opposed to the practice of quiet-sittng, he is not necessarily dependent upon this inner-oriented technique. Lu does not discuss *ch'i*[a]. For him, *hsin*[a], the mind, is by nature independent and not different from *li*[a]. Thus, it is not very remarkable that in spite of his desire for social involvement, Chu led the life of a near-recluse, while Lu, who never attained a very high position, was content to exercise the duties of minor official posts entrusted to him. The culmination of Lu's thinking would come only with Wang Yang-ming, whose life revealed the same contrary pulls between concerns for the inner and for the outer realms of existence, but whose method of self-perfection, based on a dynamic *hsin*[a], which confronts all events as they occur, would direct him to undertake social and political activities as the opportunities arose.

Lu is opposed to Chu's doctrine of reverence, which, he asserts, is not based on the classical texts and is rather "a piece of fiction."[73] In this context, he asserts: "My learning is different from others' in that I never make things up."[74]

An important difference between Chu and Lu has to do with their diverging understandings of the nature and function of *hsin*[a]. For Chu, it is the directive agent of both human nature and the emotions, but on that account, it is ambivalent, not full of goodness as is *li*[a]. For Lu, *hsin*[a] is much more. For him, the human mind, as exemplified in the minds of the sages, is the norm of being and goodness. It remains interior while assuming objective, even absolute, qualities. For Lu the transcendent is also immanent, in human minds as well as in the universe. He denies the difference between a certain "natural" state of the human being as potential sage and a higher-than-natural state, that of an actual sage. His teaching set the tone for later development especially in the Ming dynasty, with the emergence of the school of Wang Yang-ming, which saw sages everywhere.

At first sight, the philosophy of Ch'eng Yi and Chu Hsi seems to support the role of authority in the acquisition of wisdom and in the ordering of society. The harmonious universe of *li*[a] and *ch'i*[a] which revolves around the notion of *T'ai-chi*—the Great Ultimate in being and goodness—may argue well for a hierarchical structure of a strong, centralized government.[75] The appeal to the classics and to the sages, considered as lineal forebears of the exponents of this philosophy, provides another cornerstone for a regimented system of education. The truth is far more complex, since the philosophy of Ch'eng Yi and Chu Hsi was developed on the basis of their independent interpretation of the classics. The authority to which they gave adherence was higher than the state, the supposed guardian of classical exegesis, higher even than the classics. They relied primarily on their own authority, as self-appointed interpreters of the sacred message. Their claim was to solid classical learning, but particularly to their own insights into the spiritual meaning of the texts. For this reason, in the political realm, they acted as moral judges of their sovereigns rather than as dutiful ministers.[76]

Lu Chiu-yüan, on the other hand, appears to be a rebel against the entire classical tradition, and a prophet of pure insight. He proposed the recognition of *hsin*[a] as Tao (ultimate truth). He sought to internalize wisdom and virtue completely and to make the pursuit of sagehood entirely independent of classical studies. Naturally, such a rejection of external authority did not bring his teaching the favor of state power, which always relies on external sanctions. But in fact, Lu was only inferring certain logical conclusions from Ch'eng Yi and Chu Hsi's attitudes toward the classics. He clearly pointed out the significance of that "higher authority" to which appeals had been made: it was the sages' *hsin*[a], as Ch'eng and Chu also acknowledged, but it was seminally present in the *hsin*[a], a fact that neither Ch'eng nor Chu clearly demonstrated. Nearly three hundred years later, Wang Yang-ming's teachings were also attacked as heresy because they were based on private interpretation of the classics, through accommodation with Ch'an Buddhist ideas. The controversies Wang was to sustain led him to question not only the role of personal insight and of intellectual inquiry, of inner enlightenment and of a more systematic cultivation, but even the very role of authority itself, whether of the sages, the classics, or government, in the determination of truth. For if authority can be detrimental to that which it claims to defend, by what right does it continue to demand respect and adherence?

Lu pointed out the correct direction to sagehood but did not push his discoveries to their ultimate conclusions. This was done by Wang Yang-ming. Wang's teaching of sagehood reconciled the inherent tensions between the inner and outer realms of contemplation and action, the ethical and metaphysical dimensions of Confucian philosophy. It was to make clear that the authority to which the sage appeals as support for the truth of his teaching is also identical with the core of the teaching itself, namely, with *hsin*[a], the heart of all reality. Wang Yang-ming finished the work that Lu had begun, articulating a philosophy of *hsin*[a] that sees everything in relation to *hsin*[a], the self-determining agent and goal, subject and object, of the quest for wisdom. The rapid rise and later decline of Wang's school of thought came after several centuries of dominance by the school of Chu Hsi, with its emphasis on learning, and was followed by the resurgence of philology in the seventeenth century.

Conclusion

According to Kusumoto Fumio, Chu Hsi became more critical of Buddhism as he realized that Lu Chiu-yüan's philosophy was basically a rearticulation of Ch'an.[77] Indeed, in his critiques of Lu Chiu-yüan, he often speaks of Lu's philosophy simply as Ch'an. He is especially unhappy with Lu's neglect of intellectual pursuit of principles (*ch'iung-li*): "Lu Chiu-yüan does make efforts of self-cultivation. Should he also be willing to pursue principles diligently, he would have much to show for himself. Unfortunately, he is unwilling to change his ways."[78] Further: "Lu Chiu-yüan . . . is a very good person. But . . . when he speaks of the meaning of things, he acts like a private salt smuggler in central Fukien, who hides the salt underneath fish to avoid detection. For his teaching is basically Ch'an, but he covers it up by using our Confucian language."[79]

In some respects, Lu Chiu-yüan's philosophy represents what Chu Hsi would have developed had he stayed with Lin-chi influences. Lu teaches that the mind is identical to principles. For Lu, however, the mind is not just the mind of conscious activity, as is the case with the Buddhists, but also the mind as the source of moral judgments, as well as the mind as the metaphysical ground of principles. Time and again, Lu explains the "original mind" in terms of Mencius's "benevolence, rightness, propriety, and wisdom." It is the mind of moral discernment, that which tells right from wrong. And it is also the mind in which one could discover ultimate reality. Lu's problem with Chu Hsi is that while Chu knows many things, he "did not really see the Tao."[80] Presumably, that refers to Chu's not having experienced a real enlightenment that would give insight into the universal meaning of the Way.

Chu Hsi acknowledges that Lu's emphasis on the mind's being also principle marks out a metaphysical difference between Lu and Ch'an Buddhism. But he adds that Lu does not acknowledge the presence in the mind of physical endowment, which can be led astray by material desires and selfishness, and which therefore should not be simply identified with principle (li^a). In other words, Lu does not subscribe to Chu's philosophy of human nature and its explanation for the rise of moral evil. Besides, Chu explains, li^a is also present in the myriad things outside the mind. There is thus need for investigation of things to discover all the li^a in the world. To insist that the myriad li^a are all in the mind is to say virtually that the mind is empty, which is close to Ch'an.[81]

Chu's language is ambiguous. In his philosophy, the mind is constituted more by $ch'i^a$. I presume the argument here is that to see li^a alone as being present in the mind is not to see the mind as real; and to see li^a only in the mind, and not in things, is to deny the importance of the things of the world, as well as the importance of the real meaning of li^a itself.

Another contrast flows from the metaphysical difference: one concerning the doctrine of cultivation. Chu insists on the investigation of things and the extension of knowledge, with principles (li^a) as the object of spiritual, as well as intellectual, pursuit. For Lu, one can find principles by concentrating on the mind. This introvertive attention reminds us of the Ch'an teaching about pointing straight to the mind in order to find human nature. In several instances, Lu places some importance on the enlightenment experience. His disciple Yang Chien speaks of a sudden experience (on hearing Lu's words) of the brightness and spiritual intelligence of the mind.[82] With his dialectical method, he also teaches his disciples through exchanges that resemble Ch'an dialogues. His intuitive touch came to light especially in his response to a disciple who recounted to Lu his own enlightenment experience after half a month's ardent meditation. Lu replied that he already could tell what had happened. "It can be seen in your eyes."[83]

In this respect, Chu was a Confucian, not a Buddhist. Lu Chiu-yüan, on the other hand, went beyond the formal boundaries of Confucian tradition in claiming that "the Six Classics were all footnotes" to his mind.[84] However, to the extent that Lu, like Chu himself, was a moral essentialist and never abandoned his moral responsibilities in society, he too never trespassed the real boundaries that define Confucianism. Even Chu Hsi acknowledged, with some humility, that because Lu placed emphasis in his teaching on a life of virtue, his disciples tended to lead such lives, even if they lacked somewhat in their learning. Because Chu placed more emphasis on intellectual pursuit, his own disciples trailed behind Lu's in their practice of virtue.[85] For this reason, Lu can hardly be called a Buddhist in Confucian disguise, even if he showed more Buddhist influence than Chu did.

Chu's interpretation of the *T'ai-chi* as *Wu-chi*, as well as his insistence on intellectual pursuit as an integral part of spiritual and moral striving, led him to disputes with Lu Chiu-yüan over a wide range of issues. To an outsider today, theirs seems to have been a family dispute, as both were moral philosophers on a quest for spiritual enlightenment and wisdom. Chu's intuitive thinking is oriented outward, to the principles (*li*a) in things, whereas Lu Chiu-yüan's intuitive thinking is oriented inward, to the mind-and-heart.[86] Their primary philosophical principles were basically irreducible, so each believed himself to be right and criticized the other. Chu said that Lu neglected learning, while Lu thought Chu was wasting time writing commentaries and should give more attention to his own *hsin*. Their differences became almost paradigmatic, with learning posed against virtue and wisdom. Actually, within their respective philosophies, each was following a dialectical method, rising above certain dichotomies to reach a higher level of unity in thought, with Lu following more the call of action in the making of theory. Each produced a system purporting to reveal a higher reality. Both were moral essentialists, striving for the same goal of sagehood, but they differed in their first principles and, ultimately in their methods of achieving their goal.

Chu Hsi and Taoism

With leisure, my mind grows in the Way,
Vainly seeking the immortals' realm.
Bowing low, then looking up to the sublime:
I swear to sever my connections with the dust.

Chu Hsi[1]

Introduction[2]

Chu Hsi acknowledged a youthful interest in Taoism. He says that he was engrossed with "Buddhism and Taoism" for "over ten years." This lasted until he met Li T'ung and decided to concentrate on "the learning of the sages."[3]

For several decades, Chu also held sinecures involving supervision of Taoist temples. He was overseer of at least six different Taoist temples during his life.[4] What then was his understanding and evaluation of Taoism, and to what extent did Taoism influence his thinking?[5]

Speaking generally, we shall see that Chu tends to transform religious beliefs into philosophical concepts, without always succeeding completely, thereby revealing certain contradictions in his thinking. His criticism of Taoism is a selective and nuanced one and tamer than his criticism of Buddhism.[6]

Chu Hsi associated with many Taoist priests, just as he did with Buddhist monks. He made occasional sojourns in Taoist temples, exchanged words and poetry with individual priests, and sought their care in sickness.[7] Among Chu's over four hundred disciples, one has been identified as a Taoist priest versed in astrology, fortune-telling, and the art of war, who came to him through Ts'ai Yüan-ting.[8]

Chu's association with Taoist priests was different from that with Buddhist monks. We have no evidence that Chu took lessons from any Taoist priest, as we know he did from Buddhist monks. It would seem that Chu was more influenced by Ch'an Buddhism in his youth than he was by Taoism, although he showed an interest in both. With maturity, he moved away from Buddhism and, eventually, closer to Taoism, through an increasing interest in practices to ensure longevity, which he studied for practical health reasons.[9]

Chu Hsi and Taoist Philosophy

What is the "Taoist philosophy" that Chu Hsi knew, appreciated, and criticized? It has been characterized, on the one hand, as tending to regard as illusory the appearances of things that impinge on our consciousness, regarding these as epiphenomenal. On the other hand, it points out as real the substrative life forces or energies called *ch'i*[a] that underlie these appearances.[10] From this brief description, one can already see why Chu Hsi, a philosophical realist who accepts the appearances as the given, indeed, as "things," and who prefers to balance ch'i[a] (matter-energy) with *li*[a], could not be entirely comfortable with Taoist philosophy. Chu was obviously conversant with Taoist philosophical works, including *Lao-tzu* and, *Chuang-tzu*, and he commented on several selected chapters from each of these two works.

On Lao-tzu

In discussing the text *Lao-tzu*, Chu points out that he likes best the sixth chapter. He pays special attention to the two sentences "The spirit of the valley never dies. / This is called the mysterious female."[11] Chu offers a metaphysical interpretation of the passage. According to him, an empty valley, capable of transmitting echoes, represents a divinely or mysteriously transformed nature (*shen-hua chih tzu-jan*), whereas the "mysterious female" refers to what is receptive and life-giving. He even adds: "This most marvelous meaning contains the idea of *sheng-sheng* (literally, "life-giving life," "generation and regeneration"). It is what Ch'eng [Yi] learned from Lao-tzu."[12]

Chu's interpretation is actually close to that of the neo-Taoist exegete Wang Pi. Wang's comments on this chapter describe the spirit of the valley as occupying a shapeless and nameless space, "the root of Heaven and Earth," a name he also gives to "the gate of the mysterious female." His conclusion is that "all things are born of it," and yet, its "use is inexhaustible."[13]

Such a doctrine of spontaneous generation is found in the beginning of *Lao-tzu*: "The Nameless is the beginning of Heaven and Earth; / The Named is the mother of the myriad things."[14] Wang Pi explains: "Whatever is (*yu*) begins with nothing (*wu*). That is why the shapeless, nameless moment is the beginning of the myriad things, while the shaped and named moment is the mother who nurtures it and makes it grow."[15] The doctrine of spontaneous generation came from Han times. As mentioned in chapter two, the *Apocryphal Book of Changes* taught the idea of the *T'ai-yi*[a] (nothingness) producing or engendering the *T'ai-chi* (being). With Wang Pi and others, the idea grew in neo-Taoist philosophy and was to penetrate neo-Confucian thought.

In this regard, it may be no surprise that Chu should attribute to Lao-tzu Ch'eng Yi's doctrine of a dynamic universe of spontaneous generation, which presupposes a sympathetic communion with the forces of life. Ch'eng Yi had asserted that "The Way (Tao) spontaneously generates and regenerates (*sheng-sheng*) without end."[16] Chu himself is attracted to this view. His criticisms of

Taoist philosophy are generally restrained and discerning. In responding to disciples' questions, he defends Lao-tzu by saying: "Lao-tzu has said many things. How can we say there is nothing worthwhile in his book? Even in the case of Buddhism, there is much that is worthwhile. But they err regarding human destiny."[17]

Chu can appreciate *Lao-tzu* for positive teachings. In these cases, he tends to offer a Confucian interpretation of *Lao-tzu*, as Wing-tsit Chan has pointed out.[18] For example, Chu quotes from chapter 28 of *Lao-tzu*:

> Know the male
> But keep to the female
> And be a ravine to the empire. . . .
> Know the white
> But keep to the black
> And be a model to the empire.[19]

As with the spirit of the valley, Chu remarks that "the ravine and the valley both refer to a lowly place. " Lao-tzu speaks of being content in a lowly place, without seeking to move higher, which is a very rare and difficult effort. And yet, "with such effort, one could govern the country or apply strategy in warfare or take over the world without [appearing] to do anything." Here, Chu appears to shift to a practical teaching in *Lao-tzu*, that of remaining modest and humble in high office.[20]

But Chu echoes Chang Tsai's criticism of Lao-tzu for saying "being comes from nothingness." They both point out that such thinking is not to be found in the Book of Changes. And Chu Hsi adds: "In saying being comes from nothingness, Lao-tzu errs."[21] However, he admits that Lao-tzu is not a nihilist, as chapter 1 of the text also says: "Having nothing (*wu*), observe its secrets; / Having something (*yu*, i.e., "being"), observe its manifestations."[22] One is therefore to move from the manifestations of being to being itself, while observing the secrets of nothingness, hoping to unveil these as well.

Comparing Lao-tzu to the Buddhists, he claims that the latter regard Heaven and Earth as illusions, and the Four Elements as fantasy.[23] In other words, he regards the Buddhists as closer to nihilism than the Taoists.

Chu opposes the division of *Lao-tzu* into two parts under Tao and Te and disagrees with the saying:

> When the Way was lost there was virtue;
> When virtue was lost there was benevolence;
> When benevolence was lost there was righteousness.[24]

He comments: "Lao-tzu first speaks of Tao and then of Te. These are not understood but divided into two things. . . . [Besides,] without benevolence and righteousness, there is no *tao-li* (meaning). How can one yet speak of the Tao?"[25]

He criticizes Lao-tzu as a person who refuses to take responsibility, who wishes to protect his own life selfishly, and who does not care about the world around him. He also criticizes Lao-tzu's proclivity for Legalism. He points out that Lao-tzu's teachings have led to the emergence of such legalists as Shen Pu-hai and Han Fei-tzu, as well as to the military strategists connected with the *Scripture on Harmony of the Seen and Unseen* (*Yin-fu ching*).[26]

Chu also distinguishes carefully between Lao-tzu and Chuang-tzu, finding more depth in the former. Acknowledging that both teach a philosophy of withdrawal and retirement, he points out that Lao-tzu, unlike Chuang-tzu, is still concerned with social and political realities. He regards Chuang-tzu as the less rational and less responsible of the two:

> Lao-tzu's learning is generally focused on emptiness, tranquillity and non-action. . . . What is said about straddling the sun and the moon and holding up the universe . . . comes from Chuang-tzu's nonsense,[27] while what is said about that which is full of light reflecting all and penetrating all . . . comes from Buddhist empty talk. Where could you find such in the original Lao-tzu? In our own times, those who discuss Lao-tzu always mix up what is common between [Buddhism and Taoism] as though they are one school.[28]

When asked whether one should be permitted to read *Lao-tzu* and *Chuang-tzu* at all, Chu answers that there is no harm in reading them, provided that one knows one's own mind. "What is important is to understand where their meaning differs from that of the sages."[29] Here, Ch'ien Mu points out that Chu's readiness to learn from both Lao-tzu and Chuang-tzu marks a departure from Ch'eng Yi, who refused to read these texts, and shows him rather closer to Ch'eng Hao.[30]

Still, Chu's general attitude toward Taoism is a critical one. He refers to it by the term *Lao-Chuang* (Lao-tzu and Chuang-tzu), regards it as a kind of "heresy," and attacked it as Mencius had also criticized Yang Chu (for disregard of the ruler-subject relationship) and Mo Ti (for disregard of the father-son relationship). Indeed, Chu explains that if Mencius had not explicitly criticized Lao-tzu, it is because Mencius had already shown his opposition to what Lao-tzu represents in his critique of Yang Chu.[31] Thus, it may be said that Chu's own general disapproval of Taoism, like that of Buddhism, is rooted in his conviction of the primary importance of social and political responsibility. Besides this, we shall also find a critique of religious Taoism that is grounded in Chu's basically rationalist outlook.

Chu regards Lao-tzu's condemnation of rituals and music as mistaken. While less severe than Ch'eng Yi, he echoes Ch'eng's criticism of the amoral and Legalist implications of Lao-tzu's thought.[32] He singles out Lao-tzu's facile preference for survival.

On Chuang-tzu

Chu Hsi appears to have a special regard for Chuang-tzu. Chu says that while one does not know where Chuang-tzu learned what he knew, he was superior in knowledge to many scholars coming after Mencius, including Hsün-tzu. Indeed, he adds that whatever is positive in Buddhism comes from Chuang-tzu.[33] Chu praises both *Chuang-tzu* and the *Book of Mencius* for being good literature. He finds much that is positive or appealing in *Chuang-tzu*, incluing the cosmological explanations of *yin* and *yang*, which he considers to be a key to understanding the Book of Changes. And he cites particularly from the chapter "The Turning of Heaven." The cosmological questions posed there seem to have fascinated him:

> Who masterminds all this? Who pulls the strings? Who, resting inactive himself, gives the push that makes it go this way? I wonder, is there some mechanism that works it and won't let it stop? I wonder if it just rolls and turns and can't bring itself to a halt? Do the clouds make the rain, or does the rain make the clouds? Who puffs them up, who showers them down like this? Who, resting inactive himself, stirs up all this lascivious joy?[34]

Chu also cites several times with appreciation a long passage from "The Secret of Caring for Life." I quote from this famous story:

> Cook Ting was cutting up an ox for Lord Wen-hui. At every touch of his hand, every heave of his shoulder, every move of his feet, every thrust of his knee—zip! zoop! He slithered the knife along with a zing, and all was in perfect rhythm, as though he were performing the dance of the Mulberry Grove or keeping time to the Ching-shou music.[35]

When the lord expressed admiration at the cook's skill, he got the following response, which also impressed Chu:

> What I care about is the Way, which goes beyond skill. When I first began cutting up oxen, all I could see was the ox itself. After three years I no longer saw the whole ox. And now . . . I've had this knife . . . for nineteen years and I've cut up thousands of oxen with it, and yet the blade is as good as though it had just come from the grindstone.[36]

Chu sees here a hidden lesson about the gradual acquisition of *li*[a]:

> When a student first reads the text, he only sees the whole thing. After a long while he sees several pieces in it, even more than ten pieces. Only then is he making progress. This is like the cook cutting up the ox, who no longer sees the whole ox.[37]

Significantly, this corroborates Chu Hsi's preference for gradual cultivation over sudden enlightenment.

But he criticizes Chuang-tzu's exhortation in that same chapter, "The Secret of Caring for Life": "If you do good, stay away from fame. If you do evil, stay away from punishments."[38] He points out that fear of the disadvantages fame and punishment might bring causes Chuang-tzu to advocate "not doing too much good, and not doing too much evil." Philosophical Taoism is less interested in moral norms and more concerned with ensuring personal security.[39]

According to Chu, the teaching of the sages is that one should do as much real good as possible, neither seeking fame nor running away from fame. Indeed, a scholar seeking fame is not pursuing study for its own sake, especially what has been called *wei-chi chih hsüeh*:[40]

> To study for the sake of acquiring a reputation is not to study for oneself (*wei-chi*). . . . To fear that fame might injure oneself, and for that reason not to do one's best in studying, is [to show] that one's mind is already not right and has even turned slightly to evil.[41]

There are only a few sentences of criticism of Chuang-tzu in Chu Hsi's recorded conversations, although there are more in Chu's letters to friends and disciples.[42] Often, Chuang-tzu is mentioned together with Lao-tzu as "crazy," "partial," "without truth."[43] However, Chu Hsi says that Chuang-tzu was a well-educated man who understood many things but did not wish to do anything. In fact, Chuang-tzu liked to use Confucius as a mouthpiece but did not wish to imitate Confucius. Chu compares Lao-tzu and Chuang-tzu, saying that while Lao-tzu was willing to do a few things, Chuang-tzu was unwilling to do anything. It was not a case of his not being able to do anything. Rather, "he was unwilling to do anything."[44]

Lieh-tzu is another Taoist text that Chu explicitly discussed, but in only a few words. He considers Lieh-tzu to have lived before Chuang-tzu, and the latter to have modeled his writings on the former.[45] He also expresses the opinion that the hedonist teaching of Yang Chu issued out of Lao-tzu and is reflected in Chuang-tzu.[46]

A text that Chu does not appear to have discussed formally is the *Huai-nan-tzu*, with its discourses on the old Chinese concept of *ch'i*[a] that we find in Chu's philosophy. But whereas *ch'i*[a] figured in ancient philosophy independently, as "ether," matter-energy, the "stuff" of the universe, it reemerges in both Ch'eng Yi and Chu Hsi in association with *li*[a] (principle), a term with Hua-yen Buddhist overtones.

Chu Hsi and Taoist Religion

Without using such words as "philosophy" and "religion," Chu makes a careful distinction between the Taoism of Lao-tzu and Chuang-tzu and the cult of immortality that followed. He asserts that the quest for immortality came later and replaced the earlier interest in a philosophy of nonaction, until "shamans (*wu-chu*) have taken over and now only pay attention to using charms and talismans and praying for blessings and for the removal of disasters."[47] In this way, he voices greater disapproval of the latter practices, with their magicoreligious associations.

The Quest for Longevity

Living as they did during the Southern Sung period, Chu Hsi and his disciples could hardly ignore the beliefs and practices of religious Taoism. Chu's *Classi-*

fied Conversations offers us questions and answers between his disciples and himself on many subjects pertaining to the Taoist religion. Chu also appears to have better than usual knowledge of religious Taoism. Speaking generally, he shows himself to be not totally opposed to the quest for longevity, even if he had reservations about physical immortality as such.

On the question of whether there are real immortals, Chu is rational but cautious:

> People say that immortals don't die. [But I think that] it is not that they don't die, but that they pass away very gradually. . . . Since they know how to cultivate their forms and their *ch'i*ᵃ, and dissolve the sediments in this *ch'i*ᵃ, only what is pure *ch'i*ᵃ is left, so that they are enabled to levitate and change. . . . After a long time, [however,] dissipation [and death] still take place.[48]

Chu describes as strange and "uncanny" the Taoist explanations of the "apparent death" of the immortal. This refers to various explanations of what happens to the immortal at the hour of apparent death, called "liberation from the corpse." It is sometimes said that the immortal leaves his corpse behind, and other times that he only leaves behind a sword to represent his erstwhile body, so that such apparent death is called *chien-chieh*, or "liberation by sword," leaving people to guess how he died and what became of him. Chu poses here a somewhat trivial question that is nevertheless indicative of his rationalist outlook: "At the moment of death, a sword and a medicinal elixir are placed at the bedside. Should it be asked, if the sword is what became of oneself, what has the medicine become, when one's self has gone somewhere else?"[49]

Chu explains Taoist practices—presumably relating to inner or outer alchemy—as playing games with the "psyche" (*ching-shen*) and "fooling the people" to attract their faith.[50] He explains the practice of divination in similar terms, as the mind reaching out to the "contracting and expanding" *ch'i*ᵃ.[51] When told that in Taoist quiet-sitting, the effort of "making the mind force the *ch'i*ᵃ to rise up" had resulted in death by asphyxiation, Chu replied that he did not believe such was the intended result and offered another explanation according to his own investigation. He described Taoist circulation of breath (*tao-ying*) as an "inferior effort."[52] Yet he appeared reasonably familiar with Taoist meditation and even wrote a short piece on "watching the white on the nose," a Taoist technique with Buddhist antecedents that we shall explore further.[53]

Breath Regulation

Before proceeding further, we should take time to discuss breath circulation in general. Basically, there are two ways of breathing: exercising the lungs or exercising the diaphragm. Breathing with the lungs is faster paced, but breathing using the diaphragm is alleged to be more natural and relaxing. It is, indeed, what physicians in the West also counsel their patients to do. Today, most people are too rushed to attend to diaphragm breathing, but in Chu His's time, it appears to have been common practice.[54]

The practice of "watching the tip of the nose" is mentioned in a forged Buddhist classic, the *Śūrangama Sutra*. It reflects Taoist influence, recalling the "fasting of the mind" in *Chuang-tzu* and the development of the teaching of inner alchemy in the Sung dynasty.[55]

In his exchanges with his disciples, Chu Hsi criticizes Taoist practices of counting the breath and Buddhist meditation practices. His objection is the tendency to seek only peace and tranquillity while ignoring active involvement in things and affairs. In other words, he believes that there is a time for meditation and a time for action. And he prefers the kind of meditation that is morally motivated.[56] Still, this did not stop him from seeking to learn from both Buddhist and Taoist instructions and experience. His interest in "yoga" or breath regulation is a good example.

Chu mentioned the practice of "watching the tip of the nose" in his conversations with disciples. When asked what to use as a focus in quiet-sitting, he recommended the Taoist method of "counting the inhaling and exhaling of breath while watching the white tip of the nose."[57]

The very brief piece on breath circulation contains only sixty-four words, with four words in each of sixteen sentences. Entitled "*T'iao-hsi chen*," it is written in rhyme for easy remembrance:

> The nose has a white tip:
> I can see it.
> At all times and places,
> It moves with the face.
> In utmost quiet, breathe out,
> Like a fish in a spring pond.
> In utmost action, breathe in,
> Like insects between summer and fall.[58]

We find in these lines an echo of Chou Tun-yi's *Explanation of the Diagram of the Great Ultimate*, about utmost stillness being followed by utmost activity. The fish is happy to swim in a pond free of ice, and the insects prepare for hibernation between summer and autumn.[59]

To continue:

> Opening and closing—
> Who's there to move such?
> That's the work of no master.
> Its marvels are without limit.[60]

The first image is about the opening and closing of the gates of Heaven (*Ch'ien*) and Earth (*K'un*) of the Book of Changes. It also echoes what Ch'eng Yi has to say about breathing.[61] Then we find a reference to *Chuang-tzu* in "Who's there to move such?" We have earlier quoted some lines from the chapter which begins: "Does Heaven turn? Does the earth sit still? Do sun and moon compete for a place to shine? Who masterminds all this . . . ?"[62] The response to the question is that no one is in charge of the natural process of breathing.[63]

The piece goes on:

> To sleep on clouds and fly in heaven—
> That's not my problem.
> Holding the One is harmony:
> And a thousand and two hundred years' [life]!

Chu asserts that he does not expect to become immortal. But he speaks of the practice of "holding the One" and expresses his desire to live a very long life.[64]

Whereas Taoists are preoccupied with the cultivation of life, neo-Confucian philosophers have concentrated on the cultivation of the mind. Nevertheless, as human beings, they also have afflictions of the body. Should they resist Taoist methods as "heretical" or try to learn from them? Could not the cultivation of life help the cultivation of mind, and vice versa?

In a letter, Chu Hsi speaks about what to do in times of sickness: one should forget all worry and anxieties and pay attention to the cultivation of breath. This is to be done during quiet-sitting, with legs crossed, fixing one's gaze on the tip of the nose, and focusing the mind on the abdominal area. After a while, one should feel warmer and gradually experience positive effects.[65]

Two Special Taoist Treatises

Chu is the alleged author of two influential treatises, each a study of a Taoist religious text: A Study of the "Ts'an-t'ung-ch'i" (Ts'an-t'ung-ch'i k'ao-yi) and A Study of the "Yin-fu ching" (Yin-fu ching k'ao-yi).[66]

The Ts'an-t'ung-ch'i

Like the Harmony of the Seen and the Unseen (Yin-fu ching), the Harmony of the Three Ways (Ts'an-t'ung-ch'i) is a short text (one chapter). It is ascribed to the Yellow Emperor and included in the Taoist canon.[67] It purportedly shows how the Book of Changes tallies with the alleged teachings of the Yellow Emperor and of Lao-tzu, that is, with the cult of immortality. As such, it was highly regarded by the Confucian scholars of the Sung dynasty, together with Lao-tzu and Chuang-tzu.

Having apparently read many Buddhist and Taoist texts, Chu wrote a textual commentary on the Ts'an-t'ung-ch'i. He did this work when he was old and sick and officially under a cloud. It was one of his final works, together with the Ch'u Tz'u chi-chu, a commentary on the Songs of Ch'u, and the Yi-li ching-chuan t'ung-chieh, his work on the ritual text called the Ceremonials. Chu's other works on the Book of Changes had already attracted attention in Taoist and Confucian circles. Both the Ts'an-t'ung-ch'i and the Ch'u Tz'u chi-chu have Taoist concerns, the latter because of the shamanic character of some of its contents, as well as its reference to longevity and immortality. Old and sick, Chu chose to labor over these texts. The work with the ritual text represents his continual commitment to Confucian social values. The immersion in the *Ch'u Tz'u chi-chu* reminds us of his sympathies for Ch'ü Yüan, who had also experienced public disgrace in old age and allegedly searched for longevity techniques. And his interest in the *Ts'an-t'ung-ch'i* sustains the same quest, even if he found in it more cosmological understanding than anything pertaining to health and longevity.[68]

Like *A Study of the "Yin-fu ching," A study of the "Ts'an-t'ung-ch'i"* (1197) bears the pen name K'ung-t'ung tao-shih, literally, the "empty-same Taoist priest," and an assumed name, Tsou Hsi. Tsou refers to a small ancient state of the Warring States period, which could have been Chu's ancestral place, whereas Hsi is a homophone of his actual name. The title, however, merits some analysis. Taoist writers usually give their titles as well as their real or assumed names. In the case of Chu, while "emptiness" possibly signifies a Taoist belief, "empty-same" may suggest that he was *not* a real Taoist priest. Nevertheless, his use of an assumed name could be due to his preference for not openly favoring Taoism.[69]

The problem with any discussion of this work is its triple levels: it is a text about another text that in turn discusses an earlier text (i.e., the Book of Changes). And the whole task is complicated by the highly coded character of the language of both the Book of Changes and the *Chou-yi Ts'an-t'ung-ch'i*. Chu's text itself is not easy either, not only because it discusses the other two, but also because of the mathematical, or rather numerological, implications of his interpretation.

Reputed to be the first alchemical text, the *Ts'an-t'ung-ch'i* borrows the highly symbolic language of the Book of Changes to explain what appear to be alchemical processes, with *Ch'ien* and *K'un* representing the tripods, *K'an* and *Li*[b] the elixir, and the other sixty hexagrams the fire. It offers as well a system called *na-chia*, basically an elaborate correlation between the eight trigrams, which constitute the foundation of the Book of Changes and from which the Sixty-four Hexagrams are derived, and the cyclical calendrical signs called ten "heavenly stems" (*kan*), representing the various stages of the movements of the sun and moon and the supposed fluctuations of *yin* and *yang*.[70] Since the ambiguity of the language is such as to open the text to all kinds of interpretations, it has been variously understood to be teaching spiritual cultivation, sexual hygiene, or alchemy. It has been regarded by some scholars as dealing mainly with outer alchemy, that is, the quest for immortality through the making of an elixir in the furnace. It has been regarded by other scholars closer to Chu's time as dealing mainly with inner alchemy, the quest for what is euphemistically called the inner elixir. One problem is that the language of inner alchemy is basically the same as the language of outer alchemy, which it is supposed to reflect.[71]

The *Ts'an-t'ung-ch'i* played an important role in the development of Sung neo-Confucianism. It also influenced Chou Tun-yi's *Explanation of the Diagram of the Great Ultimate*, which mentions the four hexagrams Ch'ien, K'un, K'an, and *Li*[b], as well as Shao Yung's theory of numbers.[72] Chu's treatise on the *Ts'an-t'ung-ch'i* came twelve years after his treatise on the *Yin-fu-ching*.

Chu called his work *Chou-yi Ts'an-t'ung-ch'i k'ao-yi*. This is less of a textual criticism and more of a commentary. Chu probably completed it in 1197, having worked on it while he was under severe pressure from the official condemnation of his teaching. Moreover, in advancing age, he was experiencing health problems and needed advice on the cultivation of life. In this context, he also wrote the short piece on breath circulation, even though he had disdained such practices earlier.[73]

Chu worked on the text with the help of Ts'ai Yüan-ting. Chu described how he and Ts'ai discussed the treatise together, often working late at night and forgetting sleep.[74] Chu used the text that was accompanied by P'eng Hsiao's commentary (947 C.E.). He. admired the prose but acknowledged the text—with its coded language—to be extremely difficult to understand. He admitted it to be an esoteric work: "It was probably thought that a clear exposition would entail a disclosure of heavenly secrets (t'ien-chi); on the other hand, refraining completely from speaking of it would have been a pity."[75] He indicated: "I had many times wanted to study it, but, not having received any [special] transmission, I did not know [for a long time] where to begin."[76] Chu dismisses the alleged authorship of the Yellow Emperor and decides, on the basis of style, that it was probably the work of a late Han author, pointing thereby to Wei Po-yang.[77] He does not believe that the Ts'an-t'ung-ch'i was originally related to the so-called Classic of the Dragon and Tiger (Lung-hu shang-ching), which he thinks was a later forgery, very much dependent on the Ts'an-t'ung-ch'i, and attributed to Wei Po-yang.[78]

It appears that Chu was suffering from both the effects of ill health accompanying advancing age and those of political persecution when he was working on A Study of the Ts'an-t'ung-ch'i. Presumably, such work was done in the hope of finding a cure for his health problems and to calm his mind in a time of great stress. This is also reflected in Chu's commentary on the Ch'u Tz'u, which he completed 1198–99. The text, ascribed to the third-century-B.C.E. poet Ch'ü Yüan, gives expression to yearnings for immortality, especially in the chapter entitled "Far-off Journey"(Yüan-yu), a response to another chapter, "On Encountering Sorrow" (Li-sao). It describes a celestial journey and refers often to immortals and yoga techniques. In the commentary, Chu says:

> Ch'ü Yüan . . . contemplates the universe, despises the abjectness and narrowness of worldly customs, laments the shortness of the [human] life span, and so composes this section. He was hoping to control and cultivate his body and soul, sway the k'ung (emptiness) and ride the ch'i[a] (air). . . . Although this is an allegory . . . it is actually an essential teaching of longevity.[79]

He adds these words on the quest for immortality and longevity techniques:

> Where theories about immortals are concerned, it is clear that they are unreasonable and [immortality is] not to be expected. But why then did Ch'ü Yüan still show such attachment to these ideas? Because the past is no longer within reach, and the future is yet unknown, he wants to live longer while awaiting [what is yet to come].[80]

Let us, however, return to *Ts'an-t'ung-ch'i k'ao-yi*. The words *k'ao-yi* refer to a work of "examination of differences." Chu explains in an essay that he felt many persons had made arbitrary changes to Wei Po-yang's original text. Hence he himself read and compared many editions and commentaries to seek to establish a correct version.[81] However, from beginning to end, Chu was not sure he understood the text. Indeed, only twelve days before his death, he wrote to a disciple about his new work, adding: "I could not find a key to understanding this book. But I love its ancient and elegant style, and for that reason I did a study on it."[82]

Chu found the text especially ambiguous on the instructions about cultivation of life, including breath circulation and inner alchemy. He therefore turned increasingly to interpreting it in mathematical terms and in connection with the Book of Changes. In doing so, Chu tends to follow Shao Yung's judgments, understanding the language of cyclical signs to refer to seasonal and calendrical changes with which a Taoist adept must remain in harmony, especially in the careful choice of precise times at which to conduct his experiments. Chu even theorizes that Shao had learned much of what he knew from the Taoist Ch'en T'uan, who in turn had learned from the *Ts'an-t'ung ch'i* itself.[83] For example, Wei Po-yang had utilized *na-chia* to explain the making of elixirs:

Within the universe, *Ch'ien* . . . stands for Heaven above, *K'un* for Earth below, while the transformations of *yin* and *yang* and the beginning and end of the ten thousand things all occur in between them. Within the human body, *Ch'ien* as *yang* remains above, *K'un* as *yin* remains below, while the transformations of *yin* and *yang* and the beginning and end of the ten thousand things within the body all occur between them. . . . In using the word "change" (*yi*), we are always pointing to the transformations of *yin* and *yang*; in speaking of human beings, [we are referring] to what is called the golden elixir and the great medicine. Are *Ch'ien* and *K'un* not therefore the furnace and the tripod?[84]

Chu Hsi understood well this primary meaning of the text, which interprets the Book of Changes as offering the coordination of the forces of *yin* and *yang* in the universe as the explanation for cosmic change. He criticizes the then popular assumption that the text dwells mainly on outer alchemy, especially the manner of finding the right time for conducting experiments. He considers this unnatural and irrational, a later interpretation not in conformity with Wei Po-yang's original intention: "My feeling is: the essential meaning of this book dwells in the two words *K'an* and *Li*[b]. Should we obtain the crucial idea there, then we could also acquire the meaning of Wei's words about the effort (*kung-fu*)."[85]

Presumably, what the text says about the cyclical movements of *yin* and *yang* in the universe is also mirrored in the human organism. Thus, the correct method of breath circulation is implicit as well. For the order of the universe is reflected in the proper functioning of the human body. However, Chu was unable to follow through on this supposition. In the end, he would move in a direction opposite to those who were interpreting the text much more in alchemical terms.[86]

Even more than Shao Yung, Chu Hsi maintains a strictly mathematical-astronomical interpretation for such a coordination, and he uses it to interpret the basic meaning of the Book of Changes. Probably in part to better understand the mathematical context of the *Ts'an-t'ung-ch'i*, Chu worked on the "theory of numbers" (a combination of mathematics and astronomy) even after the completion of *A study of the "Ts'an-t'ung-ch'i."* His further insights were incorporated in an essay on the *Ts'an-t'ung-ch'i*. Here too, Chu acknowledges that Taoists have used the text for alchemical purposes but asserts his preference for interpreting it scientifically and cosmologically.[87]

The Yin-fu ching

The *Yin-fu ching* was attributed to the legendary Yellow Emperor and is said to have commentaries by celebrated ancient figures, the last of whom was the late T'ang military strategist Li Ch'üan (Li Quan, eighth century c.e.). It is a brief text of one *chüan*, with three hundred eighty-four characters. Li says of this book that it "first gives the Way of Immortals embracing the One, then gives the meaning of enriching the country and giving peace to the people, and finally gives the art of maintaining a strong army and gaining military victories." In this sense, it is alleged to comprehend the teachings of Taoism and Legalism as well as the art of war. For this reason, he divided the text into three parts, a practice followed by most later commentators.

Shao Yung regarded this text as coming from the Warring States period, and Ch'eng Yi dated it even earlier, in the late Shang or early Chou times. Chu Hsi, however, believed that its author was the man who allegedly "discovered" it, Li Ch'üan himself.[88] We may not agree with this opinion today, but it was a step in the right direction. Chu also made an attempt to separate the text from its various commentaries.

Before proceeding further, I would like to point out a problem with the very authorship of *both* works: the *Yin-fu ching* itself and the commentary allegedly written by Chu Hsi. This problem has been discussed by the Japanese scholar Sueki Yasuhiko, who believes the commentary to be the work of Chu's collaborator Ts'ai Yüan-ting. We have no mention of Chu's authorship of the commentary in his other writings, although we have good evidence for his authorship of *A study of the "Ts'an-t'ung-ch'i,"* which he also completed with the collaboration of Ts'ai. However, *A Study of the "Yin-fu ching"* is not usually listed as one of Ts'ai's own works either.

As for the authorship of the *Yin-fu ching* itself, Li's name is associated with two extant versions of this text, a short one (one *chüan*) and a somewhat longer one (three *chüan*). The two texts are completely different. Sueki asserts that the three-*chüan* commentary is exactly the same as Yüan Shu-chen's commentary (three *chüan*), whom he regards as the actual author of that work. Yüan probably lived in the tenth century and ascribed his own work to Li, presumably because Li was better known than he was.[89] Nevertheless, Sueki regards Li as an important link in the transmission of the text.

Li's authorship of the *Yin-fu ching* has been questioned by earlier scholars, especially the Chinese scholar Liu Shih-p'ei (Liu Shipei, 1884–1919).[90] Contemporary Chinese scholars have echoed and partly endorsed his questioning.[91] We cannot settle the issue of authorship here. But to the extent that Chu and Ts'ai were probably in agreement about what the *Yin-fu ching* represents, we may yet analyze the text as representative of opinions that Chu would support.

The preface to *A study of the "Yin-fu ching"* (1175) says of the *Yin-fu ching*:

> The three hundred words of the *Yin-fu ching* which Li Ch'üan alleged to have received in a cave are supposed to be [the words of] the Yellow Emperor which had been preserved by K'ou Ch'ien-chih. Shao [Yung] . . . thought it a work of the Warring States period; Ch'eng [Yi] . . . regarded it as coming from either the latter part of the Shang dynasty or the latter part of the Chou dynasty. On account of the long lapse of time, we know little for sure. Judging from its language and style, this could not be a very ancient text. But it must have been written by someone who had a profound knowledge of the Tao.[92]

We begin where the text begins—on the three parts of the *Yin-fu ching*. The preface asserts that, of the three hundred words making up the *Yin-fu ching*, a hundred words explain the Tao, another hundred words explain the *fa* (literally, and apparently here, "law"; in Taoist religion, often referring to ritual performance), and a third hundred words explain the *shu* ("method," i.e., political craftmanship). Should we combine these three senses, we would have a teaching that appeals to all: "Above there is the Tao of the immortals embracing the One; in the middle there is the *Fa* for enriching the country and giving peace to men; below there is the *Shu* for having a strong army and military victory."[93]

The author of *A Study of the "Yin-fu ching"* emphasizes that the "three senses" are all present—indivisibly—in the same words, and that the text should be read integrally rather than be divided into three parts.[94] He also acknowledges the text as alchemical, even though he also offers a philosophical interpretation for its content:

> Essentially it takes supreme nothingness as the principal doctrine, and the culture and principles of Heaven and Earth as *shu* (numbers), saying that in all under Heaven, being (*yu*) comes from nothingness (*wu*). Should someone be able to return being to nothingness, the universe would be in his hands.[95]

A difficult word in the text is "thief" (*tao*). The word *tao* here is not the same as that for the Way. Rather, it is another word, meaning "to steal" or "rob." Where the *Yin-fu-ching* speaks first of the Way (Tao) of Heaven and then of the "five thieves" of Heaven, *A Study* understands these to refer to the Five Phases, which produce and overcome one another.[96] A similar explanation is given to later lines in the text: "Heaven and Earth are the robbers of the myriad things;

the myriad things are the robbers of man; man is the robber of the myriad things."[97] The comment is:

> Heaven and Earth engender the myriad things and also kill the myriad things. The myriad things engender human beings and also kill human beings. Human beings engender the myriad things and also kill the myriad things. What engenders is also what kills. That is why we can reverse it and call it "thief." It is like the talk of the "five thieves." But if the engendering and the killing are each proper, then the three thieves are in harmony. And when the three thieves are in harmony, Heaven and Earth are in their proper places and the myriad things are nurtured.[98]

The text later speaks as well of "stealing the secret" (tao-chi), an expression from which Taoists derive the slogan "stealing the secret of Heaven and Earth" as characteristic of their effort to find the secret of immortality. The term chi[b] also deserves some elaboration. The Book of Changes is quoted in the text as saying that the gentleman acts according to the chi[b] that he sees, but that such chi[b] is easy to see and yet difficult to know.[99] Sueki refers to it as a sign that foretells great events. It can be perceived but needs reflection to be properly understood.[100] The comment here is: "The reason the Yellow Emperor, Yao, and Shun gained their reputations and longevity, and . . . Shen Pu-hai and Han Fei-tzu lost their lives and their clans, was all the Tao."[101] However, Sueki maintains that A Study does not support the importance of the concept of chi[b], preferring to understand the text more as a way of understanding a world which follows a pattern of regularity. He quotes from A Study:

> Heaven, Earth, and the myriad things are controlled by human beings. . . . If [human beings] can move according to the secret (chi[b]) of Heaven and Earth, the myriad transformations will be in peace. Such is the Tao of thieves. The times refer to spring and autumn, early and late. The secret refers to birth, killing, growth, and nurture.[102]

In this light, we may better appreciate why the author likes best the sentences in the Yin-fu ching near the end:

> The way of nature is quiet, producing Heaven and Earth and the myriad things; the way of Heaven and Earth is gradual, allowing yin and yang to overcome each other; the reciprocity between yin and yang permits harmonious transformation.[103]

These words influenced both Shao Yung and Chou Tun-yi before Chu. Chou's T'ai-chi t'u shuo offers a mixture of ideas coming from the Book of Changes and the Ts'an-t'ung-ch'i, and Chu would obviously have recognized this. The author of A Study of the "Yin-fu ching," whether Chu himself or Ts'ai, was a philosopher who attempted to interpret the original text cosmologically.

In Chu's own day, Taoist philosophy was no longer dominant, having been absorbed into Ch'an Buddhist philosophy, through which it continued to influence many people. But Taoist religion, known mainly as the cult of immortality, had many adherents. Several Sung emperors were patrons of Taoism, the best known being Hui-tsung, who favored the priest Lin Ling-su and promoted Lin's Shen-hsiao sect.[104] He also ordered the assembling and editing of Taoist texts, which led to the first printing (in Fukien) of the Taoist canon, with 5,481 *chüan*, a collection that survived intact during the Southern Sung and into Yüan times.[105] This was a real landmark in the history of the Taoist religion. Also, during Chu Hsi's lifetime, two Taoist "morality books" were published and began to gain wide acceptance: the *T'ai-shang kan-ying p'ien* (1164), about retribution in the life hereafter for one's actions, and the *T'ai-wei hsien-chün kung-kuo ko* (Preface 1171), about how to keep an account of our good and bad deeds.[106]

Chu Hsi's Contributions to Taoism

Chu Hsi's studies helped to make the Book of Changes and the *Ts'an-t'ung ch'i* (which is certainly a *Taoist* text) better known to Confucian scholars; they became important in Taoist circles as well. In the case of the *Ts'an-t'ung-ch'i*, his writing the study under a pen name did not prevent others from recognizing him as the author, especially as there is evidence in his other writings pointing to his authorship. The same is not true of the study on the *Yin-fu ching*, although the extant version bears the same pen name.[107]

It is worthwhile pausing here to ponder Chu's reasons for commenting upon Taoist texts, especially the *Ts'an-t'ung-ch'i*. The obvious and undeniable reason is his intellectual curiosity, which knew no bounds of orthodoxy. But was his interest also an indication of his belief in Taoist assertions? Certainly, his statements in the *Classified Conversations* and elsewhere lead us to believe that he himself did not totally discount the efficacy of Taoist practices for attaining peace of mind, health, and longevity. His use of a pen name shows his sensitivity to public expectations, and this sensitivity could also explain, if only in part, his general consistency in criticizing Taoism.

And we should not forget that Chu was struggling under persecution, being regarded officially as a "heretic," as someone not quite within the pale of Confucian orthodoxy. That was an important reason for using a pen name for his Taoist writings. After all, we have to wait for the emergence of Wang Yang-ming to find a Confucian thinker who would offer philosophical reasons for going beyond traditional limits.[108]

Basically, Chu Hsi is the original interpreter, learning from and yet transforming and making his own the ideas of those who preceded him. He did this with Chou Tun-yi's idea of *T'ai-chi*, rendering it not only transcendent and full of *li*[a] but also immanent in each particular person and thing as well as in the universe as a whole. He did this with Chang Tsai's philosophy of *ch'i*[a] and Ch'eng Yi's philosophy of *li*[a], making them consistent and giving them a central place in his own synthesis. He also did this with the text of the *Ts'an-t'ung-ch'i*, transposing its meaning to a higher level of understanding without entirely violating the literal sense of the highly ambiguous words.

Conclusion

Chu Hsi's attitude to Taoism is somewhat contradictory. As a kind of rationalist, he criticized it. But as a very curious intellectual, he was also attracted to it.
In the *Classified Conversations*, he describes the Taoist religion of his day as having evolved from a philosophy of nonaction, to an immortality cult, to the practice of shamans and "prayer-men" (*wu-chu*), who made incantations and
prognostications.[109] He describes the evolution from philosophy to religion in
negative terms, as moving from what is more credible to what is much less so.[110]
He also laments the Taoist custom of indiscriminate borrowing from Buddhism
and of setting up scriptural and doctrinal structures that parallel the Buddhist
ones:

> The Taoists have their *Lao-tzu* and *Chuang-tzu* but do not know how to
> study them. Instead, they allow them to be stolen and used by Buddhists,
> while they themselves compile scriptures and doctrines in imitation of
> Buddhism. They act like the children of a wealthy house who allow
> their own treasures to be stolen but go to others' properties to pick up
> potsherds.[111]

In discussing Chu's criticisms of both philosophical and religious Taoism, we
can see at work the mind of a man with the commitment of Confucian social
values and of a scholar with sound historical judgment as well as logical and
rationalist propensities. While Chinese ethnocentrism played a part in Chu's
displeasure with Taoist borrowings from Buddhism, we can discern his scholarly disappointment in the Taoist Three Pure Ones for lacking the philosophical
consistency of the Buddha's Three Bodies, and in the subordination of the Lord-
on-High to a divinized Lao-tzu, for missing religious sensitivity and historical
sequence:

> The . . . Primal Heavenly Celestial is not Lao-tzu's *dharmakāya* . . . ; the
> Supreme Lord Tao is not Lao- tzu's *samboghakāya*. To erect two images . . .
> and to have Lao-tzu himself as the . . . Supreme Ruler Lao is to imitate a
> Buddhist mistake and make of it another mistake.[112]

Chu claims correctly that Taoists "stole" from Buddhists such doctrines as hell
and reincarnation. He also asserts that the early-sixth-century Taoist sacred text
Chen-kao, allegedly recording fourth-century revelations, contains a chapter that
borrows heavily from the *Sutra of Forty-two Sections*:

> I once told the [Taoist] followers: You have your own precious pearl, which
> they [Buddhists] have stolen. Yet you pay no attention to that. . . . Instead,
> you steal from their corners and crevices broken cans and bottles. This is
> quite amusing.[113]

Chu criticizes the Taoists not only for borrowing from Buddhism but also for
doing so in a confused manner, with a manifest lack of logical consistency: "What

the Taoists call the Three Pure Ones is an imitation of the Three Bodies of the Buddha." Chu claims that Lao-tzu was being honored in the Three Pure Ones, without clarifying whether the first of these Pure Ones represents the *dharmakāya*, the second the *samboghakāya*, and the third the *nirmanakāya*.

> In honoring . . . the Primal Celestial [Yüan-shih T'ien-Tsun], the Supreme Lord Tao [T'ai-shang Tao-chün], and the Supreme Lord Lao [T'ai-shang Lao-chün], . . . they place below these the supreme Lord-on-High. Can one find a greater act of usurpation and treason?[114]

His reasoning was that, as a former human being, Lao-tzu should not, even when deified, rank higher than the Lord-on-High of antiquity. And he concluded that both Buddhism and Taoism should, if possible, be abrogated. If this was not possible, the Taoists could continue to pay reverence to Lao-tzu, Chuang-tzu, and other Taoist figures, but the cult honoring heavenly and earthly deities should revert to the sacrificial agencies of the government, since these deities did not legitimately belong to religious Taoism.[115]

Chu Hsi's core philosophy is governed by *li*[a] and *ch'i*[a], in whose terms he sought to explain all other concepts, be these Heaven, ghosts, or spirits. We also discern his core philosophy in the analyses of the Taoist texts, such as the *Ts'an-t'ung-ch'i* and possibly the *Yin-fu ching*, in each of which he detects a false attribution of authorship, acknowledges an alchemical content, but also seeks— and finds—a metaphysical interpretation of the universe, which he integrates into the cosmology of *li*[a] and *ch'i*[a], of the Infinite or Limitless (*Wu-chi*), which is also the Great Ultimate (*T'ai-chi*).[116]

Chu criticized Taoism, both the philosophical and the religious varieties, but his criticisms were not severe. He was essentially a moralist and worked with conventional distinctions of orthodoxy and heterodoxy. But he was not afraid to change and evolve in life. We might safely conclude that a younger Chu Hsi had been immersed for some years in reading Taoist texts as well as in Ch'an Buddhist practices, that a mature Chu Hsi became a neo-Confucian scholar and synthesizer, and that an older Chu Hsi turned more and more to Taoist practices for the cultivation of life, without giving up his basically Confucian convictions and commitments.

To the extent that Chu read Taoist texts and tested certain methods of self-cultivation, he was influenced by Taoism. But to the extent that he also transformed what he found in Taoism and incorporated it into his own thinking, Taoist influence on Chu was limited and contained. Chu turned to Taoist philosophy and religion primarily for expanding his understanding of the universe, as well as for improving his health. He integrated what he learned from them into something different: a new *Confucian Weltanschauung*, with its rational-intuitive perspective on the cosmic and the human and its unchanging commitment to social responsibility.

In this book, I have made many references to the Tao, sometimes in the Confucian context, sometimes in the Taoist. Let me conclude with a poem by Chu Hsi that is addressed to the Tao, apparently from a Taoist perspective:

Hearing the Tao, I have nothing else to do.
The hundred anxieties are all gone.
What mind is it that separates me and thee?
No place prevents the penetration of [all things].
Of yore [I was] a lad in green.
The morrow sees me old and white-haired.
The heavenly mystery is what it is:
No intended rush [marks our lives.][117]

Chu Hsi and Buddhism

The great Way (Tao) has no gate,
The thousand bypaths have a road.
Once past this pass,
Ch'ien[a] and *K'un*[a] alone march.

Tsung-shao[1]

Introduction[2]

I began chapter I with a poem about opening a door: the gate to wisdom. For this book is about the religious thought of Chu Hsi, a thinker who taught publicly and left behind a vast and coherent system that can, to a large extent, be mapped and understood. In other words, there is a door to his house, and one can go in. But a different metaphor has to be used when we talk about Ch'an Buddhism. While the Buddhist religion is also a public teaching, Ch'an prides itself on its mysterious subtlety. According to the *gatha* quoted above, the Way has no gate or, better still, no entry. What it has is a difficult pass, like that between steep mountains. We cannot speak of opening and closing the gates of Heaven and Earth, as does the Book of Changes.[3] Nevertheless, we are assured that on the other side of the pass lie the mysteries of Heaven and Earth.

How can one seek entrance when there is no entry? The answer lies in the mind, for Ch'an is about the mind and its consciousness. It is about transforming that consciousness, turning it into an entry into the mysteries of living and dying and of truth and Buddha-nature itself. It is also about a leap of consciousness, accomplished with faith and energy, without counting the consequences.

Has Chu Hsi walked on or leaped across that path of consciousness, seeking access to higher ground? To what extent was the philosopher influenced by the Buddhist religion? This question has been asked more than once. The answer will help us understand Chu's philosophy, explain his criticisms of the Buddhist religion, and assess the relative influence of the religion on neo-Confucian philosophy.[4]

There are many systems of Buddhist thought. Besides the big divisions of Theravāda and Mahāyāna, there are also diverse systems within Mahāyāna Buddhism. In discussing Chu Hsi and Buddhism, what do I mean by Buddhist philosophy? This question needs to be answered. I shall do so with the help of certain terms.

In reading Mahāyāna Buddhist texts, we come across many terms with special meaning. An important one is *k'ung* (Sanskrit, *śūnyatā*, "emptiness"). In Mahāyāna, it is sometimes called the emptiness of emptiness, since it represents the insight into the emptiness of all differentiated elements of existence, including especially suffering, impermanence, and the no-self. This concept of emptiness turns into that of compassion in relation to all sentient beings. It also underlies the hermeneutics of *upāya* (expedient means), by which Ch'an masters especially explain their teachings with the help of paradoxes. When they speak of the absolute mind, or Buddha-nature, they are not speaking of a substance with a self, whether as transcendent or immanent. They refer rather to the passing moment of actualization (presumably occuring in meditation, although not necessarily so) as both "is" and "is not." That is why realizing Buddha-nature, or becoming a Buddha in this mind or body, points to an absolute presence that vanishes even as it manifests itself.[5]

Seeing from this perspective, we may better understand Chu Hsi's metaphysical differences from Buddhism as well as his opposition to Buddhism. His Great Ultimate is rooted, albeit dialectically, in the transcendence of the infinite and limitless *Wu-chi*. As *Li*[a] more than *ch'i*[a], it has been compared metaphorically to a cosmic pillar.[6] As the substance (*t'i*) with the modes of *yin* and *yang* as function (*yung*), it possesses much more stability than the Buddha-nature. Its presence and immersion in the myriad things and affairs ensure its immanence, while its normative role as ideal goodness gives a particular Confucian character to such an ontology.[7]

Chu Hsi's Study of Buddhism

In a letter written when he was about thirty-three, Chu said to a friend: "To tell you my response to Buddhist teachings: I had a Buddhist teacher, respected Buddhist teachings, and earnestly sought to achieve its set goals. But I didn't get very far.[8]

On his deathbed, Chu's father entrusted his young son's education to three friends: Hu Hsien (Hu Xian), Liu Mien-chih (Liu Mianzhi), and Liu Tzu-hui (Liu Zihui). Of the two Lius, Mien-chih would become Chu's father-in-law. As was the case with many scholars of the time, all three, and Chu's father himself, had friends among Ch'an monks.[9]

According to Chu's Chronological Biography, he was a student of Buddhism at least during the ten years between age fifteen and age twenty-four.[10] In fact, the period of his engrossment in Ch'an was longer than a decade, as he himself indicated.[11] His name has been associated by early Buddhist sources with at least three famous monks: Yüan-wu K'en-an, Ta-hui Tsung-kao, and Ta-hui's disciple K'ai-shan Tao-ch'ien. Of the three, the best known was Ta-hui, from whom numerous scholar-officials had sought instruction.[12] Chu's association with the last one of the three, Tao-ch'ien, is certain. But his relationship with the other two requires clarification.

In the case of Yüan-wu's identity, the Japanese scholar Kusumoto Fumio mentioned both Yüan-wu K'o-ch'in, the compiler of the *Blue Cliff Dialogues* (*Pi-yen lu*), and Yüan-wu K'en-an, a younger contemporary. The first died in 1135 when Chu was five years old. But the Buddhist source Kusumoto refers to, the *K'u-ya man-lu*, speaks of K'en-an rather than K'e-ch'in, as Wing-tsit Chan has pointed out. And it is not known if the two were really one and the same person.[13] It should be mentioned, however, that the Buddhist source alleges that Yüan-wu K'en-an "taught *Confucian learning* [my italics for *ju-hsüeh*] to Chu Hsi."[14]

Scholars have also speculated about Chu's meeting with Ta-hui. According to Wing-tsit Chan and others, this definitely took place, although it is difficult to determine when. We are not certain that Ta-hui was the monk Chu met at age fifteen or so at Liu Tzu-hui's house, but Chu himself talks about meeting a monk there and using that monk's ideas with success in his own examination essay. We can put this together with the fact that, according to Liu, when Chu went to the capital Lin-an (Hangchow) for his *chin-shih* examinations in 1148, he took only one book, the *Recorded Dialogues of Ta-hui* (*Ta-hui yü-lu*).[15] Certainly, Chu acquired the *chin-shih* degree at a young age at a time when many had to take the examinations several times to pass. But his lack of ardor for the formal examination curriculum showed in the result: he was number 278 out of 330 successful candidates.[16]

Perhaps a poem written by Chu in his twenties can tell us more about his Buddhist interests:

> Living alone with nothing to do,
> Reading at times Buddhist texts,
> I rest awhile from worldly burdens
> To be with the sublime Tao.[17]

There is no doubt that Chu Hsi actually read Ta-hui's *Recorded Dialogues*. He refers to this text in his own writings:

> Not to seek the meaning of words, to play with the text without forming an opinion of it, is what recent Buddhists mean by *k'an hua-t'ou*. There is what the world calls the *Recorded Dialogues of Ta-hui*, which gives a detailed explanation of such. Try to read it, and [you will] see where all this comes from.[18]

In his conversations and writings, Chu showed a certain veneration for Ta-hui, while not fearing to express disagreements. For example, he called "silly" what Ta-hui said about Liu Tzu-hui and his brother, Liu Tzu-yü: that the former practiced cultivation without understanding Ch'an, and the latter understood Ch'an without practicing its cultivation. "[He compared them to] the so-called Mr. Chang, who had money but did not know how to use it, and the so-called Mr. Li, who knew how to use money but did not have any."[19] He also said:

The venerable [Ta-hui] talked about things that cannot be uttered and cannot be thought of. Yet when he was close to saying what matters, he did not say it right out but [substituted for it] with something rather empty. For example, if I speak of conquering the self, I would be referring to an exterior hindrance; if he said it, it would be about an interior hindrance.[20] The reason he didn't like my bothering him was my pressing him where it mattered. Others did not understand Ch'an and were despised by him. I understood Ch'an and could see his deficiency.[21]

A riddle that made a profound impression on Chu was the following saying of Ta-hui: "When an illusory thought arises, you do not need to ward it off with energy; you only have to recall the [kung-an] 'No' of [the monk] Chao-chou [778–897]."[22] In other words, keep always present in the mind the concept of wu, or nothingness. Nevertheless, Ta-hui advises against excessive reliance on the kung-an:

> There are two mistakes among the seekers of the Tao today. . . . The one is to learn too many words and sentences and seek to make something unusual with them. . . . The other is . . . to abandon all words and sentences and always keep the eyes closed, as though dead, and call it quiet-sitting, contemplating the mind and silently reflecting the light (mo-chao).[23]

There is also no doubt that Liu Tzu-hui and Ta-hui knew each other.[24] But those who assert that the monk Chu met at Liu's house was not Ta-hui claim that it was the younger Tao-ch'ien.[25] As I mentioned, there is no dispute over Chu's actually knowing, and even receiving instructions from, Tao-ch'ien. We can date Chu's contact with Tao-ch'ien to at least before he did his examinations at the capital, around age seventeen (1146). This fact is supported by Chu's acknowledged mentor, the scholar Li T'ung: "He [Chu Hsi] had first made efforts under [Tao-]ch'ien Kai-shan. That is why he understood everything from the inside."[26]

Tao-ch'ien was abbot of a monastery, Mi-an, very near where Chu grew up after his father's death. Chu wrote a number of poems about visiting Mi-an. There is a posthumous mention of Tao-ch'ien in Chu's correspondence with Lü Tsu-ch'ien (1172).[27] There is also an allusion to him in a poem.[28] Buddhist sources cite a letter from Chu to Tao-ch'ien in which Chu mentioned having "formerly received instructions from [Ta-hui] about keeping [myself] stimulated with the kung-an on the dog [and Buddha-nature]."[29] As mentioned previously, in that kung-an, the answer was a resounding "No (wu)"—an ambiguous word calling to mind the concept of "nothingness," which may well refer to absolute reality.

Chu got the response that, instead of seeking to understand this riddle, he should rather stop the act of thinking. In language demanding faith in the efficacy of sudden enlightenment, the monk says:

> It is like leaping across the Yellow River with eyes closed. Do not ask whether one could jump across or not. With all one's might, try the leap. If one succeeds in leaping across, everything will be accomplished. . . .

Don't count your gains and losses, your risks and danger. Just go ahead very courageously, putting a stop to your thoughts and hypotheses. Should you hesitate and permit a thought to arise, there will be no way out.[30]

Several years later, at age twenty-four, Chu first visited Li T'ung (1153), a student (as was Chu's own father) of Lo Ts'ung-yen. This marked a great turning point in Chu Hsi's intellectual and spiritual evolution. According to Chu's own remarks, he went to see Li because he felt that he had acquired no insights under his other teachers, Hu Hsien and Liu Tzu-hui. He was therefore seriously searching for a teacher.[31] On that occasion, he told Li about his interest in Ch'an Buddhism. Li responded: "How is it that you understand so much that is abstract, but not the things right in front of you? There is nothing mysterious to the Way. You need only to understand it in your daily concrete efforts [of cultivation]."[32]

It was Li's advice that made Chu set aside Ch'an books and study the writings of the sages. According to Chu's own words, he was to find the words of the Confucian sages more interesting than those of the Buddhists. He also explained in that context why he had been fascinated by Buddhism: because he was looking for a shortcut to enlightenment:

[I] had earnestly sought [the insights of Buddhism] but was unable to get anything. Later, on account of the master's [Li T'ung's] teachings, I reflected upon the order of what comes first and last and fast and slow. I set aside [Buddhist] teachings for the time being, and devoted myself to [Confucianism].[33]

What we may safely infer from this is Chu's youthful eagerness to achieve a certain insight into the meaning of life, to find his way to sageliness or perfection. With the help of Li T'ung, he decided not to look for shortcuts but rather to put more order into his life and do first things first.

Eventually, Chu puts special emphasis on book learning because he sees a *special* mission for the teacher of the Way, who must instruct others. He discerns a clear danger in relativizing completely the need for book learning, in the case of those who are able to acquire it. The danger lies in subjectivizing the moral law, in making of every man a law unto himself. The danger also lies in forgetting the wisdom of the ancients, in giving up an entire tradition, with its insights and merits, as well as its limitations. This could create a vacuum, an emptiness (*k'ung*) and listlessness, an intellectual iconoclasm. It is in these terms that Chu Hsi also criticizes Buddhism and Buddhist meditation: as a quest of inner enlightenment, for the sake of pure experience. Ultimately, this might mean the abandonment of the Confucian cause and its commitment to the renewal of society.

But Kusumoto Fumio insists that Buddhist influence on Chu Hsi continued while he studied under Li T'ung, who was also influenced by Ch'an teachings. Li advised Chu to seek to understand the Tao from the experience of daily living—a reflection of Hui-neng's emphasis on finding enlightenment while carrying water or firewood. Li also urged him to find, during mediation, the meaning of harmony before the rise of emotions—a teaching of the *Doctrine of the Mean*, which Confucians rediscovered after they had felt the Buddhist impetus.[34] Kusumoto thus argues that only some time after age forty did Chu begin to distance himself from Ch'an Buddhism, starting gradually to criticize Buddhism, but even then without being completely able to put away Buddhist influences.

So far, I agree with Kusumoto, although I find a few of his arguments excessive. Among other things, Kusumoto mentions that at age fifty-four, Chu built for himself a kind of hermitage called the Wu-yi ching-she (the term *ching-she* usually refers to a Buddhist retreat), where he lived much as one would in a Ch'an temple, even while he was criticizing Buddhism. I should like to point out that Chu himself commented that the term *ching-she* originally came from Confucian usage, as a place for receiving instruction, and was borrowed by Taoists and Buddhists, as a residence or hermitage. Chu's *ching-she* was rather a Confucian scholar's place of retreat, which was shared with friends and disciples.[35]

Chu Hsi's Knowledge of Buddhism

How much does Chu Hsi really know of Buddhism and Buddhist writings? As I have remarked, Chu regards himself as knowing quite a bit. But we should first recall the Ch'an dominance over Buddhism ever since the ninth or tenth century, at least where the literati were concerned. The common people preferred the Pure Land temples and the recitation of the name of the Buddha Omitofo, but the scholars were fascinated by quiet-sitting as a means to discovering the true self and the ultimate meaning of life. Ch'an Buddhism was itself a reaction to the excessive attention given to the abundance of Buddhist scriptures during an earlier, overintellectual phase in the history of Chinese Buddhism. Ch'an Buddhism discouraged those seekers of wisdom who thought the mastery of scriptural knowledge was a prior condition to salvation. It did not therefore give priority to scriptural knowledge. Instead, its followers concentrated on the practice of meditation as a way of achieving enlightenment, while the subsects that developed within Ch'an asserted their own positions regarding sudden or gradual enlightenment.

Chu made use of several terms when he discussed Buddhism. Sometimes, he called it *Fo*, sometimes *Fou-t'u*, sometimes *She-shih* (Śākyamuni), and sometimes *Ch'an*. There is not always a clear difference between his reference to Buddhism as a whole and to Ch'an in particular. A general argument is that Buddhism is a religion of alien origin without much to offer the Chinese:

> Buddhism came from the barbarians and spread into China. In the beginning, there was a language problem, and people were not so tempted by it. From the time of Chin and Sung, scholar-officials who were curious, and attracted by the unusual, took its fragmented words and rearticulated it in better style. This started to make people greatly impressed by it. It is not that Buddhism can impress people. It is the fault of those who promoted it.[36]

Most of Chu's references were, understandably, to popular Ch'an riddles (i.e., *kung-an*). He did mention a few sutras, although he did not say much about any of them. For example, he said a few generally positive things about the Theravāda anthology called the *Sutra of Forty-two Sections*, which he describes as ancient and somewhat "primitive" but containing "solid teachings"—referring, presumably, to the four noble truths and the eightfold noble path, basic Buddhist teachings. He remarked that Buddhism was introduced into China at a time when the country was experiencing a spiritual vacuum, and that its teaching evolved from that of religious discipline to that of scriptural exegesis and philosophical hermeneutics. [37]

Chu thought that all other texts, including the *Vimalakīrti Sutra*, came later and were composed with the extensive help of Chinese scholars, or perhaps by them. Indeed, he had heard that a man called Hsiao Tzu-liang, or possibly his disciples, were involved in composing the *Vimalakīrti Sutra*, although he acknowledged that he could find no information about the man. [38] He criticized the eleventh-century work *Transmission of the Lamp* (*Ch'uan-teng lu*) by Tao-yüan as a poorly written book that had been emended by the scholar-official Yang Yi (998–1022). This was a fact and attested by the preface Yang gave the text, where he explained the mandate he received from the Sung emperor Chen-tsung to emend the text. [39] This objection did not stop Chu from often citing from the text. Chu approved of the teachings in the first two or three *chüan* of the *Sutra of Perfect Enlightenment* (*Yüan-chüeh ching*), which originated in China and is not recognized as an authentic Buddhist sutra. And he pointed out that the *Śūraṅgama Sutra* is made up mainly of charms or incantations, even claiming that the other materials—which he liked—were later additions, inserted to please the Chinese. [40] Chu even thought that translators of Buddhist scriptures who could not understand Sanskrit properly made up many incantations. This shows a certain rationalism as well as ignorance on his part. [41] He criticized the *Lotus Sutra* for its mythological materials, such as in speaking of the innumerable sands of the Ganges River, the tens of thousands of *kalpas*, and so on, without giving specific dates. Presumably, he was referring to such lines as Maitreya's verse in the *Lotus Sutra*, chapter I, which exaggerates the number of Bodhisattvas in an effort to emphasize the accessibility of enlightenment in Mahāyāna Buddhist teachings: [42] "I see in that land / Bodhisattvas like Ganges' sands." [43] Other lines speak of Bodhisattvas "composing their thoughts for millions of thousands of myriads of years." [44] This is obviously an exaggerated time span, to which Indians are accustomed even if it puzzles the Chinese mind. Chu also commented on the T'ang work *Commentaries on the "Avataṃsaka sutra"* (*Hua-yen ching ho-lun*) as containing materials that stretch credibility. And he spoke about the teaching of Seng Chao (384–414) on the immutability of things in the *Book of Chao*. He describes Seng Chao's immutability correctly as pointing to a dialectic of identity between activity and tranquillity. [45]

Chu remarked that the *Greater Perfection of Wisdom* (*Prajñāpāramitā*) was too long and its content too diverse, which was why it got summarized as the *Heart Sutra*. [46] As for the *Diamond Sutra*, the favorite of the southern Ch'an school, Chu thought that its main meaning could be found in this sentence, which could be summarized in one word; "nothingness": "a noble-minded Bodhisattva should . . . frame an independent mind, which is to be framed as a mind not believing in anything, not believing in form, not believing in sound, smell, taste, and anything that can be touched."[47] These lines allegedly arrested the attention of the young Hui-neng and gave him an enlightenment experience.[48] Chu Hsi's selection of them as representative of the text is quite appropriate because the text promotes sudden and radical enlightenment in the name of the absolute emptiness of all things.

It would appear from all this that Chu had knowledge of the kind of Buddhist texts that had prepared the rise of Ch'an Buddhism (such as Seng Chao's work), as well as those texts especially favored by Chinese Mahāyāna Buddhists in general (such as the *Lotus Sutra* and the *Śūraṅgama Sutra*) or by Ch'an Buddhists in particular (such as the *Platform Sutra of the Sixth Patriarch*, which is about the monk Hui-neng, and the *Transmission of the Lamp*, which gives the stories of Ch'an monks after Hui-neng). Thus, Chu knew well the Ch'an Buddhism of his time, especially the Lin-chi lineage of transmission, with its emphasis on sudden enlightenment. It would also appear that Chu did not know very much about earlier Buddhist history or doctrinal developments. For example, he insisted that when Buddhism first entered China, it only preached a few practical things, as in the *Sutra of Forty-two Sections*. Later, it "stole" from Lao-tzu, Chuang-tzu, and Lieh-tzu—with such fourth-century monks as Hui-yüan and Tao-lin taking teachings from the Taoist texts to elaborate Buddhist doctrines.[49]

We should briefly evaluate Chu Hsi as a textual critic of Buddhist scriptures. Even if we acknowledge the influence of Taoist ideas and terminology on Buddhist developments, we should regard Chu's views as a gross exaggeration. Perhaps, we may characterize it as a *rhetorical* exaggeration, given that Chu Hsi's motive was less to discredit Buddhism as such and more to exalt Confucian teachings.[50] Chu also made a wild generalization about the rise of Ch'an Buddhism. With the advent of the first Ch'an patriarch Bodhidharma (460–534), he says, the scriptures were all swept aside by the new teaching which pointed straight to the human mind.[51]

Nevertheless, from his statements, Chu seems to be aware of differences between Theravāda and Mahāyāna, although he does not use these terms. After all, by Sung times, Theravāda was long a thing of the past for Chinese Buddhism. He seems especially conscious of the development of Ch'an as a movement within Buddhism. But he also tends to identify Ch'an with Buddhism as a whole. His criticisms of Buddhism would therefore be criticisms of the Buddhism of his time, namely, Ch'an Buddhism as he knew it in Sung times.

Chu Hsi's Criticisms of Buddhism

We move now to Chu's criticisms of Buddhist doctrines. Here, I should mention that even after his so-called conversion to Confucianism on his meeting with Li T'ung, Chu continued to articulate occasional approval of Buddhism. He said that Buddhism does have some sublime insights.[52] He remarked that Buddhist teachings like the six "roots" (sense organs), the six kinds of "dust" (qualities), the four "great" (realms or elements), the twelve *nidānas* (the chain of dependent coarising), all represent clever and precise analyses and had fascinated many people who did not find them in Confucius's teachings.[53] He was referring to the six *indriyas* (eye, ear, nose, tongue, body, mind); the six *vijñānas* (the consciousnesses that correspond to each of these organs), and the formula of dependent coarising consisting of twelve members, starting from ignorance, going through formative forces, consciousness, name-and-form, six sense fields (contact, sensation, craving, grasping, becoming, birth), and ending with old age and death.[54] The four "great" (realms) refer to the *Mahābhūta*: earth, water, fire, wind. This we can conclude from what Chu has said elsewhere: "Earth is also the body (*t'i*); water is also the lower soul (*p'o*); fire and wind are also the upper soul (*hun*)."[55] Chu talks about them generally in a letter discussing the upper (*hun*) and lower (*p'o*) souls.[56]

The *Yüan-chüeh ching* talks of the *Mahābhūta* being basically illusory and mentions the various parts of the human organism eventually returning to these four elements of the Indian Buddhist tradition: the solids like hair, nails, skin, bones, returning to earth; the fluids like blood, semen, and tears returning to water; the warm *ch'i*, or energy, returning to fire; and motion returning to wind.[57] He showed some fascination for the Buddhist differentiation of all sentient beings destined for Nirvana: the "egg-born, womb-born, spawn-born, and born by transformation," that is, the four *yoni*, or modes of birth, comprehending a whole spectrum extending from deities to moths.[58]

Nevertheless, he dislikes the mythological substrata that he found in Buddhist scriptures and rejects the teaching of *kalpas*. He derides the Buddhist description of a final conflagration, in which human beings will all be destroyed, whether by fire or storm or floods, and then a new world will come to be. He thinks that such a worldview came from not understanding the cosmology of *yin* and *yang*.[59] Generally speaking, Chu Hsi and other Confucians also reject the Buddhist assumption of rebirth (*lun-hui*). Indeed, he says disapprovingly that in seeking enlightenment, Buddhists speak of their quest for their "original countenance" before birth. They even claim that the body received from parents is only a temporary lodging, that it is like a house, which when broken down, should be abandoned in exchange for a new dwelling.[60]

Chu voices admiration for the effort of cultivation he discovered among Buddhists. But he points out that some of the great monks he had met owed their sublime character and good teachings more to their own natural endowments than to the Ch'an training. He thinks that many other scholars—like himself—neglected Confucianism for Ch'an teachings because they hoped to find a shortcut to enlightenment.[61] No doubt he was right. The many eminent monks who expounded sutras and wrote treatises on difficult and profound subjects during the more than five hundred years of Buddhist dominance showed what talent Buddhism recruited in China in the name of a higher truth and a greater enlightenment.

Chu made certain philosophical critiques of Buddhism, which reflect his concern for the basic metaphysical difference between the two schools. He says that while Confucianism maintains the central importance of the Great Ultimate (*T'ai-chi*) or heavenly principle (*T'ien-li*), Buddhism reduces everything to "emptiness." Buddhists, he claims, never see the phenomenological reality of things that Confucians affirm in the concept of *ch'i*[a] (matter-energy), which is inseparable from *li*[a] (principle, essence). As he says elsewhere, the basic difference between Confucianism and Buddhism is the difference between "realness" and "emptiness," which we may explain as accepting, or not accepting, the world as fully real. Chu opposed Buddhist philosophy for affirming the ultimate reality of only the evanescent mind, while granting a mere existential sense to the reality of appearances, reducing humans and things to subjective experiences like sensations and perceptions.[62]

Buddhism, he says, despises the world, and therefore does not understand the principles of things (*wu-li*).[63] Those who fear *saṃsāra* (the cycle of rebirth) are attracted to Buddhism. But instead of acknowledging the reality of human nature (*hsing*[a]) and the mind (*hsin*[a]), the Buddhists accept only the conscious manifestations of nature and the mind.[64] And he distinguishes between the Buddhist concept of emptiness and the Taoist concept of nothingness by saying that while Taoists make too much of a separation between being and nothingness, Buddhists are much more thoroughgoing in defining this nothingness: "Vast as the myriad affairs and things, and small as the hundred bones and nine apertures [of the body], all will return to nothingness." He continues by reducing all this to absurdity: "One eats rice every day but says [he] has not chewed a single grain of the rice. One wears clothes but says [he] has not worn a single fiber of silk."[65]

In the development of Buddhist thought, early Theravāda Buddhists had regarded as central the doctrine of nonself, which is extended to mean that things have no self-nature of their own— they are all unreal, or empty. However, since the introduction of Mahāyāna Buddhism, and with the philosophical transformations brought about by the Indian philosopher Nāgārjuna (c. 100 C.E.), Buddhists speak of emptiness in a different sense, as dialectically identical to ultimate reality. A Mahāyāna Buddhist would not accept Chu's assumption that emptiness is nonreality. On the other hand, even though Chu was aware of the dialectical recognition of reality that is found in Chinese Buddhism, he obviously regarded it as insufficiently realist. Preferring Confucianism, he perceived no real need to call the real world "empty."

Chu also criticizes the Buddhist tendency to promote the theory that mind and human nature were neither good nor evil, which is opposed to Mencius's theory of human nature as originally good.[66] Here we come to his moral critique, which is even more serious, since the parting of ways between Buddhism and Confucianism is based on the moral life as this is understood by Chu Hsi and other Confucians. Chu argues against the excessive concern shown by Buddhism for overcoming *saṃsāra*, that cycle of life and death which is regarded as punishment. He prefers the Confucian concern with human affairs, that is, with improving life in society rather than escaping from life and the world. For Chu Hsi, Buddhists' ignorance of the original goodness of human nature drives them to aim at emptying the mind, stopping thought, and opting for the kind of philosophical idealism that does not firmly acknowledge the moral character of human nature or the reality of the world. So he criticizes Buddhism for regarding conscious activity, rather than moral virtues, as the function of human nature. For him, an experience of sudden enlightenment does not necessarily achieve moral perfection. In very strong language, he has this to say:

> Although [Buddhists] regard themselves as pointing directly to the human mind, they really do not understand the mind. Although they regard themselves as seeing nature and becoming Buddhas, they really do not understand nature. That is why they destroy morality and fall into the realm of birds and beasts.[67]

Morality, for Chu Hsi, lies in human relationships. As a monastic religion, Buddhism demonstrates a flagrant neglect of social morality, which is the biggest problem he finds in the religion. He sees it as ironic that Buddhists leave their families to set up monastic orders that mimic family life:

> Such is the way with life, and no one can escape from it. Even though Buddhists and Taoists destroy human relationships, they are unable to run away from them. For example, while they neglect the father-child relationship, they acknowledge teachers and regard disciples as sons, treating the older ones as older brothers, the younger ones as younger brothers. But all that is not real, whereas sages and worthy men preserve what is real [in relationships].[68]

Referring to one of the *Jātaka* tales, in which the Buddha, in an earlier life, gave his body to feed a hungry tigress, Chu Hsi comments: "[He] abandoned his father and mother and then, meeting a hungry tigress, gave his life to feed it. What kind of moral principle does this show?"[69] This constitutes the perennial Confucian argument, with its focus on family life and ancestral veneration, against a monastic religion and its apparent belief that all sentient life, human and animal, is equally sacred.

Chu Hsi also finds fault with Buddhist spirituality, especially the doctrine of sudden enlightenment. He accuses Buddhists of neglecting the work of investigating things and extending knowledge, while wanting to leap to a higher spiritual stage without engaging in step-by-step learning of *li*ᵃ from below. He criticizes them for promoting quiet-sitting without realizing the importance of reverence, for only showing concern with "interior reverence" while neglecting "exterior rightness."[70] He says that the focus on sudden awakening tends to disregard the spiritual and moral significance of gradual cultivation, which is a lifelong task of overcoming the limitations of man's physical nature and selfishness. Where Buddhists speak of "seeing one's nature," Chu points out that Confucians speak of "knowing one's nature." The Confucian task regards self-cultivation as a gradual process that is not accomplished in a matter of one or two days, whereas Buddhists believe in sudden awakening rather than gradual cultivation.[71]

More than once, Chu refers with disdain to the well-known *kung-ans* about "three catties of hemp" and the "stool-cleaning stick." Calling "three catties of hemp" Buddha-nature is a *kung-an* from a famous Ch'an master, Fo-kuo Yüan-wu.[72] The "stool-cleaning stick" was what Indians used in place of toilet paper, hence something very dirty. The *kung-an* calling it Buddha-nature is in the recorded dialogues of the Lin-chi patriarch Hui-chao.[73] The vulgar language was used to shock the mind into some kind of enlightenment, but it repelled the scholar in Chu Hsi:

> Ch'an is only a method of concentrating idiotically on such [riddles] as "three catties of hemp" and "stool-cleaning stick." Its doctrine was not originally in such [riddles]. But the use of such [riddles] immobilized the mind, and . . . after long concentration, one would acquire sudden insights, which means enlightment. The essential is to keep the mind calm and not permit it to become distracted. After a long time, [the mind] naturally becomes bright and radiates of itself. That is why the illiterate could write *gathas* right after enlightenment. And although insights after enlightenment are similar, there can be differences of degrees in depth. I once also loved to practice Ch'an meditation, but that is all there is to it.[74]

Chu Hsi compares Buddhism unfavorably to Taoism because its doctrine of emptiness was more thoroughly nihilistic than the Taoist teaching of nothingness and also because its world-negating attitude was much more obvious: "The Buddhists' fault comes out of selfish boredom [with the world]; the Taoists' fault comes out of selfish cleverness [regarding the world]. To negate the world and withdraw from it, to regard everything as empty, is the [big] fault of Buddhism."[75]

In his critiques of Buddhist doctrines, Chu's motive was to point out differences between Confucianism and Buddhism and to show Confucian teachings to be superior. His aim was to revive Confucian teachings rather than to make a thorough or systematic criticism of Buddhist teachings. Besides, his differences with Buddhism were never personal, and he maintained friendly relations with Buddhist monks. In fact, he continued to make short sojourns in Buddhist monasteries when he traveled, including when he visited Li T'ung, in 1160 and later. These sojourns, which could be as long as a few months, gave him occasion to befriend monks. He also included individual monks in his company when he traveled with disciples, and he sometimes traveled to visit his monastic friends. These visits were all of a personal nature, although intellectual, as well as spiritual, exchanges took place.[76] These personal connections are no reason to consider Chu Hsi a Buddhist.

Chu Hsi is careful to give credit where he thinks it is due. He explains the appeal of Buddhism to different classes of people in these words:

> For its teachings on emptiness, and on not being burdened by material desires, the virtuous men of the world like it. For its abstract and metaphysical teachings, that are not entrapped in forms and things, the wise of the world like it. For its doctrine of life, death, and rebirth, which can

help people to avoid punishments [after death], the servants and slaves, the convicts and robbers, also come groveling to it.[77]

On numerous occasions, he points out what admirable people many Buddhist monks have been. The portraits of the patriarchs in the famous temples, he says, show the men's handsome miens, reveal their great personalities, and tell us how brave and strong they must have been in remaining firm in their commitments without being swayed by wealth, profit, and the pleasure of the senses.[78] Indeed, the word with which he commends Buddhists most is "bravery."[79] He is, of course, speaking of moral bravery, the courage that leads men to maintain their purity and integrity and to seek truth at the expense of everything. He thinks that the great Buddhist monks are outstanding leaders, and that, should circumstances be different, they could also become great leaders among the masses, perhaps even great "bandits." He did not intend this to be an insult, but meant it as a real expression of respect and admiration for men of great courage. Nevertheless, returning to his own preferences, he comments that the sage (Confucius) appeared on earth to fulfill a great mission, just as the Buddha also appeared on earth for the realization of a great causal event.[80] To him, it is a pity that Buddhism, rather than Confucianism, has attracted to itself so many great men.[81]

Courage or bravery is a recurring theme in Chu Hsi's conversations with his disciples. He considers reason as an arbiter of emotions, capable of guiding a person in circumstances when a false fear may arise.[82] In speaking about progress in study, he urges a disciple to have courage:

One may be groping for something, fearful that the thing might touch one's hand. . . . It's a waste of time. Go ahead bravely, with a single weapon on a lone horse. Why should one be afraid? The enemy is a man; so am I. Why should I fear him? . . . When one sees clearly the reasons, one will no longer fear the consequences, be these punishments, fortunes, or misfortunes. One would just see what is reasonable and act accordingly.[83]

Although the reference to the "enemy" may be misleading, Chu is obviously using a metaphor to encourage a fainthearted student. His words might also be understood in the context of his own life, referring, for example, to the difficulties he encountered when accused of heterodoxy. His attitude is especially interesting when we consider his admiration for the courage of Buddhist monks, who renounce everything for the sake of their religious convictions.

When asked why many scholar-officials were attracted to Ch'an Buddhism in their old age, he replies that this was due to the higher ideals in Ch'an:

Without having understood the sources of one's own tradition, [a scholar] might have read some minor texts, only for the sake of doing some writing [and] . . . to acquire a career and advantage. But once that person has seen the sublimity and mystery in [Buddhism] . . . and [realizes] that he himself is nowhere as good, . . . he may easily be tempted by Buddhist teachings.[84]

Buddhist Influence on Chu Hsi's Philosophy

Chu Hsi criticized Buddhism for its metaphysics, its theory of human nature, its weakness in moral teaching, and its doctrine of cultivation and enlightenment. But Buddhist influence on Chu Hsi is so extensive that it may be discerned in nearly all these areas: in his metaphysics, his philosophy of human nature, and his doctrine of self-cultivation.

As for his metaphysics, we recall Chu's elaboration of Chou Tun-yi's philosophy of the Great Ultimate (see chapter 2). The use of negative language to describe the *T'ai-chi* as *Wu-chi* has led to many disputes among Confucian scholars who subscribe to an ultimate norm of goodness but are disturbed when this is predicated by a word which also means "nothingness." This language has been criticized as both Taoistic and Buddhistic, for the words used and the meaning allegedly intended.

Chu Hsi, however, defends this dialectical description of the Great Ultimate, placing it in some way above differentiations of good and evil. Such language cannot but recall that of Buddhist teachings, especially that found in the *The Awakening of Faith in the Mahāyāna (Ta-sh'eng ch'i-hsin-lun)*, where we hear of the one mind and its two aspects as being empty and yet not empty, without marks yet with marks.[85] It is also an echo of the *kung-an* allegedly coming from the *Platform Sutra*, namely, "[When you] are not thinking of good and not thinking of evil, at that very moment, what is your original countenance [before your mother and father were born]?"[86] Besides, Chu identifies *T'ai-chi* with the supreme good. He also says it is present in everyone—just as, we should note, the Buddha-nature is present in all. Of course, to the extent that he chose to explain the *T'ai-chi* in terms of the *Wu-chi*, Buddhist influence on him is moderated by Taoist philosophical influence, as discussed in chapters 1 and 2.

The relationship that Chu explains between *li*[a] and *ch'i*[a] on the one hand and *Tao* and *ch'i*[b] (utensil) on the other appears parallel to what Buddhism, especially Hua-yen Buddhism, which influenced Ch'an, has to say about the noumenal and the phenomenal, emptiness and its manifestations. And his teaching that Heaven and Earth and the myriad things are all one with the self also appears similar to Ch'an teaching about the oneness of all sentient beings with all nonsentient beings. Besides, Chu Hsi emphasizes that the *T'ai-chi* is present in everyone and everything, that it is nothing other than the fullness of *li*[a].

In expounding the *Great Learning*, Chu explains "clarifying bright virtue" (*ming ming-te*) in Buddhist-like terms as *hsü-ling pu-mei* (empty, unobscured intelligence), which echoes what the T'ang monk Tsung-mi has to say about it.[87]

In his doctrine of self-cultivation, Chu approves of quiet-sitting, reminding disciples that the Ch'eng brothers and Li T'ung all taught disciples to meditate in order to recollect themselves. Meditation has nothing to do with stopping thought; rather, it means not having "bad thoughts."[88] For Chu, reverence means concentrating on one thing without distraction. This is like mindfulness in Buddhism.

All this does not mean that Chu's philosophy belongs to the same family as Hua-yen or Ch'an. On the contrary, the Buddhists tend to affirm only an existential sense of the reality of appearances, whereas Chu Hsi goes behind the appearances to affirm the things or phenomena themselves. In T'ien-t'ai and Ch'an, there is a practice called "contemplating the mind" (*kuan-hsin*), which is much recommended for beginners. It is closely associated with what is called the "one-practice *samādhi* (*yi-hsin san-mei*)." Buddhists disputed whether this mind should be the absolute mind or the deluded mind needing examination, with those favoring the former preferring pure contemplation. As the Ch'an patriarch Hung-jen, Hui-neng's master, puts it: "After the mind is made clear, when one sits, it is like being on a solitary tall mountain in the midst of a distant field. Sitting on exposed ground at the mountaintop, gazing off into the distance from all four sides. There are no limits."[89]

While Buddhists dwell principally on the mind itself, Chu is opposed to such a preoccupation. He comments on the Buddhist theory with these words:

> The mind is that which in a human being is master of the self. . . . It orders things around and does not take orders from things. That is why if the mind contemplates things, it acquires the principles of things. But then if one is to contemplate the mind itself, then one is [saying] there is another mind outside the mind that can be in charge of this mind. . . . The teaching of Buddhism uses the mind to seek the mind, uses the mind to command the mind. It is like having the mouth chew on the mouth, having the eyes look at the eyes.[90]

He continues in strong language:

> Such a course of action is precarious and oppressive, such a path is dangerous and obstructed, such a practice is empty of principles (*li*[a]) and frustrating. Although [the Buddhists] may sound like us [Confucians], they are really quite different.[91]

Elsewhere, Chu Hsi adds that Buddhists only recognize a "human mind," that is, a natural, conscious mind. When they achieve insights, they see a whole, presumably the absolute, which is beyond differentiations, including those of right and wrong. In other words, they do not recognize a "moral mind" (*tao-hsin*). That is why they cannot accept the common human relationships like rulers and subjects, fathers and sons, husbands and wives, and elder and younger brothers.[92]

A crucial difference between Chu's philosophy and Ch'an Buddhism lies in the moral intentionality of his entire thinking. Whether in his metaphysics of the Great Ultimate or *li*[a] and *ch'i*[a], in his understanding of human nature, or in his teaching of self-cultivation through the investigation of things and extension of knowledge, and even in his practice of meditation, Chu Hsi never loses sight of the moral commitment to life and society required by Confucianism. This is where he sees himself as a Confucian and not a Buddhist. This is also why he takes exception to Ch'an Buddhism, rejecting its sole concern with achieving mystical enlightenment. And this is why Chu Hsi also objects to Lu Chiu-yüan's philosophy, which he considers to make too many concessions to Ch'an Buddhism, to the extent that, in his opinion, it risks becoming more Ch'an than Confucian. As Chu once wrote to a friend:

There are similarities between us Confucians and Buddhism. But that is what one may call superficial rather than real resemblance, and we should pay attention to such. . . . What Ch'an calls enlightenment is to stop the thinking of the mind in order to see the heavenly principle. But that is not correct. The heavenly principle is there when the thinking of the mind is correct. The heavenly principle may be discovered in the flow and function [of the mind]. Why should one first stop the thinking of the mind and then see the heavenly principle? Moreover, what is the so-called heavenly principle? Are not benevolence, rightness, propriety, and wisdom all heavenly principles? Are not the relationships between ruler and subject, father and son, older and younger brothers, husband and wife, and between friends, all heavenly principles? If Buddhists really followed heavenly principles, why would they need to so transgress and destroy [moral relationships], obscuring and confusing their original minds, without even knowing it themselves?[93]

Generally, Lin-chi followers accused Ts'ao-tung of a passivity in meditation which can only enervate the mind, while Ts'ao-tung adherents accused the Lin-chi of playing dangerous games, not only with the psyche but also with the entire tradition of Buddhist spirituality, by allowing possibly illusory experiences to be mistaken for enlightenment. This is not to say that the Ts'ao-tung Buddhists ignored kung-an altogether, or that Lin-chi Buddhists did not meditate. The difference was much more in nuances of emphasis than in practice. But the nuances were important enough.

The philosophy Chu eventually developed, especially regarding self-cultivation, resembled Ts'ao-tung rather than Lin-chi. Indeed, the two schools of Chu Hsi and Lu Chiu-yüan, his rival, have sometimes been described as offering teachings on self-cultivation that are consciously parallel to the Ts'ao-tung, or "gradualist," and Lin-chi, or "subitist," schools of Ch'an Buddhism. There is much to be said for this comparison. But it does not mean Chu and Lu are newer versions of Ts'ao-tung and Lin-chi Buddhists. There are also many differences between their philosophies (grounded in their interpretations of Confucian texts) and those of the Buddhists.

It is interesting that Chu should have turned away from the "subitist" school to develop a philosophy with stronger affinities to the "gradualist" way of step-by-step cultivation, which is much closer to Tsao-tung Buddhism. Chu makes use of the metaphor of the mirror in speaking of jen[a] . He emphasizes that the light comes from within, not without:

The human being is like a mirror. Jen[a] is the brightness of the mirror. When the mirror has no dust particles, it is bright. When a human being has no selfish desire, he is humane (jen[a]). The mirror's brightness is not from the outside. The mirror originally possessed this brightness. . . . So too, jen[a] is not from the outside.[94]

He alludes to the conflict between Southern Ch'an's sixth patriarch Hui-neng and his rival Shen-hsiu, a conflict mentioned in chapter 6. He obviously prefers

Shen-hsiu's metaphor of cultivating the mind as one would polish a mirror: "Buddhists polish the mind very carefully. It is like taking something and stripping it, layer by layer, until there is nothing left to be stripped. Thus, the mind is polished until it is so bright."[95]

Elsewhere, Chu Hsi speaks of making gradual and steady efforts in investigating things and principles. "After much accumulation of [knowledge], there will naturally be insights and enlightenment."[96] As he puts it in his explanation of the *Great Learning*: "Should scholars . . . pursue [principles] exhaustively and seek to do so to the limit, after a long time of making efforts, they would one day suddenly achieve penetrating understanding."[97]

On the other hand, it would not be quite right simply to call Chu Hsi's philosophy Ts'ao-tung Buddhism. The Ts'ao-tung Buddhists were solely preoccupied with acquiring enlightenment, even if they were ready to do it gradually. Chu Hsi made a different commitment. For him, real enlightenment can only be found in the fulfillment of one's moral nature and in social interactions with others. And, as already noted, this is to be achieved in part by intellectual pursuit, which he calls investigation of things.

First a devotee and then a critic of Ch'an Buddhism, Chu Hsi retained many Buddhist influences, which he demonstrated in his use of language, his choice of metaphors, and also in his conception of truth. I have in mind his formulation of the orthodox transmission of the Confucian Tao, from the ancient sages on. It recalls the Ch'an Buddhist representation of how the Buddha passed on his "true" teaching through wordless transmission, from mind-and-heart to mind-and-heart. Chu's appropriation is especially ironic since Confucianism is so much a textual tradition. But what Chu emphasizes is the *personal* nature of the discovery of truth, even when it is passed on. The recipient is never passive but has to assimilate it actively in a spiritual dialogue carried over to personal life. Chu's formulation of orthodox transmission gains validity from the long interruption assumed between the death of Mencius and the emergence of Chou Tun-yi. Besides, given the knowledge we have of Chu's own contributions to a new view of Confucianism, we may also add that the Tao is passed on creatively, with each generation modifying its own understanding according to what it thinks are the constant norms and the changing circumstances.[98]

Chu's writings and conversations are often spiced with references to Ch'an riddles and practices. A famous one, also used by other Confucian thinkers, regards the concentration displayed by a cat intent on catching a mouse. The cat has its four feet firmly on the ground, its head and tail straight, its eyes focused, its mind without other thoughts.[99] Nevertheless Chu insists that although Confucians and Buddhists may use the same language, they refer to different ideas and practices.[100] In the present instance, if, presumably, Buddhists and Confucians are both thinking of concentration, they would concentrate on *different* things.

Conclusion

Why did Chu Hsi change from being an admirer of Buddhism to being a critic? The problems he perceived in Lu Chiu-yüan's philosophy could very well have served as a catalyst. But the real reason must be deeper. Chu had been uncomfortable with Buddhism even in those early days when he tried to learn what he could from Ch'an masters. That was why he sought out Li T'ung. And even though Li himself had been influenced by Buddhism, Li could at least direct Chu back to the inspirations of Confucianism. Like Li, Chu continued to meditate, but he practiced it, not like a Ch'an devotee, but rather as a Confucian scholar. His rational propensities led him to reject the rhetorical exaggerations and mythmaking tendencies in Buddhism, while his literary sensibilities made him shun the occasional vulgarity one finds in Buddhist writings and practices. He moved on to criticize Buddhism—especially Lin-chi practices—at times quite severely, because he was persuaded that they were misleading. He no longer believed that the whole of truth could be acquired in one moment of sudden enlightenment. He was convinced that enlightenment would take a lifetime of devoted self-cultivation. And he was eager to share his own experiences with others.

Although Chu Hsi was open to learning from Buddhist and Taoist philosophical and religious texts, he was critical of the practical thrust of Buddhist and Taoist teachings because they led to withdrawal from the world and from society or to nonrational pursuit of immortality for its own sake. Generally speaking, Chu's criticism of Buddhism was much stronger than his criticism of Taoism, since he recognized that the former had a deeper and wider influence among the populace, especially the intellectuals. However, he was much more influenced by Buddhist ideas than by Taoist ones in his philosophy—to the extent that we can distinguish one from the other.

There are extensive structural parallels between his philosophy and that of Mahāyāna Buddhism as inherited by Ch'an. There is also the common focus on self-cultivation and meditation. Are there more similarities or more differences? In my opinion, the differences outweigh the similarities. The differences go beyond methodological similarities. Chu's philosophy has an architectonic structure, covering cosmology and metaphysics, human nature, ethics, and spiritual cultivation. Buddhist systems may discuss metaphysics, human nature, and spiritual cultivation, but they pay less formal attention to ethics, which is replaced by something quite different: the rules and prescriptions of the *sangha*. Their philosophies tend to be centered on the mind and consciousness, with much less concern about social relationships. Although similarities and borrowings may be discovered in many parts of Chu's philosophical synthesis, the direction of his entire philosophy is different from that of Ch'an Buddhism. Chu Hsi was a philosophical realist and a practical moralist and his commitment was to the Confucian vision of moral and social responsibility. He followed the lifestyle of a Confucian scholar, teaching disciples the classics and the Four Books with the help of certain Buddhist ideas. He was basically a Confucian influenced by Buddhism, not a Buddhist who used Confucian terminology.

The dividing line between Confucians and Buddhists is in their metaphysical perspectives of reality and in the importance given to moral and social responsibility. This does not mean that Buddhists were "immoral," in our understanding of the word. But it does mean that, to the extent that their religion places primary importance on monastic pursuits, including that of mystical enlightenment for its own sake, it is different from Confucianism.

We shall close by quoting Chu Hsi:

Actually this business [namely, the Confucian quest for sagehood] is very much like Ch'an learning. The difference between [the two] is quite minute. Yet this minute difference is very important. Today's scholars do not know Ch'an, and Ch'an Buddhists do not know [Confucian] learning. What is quite amusing is that they attack each other, but never where it really hurts.[101]

Chu Hsi's Critics

For two thousand years since Han times, Confucianism has been
the dominant teaching. . . . There have been disputes over
orthodoxy and heterodoxy . . . as each person considers his own
thinking to be Confucius's while criticizing others for not being
Confucian.

Liang Ch'i-ch'ao[1]

Introduction

The history of Chinese thought demonstrates epochal shifts, albeit differently
from Western thought. I am speaking not just of philosophy here but of the alternation between philosophical speculation and philological interests, in a civilization dominated by book learning.[2] For example, the classical period presented
a spectrum of concerns, from morality and politics to the metaphysical Tao. The
Han period witnessed some development in metaphysicals and much textual
exegesis in an effort to absorb the legacy of the classical past. Throughout the
first thousand years after Confucius, the primary concern was grounding
human morality and establishing political order. Later periods exhibited occasional swings, with the great Mahāyāna Buddhist schools like Yogācāra, T'ien-
t'ai, and Hua-yen engaging in subtle ontological discussions with religious-
soteriological implications. These schools were absorbed into and transformed
by the eleventh- and twelfth-century Sung neo-Confucian philosophers, especially Chu Hsi, who themselves wrestled with the great ontic and deontic issues.
The fifteenth- to sixteenth-century Ming thinkers turned inward to the mind-
and-heart, only to be followed by philologists, who returned to the "outer" learning
of classical exegesis. The modern period, which witnessed the introduction of
Western ideas of science and high technology, is opening the door to yet another
period of ontic speculation and synthesis, in part fulfilled by such twentieth-
century figures as Tang Chün-i and Mou Tsung-san.

In the Chinese case, philology dominated at certain times, to the exclusion of
philosophy. I mentioned the rich classical textual heritage, which always attracted scholarly attention, whether in minute scrutiny or as an authority for
offering grand speculation. Another important reason for the concentration on

philology was political control of ideas, which drove the better minds into exegesis as an escape. Where Chu's thought is concerned, many critics from diverse perspectives react negatively to the same points. These points include especially the ontological and moral priority of *li*ᵃ over *ch'i*ᵃ, as well as of heavenly principles over human desires.

How has Chu's philosophy fared in the last thousand years? Such a test of time offers clues to the question of Chu Hsi's place in history. Chu was criticized during his lifetime and posthumously, even though his commentaries became state-sanctioned. He sought to maintain a balance between the inner concern of cultivating the mind-and-heart and investigating things in the exterior world. The posthumous criticisms came first from those who regarded his thinking as not adequately inner-directed and therefore not conducive to the goals of sagehood; Wang Yang-ming, during the Ming dynasty, was one such critic. Later, during the Manchu (Ch'ing) dynasty, critics found his teaching too inner-directed and not sufficiently oriented to the outer dimension in social and political practice. Interestingly, such Chinese soul-searching was actually paralleled by a Japanese effort to criticize Chu Hsi and the Japanese orthodoxy influenced by his ideas, and along the same lines. The Chu Hsi school tumbled more rapidly in Japan, as the country opened itself to modernizing and Westernizing influences. But these criticisms also grew in China itself, with the onslaught of Western political imperialism and the introduction of new ideas of democracy and science. Confucianism was eventually replaced by another state orthodoxy, that of Marxism-Leninism-Maoism. With the opening of Communist China to outside influences, critiques of Confucius and Chu Hsi abated, as scholarly studies on Chu's thought began to multiply and stimulate new interest.

Criticism during His Lifetime

Chu Hsi is mostly interested in normative knowledge, the knowledge of moral values. However, during much of his own lifetime, Chu's philosophy was suspected as unorthodox and possibly subversive of the social and political order by those of his contemporaries who were powerful at court. To use the words of Brian McKnight, Chu lived at "a time of peace that was haunted by war." At the time he was born, the Sung court was driven south to the seacoast in Wen-chou. At his death, the powerful imperial relative Han T'o-chou was gathering support for irridentism. In his middle years, Chu was personally involved in debates surrounding the Jürchen invasion of 1161. Responding to Emperor Hsiao-tsung's call for advice, the young man of thirty-one, a *chin-shih* at the tender age of eighteen, then out of official employ, counseled investigating things and extending knowledge to respond to changes, as well as closing the borders and focusing on internal reforms and military preparations. He was "strategically a hawk and tactically a dove." But his advice went unheeded.[3]

Chu Hsi was well known and influential for his many publications, as well as for the memorials he addressed to the throne. He did not desist from voicing his political opinions, which were not always in favor at court. In fact, Chu was the

chief example of a philosopher at odds with the state, and he spent most of his life declining official positions and asking for sinecures to support his career of writing and teaching.[4]

Chu's custom of criticizing high officials at court won him powerful enemies, especially in the circle around Han T'o-chou. Eventually, these people attacked his teachings, which they labeled "false learning," singling out the concept of the Great Ultimate as a special target. They criticized his frequent proffering of advice to the throne as "usurping imperial power." Censor Shen Chi-tsu charged Chu with crimes like "lack of loyalty, filial piety, humanity, rightness, and justice." Chu was denounced as a man who "deceived the world in order to steal a reputation." It was even suggested that he be given the death penalty.[5] Clearly, his attackers wanted to strike at his reputation as a virtuous man in order to undermine his moral authority, and they did not hesitate to fabricate charges. As a result, Chu was stripped of his official duties, and his teachings were prohibited as a "perverse and heretical doctrine" in 1196. Not only did the prohibition implicate Chu and his disciple Ts'ai Yüan-ting, but it also cast aspersions on many other scholars and intellectuals of the time who had supported Han T'o-chou's opponent, the imperial clansman Chao Ju-yü.

Chu Hsi could not have continued his work of writing and teaching without the stipends that came from his temple guardianships. He died on April 23, 1200. Although his funeral was attended by several thousand, all who went were regarded as "heretics" mourning the death of the "heresiarch."[6]

In a treatise entitled "Master Hui-an [Chu Hsi] Was Not a Recluse," the historian Li Hsin-ch'uan (Li Xinchuan, 1166–1243) offers a defense of Chu Hsi:

> In his daily life in retirement, the master continually reflected upon the mistakes of the country's policy, showing an expression of sadness and discontent. When he spoke of the weak condition of the country, he felt so sorry as to shed tears. . . . In his service of the ruler, he never lowered [the standards of] the Way in order to sell [himself]. . . . During a period of fifty years, under four successive emperors, he served outside [in local government] only nine times and stood at Court for [a total of] forty days. This shows how difficult it was [for him] to have the Way realized.[7]

In death, Chu Hsi gained a greater reputation than during his life. More ironically, it took the Mongol Yüan dynasty to give his philosophy state patronage (1313). With that, the erstwhile heresy became the dominant school of thought, as his commentaries were memorized by candidates eager to pass the civil service examinations. Elevated to state doctrine, Chu's teachings acquired a sacrosanct status that led to protection from criticism but ran the risk of gradual fossilization. The fact that state sanction proved a disservice to Chu's thought is reflected in the rigid and formalized, so-called eight-legged essay form in which students were required to write their examination essays. Any creative transformation was forestalled. The better thinkers protested either by refraining from taking the examinations or by criticizing him indirectly. This was the case with Wang Yang-ming, who developed Lu Chiu-yüan's philosophy, which centered on the human mind-and-heart as the bearer of *li*[a], the seed of goodness.

Wang Yang-ming's Criticisms[8]

Wang Yang-ming's philosophy of *hsin*[a] or *liang-chih* (literally, "innate good knowledge"), sometimes translated as "moral intuition" but going beyond that to a deeper, ontological reality, allows its followers much more freedom and spontaneity without losing its focus on the goal of sagehood. Wang was a follower of Lu Chiu-yüan, whose system he both inherited and completed. Wang realized that his own teachings clashed on many points with Chu's, whether on the primacy of human nature or of mind, of investigation of things and extension of knowledge or of sincerity of intention. Each systematically mapped out a metaphysics as well as an agenda for self-cultivation. Wang rejected Chu's agenda because it regarded personal perfection as the crowning achievement of a lifetime of diligent scholarship accompanied by the purification of passions and human desires. Wang saw personal perfection only as the purification of the sincerity of the mind.

As with so many intellectual disputes in traditional China, this one proceeded as an exercise in exegesis. Where the text of the *Great Learning* is concerned, Wang preferred the "sincerity of intention" as the essential basis for all learning and did not think it should come only after intensive and extensive investigation of all the principles of things. In 1518 he published a textual study, *The Old Version of the Great Learning*, which went back to the pre-Sung version as found in the T'ang edition of the Nine Classics. In that collection, this text formed part of the Book of Rites. Wang published it with his own brief, side commentaries in an effort to overturn Chu's emendations of the text. This effort included restoring the word *ch'in*[a] (love) to the expression *ch'in-min*, which Chu (following Ch'eng Yi) had rendered as *hsin-min* (renovate the people), and deleting a paragraph Chu had attached to the section on investigation of things and extension of knowledge.[9]

In a preface written several years earlier but published with his restored text, Wang said: "The work of making the intention sincere lies in the investigation of things. To seek such sincerity is to rest in the highest good. To rest in the highest good requires the extension of knowledge."[10] He asserts that when the text of the *Great Learning* is taken as a whole, everything falls into perspective. But when the text is divided into sections and given a commentary, as in Chu's case, the real doctrine is lost. "Fragmentation [of knowledge], emptiness [of mind], and falsehood" are the results, as the highest good disappears from sight.[11]

That same year, he also sought to reconcile Chu's teachings with his own by publishing, with his own preface, a selected collection of excerpts from twenty-four letters written by Chu Hsi to friends and disciples, purporting to show Chu in his later age articulating a reversal of some of his teachings.[12] But this backfired when it was discovered that the collection was highly selective and not sequentially organized.

In the controversy that followed, Wang acknowledged his mistakes while denying any motive to deceive:

> All my life, Chu Hsi's teachings have been like a revelation from the gods or from divination and oracles. I could hardly bear to depart from his teachings so abruptly. In my heart, I cannot bear to contradict him, and yet I cannot but contradict him, because the Way is what it is and will not be made clear unless I am forthright.[13]

Wang also made a direct appeal to the authority of Confucius:

> The old version of the *Great Learning* is the original version transmitted from generation to generation in the Confucian school. Master Chu, suspecting errors and gaps had crept in, corrected and emended it. But I believe that there had been no errors or gaps. That is why I follow the old version. Perhaps, my mistake has been in believing too much in Confucius. I did not omit Master Chu's chapter divisions or delete his commentary on purpose.
>
> By what authority did Chu Hsi decide that this paragraph should be here and that one there, that this part had been lost and should be restored . . . ? Are you not taking too seriously my divergences from Chu Hsi and not seriously Chu's rebellion against Confucius?[14]

Wang couched his disagreements with Chu Hsi in an exegetical form. But he was no true exegete. He was much more an idealist philosopher who believed in the subjective mind-and-heart as the arbiter of moral truth and wisdom:

> If [words] are examined in the *hsin*[a] and found to be wrong, then even if they have come from the mouth of Confucius, I dare not accept them as correct. How much more so for what has come from people inferior to Confucius! If [words] are examined and found to be correct, then even if they come from [the mouths of] mediocre people, I dare not regard them as incorrect. How much more so for what has come from Confucius![15]

As it happened, Wang won a partial victory on the textual level with the restoration of the expression *ch'in-min* to the standard version of the *Great Learning*. But he was never able to confirm the assertion that Confucius was somehow the author behind this text, which later scholars decided came from the Han times. His philosophy gained many adherents, not only in the Ming dynasty but also and especially among the reform-minded intellectuals toward the end of the Manchu dynasty, and even afterward. It is credited with spearheading the early stage of the Meiji restoration, which opened Japan to Western influences, and it continues to inspire contemporary Chinese philosophers following in the footsteps of the twentieth-century thinkers Tang Chün-i and Mou Tsung-san.

The Jesuit Criticisms

In the seventeenth and eighteenth centuries, missionary efforts brought China within the scope of Westerners' knowledge. The Western responses elicited were usually conditioned by the religious attitudes of the missionaries and of their informed audience in Europe. The missionaries themselves were divided; some were admirers of Chinese culture, and others were critics. The admirers were active in introducing to European readers a rich and vibrant moral tradition called Confucianism, which they compared favorably with the ethical teachings of Christianity. The best-known example is the Italian Matteo Ricci (1552–1610), who sought to accommodate the Christian message to Chinese culture. In his catechism, entitled *T'ien-chu shih-yi*, Ricci criticizes the neo-Confucian concept of *li*[a], which he renders as "reason." In the context of the Aristotelian-Thomistic category of substance and accidents, he says, "'reason' itself is accident and cannot be said to be human nature."[16]

Surprisingly for those who remember the doctrine of original sin, Ricci answers thus the question on the goodness of human nature: "If we say that the essence of human nature together with emotions are all produced by the Lord of Heaven, and if we let reason be their master, then they are lovable and desirable, and are originally good and not evil."[17]

Following Matteo Ricci, the Jesuit missionaries generally preferred early Confucianism with its belief in an anthropomorphic Heaven to the teachings of Chu Hsi or Wang Yang-ming, with their abstract vocabulary of *T'ai-chi*, *li*[a], and *ch'i*[a]. Yet they found in China an official doctrine favoring Chu Hsi and an unofficial circle of intellectuals often preferring Wang Yang-ming.

Two Jesuit works published in the seventeenth century fired the imagination of European intellectuals and added fuel to theological controversies, especially those concerning the origin of Chinese religions, the antiquity of Chinese historical chronology compared to the biblical one, and the compatibility of Confucian and Christian rites. These are Phillippe Couplet's *Confucius Sinarum Philosophus* (1687) and L. Lecomte's *Nouveaux mémoires sur l'état présent de la Chine* (1696). The latter work's extravagant praises of Chinese religious and moral teachings elicited a solemn condemnation by the faculty of Sorbonne University for questioning the uniqueness of the Christian revelation.[18]

But there were also critics of Chinese religion. Nicholas Longobardi, Ricci's immediate successor, and Antoine de Ste Marie, a Franciscan, both insisted that Chu's commentaries were essential for understanding ancient classics, which meant that China had become a land of agnostics and atheists, with no understanding of spirit as separate from matter. Longobardi's *Traité sur quelques points de la religion des chinois* and Ste Marie's *Traité sur quelque points importants de la Mission de la Chine* both appeared about 1701 and presented a vivid picture of the anxious discussions then going on among missionaries conscious of these problems. Nicolas de Malebranche, a synthesizer of Descartes and Aquinas, wrote a critique of Confucianism in the form of a dialogue: *Entretien d'un philosophe chrétien et d'un philosophe chinois*. It was the work of a Christian apologist, to help missionaries respond to arguments arising from Chinese philosophy. Less informed than Leibniz, he referred to li^a and $ch'i^a$ as reason and matter, two eternal principles of being, and then refuted these ideas as a form of atheism related to the philosophy of Spinoza.[19]

Some of Europe's best minds were led to philosophical reflections on Chinese thought. Leibniz visited and corresponded with the Jesuit J. Bouvet, from whom he derived a knowledge of the Book of Changes and neo-Confucian philosophy. In his letters and other writings, Leibniz showed his particular appreciation of Chu Hsi's teachings of li^a and $ch'i^a$, insisting that the Chinese were not materialists but had a real understanding of God and of spiritual beings. Interestingly, he read Longobardi's critical treatise only to get from it his own favorable interpretation of neo-Confucian philosophy.[20]

The Ch'ing Critics

An early critic of Chu Hsi was the iconoclastic Li Chih (Li Zhi, 1527–1602), author of *Books to Burn* (*Fen-shu*) and *Books to Hide* (*Ts'ang-shu*), so named because of their antiestablishment views. Li was against a monolithic orthodoxy. He believed that there are many ways to truth, and no one system should claim to be the correct and only "Way": "To eat and dress is human morality and the principles of things. Outside eating and dressing, there is neither human morality nor principles."[21] Li respected Chu's scholarship but was not afraid to challenge his authority or even that of Confucius. He criticized Chu's opposition of heavenly principles and human desires. For Li, human desires are natural and do not differ from heavenly principles. According to him, sages are like everyone else, and do not necessarily have anything special to teach others.[22]

As a liberal-minded thinker, Li was way ahead of his times. He thought it wrong that only rulers had the right to offer sacrifices to Heaven because, as Chu said, Heaven is li^a, and li^a is present in all. He was for gender equality and even admitted women as disciples, an action regarded as scandalous.[23]

Another critic was Wang Fu-chih (Wang Fuzhi, 1619–92), whose life straddled Ming and Ch'ing times. Interestingly, he had met Matteo Ricci, with whom he discussed whether the earth is round, or, in Chinese parlance, "egg-shaped." Chu Hsi had taught such (see chapter 3), but Wang doubted this. A philosophical follower of the school of Chang Tsai, Wang appreciated Chang's cosmological explanations regarding *T'ai-hsü* (Great Void) as full of $ch'i^a$, which he understood as matter. According to a him, li^a depends on $ch'i^a$ and cannot be found except in $ch'i^a$. When assembled, $ch'i^a$ brings forth humans and things. When dispersed, it enters the Great Void.[24]

Indeed, his preferred term is $ch'i^b$ (literally, "utensil," i.e., "material substance"). As he puts it: "All under heaven is $ch'i^b$. The Tao is the Tao of $ch'i^b$. But $ch'i^b$ cannot be called the $ch'i^b$ of Tao."[25] For this, he is much celebrated in Communist China, where dialectical materialism remains orthodox.

Wang Fu-chih opposes Chu's bifurcation of heavenly principle and human desires. He sees heavenly principles as depending on human desires for their expression: "The sage has desires. His desires are Heaven's principles. Heaven has no desires. Its principles are human desires. The scholar has both principles and desires. When principles are achieved, human desires are fulfilled."[26] On the subject of intellectual pursuits, he sees the investigation of things and the extension of knowledge as representing two steps: first sense perception and then rational apprehension. He does not agree with Chu on the need to know first before acting, preferring to see action as a vehicle of knowledge.

The concerted criticisms of Chu Hsi during the seventeenth century came with the revival of classical philological scholarship. The use of language by philosophers like Chu Hsi and Wang Yang-ming proved that both were influenced by Ch'an Buddhism. In this regard, Ku Yen-wu (Gu Yanwu, 1613–82) and Yen Jo-chü (Yan Roju, 1636–1704) both worked for the reconstruction of the specific and pristine meanings of the sages' words and utterances, as found in the classical texts. And the method they applied was called "evidential research" (k'ao-chü, literally, "investigation and evidence"), a developed form of philology, which functioned with the support of phonology, semantics, grammar, epigraphy, bibliography, geography, and even mathematics and astronomy. As Ku said: "The study of the classics *is* the study of principles (*li*ᵃ)."[27]

Yen Yüan (Yan Yuan, 1635–1704) and Li Kung (Li Gong, 1659–1733) were not to show the respect that the earlier Ch'ing scholars still accorded Chu Hsi. Both were vehement critics of the Ch'eng-Chu and of the Lu-Wang school, as representing the ascendancy of Buddhism and Taoism and as no longer representing authentic Confucianism. They preferred to go back to the study and imitation of Confucius and Mencius, for reasons of authentic scholarship, as well as for better social and political application. According to Yen: "Chu Hsi wanted to study Confucius. But he did not get the mind of Confucius and did not completely agree with Confucius's teachings. On the part of five hundred years of scholars, I regret that he did not receive the [transmission of the teachings of] Tseng-tzu and Mencius."[28] As already mentioned, Yen criticized Chu for giving meditation too much priority (see chapter 6). He also asserted that meditation wastes time and keeps the mind empty, preventing people from engaging in more practical studies that serve the world better.[29]

Yen also attacked Chu for excessive reading and for writing too many commentaries, which prevented him from constructive activity and made him "waste his life." Chu Hsi, he said, "was intoxicated with books." And this became a "different kind of heresy."[30]

Yen himself insisted on the importance of some of the practical exhortations given by the classical texts, such as the "three matters," namely, rectifying virtue, protecting life, and developing ability as given in the Book of History, and the "six functions of government," namely, defense, agriculture, economy, storage, fire and water control, and general works, as enumerated in the Book of Rites.[31] He criticized Chu Hsi for being buried in texts until his dying day. "Outside reading books, Chu had nothing to say. In fact, he talked Ch'an Buddhism while holding the Five Classics, the *Analects*, and the *Book of Mencius* in his hands."[32] "[Chu] spoke only of words and texts, and only discussed theory, without repenting of such till death. He abandoned completely Confucius's teachings about ordering the world and its affairs."[33]

Li disputed Chu's interpretation of the *Great Learning*. For him, *ko-wu* is no investigation of things or intellectual pursuit but refers to "making virtue manifest, loving the people, rendering the intention sincere, rectifying the mind, cultivating the self, ordering the family, governing the state, and giving peace to the world." And these tasks require learning the ancient six arts, namely, such practical pursuits as ritual, music, archery, charioteering, writing, and mathematics.[34]

Then came Tai Chen (Dai Zhen, 1724–77), the greatest classical scholar of the Ch'ing period. He used philology to discover "the mind of the sages." He did a special study of the text of *Mencius* and exposed, through this, the great amount of Buddhist influence on Chu Hsi and other philosophers of nature and principle, who basically used ideas from *Mencius* for their own purposes. With passion and urgency, he decried their ideas and research methods. He opposed the concept of *li*[a] as principle transcending *ch'i*[a] and change, a concept that had become in his time an instrument of oppression. In its place, he and others preferred *ch'i*[a] and, with it, attempted to rehabilitate human desires (*jen-yü*) that Chu and his followers had waged war against:[35]

> The word *li*[a] (principle) does not appear often in the Six Classics, in the works of Confucius and Mencius, or in commentaries, records, and other texts. But today even the most foolish and brutal appeal to principles in making decisions or criticisms. . . . Personal opinion is taken to be principle. . . . Isn't it against reason (*li*[a]) to use this to manipulate things and also control people?[36]

Tai said that Chu and other Sung thinkers caused much confusion because they "interpreted the words of the Six Classics, Confucius, and Mencius in terms of the ideas of Lao Tzu, Chuang Tzu, and the Buddhists. How can we tell one from the other today?"[37] "[W]hat they call 'principle' is similar in meaning to what the Buddhists call 'original countenance,' and what they describe as 'preserving principle' (*ts'un-li*) is quite like the Buddhist saying 'be always alert' (*ch'ang hsing-hsing*)."[38] Tai is especially adamant about their disparagement of human emotions and desires: "The ancients who discussed *li*[a] looked for it in human emotions, seeking to render these without fault. . . . The moderns who discuss *li*[a] seek it outside human emotions, considering it to be uncaring."[39]

The Ch'ing critics were scholars and specialists spearheading a new literary movement, a return to philological studies of the Five Classics. Although they admitted the partly Buddho-Taoist character of the whole of neo-Confucian thinking—whether Chu Hsi's or Wang Yang-ming's—their movement never took root among a larger following. The government, in the meantime, continued to sponsor Chu Hsi's philosophy as state orthodoxy, while philology replaced independent thinking in the academic world, preventing any danger of intellectual subversion of the state. Nevertheless, the Ch'ing critics were effective to the extent that the philosophers who came later tended to favor Wang Yang-ming for his protest against a status quo, his exaltation of conscience (and, implicitly, of individual freedom), and his emphasis on the unity of action and knowledge. This does not mean that Chu's thought disappeared. It remained powerful and was especially reflected in late Ch'ing scholarship, whether by those in official positions like Tseng Kuo-fan (Zeng Guofan) or by private scholars like Liu Shih-p'ei and others.[40]

The Japanese Critics: Itō Jinsai and Ogyū Sorai

Itō Jinsai (1627–1705) and Ogyū Sorai (1666–1728) were older contemporaries of Yen Yüan and Li Kung. They articulated certain criticisms of Chu Hsi and his school that were in general agreement with the Ch'ing critics. They encouraged philological studies on earlier texts and moved away from abstract philosophizing. They also decried *li*[a] and exalted *ch'i*[a] and, with it, human desires (*jen-yü*). But apparently, the early Ch'ing Chinese scholars like Yen and Li and Japanese scholars like Jinsai and Sorai did not even know of each other's existence, although some modern Japanese scholars see them—especially Sorai—as having prepared the way for Tai Chen.[41]

In his study of Tai Chen and Chang Hsüeh-ch'eng (Zhang Xuecheng), Yü Ying-shih claims the parallels were more incidental than intentional, although he points out historical interaction between Chinese and Japanese scholars in the middle period of the Ch'ing dynasty. The Chinese scholar Liu Pao-nan (1791–1855), for example, twice cited Ogyū Sorai in his own commentary on the *Analects*. The degree of similarity between Ogyū Sorai and Tai Chen is nevertheless astonishing. The former published a textual study of the *Analects*, and the latter did a similar work on *Mencius*.[42]

By Jinsai's and Sorai's time, the Chu Hsi school, or Shushigaku, had been in Japan for about a century and had become the dominant school of thought. It had produced thinkers like Fujiwara Seika, Hayashi Razan, and Yamazaki Ansai, each of whom sought to adapt it to the Japanese cultural landscape, especially by incorporating Shinto elements. To criticize Shushigaku or its Chinese founder was to attack the intellectual establishment. Both Jinsai and Sorai were once Shushigaku followers, and each had become dissatisfied with it. At the root was some discomfort with a philosophical system coming from outside that did not exactly respond to Japan's perceived psychological conditions and intellectual needs. Their efforts, combined, would signal a new movement, the Kogaku, or school of ancient learning, which returned to the origins of Confucianism for its inspiration and eventually led to the study of Japan's own ancient culture and the nationalist sentiments accompanying that new interest.

Jinsai rejected Chu's metaphysical structure based on both *li*[a] and *ch'i*[a]. He accepted only the more ancient notion of *ch'i*[a] (in Japanese, *ki*) as the life force in humans and in the universe. He advocated cultivating *ki* and developing the Confucian virtue of *jen*[a], which, for him, meant "love," as expressed in particular virtues like loyalty, faithfulness, reverence, and forgiveness.[43] By criticizing Chu Hsi and others for radically altering the original teachings of Confucianism,

Jinsai also directed the return to the study of ancient Chinese classics. In the words of his son, Itō Tōgai:

> My father's belief in returning to the ancient source [of Confucianism] was not the blithe expression of a momentary personal fancy. He had been under the spell of the philosophy of "human nature and principle" for years. . . . He studied a few doubtful points from all angles . . . until at long last he became aware of the fact that present-day Confucianism was no longer the Way of the Three Dynasties.[44]

While Jinsai did not object to human perfectibility as taught by Mencius, he did not like Chu Hsi's method for awakening to the seeds of sagehood within:

> [This] teaching has not been in accord with the original aim of the Sages. Humanity, rightness, decorum and wisdom are considered to be complete in original human nature . . . [and] do not need to be acquired through cultivation. . . . [But] how could sagehood be attained by nothing more than a return to one's original nature?[45]

Sorai had also experienced a profound dissatisfaction with Chu Hsi and preferred to immerse himself in the study of ancient Chinese texts. He strongly criticized Chu and his school for having moved away from the study of the early sage-kings and Confucius. Indeed, he claimed that Chu and others were unable to engage in such, as they no longer understood the written language of the classical texts. In his first major treatise, *Distinguishing the Way* (*Bendō*), Sorai gave what he thought were the problems with post-Confucius scholars. He drew a line between Confucius and those coming after him, like Tzu-ssu and Mencius. He honored Confucius for studying the way of the early kings but thought the others had diverged from the master, for example, in teaching that sagehood was attainable: "The virtues of wisdom and perspicacity were received by the early kings in their Heaven[-endowed] natures. It is not that which common people can attain. Therefore, there was no doctrine in ancient times saying that learning makes a sage."[46]

Acknowledged as Japan's best China scholar, Sorai was a religious man who respected the place of Heaven in the ancient Chinese texts and saw in it a means for pacifying the country. He attacked the union between the inner and the outer, especially inner cultivation as a way of attaining correct ethical and political behavior. Sorai believed that sages are born, not made, and that the historical sages, with the exception of Confucius, were dynastic founders who instituted rites and music. He objected to Chu Hsi as a proud man eager only to perfect himself while neglecting to submit to the way of the early kings. He opposed Chu's program of investigating things and extending knowledge, aimed at finding *li*[a] rather than the Way of the early kings. For him, principles were too abstract to convey the concreteness and complexity of things. One should rather study the rituals of the ancient sages. Without mentioning Chu Hsi by name, Sorai criticized Chu's interpretation of investigating things in the context of the *Great Learn-*

ing and advocated a return to the ancient six arts, as did his Chinese contemporaries Yen Yüan and Li Kung:

> "Things" refers to the concrete meaning of the teachings. The ancients studied in order to complete the virtues that existed within them. . . . The "six arts" all include "things" which are the regulations of completing virtues. If one practices these "things" for a long time, then the virtues one seeks to preserve will be completed. This is what is called "things being arrived at."[47]

Much more akin to Mencius's third-century-B.C.E. opponent Hsün-tzu and to the ancient Chinese legalists, Sorai desired a system of thought that could be applied to Japan's practical, social, and political needs. By his time, the Shushigaku had basically run its course in Japan. Sorai himself unleashed an intellectual revolution that favored the study of Chinese antiquity. Ironically, it would lead to Kokugaku, or National Learning, and the study of Japan and its own native tradition, especially Shinto, nurturing an intense nationalism. Ironically also, the later nationalist thinkers would find Sorai himself too backward-looking as well as too friendly to Chinese values.

The Modern Critics

Already before the Communist victory in China (1949), attacks were made on Chu Hsi's form of state orthodoxy as having led to a fossilization of thought and morals in Chinese society. One well-known but moderate critic was the American-educated philosopher and scholar Hu Shih (1891–1962).[48] Whether this fossilization was Chu's fault, or that of the government which made use of his ideas without seeking to fully understand their import, is not our problem here. But criticisms have been abundant and were articulated long before the concerted political effort to discredit Confucius himself in the 1973–74 campaign that has since been itself discredited.[49]

There is a tendency to see the school of Chu Hsi mainly as a vehicle to strengthen state control on intellectual and social life. The Chinese were the first to point this out, especially during the iconoclastic May Fourth Movement (1919), when many intellectuals and students condemned Confucius and Chu Hsi for the intellectual and social shackles that had been placed on their individual freedom and the perceived modernization of the country. With the adulation for the West, and for "Mr. Democracy" and "Mr. Science," came the cries against the Confucian establishment: "Down with Confucius & Sons!"

The writer Lu Hsün was the fiercest critic of Confucianism, whether ancient or of a Chu Hsi variety. He attacked the social and ethical system it allegedly created, the *li-chiao* (literally, "ritual religion"), as inhuman, even cannibalistic, and urged that people live for themselves, not their ancestors.[50]

As this phenomenon is well studied, I shall not give it much space in this book. The problem is also well articulated in English by such scholars as Joseph

Levenson. Levenson finds fault with a traditionalist system that showed too much respect for historical precedent and exhibited a "constant will to narrow the vision." For him and for others, certain aspects of Chu's thinking lent stability to the established order. For example, the concept of the Great Ultimate is seen as an axis supporting the status quo: "Absolute traditionalism is a completely hypothetical, self-destructive concept; a sense of the past that can never develop if an original unmitigated reverence for 'what is' precludes its ever becoming past."[51]

The Communist party was born in the aftermath of the May Fourth Movement, and its ideas and values were in part shaped by the iconoclastic stance it represented. Criticisms of Confucius and his teachings, as well as of Chu Hsi and his school, continued among the leftist intellectuals, and the flame spread under Communist rule after 1949, with diatribes against Confucius turning vitriolic during the Cultural Revolution (1966–76).

The problem became how to assign thinkers to the right categories in order to pronounce judgment on their teachings. In all cases, the Marxist classics together with the beliefs of dialectical materialism are regarded as an absolute test and a normative guide (*ching*) for all relative and secondary truths. Taking their cues from A. A. Zhdanov (d. 1948), the cultural spokesman of Stalinist days in the Soviet Union, who made his analysis of Russian intellectual history in the light of Marxist categories, the students of Chinese philosophy were required to apply materialist-idealist antithesis to the understanding of traditional philosophy.[52] It was understood, of course, that materialism is right and idealism wrong. In fact, idealist philosophies are regarded as possessing other negative qualities, such as being oppressive of the people. Hou Wailu and others produced a monumental five-volume work, *A General History of Chinese Thought*, completed in 1960. The work tends to be more critical of neo-Confucian philosophy, labeling the Chu Hsi school as a politically reactionary movement. It is described as an objective idealism for recognizing an underlying metaphysical reality in the world of manifold objects. And it is criticized for a near-monastic cultivation of religiosity and for a philosophical scholasticism serving the establishment.[53]

Chinese Marxist scholars have consistently favored *ch'i*[a] over *li*[a], constantly attempting to discover in *ch'i*[a] a materialist ancestry for Chinese Marxism. This appears to be the intention of Hou Wai-lu's monumental five-volume work, as well as of those authors who became prominent during the Anti-Confucius campaign in 1973–74, including Yang Rongguo and Ren Jiyu.

I shall offer examples of criticisms made before and during the Cultural Revolution, according to subject matter. I wish to note here that Hou Wailu, whose criticisms were articulated in the 1950s, himself suffered humiliations during the Cultural Revolution when he was deemed not leftist enough. On the other hand, Yang Rongguo came into the limelight during the Cultural Revolution as a staunch critic of traditional Chinese thought, although he is hardly remembered today. When we compare the two critics, Yang comes forth as less reserved and more political.

According to Yang, Chu apparently served the wrong cause—a regressive one, that of the "feudal moral and social order." And Yang's criticisms, like others, usually allude to the so-called worship of Chu on the part of later governments, from Yüan to Ch'ing (the thirteenth century to the early twentieth), from Tseng Kuo-fan, the nineteenth-century conqueror of the T'ai-p'ing rebels, to Chiang Kai-shek, the twentieth-century Nationalist leader, as evidence of the reactionary character of his philosophy.[54]

In attacking Chu's li[a]/ch'i[a] philosophy, Hou's book gives the example of a fan, to discuss the relationship between li[a] and ch'i[b], the material thing itself. As Chu himself explains: "The fan is made in a certain way and should be used in this way. This is the li[a] above shapes. . . . In each of the ch'i[b] within shapes, there is such a principle. This is the tao[a] above shapes."[55] Hou comments:

> [For Chu], the concrete fan is not what counts as existing. Whether you put it down or use it to fan yourself, it is the same "principle of the fan" . . . that is manifest. For Chu, the ordinary variety of fans, whether round in shape, made of rushes or goose feathers or sandalwood, is only the manifestation of "the principle of fans". . . .
>
> Not only so, but Chu says that the fan . . . is also a direct manifestation of the Great Ultimate, the whole of li[a] in the universe. Here he is influenced by Hua-yen Buddhism.[56]

In the context of the Great Ultimate, Hou calls li[a] the "sovereign ruler of all things," "the primary reason for the mystery of why the universe exists as it does and changes as it does." "Li[a] is the ruler of the world. It is not subject to any restraint and has the power to show its greatness and bestow fortune or misfortune."[57]

Because of his metaphysics of li[a] and ch'i[a], Chu has been described as a dualist. Yang points out, however, that his philosophy is basically monist—based on li[a] and, especially, T'ai-chi, the fullness of li[a]. This is a spiritual substance, first principle of the universe, source of all being and life. As Ren Jiyu also emphasizes, the realm of li[a] represents the highest, eternal, and absolute being. Li[a] fills the universe and is the cause of the creative transformation of all things. And li[a] is prior to ch'i[a], which it produces. Thus, they say Chu makes use of a materialist notion to build up a system that is best described as objective idealism. It is said to be a "cunning" kind of idealism and reveals a closeness to Hegel's metaphysics.[58]

Chu also speaks of li[a] and ch'i[a] in his theory of human nature, of the human body and spirit. Where li[a] corresponds to the metaphysical (human nature), ch'i[a] corresponds to the physical (the shape). Hence, his critics say the human, too, is a product of the absolute spirit. But if one is to ask—as did Yang Rongguo—how the objective spirit li[a] can produce humanity and the myriad things, the answer is that it merely represents another way of saying that God (Lord-on-High, Shang-ti) is creator of the universe. Even Chu Hsi seems to admit this when he says that "the Lord is principle (li[a]) and ruler." Following this logic, the Lord is li[a], the Lord is also ruler of the universe, and idealism is finally directed toward theism.[59]

At other times, Chu is said to have associated his philosophy of li[a] directly with feudal morality. He speaks of ch'i[a] as the source of the material elements, such as metal, wood, water, fire, and earth, while li^a is the source of the moral virtues, of benevolence, rightness, propriety, wisdom, and faithfulness. He also says that the realm of li^a includes the ethical relationship between ruler and subject, father and son, husband and wife, elder and younger brothers, friend and friend. But since for these critics, li^a is absolute spirit, and also prior to $ch'i^a$, Chu Hsi has obviously proposed the priority of feudal morality and of the feudal political order before even the emergence of the human race and of society. His objective idealist philosophy is oriented to the service of centralized authority and of feudal government.[60]

The criticisms continue. Besides proposing an a priori, eternal, and absolute li^a, Chu Hsi has also taught that while li^a is one, its manifestations are many, and that everything has its own $T'ai$-chi. In this sense, everything looks to $T'ai$-chi, the highest li^a, as the ground of its own being.

Referring to this same theory, Hou quotes the Buddhist metaphor of the moon reflected on the water everywhere in order to ridicule Chu's abstract philosophy of li^a, which he calls a "castle in the air."

> From this we can uncover Chu Hsi's secret. He creates a supernatural Tao—li^a or $T'ai$-chi—from the real $ch'i^b$. Then he puts aside the abstraction, to return to the real world of $ch'i^b$. Here he seems to be affirming the existence of $ch'i^b$ or the fan, but actually he completed his creation, making out of the absolute subject li^a a natural fan.[61]

Applied to the ethical sphere, it means that although there is only one li^a, it is manifest differently in the ruler-subject relationship compared with the father-son relationship. But everyone is thereby obliged to adhere to these moral principles in human relationships as eternal, unchanging norms, with an absolute binding force. This implies also the permanence of a feudal governmental structure. The positions of ruler and subject, father and son, are unchanging, because rooted in ontological ground. Hence, even if he acknowledges a certain contradiction and tension between things and affairs, he denies the possibility of changing the established order of things.[62]

Chu Hsi took over from Ch'eng Yi his doctrine of cultivation in terms of investigating things and extending knowledge. We are told that this implies an a priori epistemology, not to penetrate into the special principle governing each individual thing but to comprehend the one li^a that underlies all things. Hence, even the li^a that he describes as present in each individual thing is less the principle of the thing in itself than the manifestation of the a priori heavenly principle ($T'ien$-li).

In his theory of human nature, Chu Hsi confirms the presence in the human of "heavenly nature" and of "physical nature." One refers to li^a, the other to $ch'i^a$. Chu refers to sages as having the purest $ch'i^a$, without the contamination of material desires, and to the foolish people ("the oppressed classes") as having a dull quality of $ch'i^a$ and being hindered by material desires. Thus, he is said to make human desires the root of all evil, that which must be controlled by heavenly principle in order to ensure the recovery of an originally good nature. Such a theory of human nature allegedly serves well as "opium of the people," to help the cause of feudal order. Moreover, it offers a philosophical explanation for the social and economic differentiation between social classes.[63]

With the end of the Cultural Revolution, China has opened itself to the outside world and departed officially from the critical stance I have been describing. I have nevertheless given an account of it because the criticisms lasted for about twenty-five years and have presumably influenced many minds. They ought to be recalled for whatever merits or demerits they had and as a sign of a time that was with us only recently. Moreover, they offer an independent affirmation of the religious character of Chu's thought, and even of the entire Confucian tradition.

I should mention that Chu Hsi's "objective idealism" fared a little better than Wang Yang-ming's "subjective idealism" under Marxist and Maoist scrutiny. Moreover, these criticisms have since abated, as a new generation of mainland Chinese philosophers has emerged who reinterpret more objectively and even favorably the Confucian legacy, including the philosophy of Chu Hsi. I am speaking of such persons as Chang Liwen, Chen Lai, and Li Zhehou, some of whom might have studied with and certainly knew about the now deceased Feng Youlan, also known as Fung Yu-lan (1895–1990), himself a follower of Chu Hsi, in spite of the twists and turns of his own intellectual evolution under the Communist regime.[64]

Among Chinese outside the mainland, the scholar best known for affinities with Chu Hsi is the now deceased intellectual historian Ch'ien Mu (1895–1990), the author of *Chu-tzu hsin hsüeh-an*. The philosophers Tang Chün-i and Mou Tsung-san both contributed to a new knowledge of and interest in China's spiritual and philosophical heritage while showing their preference for Wang Yang-ming over Chu Hsi. Indeed, if Tang, together with Hsü Fu-kuan, seeks to point out those differences between Chu Hsi and Ch'eng Yi that permit Chu to keep a stronger dimension of transcendence in his thinking, Mou attacks Chu Hsi for rendering transcendent notions immanent and for the placidity of his intentions and goals, which pale next to Lu Chiu-yüan's and Wang Yang-ming's more dynamic quest for wisdom and enlightenment.

Ch'ien Mu showed little interest in the religious aspect of Chinese philosophy. But both Mou and Tang deal with the religious character of the Confucian tradition, often sympathetically, and in the light of Western philosophy. In Mou's case, his philosophical discourse is done especially as a dialogue with Kant, whom he both respects and criticizes. He characterizes Chinese religious thought as a "concerned consciousness," an axiological reading of the world and human existence. He is also forthright in his criticisms of those philosophers he regards as deviating from the Mencian way, such as Hsün-tzu, Ch'eng Yi, and Chu Hsi. He even rejects the *Great Learning* as a canonical text because he considers it closer to Hsün-tzu's philosophy, and because of Chu's editorial changes to the text. His preference is for the Hunan school, to which Chang Shih belonged, and he especially honors Chang's mentor, the obscure Hu Hung, whom he exalts as a mainline transmitter of the philosophies of Chou Tun-yi, Chang Tsai, and Ch'eng Hao.[65]

In discussing the question of the Great Ultimate, Tang Chün-i agrees that some ancients perceived *chi*[a] as "middle," although Chu Hsi prefers to understand it as "pole," in line with the Pole Star, or as "ultimate," as the pivot of creative transformation. Tang suggests that Lu's emphasis keeps *chi*[a] within the realm of *yin* and *yang*, maintaining that the ultimate reality, or Tao, dwells in the realm of flux, whereas Chu's interpretation points to his own fundamental belief that the Tao transcends *yin* and *yang*.[66] Mou Tsung-san generally agrees with this etymology but asserts that for Lu Chiu-yüan, the dispute on *Wu-chi* and *T'ai-chi* was less on the subject itself and more of a rebuke to Chu for his philosophical verbosity. Interestingly, Mou even indicates that on the subject of the Great Ultimate being the *Wu-chi*, "Lu Chiu-yüan might not have been right."[67] Here, I presume Mou sees some validity in the need to protect the transcendence of the Great Ultimate through the *via negationis*.

Mou contrasts the vertical or transcendent systems of thought with the horizontal ones. For him, Hu and Lu Chiu-yüan teach more self-transcendence, whereas Chu represents a naturalism with a strong dose of rationalism. He asserts that Chu interprets metaphysical reality only as existing, without any dynamic activity, and in a passive and horizontal system. For him, Chu misinterprets Chou's concept of *T'ai-chi*, reducing it to Ch'eng Yi's *li*[a]. Chu also confuses cognitive and epistemological questions with ethical ones, developing an overly formal and intellectual system that obscures moral metaphysics. Chu's *li*[a] is too much a particular principle of existence or actualization, and not the creativity that it should be. Chu's *hsin*[a] is no creative mind; his *jen*[a] became an abstract principle rather than a mode of creative being.[68]

For example, in opposition to Yen Yüan, Mou criticizes Chu for not really understanding Li T'ung's deeper intentions for meditating, regarding the practice as "empty" cultivation: "[Chu] did not know that within the transcending personal experience resides a transcendent awareness."[69] According to Mou, Chu gradually developed a dislike for anything resembling Ch'an meditation, regarding its goals as "too sublime." From disliking so-called empty conversations, Chu moved away from a truly interior life. Rather, he concentrated on following *jen*[a] as the "character of the mind and the principle of love" and on investigating things and extending knowledge, reducing even this to "book learning."[70]

Mou soundly criticizes Chu for having gone in the wrong direction, turning away from Ch'eng Hao's and Hu Hung's understanding of *Jen*[a] and breaking with Li T'ung's teachings. In very strong language, Mou upbraids Chu for "having placed his emphasis in teaching on extending knowledge and investigating things, rather than on spiritual cultivation, and regarding [cultivation] in terms of emptiness."[71]

In his book *Development and Completion of Chu Hsi's Thought*, Liu Shu-hsien offers appraisals of Chu's philosophy. Following Mou, he invokes Kant, but seems to favor Ernst Cassirer's philosophy of symbolic forms. Liu points out the inadequacy of Chu's moral metaphysics, for not distinguishing clearly between ordinary knowledge and moral knowledge. He also finds shortcomings in Chu's cosmology for lacking a proper scientific basis. But he praises Chu's explanation of evil, his teaching of spiritual cultivation, and his emphasis on political ethics, seeing the latter as having potential to prepare for modern ideas of freedom and democracy.[72]

Without mentioning Mou's name, Ch'ien Mu defends Chu quietly. For example, Ch'ien asserts that it is in opposition to the Buddhist theory of emptiness that Chu emphasizes li^a as real and defines jen^a as the li^a of the mind. For him, Chu remains a follower of Mencius in his broad understanding of mind.[73]

In the West, Chu Hsi was appreciated by Joseph Needham (1900–95) and others because his emphasis on investigation of things and extension of knowledge—the teachings of the *Great Learning*—contributed to a spirit of scientific inquiry.[74] Chu Hsi has also been well served by Wing-tsit Chan (1901–94), who labored tirelessly to make known in English to generations of students and scholars Chu's works and teachings, which he obviously admired.[75]

Conclusion

The list of critics is long. In most cases, the criticisms could be expected. Each critic usually started with a different perspective on reality and used a different starting point in philosophical principle. Often, the methods are completely different, especially in the case of the philologists. Nevertheless, what they have said has some importance because of the influence they have had, especially in the recent centuries and decades.

We should note that both during and after his life, Chu was criticized more often for political than for philosophical reasons. In that sense, concerns of orthodoxy have dominated time and again, even if the orthodoxy itself changed. In these cases, many of the critics had little philosophical stature. Today, we need not take such assessments very seriously. Still, in their own time, some critics had real grounds for their misgivings. Yen, Li, and Tai together pointed out the immense and undeniable Buddhist influence manifest in his thought, an influence without which Chu's system would not exist. We must take this seriously in the name of truth, if not that of orthodoxy. Chu transformed Buddhist ideas and incorporated them into his own system, but without acknowledging them, and even while criticizing Buddhism. Although Yen and Li had antitheoretical prejudices, they were correct in discerning the differences between Chu's teachings and those of Confucius in the sixth century B.C.E.

Modern critics had a different point of departure. Those who attacked both Confucius and Chu Hsi in the earlier part of the twentieth century were unhappy with the patriarchal Confucian social order, with its emphases on ritual and its restrictions on individual liberty. These criticisms were enhanced under Communist rule, when the orthodoxy became Marxism-Leninism-Maoism and increasingly political.

We could say that the critics were often thinkers of an inferior order, and then dismiss them. But that is not altogether fair or useful. Their criticisms contribute to our enhanced understanding and even appreciation of Chu Hsi. For example, quite surprisingly, the voices of criticism, while differently motivated, focused on certain issues, like the priority of li^a over $ch'i^a$ and the negative treatment of human desires. In certain instances, they betray a preference for dialectical materialism. But by attacking Chu for his religious and spiritual concerns, Marxist thinkers confirm the presence of those concerns and their overall importance in Chu's system. For a Western philosopher like Leibniz, these are much appreciated. But for the contemporary thinker Mou Tsung-san, they are regarded as not deep enough.

There is irony, too, in Chu's critical concern for words and their meaning and his tendency to broaden the meaning of words to suit his philosophical interpretation. This occurs especially with the difficult problem of ghosts (*kuei*) and spirits (*shen*[a]). He interpreted the words with ingenuity, if without concern to their semantic etymology: "*Shen*[a] means to stretch (*shen*[b] [a homophone]); *Kuei* means to contract (*ch'ü*)." Referring to the stretching and contracting of *ch'i*[a], he applies it in the first instance to the occurrence of natural phenomena like rain or wind, in the second instance to unusual but still natural phenomena, like sudden storms, attributed to incorrect and evil *kuei-shen*, and in the third instance, *kuei-shen* recover their original meaning, as ghosts and spirits, reached by sacrificial offerings and human prayers (see chapter 3).

There is another dimension that emerges in Chu Hsi's thought as it matured: his growing self-confidence. He was ready, not only to teach his own theories, but also to correct those of his contemporaries and even his predecessors, yes, even the ancient sages, in part through the editing of their texts. This took place in spite of Chu's own reputation as a critical scholar who could discern the authenticity or lack of authenticity of certain ancient texts. Early in life, Chu edited the writings of Hsieh Liang-tso, using generously his editorial privileges in reducing them to size. Chu did it again to Hu Hung, by striking out what he did not like in Hu's texts, in spite of opposition from Chang Shih and Lü Tsu-ch'ien, who counseled respect for textual integrity. In the end, his edition of Hu's *Understanding Words* (*Chih-yen*) also became the established edition.[76] Possibly, he changed the wording of the first line in Chou Tun-yi's explanatory text to the *Diagram of the Great Ultimate*, to ensure greater philosophical consistency in his own exposition. He moved to the editing of the writings attributed to the sages, especially the text of the *Great Learning*, publishing the Four Books with his commentaries and textual changes in 1190. In reflecting on Chu as textual editor, I could not help seeing a certain affinity between him and Lu Chiu-yüan, who referred to the classics as his "footnotes."[77] Chu was ingenious in bending words and texts to his interpretations. Yet, he depended on these same words and texts for their authority. He differed from Lu Chiu-yüan to the extent that he *also* believed in, and taught, the importance of textual study and of the path of knowledge and inquiry. Here, too, in a strange way, Chu sought to maintain a certain balance between manipulating the given texts and yet respecting them as a heritage to be preserved and studied.

Every thinker is vulnerable to criticism. Chu Hsi's overarching and comprehensive system exposes him all the more to criticisms from every side. This is inevitable, and a further testimony to his real contributions. But these disagreements have not yet stimulated anyone to replace his system with a better one of the same architectonic scale. This fact should help us put in perspective the philosophical criticisms themselves.

Chu Hsi's Relevance

The meaning to be savored is limitless. [The *Doctrine of the Mean*]
is full of real learning (*shih-hsüeh*). The good reader will make
discoveries by meditating on it and retain something for use
throughout life without ever exhausting its wealth.

Chu Hsi[1]

Introduction: Orthodoxy and Relevance

Long before Chu Hsi's system was declared state orthodoxy, Chu himself asserted his inheritance of the true mantle of the ancient sages, which had been lost since Mencius but was rediscovered by Chou Tun-yi and the Ch'eng brothers.[2] He speaks of this in several places, being the first person to refer to the "orthodox line of the Tao" (*Tao-t'ung*).[3] Especially in his preface to the annotated edition of the *Doctrine of the Mean*, he offers Tzu-ssu, Confucius's grandson, as author of the *Doctrine of the Mean*. It was compiled, according to him, to safeguard Confucius's spiritual legacy, derived from the ancient sage-kings:[4]

> This was passed to Mencius, who was able to elaborate on what this text teaches and continue the transmission of the earlier sages. But after his death the transmission was lost. . . . The disciples of Lao-tzu and the Buddha emerged, with a teaching that is close to ours, and so confused the truth. Fortunately, this book survived, and the Ch'eng brothers were able to rely on it, to resume the transmission interrupted by [over] a thousand years, and have the support to rebuke Taoists and Buddhists for their incorrect teachings that so resembled the correct.[5]

As an orthodoxy, Chu's system represented perennial truth, as did Aquinas's for the Catholic Church. But orthodoxies change with political climates, while the question of relevance remains. So the question has arisen time and again: are Chu's ideas and values still relevant in our own times? This question gathered steam in China especially during recent decades, when his influence was waning and a new orthodoxy in the form of Marxism-Leninism-Maoism held sway.

Chu Hsi's Core Thinking

By the core of Chu's teaching, I refer to its heart, that by which it lives and in-spires. Chu Hsi points out Mencius as the crucial figure in his line of transmission of the orthodox Confucian Way. Although the *Book of Mencius* is an important text in this transmission, the text that appears even more important is the *Doctrine of the Mean*, which allegedly came from Tzu-ssu, Confucius's grandson, regarded as Mencius's teacher. Chu gives his own role regarding the text of the *Doctrine of the Mean* in these words:

> From an early age, I was instructed in this text but privately doubted [its importance]. Reflecting on it for many years, one day I suddenly felt as though I got its essential message and so dared to put together the theories of many and harmonize them. In this way, I completed one volume of an annotated edition.[6]

The *Doctrine of the Mean* presents emotional equilibrium and harmony as its core teaching. As pointed out in chapter 5, the term "Mean" refers to the moral mind, *tao-hsin*, that the ancient sages passed on to one another, from mind-and-heart to mind-and-heart. This is what Confucius, Mencius, and their true disciples received in a disposition of reverence and caution lest they spoil or lose it on account of human frailty.

All in all, we are speaking more of a spiritual message than a dispassionate and rational formulation of philosophical truth. The very *personal*, even secret, character of the transmission strengthens this opinion. Obviously, there is Ch'an Buddhist influence in the idea of a transmission that takes place outside "established teaching" (*chiao-wai*). This is alluded to in Chu's poetry. I offer an example:

> When the ink leaves the lines you're reading,
> You'll see the "mind" passed down outside the teaching (*chiao-wai hsin*).
> This is our family's true treasure:
> No need to covet a full basket of gold.[7]

The implication is *to read between the lines*, to grasp that moral mind, passed down from long ago, outside the established teaching. This refers to the extraordinary mode of transmission, from mind-and-heart to mind-and-heart rather than from words and texts. To emphasize this is not to deny Chu Hsi's status as a philosopher. Rather, I am emphasizing the spiritual character of his philosophical discoveries. As we know from chapter 6, Chu moved from an old to a new theory of psychic equilibrium and harmony, based on the *Doctrine of the Mean*, after reading Ch'eng Yi. He begins his philosophy with the Great Ultimate and concerns of cosmology, but he builds it very much on these central teachings of equilibrium and harmony, as well as on related methods of personal and spiritual cultivation.

There is the other question of the line of transmission itself. According to Chu, Chou Tun-yi and the Ch'eng brothers resumed Mencius's transmission of the

Confucian Tao. However, there is plenty of evidence that Chou Tun-yi, Chang Tsai, and the Ch'eng brothers did not pass on the same teaching. Chou's place in history came from Chu, not from the Ch'engs. But even their—especially Ch'eng Yi's—place in history also came largely from Chu's establishment of the "orthodox line of transmission," which, historically speaking, is more fiction than fact. Chu needed to appeal to authority, and he built up the moral authority of Chou and the Ch'engs to enhance his own teachings. He needed Chou because of his cosmology and the transcendent *T'ai-chi*, and he depended on Ch'eng Yi and even Chang Tsai—whose cosmology he basically rejected—for his own metaphysics and theory of human nature.

This does not mean that Chu was arbitrary in choosing his inheritance from the past. He weighed the issues, even struggled with them, for many years, waiting for insights while reading ceaselessly. As Chu himself said in the preface to the annotated edition of the *Doctrine of the Mean*, he mediated between his intellectual predecessors, "putting together the theories of many and harmonizing them," before coming to a final judgment as to what he accepted.[8]

We cannot forget the Buddhist and Taoist influences on Chu's thought, which would be pointed out especially by his critics in the Ch'ing dynasty. Taoist concerns served as a stimulus to his thinking, especially his cosmological thinking, and Taoist methods of yoga or breath circulation assisted him in his efforts to maintain health. Nevertheless, Taoist influences helped to expand his thinking without affecting too much the structure of his thought. This is where Buddhist influences came into play. His metaphysics of within and without, of *Li*[a] being one with many manifestations, of *li*[a] and *ch'i*[a] as the structural concepts tying together his entire system, all reflect a profound influence from Chinese Buddhism, starting from the fifth-century Seng Chao, the disciple of Kumārajīva, through the T'ien-t'ai and Hua-yen schools, and especially as all is summed up in Ch'an.

A thinker with a mission, Chu wanted to rebuild Confucian thinking in his image and likeness. He did so with the help of the philosophies of Chou, Chang, and Ch'eng Yi, selecting what suited his own ideas and inclinations. He established a new canon in the Four Books and sought to pass on his teaching through his commentaries on these works, as well as on the other thinkers who were his chosen predecessors. We need to acknowledge that he placed great value on spiritual truths.

Chu Hsi's Method of Thinking

Chu Hsi's philosophy flows from the Great Ultimate, or supreme *li*[a], his one comprehensive principle that determines the form of his entire philosophy. We may repeat with him: "*Li*[a] is one but its manifestations are many." This is his way of resolving the problem of the one and the many, by regarding the one as interior and latent (*wei*), and also as reality per se (*t'i*), and the many as exterior and manifest (*hsien*) or as functioning reality (*yung*). If he goes on to speak of *ch'i*[a], it is to give manifest shape to *li*[a] rather than to render reality dualistic.[9] So far, everything seems straightforward, except to recall that the Great Ultimate also represents the movement of reversal of the Tao in an ongoing creative process in which *yin* and *yang*, rest and motion, alternate. But this is more implicit than explicit, and Chu insists that the Great Ultimate remains somehow transcendent.

All this goes to say that Chu Hsi's method tends to be dialectical, as he attempts to unite seemingly opposing ideas, integrating them into a higher unity. He frequently proceeds with dialogues, whether in his *Classified Conversations* or through correspondence, as in his defense of Chou Tun-yi's statement that the *Wu-chi* is also the *T'ai-chi*. Always interacting with a diversity of views and opinions, he seeks to incorporate as much as possible into his own eclectic system. In doing so, he is not shy about emending words and texts to render the meaning more suitable to his own purposes.

Chu's perspective of reality is diaphanous, regarding all things as manifestations of a greater, transcendent reality. He usually makes immanent what is transcendent, so that he also sees reality as "essentialist," that is, accepting the reality of particular things on the strength of their particular *li*[a]. If this appears unusual, we should remember the indelible Ch'an Buddhist influence which strengthens his dialectical logic and helps him to go beyond the subject-object opposition. Besides, to the extent that particular things are manifestations of the greater *Li*[a], I return to the recognition of a great noumenon behind all phenomena. The problem is complex, as this noumenon, the Great Ultimate, is not just an unmoved Mover. It is the source and origin, as well as an inherent part of the cosmic process of change and transformation. However, Chu spent more time and energy defending the Great Ultimate as the source of all things than he did in arguing for it as part of flux itself. Indeed, if we take the immanence of the Great Ultimate as indicative of the diaphanous character of flux, revealing a transcendent principle behind all, then we are once more back where we began, with a noumenal interpretation of reality.

My difficulties with analyzing Chu's philosophical principle and methodology have to do with who Chu was: a man and a thinker of his time. He used the scholarly and philosophical tools of his time to pursue knowledge and understanding. His method of thinking belongs to medieval China, not the modern West. Certain differences are easier to explain when we remember that in English, the word "mind" has only an intellectual reference. In Chinese, as noted in chapter 5, the equivalent word, *hsin*[a], has a much broader range of meanings, as both mind and heart, since it not only thinks but also feels and even wills. The word "enlightenment" also has a different meaning in the East. For the westerner, it usually refers to scientific rationalism overcoming the darkness of medieval ignorance. For the Chinese, it has to do with a mystical breakthrough that is an experience of the whole self, not just of the mind.[10] In Chu Hsi's case, many moderns (including Joseph Needham) regard him as a rationalist and hail his "investigation of things" as representing a scientific spirit. That may be so, but not entirely. Chu is a rationalist, to the extent that he prefers reason to blind faith. But he is also a seeker of the Confucian Tao. Fung Yu-lan points out that Chu intends the investigation of things to be a method of personal cultivation rather than of scientific inquiry.[11] Indeed, it is the inadequacy of this method for reaching sagehood that has drawn the wrath of critics like Mou Tsung-san.

The twentieth-century philosopher Ho Lin asserts that Chu's love of learning also shows something of a scientific spirit. Ho says Chu's method of investigating things, aimed at acquiring *li*[a], has a strong intellectual component even if the goal is to understand the mind in its entire substance (*ch'üan-t'i*), that is, as the Great Ultimate, and in its "large function" (*ta-yung*), directing behavior with *li*[a]. And the final goal of these efforts is always personal cultivation, the ordering of the family and the state, and giving peace to the world—to cite the words of the *Great Learning*.[12] So Chu's truth is spiritual truth, the truth that inspires human hearts, the knowledge of the norm or value of things, which is attained through intuition or moral and spiritual sensibility.

Intuition suggests immediacy, the immediate knowledge of concepts without inference. It seems strange to speak therefore of "intuitive reasoning" except to point out that immediate apprehension of truths may be followed by some form of rational thinking. This is more comprehensible to us today with the discoveries of how the brain works, for example, in so-called waves, as those propelling intuition and others driving reason come very close together. In this context, we may better understand Chu's parable comparing knowing to awaking from sleep:

> When our mind-and-heart is not clear and bright, we may be compared to someone in deep sleep, who doesn't even know he has a body. He has to be awakened to know this. . . . I see that the essential task is in awakening. So in these things, in order to understand, we must have experience.[13]

The essential task is in awakening. Knowledge follows. The whole person awakens, but the awakened mind thinks better. This is what I mean by "intuitive reasoning," a reasoning that follows intuition. It is like faith coming first in Western theology, followed by reasoning, explaining what can be explained. Ho Lin calls this kind of cognitive experience "intellectual sympathy."[14]

Presumably, it is this intellectual sympathy for the truth at hand, as preserved in the sacred texts, that assists in understanding the message of the sages, in an experiential process that is both illuminating and transformative. When light comes, the person feels as though he or she is awakening from slumber and wonders at his or her own earlier dullness, as Chu Hsi did before he arrived at several of his important positions regarding emotional equilibrium and harmony and the important role of reverence in self-cultivation.

But then, what value have such intuitions, whether into the nature of truth or wisdom itself or into the ways by which this may be acquired? If Chu Hsi has his own conclusions, based on such intuitive reasoning, so does Lu Chiu-yüan, based on his—even if the two thinkers do not entirely operate along the same lines in such reasoning. Their conclusions are not the same and are difficult to verify because they are based in large part on experience, which varies from individual to individual. We need more objective norms as a basis for making judgments of relevance.

The Constant (*Ch'ang*) and the Varying (*Pien*): The Teachings

In Confucius's *Analects* 9:29, we find this passage, which appears, at first sight, to be about how to judge human nature:

> Someone good enough as a fellow student may not be suitable as a fellow traveler in the pursuit of the [moral] Way; someone suitable as such a fellow traveler may not be suitable as a collaborator in a common stand [taken in particular circumstances]; someone suitable to be this may not be the right partner in the exercise of moral discretion (*ch'üan*).[15]

The intended meaning here is not transparent. The impression is that various pursuits require different kinds of people, with the implied lesson being the importance of judging character. For centuries, however, commentators have focused on the last words: *moral discretion*, also translated as "the morally expedient."[16] The master appears to think that the exercise of this characteristic is difficult.

In the Kung-yang commentary to the Spring and Autumn Annals, it is said, "The expedient is that which, while opposed to the norm (*ching*b), is good." We have here the polarity between the norm or standard and the expedient or the variant, a polarity that demonstrates the recognition in Confucian thought of moral conflicts requiring resolution according to circumstances.

The "expedient" (*ch'üan*) is a term that has aroused much discussion through the ages. In conventional usage, it may refer to a scale that determines weights, with the extended meaning of the mental power of weighing moral issues, and also of exercising power. According to the Han lexicon, the *Shuo-wen*, the word, with a wood radical, has among other meanings that of being opposed to the constant.[17] The norm or standard (*ching*b), on the other hand, refers etymologically to the warp of a fabric and is used to refer to classical texts because of their normative value. In other words, while the classics, attributed to the sages as authors, contain sublime moral values to be treasured and lived by, these are not absolute values. Depending on circumstances, moral discretion may be required in seeking to apply their teachings.

But interpreters of the classical texts and their commentaries have not spoken in unison. Chu Hsi's predecessor Ch'eng Yi asserted that the expedient does not differ from the norm, standard, or constant. This means a rejection of the expedient and support for what may be called "absolute morality."[18]

But Tung Chung-shu, the great Han Confucian, had said before him: "although the expedient is at variance with the norm, it must be within the scope of what can be allowed. . . . The expedient is a tactful measure. It would be better if we can return to the norm."[19] And so, if the norm remains the usual measure, the expedient may have to serve in unusual situations.

Chu Hsi appears to have hesitated in deciding whether such a distinction should be made. In explaining the *Analects*, he repeats Ch'eng Yi's commentary, but he has also diverged from it. For him, the norm and the expedient are both subordinate to a higher moral norm: the transcendent Way, or Tao. In some circumstances, it is even possible for the expedient to be closer to the Way.[20]

In his recorded conversations, Chu articulated his preference for the views of Tung Chung-shu, while also defending what he thought to be Ch'eng Yi's intentions. "That which is at variance with the norm and complies with the Way is called the expedient," citing the Han scholar.[21] Chu asserts that "the norm is the constant principle and the expedient is the varying principle when the constant . . . does not work."[22] This does not mean he supports a relativist morality. It does mean that he is for flexibility and adaptability: "Ch'eng Yi said the expedient is nothing other than the norm. This teaching is more dead than alive [i.e., not flexible]. What I say is not to contradict him but to make distinctions for him."[23]

Paradigmatic Examples

Moving to examples, I shall choose a few that I call paradigmatic because they discuss cases drawn from classical sources, and because they have been discussed over and over again by a number of philosophers through the centuries. In the first example, we have a dialogue between the fifth-century-B.C.E. Mencius and his "Sophist" interlocutor about the ritual law governing gender relations:

> "Don't the rites prescribe that in giving and receiving, man and woman should not touch each other?"
> "Yes, they do," Mencius answered.
> "Then: if one's sister-in-law is drowning, should one extend a hand to help her?"[24]

The conflict here is obvious. Ordinarily, a brother may not touch his sister-in-law. But what if her life is in danger and he can make a difference? Which is more important: the ritual law or her life? With his characteristic emphasis, Mencius replied:

> "He who doesn't help a drowning sister-in-law is an animal [literally, a wolf]. The rites prescribe that men and women not touch each other in giving or receiving. But extending a helping hand to a drowning sister-in-law is an exercise of moral discretion (*ch'üan*)."[25]

Chu's comment is in favor of Mencius's decision: "he who extends his hand to save his drowning sister-in-law is exercising *the expedient*." He agrees that while ritual law stipulates that a brother should not touch a sister-in-law, a higher law compels him to save her from drowning by removing her physically from the danger.

This case of saving a drowning woman is clear in regard to the possible choices: between a moral obligation and a simply ritual one. But another oft-cited case is less clear. Taken from the classics, it is about the legendary Shun marrying the daughters of Emperor Yao without first telling his own parents, who were most probably opposed to the union. The story is not historical and may be mythical.

Shun was *the* filial son, ever loyal to his blind father in spite of the deadly machinations of a wicked stepmother and a spoiled stepbrother. He was summoned to court by an emperor attracted to filial virtue, who promptly offered him the two princesses in marriage. Eventually, he would be given the throne as well.

Ritual law prescribes that the son at least request parental permission before marrying. In fact, in traditional families parents arranged the marriages of their children. In Shun's case, it would appear that his parents had neglected to do so for him. Here, the higher good, which refers to moral law, lies in the production of progeny to continue the family line and the veneration of ancestors. Generations of Confucian thinkers excused Shun's seemingly unfilial behavior in the choice of wives by referring to such. It could be added that Shun was also obeying the wishes of his sovereign.

My problem is that the production of progeny for the protection of the family line and the ancestral cult is not so obviously the reason for marriage here— certainly not today. Today, children who marry without parental permission do so rather in the name of their own autonomy as individuals looking for happiness, as well as of a greater loyalty to each other than to the parents.

Of course, it could be that Shun himself felt like the children today who do not request parental permission. We have no evidence to the contrary. We are only judging the case as Chu Hsi did before us, in approving Shun's action. It would appear that the higher reason Chu gave for disobeying ritual law in this case is itself a ritual obligation rather than a moral one. In other words, this is no constant norm.

The importance, though, is that he made such a distinction: between a higher and a lower loyalty, between the constant and the varying. Chu sought to reform ancient rituals for his own times. This distinction between the standard and the expedient, or the constant norm and changing circumstances, was the leading inspiration for him as a thinker and reformer, without which he could not have made his mark on the history of Chinese thought and culture.

On the other hand, Chu describes this as an exceptional case. It should not be made into a standard norm, or else everyone might marry without notifying their parents and so disturb the conventional moral law governing filial piety. The same, of course may be said about the ruler-subject relationship, where obedience is usually expected of the subject but exceptions may occur.[26]

Here, we can return to the dialogue in Mencius about saving the drowning sister-in-law. It appears that Mencius's interlocutor had another reason to question him besides the conflict between ritual and morals. The conversation continues as follows: "Now the whole world is drowning. Why is it that you, Master, are not helping it?"[27] The meaning is more obscure. The interlocutor is turning to analogy to ask why Mencius isn't "helping a drowning world." He seems preoccupied either with Mencius's not doing anything personal, such as taking a personal stand on certain issues (to return to *Analects* 9:29) and, perhaps, finding partners to do so, or with criticizing Mencius for somehow neglecting a higher good in confining himself to teaching moral principles rather than participating in political action.

Mencius's answer seems ironic and even irritated. "When your sister-in-law is drowning, you help her with your hands. When the whole world is drowning, you help it with the Way. Do you expect me to help the world with my hands?"[28] There is a contrast of hands and the Way, giving priority to the Way.

Here Chu Hsi comes to our rescue, to enlighten us with the context:

> [The interlocutor is saying that] with the world in chaos, and the people's suffering comparable to drowning, you cannot just abide by the correct Way of the ancient kings. . . .
>
> The drowning world can only be saved by the moral Way. But you would have me violate such and seek a compromise, thus losing the means by which the world might be rescued. . . .
>
> This chapter says that to keep personal integrity and abide by the Way is the means by which one may save the times. To go against the Way and sacrifice human lives is only to lose oneself.[29]

We are now moving from a discussion of the private realm of saving a family member from drowning to a discussion of political participation. According to Chu Hsi, Mencius's answer is adamant: personal integrity comes first. The follower of Confucius may try to help save the world only if he does not compromise important principles. There is no question of adaptation or compromise here, as there can be with ritual law.

Answers from Chu Hsi

As mentioned, Chu Hsi makes a philosophical distinction between a metaphysical world "above shapes" made up of li^a and a world "within shapes" dependent upon $ch'i^a$ (energy). Chu's metaphysics inevitably affected his theory of gender, as well as of history and politics.

On Gender

First of all, the superiority of men over women was considered a "constant principle" by Chu Hsi and others throughout most of China's history. It flows from the analogy between Heaven's superiority and Earth's lowliness, as derived from the *Great Commentary to the Book of Changes*: "Heaven is high, Earth is low . . . / Inferior and superior places are established."[30] Chu Hsi has this to say: "There is a natural order of hierarchy. That is why when they are alive, the husband may have a wife and also concubines, while the wife is not permitted two [spouses], as her [husband is to her] like Heaven is [to Earth]."[31] I now quote from his *Chinssu lu*: "Between man and woman, there is an order of superiority and inferiority, and between husband and wife, there is the principle of who leads and who follows. This is a constant principle."[32] Male superiority is therefore a "*constant principle*," which Chu did not envisage would change with circumstances, because it is based on a higher, ontological order.

Of course, within the framework of Confucian thinking, the individual was always regarded as a member of a much more important, larger group, be that family or society. The gender question therefore was part of a larger complex of questions involving the "five relationships," namely, husband and wife, father and son, ruler and subject, elder and younger sibling, and friend and friend.[33] Although the relationships call for reciprocity, they also posit the presence of a senior and superior partner as a constant principle. From this perspective, Chu Hsi's philosophy has no place for political democracy either. But of course, we should not expect that a twelfth-century Chinese thinker would be receptive to such thinking.

Chu Hsi was twice in southern Fukien: the first time, as a young man of twenty-two, as a magistrate in T'ung-an Prefecture in Ch'üan-chou, for three years (1153–56); the second time, as prefect of Chang-chou (1190–91), for about a year. Although his total sojourn was not long, the influence he exerted on the morals and customs there was strong. And this included customs regarding women and marriage. It appears that the local people in T'ung-an, for example, were choosing their own partners and practicing cohabitation. This displeased Chu Hsi, who decided to put an end to such customs:

> The ritual and legal texts place emphasis on marriage. It is what differentiates men from women, regularizes the relationship between husband and wife, rectifies the customs, and prevents the beginnings of disorders and disasters. I hear that this prefecture has not had a tradition of marriage rituals. The people in the alleys and neighborhoods who are too poor to be able to make betrothal gifts often practice elopement and call it "getting a companion as wife." This has become a tradition, so much so that even the educated and the rich sometimes do it without scruple or anxiety. Such illicit acts not only transgress the rituals and ceremonies and the laws of the land but also give rise to jealousies which could cause violence, leading sometimes to death.[34]

In his third year in T'ung-an, Chu Hsi forbade these practices and appealed to higher officials to enforce marriage rituals. According to the local gazetteer, he even made sure that women only appeared in public with their faces covered.

Obviously, thinkers like Chu Hsi did not find women to be men's intellectual equals. Where personal qualities are concerned, they also regarded women as being too emotional. There is, however, no evidence that they considered women as being less than human, as incapable, for example, of understanding and acting according to moral principles.[35] Indeed, with hindsight, we might say today that men expected much more of women than of themselves. Perhaps, this remains true even today.

We know Chu's positions on gender relations, particularly his approval of polygamy and disapproval of cohabitation without marriage and of women's public roles.[36] Indeed, female chastity and faithfulness to one spouse became such an overriding virtue in that region that many women committed suicide after their husbands' deaths or preferred death to being raped. The gazetteer gives honorable mention to these "virtuous women."[37]

On Political Conduct

Sage-kings are presumed to have ruled in China's past. They are also supposed to return, after long intervals. Mencius was pained by the absence of any sage-king after seven hundred years of Chou rule.[38] Han scholars were also puzzled by the fact that Confucius, the sage par excellence, was never king. In order to lend more credence to the doctrine of Heaven's mandate, they gave him the unique honor of having been "uncrowned king" (*su-wang*) and even made him the founder of a fictitious dynasty.[39] Before him Tung Chung-shu had already postulated Confucius's foundation, by heavenly mandate, of a fictitious dynasty of Lu through his compilation of his Spring and Autumn Annals, in which he passed moral judgments on historical rulers.[40]

It has indeed been the irony of history that no king or emperor of the Han dynasty or after should have been "sage," even if every dynasty sought to provide itself with fictitious ancestral lines claiming descent from some sage-king of antiquity. While it is true that certain sages of antiquity were not kings but ministers, such as Yi-yin and the duke of Chou, they were ministers to sage-kings—King T'ang of Shang and King Wu of Chou—who had received the mandate for themselves and their families. What seems inconceivable is the withholding of the mandate from sages like Confucius and Mencius in a time of real decadence when a sage could have done so much good as a ruler.

Chu's personal uninvolvement in politics does not mean that he considered political life irrelevant for the seeker of sageliness. Far from it. There is reason to think that he aspired to high political office, although he never attained it. And there is clear evidence of political thinking in his philosophy. Chu also developed the theory of an ideal polity, which is to be found in the remote past—the Golden Age of sage-kings. According to him, such a state of bliss may be restored, not by reverting to outmoded institutions but by the ruler's attention to his own duty of self-cultivation and to the careful selection of ministers who share these concerns. However, Chu himself was never selected for high office.

With his metaphysics of li^a and $ch'i^a$, Chu also draws an opposition between T'ien-li (heavenly principle) and jen-yü (human passions) in his dualistic interpretation of antiquity and modernity. He speaks of antiquity, represented by the pre-Ch'in age of "kings," as the age dominated by the heavenly principle, and the post-Ch'in age of "tyrants" as dominated by human passions or caprice. The best days of the glorious dynasties of Han and T'ang are included in the second category, in the time when the way of virtue was forgotten. His avowed aim was therefore to restore to society and human consciousness the lost "Way" of Confucian virtue, including Confucian political virtues: a government by moral suasion.

This dichotomy, with its implicit condemnation of all of history after the three dynasties of Hsia, Shang, and Chou (ended 249 B.C.E.), aroused the dissatisfaction of Ch'en Liang (1143–93), the advocate of pragmatic statesmanship. Ch'en disputed with Chu on this subject in a series of letters. Ch'en was an admirer of the institutions of Han and T'ang, in particular of the political and military achievements of Emperors Kao-tsu (r. 206–195 B.C.E.) and T'ai-tsung (r. 626–49).

He considered that their ways of governing the country were fundamentally correct, that is, "kingly," although they might be said to have mingled certain principles of "tyranny" with those of "kingliness."[41]

Chu Hsi remained unmoved by such arguments. For him, the morality of "means" was just as important as that of "ends," and the latter could never be used to justify the former. Besides, success was no criterion in the judgment of a ruler's moral character, which should be analyzed solely in terms of motivations. Famous rulers like the Han dynastic founder and the second T'ang emperor were both ruthless in the pursuit of power. The T'ang emperor, a younger son, killed two siblings to ensure his own imperial succession. Chu found such action abominable:

> In the case of Emperor Kao-tsu of Han, the selfish motive might not have been so manifest, but you cannot deny its presence. In the case of Emperor T'ai-tsung of T'ang, his actions were certainly motivated by human passion. . . . If his rightness is justified merely on the grounds that he left the world in a long period of peace and order, this would be to define rightness in terms of success. . . . You should use your enthusiasm to appreciate the work of men who lived up to the standards of the Three Dynasties and not waste your time in the defense of Han and T'ang dynasties.[42]

That Chu Hsi objected to praising the two great emperors of Han and T'ang on the ground of their despotic actions and moral transgressions is evident from what he said to Ch'en in another letter.[43] Admitting that Emperor Kao-tsu's treatment of the conquered population of Ch'in had been correct and generous, he criticized the continuation of certain penal measures which the Han dynasty had inherited from the preceding period, as well as Emperor Kao-tsu's cruelty and disloyalty toward those of his ministers who had assisted him in gaining the throne. Emperor T'ai-tsung was similarly criticized for his transgressions of the principles of moral relationships, especially those governing the family.

Holding high the norm of sageliness to judge the character of past rulers, Chu Hsi said: "The sage is like the gold of gold. Those who seek sagehood without achieving it have yet some iron in their gold. And [some] . . . are only iron. Emperors and kings are no different."[44]

While he upheld that the same moral principles should prevail in the present as in the past, Chu did not propose the reestablishment of political feudalism or of the well-field system. According to him, the sage may not always act in the same way were he to live in different epochs. In his own time, circumstances were such that a restoration of past institutions would cause more harm than good:

> Feudalism and the well-field system were instituted by the sage-kings in order to share the world with all. How dare I consider that as not good? Yet, given our situation today, I fear it is difficult to restore these institutions. If we should enforce such a restoration, I fear, too, that other evils will arise which we cannot predict, and so things will become worse than they are, and even more difficult to manage.[45]

Did philosophers like Chu really consider it possible to restore the golden past? Certainly, this must have been a question that often occupied their minds. Perhaps, it might be better to ask first: what were the conditions that could make such a restoration possible? The answer would be: when the ruler becomes a sage, or when the sage becomes a ruler. However, sage-rulers only existed in remote antiquity and have not been heard of since, as the distinction between the age of kingliness or principle of Heaven and that of tyranny or selfish desire makes clear. For the philosophers, the hope lay either in converting the ruler into a sage or in becoming the ruler's chief minister, assisting him in the government of the country and also in the rectification of his own mind-and-heart! However, neither of these alternatives was ever achieved. It is, therefore, to the credit of Chu and others that they never gave up hoping that the utopia might still be restored.

Chu Hsi and other philosophers spoke on two levels whenever they discussed utopian theories. These existed as moral ideals, not as immediate, practical goals. Their proximate aim was not to overthrow the existing social order and to inaugurate a new form of social organization but to transform the status quo from within—from within the hearts of men, especially the hearts of rulers. That was why many memorials, even those written by scholars who did not claim to be philosophers, often began by referring to the Three Dynasties, to Yao and Shun, or at least to Confucius. It was essential that the moral ideals—or, in some cases, the purported moral ideals—be expressed, in order that the scholars might get a hearing by presenting themselves within the safe boundaries of orthodoxy. But once this had been done, they were free to propose almost any kind of reform they desired, be that the reform of the sovereign's private life or that of tax-farming, provided, of course, that they also had the courage to suffer for their views, in case those views did not please the imperial ears.

The Applications

Besides a distinction between the constant and the varying, there is also a difference between beliefs and their applications. Chu Hsi displays more flexibility when it comes to practice or application of his norms, even after having taken into consideration moral discretion in modifying such norms.

On Gender

Actually, in their own lifetimes, neither Ch'eng Yi nor Chu Hsi was rigid in applying in real life their convictions regarding women's role in marriage. Ch'eng Yi mentioned his own father having arranged the remarriage of a widowed niece in order to lessen her mother's sorrow. This implies Ch'eng's lack of disapproval.[46] Chu Hsi commented on the contradiction between this situation and Ch'eng Yi's proscription against the remarriage of widows. "There is the question of a norm. But people cannot always live up to it."[47] The expedient, therefore, is permitted not only when it is considered to be a better choice than the norm but also when it is a realistic alternative to an unachievable ideal.

In one case, a woman was granted permission by the local magistrate to accede to the wishes of her parents and return to her parental home. The reason was that her husband was too poor to support her. A disciple of Chu Hsi's criticized this official decision. But Chu responded: "If the husband is not capable . . . of supporting his wife, and the wife has no means to support herself, what can one do? In a case like this, one should not be bound by great moral principles."[48] Chu shows here real flexibility, supporting the reciprocal character of the conjugal relationship. He is asserting that a wife should not always act like a martyr. On the other hand, it is interesting that the disciple should be more rigid than the master. This is indicative of the increasing rigidity that would develop after Sung times.

In discussing the remarriage of widows, we should keep in mind the parallel problem of the remarriage of widowers. Here, the opinions voiced were actually just as parallel. Widowers were permitted to marry only as a concession to the needs of the family, rather than as an individual right. Chang Tsai refers to the fact that only one husband and one wife were buried together and received sacrifice together but then explains:

When the two first married, they made no arrangement of remarrying. Hence, the husband should marry only one wife, and the wife should marry only one husband. Nowadays, when a woman loses her husband to death, it is like a great virtue of Heaven and Earth that she not be permitted to remarry. But why should the husband also remarry? When we calculate the priorities, we see that things like the support of parents and the maintenance of the family and its sacrifices cannot be discontinued. Thus, remarriage is permitted [to the husband].[49]

Ch'eng Yi did not favor widowers' remarrying either, although he allowed it. He too asserted a certain ritual equality of the sexes in this matter. What he said echoes Chang Tsai's words: "At the time that the couple marry, how can they promise that should one die first, the other could remarry . . . ? What they promise is only that the two will remain married all their lives."[50]

We are referring here to marrying another "first wife." Men always had the right to take concubines, outside marriage rites. Thus, there is a formal equality between husband and wife, with the understanding that the husband may have secondary wives who remain her inferiors as well as his.

Remarriage is permitted to the husband out of tolerance, or expediency, rather than as a moral norm. Where the widow is concerned, Ch'eng Yi is remembered for having said that, in principle, it is better to starve than to remarry, which is what Chu Hsi has reiterated. After all, "To starve to death is a very small matter, but to lose one's virtue is a very serious matter."[51] This was said in answer to a question regarding whether a man should marry a widow. Chu's answer was: "to marry is to take a mate to oneself. To take as mate someone who has lost virtue is to lose virtue oneself."[52]

This means, among other things, that men are discouraged from marrying widows.[53] In actual fact, neither Ch'eng Yi nor Chu Hsi was rigid in applications.

For example, Ch'eng Yi remarked that while a husband may divorce his wife when she is judged to be "not good," a divorced woman's serious faults should not be made public in order not to make it impossible for her to remarry. Indeed, Ch'eng Yi quoted an ancient saying: "When divorcing a wife, one should make it possible for her to remarry."[54]

Presumably, a divorced woman no longer owes loyalty to her husband and is therefore permitted to remarry. Presumably also, she might have to remarry in order "not to starve." But she is not a widow.[55] Chu Hsi took Ch'eng Yi's ideas seriously enough to write to a disciple to urge him to counsel his widowed younger sister not to remarry:

> [L]et her understand that [just as when a dynasty falls,] the minister must remain loyal, so too . . . the widow must remain chaste. . . . From the popular point of view, this is truly unrealistic, but in the eyes of a gentleman who knows the classics and understands principles, this is something that cannot change.[56]

Note here once more the important parallel drawn between a widow's remarriage and the disloyalty of a government official to his ruler. As Wang Fu (1692–1759) has commented: "If a woman sacrifices her virtue because of fear of hunger, how different is she from the minister who surrenders to the enemy because of fear of battle?"[57]

There appears no doubt that the increasing subjugation of women by men from Sung times on was based on philosophical presuppositions going back to classical times. The contributing cause for the strengthening of these philosophical beliefs appears to have been the unhappiness of intellectuals with the period of disorder and instability that immediately preceded the Sung, which witnessed a decline of authority and moral values in general, especially family values. Confucian scholars were not all so rigid; in an earlier period, several leading scholars showed an astonishing flexibility on such questions as the remarriage of widows. But the philosophers contributed to the tendency toward rigidity in their revival of interest in such texts as the Book of Changes and in their insistence on Confucian ritualism.

What we might today call the assault on women's position in society can be much better understood when we see it in the context of the general trend to strengthen authority: the authority of the ruler vis-à-vis the minister, as well as the authority of the husband vis-à-vis the wife. Like other Sung philosophers, Chu regarded himself as tightening the moral fiber of Sung society in the face of perceived threats from the negative examples of the T'ang dynasty and the time that followed, especially the Five Dynasties period. In opting for the strengthening of the ruler-minister bond, he and others were also seeking to improve their own social position. Chu was often in disagreement with the government on various issues. But he basically supported the authority of the state and perceived himself as a potential or actual advisor to the rulers.

Here, it is interesting to speak a little about social rituals distinguishing men and women. Chu Hsi was asked, for example, why women of his times did not have to prostrate themselves to guests. Instead, they performed "curtsies," either bending their knees or even lowering their hands to the floor while kneeling, but without lowering their heads. His answer was that they wore too much jewelry in their hair! Perhaps other reasons include their being less of a physical threat as potential assassins. The men often had to humiliate themselves more: to lower their heads to the floor as well, especially in front of the ruler.[58]

It appears that in antiquity, rulers also returned their ministers' bows or prostrations, as husbands returned their wives', and parents-in-law their daughters-in-law's. In Han times, rulers would stand up when their prime ministers arrived. Even in T'ang times, ministers sat while conversing with rulers. But by Chu's day, the prime minister had to remain standing while speaking, and men no longer treated women like near-equals.[59]

In discussing these changes, Chu appears to favor the older customs. However, the degradation of the scholar-minister would continue after his times. In Ming times, ministers were further humiliated, sometimes punished at court by public caning. Indeed, the evolution of rituals governing men and women, as well as rulers and ministers, is indicative of the gradual erosion of the privileges that once belonged to the women as wives and to the men as ministers. Instead of moving toward egalitarianism, society moved the other way, raising the ruler above everyone else, until he became isolated from good advice and subject to the whims of his inner court, especially the palace eunuchs. The same happened to the husband as patriarch at home with his subordinate wife and often a circle of concubines.

All this comes from the metaphysical order of *yang* over *yin*, of Heaven over Earth, as given in the Great Commentary to the Book of Changes. In the order of nature, the husband-wife relationship precedes even that of the father-son, and certainly, that of the ruler-subject. In the order of social realities, however, the relationship of the wife to the husband is patterned on that of the minister to the sovereign. After Sung times, Chinese history witnessed an increasing centralization of state power in the hands of the ruler, who regarded his ministers as servants rather than as partners, just as the women of his harem were all his concubines. A forged classic, the *Classic of Loyalty* (*Chung-ching*), discussed below, contributed to this climate of opinion.

On Political Conduct

When we examine his teachings closely, we find that Chu Hsi was more interested in the metaphysics of *li*[a] and *ch'i*[a] and questions of self-cultivation. Indeed, Chu's definition of the "political loyalty" (*chung*[b]) was much more in terms of loyalty to one's own conscience than loyalty to the ruler. In discussing the ruler's position and powers, he also discusses the importance for the ruler to "rectify his mind-and-heart," thus effectively asking the ruler to limit his own powers by careful self-cultivation.[60] These views differed from those offered by the forged *Classic of Loyalty*, which appeared in early Sung times and emphasized exclusively the minister's obligations to the ruler.[61] After all, Chu regarded himself as the moral arbiter of society and, in that sense, enjoyed a certain freedom of expression vis-à-vis the state.

Chu agreed that the ruler was invested with absolute power and authority, but Chu also thought that the ruler had tremendous responsibilities. He had to model not only his government, but also his own behavior on the operations of Heaven. He had to procure the welfare of his people and guide them on the way to sagehood. He had to strive to bring about the realization of a great peace and a great unity to the world. Any grave failure on his part to fulfill these duties might shake the confidence placed in his imperial mandate and even lead to the overthrow of his rule. Ultimately, it was the support of the people that determined for him the good graces of Heaven and the success of his government.

For Chu and men like him, the office of ruler belonged rightfully to the sage: the man who lived not for himself but for others. And yet, as already mentioned, no king or emperor of historical times had been a "sage." Still, a ruler usually allowed himself to be addressed as his "sagely Majesty," while every minister knew in his heart that the title was undeserved. The burden of Chu's work, and of those like him, was therefore to place moral limits on the ruler's power rather than to increase it.[62]

It has been alleged that philosophers like Chu Hsi reinforced social rigidity after the interval of several centuries of Buddhist and Taoist dominance in Chinese thought and life, which disrupted the supremacy of Confucian social values. The truth, however, is much more complex. The "three bonds" and the "five relationships" were accepted explicitly,[63] although little discussed by the great thinkers. Chu's great contribution to Chinese thought is the restoration of another dimension to these "bonds" and "relationships"—the primary bond or relationship of the person to himself, in personal integrity, as this was present in the *Analects*.[64] And the need of "reverence" in self-cultivation, so much emphasized by Chu, is socially and politically consequential, since it brings to light that part of man independent of all external authority—his spiritual freedom.

Chu does not omit to point out the warning inherent in Confucius's saying that "the ruler should regard his minister with propriety or respect; the minister should serve the ruler with faithfulness"; even citing Mencius, who said that "when the prince regards the minister as a dog or horse, the minister will regard the prince as his greatest enemy."[65] In this context, he also praises unequivocally the achievements of Kuan Chung (d. 645 B.C.E.), who had abandoned his first master, Lord Chiu, in order to serve Chiu's brother and murderer, Duke Huan of Ch'i.[66] In other words, Chu is against a narrow sense of loyalty to the sovereign.

Contrary to the conventional impression of Chu Hsi as the loyal supporter of the ruler's dignity and absolute authority, Chu considered himself rather as the ruler's teacher and judge, either through word or action. His profound awareness of the unity that should exist between ethics and politics made him the bearer and spokesman of the Confucian conscience. Like Confucius and Mencius, he thought it his mission from Heaven to stand up to the kings and to offer them counsels and criticisms on behalf of the people for whom the state existed. He saw clearly the important position of the ruler in the absolute imperial system.

Although he did not directly criticize the system itself, he was extravagant in his praise of the golden past, when rulers were sages who governed by moral suasion. He was also persevering and courageous in his repeated efforts, in and out of office, to convert the ruler's mind-and-heart, to make him into a true sage-king. He regarded the ruler's responsibility of loving the people to be infinitely heavier than the subject's duty to show loyalty—a duty only conditional to the ruler's merits and virtues.

Chu continually reminded his sovereigns—indeed, he did so ad nauseam—that the ruler's mind "is the great root of the world." "If the sovereign's mind is upright, all the affairs of the world will be correct. If the sovereign's mind is not upright, none of the affairs of the world can be correct."[67] He once added this postscript to a memorial submitted to Emperor Hsiao-tsung:

> People in the streets falsely say that Your Majesty detests hearing talks on the rectification of the mind and the sincerity of thought, and that your ministers are therefore warning one another against saying such things. I, your servant, know that this cannot be true.[68]

It struck me that the American news media were saying much the same about President Richard Nixon in the days of the Watergate scandal leading to his resignation in 1974, and said similar things about President Bill Clinton regarding the sex scandal in 1998. Perhaps East and West do agree on certain basic issues.

Conclusion

How relevant are Chu Hsi's ideas today? This is a big question and deserves consideration. Returning to the yardstick offered by the creative tension between the constant and the varying, I find that Chu Hsi's system is not a closed one but remains open to change. This gives it a universal thrust, ensuring it a relevance and timeliness that should endure. Today, we may disagree with him about male superiority as a constant principle. We may also find his hopes for a sage-ruler naive and prefer to see changes in the political order that grant more freedom and popular participation. But we should also acknowledge the positive aspects in his ideas, some of which came to him from the Confucian tradition itself. I refer here to the belief in human perfectibility, which presumes a measure of human freedom and equality, and which made possible, even in the traditional past, political participation through the merit principle. I would applaud him, too, for his central concern for spiritual self-cultivation, so very important for personal and social fulfillment.

After following Chu Hsi in his religious thinking, I remain respectful of him for even attempting what he did. He struggled to understand and make relevant for his own time the traditions he received, both intellectual and popular, with all their contradictions. He has left us a creative synthesis of the entire Confucian legacy in response to Buddhist and Taoist challenges. Its comprehensive range and its efforts to deal with a host of difficult religious problems alone merit sympathetic attention. He used concepts from Buddhist thought, such as *li*[a], to reinterpret the Confucian tradition for a transformed intellectual world. It is not always fair to judge him, as does Mou Tsung-san, for a lack of faithfulness to Mencius. Tai Chen has shown that all the schools of neo-Confucian thought reinterpreted Mencius's words and terms. Rather, we should judge Chu's system on its own merits. We remain free to prefer others.

Take, for example, the oft-posed question as to why Ch'eng Yi did not teach Chou Tun-yi's Great Ultimate. I would repeat that Ch'eng's interests were more focused on the metaphysics of *li*[a] and *ch'i*[a], which he developed. It is obvious that Chu himself learned something from *each* person: from Chou and from the Ch'engs, especially Ch'eng Yi. His synthesis was both selective and creative, as he added to it new ideas of his own.

I don't deny that in the Confucian social order, human relationships tend to become hierarchically rigid, with superior partners—fathers, husbands, rulers—exercising more right and privilege and inferior partners performing more duty and submission. Such were the results of the merging of Confucian thought with *yin-yang* ideas and their arbitrary correlation of cosmic forces and human relations. Such is the defect, by excess, of the microcosm/macrocosm outlook, the result of a desire to give order to every aspect of reality by a system of correspondence that was at times mechanical. Chu Hsi belonged to such a social order and did not question its correctness.

Chu's philosophy is consistent on every level. For example, consider the concept of the Great Ultimate. It is both *Li*[a] and *Li*[a] in *ch'i*[a]. It is Being; it is also Being-in-becoming. It sums up within itself the transcendent horizon of his system while also keeping an immanent dimension. For those who find that Chu Hsi compromises the transcendent, I would respond that he is elevating the particular things, the ordinary creatures and events of life, to a higher level, as he discovers in them the unitary vision of *T'ai-chi*.

The Great Ultimate has been much criticized by the Marxists as offering metaphysical support to a feudal structure. Chu interprets the Great Ultimate also as the heavenly principle (*T'ien-li*), sometimes called the moral Way. He regards it as present in the starry skies above and in human hearts below. It is the absolute constant against which moral discretion is exercised. In the case of the drowning sister-in-law, it asserts the value of a single human life as being above any ritual law; in the case of the autonomy of marriage, it protects the freedom of individual choice over parental obstruction. A good equivalent to it on one level would be Natural Law, understood as a universal moral law, reflected in the human conscience in its choice of good and rejection of evil. I make this comparison in good company, with Hu Shih, otherwise a critic of Chu Hsi.[69] This freedom of choice points to an openness of the human spirit that reaffirms its own dignity and makes possible personal, as well as sociopolitical, transformation in the name of a greater freedom, as well as a greater responsibility.[70]

It has been said that China's Natural Law tradition is weak, on account of the absence of a transcendent Lawgiver. However, the Marxist critics have singled out the heavenly principle for criticism because of its transcendent character. Some of them even claim that Chu's transcendent *li*[a] is only another name for a creator God. Although this remains a subject of dispute, it is interesting for the claim that "idealism points to theism." In the case of continental Western philosophers, this claim is justifiable. In the Chinese case, this claim also deserves more scrutiny, as the Marxist critics have actually helped to bring to light the religious character of Chu's thought. I would like to point out that this religious character has a strong redeeming quality, since the presence of the transcendent principle as constant may permit later changes made according to the needs of correct, moral expediency, which may render as relative everything that is not heavenly principle.

In the Great Ultimate, Chu Hsi has a comprehensive principle around which his entire system revolves. Chu also uses a dialectical method that transforms and integrates opposing views and takes them to a higher level, as he does with the paradoxical statement of *Wu-chi erh T'ai-chi*, about Being as Becoming, transcendence as immanence. On another level, he reconciles the apparent dichotomy of *wei-fa* and *yi-fa* in the *Doctrine of the Mean*, thus giving his system a great inner consistency. He also possesses an essentialist sense of reality common to the Confucian school, accepting freedom and moral responsibility, as in his theory of human perfectibility and his focus on personal cultivation through reverence and intellectual pursuit. Human perfection is possible through the presence of the transcendent heavenly principle in all, which can elevate the petty events of our daily lives into meaningful Tao.

In metaphysical terms, Chu Hsi's philosophy revolves around the dialectical structure of *li*[a] and *ch'i*[a], involving both a vertical (transcendent) and a horizontal (immanent) plane, as well as their synthesis, and permitting these planes to each have its own *li*[a]/*ch'i*[a] structure, as well as to intersect with each other in a creative and dynamic pattern. He absorbs Buddhist metaphysical and logical structures of the one *Li*[a] with multiple manifestations, of the Buddho-Taoist *t'i*/*yung* tensions, as well as of very early Chinese conceptions of *ch'i*[a]. But he grounds all in the Confucian *Doctrine of the Mean*, in the dialectical structure of *chung*[a] and *ho*, of *wei-fa* and *yi-fa*, as well as in sincerity (*ch'eng*), seeing in this doctrine of the Mean the meeting point of the cosmic and human orders. He should not be criticized for borrowing from other traditions but appreciated for his ability to transform ideas from all sources and create a new and greater synthesis, one that works out the relations between the moral and rational orders of *li*[a] and the physical and emotional order of *ch'i*[a], and the relations between the intellectual and cognitive domain of investigating things and extending knowledge and the domain of spiritual cultivation in *hsiu-sheng*.[71]

I mentioned just now a greater responsibility, as well as a greater freedom, as it is my belief that true freedom brings with it responsibility. In our day, we speak of global responsibility, of protecting the earth and the environment. The Chinese philosophical tradition considered itself a universal tradition, intended for "all under Heaven." Chu spoke of *T'ien-li* as an all-embracing, transcendent absolute that is somehow immanent in human minds and hearts. For this reason, he and others like him also regarded their mission as that of "saving a world at risk of drowning." To do so, they not only extend their hands but also share with all their discovery of the timeless treasure, the heavenly principle, the moral Tao.

To conclude, let us reflect on the words of an eclectic late-sixteenth-century Chu Hsi follower, who accepted Taoism and Buddhism as well as Chu's teachings:

> My body is a small universe:
> Should joy and anger not exceed measure,
> And likes and dislikes follow the rules,
> That's the work of harmonizing *li*ᵃ.

> Heaven and Earth are our great parents:
> Should people have no complaints,
> And things suffer no ill symptoms,
> Then the mind and nature are at peace.[72]

The Confucian task remains that of helping people live in peace and harmony with no complaints and ensuring that the myriad things of the universe are respected, as fellow travelers in this life, and as beloved brothers and sisters in our large cosmic family, under the guidance of the great parental symbols of *Ch'ien* and *K'un*.

Appendix A

A Chronology of Chu Hsi's Life and Works

This outline is based mainly on Wang Mao-hung's *Chronological Biography*, with reference also to the other biographies cited in this book.

1130	Birth of Chu Hsi (15th day, 9th moon, or October 18) in Yu-hsi, Fukien, to a district sheriff, Chu Sung, and his wife.
1140	Family moved to Chien-yang, Fukien, when Chu Sung resigned from post as assistant director in ministry of personnel.
1143	Death of father. The young boy is entrusted to three friends as teachers: Liu Tzu-hui, Liu Mien-chih, and Hu Hsien. Chu would marry the daughter of Liu Mien-chih.
1148	At age eighteen, Chu obtains the *chin-shih* degree.
1153–56	Magistrate of T'ung-an, Fukien.
1153	First visit to Li T'ung.
1158	Second visit to Li T'ung.
1158–63	Superintendent of Nan-yüeh Temple, T'an-chou, Hunan.
1159	Edited *The Recorded Conversations of Hsieh Liang-tso* (*Shang-ts'ai yü-lu*).
1160	Third visit to Li T'ung; became his disciple.
1162	Fourth visit to Li T'ung. Wrote memorial to Hsiao-tsung, the new emperor.
1163	Death of Li T'ung. Chu summoned to the capital at Ling-an and had three audiences with the emperor.
1165	Briefly, professor in the military academy; then returned to Ch'ung-an, Fukien.
1165–67	Reappointed to the Nan-yüeh Temple.
1166–69	Corresponded with Chang Shih and others in Hunan on equilibrium and harmony (*chung-ho*).

231

1167   Inspected flood areas in Ch'ung-an. Visited Chang Shih at T'an-chou.

1168   Compiled *Surviving Writings of the Ch'eng Brothers of Honan* (*Honan Ch'eng-shih yi-shu*).

1169   Birth of his first son. Wrote on *wei-fa* and *yi-fa* in the context of his new theory of equilibrium and harmony. Death of his mother.

1170   Corresponded with Lü Tsu-ch'ien and others on Ch'eng Yi's teaching of reverence.

1171   Started granary in Wu-fa-li, Ch'ung-an.

1172   Published *Essential Meaning of "Analects" and "Mencius"* (*Yü-Meng yao-yi*); finished *Outline of "Tzu-chih t'ung-chien"* (*Tzu-chih t'ung-chien kang-mu*); *Words and Deeds of Famous Ministers under Eight Dynasties* (*Pa-ch'ao ming-ch'en yen-hsing lu*); *Explaining the "Western Inscription"* (*Hsi-ming chieh-yi*).

1173   Wrote the *Explanations to the Diagram of the Great Ultimate* (*T'ai-chi-t'u shuo-chieh*); *Explanations to Penetrating the Book of Changes* (*T'ung-shu chieh*). Edited the *Supplement to the Writings of the Ch'eng Brothers* (*Ch'eng-shih wai-shu*); *The Transmission of the Teachings of Chou Tun-yi and the Ch'engs* (*Yi-lo yüan-yüan lu*).

1174–76   Director of Ch'ung-tao Temple, T'ai-chou, Chekiang.

1174   Edited the *Family Rituals, Ancient and Modern* (*Ku-ching chia-chi li*).

1175   Visit of Lü Tsu-ch'ien; they compiled *Reflections on Things at Hand* (*Chin-ssu lu*). Goose Lake Monastery Debates with Lu Chiu-yüan.

1176   Death of his wife, with whom he had three sons and five daughters.

1176–78   Director of Ch'ung-yu Temple, Mount Wu-yi, Fukien.

1177   Annotated the *Analects* and the *Book of Mencius* (*Lun Meng chi-chu* and *Huo-wen*); the *Historical Annals* (*Shih-chi ch'uan*); the *Chou-yi pen-yi* (*Inquiry into the Original Meaning of the Book of Changes*).

1179   Prefect of Nan-k'ang, Kiangsi, where he reestablished the White Deer Cave Academy.

1180   Drought; prayed to spirits of mountains and rivers.

1181   Opened granaries with imperial assistance to feed the poor in thirty-five locations; helped 127,607 adults and 90,276 children among the starving population. Lu Chiu-yüan invited to the White Deer Cave Academy to lecture. Mourned the death of Lü Tsu-ch'ien. Received in imperial audience by Hsiao-tsung, who granted further requests for famine relief.

1182	Inspected two prefectures in Shao-hsing for famine relief; reported on drought and locust plagues and corrupt local officials.
1183–85	Director of Ch'ung-tao Temple, T'ai-chou, Chekiang; built Wu-yi ching-she where he resided.
1184	Visited eastern Chekiang for several months.
1185	Criticized Lu Chiu-yüan's ideas in correspondence with him; also criticized Ch'en Liang's ideas in correspondence.
1185–87	Director of Yün-t'ai Temple, Hua-chou, Shensi.
1186	Completed *Introduction to the Book of Changes* (*Yi-hsüeh ch'i-meng*) and *Correcting Errors in the Book of Filial Piety* (*Hsiao-ching K'an-wu*).
1187	Director of Hung-ch'ing Temple, Ying-t'ien. Completed *Elementary Learning* (*Hsiao-hsüeh*).
1187–89	Director of Ch'ung-fu Temple, Mount Sung, Honan.
1188	Imperial audience; addressed a very lengthy memorial to the throne emphasizing the importance of the ruler's having a correct mind; read by the emperor personally under candlelight. Published *Explanations to the Diagram of the Great Ultimate* (*T'ai-chi-t'u shuo chieh*) and *Explanations on the "Western Inscription"* (*Hsi-ming chieh-yi*).
1188–89	Director of Ch'ung-fu Temple, Mount Sung, Honan.
1189	Retirement of Emperor Hsiao-tsung and succession of Kuang-tsung. Completed prefaces to the *Great Learning* (*Ta-hsüeh chang-chü hsü*) and to the *Doctrine of the Mean* (*Chung-yung chang-chü hsü*).
1190	Published the *Collected Commentaries on the Four Books* (*Ssu-shu chi-chu*).
1190–91	Prefect of Chang-chou, Fukien; emphasized rituals of mourning, funeral, marriage; forbade unmarried women to live in private nunneries. Published work on Four Classics (Book of Changes, Book of Poetry, Book of History, Spring and Autumn Annals).
1191–93	Director of Hung-ch'ing Temple, Ying-t'ien.
1191	Death of eldest son, Chu Shu.
1192	Completed *Essential Meaning of Mencius* (*Meng-tzu yao-yi*).
1194	Pacification commissioner of Ching-hu South, T'an-chou, Hunan; repaired Yüeh-lu Academy. Resignation of Kuang-tsung and succession of Ning-tsung as emperor. Appointed Junior Lecturer-in-Waiting; wrote memorial to the throne; had imperial audiences.

1194–96   Supervisor of Hung-ch'ing Temple, Ying-t'ien.

1196   Official proscription of the teachings of Ch'eng Yi. Censor Shen Chi-tsu impeached Chu for ten crimes, including "false learning." Chu was dismissed from appointment as compiler and from temple guardianships. Started (*A Comprehensive Explanation of the Classic "Yi-li" and Its Commentaries*) (*Yi-li ching-chuan t'ung-chieh*).

1197–98   Further attacks on "false learning." Disciple Ts'ai Yüan-ting exiled. Completed the *Inquiry into Han Yü* (*Han Wen k'ao-yi*).

1199   Completed *Collected Commentaries to the "Songs of the South"* (*Ch'u-tz'u chi-chu*).

1200   Amended the *Great Learning*'s chapter on sincerity of intention; responded to questions on ritual. Died in the presence of son Tsai and disciples Huang Kan and others. Funeral attended by three thousand.

1313   The *Collected Commentaries on the Four Books* (*Ssu-shu chi-chu*) made the basis of civil service examinations.

Appendix B

Some Controversies over Chou Tun-yi's *Diagram* *of the Great Ultimate*

Many controversies surround Chou Tun-yi's *Diagram of the Great Ultimate* (*T'ai-chi t'u*) and Chu Hsi's interpretation of this *Diagram*. I shall try to clarify three principal problems. First, however, it should be pointed out that because of political disunity, many philosophical texts and records were scattered at Chu's time. In addition, Chu's philosophical predecessors lived in north China, but the center of gravity had shifted to the south, where Chu lived. Chou's *Diagram* and *Explanation* were not mentioned by the Ch'engs or Shao Yung. When Chu's editions of Chou's work first came out, apparently many of his contemporaries did not accept either the *Diagram* or the *Explanation* as authentic. There was speculation that Chou had derived his diagram from a Taoist diagram that looks very similar. The fact that an earlier, Buddhist source existed, the *Diagram of Ālaya-vijñāna*, was also brought up. There were disputes too regarding the exact wording in Chou's *Explanation*, as prepared for publication by Chu Hsi, because a different wording was found in a draft biography of Chou, which yields a different philosophical interpretation.

I shall start with the better-known controversy regarding a Taoist origin for Chou's *Diagram* and shall move then to the question of a Buddhist origin. After that, I shall deal with problems arising from the wordings in the explanatory text.

The Claims for Possible Taoist Sources

The following claims have been made regarding a Taoist origin for Chou Tun-yi's *Diagram*.

1. The earliest known claim came from Chu's older contemporary Chu Chen's *Han-shang Yi-chi chuan* (c. 1134), which mentions Mu Hsiu (979–1032) transmitting a Taoist diagram to Chou, who passed it on to the two Ch'eng brothers. Apparently, Lu Chiu-yüan and others knew of this. Among other things, Lu refers to Chu Chen's claim that Chou received his *Diagram* from the Taoists Mu Hsiu and Ch'en T'uan.[1] On his part, Chu Hsi claims that he does not know where the *Diagram* comes from and generally maintains that it represents solely Chou's work.[2]

2. Next came Huang Tsung-yen (1616–86), who asserted that Chou's *Diagram* was originally entitled *Wu-chi t'u*. Reportedly, Ch'en T'uan, the Taoist re-

cluse, had the *Wu-chi t'u* carved into the face of a cliff on the sacred Mount Hua. This was the diagram Mu Hsiu received. It consists of a series of circles basically similar to those of Chou's *Diagram*, which should be read from the bottom up. To the bottom circle belongs the label "Doorway of the Mysterious Female," to the one above that, "Transmuting Essence into Energy, transmuting Energy into Spirit." In the middle is the group of five circles representing the Five Agents and bearing the title, "Five Agents assembled at the Source." Above these are two larger circles, the lower of which is made up of interlocking black and white areas and bears the caption "Taking from [Hexagram] *K'an* to supplement [Hexagram] *Li*[b]," and the higher of which carries the title "Transmuting Spirit to return to Emptiness; reversion to the *Wu-chi*."[3] Allegedly, Ch'en T'uan passed this diagram and its secrets to Mu Hsiu, who passed it to Chou Tun-yi.[4]

3. Other sources say that this Taoist diagram came originally from the legendary Ho-shang-kung. It passed to the second-century Wei Po-yang, who used it to compile the *Ts'an-t'ung-ch'i*, and then to Chung-li Ch'üan (dates uncertain, Han dynasty), through whom it eventually got to Lü Tung-pin (b. 798), who in turn passed it to Ch'en T'uan, who gave it to Mu Hsiu when both were hermits on Mount Hua in Shensi.[5] The problem is the gaps in time: between the second and the early ninth century, and then between that and the tenth century, when Ch'en, Mu, and Chou lived.

4. Mao Ch'i-ling (1623–1716) asserts that the *Ts'an-t'ung-ch'i* edition from the early-tenth-century scholar P'eng Hsiao originally contained several diagrams, which are no longer present in the later editions that appeared after Chu Hsi's own study of this text, the *Ts'an-t'ung-ch'i k'ao-yi*. These diagrams included the Diagram of the Outline of [the Forces] Water and Fire and the Diagram of the Three-and-Five Supreme Essences. According to him, the former supplied the basis for Chou's second circle from the top, representing *yin* and *yang*, while the latter was the source for Chou's circles depicting the Five Agents.[6]

5. As mentioned in chapter 1, some have confused Chou's *Diagram* with the *Hsien-t'ien-t'u*. This appears to be a very different diagram that was transmitted from Taoist circles to Shao Yung and demonstrates, in circular sequence, the order of the trigrams of the Book of Changes.[7]

Whether Chou Tun-yi acquired knowledge of the *Diagram of the Great Ultimate* from Taoist circles has been contested time and again, including recently. The Japanese scholar Azuma Jūji disputes it, among other reasons, on the ground of Chou's relative youth (age fifteen) at the time of Mu Hsiu's death. This may not be a strong argument, since Chou could well have been a precocious youth.

Actually there were several Taoist diagrams preceding Chou's. Azuma Jūji points out that the so-called *Wu-chi t'u*, or the *Hsien-t'ien T'ai-chi t'u* (*Diagram of the Ante-Heaven Great Ultimate*), which so resembles Chou's *Diagram of the Great Ultimate*, was established only long after the time of Chou Tun-yi, that is, during the Southern Sung period, and cannot therefore be the ancestor to Chou's *Diagram*.[8] Azuma relies heavily on the work of Imai Usaburō. What he does support is a certain measure of influence from inner-alchemy circles on Chou's *Diagram*.[9]

The *Wu-chi t'u*

Ambiguity surrounds the meaning of *Wu-chi* and even *T'ai-chi* in the context of Taoist cultivation.

The Meaning of Terms

For Taoist practitioners of inner alchemy, the *Wu-chi* refers to the cavity in the human organism between the two eyes. Sometimes it also refers to what is represented in the *Diagram* by the lowest circle: the Gateway of the Mysterious Female.

The Great Ultimate, or *T'ai-chi*, however, refers to the inner light perceived in meditation, an image of *ch'i*[a], or inner energy, or even the elixir itself, formed near the above-mentioned cavity between the eyes or in the very middle of the human organism, just under the navel.

There are times when *Wu-chi* and *T'ai-chi* refer to the same thing—the golden elixir, a name for the achievement of inner enlightenment.[10]

The Reading of the Taoist Diagram

For the religious Taoist eager to explore the hidden recesses of his own self, for reasons of health, longevity, or inner enlightenment, *Wu-chi t'u* is a symbolic representation of the human organism, following the macrocosm/microcosm idea. From the bottom up, the three groups of circles in the *Diagram* represent the three Cinnabar Fields in the human body—in the abdomen, chest, and heart.[11] The middle group of five circles represents the five viscera, and the lowest, unnamed circle to which they are joined could represent the locus for enlightenment, somewhere in the middle of the second Cinnabar Field, presumably 1.3 Chinese inches just inside the navel.

A Possible Buddhist Inspiration

As mentioned in chapter 1, there is a possible Buddhist source for Chou Tun-yi's *Diagram*. This is the Ch'an patriarch Tsung-mi's so-called *Diagram of Ālaya-vijñāna* (storehouse consciousness). It is part of a much larger chart illustrating the interrelationships of various Ch'an schools through their doctrinal differences, characterized by proximity or distance to truth or illusion.

The top-center position of the entire chart is occupied by a representation of the mind of all sentient beings, accompanied by a small black dot (symbol of ignorance) and a large blank circle (symbol of awakening to truth) $\overset{\bullet}{\bigcirc}$. According to Tsung-mi:

> This chart has its head in the middle, with the three words *chung-sheng hsin*[a] (mind of all sentient beings). Starting from these words, going to its

two sides, . . . the red [dot] [i.e., blank circle] ○ records the ten stages of pure *dharmas*, the dark dot ● expresses the ten stages of defiled *dharmas*.[12]

Generally speaking, the headings given are taken from the text of the Buddhist sastra *Awakening of Faith in the Mahāyāna* (*Ta-sheng ch'i-hsin lun*), and comments under the headings are discussions of principles in that text.

To return to Tsung-mi's words:

> I have described in detail here the delusion sequence of the ten stages and the awakening sequence of the ten stages. I have used the sutras and sāstras to bring together the three types of [teachings], from the shallow to the profound. . . .
>
> Using a stream and its source as a clear mirror . . . , one is made to see the difference between identity and identity-in-difference. Although a thousand variegated images [may be reflected] in the mirror, do not take some as beautiful and others as ugly. While the mirror is uniformly bright, do not shun [looking at] the multicolored [images reflected there].[13]

What is particularly interesting is his use of small circles to represent the ten stages of decreasing delusion, ranging from a small dark dot to larger dots bearing crescent-shaped blankness, or "light," and gradually moving to circles where half or more is occupied by light, and finally, to a completely blank, or bright, dot. Obviously, what is represented is the process by which, step by step, one may reverse ignorance and recover original enlightenment, as outlined in his treatise. Buddhists respect the full moon as a symbol of enlightenment, and Tsung-mi offers in his chart various phases of the moon in a symbolic sequence showing how one might systematically reverse ignorance and retrieve original enlightenment.

Under the top center position come the two big symbols of delusion, represented by a dark dot ●, and truth, represented by a bright dot enclosing a small dark dot ⊙. Each of these is further subdivided into two, every time accompanied by a pair of circles, one of which encloses much darkness and the other is completely blank. These are somehow joined and then further subdivided, eventually with the delusion side joined to the *ālaya-vijñāna*, itself subdivided into nonawakening (a dot with shaded and unshaded areas ◎) and awakening (a dot with a small dark core ⊙), leading respectively to ten kinds of nonawakening, each accompanied by a dark dot, and ten kinds of awakening, each accompanied by a bright dot.[14]

In the chart, the *Diagram of Ālaya-vijñāna* appears as part of the grand whole. Here, it is interesting to note that the ninth-century Tsung-mi was already influenced by the Book of Changes. In the chart, he uses, as mentioned, a small circle with interlocking shaded and unshaded areas much like the *T'ai-chi* ◑. This symbol illustrates the inclusion of both truth and illusion in the *ālaya* consciousness. As mentioned in chapter 1, it can be spelled out as embracing the trigram *Li*[b] on the left and the trigram *K'an* on the right. *Li*[b] illustrates the moon rising into the sky and refers to fire, brightness, and the mind, which is written with a flame symbol. Its opposite, *K'an*, illustrates the sun going down into the sea and refers to water, darkness, and (like *Li*[b]) the mind. Both trigrams point therefore to the mind. Both are also important in Chou Tun-yi's *Diagram of the Great Ultimate*, but with one small difference: the blank, central circle present in Chou's second large circle, representing the immanence of the Great Ultimate in *yin* and *yang*, is absent in the Buddhist symbol, which is divided into two halves.[15]

Presumably, in the Buddhist diagram, the symbol *Li*[b] also represents ultimate truth in the undifferentiated mind and that of *K'an* represents relative truth, the mind as it is experienced and as it reflects flux. This is a very early reference to these trigrams, preceding the Taoist circle of Ch'en T'uan and Mu Hsiu by a few centuries.

Two parts of Tsung-mi's chart are shown in figure 3 (see chapter 1), both including the *ālaya* consciousness as represented by a circle of interlocking shaded and unshaded areas.

The Question of Chou Tun-yi's Draft Biography

As it exists, the first sentence in Chou's *Explanation of the Diagram of the Great Ultimate* says, *Wu-chi erh T'ai-chi*, "the *Wu-chi* which is also the *T'ai-chi*." On Chu's own testimony, there existed an old biography of Chou Tun-yi which gives the words differently, as *Tzu Wu-chi erh-wei T'ai-chi*; that is, "from *Wu-chi* until it becomes *T'ai-chi*." It was drafted for the official history by the famous historian Hung Mai (Hong Mai, 1123–1202).[16]

By chance, Chu Hsi saw the draft biography in 1188 and insisted that it was wrong:

> I borrowed his [Hung's] work on the dynasty's history. It included biographies of Chou Tun-yi, the Ch'engs, and Chang Tsai. The entire *Explanation of the Diagram of the Great Ultimate* is given. . . . But where the first sentence should be *Wu-chi erh T'ai-chi*, it says *Tzu Wu-chi erh-wei T'ai-chi*. I don't know on what basis two words [*Tzu* and *wei*] are added. . . .
>
> Some say this should be changed; others say no. But formerly, to clear a slander, Su Sung [Su Song] had requested a change of words . . . in the official historical [biography] of his father. Our deceased emperor agreed. And this is a case on which hinges the transmission of the Tao for a hundred generations. We should refer to the precedent, and there is no reason not to change it.[17]

That Chu Hsi sought to have the words changed is recorded by himself in the following year. After once more describing the different wordings, he adds: "I wanted to use the former prime minister Su's case as a precedent . . . to correct the mistake. I regret that I wasn't able to do so."[18]

The different wordings gave rise to many controversies, including an exchange of correspondence between Chu Hsi and Lu Chiu-yüan. In Chu's response (1189) to Lu, near the end of the letter, he refers to this difference:

Recently I saw Chou Tun-yi's [draft] biography. . . . According to that account, [the words] are *Tzu Wu-chi erh-wei T'ai-chi*. Should Chou's own text really contain these words, I would agree with you and stop arguing. But because those words were added [to the original *Explanation*], it goes to show even more clearly the intended meaning of the wording without the additions. Please reflect upon this.[19]

We, too, shall reflect upon this further before concluding this appendix.

Some Conclusions

The Taoist diagram is useful for instructing us in the techniques of what is called inner alchemy. It outlines the various stages through which a human being may rise in his ascent to the status of the immortal, with the help of specific techniques developed for the manipulation of nature. These techniques include the making of the outer elixir through practices of alchemy and, more important, the discovery of the inner elixir through yoga and meditation. Such is the goal of an interiorized quest for mystical enlightenment, a symbol of spiritual immortality.[20]

Was Chou's *Diagram* derived from a Taoist diagram? The visual similarities between Chou's *Diagram* and the *Wu-chi t'u* are such that I would personally say yes. But Tsung-mi's diagram (really part of a chart) is visually very different from Chou's, and the purported messages appear different. For the Mahāyāna Buddhist, it is important to establish the relative truth presented by the external universe, but it is even more important to affirm the higher truth of *tathatā (chen-ju)*. For Chou Tun-yi or Chu Hsi, the reality of the external world is a given. Chou's interest is less in establishing and analyzing the two kinds of truth and more in affirming the transcendent nature of the great principle behind the cosmic process, the *T'ai-chi*, as well as its presence in change, that is, its immanence. There is a parallel to the Buddhist teachings, and Chou could very well have had Buddhist influences.[21] We know that he was not given to criticizing either Taoism or Buddhism as did Chang Tsai, the Ch'eng brothers (who were Chang's nephews), and Chu Hsi. But judging from his *Diagram* and its *Explanation*, Buddhist influences merged well with philosophical Taoist influences in a thinker who was thoroughly syncretistic, transforming what he learned from other sources into his own philosophy.

Only in late 1188 did Chu begin to teach Chou's *Diagram* in public. For years before that, he was engaged in the editing and publishing of Chou's *Diagram* and his *Penetrating the Book of Changes*. That same year, before he read Hung's draft biography, he had written a "Postscript to the *Explanation of the Great Ultimate* and the 'Western Inscription.'"[22] Did Chu Hsi himself change the wording in Chou's *Explanation of the Diagram*? Historically, this is difficult to ascertain. Clearly, Chou Tun-yi's biography in the later *Sung Dynastic History* gives the first words for the *Explanation* as *Wu-chi erh T'ai-chi*, as in Chu's version. But this later work, completed in the thirteenth century, probably accepted the wording on Chu's authority.[23] Was the reading of Chou's draft biography an occasion for Chu's decision to teach the *Diagram* openly, to establish his version of things, and especially his philosophical interpretation?

Clearly, Chu's version of the wording offers the possibility for an interpretation such as his, which is also logically consistent with the rest of his philosophy. Clearly too, Chu acknowledged having altered other texts, such as the *Great Learning*. But what of this text? A historical answer is hard to establish, as our evidence is only circumstantial.

Chu has presented a cosmological basis for his own philosophical system through his interpretation of Chou's *Diagram of the Great Ultimate*. It gives his preference for *li*[a] over *ch'i*[a], which is also the essential difference between Chu's cosmology and that behind any Taoist diagram, where *ch'i*[a], and only *ch'i*[a], would be the first cause of, as well as the substrative reality behind, the universe and the myriad things.

Appendix C

Chu Hsi and Whitehead: God and the World

Introduction[1]

Because of Chu Hsi's metaphysics of li^a and $ch'i^a$, which bears a structural resemblance to Aristotelian-Thomist form and matter, one might think that Chu can be usefully compared to the Greek philosopher Aristotle or to his great medieval Christian interpreter and heir Thomas Aquinas. Besides, Chu stands historically closer to Aquinas, and the two resemble each other for their efforts to produce philosophical syntheses with strong religious overtones. On closer examination, however, one finds that the intellectual and cultural contexts in which each worked and thought also offer serious differences, leading to diverging interpretations of philosophical terms that appear to share similar structural functions. For example, for Chu Hsi, $hsing^a$, the nature of all things, including humans, is full of li^a, often translated as "principle." This may remind us of the Aristotelian-Thomist idea of essence *(essentia)*, except that essence refers to the quiddity of things, which, in the Chinese context, might refer rather to $ch'i^a$, often translated as "matter-energy."[2]

Chu Hsi's philosophy has been compared to those of Aristotle, Aquinas, Spinoza, Leibniz, Spencer, and Whitehead.[3] Obviously, the philosophies of these six Western thinkers are not all alike. With regard to "God and the world," for example, Whitehead has developed his thinking somewhat in opposition to that of Thomas Aquinas. And yet, it is not incorrect to assert that Chu Hsi shares common ground with both Aquinas and Whitehead, agreeing with the former that God or the Ultimate is in some respects above change, while also insisting, with the latter, that the Ultimate or God is immersed in change itself. Comparative studies of Eastern and Western philosophers are always relative, especially in the case of thinkers who were ignorant of each other. Their philosophies grew out of different cultural matrices with divergent basic concerns. To see one Chinese philosopher only in the light of one Western philosopher may involve too many risks to prove rewarding, the best-known risk being the imposition of alien categories on a different tradition. It would be foolish, for example, to say that one can only understand Chu Hsi after one has understood Aristotle, Aquinas, or Whitehead, and that one cannot discuss Chu's philosophy except in terms of ideas and language that belong to the Aristotelian, Thomistic, or Whiteheadian systems. This is tantamount to saying that the Chinese philosophical tradition is unintelligible to the Western philosopher except in *the westerner's* terms—an assertion amounting to cultural chauvinism.

Another difficulty in comparative philosophy lies in the meaning of words, not only between Chinese and English but also between different thinkers in each civilization, Chinese as well as Western. What Chu Hsi means by *li*ᵃ, for example, is not exactly what Lu Chiu-yüan means. Nevertheless, I am not ruling out the possibility or value of comparative studies. I am only pointing out an inherent circumstance of limitation that cannot be overlooked. On the other hand, I also see a distinct usefulness in comparative studies. I think that the study of one philosophy in dialectical relationship with one from a very different tradition can yield fruitful insights, primarily into one's own tradition. I hope that the study I undertake will contribute to my own understanding of Chu Hsi's philosophy, by discovery of a richness of depth hitherto unsuspected, and I hope that students of Whitehead may also gain insight into his philosophy because of the trouble they take to examine certain issues common to Whitehead's philosophy and what we call Chinese philosophy—a tradition representing four thousand years of scholarship, reflection, and wisdom and expressed in a language diametrically different from Greek, Latin, German, or English.

A comparative study of Chu Hsi and Whitehead is especially appropriate and useful for several reasons. Whitehead was personally conscious of possible resemblances between his philosophy and that of China or East Asia—of which Chu remains an important representative. Chu Hsi and Whitehead shared a common interest in the world of nature—the starting point in their respective philosophies. Each was a systematic thinker who constructed a metaphysical doctrine as a manner of inheriting critically from the entire legacy of tradition and of opening new horizons to the future. Each evolved a philosophy that bears striking resemblances in structure and content to that of the other. I affirm all this while realizing that the common ground between the two philosophies is more of correlation than of coincidence, and that many ambiguities remain. I know, too, for example, that my use of the word "God" in the case of Chu Hsi may be regarded as questionable. I shall show that I have good reasons for doing so and that Chu's philosophy and Whitehead's show many points of convergence, especially in their respective treatments of the problem of interrelation between God and the world. I hope also that their convergence of mind on this question will itself serve as an exemplification of the basic concurrence of their philosophical outlooks.

I shall begin with the general dissimilarities and similarities in structure between the two philosophies. Some of these are shared between Whitehead's philosophy and Chinese philosophy in general; others, between Whitehead and Chu Hsi in particular.

Structural Comparison

On first reading, more differences than similarities will emerge between Whitehead and Chinese philosophy. Take, for example, *Process and Reality*. The reader is given at once a definition of speculative philosophy with emphasis on logical coherence, a method that includes induction and "imaginative rationalization," and a redesigned philosophical language.[4] This is alien to persons accustomed to traditional Chinese philosophy, which offers no definition of metaphysics or ethics and no methodological analyses, and prefers a language that is more vernacular than specialized (albeit not without a minimal technical vocabulary). Also, Whitehead's categoreal scheme will appear excessively complex and determinate to the Chinese philosopher—in spite of his assertions that they remain "tentative formulations of ultimate generalities." The question that arises is: why such a complicated schema if the enterprise is merely tentative? Whitehead gives the impression that he remains the scrupulous mathematician, with a penchant for scientific categories and logical deductions. He seems to place excessive confidence in reason even when he knows he is attempting to express the unutterable. If he emphasizes experience, it is the kind that makes up prehensions and apprehensions—modes of knowledge and perception that have generally been neglected by the mainstream of Chinese philosophy outside Buddhism. We need, of course, to go underneath the skin of Whitehead's language and schema to understand the purpose of his enterprise. We shall then recognize that the prehensions and apprehensions refer to the real structures of life rather than the logical structures of propositions. Indeed, these structures belong to the content of what is known as common sense experience and are easily taken for granted and overlooked by the average speculative philosopher.[5] He says: "Our datum is the actual world, including ourselves; and this actual world spreads itself for observation in the guise of the topic of our immediate experience."[6] Such a starting point is also that of the Taoists, with their interest in the natural world, and of the Confucians, whose fascination is with the events of human life itself. Lin Yutang once said that Chinese thought has always remained "on the periphery of the visible world, and this helps a sense of fact which is the foundation of experience and wisdom."[7] He might have had in mind these words from the Great Commentary to the Book of Changes, which so impressed Chu Hsi's rival Lu Chiu-yüan: "It is by means of the easy and the simple that we grasp the laws of the whole world"; and again, that this is what "the common people make use of day by day and are not aware of, for the way of the gentleman is rare."[8]

Whitehead's use of language can also offer a certain parallel to the known practice in the Chinese tradition. I refer here not to his familiarity with the technical scientific vocabulary of quantum theory and electromagnetic waves, and his effort of transposing such into his philosophy, but to his occasional "lapses" into the evocative language of metaphors and cryptic sayings so characteristic of Chinese thinkers who prefer the allusion of paradoxes and riddles and an almost poetic medium.[9] Besides, for Whitehead himself, even the technical terms themselves remain "metaphors mutely appealing for an imaginative leap."[10] The final summary of his philosophical views on God and the world is presented in a series of antitheses in each of which a shift of meaning converts the opposition into a contrast. The intended effect is the emphasis on relational significance rather than underlying substance. And this is the effect of the ideographic Chinese language, where the absence of a proper copula has made of metaphorical suggestiveness a substitute for equations, thus enforcing what is known as the logic of correlative duality, in which the dialectical opposition of terms has been put to maximum use.

There is, besides, a cyclical movement in Whitehead's thought, as well as language, that cannot go unnoticed. He speaks in a language of reenaction. His exposition has been described as corresponding to three phases of an airplane flight, with which he himself compares speculative philosophy: it begins on the ground; it rises into the air; it *returns* to earth. There is "a spilling-over of immediacy from one occasion into another. . . . The cause passes on its feeling to be reproduced by the new subject as its own, and yet is inseparable from the cause. There is a flow of feeling."[11] The "flow of feeling" comes to Whitehead from the notion of the flux of energy in the quantum field theory. That it bears similarity to the Chinese *yin-yang* philosophy has been pointed out especially by Joseph Needham. We see it to be especially true of Chu Hsi's interpretation of change: how in the case of *yin* and *yang*, as the two modes of becoming, each rises to its maximum and then falls away, leaving the field to its opposite.[12]

I have already mentioned Whitehead's goal of systematic unity in all his writings as a particular resemblance he bears to Chu Hsi. *Process and Reality*, for example, is written "to state a condensed scheme of cosmological ideas, to develop their meaning by confrontation with the various topics of experience, and finally to elaborate an adequate cosmology in terms of which all particular topics find their intercommunications."[13] This stated aim is similar to that expressed by Chu Hsi in his anthology of the Sung masters, in which he incorporated his own commentary on their ideas—*Reflections on Things at Hand* (*Chin-ssu lu*). Although originally without subject titles, the book systematically unfolds ideas on cosmology and their relevance to personal and social life and, indeed, to the highest ideals and values of human fulfillment.

A question might now be raised regarding Whitehead's categoreal scheme and the place of his category of the ultimate: creativity. Has Chu Hsi developed his ideas in a manner comparable to Whitehead, proceeding from a clearly postulated starting point to the analysis of certain derived notions? And if so, what is the category in Chu's metaphysics that might be said to correspond to Whitehead's creativity?

The Categoreal Scheme

In the first part of *Process and Reality*, Whitehead maps out the groundwork of his metaphysical system with one category of the ultimate, eight categories of existence, twenty-seven categories of explanation, and nine categoreal obligations. According to him, the category of the ultimate expresses the general principle presupposed in the three more specialized categories. Together, they offer a summary of the ideas that are fundamental to his philosophy—ideas, nevertheless, that do not serve as clear and certain premises from which conclusions may be derived, that are rather themselves derived from a reflection of lived experiences.

For Whitehead, the category of the ultimate refers to "creativity"—an ultimate matter of *fact*, the principle by which the many enter into complex unity. He speaks of the many becoming one, and being also increased by one. He sees the introduction of novelty into the content of the many. As the "universal of universals," the creative advance he proposes as the starting point for his philosophy is a notion transcending all "entities"—including God. It is also the hallmark of his entire philosophy. Let me quote Charles Hartshorne here: "Process is creative synthesis, the many into a new one producing a new many—and so on forever."[14]

To understand the role that Creativity serves in his system, we may turn to a pair of technical terms: events and objects or, rather, "actual entities" and "eternal objects." They are the concrete and abstract poles around which his whole system revolves. Actual entities are the real things (*res verae*) that constitute the universe. An actual entity is an experiencing subject and is in turn constituted by its experience. Eternal objects, on the other hand, are merely possibilities—potential forms of definiteness. They represent the abstract or conceptual pole, in contrast to the concrete and physical entities. The actual entities safeguard the plurality of the real things of the universe, as well as their interrelatedness; the eternal objects make sure of the possibilities of novelty that are not yet actual but that are required by a philosophy of creativity.[15]

Let us turn now to the philosophy of Chu Hsi. Does it offer any correlates to these basic ideas? If so, is the correlation mainly functional, or does it also suggest similarity in thought content? The answers to these preliminary questions are important to situating the central problem of "God and the world" in the respective philosophies of Chu Hsi and Whitehead.

At first sight, we may discover very inadequate correlation. Examining the writings of Chu Hsi, we find that he begins at once with his cosmology of the Great Ultimate. But this is a notion with a certain definiteness. It is not an ultimate matter of fact corresponding to the notion of Creativity. With all his systematic inquiry, Chu Hsi did not articulate clearly for us his categoreal scheme.

Indeed, we can only discover Chu Hsi's "category of the ultimate" after having begun a study of his cosmology itself. By situating both the term and the idea of the Great Ultimate in their respective textual and philosophical contexts, we can uncover Chu Hsi's own categoreal scheme, that around which his system revolves. I refer here specifically to the Book of Changes and what it represents. I consider the comprehensive yet dialectical concept of *Wu-chi erh T'ai-chi* as providing the basic thrust for Chu's philosophy, somewhat as the principle of creativity does for Whitehead's. *Wu-chi erh T'ai-chi* is about Being as Becoming and therefore underlines change. I believe that I have good reasons for thinking so.

The reasons are both textual and philosophical. Chu Hsi's Great Ultimate came to him originally from the Great Commentary to the Book of Changes, that portion of the classic which provides a key to the interpretation of the entire work, and which has been accepted as such by generations of Chinese thinkers and scholars. Now, change refers to a primordial creative activity—that "great pervasive power of Heaven and Earth" (*sheng-sheng chih hsin*).[16] The process of differentiation from nondifferentiation, as found in the Book of Changes and the *Lao-tzu*, is a Chinese expression of the notion of change and creativity as this is given in Whitehead. I agree essentially with both of them, by asserting that the notion of change and creativity given in the Book of Changes provides the ultimate perspective against which we are to understand Chu Hsi's philosophy of what is equivalent to Whitehead's God and world. But I wish to point out something else: that the Chinese notion of change appears to lack the emphasis on creative advance, which is oriented to an ever-better and greater future, as this is expressed by Whitehead. In other words, creativity remains more cyclical than linear in the Chinese tradition, and more linear than cyclical in the Whiteheadian and, I may add, the Teilhardian. This is an oversimplification, but the scope of this study does not allow a proper development of the similarities and differences between "creativity" as it is understood in the Book of Changes and by Whitehead.

In both the Book of Changes and Chu Hsi's philosophy, we can clearly discern a dipolar approach to the understanding of the process of becoming. An article by Tong Lik-kuen points out the function of the two primal trigrams, *Ch'ien*[a] (Heaven) and *K'un*[a] (Earth), which serve as abstract and concrete (or, perhaps, ideal and real) poles, the realms of heavenly and earthly forms, especially in the interpretation of the nature of the absolute or God-equivalent.[17] In the context of Chu Hsi's philosophy, we have the dipolar *li*[a] (principle) and *ch'i*[a] (energy, vital force). The *li*[a] par excellence is none other than the *T'ien-li*, the heavenly principle. One can therefore find a clear functional correlation between *Ch'ien*[a] and *K'un*[a], on the one hand, and *li*[a] and *ch'i*[a], on the other. For *li*[a] represents the ideal pole, that which is "above shapes" (*hsing-erh-shang*); and *ch'i*[a] represents the real pole, that which is "within shapes" (*hsing-erh-hsia*). And Chu Hsi emphasizes that while *li*[a] may be, logically speaking, "prior" to *ch'i*[a], the two are never separate in reality, as *li*[a] is never manifest except through *ch'i*[a]. Frequently, *li*[a] is regarded as the formal principle, and *ch'i*[a] the material principle. This analogy is valid to some extent. But we must keep in mind that *ch'i*[a] is not just matter in a passive and receptive state, ready to receive the impression of forms. On the contrary, *ch'i*[a] is a dynamic principle, which gives shape and actuality to *li*[a], to which, in turn, the "myriad creatures" (*wan-wu*) owe their formal organization and their participation in the plenitude of being and goodness. In this book, I translate *ch'i*[a] mainly as "energy," without any intention of restricting it to the realm of living, organic beings. But each is at the same time transcendent of, and yet immanent in, the other. The Great Ultimate, for example, as that which is above form and shape, is *li*[a] (see chapter 2). But since it is also involved in change and becoming, through the two modes of *yin* and *yang*, it is involved in *ch'i*[a]. And then, according to Chu Hsi, the interaction of the two modes with the Five Phases of Fire, Water, Wood, Metal, and Earth, which represent the "material substances" (*chih*) as agents of change, cause the "myriad creatures" to come into existence.

There are various ways of correlating Chu Hsi's basic ideas with Whitehead's categories. One way is to match "principles" (*li*[a]) with "eternal objects," since principles both transcend the actual things while also being immanent in them.

The "myriad creatures" (*wan-wu*) can be regarded as "actual occasions." This is all the more so as they themselves are immersed in becoming, organically inter-related, and refer to the whole continuum of actual entities in our universe, in-cluding humans, animals, plants, and stones.[18] Therefore, by definition, they need not exclude electrons and protons, had Chu Hsi known of these. The dy-namic character of "creatures" (*wu*) is better seen when we remember that the term refers also to "affairs" (*shih*) and, in the case of a later philosopher, Wang Yang-ming, to "affairs of the mind."[19] *Ch'i*ᵃ, the essential constituent of all "crea-tures," may be better appreciated as that through which the actual occasions create themselves, in the dynamic process of becoming, by which the many "data" (*chih*), as, for example, represented by the Five Agents, or Phases, are in Whitehead's terms "prehended" and absorbed into the unity of a "satisfaction." Indeed, actual occasions are manifest only through *ch'i*ᵃ; and if the *yin* mode of *ch'i*ᵃ represents the physical prehensions of objectified actual entities, the *yang* mode of *ch'i*ᵃ may be said to represent the conceptual prehensions of eternal objects.

The Problem of God

The question now is: where do we see God? Is God one of the "myriad creatures" in Chu Hsi's system, as it is an actual entity in that of Whitehead? Have we even any justification for using the word "God" at all when discussing the philoso-phy of Chu Hsi? These are questions that I shall attempt to answer as I turn now to an examination of the problem of God in the Chinese tradition.

In *Process and Reality*, Whitehead speaks of the various images of God found in the development of theistic philosophy: that of an imperial ruler, as with the Roman Empire and its divine caesars, as well as with the Muslims; the personi-fication of moral energy, as with the Hebrew prophets; and an ultimate philo-sophical principle, as with Aristotle's Unmoved Mover and in Indian Buddhism.[20] This is not the place to comment much upon or criticize this interpretation, ex-cept to point out that Whitehead consciously exaggerated the contours of these images in his polemical effort to attack the notion of God in classical Christian theism, which, according to him, is a combination especially of the imperial ruler and the Unmoved Mover. I shall have something to say about these images in the context of the Chinese tradition later on. At present, I wish to recall what Whitehead said a little earlier about the concept of God and its various inter-pretations "before the world." In *Religion in the Making*, they are, in the order enumerated by himself: the "Eastern Asiatic" concept of an impersonal but self-ordering order to which the world conforms, or an extreme form of "imma-nence"; the Semitic idea of a personal deity whose fiat created the world, or an extreme form of "transcendence"; and the "pantheistic" concept, which regards the world itself as illusion, with reality only in God, an extreme doctrine of "monism."[21]

There are differences between the two sets of threes, and understandably so, as the differences stem from the varying purposes of Whitehead's enterprise in the two works. *Religion in the Making* already contains the germ of the concept of God that Whitehead is to propose with more explicitness in *Process and Reality*, and he is to do so in conscious opposition to other concepts of God accepted in earlier periods of history. For our purposes, however, what is important is to examine the concept of God in China and see to what extent Whitehead has been accurate or inaccurate in his assessment of the East Asian situation. Briefly, does the Chinese God represent an extreme form of "immanence"? I approach this issue by discussing the concept of God found in the Confucian classics—the locus classicus for China's major tradition and especially for Chu Hsi, the conscious heir and interpreter of the Confucian heritage. I shall then discuss Chu Hsi's interpretation itself to determine how far it has diverged from the original concept, and go on, from there, to compare Chu Hsi's concept with Whitehead's.

Is the Chinese God a totally immanent one, or does the question itself contain a contradiction? Indeed, does the Chinese tradition know of a God at all? An answer to this fundamental question should enlighten us regarding the immanence or transcendence of this deity, should one exist.

On this question of the existence of God in the Chinese tradition, some of the greatest scholars of the West have been mistaken. From the French *philosophes* of the Enlightenment to such justly renowned writers of our own day, such as F. S. C. Northrop and Joseph Needham, the answer has been no. Northrop discusses the immediate aesthetic quality of the Chinese language, reaching the conclusion that it can only represent a nominalist and positivist philosophy, and goes on to declare that Chinese religions are not theistic, since they regard the divine as indeterminate.[22] Needham is justly renowned, among other accomplishments, for pointing out the organismic character of Chu Hsi's philosophy and its resemblance to Whitehead's thought, but he says that he knows of no personal deity, Creator and Lawgiver, in the Chinese tradition.[23]

In this regard, some of China's best scholars have been much less hasty. Before the 1930s, it was the fashion among Chinese intellectuals to emphasize the secular, rather than religious, character of Chinese culture. But even then, an agnostic like Hu Shih, philosopher and classical scholar and student of John Dewey, acknowledged the belief in a supreme deity in early Chinese civilization.[24] In the 1930s and after, the historians of the School of Higher Criticism, Ku Chieh-kang and others, confirmed this assertion when they demythologized China's remote antiquity and proposed that the legendary sages—the Yellow Emperor, Yao, Shun, and Yü—were originally mythical symbols of the supreme deity.[25] Archeological findings have strengthened these assertions. Today, historians of early Chinese religion speak with some assurance of both the "Lord-on-High" and "Heaven" of the oracle bones and the Confucian classics as representing a supreme God with clearly personal attributes, exalted above all other gods, lord of the universe and of history, and judge of human consciences.[26] To use Whitehead's vocabulary, the image projected is that of a God who is simultaneously imperial ruler and personification of moral power.

If the Chinese had an image of God that was at once personal, because based on analogy to the human being, and transcendent, because regarded as ruler and personification of moral power, they did not, nevertheless, develop a doctrine of God comparable to the classical theism of the West. I refer here to that system which Whitehead describes as a union of the Roman imperial idea and the early Semitic moral force with the Aristotelian notion of Unmoved Mover—a union that he asserts did not take sufficiently into account the "Galilean" emphasis of the New Testament upon love. It is, of course, characteristic of the Chinese tradition to prefer images to doctrines and to present doctrines in terms of images—in a metaphorical and highly symbolic form, joining language to diagram, as in the case of Chu Hsi himself.

One instance of a Chinese symbol for the divine with some relevance for our subject is that of the Pole Star, which appears to be above motion and yet "governs" the circumpolar stars. Confucius referred to this symbol as an analogy for imperial authority on earth: "He who exercises government by means of his virtue may be compared to the (Pole) Star of the North, which keeps to its own place, and yet all the (other) stars turn toward it."[27] The pole star was regarded as the residence of the Great One (*T'ai-yi*[b]), a new name for the supreme deity that emerged some time before the Han dynasty. It is important to note here that the Great One presents a clear association of meaning with the Great Ultimate (*T'ai-chi*), the first principle, Supreme Exemplar, and "ground of being and becoming" in Chu Hsi's philosophy, an association that entails a consequent importance for our understanding of the simultaneous transcendence and immanence of the Great Ultimate.[28]

Chu Hsi was a meticulous student of the classics and a prolific writer of commentaries. He knew that such designations as Lord-on-High and Heaven were used in the classics to refer to the supreme deity. He did not ignore their meaning for philosophy. In dialogues with his disciples, he pointed out that the word "Heaven" must be understood according to its varying contexts. In some passages, it refers to the sky above, in others, to a ruler or master (*chu-tsai*), and in still others, to "principle" (*li*[a]) (see chapter 3).

That Heaven refers to the sky above in certain classical contexts will present no problem to the student. That it also refers to the "ruler," and that this "ruler" is none other than "principle" (*li*[a]) is Chu Hsi's own assertion. He claims that while it is not correct to maintain there is "a man in Heaven, commanding this [and that]" as lord and ruler of the universe, it is equally incorrect to say that there is no such ruler. For "there is nothing more eminent under Heaven [i.e., in the universe] than principle. Hence it is called ruler."[29]

Chu Hsi also paid some attention to the question of sacrifices offered to the powers above. In the course of history, the Chinese have instituted many sacrifices, offered to a multiplicity of deity-symbols, including earth and grain, in addition to the earlier sacrifice offered to the Lord-on-High, also known as Heaven. Chu Hsi lamented this development, recalling to his disciples that the Great One (*T'ai-yi*[b]) was earlier worshiped as the supreme Lord, and insisting also that Heaven can have only one such Lord, just as the state should have only one supreme ruler. He added explicitly that the Great One should not be confused with the Pole Star, its symbol, which offers the analogy of a divine court—the Lord surrounded by lesser lords, as an exemplar for the human court.[30]

Thus, if Chu Hsi agrees with ancient traditions that such words as "Lord-on-High," "Heaven," and "Great One" all refer to the same ruler, God, he has obviously moved beyond them by endeavoring to remove the prereflective, anthropomorphic overtones from these words, discerning symbol from myth. But what is his position regarding the personal Absolute? Does he recognize consciousness in God?

At this point we must introduce yet another term into our study: that of "mind," particularly, "the mind-and-heart (hsin^a) of Heaven and Earth." The following dialogue between Chu Hsi and a disciple will throw light on Chu Hsi's position in this regard:

> Question: Is the mind (hsin^a) of Heaven and Earth conscious (ling) or is it different and without action (wu-wei)?
> Answer: The mind of Heaven and Earth cannot be said to be unconscious, but it is not like that of the human being. . . . The mind has the meaning of ruler. But what is called ruler is principle. It is not as though there is another principle outside the mind, another mind outside principle.[31]

And then comes the statement I've already quoted in chapter 3:

> Should [Heaven and Earth] have no mind, then cows would give birth to sheep, and the peach tree would produce pears.[32]

Chu Hsi identifies mind—the mind of Heaven and Earth—with ruler and principle. And he also attributes to this mind certain qualities of consciousness and the power of ensuring that an order will prevail in the process of creativity. It is difficult to reason at once from this that Chu's God is a personal Absolute, as Chinese thinking does not clearly separate the notion of personality from that of humanity. But the Chinese tradition often refers to man as the "mind" of Heaven and Earth, because he gives the universe consciousness by his own powers of mind. Chu's words may therefore imply an analogy of proper proportionality, by which the mind of the universe is said to be Lord and ruler on high, that is, God. This would bring us closer to the analogy proposed by Schubert M. Ogden and others, that God is to the world as the self is to the body,[33] each as a principle of consciousness for the other. Chu Hsi's God may then be said to resemble more the "personal God" of panentheistic theology, while differing in important respects from the personal God of classical theism.

This will become clearer, I hope, with a closer examination of the place of the Great Ultimate in Chu Hsi's philosophy. The notion of the Great Ultimate approximates most the notion of God in Western theistic philosophy, and it serves as foundation and center of Chu's entire metaphysical system, the explanation of the organic interrelatedness of all things. I see Chu Hsi's philosophy of the Great Ultimate as an effort to present the notion of God as the chief exemplification of his metaphysical principles, an effort similar to Whitehead's. I find it all the more remarkable since Chinese philosophers have usually refrained from invoking God as the final explanation of all that they are unable to explain rationally. They have preferred either to remain silent on the question of God, as did Confucius himself, or to offer a metaphysical system in which this notion of God itself is given a logical and coherent explanation, as in the case of Chu Hsi.

A Dipolar Ultimate?

Does the philosophy of Chu Hsi offer a dipolar (Whitehead's term) God— transcendent of change and yet immanent in change itself? Does not the strong "process-orientation" of Chinese philosophy incline one to think that the Chinese God would be more "consequent" than "primordial," more immanent than transcendent? To find answers to these questions, let us turn to Chu Hsi himself.

The starting point in Chu Hsi's philosophy is not the concept of principle (*li*[a]), a word with Buddhistic overtones, as the constitutive principle of human nature, as well as the universe, but rather the concept of the Great Ultimate (*T'ai-chi*), with its Taoistic associations, as source, as well as ground, of all things, that which holds the universe together. Chu Hsi's synthetic genius is manifest in the inheritance of the concept of the Great Ultimate from the philosopher Chou Tun-yi and of the concept of principle from Ch'eng Yi, and in his successful enterprise of interpreting the Great Ultimate in terms of principle.

The term "Great Ultimate" is usually recognized as stemming from the Great Commentary to the Book of Changes, a nominally Confucian work. But Chinese scholars have also associated it with the term "Great One" (*T'ai-yi*[b]), a designation, first, of the supreme deity and, then, of one of the gods, assimilated especially into the pantheon of Taoist religion. This is significant in our study of Chu Hsi, being symbolic of the philosophical transformation of religious beliefs. It appears, indeed, that the term "Great One" early assumed philosophical meaning, coming to represent the fullness of *ch'i*[a] that was present before the separation of Heaven and Earth and that is to fill the entire universe.[34]

According to the Great Commentary to the Book of Changes, the Great Ultimate produces the two modes, presumably of *yin* and *yang*, before these, in turn, produce the Four Images, who, in turn, produce the Eight Trigrams (see chapter 1).

Obviously, the use of progression in numbers suggests the process of differentiation flowing from non-differentiation, showing how the diverse modes of existence all emanate from the unity of the Ultimate. But numbers here refer also to certain linear symbols: trigrams and hexagrams, themselves representations of a cosmic process mirrored in the human psyche, the reason for their effectiveness also in divination. Interestingly, in *Lao-tzu* (ch. 42), we find a similar use of numbers, with no explicit reference to trigrams and hexagrams, but with mention of *yin* and *yang* as modes of change.[35]

Chou Tun-yi's and Chu Hsi's Great Ultimate differs, however, from that of the Great Commentary to the Book of Changes because of their introduction of another term, which first appeared in *Lao-tzu* (ch. 28): the Limitless (*Wu-chi*). The full title of the "Great Ultimate" is therefore "Limitless and yet Great Ultimate," as explained in chapter 2.

The term "Great Ultimate" itself may not be too difficult to understand. Its usage in the Great Commentary to the Book of Changes is also indicative of its philosophical meaning, as the first principle of the universe. But the paradoxical description of the Great Ultimate as Limitless can be a puzzling one. Here I repeat some ideas already mentioned in chapter 1. The Chinese term *Wu-chi* (Limitless) is itself capable of many interpretations all at the same time. One possible meaning is the Infinite or Limitless; another is "No-Ultimate," the negation of the validity of the first principle itself. Still another possibility is "Ultimate of Nothingness." In each case, the meaning depends on one's interpretation of nothingness (*wu*). Does it represent a *via negationis*, by which plenitude is described in negative terms, or a philosophical nihilism?

It is my contention that Chu Hsi's insistence on keeping the Limitless in the description of the Great Ultimate is an expression of his dipolar characterization of the Great Ultimate itself—his philosophical equivalent to the God of classical religion. I support this contention by appealing to Chu Hsi's own explanations of this paradoxical description. Chu Hsi asserts that the Limitless refers to the limitless: that beyond which the mind can go no further. But he insists that the Great Ultimate is also a principle of plenitude: it is full of *li*[a] (principle), that which constitutes the myriad things, that which helps the determination of good and evil.[36] Defending Chou Tun-yi for having proposed the dipolar description of the first principle, incorporating, therefore, insights from Taoism into Confucian metaphysics, Chu Hsi speaks with religious reverence of the discovery itself: that Chou has seen the Tao-in-itself and knows it to be beyond ordinary conceptions. This was discussed in chapter 2. Here, I wish to resume where the quotation there, on page 43, ends:

> One can know that this venerable man has really received the secret which has not been transmitted since the time of the thousand sages. . . . Chou described it as Limitless, precisely because it is not bound by space or shape, it is prior to things and yet also after the creation of things, it is outside *yin* and *yang*, and yet operates in the midst of *yin* and *yang*; it penetrates all things, is absent nowhere, and yet is originally without sound, smell, shadow, or echo.[37]

Chu Hsi feared that the dipolar dimensions of emptiness and plenitude, transcendence and immanence, which characterize the first principle, would be lost in a philosophy of monism, as represented by his rival, Lu Chiu-yüan. In this regard, the Limitless and the Great Ultimate approximate Whitehead's proposal of the primordial and consequent natures of the deity: of God as ground of all possibilities, eternal and unchanging, and yet ever in "process" of further creation. Let us turn to Whitehead's own words:

> The nature of God is dipolar. He has a primordial nature and a consequent nature. The consequent nature of God is conscious; and it is the realization of the actual world in the unity of his nature, and through the transformation of his wisdom. The primordial nature is conceptual. (He is the unlimited conceptual realization of the absolute wealth of potentiality.) The consequent nature is the weaving of God's physical feelings upon his primordial concepts.[38]

For Chu Hsi, the dipolar character of the Great Ultimate is especially explained in terms of li^a and $ch'i^a$. I mentioned earlier that the term "Great One," which is closely associated with the "Great Ultimate," refers to the plenitude of $ch'i^a$ in a chapter of the Book of Rites. Yet Chu Hsi himself refrains from describing the Great Ultimate *directly* in terms of li^a and $ch'i^a$. He prefers to describe it primarily as the fullness of li^a. Speaking paradoxically, he maintains that the Great Ultimate itself does not "move," although it is also found in change and becoming— in the two modes of *yin* and *yang*, in the interaction of the Five Phases with the two modes, which results in the production of the "myriad creatures." [39] It would seem that he was anxious to preserve its transcendence over change while also acknowledging its immanence in change.

Put into Whiteheadian terms, the li^a and $ch'i^a$ of Chu Hsi approximate Whitehead's "conceptual" and "physical" poles of realization, in the interaction between God and the world. Li^a serves as the principle of permanence amid flux, which brings multiplicity into unity, while $ch'i^a$ serves as the principle of change and multiplicity, because of which creativity is immersed in the process of concrescence. According to Whitehead:

> For God the conceptual is prior to the physical, for the World the physical poles are prior to the conceptual. . . . Thus, by reason of his priority of appetition, there can be but one primordial nature for God; and, by reason of their priority of enjoyment, there must be one history of many actualities in the physical world. [40]

The movement from the conceptual to the physical pole of realization, as this is conceived in the dipolar nature of God, is none other than the order of creativity itself. It is also envisaged in the interpretation of the notion of the Great Ultimate—with the myriad creatures coming forth from the Great Ultimate and then returning to the Great Ultimate, which is also the Limitless. I think Chu Hsi can agree with Whitehead in saying: "In God's nature, permanence is primordial and flux is derivative from the World; in the World's nature, flux is primordial and permanence is derivative from God." [41]

However, the "Limitless and yet Great Ultimate" characterization of this first principle remains an ambiguous one. It seems, in some ways, more a logical than an ontological characterization to insist that the Great Ultimate is "limitless"— that beyond which the mind cannot conceptualize. Chu Hsi never clearly explained the Limitless in terms of $ch'i^a$, to oppose it to the Great Ultimate, which he repeatedly identifies with li^a . According to his own metaphysical structure, this might mean a God more primordial than consequent. And yet, he has said quite clearly that the "Limitless and yet Great Ultimate" is "prior to things and yet also after the creation of things." He seems to give a great importance to such dipolarity, even if he has not integrated it clearly into his interpretation of the Great Ultimate. Other thinkers have done so. Fung Yu-lan, a modern follower and reinterpreter of Chu Hsi's philosophy, has explained this dipolarity of Great Ultimate and Limitless in terms of the plenitude of li^a and of *chi*. [42] Nevertheless, I think we have enough evidence for considering that Chu has an appreciation of the Great Ultimate as a dipolar concept, even if he has not formulated it in unambiguous terms.

We return now to a problem stated much earlier: can the Great Ultimate of Chu Hsi be described as one of the myriad creatures, the counterpart of an "actual entity" in the Whiteheadian system? The answer to this question will show us even more the affinity of spirit between Chu Hsi and Whitehead, as well as some important differences. The Great Ultimate is first and foremost a principle of unity and of wholeness. In its "primordial nature"—as the fullness of *li*[a]—it may be described as the mind of the universe. In its "consequent nature"—becoming immanent through *ch'i*[a]—it is manifest in the world of the myriad creatures, not only in the totality of multiplicity but also in each and every individual "creature." It is thus possible to say that each individual entity, each actual occasion, offers a certain reflection of God or the Ultimate. But it will not be possible to say with Whitehead that the Great Ultimate is itself also an individual, an actual entity, albeit a very unique one.

Conclusion

There is much more that one can say about "God and the world" in this comparative study of Chu Hsi and Whitehead. We have not yet discussed, for example, what Whitehead refers to as the "tender elements" in our understanding of God, relating especially to the historical manifestations of love and compassion so central to Christian doctrine. Now, although the historicity of God as expressed in the theology of Incarnation and Redemption is quite alien to the Chinese tradition, the "tender elements" of the divinity have not been completely overlooked.[43] In the case of Chu Hsi, we have mentioned his discussion of God as the "mind" of the universe. Much more can be said about this. I see possibilities especially for postulating an idea of God in which "mind" would represent the "primordial" nature, while its manifestation of creativity and even a loving Providence would be represented by *jen*[a]—the "consequent" nature. The whole evolution of the concept of *jen*[a] is worthy of investigation. In the case of Chu Hsi, it is an example of his effort to incorporate the philosophy of Ch'eng Hao, whose starting point is the self as found in human relations. As a life-giving principle, *jen*[a] is thus a metaphysical elaboration of human love, which becomes the symbol for creativity in the universe as well. Hence, the incorporation of both *li*[a] (taken from Ch'eng Yi) and *jen*[a] (taken from Ch'eng Hao but reinterpreted by Chu) into Chu's metaphysical system can demonstrate for us Chu Hsi's relative success in overcoming the dichotomy between the world and the self. This is a success made possible by the fundamentally microcosm/macrocosm outlook so characteristic of the entire Chinese tradition and by the dialectical method he uses, which, incidentally, is also Whitehead's method.[44] If the Great Ultimate is order or principle (*li*[a]) as well as creativity and plurality (*ch'i*[a]), it is also mind (*hsin*[a]) and love (*jen*[a]).

Let me give here a summary of the similarities and differences that I have found in this study of Chu Hsi and Whitehead. Chu Hsi's metaphysical model—

as given in his commentaries on Chou Tun-yi's *Diagram of the Great Ultimate*—is a much less determinate, and therefore much more ambiguous, one than Whitehead's. Where both men make use of a paradoxical language, Chu Hsi's remains much more symbolic because of its reference to a *Diagram* that is itself a symbolic structure. Whitehead's language tends to be more rationalistic, with its reference to ideas taken from modern physics and with its concern for making God simultaneously a supreme exemplification of most of its principles as well as a supreme exception from some of its principles.

I mentioned earlier Whitehead's discussion of the various images of God found in the development of theistic philosophy, as well as his discussion of the other "three ways" of interpreting the concept of God, which he also singled out elsewhere. I do not find them, however, adequately clear for our purposes of comparative study. I prefer Charles Hartshorne's three alternatives for describing the relation between God and the world: the way of classical theism, with a totally transcendent God related only extrinsically to the world; the way of pantheism, in which God and the world are identified; and the way of panentheism, in which God is at the same time transcendent of the world and also immanent in the world, because he includes the world without being one with the world.[45] I think, with him and others, that Whitehead is essentially closer to the way of panentheism than he is to the way of classical theism, although I also agree with William Christian that Whitehead's God is not far removed from the classical model.[46] But if this is so, I should like to situate Chu Hsi in the panentheist way itself, sympathetic to the theists in his insistence upon the transcendence of the Great Ultimate as Limitless and in his attribution of consciousness to the Ultimate, while open also to the pantheists in his equal insistence upon the immanence of the Great Ultimate as this is found in the interaction of *yin* and *yang* with the Five Phases.

Fundamentally, Chu Hsi's metaphysical choice is similar to Whitehead's. He has rejected the anthropomorphic image of the deity as this is given in classical Chinese religion. He has also found unacceptable certain pantheistic philosophies that identify God and the world, as for example in Buddhism. He has therefore elaborated his own alternative, his own version of a middle way.

Appendix D

An Explanation of Key Terms

This appendix explains more succinctly certain terms and pairs of terms that have special importance in this book. Their sequential order generally follows the order of their appearance in the book, to the extent that this is possible. As one may expect, the terms are often intertwined in meaning.

Tao / tao-t'ung 道 / 道統

Tao refers to the unnameable ultimate reality. In this book, it often represents the Confucian Way, that is, as spelled out by Confucian moral values.

Chu is the first person to refer to *tao-t'ung*, or the "orthodox line of the Tao." In his preface to the annotated edition of the *Doctrine of the Mean*, he offers Tzu-ssu, Confucius's grandson, as author of the *Doctrine of the Mean*, compiled to safeguard Confucius's spiritual legacy and derived from the ancient sage kings. The Confucian Way was then transmitted to Mencius, after which the transmission was interrupted for many centuries, until the Tao was rediscovered by Chou Tun-yi, Chang Tsai, and the two Ch'engs, Hao and Yi, after which it passed to Chu Hsi.

T'ai-chi / Wu-chi 太極 / 無極

T'ai-chi, literally, the "Great Ultimate." For Chou Tun-yi, it refers to ultimate reality, the source and principle of all being and goodness, the one behind the many. For Chu Hsi, it is also the *T'ien-li*, or Heavenly principle, the transcendent that is also immanent in the universe and in every individual human and thing. Yet humans and other creatures are different, according to what each has received of *ch'i*[a].

Chu says that as *li*[a], the Great Ultimate is also nature (*hsing*[a]) in human beings. He also calls the Great Ultimate the *T'ien-li*, literally, "Heavenly principle."

This interpretation is different from that of the Taoists, for whom the Great Ultimate is full of *ch'i*[a], that substantive reality translated sometimes as "matter-energy."

For Chu Hsi, *Wu-chi*, literally, the "Infinite and Limitless," that which is beyond concept and language, because beyond determination, is the "other face" of the Great Ultimate, which explains and supports its transcendence.

Li[a] / *ch'i*[a] 理 / 氣

The two coordinate principles which constitute all things. The *Shuo-wen* explains *li*[a] in terms of patterns in jade. In *Mo-tzu* it refers usually to principle or reason. In *Hsün-tzu*, the *li*[a] of a particular thing is its configuration, its specific form, and all *li*[a]s are subsumed in the great Tao and present also in all things. In the "Record on Music" of the Book of Rites, the term occurs frequently, usually as the verb *to order*. The expression "heavenly principle" (*T'ien-li*), so much favored by Chu Hsi, also occurs in this text. In Hua-yen Buddhism, the distinction is made between the two realms of *li*[a] (the noumenal) and *shih* (the phenomenal). The Ch'eng brothers Hao and Yi identify the *li*[a] of one thing with the *Li*[a] of all things. For Chu Hsi, *li*[a] is the principle that makes all things what they are, with their being and goodness, as well as the principle that makes the universe what it is, with its being and goodness. Chu speaks of the one *Li*[a] between Heaven and earth that has multiple manifestations.

The much older concept *ch'i*[a] is often translated as "breath," "energy," "ether," or "material force," but is better rendered as "matter-energy." Present in many ancient texts, often with a cosmological reference, *ch'i*[a] is pervasive in the universe, giving rise to all things, endowing them with life and energy. We are speaking here of a substantive psycho-physical reality, underlying the world as it appears to our consciousness and corresponding in a way to the pneuma of the ancient Greeks. Ch'eng Yi distinguishes between *li*[a] (principle, being, goodness), which belongs to the realm as that which belongs to the realm "above shapes" (*hsing-erh-shang*), and *ch'i*[a] (matter/energy), which belongs to the realm "within shapes" (*hsing-erh-hsia*), establishing a metaphysical structure that Chu His accepted. For Chu, all things are made of both *li*[a] and *ch'i*[a]. He gives logical, though not temporal, priority to *li*[a] over *ch'i*[a].

Hsing[a] / *hsin*[a] 性 / 心

Hsing[a] is a character compounded of two words, the "mind" (or "heart") and "life." It refers primarily to human nature, that which we receive with life. But it also refers to the natures of other creatures. All things, indeed, have been endowed from Heaven with *hsing*[a], or nature, that by which they are what they are. And while nature is regarded as originally good, it cannot be separated from physical form, which comes with matter-energy (*ch'i*[a]), and is, depending on its quality, prone to both good and evil.

Chang Tsai distinguished between the heavenly nature, which is good, and the physical nature, which individuates it and makes it capable of evil. An individual's nature is what it is depending on the quality of the *ch'i*[a] with which it is endowed. Chu accepted this enthusiastically as an explanation for the problem of evil in human nature.

Etymologically represented as a flame symbol, pointing to dynamism, *hsin*[a] is usually translated as "mind" and sometimes as "mind and heart." It is the meeting point of the intellect and the will. In Mencius it refers to the center of being that is the self-reflective source of all our conscious and moral activities: the heart as well as the mind as source of moral principles. In the *Great Learning* and the *Doctrine of the Mean*, the moral mind is what is prominent. In Buddhist, especially Ch'an texts, it signifies being, reality, even ultimate reality. It may be better rendered by the Latin *mens*, as the "apex of the soul," as its "innermost sanctuary," or by the French *coeur* in the sense assigned it by Blaise Pascal— although even these words do not capture all its meaning.

Just as nature (*hsing*[a]) is full of principle (*li*[a]), so too is the mind (*hsin*[a]) full of *ch'i*[a]. According to Chu, nature transcends mind while being inseparable from it; the way *li*[a] transcends *ch'i*[a] without being separate from it. But where nature is passive, mind is dynamic. The mind is in charge of the human person, of his nature and his emotions.

Chung / ho 中 / 和

These terms come from the *Doctrine of the Mean*. Following James Legge, I translate *chung* as "equilibrium" and *ho* as "harmony." In Chinese, *chung* is the same word as the "middle," the "Mean," while *ho* refers to peace and harmony.

Chu's thought on *chung* and *ho* evolved in stages. After abandoning Li T'ung's quest for the *wei-fa*, Chu consulted with Chang Shih. He first thought that the *wei-fa* is present in the *yi-fa* and, therefore, that prolonged meditation is unnecessary. This also entailed metaphysically his associating the *wei-fa* to human nature and the *yi-fa* to the mind and heart. This emerged around 1166 and is what he calls his "Old Theory [or "Doctrine"] on Equilibrium and Harmony [*chung/ho*]."

In his mature thinking, Chu decided around 1170 that the *wei-fa* is present in the *yi-fa* and that the two states belong both to the same reality, the mind, rather than to nature and the mind respectively. This represents his "New Theory," which correlates with his interpretation of *Wu-chi*'s being also *T'ai-chi*. It is a clear instance of his preference for accepting both transcendence and immanence in a dialectical manner.

Wei-fa / yi-fa 未發 / 已發

The description is of two states of consciousness, before and after the rise of emotions. The *wei-fa* is free of emotions, concepts, and images. It is a state of pure experience, or pure consciousness, when the mind and heart is fully present to, and focused on, itself. The *yi-fa* represents a state of emotions in harmony. The language of *wei-fa* suggests something hypothetical, and that of *yi-fa* something that can be actualized.

T'i / yung 體 / 用

These terms come from the neo-Taoist philosopher Wang Pi. *T'i*, literally, the "body," and by extension, "substance," refers to the Tao-in-itself, in opposition to *yung* (literally, "use" or "function"). Sometimes translated as "substance/function," *t'i* and *yung* represent a pair of coordinate concepts referring to reality and its manifestation, or the latent and the manifest. These also acquired later Buddhist overtones as "ultimate" and "mundane" truths. Frequently, the inner, or latent, is called *t'i*, while the outer, or manifest, is called *yung*. Often *t'i* refers to a deeper reality in a still mode, whereas *yung* refers to its active manifestation.

Tao-hsin / jen-hsin 道心 / 人心

These terms refer to the "moral mind" versus the "human mind." For Chu, they sum up the spiritual legacy transmitted by the sages. Chu associates the *tao-hsin* with *T'ien-li* and the *jen-hsin* with *jen-yü* (human desires), emphasizing the need of the one dominating over the other. This theme of spiritual struggle became central to his system of "orthodox transmission" of the Confucian truth, which he considered lost since Mencius and only rediscovered by Ch'ou Tun-yi and the Ch'eng brothers. And Chu regarded himself as an heir in this intellectual lineage, with the mission of passing to later generations the important message.

Notes

The following abbreviations have been used throughout the notes section.

CTCS   *Chang-tzu ch'üan-shu (Complete Works of Chang Tsai).*

CTNP   *Chu-tzu nien-p'u (Chu Hsi's Chronological Biography).*

CTTC   *Chu-tzu ta-ch'üan (Collected Writings of Chu-Hsi).*

CTYL   *Chu-tzu yü-lei (Classified Conversations).*

CTYS   *Chu-tzu yi-shu (Surviving Writings of Chu Hsi).*

CYCC   *Chung-yung chang-chü (Annotated Edition of the Great Learning).*

CYCY   *Chou-yi cheng-yi (Correct Meaning of the Book of Changes).*

ECCS   *Erh-Ch'eng ch'üan-shu (Complete Writings of the Two Ch'engs).*

HSCC   *Hsiang-shan ch'üan-chi (Collected Writings of Lu Chiu-yüan).*

HTHT   *Hsin-t'i yü Hsing-t'i (On Mind-in-Itself and Nature-in-Itself).*

LCCC   *Li-chi Cheng-chu (Book of Rites with Cheng Hsüan's Commentary).*

PR   Alfred North Whitehead. *Process and Reality.* 1929. Reprint, New York, Free Press, 1969.

SK   *Ssu-k'u ch'üan-shu tsung-mu t'i-yao (Essentials of the Catalog of the Four Libraries Series).* Taipei, Yi-wen reprint, 1972.

SPPY   *Ssu-pu pei-yao (Essentials of the Four Libraries Series).*

SPTK   *Ssu-pu ts'ung-k'an (Collection of the Four Libraries Series).*

SSCC   *Ssu-shu chi-chu (Collected Commentaries on the Four Books).*

SYHA   Huang Tsung-hsi et al., eds., *Sung-Yüan hsüeh-an (Records of Sung and Yüan Scholars).* Taipei, World Bookstore, 1966.

T   *Taishō shinshu Daizōkyō (Taishō edition of the Buddhist Canon).*

TLP   *Chung-kuo che-hsüeh yüan-lun: Tao-lun p'ien (An Inquiry into Chinese Philosophy).*

TLTL   *Ts'ung Lu Hsiang-shan tao Liu Chi-shan (From Lu Chiu-yüan to Liu Tsung-chou).* Taipei, Student Bookstore, 1979.

TSCC   *Ts'ung-shu chi-ch'eng (Collected Series of Books).*

TT   *Tao-tsang (Taoist Canon).*

WWKC   *Wang Wen-ch'eng kung ch'üan-shu (Complete Writings of Wang Yang-ming).* SPTK ed.

YCP   *Chung-kuo che-hsüeh yüan-lun: Yüan-chiao p'ien (An Inquiry into Chinese Philosophy: On the Original Teaching).*

YHP   *Chung-kuo che-hsüeh yüan-lun: Yüan-hsing-p'ien (An Inquiry into Chinese Philosophy: On Original Nature).*

YTP   *Chung-kuo che-hsüeh yüan-lun: Yüan-tao-p'ien (An Inquiry into Chinese Philosophy: The Original Tao).*

Chapter 1

1. Literally, what is "expedient."
2. Chou Tun-yi posted this poem on his door. See his *Complete Writings: Chou Chang ch'üan-shu (The Complete Works of Chou Tun-yi and Chang Tsai)*, in Okada Takehiko, ed., *Chin-shih Han-chi ts'ung-k'an (Collected Chinese Texts from Recent Times)* (Taipei, Chung-wen, 1972), vol. 1, 4:4a. "Opening" and "closing" refer to *yang* and *yin*, motion and rest. The metaphor comes from an appendix to the Book of Changes. See also chapter 8.
3. On opening and closing the gate of wisdom with regard to the Book of Changes, consult chapter 8 in the present work.
4. Consult James T. C. Liu, *China Turning Inward: Intellectual-Political Changes in the Early Twelfth Century* (Cambridge, Council on East Asian Studies, Harvard University, 1988), ch. 7; Robert P. Hymes and Conrad Shirokauer, eds., *Ordering the World: Approaches to State and Society in Sung Dynasty China* (Berkeley, University of California Press, 1993).
5. Min is another name for the Fukien region.
6. Stanislas LeGall, *Chu Hsi: Sa doctrine, son influence* (Shanghai, La Mission Catholique, 1923), p. 1. The French says: "a fine talker and a detestable philosopher, this man succeeded, for over seven centuries, in imposing on his many compatriots a completely materialist explanation of the old texts."
7. Carsun Chang, *The Development of Neo-Confucian Thought* (New York, Bookman Associates, 1957–62), vol. 2, appendix.
8. This has been the joint work of Western and Chinese scholars especially in the United States. Wing-tsit Chan contributed the most, through his translations and other works. Others include William Theodore de Bary, Liu Shu-hsien, and Tu Weiming.
9. I am referring especially to the work of Hou Wailu, Zhao Jibin, and Du Guoxiang: *Chung-kuo ssu-hsiang t'ung-shih (A History of Chinese Thought)* (Peking, Jen-min, 1957–60), vol. 4A, chs. 10–12; vol. 4B, ch. 13.
10. I shall discuss the Four Books later, especially in chapters 5–6.
11. See Carl Jung's foreword to *The I Ching, or Book of Changes* trans. R. Wilhelm and C. F. Baynes (Princeton University Press, 1967), xxi–xxxix.
12. Both of these works can be found in the final volume of *CTYS*.
13. *Chou-yi Wang-Han chu (Book of Changes with Commentaries by Wang Pi and Han K'ang-po)*, SPPY ed., 7:3b; Marcel Granet, *La pensée chinoise* (Paris, Albin Michel, 1968), pp. 111–48; Anne Cheng, *Histoire de la pensée chinoise* (Paris, Seuil, 1997), p. 242.
14. Joseph Needham, *Science and Civilisation in China* (Cambridge University Press, 1959–61), vol. 2, p. 467.
15. Ibid., vol. 3, pp. 229–33; Carl Hentze, *Mythes et symboles lunaires* (Anvers, 1932), especially chs. 2 and 3.
16. James Legge, trans., *The Chinese Classics* (Oxford, Clarendon, 1893–95), vol. 3, pp. 325–26. Consult John S. Major, "Note on the Translation of Two Technical Terms in Chinese Science: *Wu-hsing* and *Hsiu*," *Early China* 2 (1976), 1–3; Anne Cheng, *Histoire*, p. 244.

17. Anne Cheng, *Histoire*, p. 249. See also Michael Loewe, on the symbols water, earth, and fire, in *Divination, Mythology, and Monarchy in China* (Cambridge University Press, 1994), p. 57.

18. Anne Cheng, *Histoire*, pp. 248–49; John B. Henderson, *The Development and Decline of Chinese Cosmological Thought* (New York, Columbia University Press, 1984), ch. 1.

19. *Lü-shih ch'un-ch'iu* (*Lü's Spring and Autumn Annals*), SPPY ed., 13:3b. Eng. translation adapted from Fung Yu-lan, *A History of Chinese Philosophy*, trans. Derk Bodde (Princeton University Press, 1952–53), vol. 1, p. 168.

20. *Ch'un-ch'iu fan-lu* (*Luxuriant Gems of the Spring and Autumn Annals*), SPPY ed., sect. 56, 13:1b–2a. English translation adapted from Wing-tsit Chan, trans., *A Source Book in Chinese Philosophy* (Princeton University Press, 1963), pp. 280–81.

21. The T'ang edition was called the *Wu-ching cheng-yi* (*Correct Meaning of the Five Classics*) and was done under the supervision of K'ung Ying-ta (574–648). As it included the three ritual texts (see n. 23) and the three commentaries to the Spring and Autumn Annals, there were nine classics involved. These were inscribed in stone, together with the *Classic of Filial Piety* (*Hsiao-ching*), the *Analects* (*Lun-yü*), and the ancient glossary, the *Erh-ya*. During Sung times, the *Book of Mencius* was also elevated to a classic, making up a total of thirteen. See P'i Hsi-jui, *Ching-hsüeh li-shih* (*A History of Classical Studies*), annotated by Chou Yü-t'ung (Taipei, Wen-hai, 1964), pp. 42–45.

22. These are chapters from the classical Book of Rites, which were given independent status. Recently, in 1993, archaeologists uncovered lost texts, now attributed to Confucius's grandson, Tzu-ssu, and his circle, which articulate concepts of human nature and the human mind. These texts testify to an early origin for ideas that Chu Hsi and his immediate predecessors and successors developed. Consult the texts on bamboo collected from Guodian and published by the Chingmen, or Jingmen, City Museum in *Kuo-tien Ch'u-mu chu-chien* (Peking, Wenwu, 1998).

23. Kidder Smith, Jr., et al., eds., *Sung Dynasty Uses of the I-Ching* (Princeton University Press, 1990), pp. 46–55. In the classical corpus, the ritual texts complicate matters because they are really three texts: the so-called Book of Rites (Li-chi), the Ceremonials (Yi-li), and the Institutes of Chou (Chou-li). The laconic Spring and Autumn Annals usually have associated to them the *Annals of Tso*, a longer, narrative account, and the *Kung-yang* and *Ku-liang* commentaries, which are catechetical in formula.

24. For the *Great Learning*, Chu incorporated Ch'eng Yi's substitution of a word in the text, changing *ch'in-min* (loving the people) to *hsin-min* (renovate the people).

25. Ōtsuki Nobuyoshi, *Chu-tzu Ssu-shu chi-chu tien-chü k'ao* (*On the Sources of Chu Hsi's Collected Commentaries on the Four Books*) (Taipei, Student Bookstore, 1976).

26. This refers to the sentence *Yin wu-suo-chu erh-sheng ch'i-hsin*. See *Chin-kang p'an-jo po-lo-mi ching* (*The Diamond Prajñāpāramitā Sutra*), T 8, no. 235, p. 749c. English translation from F. Max Müller, ed., *The Vagrakkhedika, or Diamond-Cutter*, in *Buddhist Mahayana Texts*, Sacred Books of the East Series, vol. 49, ed. F. Max Müller (London, Oxford University Press, 1894), p. 122.

27. D. C. Lau, trans., *Lao Tzu: Tao-te ching* (Harmondsworth, Penguin Books, 1963), p. 60.

28. *Lao-tzu,* with Wang Pi's commentary, *SPPY* ed., 4:3a.

29. Walter Liebenthal, trans., *Chao Lun: The Treatises of Seng Chao* (Hong Kong University Press, 1968), pp. 18–28.

30. Consult *Tsu-t'ing shih-yüan* (*Events from the Patriarchs' Courts*) (1108), *Hsü tsang-ching* (*Supplement to the Buddhhist Canon*) (Korean: *Sokchanggyong*) (*Supplement to the Tripitaka*) (reprint, Seoul, Poryonguk, 1981), vol. 138, 5:66b (p. 132). The statement is attributed to the legendary Bodhidharma. The English is adapted from D. T. Suzuki, *Zen Buddhism: Selected Writings of D. T. Suzuki,* ed. William Barrett (New York, Doubleday/Anchor, 1956), p. 61.

31. See Tsung-mi, *Ch'an-yüan suo-ch'üan chi-tu hsü* (*A Preface to the Collected Writings on the Sources of Ch'an*), *T* 48, no. 2015. This work collects teachings from Ch'an and non-Ch'an masters that corroborate one another. Consult also Takeuchi Yoshio, *Takeuchi Yoshio zenshū,* ed. Kōjirō Yoshikawa et al. (Tokyo, Kadokawa shoten, 1985), vol. 8, pp. 162–63.

32. Tsung-mi, *Yüan-jen lun* (*On Original Human Nature*), *T* 45, no. 1886, pp. 708–10; Tsung-mi, *Ch'an-yüan;* Feng Yu-lan, *Chung-kuo che-hsüeh-shih* (Shanghai, Commercial Press, 1934), p. 792. This part of Fung was not included in the edition translated by Derk Bodde.

33. Tsung-mi, *Yüan-jen lun;* Feng, *Chung-kuo che-hsüeh-shih,* pp. 798–99.

34. See *Hung-chih Ch'an-shih kuang-lu* (*The Recorded Dialogues of Ch'an Master Hung-chih*), *T* 48, no. 2001, ch. 5, p. 72c.

35. See Ta-hui's recorded dialogues, *Ta-hui P'u-chüeh ch'an-shih yü-lu, T* 47, no. 1998A, ch. 30, pp. 881–942. The original story is given in the *Wu-men kuan* (*The Pass without a Gate*), *T* 48, no. 2005, p. 292. See also the biographies in the *Hsü Ch'uan-teng lu* (*Supplement to the Transmission of the Lamp*), *T* 51, no. 2077, ch. 27, pp. 649–54, and ch. 17, p. 579. Consult Koichi Shinohara, "Ta-hui's Instructions to Tseng K'ai: Buddhist 'Freedom' in the Neo-Confucian Context," in Irene Bloom and Joshua A. Fogel, eds., *The Meeting of Minds: Intellectual and Religious Interaction in East Asian Traditions of Thought* (New York, Columbia University Press, 1997), pp. 175–208; Heinrich Dumoulin, *A History of Zen Buddhism,* trans. James W. Heisig and Paul Knitter (London, Macmillan, 1988–90), vol. 1, pt. 2, ch. 8. See also chapter 9, below.

36. Whalen W. Lai, "Sinitic Mandalas: The *Wu-wei-t'u* of Ts'ao-shan," in Whalen W. Lai and Lewis Lancaster, eds., *Early Ch'an in China and Tibet,* Berkeley Buddhist Studies Series (Berkeley, Asian Humanities Press, 1983), p. 237.

37. See Isabelle Robinet, *Introduction à l'alchimie intérieure taoiste de l'unité et de la multiplicité* (Paris, Cerf, 1995); Ho Peng-yoke, *Li, Qi, and Shu: An Introduction to Science and Civilisation in China* (Hong Kong University Press, 1985), ch. 5, on alchemy and literati in Sung dynasty China. Taoist texts dealing with inner alchemy or related subjects current in Sung times include *Mi-ch'uan Cheng-yang cheng-jen ling-pao pi-fa* (*The Secretly Transmitted Ling-pao Method of Chung-li Ch'üan*), 3 chs. in *TT,* vol. 47; *Chung-Lü ch'uan-tao chi* (*Collected Texts on the Teachings of Chung-li Ch'üan and Lü Tung-pin*), 3 chs. in *TT,* vol. 7; and *Hsi-shan chün-hsien hui-chen chi* (*Record on the Immortals' Assembly in Hsi-shan*), 5 chs. in *TT,* vol. 7. In the Southern Sung period, see Tseng Ts'ao, *Tao-shu,* 42 chs. in *TT,* vols. 34–35; Chang Po-tuan, *Wu-chen p'ien* (*On Awakening to Truth*), which appeared with Wen Pao-kuang's commentary as *Wu-chen p'ien chu-shu, TT,* vol. 4.

38. This is given in Chen Kaiguo, *Ta-Tao hsing* (Peking, Hua-hsia, 1993), a lengthy story of Wang Liping, a contemporary Taoist master trained by hermits in the

Dragon Gate lineage established by the thirteenth-century patriarch Ch'iu Ch'u-chi.

39. Consult *Chou-Yi Wang-Han chu, SPPY* ed., 7:9b; Wilhelm and Baynes, *I Ching,* p. 320.

40. See Lü Ssu-mien et al., *Ku-shih pien (Debates on Ancient History)* (1941; Hong Kong reprint, Taiping, 1963), vol. 7, pp. 231–32; Needham, *Science and Civilisation,* vol. 3, p. 57. See figure 1 for the River Chart and the Lo Writing given in Chu Hsi's *Yi-hsüeh ch'i-meng, CTYS,* vol. 12.

41. The source of Chou Tun-yi's *Diagram* is treated more fully in appendix B.

42. This statement is from eighteenth-century Europe but is very descriptive of the Chinese Taoist quest as well. See Mircea Eliade, *Yoga: Immortality and Freedom* (Princeton University Press, 1969), p. 291.

43. Consult Chu Hsi's *Yin-fu ching k'ao-yi (Inquiry into the Yin-fu ching), CTYS,* vol. 12, p. 6a.

44. *ECCS, Yi-shu,* 6:4a.

45. *Chou Lien-hsi chi (Collected Writings of Chou Tun-yi),* in Chang Po-hsing, comp., *Cheng-yi-t'ang ch'üan-shu* (Shanghai, Commercial Press reprint, 1936), ch. 8, p. 151; see also Lao Ssu-kuang, *Chung-kuo che-hsüeh shih (A History of Chinese Philosophy)* (Taipei, San-min, 1981), vol. 3A, p. 142.

46. See Azuma Jūji, "Taikyokuzu no keisei: Ju butsu dō sankyō o meguru saikentō" (The Formation of the *Diagram of the Great Ultimate*: A Reexamination of the Three Teachings of Confucianism, Taoism, Buddhism), *Nippon Chūgoku gakkaihō* 46 (1994), 73–86.

47. Edward J. Thomas, *The History of Buddhist Thought* (London, Routledge and Kegan Paul, 1933; reprint, 1971), pp. 233–35.

48. Azuma, "Taikyokuzu no keisei," pp. 79–80; consult Tsung-mi's *Ch'an-yüan,* pp. 397–414. The chart(s) in question take up pp. 410–13. See figure 3.

49. See Tsung-mi, *Ch'an-yüan.*

50. For the different wordings, consult *CTTC* 71:4a.

51. Imai Usaburō, *Sōdai ekigaku no kenkyū (The Study of the Book of Changes during the Sung Dynasty)* (Tokyo, Meiji shoin, 1958), ch. 5.

52. Ibid., pp. 353–57.

53. For the diagram itself and the text of the *T'ai-chi-t'u shuo (Explanations of the Diagram of the Great Ultimate),* see *Chou-tzu ch'üan-shu (Complete Works of Chou Tun-yi)* in *Chou-Chang ch'üan-shu,* in Okada Takehiko, ed., *Chin-shih Han-chi ts'ung-k'an* (Taipei, Chung-wen, 1972), vol. 1, 1:1a–7b.

54. Consult Tung Chung-shu, *Ch'un-ch'iu fan-lu, SPPY* ed. ch. 11, sec. 42, 2a–b. Consult also Fung, *History,* vol. 2, pp. 20–21. Tung's sequence gives Wood, Fire, Earth, Metal, Water. This is the sequence of mutual generation.

55. Consult Chu Hsi's commentary on the *Diagram of the Great Ultimate* (Chou Tun-yi, *Chou-tzu ch'üan-shu* 1:15b) in *Chou-Chang ch'üan-shu,* vol. 1. I thank Whalen Lai for his assistance on this subject.

56. Imai, *Sōdai ekigaku,* pp. 389–91.

57. *Mencius* 6A:6.

58. Prudence, or "practical wisdom," is an important virtue for both Aristotle and Thomas Aquinas. See Lee H. Yearley, *Mencius and Aquinas: Theories of Virtue and Conceptions of Courage* (Albany, State University of New York Press, 1990), p. 77.

59. The *Diagram* and *Explanation* should be studied together with Chou's treatise *Penetrating the Book of Changes (Yi-t'ung),* a brief work purporting to interpret the classical text in terms of the philosophy of the *Doctrine of the Mean (Chung-*

yung). Consult William Theodore de Bary and Irene Bloom, eds., *Sources of Chinese Tradition* (New York, Columbia University Press, 1999), vol. I, pp. 672–76.

60. Don J. Wyatt, "Chu Hsi's Critique of Shao Yung: One Instance of the Stand against Fatalism," *Harvard Journal of Asiatic Studies* 45 (1995), 649–66.

61. *CTYL* 94:2b–3a.

62. See Julia Ching and Willard G. Oxtoby, *Moral Enlightenment: Leibniz and Wolff on China*, Monumenta Serica Monograph Series, no. 26 (Nettetal, Steyler Verlag, 1992), pp. 81–141. See also Helmut Wilhelm, *Eight Lectures on the I-ching* (Princeton University Press, 1960), pp. 90–91. See Shao's epitaph by Ch'eng Hao, in Chu Hsi, comp., *Yi-Lo yüan-yüan lu* (*The Origins of the Schools of Chou Tun-yi and the Ch'eng Brothers*), *CTYS*, vol. 6, 5:2a–b. See also Anne D. Birdwhistell, *Transition to Neo-Confucianism: Shao Yung on Knowledge and Symbols of Reality* (Stanford University Press, 1989); Don J. Wyatt, *The Recluse of Loyang: Shao Yung and the Moral Evolution of Early Sung Thought* (Honolulu, University of Hawaii Press, 1996), ch. 7.

63. *CTCS*; Chang Tsai, *Cheng-meng* (*Correcting Youthful Ignorance*) SPPY ed., 2:2a–3b. Consult Ira E. Kasoff, *The Thought of Chang Tsai, 1020–1077* (Cambridge University Press, 1984), especially ch. 2.

64. *CTCS* 1:2a. English translation adapted from Wing-tsit Chan, *Source Book*, p. 497.

65. See Hsü Shen, *Shuo-wen chieh-tzu Tuan-chu* (*A Lexicon with Tuan Yü-ts'ai's Commentary*), SPPY ed., 1A:21a; Wing-tsit Chan, "The Evolution of the Neo-Confucian Concept *Li* as Principle," in Chan, *Neo-Confucianism Etc.: Essays by Wing-tsit Chan*, comp. Charles K. H. Chen (Hong Kong, Oriental Society, 1969), pp. 45–87, especially 46–48; Paul Demiéville, "La pénétration du bouddhisme dans la tradition philosophique chinoise," *Cahiers d'histoire mondiale* 3 (1956), 28.

66. *Mo-tzu*, SPPY ed., sec. 3, 1:6a.

67. *Kuan-tzu*, SPPY ed., sec. 55, 18:4a. English translation adapted from Needham, *Science and Civilisation*, vol. 2, p. 477.

68. *Mencius* 5B:1.6.

69. *Hsün-tzu*, SPPY ed., sec. 17, 11:13b; sec. 19, 13:2b; sec. 22, 16:7a–10b; sec. 23, 17:1a. Consult *TLP*, introductory vol., ch. 1, pp. 1–39, especially pp. 5–6, 11–16.

70. *LCCC*, sec. 19, 11:8a.

71. *Chuang-tzu*, SPPY ed., sec. 14, 5:20b. English translation adapted from Burton Watson, trans., *The Complete Works of Chuang Tzu* (New York, Columbia University Press, 1968), p. 156.

72. *CYCY* 7:3a, 9:2b; *Chou Yi Wang Han chu*, 7:1b, 9:1a; *TLP*, p. 23.

73. Tsung-mi, *Chu Hua-yen fa-chieh kuan-men*, T 45, no. 1884, pp. 683–92; *TLP*, pp. 40–49. Consult also *TLP*, pp. 26–39; Needham, *Science and Civilisation*, vol. 2, pp. 472–78; William Ernest Hocking, "Chu Hsi's Theory of Knowledge," *Harvard Journal of Asiatic Studies* 1 (April 1936), 109–27, especially p. 114.

74. *Chou-tzu T'ung-shu* (*Penetrating into [the Book of Changes]*), SPPY ed., ch. 13, p. 3a; ch. 22, p. 5a.

75. See, e.g., *CTCS* 2:18a–19b, 20b–21a.

76. *ECCS*, *Yi-shu*, 2A:21–22, 11:3b, 5a.

77. *CTCS* 1:7a–b gives Chu's commentary. Consult *TLP*, pp. 49–54. Tang discusses the meaning of *li*[a] in the later Ch'ing thinkers, especially Tai Chen; see pp. 55–69.

78. *Hsün-tzu*, sec. 2, 1:9a; *Huai-nan-tzu*, SPPY ed., especially chs. 2–3; *Lieh-tzu*, SPPY ed., ch. 1; *Kuan-tzu*, ch. 4, sec. 12. Consult Onozawa Seiichi et al., eds., *Ki no shisō: Chūgoku ni okeru jigenkan to ningenkan no tenkai* (*The Concept of Ch'i*[a]: *The*

Development of Naturalism and Humanism in China) (Tokyo University Press, 1978), chs. 1–2. This book contains chapters written by specialists discussing the transmission and evolution of the early and Taoist concepts of *ch'i*[a] into neo-Confucian philosophy.

79. *Kuan-tzu*, ch. 16, sec. 49, p. 1. English translation adapted from W. Allyn Rickett, *Kuan Tzu* (Hong Kong University Press, 1965), vol. 2, p. 99.

80. Charles Le Blanc, *Huai-nan-tzu: Philosophical Synthesis in Early Han Thought* (Hong Kong University Press, 1985), p. 14; Feng Youlan, *Chung-kuo che-hsüeh-shih hsin-pien* (*A New History of Chinese Philosophy*) (Peking, Jen-min, 1964), vol. 2, 146–50; Hsü Fu-kuan, *Liang Han ssu-hsiang-shih* (*A History of the Thought of the Han Times*) (Taipei, Student Bookstore, 1976), pp. 175–284.

81. Walter Watson, *The Architectonics of Meaning: Foundations of a New Pluralism* (Albany, State University of New York Press, 1985), pp. 50–51.

82. Needham, *Science and Civilisation*, vol. 2, p. 472.

83. Ho Peng-yoke, *Li, Qi, and Shu*, p. 3. We may also mention in this connection the Latin *spiritus* and the Hebrew *ruah* (air, breath, spirit): "In the beginning God created the heavens and the earth. The earth was without form and void . . . and the Spirit (*ruah*) of God was moving over the face of the waters" (Genesis 1:1–2).

84. See Tsung-mi, *Yüan-jen lun*, pp. 707–10; Fung, *History*, vol. 2, pp. 304–38; Onozawa et al., *Kino shisō*, pp. 333–51.

85. In Onozawa et al.'s book, a section by Tsuchida Kenjirō in pt. 3, ch. 1, points out Taoist religious influences on Ch'eng Hao's and Ch'eng Yi's conceptions of *ch'i*[a]. See *Kino shisō*, pp. 417–37.

86. *CTYL* 1:1b.

87. Ibid.

88. *CTYL* 1:2a–b. See Yamanoi Yū's contribution in Onozawa et al., *Kino shisō*, pt. 3, ch. 2, pp. 438–52, on *ch'i*[a] in Chu Hsi.

89. Sun Cheng-ch'ing, "Chu Hsi te li/ch'i kai-nien yü Ya-li-ssu-tuo-te (Aristotle) te hsing-chih kai-nien chih pi-chiao" (Chu Hsi's Li/Ch'i Concept Compared to Aristotle's Idea of Form and Matter), in Chung Ts'ai-chün, ed., *Kuo-chi Chu-tzu hsüeh hui-yi lun-wen chi* (*Collected Papers from the International Symposium on Chu Hsi*) (Taipei, Academia Sinica, 1993), pp. 751–68.

90. Chang Tung-sun, "A Chinese Philosopher's Theory of Knowledge," *Etc.: A Review of General Semantics* 9 (1952), 203–26; Needham, *Science and Civilisation*, vol. 2, p. 478.

91. *CTYL* 1:1b.

92. Consult *YTP*, vol. 3, suppl., pp. 438–56.

93. See Lou-ying, comp., *Shan-hui ta-shih yü-lu* (*Recorded Dialogue of Master Shan-hui*), in *Hsü tsang-ching*, vol. 120, ch. 4, 27b (p. 53); *SYHA*, ch. 12, p. 307. This *gatha* was composed by the Buddhist Fu Ta-shih; it is given in the *SYHA* as what Chou Tun-yi received from the monk Shou-ya. The English translation is my own.

Chapter 2

1. Chu's poem refers to Heavenly Pillar Peak, in the sacred Wu-yi Mountains. See *CTTC* 6:23a. *Ch'ien* (Heaven) and *K'un*[a] (Earth) are the two great trigrams, the parents of all the others.

2. *CTNP*, ch. 1A, p. 2.

3. *CTNP*, ch. 1A, pp. 1–2.

4. See chapter 1.

5. Chu Hsi and Lü Tsu-ch'ien, eds., *Chin-ssu lu*, in *CTYS*, (Taipei reprint, Yi-wen, 1969). For an English translation, see Wing-tsit Chan, trans., *Reflections on Things at Hand* (New York, Columbia University Press, 1967).

6. Consult Azuma Jūji, "Shushi no sūshōeki shisō to sono igi" (Significance of Chu Hsi's Thought on the Symbols and Numbers in the Book of Changes), *Firosofia* 68 (1980), 145–75; Julia Ching, *Mysticism and Kingship in China: The Heart of Chinese Wisdom* (Cambridge University Press, 1997), ch. 4; Chiu Hansheng, "Zhu Xi's Doctrine of Principle," in Wing-tsit Chan, ed., *Chu Hsi and Neo-Confucianism* (Honolulu, University of Hawaii Press, 1986), pp. 116–37; Tang Chün-i, *TLP*; Yamanoi Yū, "The Great Ultimate and Heaven in Chu Hsi's Philosophy," in Wing-tsit Chan, *Chu Hsi and Neo-Confucianism*, pp. 79–92, especially 79–87; Teng Ai-min, "Zhu Xi's Theory of the Great Ultimate," in Wing-tsit Chan, *Chu Hsi and Neo-Confucianism*, pp. 93–115.

7. For primary sources, consult Chu Hsi and Lü Tsu-ch'ien, *Chin-ssu lu*, vol. 1, ch. 1; Wing-tsit Chan, *Reflections*; *CTYL*, especially ch. 1, pp. 94 and 116; and certain letters and essays from the *CTTC*, especially ch. 36, which contains Chu's correspondence with the Lu brothers, and from *HSCC*, ch. 2. Consult also Chu Hsi, *Yi-hsüeh ch'i-meng*, 2:2a.

8. See also Wilhelm and Baynes, *I Ching*, pp. 318–19.

9. See Chang Chung-yüan, "Creativity as Process in Taoism," *Eranos Jahrbuch* 25 (1963), 392.

10. *Lao-tzu*, ch. 42. English translation from Lau, *Lao-tzu*, p. 103.

11. Lao-tzu, ch. 28. English translation from Lau, *Lao-tzu*, p. 85.

12. See Chu's letter to Lu Chiu-yüan, *CTTC* 36:10b.

13. From the *Yi-wei ch'ien-k'un tso-tu* (*Fragments from the Apocryphal Book of Changes*), in *Yi-wei shih-lei mou chi ch'i-ta wu-chung* (*A Collection of Five Fragments from the Apocryphal Book of Changes*, with Cheng Hsüan's Commentary), *TSCC* ed., 1st ser. (Changsha, Commercial Press, 1937), pt. 1, p. 2b.

14. Ibid., p. 3a.

15. Ibid., p. 2b.

16. Consult Imai, *Sōdai ekigaku*, p. 359.

17. Consult *Chuang-tzu*, sec. F, 3:19a–b; *Yi-wei Ch'ien/K'un tso-tu*, pt. 1, p. 4b; Norman J. Girardot, *Myth and Meaning in Early China: The Theme of Chaos (Huntun)* (Berkeley, University of California Press, 1983), especially chs. 5–6.

18. *Yi-wei Ch'ien/K'un tso-tu*, pt. 2, p. 30; Fung, *History*, vol. 2, p. 101.

19. *Huai-nan-tzu*, 14:1a.

20. Ibid.

21. This becomes all the more interesting when we remember that the Moon, Earth, and Heaven—like the Pole Star—have each served at one time or another, and sometimes simultaneously, as the symbol for the supreme deity in ancient China. See also Joseph Shih, "The Notions of 'God' in Ancient Chinese Religion," *Numen* 16 (1969), 99–138, especially 131–37.

22. Ibid.

23. Mircea Eliade, *The Sacred and the Profane* (New York, Harcourt Brace, 1959), pp. 35–37.

24. K'an and *Li*[b] play an especially important role in Taoist alchemy and yoga, representing the kidneys and the heart in the human organism. In breath circulation, it is believed that the heart or mind can be calmed by properly directed waters from the kidneys.

25. *CTYL* 1:4b.
26. *HSCC* 22:5a.
27. *CTYL* 94:5b.
28. Consult chapter 1.
29. Chou Tun-Yi, *T'ai-chi-t'u shuo* (*Explanations of the Diagram of the Great Ultimate*), in *Chou-tzu ch'üan-shu*; Chu Hsi, "T'ai-chi shuo" (On the Great Ultimate), *CTTC* 67:16a–b; Chu Hsi, "Chou-tzu 'T'ai-chi/T'ung-shu' hou-hsü" (Epilogue to Master Chou's *Great Ultimate* and *Book of Penetration*), *CTTC* 75:18a–19b; Chu Hsi, "Tsai-ting T'ai-chi T'ung-shu hou-hsü" (Another Epilogue to the [Explanations on] the *Great Ultimate* and *Penetrating into the Book of Changes*), *CTTC* 76:4a–6b; Chu Hsi, "T'i *T'ai-chi/Hsi-ming chieh hou*" (Postscript to the *Explanation of the Great Ultimate* and the "Western Inscription"), *CTTC* 82:14a.
30. *Chuang-tzu*, sec. 3, ch. 2:1b–2a. English translation in Burton Watson, *Chuang Tzu*, pp. 50–51. For Chu on this story, see chapter 8.
31. See *CTNP* 1B:30; Ch'ien Mu, *Chu-tzu hsin hsüeh-an* (*A New Scholarly Record of Chu Hsi*) (Taipei, San-min, 1971), vol. 3, p. 54.
32. *CTNP* 1B:53.
33. Chu Hsi, "T'i *T'ai-chi Hsi-ming chieh* hou," *CTTC* 82:14a; *CTNP* 3B:166.
34. Chu Hsi, "Chu-tzu *T'ai-chi t'u* shuo-chieh" (*Chu Hsi's Explanation of the Diagram of the Great Ultimate*), in *Chou Lien-hsi chi*, ch. 1, pp. 28–29. Interestingly, the wording is different in the letter collected in *CTTC*, ch. 31, although the meaning does not change much. See also *CTYL* 93:7a. Consult *TLP*, pp. 400–401; Angus C. Graham, *Two Chinese Philosophers: Ch'eng Ming-tao and Ch'eng Yi-ch'uan* (London, Lund Humphries, 1958), p. 144; Julia Ching, "Truth and Ideology: The Confucian Way (*Tao*) and Its Transmission (*Tao-t'ung*)," *Journal of the History of Ideas* 35 (1974), 371–88.
35. *ECCS*, *Yi-ch'uan Yi-chuan hsü* (*Ch'eng Yi's Preface to the Great Commentary on the Book of Changes*), p. 4a.
36. *CTYL* 94:18b.
37. *CTNP*, ch. 4, p. 342.
38. For the *Doctrine of the Mean*, see especially chapter 6.
39. Olaf Graf, *Tao und Jen: Sein und Sollen im sungchinesischen Monismus* (Wiesbaden, Otto Harrassowitz, 1970), p. 22.
40. *Lieh-tzu*, 1:3b. The word *yi* is the same as in the *Yi-ching*, or Book of Changes.
41. *CTYL* 94:13a.
42. *CTYL* 98:1b.
43. *CTYL* 99:2a, p. 4025.
44. *CTYL* 99:2b, p. 4026.
45. *CTYL* 99:3a, p. 4027.
46. For Chang's "Western Inscription," see *CTCS* 1:2a.
47. *CTYL* 98:12b–17b.
48. *CTYL* 94:18b–19a.
49. *CTYL* 94:4b–5a.
50. Letter to Lu Chiu-yüan (1183), in *CTTC* 36:9b.
51. Consult Teng, "Zhu Xi's Theory," p. 94.
52. *CTYL* 1:1a.
53. *HSCC* 2:11a.
54. *CTYL* 94:1b.

55. *Chou-tzu T'ung-shu*, ch. 22, p. 5; consult the English translation in Wing-tsit Chan, *Source Book*, p. 474.
56. Fung, *History*, vol. 2, p. 444.
57. *CTYL* 94:6a.
58. Fung, *History*, vol. 2, p. 537.
59. *CTYL* 1:1b–2a, pp. 2–3.
60. *CTYL* 94:1b–2b.
61. *CTYL* 94:1b.
62. *CTYL* 94:6a.
63. *CTYL* 94:10a, p. 3773; *TLP*, pp. 453–54; Whalen W. Lai, "How Principle Rides on Ether: Chu Hsi's Non-Buddhistic Resolution of Nature and Emotion," *Journal of Chinese Philosophy* 11 (1984), 31–65.
64. *CTYL* 94:11a–b. Consult Chiu Hansheng, "Zhu Xi's Doctrine of Principle," in Wing-tsit Chan, *Chu Hsi*, pp. 120–21.
65. The reference is to the monk Yung-chia's *Cheng-tao ko* (*Song on Witnessing the Way*). See *T* 48, no. 2014, p. 396b; *CTYL* 18:8b.
66. *CTYL* 94:6a.
67. *CTYL* 94:13b.
68. This question is also raised by Shimada Kenji, *Shushigaku to Yōmeigaku* (Tokyo, Iwanami, 1984), pp. 87–88.
69. *CTYL* 94:35b.
70. Fung, *History*, vol. 2, p. 541.
71. Nicolaus Cusanus, *Of Learned Ignorance*, trans. Fr. Germain Stark (London, Routledge and Kegan Paul, 1954), bk. 2, pp. 81–82.
72. Ibid., p. 83.
73. See his letter to Cardinal Julian [Cesarini], in Cusanus, *Of Learned Ignorance*, p. 173.
74. *CTYL* 94:3b–4a, pp. 3760–61.
75. *CTYL* 94:2b–3a, pp. 3758–59. For Shao Yung, see "Kuan-wu p'ien" (On Contemplating Things), ch. 6, sec. 60, 11a–14a, in Shao Yung, *Huang-chi ching-shih shu* (*Supreme Principles for Governing the World*), SPPY ed.; Fung, *History*, vol. 2, p. 470.
76. *CTYL* 1:6a, p. 11.
77. Chiang Kuang-hui, "Chu Hsi che-hsüeh yü-lun" (On Other Questions in Chu Hsi's Philosophy), in Chung, *Kuo-chi Chu-tzu hsüeh-hui*, pp. 771–75.
78. There are nine extant letters on the subject: two from Lu Chiu-shao (Liu Jiushao) to Chu Hsi and two from Chu Hsi to Lu Chiu-shao, three from Lu Chiu-yüan to Chu Hsi and two from Chu Hsi to Lu Chiu-yüan. The longest and most important correspondence remains the exchange between Chu Hsi and Lu Chiu-yüan. See two letters from each in *CTTC* 36:7a–16b and *HSCC* 2:4b–11b.
79. *HSCC* 2:9a–10a.
80. *CTYL* 94:8b, p. 3770; 94:12a, p. 3777; *CTTC* 36:8b–9a.
81. Letter to Lu Chiu-shao, *CTTC* 36:3b.
82. *CTTC* 36:4b–5a.
83. Lu Chiu-yüan refers to Chiu-shao's views in *HSCC* 2:5b, in his letter to Chu.
84. *CTTC* 36:8a.
85. *CTTC* 36:9a.
86. *HSCC* 2:6a.
87. *HSCC* 2:6b.
88. *HSCC* 2:9b.
89. *CTTC* 36:9b–10a.

90. *CTTC* 36:11b–12a.
91. Imai, *Sōdai ekigaku*, p. 461.
92. See Julia Ching, *To Acquire Wisdom: The Way of Wang Yang-ming* (New York, Columbia University Press, 1976), introduction.
93. Yamanoi, "Great Ultimate," in Wing-tsit Chan, *Chu Hsi*, pp. 83–86.
94. *CTTC* 4:6b. The English translation given in the text was adapted from Li Chi, "Chu Hsi the Poet," *T'oung Pao* 58 (1972), 86–87.
95. Ernst Cassirer, "Myth and Religion," in *An Essay on Man: An Introduction to a Philosophy of Human Culture* (New Haven, Yale University Press, 1944), p. 94.

Chapter 3

1. *CTTC* 2:10b.
2. For a primary source, consult especially *CTYL*, ch. 3. A selected English translation of this can be found in Daniel K. Gardner, "Zhu Xi on Spirit Beings," in Donald S. Lopez, Jr., ed., *Chinese Religions in Practice* (Princeton University Press, 1996), pp. 106–22.
3. For Ch'eng's philosophy, consult Graham, *Two Chinese Philosophers*, especially pt. 1.
4. The secondary literature on this subject includes Wing-tsit Chan, *Chu Hsi: New Studies* (Honolulu, University of Hawaii Press, 1989); Wing-tsit Chan, *Chu Hsi: Life and Thought* (Hong Kong, Chinese University Press, 1987); Carsun Chang, *Development of Neo-Confucian Thought*, vols. 1–2; Julia Ching, *Chinese Religions* (London, Macmillan, 1993), chs. 1–2; Yung-sik Kim, "*Kuei-shen* in Terms of *Ch'i*: Chu Hsi's Discussion of *Kuei-shen*," *Tsing-Hua Journal of Chinese Studies* 17 (1985), 149–62; Gardner, "Zhu Xi on Spirit Beings," pp. 106–22. See also Daniel K. Gardner, "Ghosts and Spirits in the Sung Neo-Confucian World: Chu Hsi on *Kuei-shen*," *Journal of the American Oriental Society* 115 (1995), 598–611; Miura Kunio, "Shushi kijinron no rinkaku" (An Outline Description of Chu Hsi's Theory of Ghosts and Spirits), in *Jinkannen no hijōbunkaron teki kenkyū* (*A Study of the Notion of God in Comparative Culture*) (Tokyo, Kōdansha, 1981), pp. 741–84; Miura Kunio, "Shushi kijinron-ho" (A Supplement to Chu Hsi's Theory of Ghosts and Spirits), *Jinbun kenkyū* 37 (1985), 185–203; *YCP*, vol. 1; Hoyt C. Tillman, "Consciousness of *T'ien* in Chu Hsi's *i* Thought," *Harvard Journal of Asiatic Studies* 47 (1987), 31–50.
5. *CTYL* 1:4b.
6. Hsü Fu-kuan, "Ch'eng-Chu yi-t'ung ch'u-kao" (A Preliminary Study of Similarities and Differences between the Ch'engs and Chu Hsi), *Ta-lu tsa-chih* 64 (1982), 1–20, especially 6–10. See also Hsü Fu-kuan, "A Comparative Study of Chu Hsi and the Ch'eng Brothers," in Wing-tsit Chan, *Chu Hsi and Neo-Confucianism*, pp. 48–54.
7. *YCP*, vol. 1, pp. 150–63. This book has as subtitle "The Development of Sung-Ming Confucianism."
8. Consult Yamanoi Yū, "The Great Ultimate and Heaven in Chu Hsi's Philosophy," in Wing-tsit Chan, *Chu Hsi and Neo-Confucianism*, pp. 87–90; Yamane Mitsuyoshi, "Shushi no ten ni tsuite" (Chu Hsi on Heaven), *Tōhō Shūkyō* 26 (1965), 34–54; Yamane Mitsuyoshi, *Shushi rinri shisōkenkyū* (*A Study of Chu Hsi's Ethics*) (Tokyo, Tōkai University Press, 1983).
9. *CTYL* 1:5a.
10. *CTYL* 2:3b. Ts'ai is supposed to have followed Chu the longest and was regarded more as a friend than a disciple because of his own wide learning. See Wing-

tsit Chan, *Chu-tzu meng-jen (Chu Hsi's Disciples)* (Taipei, Student Bookstore, 1982), pp. 331–32.

11. Consult Tomoeda Ryūtarō, "The System of Chu Hsi's Philosophy," in Wing-tsit Chan, *Chu Hsi and Neo-Confucianism*, pp. 162–63.

12. In a letter to Ts'ai Yüan-ting, Chu even devised a planetarium. See *CTTC*, supplementary collection, 3:7a.

13. Needham, *Science and Civilisation*, vol. 3, pp. 439–42.

14. Ibid., 229–31.

15. Consult *CTYL*, ch. 7.

16. *CTYL* 1:5b.

17. *CTYL* 1:4b.

18. The mythical Eight Cords allegedly hold together the universe. See *Huai-nan-tzu* 1:1a.

19. *CTTC* 4:7b. English translation adapted from Li Chi, "Chu Hsi the Poet," p. 87. For the myth of *Hun-tun* (Chaos), see *Chuang-tzu*, sec. 7, 3:19a–b; see also Girardot, *Myth and Meaning in Early Taoism*, chs. 5–6. Here, Chu is probably thinking of the indeterminate character of the *Wu-chi*.

20. Yung-sik Kim, "*Kuei-shen*," p. 163.

21. *CTYL* 1:7a.

22. *CTYL* 1:7b.

23. *CTYL* 1:7a.

24. *CTYL* 1:8a. See also chapters 1 and 2.

25. Yung-sik Kim, "*Kuei-shen*," pp. 166–71. It may be noted that much of *CTYL*, ch. 2, is devoted to calendrical calculations.

26. *CTYL* 1:4b; Wing-tsit Chan, *New Studies*, p. 187.

27. *CTYL* 1:4b. Consult Julia Ching, *Confucianism and Christianity: A Comparative Study* (Tokyo, Kodansha International, 1977), p. 134.

28. Chu Hsi, *Lun-yü chi-chu (Collected Commentaries on the Analects)*, in *SSCC, SPPY* ed., 2:4b.

29. *CTCS* 2:21a; Kasoff, *Chang Tsai*, p. 57.

30. Consult Tillman, "Consciousness of *T'ien*," pp. 31–50.

31. *CTYL* 98:11a–b, pp. 4002–3.

32. *CTYL* 1:3b.

33. *CTYL* 1:3a.

34. *CTYL* 1:3b.

35. *CTYL* 1:3b.

36. *CTYL* 87:14b, p. 8560.

37. *LCCC* 11:9a.

38. *Huai-nan-tzu* 1:4a.

39. *CTYL* 97:11, p. 4001. See *ECCS, Wai-shu* (Supplements), 12:4a.

40. Ch'eng Hao, "On the Difference between Kings and Hegemons," in *Ming-tao wen-chi (Ch'eng Hao's Collected Writings)* (2:1a); Ch'eng Yi, *Yi-shu (Surviving Writings)* (15:1b); both from *ECCS*. See also *TLP*, pp. 425–32.

41. Consult Legge, *Chinese Classics*, vol. 4, p. 431. Chu's quotation is taken from the Decade of King Wen.

42. Chu Hsi's commentary on the Diagram, in *Chou-tzu ch'üan-shu* op. cit., 1:3a.

43. *CTYL* 90:3a, p. 3635.

44. *CTTC* 70:5a.

45. *CTYL* 13:2a–3a.

46. On this subject, consult Julia Ching, "Philosophy, Law, and Human Rights in

China," *East Asian Review* I (1997), I–20; Julia Ching, "Human Rights: A Valid Chinese Concept?" in William Theodore de Bary, ed., *Confucianism and Human Rights* (New York, Columbia University Press, 1998), pp. 67–82.

47. Chu Hsi, *Meng-tzu chi-chu* (*Collected Commentaries on the Book of Mencius*), in SSCC, SPPY ed. The comment is on *Mencius* 6A:3.

48. *CTYL* 13:2a.

49. *CTYL* 13:2a.

50. *CTYL* 13:7b.

51. *CTYL* 1:1a.

52. *CTYL* 1:1b.

53. Fukuda Shoku, "Chu Hsi te ssu-sheng kuan" (Chu Hsi on Life and After-life), in Chung, *Kuo-chi Chu-tzu hsüeh-hui*, pp. 879–906; Shibata Atsushi, "Inyō no rei to shite no kijin: Shushi kijin kaikonron no jomaku" (Ghosts and Spirits in the Light of Yin and Yang: A Preface to Chu Hsi's Theory of Ghosts and Spirits), *Tetsugaku nenpō* 50 (1991), 71–91.

54. *ECCS, Yi-shu* 3:1a.

55. *ECCS, Yi-shu*, 2B:3a

56. *ECCS, Yi-shu*, 18:6b–7a.

57. *CTYL* 3:14b.

58. *CTYL* 3:1a.

59. *CTYL* 3:1b.

60. *CTYL* 3:1b.

61. *LCCC* 14:1b–2a.

62. *Chou-li Cheng-chu* (*The Institutes of Chou with Cheng Hsüan's Commentary*), SPPY ed., ch. 18; Miura, "Shushi kijinron no rinkaku," p. 741; Julia Ching, *Chinese Religions*, chs. 1–2.

63. Consult Tomoeda Ryutarō, *Shushi no shisō keisei* (*The Formation of Chu Hsi's Thought*) rev. ed. (Tokyo, Shunjūsha, 1979), ch. 2, p. 889; Miura, "Shushi kijinron no rinkaku," pp. 741–84; Miura, "Shushi kijinron-ho," pp. 185–203.

64. Miura, "Shushi kijinron no rinkaku," pp. 741–43.

65. Letter to Tung Shu-chung, *CTTC* 51:10a. On this subject, consult Yung-sik Kim, "The World View of Chu Hsi (1130–1200): Knowledge about the Natural World in *Chu Tzu Ch'üan Shu*" (Ph.D. diss., Princeton University, 1979), especially ch. 3.

66. *CTYL* 3:1b.

67. *Ch'un-ch'iu Tso-shih-chuan Tu-shih chi-chieh* (*The Spring and Autumn Annals with the Tso Commentary and Tu's Collected Explanations*), SPPY ed., 21:27a.

68. See ibid.

69. *LCCC* 14:10a. See also James Legge, trans., *Li Ki*, Sacred Books of the East, vol. 28, ed. F. Max Müller (Oxford, Clarendon, 1886), p. 220.

70. *LCCC* 14:10b.

71. Ibid.

72. *CTYL* 3:4a, 7a–b; 63:22a–b; *ECCS, Yi-shu*, 18:13a. Consult Zhang Liwen, *Chu Hsi ssu-hsiang yen-chiu* (*A Study of Chu Hsi's Thought*) (Peking, Chinese Social Science Publications, 1981), pp. 309–10.

73. *Li-chi Cheng-yi* (*Correct Meaning of the Book of Rites*), SPPY ed., 26:12b.

74. *CTYL* 63:21b.

75. *CTYL* 3:4a.

76. Reply to Liao Tzu-hui, in *CTTC* 45:19b.

77. *ECCS, Ts'ui-yen* (*Selected Words*), 2:1b–3b; *Yi-shu*, 11:3a–4b.

78. *CTCS* 2:4a.
79. *CTYL* 3:4a–6b.
80. *CTYL* 3:2a.
81. *CTYL* 3:1b–2a.
82. *CTYL* 3:1b.
83. Wang Ch'ung, *Lun-heng, SPPY* ed., sec. 4, 1:10b; also 2:4b, 7b; 21:5a–6b.
84. *CTYL* 3:2a; Ch'ien, *Chu-tzu hsin hsüeh-an*, vol. 1, p. 298.
85. See his letter to Tu Jen-chung, in *CTTC* 62:16b.
86. *CTYL* 2:10a–b, 37–38; 3:3a, 55.
87. *CTYL* 3:12b.
88. *CTYL* 3:5b–6a.
89. *CTYL* 3:4b, 58. Ghost fires refer to flashes of light hovering over dark and humid graveyards, possibly due to gases from decayed corpses; ghost whistles probably refer to the whistling of winds in such places.
90. *CTYL* 3:2a, 12a.
91. *CTYL* 3:16b.
92. *CTYL* 3:6a, 10b, 19.
93. *CTYL* 3:9b. Consult Miura, "Shushi kijinron-ho," pp. 186–88.
94. *CTYL* 3:19b.
95. English translation adapted from Legge, *Chinese Classics*, vol. 1, pp. 397–98.
96. *Doctrine of the Mean*, ch. 19. English translation adapted from Legge, *Chinese Classics*, vol. 1, pp. 403–4.
97. *CTYL* 3:5b.
98. *CTYL* 3:14a–16a.
99. *CTYL* 3:12a–13a.
100. *CTYL* 3:4a.
101. *CTYL* 90:18b, p. 3666.
102. Shimada, *Shushigaku to Yōmeigaku*, p. 86. The emphasis on descendants and ancestors sharing the same *ch'i* brings to mind recent discoveries about DNA, the complex molecule carrying coded genetic information that is present in human cells and can be used to identify individuals and their genetic relationships. Chu was no party to such scientific research but would have been, like many other Chinese, predisposed to accept the validity of this discovery.
103. *CTYL* 3:4a.
104. *CTYL* 3:17a. See also 3:11b.
105. *CTYL* 3:15b.
106. *CTYL* 86:3a.
107. *ECCS, Yi-shu*, 2B:3b.
108. *CTYL* 90:18b, p. 3666.
109. Chu Hsi, *Ch'u-tz'u chi-chu* (*Collected Commentaries on the Songs of the South*), T'ing-yü-chai ed. [1900], 2:1b–2a. Consult also Wang Ching-hsien, "Chu-tzu chiu-ko ch'uang-yi-k'ao" (An Inquiry into the Creative Meaning of Chu Hsi's Interpretation of the *Nine Songs*), in Chung, *Kuo-chi Chu-tzu hsüeh-hui*, pp. 1141–56.
110. Chu Hsi, *Ch'u Tz'u chi-chu* 2:4a.
111. *CTYL* 3:2b.
112. *CTYL* 3:20a–b.
113. Ibid. The explanatory note about the origin of the Lo Writing came from K'ung Ying-ta, the exegete for the Book of History.
114. *CTYL* 65:9a. Consult *CTTC* 38:1a–2b.

115. We have about forty-five extant letters from Chu to Ts'ai, in *CTTC*, ch. 44.
116. For more on Ts'ai, see *Sung-shih* (*Sung Dynastic History*), in *Erh-shih-wu shih* (*Twenty-Five Dynastic Histories*), K'ai-ming ed., ch. 434, pp. 5595–96; *SYHA*, ch. 56.
117. See Liu Ts'un-yan, "Chu Hsi yü *Ts'an-t'ung-ch'i*" (Chu Hsi and the *Ts'an-t'ung-ch'i*), in *Ho-feng-t'ang hsin-chi* (*A New Collection from the Hall of Harmonious Winds*) (Taipei, Hsin-wen-feng, 1997), vol. 2, 481. See also Chang Li-wen's article, "An Analysis of Chu Hsi's System of the Thought of *I*," in Wing-tsit Chan, *Chu Hsi and Neo-Confucianism*, p. 293. The other seven diagrams are various versions of the Eight Trigrams and the Sixty-four Hexagrams.
118. *Shang-shu cheng-yi* (*Correct Meaning of the Book of History*), *SPPY* ed., 12:2a, 18:11b; Chu-Hsi, *Chou-yi pen-yi* (*Original Meaning of the Book of Changes*), Four Libraries ed., 6th Collection, no. 001, Appended Remarks, pt. 1, 7:12b.
119. Chu Hsi, *Chou-yi pen-yi*, ch. 3, commentary on Appended Remarks, pt. 1, ch. 9.
120. See *CTTC* 38:1a–5a; 84:3b–4a. Consult Hu Wei, *Yi-t'u ming-pien* (*An Explanation of the Diagrams of the Book of Changes*), *TSCC* ed., 1st ser., ch. 1; Chang Liwen, "Analysis of Chu Hsi's System," in Wing-tsit Chan, *Chu Hsi and Neo-Confucianism*, pp. 301–6.
121. *CTTC* 85:5b. "Facing" translates *tui-yuëh*, an expression with ritual overtones in the context of the worship of the Lord-on-High. See *Sung-shih*, Treatise on Ritual, pt. 2, p. 4734b.
122. Yamanoi, "The Great Ultimate," in Wing-tsit Chan, *Chu Hsi and Neo-Confucianism*, pp. 87–90.
123. Shibata Atsushi, "Li Ma-tou yü Chu-tzu hsüeh" (Matteo Ricci and the Chu Hsi School), in Chung, *Kuo-chi Chu-tzu hsüeh-hui*, pp. 909–22, especially pp. 913–17.
124. Mou Tsung-san, *Hsin-t'i yü hsing-t'i* (*On Mind-in-Itself and Nature-in-Itself*) (Taipei, Cheng-chung, 1981), vol. 3, pp. 484–85.
125. *CTTC* 4:11a.

Chapter 4

1. This self-admonition attached to his portrait (see *CTTC* 85:11a) reveals Chu's commitment to the knowledge and practice of ritual, as well as to other Confucian virtues.
This chapter is a corrected, revised, and expanded version of my article "Chu Hsi and Ritual," in Anne-Marie Blondel and Kristofer Schipper, eds., *Essai sur le rituel*, vol. 2, Bibliothèque de l'École des Hautes Études, Section des Sciences Religieuses, vol. 95 (Louvain-Paris, Peeters [1990]).
2. According to Chinese calculation.
3. *CTYL* 90:93b–94a.
4. Consult Chu Hsi's massive *Yi-li ching-chuan t'ung-chieh* (*A Comprehensive Explanation of the Classic Yi-li and Its Commentaries*), Four Libraries Rare Books, Series 10 (Taipei reprint, Commercial Press, 1980), ch. 26. This will be cited as *Yi-li ching-chuan*. The *Wen-kung chia-li* (*The Family Rituals of Chu Hsi*) (8 chs.) has been translated into French: Charles de Harlez, *Kia Li: Livre des rites domestiques chinois* (Paris: E. Leroux, 1889). The *Chia-li* (in 5 chs.) has been translated by Patricia Buckley Ebrey, *Chu Hsi's Family Rituals: A Twelfth-Century Manual for the Performance of Cappings, Weddings, Funerals, and Ancestral Rites* (Princeton University Press, 1991). Consult also Li Kuang-ti's compilation, *Chu-tzu li-tsuan* (5 chs.), which organizes materials according

to ritual categories, assembling Chu's expressed opinions on rituals and related subjects from Chu's *Classified Conversations* (*CTYL* 84–91) and from the *Collected Writings* but not from the *Yi-li ching-chuan*. Cf. Li's *Jung-ts'un ch'üan-chi* (*Collected Writings*) (Taipei Prefecture, Yung-ho County, Wen-yu Publications reprint, 1972), vol. 15. Consult also *SK*, ch. 22, p. 471. A short treatise, *Shih kung* (*Explaining Palaces*) (1 ch.), was formerly and erroneously included in Chu's *Collected Writings* but appears to have been compiled by Li Ju-kuei; see *SK* ch. 23, p. 489; ch. 20, pp. 422–23. Li compiled *Yi-li chi-shih* (*Collected Explanations of the Ceremonials*) (30 chs.); see *SK* ch. 20, pp. 421–22. Consult also *CTYL*, especially chs. 55–77, 91–92; and certain letters and essays from *CTTC*.

5. For secondary sources, consult the chapter in Ch'ien Mu's *Chu-tzu hsin-hsüeh-an* entitled "Chu-tzu yü li-hsüeh" (Chu Hsi and the Study of Ritual), vol. 4, pp. 112–79; Patricia Ebrey, "Education through Ritual: Efforts to Formulate Family Rituals during the Sung Period," in William Theodore de Bary and John W. Chaffee, eds., *Neo-Confucian Education: The Formative Stage* (Berkeley, University of California Press, 1989), pp. 285–86; Kao Ming, "Chu Hsi's Discipline of Propriety," in Wing-tsit Chan, *Chu Hsi and Neo-Confucianism*, 312–35; Choe Kan-tok, "*Chu-tzu chia-li* tsai Han-kuo chih shou-jung yü chan-k'ai" (The Acceptance and Development of Chu Hsi's *Family Rituals* in Korea), in Chung, *Kuo-chi Chu-tzu hsüeh-hui*, pp. 235–48; Uno Seiichi, "Shushi to rei" (Chu Hsi and Ritual), in the compendium on Chu Hsi compiled by Morohashi Tetsuji and Yasuoka Masatsugu, *Shushigaku taikei*, vol. 1, *Shushigaku nyūmon* (An Introduction to the School of Chu Hsi) (Tokyo, Meitoku, 1974), pp. 272–82.

6. *Li-chi Cheng-yi*, 3:3b. For an English translation, see Legge, *Li Ki*, vol. 27, p. 90.

7. They were replaced by the revised and comprehensive *New Forms for the Five Rites of the Cheng-ho Period* (*Cheng-ho wu-li hsin-yi*) (1107–13). This is in 37 chapters. See Four Libraries Rare Books, ser. 10 (Taipei reprint, Commercial Press, 1980).

8. *CTYL* 41:6a.

9. See Chu Hsi's reply to Li Hui-shu, *CTTC*, 62:22a, where he points out disagreements with Ch'eng Yi on ritual matters; see also, in reply to Kuo Tzu-ch'ung, *CTTC* 64:12a–15a, where he says Ssu-ma's work is better than Ch'eng Yi's. Ssu-ma Kuang also wrote a larger work, *Shu-yi* (*On Etiquette*); see Patricia Buckley Ebrey, *Family and Property in Sung China: Yüan Ts'ai's Precepts for Social Life* (Princeton University Press, 1984), pp. 31–42.

10. Letter to Ou-yang Hsi-hsün, *CTTC* 61:21b–22a.

11. *CTYL* 83:26b, 14:26a–27b.

12. *CTYL* 87:1a–b.

13. *CTYL* 86:1a–b.

14. *CTYL* 86:1b.

15. *CTYL* 85:1b–2a.

16. *CTYL* 85:4a.

17. *CTYL* 87:5b.

18. *CTTC* 14:26a–27b.

19. *CTYL* 27:2b.

20. See *SSCC*, *Ta-hsüeh chang-chü*, 4b–5a. See also Julia Ching, *To Acquire Wisdom*, ch. 3.

21. *CTYL* 84:1b.

22. Uno, "Shushi to rei," p. 277.

23. See Wing-tsit Chan, *New Studies*, pp. 74–75, 347–51; *Chu-tzu men-jen*, 261–62.
24. HSCC 36:9a–b; Hoyt C. Tillman, *Confucian Discourse and Chu Hsi's Ascendancy* (Honolulu, University of Hawaii Press, 1992), chs. 4–5.
25. *CTTC* 74:12a–13a.
26. *CTTC* 46:32a–36a, 29:22b–23a.
27. *CTYL* 83:28a.
28. *CTTC* 14:26a–27b.
29. Ibid.
30. Letter to Li Chi-chang, in *CTTC* 38:41a–b.
31. As it now stands, the work includes such parts as *Family Rituals* (5 chs.), which should not be confused with the independent treatise of the same title; *Village Rituals* (3 chs.); *School Rituals* (11 chs.); and *State Rituals* (4 chs.), a total of 23 chapters in 42 sections. Besides that, we have 18 sections (chs. 24–37) under an older title, *Yi-li chi-chuan chi-chieh* (*The Ceremonials with Collected Commentaries and Collected Explanations*), including Chu Hsi's treatment of court ceremonials but without a discussion of divination. Among these, several prefaces to the sections are also missing, and the arrangement of subject matter is not as originally planned.
32. Huang's supplement to Chu's work includes the treatment of mourning (15 chs.)
33. See Chi Yün's foreword to *Yi-li ching-chuan*, 1a–3a; see also Kao, "Chu Hsi's Discipline of Propriety," pp. 315–16.
34. See *Yi-li ching-chuan*, 3a–4a.
35. Chu's large compendium, the *Yi-li ching-chuan*, also includes five chapters on family ritual.
36. See Ebrey, *Chu Hsi's Family Rituals*.
37. Tai Hsien, *Chu-tzu shih-chi* (*A True Record of Chu Hsi*), 2:13b, in Okada Takehiko, comp., *Chin-shih Han-chi ts'ung-k'an* (*Early Modern Chinese Texts Series*) (Taipei, Chung-wen reprint, 1972), vol. 22, p. 100.
38. *CTTC* 75:16b–17a. Chu had early expressed an interest in the subject of family rituals, mentioning his own experience at age fourteen when he mourned his father's death and his youthful efforts to assemble information. *CTYL* 90:93b–94a.
39. Huang Kan, *Chu-tzu hsing-chuang*, in Okada, *Chin-shih Han-chi ts'ung-k'an*, vol. 21, p. 126. The exact words used are *Ku-chin chia-chi-li* (*Family Sacrificial Rituals, Ancient and Modern*).
40. Yeh Kung-hui, comp., *Chu-tzu nien-p'u* (in the same volume as the official biography but with different pagination), in Okada, *Chin-shih Han-chi ts'ung-k'an*, vol. 21, p. 91.
41. Consult "*Chia-li k'ao,*" "*Chia-li hou k'ao,*" and "*Chia-li k'ao-wu,*" in *Pai-t'ien ts'ung-kao* (*Miscellaneous Writings*), in Ch'ang Pi-te, comp., *Ch'ing ming-chia chi-hui-k'an* (*Collected Writings of Famous Ch'ing Writers*) (Taipei, Han-wen wen-hua shih-yeh, 1972), ch. 2, pp. 1a–22b. Rather than using Wang's well-known Chronological Biography, written much later, I prefer to consult Chu's earlier biographies on this point.
42. Huang Kan, *Chu-tzu hsing-chuang*, p. 127; cited also by Chi Yün, *SK*, pp. 469–70.
43. Uno, "Shushi to rei," pp. 281–82.
44. Ch'ien Mu refers to Chiu Chün's *Wen-kung Chia-li yi-chieh* (*On Chu Hsi's Family Rituals*); see *Chu-tzu hsin hsüeh-an*, vol. 4, p. 167.
45. *CTTC* 81:5b–6a, 83:14a.
46. Ebrey, "Education through Ritual," pp. 285–86.

47. Chu Hsi's preface to the Book of Rites, in *CTTC* 74:16a–b.
48. *CYCC* 17a–b.
49. See Jung's foreword to Wilhelm and Baynes, *I Ching*, p. xxiv.
50. Ibid.
51. *ECCS*, *Yi-shu*, 2B:3a. Such an attitude toward divination characterized most Chinese scholars.
52. Consult *Yi-ch'uan yi-chuan* (4 chs.), in *ECCS*. See especially Ch'eng Yi's preface. Consult Hsü Fu-kuan, "Chu Hsi and the Ch'eng Brothers," pp. 52–53.
53. *CTYL* 65:5a, p. 2553.
54. Letter to Lü Tsu-ch'ien, *CTTC* 33:32b.
55. See Hsü Fu-kuan, "Chu Hsi and the Ch'eng Brothers," in Wing-tsit Chan, *Chu Hsi and Neo-Confucianism*, pp. 52–53.
56. Tillman, *Confucian Discourse*, pp. 121–22.
57. *CYCC* 17b. Smith et al., *Sung Dynasty Uses of the I-Ching*, pp. 169–205. This chapter was written by Joseph Adler.
58. *CTYL* 66:6b.
59. Chu Hsi, "Shih-yi" (Divination Ritual), in *Chou-yi pen-yi*. For Chu Hsi's *Yi-hsüeh ch'i-meng*, I have consulted the edition in *CTYS*, vol. 12.
60. Patricia Buckley Ebrey, "Sung Neo-Confucian Views on Geomancy," in Bloom and Fogel, *Meeting of Minds*, pp. 75–107, especially pp. 92–97.
61. *CTTC* 15:34a–b.
62. Ebrey, "Neo-Confucian Views," p. 86.
63. *CTTC* 15:34b.
64. *CTTC* 15:33b; Ebrey, "Neo-Confucian Views," p. 89.
65. *CTTC* 15:35a. For more on the subject, we await Ron-guey Chu's ongoing study of Chu Hsi as a *feng-shui* master, which utilizes major *feng-shui* texts to show Chu Hsi's high status in the *feng-shui* tradition.
66. That Chu Hsi permitted his disciples to divine for him is interesting. It may signify that he wanted to distance himself from the practice, even though he accepts the result. This happened, even though he suggested (p. 175) that he divined for himself.
67. See letter to Vice-Minister Chang, in *CTTC*, supplements, 5:6a.
68. Consult Huang Kan, *Chu-tzu hsing-chuang*, 48b, p. 96; Wing-tsit Chan, *New Studies*, pp. 112–13.
69. *CTYL* 107:10b–11b.
70. *CTNP* 4:341–42; Wing-tsit Chan, *New Studies*, pp. 114–15.
71. *CTYL* 89:11b.
72. Consult *LCCC*, ch. 12, sec. 20, *Tsa-chi* (*Miscellaneous Records*), pt. 1; Legge, *Li Ki*, pp. 132–36. See also Yu Ying-shih, "'O Soul, Come Back!' A Story in the Changing Conception of the Soul and After-Life in Pre-Buddhist China," *Harvard Journal of Asiatic Studies* 47 (1987), 363–95.
73. Chu Hsi, *Ch'u Tz'u chi-chu*, sec. 9, 7:4a–6b. The English is adapted from David Hawkes, trans., *The Songs of the South: An Ancient Chinese Anthology* (London, Oxford University Press, 1959), pp. 104–5.
74. Chu Hsi, *Ch'u Tz'u chi-chu*, 7:2a.
75. See *LCCC*, pt. 2, 12a–b; English translation in Legge, *Li Ki*, p. 152.
76. *CTYL* 90:17b, p. 3664.
77. See Tu Yu's survey of Chinese political institutions, *T'ung-tien* (Preface 1896), 48:19b–21a.
78. *CTYL* 90:17b–18a, pp. 3664–65.

79. Ibid.
80. *CTTC* 86:2b–3a.
81. *CTYL* 3:17a.
82. *CTYL* 12a.
83. *CTYL* 89:8b.
84. *CTTC* 75:17a.
85. *CTYL* 3:16a.
86. *CTTC* 86:12b–16a; *CTYL* 3:17a. See also Wing-tsit Chan, "Chu-tzu chih tsung-chiao shih-chien" (Chu Hsi's Practice of Religion), in *Chu-hsüeh lun-chi* (*Collected Essays on Chu Hsi's Philosophy*) (Taipei, Student Bookstore, 1982), pp. 181–97.
87. *CTTC* 83:19b.
88. *CTTC* 100:4a–b.
89. Chu's chronological biography seems to indicate that they were Buddhists. See Yeh, *Chu-tzu nien-p'u*, p. 179.
90. *CTYL* 3:18a.; Tai Hsien, *Chu-tzu shih-chi*, 2:5a, p. 83.
91. Ibid.
92. *CTYL* 107:14b–15b; Wing-tsit Chan, *Life and Thought*, pp. 139–61.
93. Ibid.
94. Consult *Sung-shih*, ch. 107/108, which describes these rituals.
95. *Sung-shih*, ch. 36, pp. 83–84.
96. Consult Chu's chronological biography, pt. 3, p. 198.
97. *Sung-shih*, ch. 37, p. 84. See Chu's chronological biography, pt. 3, p. 198.
98. See *CTTC* 15:19b–32b, which includes his explanatory diagrams.
99. *CTYL* 84:7a.
100. *Lun-yü chi-chu*, 9:4a, in *SSCC*.
101. *CTYL* 22:10a–10b.
102. *CTYL* 87:24a.
103. Consult *Chou-tzu T'ung-shu*, 3a; *CTYL* 87:24a–b; Chiang Yi-pin, "Chu-tzu te yüeh-lun" (Chu Hsi on Music), in Chung Ts'ai-chün, *Kuo-chi Chu-tzu hsüeh-hui*, pp. 15–16.
104. *CTYL* 86:17a.
105. *CTYL* 92:6b, p. 3720.
106. Chou Tun-yi, *T'ung-shu*, p. 4a.
107. Ibid., 3a. See also *CTYL* 87:23b–24b.
108. *CTYL* 84:1a–b.
109. *CTTC* 1:3b–4b. *Chao-yin* means "summoning the hermit." *Fan Chao-yin* refers to a response to the *chao-yin*.

Chapter 5

1. *CTTC* 2:10b. Chinese mirrors were often made of bronze and reflect only on one side. A *mou* is a Chinese acre. This poem was written in 1166.
2. I refer here especially to the behaviorist school; see B. F. Skinner, *Science and Human Behavior* (New York, Macmillan, 1953). See also Seymour W. Itzkoff, *Ernst Cassirer: Scientific Knowledge and the Concept of Man* (University of Notre Dame Press, 1971), pp. 150–52. Their opposition includes the personalists and existentialists. Consult Jacques Maritain, *Integral Humanism*, trans. Joseph W. Evans (New York, Scribner's Sons, 1968), ch. 1; Emmanuel Mounier, *Personalism*, trans. Philip Mairet (New York, Grove Press, 1952); Martin Heidegger, *Being*

and Time, trans. J. Macquarrie et al. (New York, Harper and Row, 1962), pt. 1. For the "symbolist" view, as articulated by Ernst Cassirer, see his *Essay on Man*, especially chs. 1, 2, and 12. Cassirer defines the human as a symbolic animal, and as such, different from the instinctual ones. There is also the "panpsychist" view, which permits a hierarchy of psychic "monads" or "societies" and "nexuses" of "actual occasions," to use the language of Leibniz and A. N. Whitehead. Consult Julia Ching and W. G. Oxtoby, *Moral Enlightenment*. See also appendix C in this book.

3. Consult Wing-cheuk Chan, "Confucian Moral Metaphysics and Heidegger's Fundamental Ontology," *Analecta Husserliana* 17 (1984), 187–202.

4. Consult Chu Hsi, "Ming-tao *lun-hsing shuo*" (*A Treatise on Ch'eng Hao's "Discourse on Nature"*), in *CTTC* 67:16b–18a. An English translation can be found in Wing-tsit Chan, *Source Book*, pp. 597–99.

5. *CTTC* 67:17b.

6. Wing-tsit Chan, *Chin-ssu lu hsiang-chu chi-p'ing* (*Reflections on Things at Hand with Detailed Commentaries and Collected Opinions*) (Taipei, Student Bookstore, 1992), p. 557.

7. *CTYL* 104:1a, p. 4151. The reference to Mencius is to 6A:7.

8. For primary sources, see *CTYL*, especially chs. 5, 94, 98. See also Chu Hsi's correspondence with Chang Shih, especially in *CTTC*, chs. 30–32, and several of Chu's treatises, including "On Calming Nature," "On Contemplating the Mind," and "On Jen," in *CTTC*, ch. 67.

9. For secondary works, consult John H. Berthrong, "Chu Hsi's Ethics: *Jen* and *Ch'eng*," *Journal of Chinese Philosophy* 14 (1987), 161–77; Irene Bloom, "Three Visions of Jen," in Bloom and Fogel, *Meeting of Minds*, pp. 8–42, especially pp. 23–30; Wing-tsit Chan, *New Studies*, ch. 11; Zhang Liwen, "Wei-fa yi-fa lun chih tsung-kuan: Chu-tzu ts'an-chiu wei-fa yi-fa lun chih ts'e-ts'o, chuan-pien ho yin-hsiang" (The Theories of *yi-fa* and *wei-fa* in Chu Hsi: Their Evolution and Influence), in Chung, *Kuo-chi Chu-tzu hsüeh-hui*, pp. 497–520; Ch'en Chün-min, "Chu-tzu te sheng-hsien jen-ko li-hsiang" (Chu Hsi's Ideal of Sagehood), in Chung, *Kuo-chi Chu-tzu hsüeh-hui*, pp. 659–76; Julia Ching, "Chu Hsi's Theory of Human Nature," *Humanitas* 20 (1979), 77–100; Julia Ching, *Mysticism and Kingship*, ch. 4; Chung Ts'ai-chün, "Chu-tzu hsüeh-p'ai tsun-te-hsing tao-wen-hsüeh wen-t'i yen-chiu" (A Study of Honoring Moral Nature and Following Intellectual Pursuits in Chu Hsi's School), in Chung, *Kuo-chi Chu-tzu hsüeh-hui*, pp. 1271–300; A. C. Graham, "What Was New in the Ch'eng-Chu Theory of Human Nature?" in Wing-tsit Chan, *Chu Hsi and Neo-Confucianism*, pp. 138–57; Liu Shu-hsien, *Chu Hsi che-hsüeh ssu-hsiang te fa-chan yü wan-ch'eng* (*The Development and Completion of Chu Hsi's Philosophical Thought*) (Taipei, Student Bookstore, 1982), chs. 4–5; Meng P'ei-yüan, "Chu Hsi te hsin-ling chin-chieh shuo" (Chu Hsi on Spiritual Dispositions), in Chung, *Kuo-chi Chu-tzu hsüeh-hui*, pp. 417–36; Donald J. Munro, *Images of Human Nature: A Sung Portrait* (Princeton University Press, 1988); *HTHT*, vol. 3, ch. 4; Satō Hitoshi, "Chu Hsi's 'Treatise on Jen,'" in Wing-tsit Chan, *Chu Hsi and Neo-Confucianism*, pp. 212–27.

10. *CTYL* 94:12a.

11. *CTYL* 94:11b–12a.

12. Yamanoi Yū, "The Great Ultimate and Heaven in Chu Hsi's Philosophy," in Chan, *Chu Hsi and Neo-Confucianism*, pp. 82–83.

13. *CTYL* 4:1b; *CTTC* 39:24b.

14. *CTYL* 4:1a–6b, pp. 89–100.

15. *CTYL* 4:2a, p. 91.
16. *CTTC* 61:28b–29a.
17. *CTTC* 58:13a.
18. *CTTC* 58:13a–b. Consult *YHP*, p. 373. The Mencian theory of four beginnings will be discussed later in this chapter.
19. *YHP*, pp. 369–72.
20. See Fung, *History*, vol. 1, pp. 395–98, vol. 2, pp. 340–42; Yamanoi Yū, "Shushi no shisō ni okeru ki" (Ch'i[a] in Chu Hsi's Thought), in Onozawa et al., *Ki no shisō*, pp. 438–52.
21. Julia Ching, *To Acquire Wisdom*, p. 57. Consult *Mencius* 7A:1–2, 4; *Leng-chia o-po-tuo-lo pao-ching* (Lankavatāra sūtra), *T* 16, no. 670, pp. 480–514; Shih Tao-yüan, *Original Teachings of Ch'an Buddhism, Selected from the Transmission of the Lamp*, trans. Chang Chung-yüan (New York, Vintage Press, 1971), introduction, pp. 4–14; *TLP*, pp. 70–84; *YCP*, vol. 2, ch. 19.
22. *CTYL* 5:1b.
23. *CTYL* 5:5a–b.
24. *SSCC, Ta-hsüeh chang-chü*, 1a.
25. *SSCC, Meng-tzu chi-chu*, 1a.
26. Chu Hsi, "A Treatise on the Examination of the Mind," *CTTC* 67:18b. Consult *YHP*, ch. 13, pp. 378–84; Liu Shu-hsien, "The Function of the Mind in Chu Hsi's Philosophy," *Journal of Chinese Philosophy* 5 (1978), 195–208.
27. *CTYL* 98:7b, p. 3994. Consult also *CTYL* 5:9a, *CTTC* 73:40b.
28. *CTYL* 98:7a.
29. *CTYL* 98:6b–8a. For Chang Tsai, see *CTCS*, 14:2a.
30. *CTYL* 5:5b, 6b; Ch'ien, *Chu-tzu hsin hsüeh-an*, vol. 2, p. 35.
31. *CTTC* 4:1.6b–9a. The nine extremes refer to the highest reaches of Heaven. See *Huai-nan-tzu*, 12:15b. English translation adapted from Li Chi, "Chu Hsi the Poet," p. 89.
32. *CTYL* 94:35a–b.
33. *CTYL* 4:2a.
34. *CTYL* 94:35b.
35. *CTYL* 1:1a.
36. *CTYL* 94:6a; p. 3765.
37. Fung, *History*, vol. 2, p. 559.
38. Consult Julia Ching, "The Problem of Evil as a Possible Dialogue between Neo-Confucianism and Christianity," *Contemporary Religions in Japan* 9 (September 1968), 161–93.
39. See *CTCS* 5:4a–b.
40. *CTYL* 4:12b–13a.
41. *Mencius* 2A:6.
42. *ECCS, Yi-shu*, 19:4b.
43. *CTYL* 5:13a.
44. *CTYL* 5:10b. See *CTCS* 14:2a, regarding the mind controlling human nature and the emotions.
45. *CTYL* 5:6a.
46. *CTYL* 4:11b–12a. For Han Yü, see "Yüan-hsing" (Inquiry on Human Nature), in *Han Ch'ang-li ch'üan-chi* (*Complete Works of Han Yü*) (Taipei, Hsin-wen-feng, 1977), vol. 2, pp. 59–60.
47. Ronald de Sousa, *The Rationality of Emotions* (Cambridge, MIT Press, 1987), p. 17.

48. Legge, *Li Ki*, vol. 27, p. 379.
49. *Doctrine of the Mean*, ch. 1; see *SSCC* (*CYCC*) 1:2a.
50. *CTYL* 94:7a.
51. *CTYL* 5:7a.
52. *Mencius* 2A:6.
53. *Mencius* 6A:6.
54. *CTCS* 14:2a.
55. *CTYL* 5:9a.
56. *CTYL* 60:4a.
57. *CTYL* 5:7a.
58. *Doctrine of the Mean*, ch. 1.
59. *CTYL* 53:17b.
60. Consult Julia Ching, "Yi Yulgok and the Four-Seven Debate," in William Theodore de Bary et al., eds., *The Rise of Neo-Confucianism in Korea* (New York, Columbia University Press, 1985), pp. 303–22.
61. Consult Kirile Ole Thompson, "How to Rejuvenate Ethics: Suggestions from Chu Hsi," *Philosophy East and West* 41 (1991), 493–513.
62. See *Analects* 16:9.
63. Consult *HTHT*, chs. 4–6.
64. Satō, "Chu Hsi's 'Treatise on *Jen*,'" pp. 212–27.
65. Chu Hsi, "Treatise on *Jen*," in *CTTC* 67:21a.
66. *CTYL* 121:17a, 6:13a.
67. Han Yü, "Yüan-tao" (Inquiry on the Way), in *Han Ch'ang-li ch'üan-chi*, vol. 2, p. 55.
68. *ECCS*, *Yi-shu*, 18:1a.
69. Consult Lao, *Chung-kuo che-hsüeh-shih*, in Chan, ed., *Chu Hsi and Neo-Confucianism*, vol. 3A, p. 291.
70. Shirokauer, "Chu Hsi and Hu Hung," op. cit., pp. 482–97; Tillman, *Confucian Discourse*, pp. 30–36.
71. Sixth letter to Chang Ching-fu, in *CTTC* 31:5a.
72. *CTTC* 42:9a, fifth letter to Hu Kuang-chung.
73. *CTTC* 67:20a.
74. *CTTC* 67:20a–b.
75. *CTYL* 20:15b–17b. Consult also Satō, "Chu Hsi's 'Treatise on *Jen*,'" p. 224.
76. *CTYL* 20:17a–20b.
77. See *CTYL* 1:3b–4a, 69:16a–17a; Wing-tsit Chan, *New Studies*, pp. 188–89.
78. *ECCS*, *Yi-shu*, 2A:2a.
79. *CTTC* 32:18a–b, 19a–b, 21a.
80. The exchange of treatises occurred around 1172, when Chu was forty-three years old. His own treatise was revised many times and is now included in his *Collected Works* (*CTTC* 67).
81. *CTTC* 42:14b–15a, 20a.
82. *CTTC* 32:20b.
83. *Analects* 6:21; *CTTC* 67:23a; Satō, "Chu Hsi's 'Treatise on *Jen*,'" p. 223; Tillman, *Confucian Discourse*, pp. 74–78.
84. Shirokauer, "Chu Hsi and Hu Hung," op. cit., pp. 490–95.
85. Consult *Nan-hsüan hsien-sheng wen-chi* (*Collected Writings of Chang Shih*), Sung Dynasty ed. (Taipei, National Palace Museum reprint, 1981), 18:1a–b.
86. See Liu Shu-hsien, "Chu Hsi te jen-shuo, t'ai-chi kuan-nien yü tao-t'ung wen-t'i te tsai hsing-ch'a" (A New Examination of Chu Hsi on *Jen*, *T'ai-chi*, and *Tao-t'ung*),

Shih-hsüeh p'ing-lun 5 (1983), 173–88; and Wing-tsit Chan's response in *New Studies*, pp. 173–75. For Hu Hung's *Chih-yen*, see *Po-tzu ch'üan-shu* ed. (Shanghai, Shao-yeh shan-fang, 1927).

87. Berthrong, "Chu Hsi's Ethics," p. 167.

88. *Shuo-wen*, 3B:9b.

89. *Doctrine of the Mean*, ch. 21. English translation adapted from Legge, *Chinese Classics*, vol. 1, pp. 414–15.

90. Chu Hsi, *CYCC*, in *SSCC*, p. 20.

91. *Doctrine of the Mean*, ch. 24.

92. Ibid.

93. Ibid., ch. 25.

94. *CYCC*, in *SSCC*, p. 22.

95. Berthrong, "Chu Hsi's Ethics," p. 169.

Chapter 6

1. This poem of Chu Hsi's is collected in Ch'en Hung-mou, ed., *Wu-chung yi-kuei* (*Five Kinds of Traditional Rules*), SPPY ed., vol. 1, p. 22a.

2. This chapter is a thoroughly revised version of an earlier study. Consult Julia Ching, "Chu Hsi on Personal Cultivation," in Chan, *Chu Hsi and Neo-Confucianism*, pp. 273–91. Consult also Julia Ching, "What Is Confucian Spirituality?" in Irene Eber, ed., *Confucianism: The Dynamics of Tradition* (New York, Macmillan, 1986), pp. 63–80.

3. The three bonds and five relationships refer to the ruler, father, and husband as superior partners, to be respected and obeyed as norms or models by the subject, son, and wife with whom they are "bonded." The five relationships add the bonds between older and younger brothers and between friends; here, seniority of one partner is also acknowledged, but not to the same extent.

4. For primary sources, consult *CTYL*, especially chs. 5–13 and 104. Many, if not most, of the other chapters from the two collections *CTYL* and *CTTC* treat the subject of self-cultivation; see especially *CTYL*, chs. 6–13. Many of the chapters commenting on the Four Books, that is, *CTTC* 5:14–64, and much of the correspondence in the *CTTC* treats or touches on this subject as well.

5. See chapter 10 on this point. For secondary sources, consult William Theodore de Bary, "Neo-Confucian Cultivation and the Seventeenth Century 'Enlightenment,'" in William Theodore de Bary, ed., *The Unfolding of Neo-Confucianism* (New York, Columbia University Press, 1975), pp. 1–66; Wing-tsit Chan, "Chu Hsi and Quiet-Sitting," in Wing-tsit Chan, *New Studies*, pp. 255–70; Chen Lai, *Chu Hsi che-hsüeh yen-chiu* (*A Study of Chu Hsi's Philosophy*) (Peking, Social Science Publications, 1988), pt. 2, ch. 1; Cheng Chung-ying, *New Dimensions of Confucian and Neo-Confucian Philosophy* (Albany, State University of New York Press, 1991); Chung Ts'ai-chün, *The Development of the Concepts of Heaven and of Man in the Philosophy of Chu Hsi* (Taipei, Academia Sinica, 1993), ch. 3; Daniel K. Gardner, *Chu Hsi and the Ta-hsüeh: Neo-Confucian Reflection on the Confucian Canon* (Cambridge, Council on East Asian Studies, Harvard University, 1986); Daniel K. Gardner, "Chu Hsi's Reading of the Ta-hsüeh: A Confucian's Quest for Truth," *Journal of Chinese Philosophy* 10 (September 1983), 182–204; Daniel P. Gardner, "Transmitting the Way: Chu Hsi and His Program of Learning," *Harvard Journal of Asiatic Studies* 49 (1989), 141–72; and Daniel K. Gardner, trans., *Learning to be a Sage: Selections from the Conversations of Master Chu, Ar-*

ranged Topically (Berkeley, University of California Press, 1990); Huang Chün-chieh, "The Synthesis of Old Pursuits and New Knowledge: Chu Hsi's Interpretation of Mencian Morality," *New Asia Academic Bulletin* 3 (1982), 197–222; Philip J. Ivanhoe, *Confucian Moral Self-Cultivation* (New York, Peter Lang, 1993); Li Ming-hui, "Chu-tzu lun-o chih ken-yüan" (Chu Hsi on the Origin of Evil), in Chung, *Kuo-chi Chu-tzu hsüeh-hui*, pp. 553–79; Okada Takehiko, *Zazen to Seiza* (*Zen Meditation and Confucian Quiet-Sitting*) (Tokyo, Ofusha, 1972); Liu Shu-hsien, *Chu-tzu che-hsüeh ssu-hsiang*, ch. 3; *HTHT*, vol. 3; Takahata Tsunenobu, "Chō Nanken no shisō hensen" (Evolution of Chang Shih's Thought), in his book, *Chō Nanken shū jinmei sakuin* (*Index to Names in Chang Shih's Collected Writings*) (Nagoya, Saika shorin, 1976); *YCP*, vol. 1, chs. 10–11; Rodney Taylor, "Chu Hsi and Meditation," in Bloom and Fogel, *Meeting of Minds*, pp. 43–74; Rodney Taylor, *The Confucian Way of Contemplation: Okada Takehiko and the Tradition of Quiet Sitting* (Columbia, University of South Carolina Press, 1988); Tillman, *Confucian Discourse*; Tian Hao [Hoyt C. Tillman], *Chu Hsi te ssu-we shih-chieh* (*Chu Hsi's World of Thought*) (Taipei, Yun-ch'eng, 1996), especially chs. 3, 5; Ts'ai Jen-hou, "Chu-tzu te kung-fu lun" (Chu Hsi's Theory of Self-Cultivation), in Chung, *Kuo-chi Chu-tzu hsüeh-hui*, pp. 581–98; Allen Wittenborn, "Some Aspects of Mind and Problems of Knowledge in Chu Hsi's Philosophy," *Journal of Chinese Philosophy* 9 (1982), 13–48; Yu Ying-shih, "Morality and Knowledge in Chu Hsi's Philosophical System," in Wing-tsit Chan, *Chu Hsi and Neo-Confucianism*, pp. 228–54; Conrad Shirokauer, "Chu Hsi and Hu Hung," in Wing-tsit Chan, *Chu Hsi and Neo-Confucianism*, pp. 480–502.

6. *CTYL* 13:2a–3b; Fung, *History*, vol. 2, pp. 560–63.

7. Chu Hsi's preface, p. 1a, in *SSCC*, *CYCC*. See also Book of History, ch. 3. English translation adapted from Legge, *Chinese Classics*, vol. 3, p. 61.

8. Consult Chu Hsi's preface, p. 1a, in *SSCC*, *CYCC*. Also see Wing-tsit Chan, "Chu Hsi's Completion of Neo-Confucianism," in Françoise Aubin, ed., *Études Song, Sung Studies: In Memoriam Étienne Balazs*, ser. 2, no. 1 (Paris, Mouton, 1971), pp. 60–87. Julia Ching, "Truth and Ideology," pp. 371–88.

9. *CTTC* 2:10a. This poem is entitled "Self-Conquest." Dust can refer to defilement (Sanskrit, *guna*).

10. *CTYL* 5:10a–b. English translation adapted from Wing-tsit Chan, *Source Book*, p. 631.

11. *Doctrine of the Mean*, ch. 1.

12. Chu's intellectual evolution and the development of his doctrine of psychic equilibrium and harmony are discussed thoroughly in *HTHT*, vol. 3.

13. Literally, the "six points" (*liu-ho*), namely, the four directions, the summit, and the nadir.

14. *SSCC*, *CYCC*, p. 1a.

15. Chu Hsi, "Yi-fa/wei-fa shuo" (On *Yi-fa* and *Wei-fa*), in *CTTC* 67:11b. Consult *HTHT*, vol. 3, p. 132.

16. *CTTC* 64:28b–29a; *HTHT*, vol. 3, pp. 147–48.

17. See W. T. Stace, *Mysticism and Philosophy* (Philadelphia, Lippincott, 1960). On the question of pure consciousness, see also Robert K. C. Forman, ed., *The Problem of Pure Consciousness: Mysticism and Philosophy* (New York, Oxford University Press, 1990), introduction, pp. 8–9. However, as I say below, I am not limiting the term only to so-called introvertive mysticism.

18. William James, *The Varieties of Religious Experience* (New York, Mentor Books, 1958), p. 306. He is quoting from R. M. Bucke. The edition I consulted is Rich-

ard M. Bucke, *Cosmic Consciousness: A Study in the Evolution of the Human Mind* (New York, Dutton, 1923), p. 2.

19. Bucke, *Cosmic Consciousness,* pp. 7–8; James, *Religious Experience,* p. 307.

20. See Chu Hsi's biography of Li T'ung, *CTTC* 97: 26b–30a.

21. *Yen-p'ing ta-wen,* in *Shang Ts'ai yü-lu/Yen-p'ing ta-wen fu pu-lu (Recorded Conversations of Hsieh Liang-tso/Li T'ung's Answers to Questions, with Supplement),* in Okada Takehiko, ed., *Chin-shih Han-chi ts'ung-k'an (Collected Chinese Texts from Recent Ages)* (Taipei, Chung-wen reprint, 1972), pt. 1, 17b (p. 64).

22. Chu Hsi, "Preface to the Old Doctrine of Equilibrium and Harmony," *CTTC* 75:22b–23a. This preface gives an account of the evolution of his theories of harmony and equilibrium.

23. Consult *CTNP,* 1B:23–24; consult also *CTTC* 64:28b–29b. For the dating of the letters and his doctrinal evolution, see Chen Lai, *Chu Hsi che-hsüeh yen-chiu,* pp. 97–115; Chung, *Development,* ch. 3.

24. *CTTC* 30:19a.

25. *CTTC* 30:19a.

26. "Preface to the Old Theory of Equilibrium and Harmony," *CTTC* 75:23a–24a.

27. Consult *HTHT,* vol. 3, ch. 3, pp. 210–28, especially for his criticisms of Chu.

28. *CTTC* 62:6a.

29. See *HTHT,* vol. 3, chs. 1–3.

30. *SSCC, CYCC,* 2a–b.

31. See Chu Hsi's first letter to the Hunan gentlemen on equilibrium and harmony, *CTTC,* chs. 31–33. Consult Wing-tsit Chan, *Source Book,* pp. 600–602. This letter was allegedly written in 1169, when Chu was forty.

32. See Chapter 5. See also *HTHT,* vol. 3, ch. 4.

33. *Chuang-tzu,* ch. 6.

34. *CTTC* 85:6b.

35. *CTYL* 12:15a–b; *HTHT,* vol. 3, p. 226.

36. *CTYL* 45:11b.

37. Yen Yüan, *Chu-tzu yü-lei p'ing (A Critique of Chu Hsi's Classified Conversations),* in *Yen-Li ts'ung-shu (Collected Writings of Yen Yüan and Li Kung)* (n.p., Ssu-ts'un hsüeh-hui, [1923]), pp. 2b, 18b, 22a, 24a.

38. *CTYL* 116:17b.

39. *CTYL* 116:17b, p. 4474.

40. *CTYL* 62:25b.

41. See Chu Hsi's biography by his disciple Huang Kan *(Chu-tzu hsing-chuang).* See also Conrad M. Shirokauer, "Chu Hsi's Political Career: A Study in Ambivalence," in Arthur F. Wright, ed., *Confucian Personalities* (Stanford University Press, 1962), pp. 162–88.

42. *CTYL* 9:1a, p. 235.

43. See Chu's first letter to the gentlemen of Hunan on equilibrium and harmony, *CTTC,* ch. 31. An English translation is given in Wing-tsit Chan, *Source Book,* pp. 600–602.

44. Consult *Liu-tsu ta-shih fa-pao t'an-ching, T* 48, no. 2008, 348–49. For an English translation, see Philip B. Yampolsky, *The Platform Sutra of the Sixth Patriarch* (New York, Columbia University Press, 1967), pp. 130–32.

45. *CTYL* 12:7a.

46. *CTYL* 12:7b–18b, 15:1a–13b. Chu Hsi also elaborated on this in his commentary on the *Great Learning.*

47. Hsü Fu-kuan, "Ch'eng Chu yi-t'ung ch'u-kao," op. cit., 1–20.

48. *CTYL* 94:17a.
49. *Analects* 12:19.
50. Commentary on Hexagram 2, *K'un*. Consult Richard John Lynn, trans., *The Classic of Changes: A New Translation of the I-ching, as Interpreted by Wang Bi* (New York, Columbia University Press, 1994), p. 147. The English translation here is my own.
51. Chu Hsi and Lü Tsu-ch'ien, *Chin-ssu lu* 2:3b.
52. See Satō Hitoshi, "Kuan-yü Chu Hsi ching-shuo te yi-ko k'ao-ch'a" (An Enquiry into the Word *Ching* in Chu Hsi), in Chung, *Kuo-chi Chu-tzu hsüeh-hui*, pp. 615–58, especially pp. 615–19.
53. *CTYL* 12:10b.
54. *CTYL* 19:7b.
55. *CTYL* 59:29a–b.
56. *ECCS, Yi-shu*, 18:5b.
57. Jacques Leclerq, *The Interior Life*, trans. F. Murphy (New York, P. J. Kenedy, 1961), p. 118.
58. *CTYL* 12:2b.
59. *Analects* 12:1.
60. *CTYL* 6:12a; consult Berthrong, "Chu Hsi's Ethics," pp. 161–77, especially p. 166.
61. *CTYL* 9:3b.
62. *CTYL* 60:10b.
63. *CTYL* 42:4a.
64. *CTYL* 41:1a–16b.
65. *CTTC* 4:9b.
66. *Shuo-wen*, sec. 12B, 29b.
67. Chu Hsi, "Essay on Calming [Human] Nature," *CTTC* 67:6a.
68. *CTYL* 6:6a.
69. *CTYL* 6:9a.
70. *ECCS, Yi-shu*, 18:5b.
71. See Chu Hsi, *Ta-hsüeh chang-chü*, in *SSCC, SPPY* ed., p. 6a–b. English tranlation adapted from Legge, *Chinese Classics*, vol. I, p. 365. This is from the famous passage that Chu added to the text of the *Great Learning*.
72. Chu Hsi, *Ta-hsüeh chang-chü*, p. 6a–b; Legge, *Chinese Classics*, vol. I, pp. 365–66.
73. *Mencius* 7A:1.
74. On studying in general, see *CTYL*, chs. 7–13; on book learning, see chs. 10–11, which give specific suggestions for reading books.
75. Reply to Chiang Tuan-po, in *CTTC* 64:23b.
76. *CTYL* 10:1b.
77. *CTYL* 10:3a.
78. *CTYL* 10:1b.
79. Entitled "The Pleasures of Study during the Four Seasons," this poem is also found in Ch'en Hung-mou, *Wu-chung yi-kuei*, p. 22a; English translation adapted from Li Chi, "Chu Hsi the Poet," pp. 55–119, especially pp. 117–18.
80. Ch'en Hung-mou, *Wu-chung yi-kuei*, p. 22a; Li Chi, "Chu Hsi the Poet," pp. 117–19.
81. *CTYL* 10:1a.
82. *CTTC* 14:11a. Consult Yu Ying-shih, "Morality and Knowledge in Chu Hsi's

Philosophical System," in Wing-tsit Chan, *Chu Hsi and Neo-Confucianism*, pp. 228–54.

83. Fung, *History*, vol. 2, pp. 561, 573–629. See also Julia Ching, *To Acquire Wisdom*, especially ch. 3.

84. Chu Hsi, "A Record on the Temple Commemorating Chou Tun-yi in the Lung-hsing-fu School," *CTTC* 7:18b–19a.

85. *HTHT*; Hsü Fu-kuan, "Chu Hsi and the Ch'eng Brothers," pp. 54–55.

Chapter 7

1. *HSCC* 36:3b.

2. My first and somewhat general study of this subject appeared a number of years ago. Consult Julia Ching, "The Goose Lake Monastery Debates," *Journal of Chinese Philosophy* 1 (1974), 161–78. This chapter presents a much more thorough review.

3. The primary sources for this chapter include *CTYL*, especially ch. 124; *HSCC*, especially chs. 2, 34, and 36; and Chu's correspondence with the Lu brothers, in *CTTC*, ch. 36. The *SYHA* 12:293–94 also gives selections from the correspondence.

4. For secondary sources, consult Wing-tsit Chan, *Chu-hsüeh lun-chi*, pp. 205–50; Carsun Chang, *Development of Neo-Confucian Thought*, vol. 1, pp. 270–75; Ch'ien Mu, *Chu-tzu hsin hsüeh-an*, vol. 3, 293–488; Ho Lin (He Lin), "Sung-ju te ssu-hsiang fang-fa" (Method of Thinking of Sung Dynasty Confucians), in Symposium on Sung History, ed., *Sung-shih yen-chiu-chi* (*Collected Essays on Sung History*), 2nd collection (Taipei, Sung-shih ts'ung-shu, 1964), pp. 39–66, especially pp. 54–56; Hsü Fu-kuan, *Chung-kuo ssu-hsiang-shih lun-chi* (*Essays on the Chinese History of Ideas*) (Taipei, Student Bookstore, 1975); Huang Chin-hsing, "Chu Hsi versus Lu Hsiang-shan: A Philosophical Interpretation," *Journal of Chinese Philosophy* 14 (1987), 179–208; Huang Chang-chien, "O-hu chih-hui Chu Lu yi-t'ung lüeh-shuo" (The Goose Lake Meeting and the Differences between Chu Hsi and Lu Chiu-yüan), in Symposium on Chung History, *Sung-shih yen-chiu-chi*, pp. 31–38; Huang Siu-chi, "Chu Hsi's Ethical Rationalism," *Journal of Chinese Philosophy* 5 (1978), 175–93; Huang Siu-chi, *Lu Hsiang-shan, A Twelfth-Century Chinese Idealist Philosopher* (New Haven, American Oriental Society, 1944); Oaksoon Chun Kim, "Chu Hsi and Lu Hsiang-shan: A Study of Philosophical Achievements and Controversy in Neo-Confucianism" (Ph.D. diss., University of Iowa, 1980); Kusumoto Masatsugu, *Sō-Min jidai jugaku shisō no kenkyū* (*A Study of Sung-Ming Confucianism*) (Tokyo, Hiroike Gakuen Press, 1972); Lao Ssu-kuang, *Chung-kuo che-hsüeh-shih*, vol. 3, pp. 409–14; Lin Chi-p'ing, *Lu Hsiang-shan yen-chiu* (*A Study of Lu Chiu-yüan*) (Taipei, Shang-wu, 1983); Liu Shu-hsien, "The Function of Mind in Chu Hsi's Philosophy," *Journal of Chinese Philosophy* 5 (1978), 195–208; *TLTL*, chs. 1–2; Okada Takehiko, "Shu-Riku dōiron genryō kō" (An Examination of Comparative Studies on Chu Hsi and Lu Chiu-yüan), in *Mekada Makoto hakushi kanreki kinen Chūgokugaku ronshū* (*Festschrift on Chinese Studies in Honor of Dr. Mekada Makoto*) (Tokyo, Daian, 1964), pp. 69–89; *YHP*, pp. 531–643; Tang Chün-i, "Chu-Lu yi-t'ung t'an-yüan" (A Study of the Sources of Differences and Similarities between Chu Hsi and Lu Chiu-yüan), *Hsin-ya hsüeh-pao* 8 (February 1967), 1–100; Tillman, *Confucian Discourse*, chs. 8–9; Tian, *Chu Hsi te ssu-wei shih-chieh*, chs. 8–9; Yu Ying-shih, "Morality and Knowledge in Chu

Hsi's Philosophical System," in Wing-tsit Chan, *Chu Hsi and Neo-Confucianism,*
pp. 228–54.

5. *CTTC* 54:5b.
6. *CTNP* 2a:59. See especially Wing-tsit Chan, *Reflections,* p. 1, n. 6.
7. *HSCC* 34:24a–b.
8. *HSCC* 36:9b; *CTNP* 2a:60; Lü's biography in *Lü Tung-lai wen-chi,* TSCC ed., p. 1; *HSCC* 36:9a.
9. Wing-tsit Chan, *New Studies,* p. 436. See the gazetteer *Kwang-hsin fu-chih* (1872), 2B:19a–20a.
10. See *Kwang-hsin fu-chih* 2B:20a. In the mid–eleventh century, Chu's older contemporary the poet Tseng Kung (1019–83) visited the monastery and wrote a poem to mark the occasion. Later, another poet, Chu's younger contemporary Hsin Ch'i-chi (1140–1207), also visited the place and wrote a patriotic poem in its honor.
11. *Kwang-hsin fu-chih* 4B:27b–36a; Wing-tsit Chan, *New Studies,* p. 436.
12. See Shirokauer, "Chu Hsi's Political Career," pp. 162–69.
13. *CTNP* 2A:59–65.
14. *HSCC* 36:6a–b.
15. Ibid.
16. *TLTL,* p. 139. Mou Tsung-san criticizes Chu even more for labeling Lu from then on as a Ch'an Buddhist.
17. *SYHA,* ch. 51.
18. *SYHA* 36:8b.11.
19. *HSCC* 36:9b.
20. This is an allusion to the legacy of the ancient sages.
21. The poem is found in *HSCC* 34:24a.
22. *HSCC* 34:24b.
23. Mount T'ai is in Shantung; Mount Hua is in Kiangsu.
24. The allusion here is to the *Great Commentary to the Book of Changes.* See *CYCY* 7:2a–b.
25. *HSCC* 34:24b.
26. *CTYL* 64:22b; 124:1b, 2a–b, 4a.
27. *HSCC* 22:5a.
28. *CYCY* 7:2a. The translations from the Book of Changes are adapted from Cary F. Baynes's English translation of Richard Wilhelm's *I Ching,* p. 286.
29. *CYCY* 7:2b. Wilhelm and Baynes, *I Ching,* p. 286.
30. *CYCY* 7:3a; Wilhelm and Baynes, *I Ching* p. 287.
31. *HSCC* 36:9b.
32. For Lu Chiu-yüan's letter, see *HSCC* 1:2b–3b. He quotes *Mencius* 4A:2 (Legge, *Chinese Classics,* vol. 2, p. 293).
33. *HSCC* 36:9b.
34. *Mencius* 7A:4.
35. *SYHA,* ch. 58, p. 1084.
36. Tokiwa Daijō, *Shina ni okeru Bukkyō to Jūkyō Dōkyō (Buddhism in Relation to Confucianism and Taoism in China)* (Tokyo, Tōyō bunko, 1930), pp. 389–96 passim.
37. *HSCC* 2:9a–b.
38. *CTTC* 43:7a.
39. *HSCC* 34:16a–17b.

40. See Wilhelm and Baynes, *I Ching*, pp. 345–48.
41. Ibid., p. 346.
42. For the Nine Hexagrams, see *Chou-yi chen-yi* 8:10a–11a. English translation adapted from Wilhelm and Baynes, *I Ching*, p. 346. See also *HSCC* 36:9a, 34:16a–b.
43. *CTNP* 2a:72–74.
44. *CTYL* 76:11b, p. 3103.
45. *CTYL* 76:10b–11b, pp. 3102–4.
46. *HSCC* 36:9a–b. See also *HSCC* 34:16a–17b.
47. *HSCC* 34:4a.
48. *CTTC* 4:10a. See also *HSCC* 36:8b–9a.
49. Wing-tsit Chan, *Chu-hsüeh lun-chi*, p. 261.
50. See Lu's chronological biography in *HSCC* 36:10b.
51. *HSCC* 23:1a–b.
52. *HSCC* 23:1b–2a, 36:10a; *CTNP* 2B:96–99.
53. *ECCS, Ts'ui-yen*, 2:34a.
54. *CTYL* 124:1b–2a.
55. Wang Mao-hung, *Chu-tzu nien-p'u* 3A:124–25; *HSCC* 35:5a–b; Lao, *Chung-kuo che-hsüeh-shih*, vol. 3A, pp. 346–47.
56. Letter to Sun Ching-fu, quoted in *CTNP* 3A:132–33.
57. Wing-tsit Chan, *New Studies*, pp. 442–43.
58. Quoted by Ho, "Sung-ju te ssu-hsiang fang-fa," p. 58. Although Ho says he read it in Lu's *Chronological Biography*, I am unable to find it there.
59. Ho, "Sung-ju te ssu-hsiang fang-fa," p. 58.
60. Chen Lai, *Chu-tzu che-hsüeh yen-chiu*, pt. 4, chs. 1–3; T'ian Hao, *Chu Hsi te ssu-wei shih-chieh*, ch. 9.
61. *CTYL* 124:10b.
62. For humanity or goodness as original, see *Mencius* 6A:1–3, 6. For rightness as external, see *Mencius* 6A:4–5.
63. *CTYL* 124:5a.
64. *CTYL* 124:5b, 52:5b.
65. *CTYL* 124:7b–8a.
66. *Mencius* 6A:6.
67. *YCP* 10A:202–3; *YHP* 531–38.
68. *CTYL* 18:2a, p. 627.
69. *HSCC* 34:14b.
70. *HSCC* 34:4b–5a.
71. *Mencius* 6A:15.
72. *Mencius* 4B:19.
73. *HSCC* 1:2b–3a.
74. *HSCC* 34:5a.
75. Joseph Levenson, *Confucian China and Its Modern Fate* (Berkeley, University of California Press, 1965), vol. 2, pp. 65–66.
76. See Shirokauer, "Chu Hsi's Political Career," pp. 187–88.
77. Kusumoto, *Sō-Min jidai jugaku shisō no kenkyū*, p. 355.
78. *CTYL* 124:15a.
79. *CTYL* 9b.
80. *HSCC* 34:14b.
81. *CTYL* 126:8a–b.
82. See the preface by Yang Chien to *HSCC*, third preface, p. 1.

83. *HSCC* 35:28b.
84. *HSCC* 34:4a.
85. See *HSCC* 34:4b.
86. Ho, "Sung-ju te ssu-hsiang fang-fa," pp. 65–66.

Chapter 8

1. *CTTC* 1:8a. This poem was written during a visit to a Taoist temple on Mount Wu-yi. Chu Hsi was then in his twenties. The English translation was adapted from Li Chi, "Chu Hsi the Poet," p. 74.
2. Consult Julia Ching, "Chu Hsi and Taoism," in Bloom and Fogel, *Meeting of Minds,* pp. 108–43. This chapter is a revised version of that study.
3. *CTYL* 104:8b.
4. See his *Chronological Biography,* in *CTNP,* chs. 2–3.
5. I have consulted especially *CTYL,* ch. 25, a very long chapter, far longer than the one on Buddhism; relevant parts in the *CTTC,* especially Chu's poetry; as well as Chu's studies on *Yin-fu ching* and *Ts'an-t'ung-ch'i,* both in *CTYS.*
6. For secondary sources, consult Wing-tsit Chan on Chu and Taoist philosophy in "Chu Hsi's Appraisal of Lao-tzu," *Philosophy East and West* 25 (1975), 131–44; *Chu-tzu hsin t'an-so (A New Exploratory Study of Chu Hsi)* (Taipei, Student Bookstore, 1981); and *New Studies,* pp. 486–503. The Japanese scholar Sakai Tadao concentrated on Chu Hsi and Taoist religion in "Shushi to dōkyo" (Chu Hsi and Religious Taoism), in *Shushigaku nyūmon (Introduction to the School of Chu Hsi),* in Morohashi Tetsuji et al., comps., *Shushigaku taikei* (Tokyo, Meitoku, 1974), vol. I, pp. 411–27. An older Japanese work deals with both Taoist philosophy and Taoist religion in a wider context: Tokiwa, *Shina ni okeru bukkyo to jukyo dōkyo.* Consult also Yoshikawa Kōjirō and Miura Kunio, *Shushi shū* (Tokyo, Asahi Shinbunsha, 1976), ch. 6.
7. *CTTC* 6:22b, 76:27a–b, 9:10b.
8. Wang Tzu-ts'ai et al., *Sung-Yüan hsüeh-an pu-yi (Supplement to the Records of Sung and Yüan Scholars),* *Ssu-ming ts'ung-shu* ed. (Taipei, National Defense Academy, [1966]), ch. 69, p. 176a–b; see Wing-tsit Chan, *Chu-tzu meng-jen,* p. 99.
9. If we compare Chu Hsi with the later Wang Yang-ming, we find that in his youth, Wang had a much stronger interest in Taoism. Indeed, he was engrossed in Taoist practices promoting longevity. With age, however, he moved closer to Ch'an Buddhist ideas.
10. David A. Dilworth, *Philosophy in World Perspective: A Comparative Hermeneutic of the Major Theories* (New Haven, Yale University Press, 1989), p. 28.
11. *Lao-tzu* 1.6:4a. This version comes with Wang Pi's commentary. English translation from Lau, *Lao Tzu,* p. 62.
12. *CTYL* 125:9a.
13. See Wang's commentary on *Lao-tzu,* 1.6:4a.
14. *Lao-tzu* 1:1a.
15. Ibid.
16. *ECCS, Yi-shu,* 12:5b.
17. *CTYL* 125:7b.
18. Wing-tsit Chan, *Chu-tzu hsin t'an-so,* pp. 615–16; Wing-tsit Chan, *New Studies,* pp. 494–97.
19. *Lao-tzu* 28:16a–b. English translation adapted from Lau, *Lao Tzu,* p. 85.
20. *CTYL* 125:9a.

21. *CTYL* 125:10a; *CTCS* 3:11a. The reference is to *Lao-tzu* 2.40:4a.
22. *Lao-tzu* 1:1a.
23. *CTYL* 126:5b. The Four Elements are earth, water, fire, and wind.
24. *Lao-tzu*, ch. 38. English translation adapted from Lau, *Lao Tzu*, p. 99.
25. *CTYL* 13:8b.
26. *CTYL* 126:9b.
27. Chu Hsi alludes to the description of the Perfect Man in *Chuang-tzu*, ch. 2. "On Making All Things Equal"; see Burton Watson's translation, *Chuang Tzu*, p. 46.
28. *CTYL* 125:1b.
29. *CTYL* 97:16b.
30. Ch'ien Mu, *Chu-tzu hsin hsüeh-an*, p. 612.
31. *CTYL* 126:1a–b.
32. See *CTYL* 125:3b; *ECCS*, *Ts'ui-yen*, 1:8a–b, 9a; *ECCS*, *Yi-shu*, 18:39b.
33. *CTYL* 16:44b–45a. Wing-tsit Chan, *New Studies*, pp. 498–502.
34. English translation from Burton Watson, *Chuang Tzu*, p. 154.
35. English translation from ibid., p. 50.
36. Ibid., pp. 50–51. For Chu, see *CTYL* 20:9a–b, 125:11a–b.
37. *CTYL* 10:2a. See also 57:6a.
38. *Chuang-tzu*, ch. 2. See Burton Watson, *Chuang Tzu*, p. 50.
39. Chu Hsi, "Yang-sheng chu shuo" (On Cultivating Life), in *CTTC* 67:23b–24b.
40. Ibid.
41. *CTTC* 67:24a. To study for one's own sake is very close to discovering truth for oneself (*tzu-te*), which William Theodore de Bary highlights in several thinkers, including Chu Hsi, in *Neo-Confucian Orthodoxy and the Learning of the Mind-and-Heart* (New York, Columbia University Press, 1981).
42. Wing-tsit Chan, *Chu-tzu hsin-t'an-so*, p. 627.
43. *CTTC* 46:16b, 67:23b, 38:35a.
44. *CTYL* 125:3b.
45. *CTYL* 126:2a.
46. *CTYL* 125:2a. There is a chapter on Yang Chu's hedonism in the text *Lieh-tzu*.
47. *CTYL* 12:14b.
48. *CTYL* 125:13a–b.
49. *CTYL* 125:16a. For the problems of "liberation from the corpse" or "liberation by sword," see Michel Strickmann, "On the Alchemy of T'ao Hung-ching," in Holmes Welch and Anna Seidel, eds., *Facets of Taoism: Essays in Chinese Religion* (New Haven, Yale University Press, 1979), pp. 130–31.
50. *CTYL* 128:15b.
51. Chu has written on the practice of divination according to the Book of Changes. See *CTTC* 66:11b–27b.
52. *CTYL* 125:13b.
53. See Chu Hsi, "T'iao-hsi chen" (On Regulating Breath), in *CTTC* 85:6a. For more information on this subject, consult Miura Kunio, "Shushi to kokyū" (Chu Hsi and Breath Control), in Osamu Kanaya, ed., *Chūgoku ni okeru ningensei no kenkyū* (*Researches on the Problem of Human Existence in China*) (Tokyo, Sōbunsha, 1983), pp. 499–521.
54. *CTYL* 1:6b. For more information about Taoist cultivation of health through breath circulation, consult Chiang Wei-ch'iao's autobiographical treatise, *Ying-shih-tzu ching-tso fa* (*Master Ying-shih's Method of Meditation*), in Hsiao T'ien-shih, comp. *Tao-tsang ching-hua*, 2nd Collection, no. 9 (Taipei, Tzu-yu ch'u-pan she, 1984).

55. For the Buddhist source, consult *T* 19, no. 945, p. 126c. For the fasting of the mind, see *Chuang-tzu*, "In the World of Men," English translation in Burton Watson, *Chuang Tzu*, pp. 57–58.
56. *CTYL* 126:10b.
57. *CTYL* 120:3b.
58. *CTTC* 85:6a.
59. For Chou Tun-yi, see *SYHA*, ch. 9. The last two sentences hide a reference to a Taoist work on inner alchemy, the *Hsing-ming kuei-chih* (*The Essential Meaning of Nature and Destiny*), ascribed to the school of the Taoist Yin, in Hsiao T'ien-shih, comp., *Tao-tsang ching-hua*, 1st Collection, no. 5 (Taipei, Ta-yu ch'u-pan-she, 1981), part "heng," p. 175. The last sentence also refers to dragons and serpents hibernating. See the Book of Changes, Appended Remarks, pt. 2; See *Chou-yi pen-yi, K'ao yü ch'i-ta* (Changsha, Commercial Press, 1937), 8:4a.
60. *CTTC* 85:6a.
61. See *Chou-yi pen-yi*, Appended Remarks, 1.7:12a. Consult *ECCS, Yi-shu*, ch. 15.
62. Consult Burton Watson, *Chuang Tzu*, p. 154. Reference to Lau, *Lao-tzu*, ch. 51, p. 112, and to Ch'u Tz'u, *T'ien-wen* (The Heavenly Questions). Consult Chu's *Ch'u-tz'u chi-chu*, ch. 3.
63. *ECCS, Yi-shu*, ch. 11.
64. For "holding the One," which became a method of meditation, see *Lao-tzu*, ch. 10 (Lau, *Lao-tzu*, p. 66). Also see *Pao-p'u-tzu, SPPY* ed., ch. 18; English translation by James Ware, trans., *Alchemy, Medicine, Religion in the China of* A.D. *320: The Nei-p'ien of Ko Hung* (Cambridge, MIT Press, 1966), pp. 303–4. Among the famed immortals, Kuang-ch'eng *tzu* was a legendary ancient described in *Chuang-tzu*. See Burton Watson, *Chuang Tzu*, pp. 118–20.
65. *CTTC* 51:27a.
66. See Azuma Jūji, "Shuki 'Shueki sandōkei kōi' ni tsuite" (A Study of the *Chou-yi Ts'an-t'ung-ch'i k'ao-yi* by Chu Hsi), *Nippon Chūgoku gakkaiho* 36 (1984), 175–90; and Sueki Yasuhiko's three articles: "Shushi to dōkyō wo meguru ichisokumen: 'Inpukyō kōi' kō" (On Chu Hsi and Taoism: The *Yin-fu ching k'ao-yi*), *Tōhōgaku* 60 (1980), 81–95; "Inpukyō kōi no shisō" (The Thought of *Yin-fu-ching k'ao-yi*), *Nippon Chūgoku gakkaihō* 36 (1984), 163–73; and "'Inpukyō kōi' senjakō" (An Inquiry into the Authorship of *Yin-fu ching k'ao-yi*), in *Chūgoku tetsubunka gaku kaihō* 10 (1985), 50–69. In the last-cited article, Sueki expresses the opinion that the *Yin-fu-ching k'ao-yi* is not from Chu's pen but is the work of his friend and contemporary Ts'ai Yüan-ting.
67. The "Three Ways" refer to the Yellow Emperor, Lao-tzu, and the Book of Changes. For the Yellow Emperor, consult Yün-hua Jan, "The Change of Images: Yellow Emperor in Ancient Chinese Literature," *Journal of Oriental Studies* 19 (1981), 117–37.
68. Miura mentions this fact and asserts that to the end of his life, Chu balanced his concern for the physical self with his effort to transcend the self. See "Shushi to kokyū," pp. 517–18.
69. For the *Ts'an-t'ung-ch'i k'ao-yi*, I have consulted the edition in the *CTYS*, vol. 12.
70. See Needham, *Science and Civilisation*, vol. 2, p. 441; Henderson, *Chinese Cosmological Thought*, pp. 16–20, especially the diagram on p. 17 illustrating the correlation of the trigrams with the phases of the moon and the days of the lunar month.

71. The scholarly divergence continues today. Azuma supports Ch'en Kuo-fu, who prefers to understand the text more in terms of inner alchemy. See Azuma, "Shu Ki 'Shueki sandōkei kōi' ni tsuite," pp. 188–89, n. 2; Ch'en Kuo-fu, *Tao-tsang yüan-liu k'ao* (*An Examination of the Sources and Transmission of the Taoist Canon*) (Peking, Chung-hua, 1963), appendix 6, pp. 438–53.

72. Sakai, "Shushi to dokyō," p. 417.

73. Azuma, "Shu Ki 'Shueki sandokei koi' ni tsuite," pp. 179–80. For Taoist cultivation of life, see Sakade Yoshinobu, *Dōkyō to yōjō shisō* (*Taoism and the Cultivation of Life*) (Tokyo, Perikansha, 1992).

74. *Ts'an-t'ung-ch'i k'ao-yi*, preface, 3a. For Ts'ai, see Wing-tsit Chan, *Chu-tzu meng-jen* pp. 331–32.

75. *Ts'an-t'ung-ch'i k'ao-yi* 1b–2a. The reference to transmission alludes to Chu's not belonging to any esoteric circle in which such texts were orally transmitted.

76. Ibid.

77. *CTYL* 125:13a.

78. *CTYL* 5a–b. Chu's judgment is based upon mistakes he found in the *Classic of the Dragon and Tiger*. As far as the authorship of the *Ts'an-t'ung-ch'i* is concerned, Kristofer Schipper thinks it could be an apocryphal text of the Han dynasty appended to the Book of Changes. For this and other opinions, see Fukui Kōjun, "A Study of Chou-i Ts'an-t'ung-ch'i," *Acta Asiatica* 27 (1974), 19–32.

79. Chu Hsi, *Ch'u Tz'u chi-chu* 5:2a. For an English translation of the *Ch'u-tz'u*, see Hawkes, *Songs of the South*.

80. Chu Hsi, *Ch'u-tz'u chi-chu* 5:1a.

81. *CTTC* 84:26b.

82. *CTTC* 45:15a.

83. Actually, Shao had studied with Li Chih-ts'ai, a Taoist from Ch'en's circle. See *Sung-shih*, ch. 427, pp. 5580–81. For Ch'en T'uan, see also Livia Knaul, *Leben und Legende des Ch'en T'uan*, Würzburger Sino-Japonica, vol. 9 (Frankfurt, Peter Lang, 1981).

84. *Ts'an-t'ung-ch'i k'ao-yi* 2 b.

85. *Ts'an-t'ung-ch'i k'ao-yi*, in *CTYS* 2a.

86. Azuma, "Shu Ki 'Shueki sandokei koi' ni tsuite," pp. 187–88.

87. See *CTTC* 67:25a–26b.

88. Ibid.

89. Sueki, "Yinkokyō Impukyō kōi no shisō," pp. 163–64.

90. Liu Shih-p'ei, *Tu Tao-tsang chi* (*Reading Notes on the Taoist Canon*), in *Liu Sheng-shu hsien-sheng yi-shu* (*Surviving Works of Liu Shih-p'ei*) (1936).

91. Sueki refers to Wang Ming and Chang Dainian, who doubt Li's authorship at least for part of that work. See "Impukyō," p. 173, nn. 4 and 6.

92. *Yin-fu-ching k'ao-yi* 1b. For more information on that text, see Needham, *Science and Civilisation*, vol. 2, pp. 447–48.

93. Preface to *Yin-fu ching k'ao-yi*, in *CTYS*, vol. 12. See p. 1a.

94. Ibid.

95. Ibid., 6a.

96. Ibid., 4a.

97. Ibid., 6a.

98. Ibid. See also *CTYL* 125:14a–b.

99. *Yin-fu ching k'ao-yi*, 6b. Reference is to the appendices (pt. 2) to the Book of Changes. See Chu Hsi, *Chou-yi pen-yi* 8:5b.

100. Sueki, "Impukyō kōi no shisō," pp. 166–67.
101. *Yin-fu ching k'ao-yi* 7a.
102. Ibid., 6a.
103. Ibid., 9a.
104. See Chin Chung-shu, "Lun Pei-Sung mo-nien chih ch'ung-shang Tao-chiao" (On the Favoring of Religious Taoism during the Last Years of the Northern Sung), in Symposium on Sung History, ed., *Sung-shih yen-chiu chi (Collected Essays on Sung History)* (Taipei, Chung-hua ts'ung-shu pien-sheng wei-yüan-hui, 1974/76), vol. 7, pp. 291–392, and vol. 8, 207–78.
105. Ch'en Kuo-fu, *Tao-tsang yüan-liu k'ao*, vol. 1, pp. 135–36, 147–49.
106. Sakai Tadao, "Shushi to dōkyō," pp. 426–27. Chu Hsi said nothing about these two texts, although a later scholar of his school, Chen Te-hsiu (1178–1235), would write a preface for the *T'ai-shang kan-ying p'ien*.
107. Chu had been criticized by others, including the Ming scholar Hu Chü-jen (1434–84), for advocating "watching the tip of the nose" and writing these treatises on Taoist texts, that is, for leading others "into heresy." See Hu Chü-jen, *Chü-yeh lu (Record of Self-Cultivation)* (1633), 3:10a–11b, 7:11b–12a.
108. Julia Ching, *To Acquire Wisdom*.
109. *CTYL* 125:14b.
110. *CTYL* 125:14a.
111. *CTYL* 125:15a.
112. *CTYL* 125:15a–b.
113. *CTYL* 126:4a–b.
114. *CTYL* 128:15a.
115. *CTYL* 128:15b.
116. Consult Liu Ts'un-yan, "Chu Hsi yü *Ts'an-t'ung ch'i*."
117. *CTTC* 3:13b.

Chapter 9

1. *Wu-men kuan*, p. 292b.
2. This present study is a much-expanded version of my article Ching Chia-yi, "Shushi to Bukkyō" (Chu Hsi and Buddhism), in *Shushigaku nyūmon*, in Morohashi Tetsuji et al., eds., *Shushigaku taikei* (Tokyo, Meitoku, 1974), vol. 1, pp. 397–410; and my article Ching Chia-yi, "Chu-tzu yü fo-chiao" (Chu Hsi and Buddhism), *Hsin-ya hsüeh-shu chi-k'an* 3 (1982), 135–41.
3. See Chu Hsi, *Chou-yi pen-yi*, Appended Remarks, 1.7:12a.
4. Where Chu's own writings are concerned, I have consulted *CTYL*, especially ch. 126, and *CTTC*. Chu's poetry often shows more Buddhist and Taoist sentiments than do his prose or recorded dialogues. *SYHA* is a useful text; another important Ming dynasty text is Huang Wan's *Ming-tao p'ien*, ed. Hou Wai-lu (Peking, Chung-hua, 1959). Consult especially ch. 1, pp. 11–14. *T* 47 includes the recorded dialogue of the monk Ta-hui Tsung-kao, who allegedly influenced Chu in his youth. Other Buddhist sources consulted will be given in the notes.
5. Consult Dilworth, *Philosophy in World Perspective*, pp. 147–49.
6. See the poem at the beginning of chapter 2.
7. As secondary references, I have consulted the following works: Araki Kengo, *Bukkyō to jukyō (Buddhism and Confucianism)* (Kyoto, Heirakuji shoten, 1963); Derk Bodde, "The Chinese View of Immortality: Its Expression by Chu Hsi and

Its Relationship to Buddhist Thought," in Charles Le Blanc and Dorothy Borei, eds., *Essays on Chinese Civilization* (Princeton University Press, 1981); Wing-tsit Chan, *Chu-tzu hsin t'an-so*; Ch'ien Mu, *Chu-tzu hsin hsüeh-an*, vol. 3; Charles Weihsun Fu, "Chu Hsi and Buddhism," in Wing-tsit Chan, ed., *Chu Hsi and Neo-Confucianism*; Wing-tsit Chan, *New Studies*; Ichiki Tsuyuhiko, "Shushi no 'Zatsugabuken' to sono shūhen" (Chu Hsi's "On Miscellaneous Learning" and Its Circumstances), in Sōdaishi kenkyūsha, ed., *Sōdai no shakai to shūkyō (Society and Religion in Sung China)* (Tokyo, Kyūko shōin, 1985), pp. 7–10; Kusumoto Fumio, *Sōdai jugaku no zen shisō kenkyū (A Study of Zen Thought in Sung Confucianism)* (Nagoya, Nisseido, 1980); Galen Eugene Sargent, *Tchou Hi contre le bouddhisme* (Paris: Imprimerie Nationale, 1955); Koichi Shinohara, "Ta-hui's Instructions to Tseng K'ai: Buddhist 'Freedom' in the Neo-Confucian Context," in Bloom and Fogel, *Meeting of Minds*, pp. 175–208, especially pp. 189–94; Tokiwa Daijō, *Shina ni okeru Bukkyō to jukyō dōkyō*; Yanagida Seizan, "Bukkyō to Shushi no shūhen" (Buddhism and Those around Chu Hsi), *Zen bunka kenkyūjo kiyō (Studies on Zen Culture)* 8 (1976), 1–30.

8. *CTTC* 30:3a.

9. Ch'en Chien, *Hsüeh-pu t'ung-p'ien*, in Chang Po-hsing, comp., *Cheng-yi t'ang ch'üan-shu* (Shanghai, Commercial Press, 1936), suppl., ch. 2; *SYHA*, ch. 34. Consult Satō Hitoshi, *Shushi: Oi yasuku gaku narigatashi (Chu Hsi: Easy to Grow Old but Hard to Learn)* (Tokyo, Shūeisha, 1985), 55–71.

10. *CTNP* 1A:1.

11. *CTTC* 38:34b.

12. See *CTNP* 1A:16; Wing-tsit Chan, *Chu-tzu hsin-t'an-so*, pp. 633–39, 641–50; Wing-tsit Chan, *New Studies*, pp. 510–11.

13. *K'u-ya man-lu (Notes by [the Monk] K'u-ya)*, in *Hsü Tsang-ching*, vol. 148, preface 1272, 2:81b. See Kusumoto Fumio, *Sōdai jugaku no zen shisō kenkyū*, p. 327; Wing-tsit Chan, *Chu-tzu hsin-t'an-so*, p. 636; Wing-tsit Chan, *New Studies*, pp. 518–19.

14. *K'u-ya man-lu* 15:81b.

15. Liu Tzu-hui *Fo-fa chin-t'ang p'ien (An Account of Buddhism [in China])*, preface 1391 in *Hsü Tsang-ching*, Pao-lien-t'ang ed., 15:484. See also Wing-tsit Chan, *New Studies*, pp. 515–18. For Chu's own comments, see Wang, *CTNP* 1A:16.

16. Satō, *Shushi*, p. 76.

17. *CTTC* 1:8b.

18. Letter to a disciple, *CTTC* 60:5a.

19. *CTYL* 126:20b.

20. The word "hindrance" (*chang*; Sanskrit, *varana*) refers to passions or delusions hindering enlightenment.

21. *CTYL* 41:14a, p. 1687.

22. See *Recorded Dialogues of Ta-hui*, T 47, no. 1998A, ch. 21, p. 899a. See also *Wumen kuan*, pp. 292c–294a; English translation in Zenkei Shibayama, *Zen Comments on the Mumonkan*, trans. Sumiko Kudo (New York, New American Library, 1974).

23. *Recorded Dialogues of Ta-hui*, T 47, no. 1998A, ch. 20, p. 895b.

24. *CTYL* 126:19a; Wing-tsit Chan, *New Studies*, pp. 511–13.

25. Yoshikawa and Miura, *Shushi shū*, p. 374; Tomoeda, *Shushi no shisō keisei*, pp. 45–47; Satō, *Shushi*, pp. 71–73; Wing-tsit Chan, *Chu-tzu hsin-t'an-so*, pp. 638–39; Wing-tsit Chan, *New Studies*, pp. 515–17.

26. See Li T'ung's letter to a friend, in *Li Yen-p'ing chi (Collected Writings of Li T'ung)*,

comp. Chang Po-hsing, *TSCC* ed., ch. 1, p. 4. Actually, Li wrote very little. This collection presents some records of Li's conversations with Chu Hsi and a few letters from Li to various persons. For Chu's sacrificial essay in memory of Tao-ch'ien, see *Fo-fa chin-t'ang p'ien* 15:84a.

27. *CTTC* 33:12a.
28. Yan Yaozhong, "Chu Hsi yü Mi-an" (Chu Hsi and the Mi-an Monastery), *Chung-hua wen-shih lun-ts'ung* 57 (1998), 241–54.
29. *Fo-fa chin-t'ang p'ien* 48:84a. Chu used Ta-hui's other name, Miao-hsi.
30. *K'u-ya man-lu* 2:80b.
31. *Li Yen-p'ing chi*, ch. 3, p. 49. According to the *K'u-ya man-lu* (2:80b), when Chu first visited Li T'ung, he had with him only the *Book of Mencius* and that same *Recorded Dialogues of Ta-hui*.
32. *Li Yen-p'ing chi*, ch. 3, 41–42.
33. *CTTC* 30:3a.
34. *Li Yen-p'ing chi*, ch. 2, p. 18.
35. Kusumoto Fumio, *Sōdai jugaku no zen shisō kenkyū*, p. 351, referring to Wang, *CTNP* 3A:121; for my point, see *CTYL* 126:16b; see also Wing-tsit Chan, *Chu-tzu hsin-t'an-so*, pp. 463–85; Wing-tsit Chan, *New Studies*, ch. 21.
36. *CTTC* 72:45b.
37. *CTYL* 126:3b–4a, 16a.
38. *CTYL* 126:18b.
39. *CTYL* 126:18b. Consult *Ching-te ch'uan-teng lu*, T 51, no. 2076, p. 196b–c.
40. Consult *Ta-fo ting ju-lai mi-ying hsiu-cheng liao-yi chu p'u-sa wan-hsing shou Leng-yen ching* (*Surangama Sutra*), T 19, no. 945. As a matter of fact, this sutra is today considered a Chinese forgery.
41. See *CTYL* 126:18a, 125:5a.
42. *CTYL* 126:27b.
43. Consult Leon Hurvitz, trans., *Scripture of the Lotus Blossom of the Fine Dharma* (*The Lotus Sutra*) (New York, Columbia University Press, 1976), p. 7.
44. Ibid., p. 9.
45. *CTYL* 126:3a, 17a. Consult *Chao Lun*, op. cit.
46. *CTYL* 126:16a. The very short *Heart Sutra* does belong to the big corpus called the *Perfection of Wisdom Sutras*. It speaks especially of emptiness, presumably the emptiness of signs or *laksas*. Consult Edward Conze, *The Prajñāpāramitā Literature* (The Hague, Mouton, 1960); Leon Hurvitz, "Hsüan Tsang (602–664) and the Heart Scripture," in Lewis Lancaster et al., eds., *The Prajñāpāramitā and Related Systems: Studies in Honor of Edward Conze*, Berkeley Buddhist Studies Series (Berkeley, Asian Humanities Press, 1977), p. 105.
47. *Ching-kang po-je po-lo-mi ching*, T 8, no. 235, p. 749c; English translation from Müller, *The Vagrakkhedika, or Diamond-Cutter*, p. 122. Chu referred to these lines in *CTYL* 126:17a. See also chapter 1.
48. *Liu-tsu ta-shih fa-pao t'an-ching*, p. 348, n. 3.
49. *CTYL* 126:16a. The *Sutra of Forty-two Sections* was attributed to the first Indian monks to officially arrive in China. It represents Theravāda teachings and has various editions and commentaries.
50. The Japanese scholar Tokiwa Daijō considers this Chu's weakest argument, indeed, a slander on Buddhism and proof that he did not know very much about the religion.
51. *CTYL* 126:2a, 4b, 24b–25a.

52. *CTYL* 126:6a.
53. *CTYL* 126:16b.
54. Consult Takasaki Jikido, *An Introduction to Buddhism*, trans. Rolf W. Giebel (Tokyo, Tōhō Gakkai, 1987), pp. 77, 109, 150.
55. *CTYL* 126:21a.
56. See *CTTC* 45:15b.
57. Consult *T* 17, no. 842, pp. 913b, 914b.
58. *CTYL* 126:17a.
59. *CTYL* 126:16b.
60. *CTYL* 126:6a.
61. *CTYL* 126:25b.
62. Consult Dilworth, *Philosophy in World Perspective*, p. 22.
63. See *CTYL* 126:6a.
64. *CTTC* 43:8a–9a.
65. *CTYL* 126:5a–b.
66. *CTTC* 52:4a.
67. *CTTC* 70:5b.
68. *CTYL* 126:7a.
69. *CTYL* 126:21b.
70. *CTYL* 126:17b–18a.
71. *CTTC* 45:15b, 72:43a–b.
72. A catty is a unit of weight. See the *Fo-kuo Yüan-wu Ch'an-shih Pi-yen lu* (*The Blue Cliff Dialogues of Ch'an Master Fo-kuo Yüan-wu*), *T* 48, no. 2003, p. 152c. It is also mentioned in *Wu-men kuan*, p. 295.
73. Consult *Cheng-chou Lin-chi Hui-chao Ch'an-shih yü-lu* (*Recorded Dialogues of Ch'an Master Lin-chi Hui-chao*), *T* 47, no. 1985, p. 496c. The *Kung-an* is also mentioned in the *Wu-men kuan*, p. 295c.
74. *CTYL* 126:19b. See also *CTYL* 126:10a.
75. *CTYL* 126:5b.
76. Wing-tsit Chan, *Chu-tzu hsin-t'an-so*, pp. 633–37.
77. *CTTC* 70:6b.
78. *CTYL* 4:9b.
79. *CTYL* 132:17a–18a.
80. *CTYL* 13:7a. Consult the *Miao-fa lien-hua ching* (*Lotus sutra*), Kumārajīva's translation, in *T* 9, no. 261, p. 7a.
81. *CTYL* 132:17a.
82. *CTYL* 120:3a.
83. *CTYL* 120:7b.
84. *CTYL* 126:25b. Consult *Fo-fa chin-t'ang p'ien* 15:84a.
85. *Ta-sh'eng ch'i-hsin lun*, *T* 32, no. 1666, pp. 576a–b. English translation in Yoshito S. Hakeda, trans., *The Awakening of Faith, Attributed to Aśvaghosha* (New York, Columbia University Press, 1967), pp. 34–35.
86. See *T'an-ching*, op. cit., p. 349b. This *kung-an* is from a later version of the *Platform Sutra*. Consult Yampolsky, *Platform Sutra*, p. 134, n. 48.
87. See Chu's *Ta-hsüeh chang-chü*, p. 1a. For the Buddhist parallel, see Tsung-mi's essay in *Yüan-jen lun*, p. 710a, where the expression is *chao-chao pu-mei* (i.e., bright and without obscurity).
88. *CTYL* 12:16a.
89. Ching-chüeh, *Leng-chia shih-chih chi*, *T* 85, no. 2837, pp. 1287c–1290a. Consult

Bernard Faure, "The Concept of One Practice Samādhi in Early Ch'an," in Peter N. Gregory, ed., *Traditions of Meditation in Chinese Buddhism* (Honolulu, University of Hawaii Press, 1986), pp. 114–15.

90. Chu Hsi, "Kuan-hsin shuo" (On Contemplating the Mind), in *CTTC* 67:20a.

91. *CTTC* 67:21b. To have the mind contemplate itself is a reflexive process suggesting a pure experience of consciousness, which is sometimes called introvertive mysticism, as I have mentioned.

92. *CTYL* 126:12a, 13a.

93. *CTTC* 59:23b.

94. *CTYL* 95:13b.

95. *CTYL* 126:11b. Consult *Liu-tsu ta-shih fa-pao t'an-ching*, pp. 348–49.

96. *CTYL* 18:5a.

97. Chu Hsi, *Ta-hsüeh chang-chü*, p. 6b.

98. For a fuller discussion, see chapters 6 and 11.

99. *CTTC* 71:6B. The reference is to the Ch'an text *Wu-teng hui-yüan* (*The Gathering of Five Lamps*), in *Hsü Tsang-ching*, vol. 138, 17:335a. Wang Yang-ming also used this *kung-an* in teaching concentration.

100. *CTYL* 126:11a.

101. This letter (1166) is cited in Wang, *CTNP* 1A:27.

Chapter 10

1. Liang Ch'i-ch'ao, *Yin-ping-shih ho-chi, wen-chi* (*Collected Writings of Liang Ch'i-ch'ao*) (Shanghai, Chung-hua, 1941), 9:55–56.

2. Fung, *History*, vol. 1, introduction. Fung's history of Chinese philosophy alternates between the periods of philosophical speculation and those of classical exegesis. This is even clearer in the Chinese original. See Feng Yu-lan, *Chung-kuo che-hsüeh-u shih* (Shanghai, Commercial Press, 1935). Consult also Benjamin A. Elman, *From Philosophy to Philology* (Cambridge, Harvard University Press, 1984); John B. Henderson, *Scripture, Canon, and Commentary: A Comparison of Confucian and Western Exegesis* (Princeton University Press, 1991).

3. Consult Tai Hsien, *Chu-tzu shih-chi* 2:9b–10a, pp. 92–93; Brian McKnight, "Chu Hsi and His World," in Wing-tsit Chan, *Chu Hsi and Neo-Confucianism*, pp. 408–24.

4. See *CTNP*, ch. 1–4.

5. *CTNP* 4B:218–20; Tai Hsien, *Chu-tzu shih-chi* 4:19a–b, pp. 197–98.

6. *CTNP* 4B:230–31; Shirokauer, "Chu Hsi's Political Career," pp. 184–85.

7. See Li Hsin-ch'uan, "Hui-an hsien-sheng fei su-yin" (Master Chu Hsi Was Not a Recluse), in *Chien-yen yi-lai ch'ao-yeh tsa-chi* (*Miscellaneous Records of Court and Country since 1127*), TSCC ed., pt. 2, p. 445.

8. Consult Julia Ching, *To Acquire Wisdom*, ch. 3.

9. I'm referring to *Ta-hsüeh ku-pen p'ang-chu* (*The Old Version of the "Great Learning"*), in *WWKC*. Wang excluded Chu's preface as well as his chapter divisions.

10. *WWKC* 7:241a–b.

11. *WWKC* 7:241a–b.

12. *Chu-tzu wan-nien ting-lun* (*Definitive Ideas of Chu Hsi in His Later Life*). This was published with a passage from Wu Ch'eng (1249–1333) expressing regret at the degeneration of Chu's school. See *WWKC* 3:168a–69a.

13. *WWKC* 2:119b.

14. *WWKC* 2:117a.

15. *WWKC* 2:117a.

16. Matteo Ricci, *The True Meaning of the Lord of Heaven*, trans., with the original Chinese, by Douglas Lancashire and Peter Hu Kuo-chen, S.J., ed. Edward J. Malatesta, S.J. (St. Louis, Institute of Jesuit Sources, 1985), p. 351. Consult Shibata Atsushi, "Minmatsu tenshukyō no reikonkan—Chūgoku shisō to no taiwa wo megutte," *Tōhōgaku* 76 (1988), 1–13.

17. Ricci, *True Meaning*, p. 351.

18. Consult Jerome Heyndrickx, *Philippe Couplet, S.J. (1623–1693): The Man Who Brought China to Europe* (Nettetal, Steyler Verlag, 1990).

19. Virgile Pinot, *La Chine et la formation de l'esprit philosophique en France, 1640–1740* (Geneva, Slakine reprint, 1971), pp. 305–13, 329–31.

20. Julia Ching and Willard Oxtoby, *Moral Enlightenment*, pp. 45–46; see also Leibniz, "Discourse on the Natural Theology of the Chinese," in ibid., pp. 91–94. For Bouvet, consult Claudia von Collani, *P. Joachim Bouvet, s.j.: Sein Leben und sein Werk* (Nettetal, Steyler Verlag, 1985).

21. This quotation is taken from his correspondence. See Li Chih, *Fen-shu*, in *Fen-shu/Hsü Fen-shu (Books to Burn/Supplement to Books to Burn)* (Peking, Chung-hua, 1974), vol. 1, ch. 1, p. 10.

22. Ibid., pp. 84–85.

23. Ibid., introduction.

24. Wang Fu-chih, *Chang-tzu Cheng-meng chu (Commentary on Chang Tsai's "Correcting the Ignorant")* (Peking, Chung-hua, 1975), ch. 1, pp. 5–7. Consult Alison H. Black, *Man and Nature in the Philosophic Thought of Wang Fu-chih* (Seattle, University of Washington Press, 1989).

25. *Chou-yi wai-chuan (On the Supplement to the Appendix to the Book of Changes)* (Peking, Chung-hua, 1977), pt. 1, ch. 12, p. 203.

26. Wang Fu-chih, *Tu Ssu-shu ta-ch'üan shuo (On the Collected Commentaries of the Four Books)* (Peking, Chung-hua, 1975), vol. 1, ch. 4, p. 248.

27. Ku Yen-wu, *T'ing-lin shih-wen chi (Collected Writings of Ku Yen-wu)*, SPTK, 1st ser. ed., 3:102; Julia Ching, *Mysticism and Kingship*, p. 161; consult Chung-ying Cheng, "Practical Learning in Yen Yüan, Chu Hsi, and Wang Yang-ming," in William Theodore de Bary et al., eds., *Principle and Practicality: Essays in Neo-Confucianism and Practical Learning* (New York, Columbia University Press, 1979), pp. 37–68.

28. Yen Yüan, *Ts'un-hsüeh p'ien (On Preserving Learning)* (n.p., Ssu-ts'un hsüeh-hui, [1923]), 3:8.

29. Yen, *Chu-tzu yü-lei p'ing*, pp. 2b, 18b.

30. Ibid., 19b, 7b, 8a.

31. Cheng Chung-ying, "Yen Yüan, Chu Hsi and Wang Yang-ming," p. 39.

32. Yen, *Chu-tzu yü-lei p'ing*, 8b.

33. Ibid., 9a.

34. Li Kung, *Ta-hsüeh pien-yeh (Analysis of the "Great Learning")*, in *Yen-Li ts'ung-shu (Collected Writings of Yen Yüan and Li Kung)* (n.p., Ssu-ts'un hsüeh-hui, [1923]), 2:8; Julia Ching, *Mysticism and Kingship*, p. 162.

35. Ann-ping Chin et al., trans., *Tai Chen on Mencius: Explorations in Words and Meaning, a Translation of Meng-tzu tzu-i shu-cheng with a Critical Introduction* (New Haven, Yale University Press, 1990), pp. 38–39.

36. Tai Chen, *Meng-tzu tzu-yi shu-cheng (A Study of the Meaning of Words in Mencius)* (Taipei, Kuang-wen reprint, 1978), 1:1b. Consult Ann-ping Chin, op. cit., p. 74.

37. Tai Chen, *Meng-tzu* 1:8a; Ann-ping Chin, op. cit., p. 89.
38. Tai Chen, *Meng-tzu* 1:9a; Ann-ping Chin, op. cit., p. 91.
39. Tai Chen, *Meng-tzu* 3:14a.
40. See Arita Kazuo and Oshima Akeru ed., *Shushigaku teki shii: Chūgoku shisōshi ni okeru dentō to kakushin* (*The Thought of Chu Hsi's School: Tradition and Change in the History of Chinese Thought*) (Tokyo, Kyūko shoin, 1990), pt. 1, ch. 1, suppl.
41. For Itō Jinsai and Ogyū Sorai, see Yoshikawa Kōjirō, *Jinsai, Sorai, Norinaga: Three Classical Philologists of Mid-Tokugawa Japan* (Tokyo, Tōhō Gakkai, 1983), pp. 9–260.
42. Yü Ying-shih, *Lun Tai Chen yü Chang Hsüeh-ch'eng* (*On Tai Chen and Chang Hsüeh-ch'eng*) (Taipei, Hua-shih, 1977), pp. 191–96; consult Robert N. Bellah, "Baigan and Sorai: Continuities and Discontinuities in Eighteenth-Century Japanese Thought," in Tetsuo Najita et al., eds., *Japanese Thought in the Tokugawa Period, 1600–1869* (University of Chicago Press, 1978), pp. 137–52; Charles Wing-hoi Chan, "The 'Benevolent Person' versus the 'Sage': Ogyū Sorai's Critiques of Chu Hsi" (Ph.D. diss., University of Toronto, 1994), pp. 36–37.
43. Ryusaku Tsunoda, ed., *Sources of Japanese Tradition* (New York, Columbia University Press, 1958), p. 411.
44. The Three Dynasties refer to the ancient Hsia, Shang, and Chou. See ibid., p. 415.
45. Ibid., p. 418.
46. Olof G. Lidin, trans., *Distinguishing the Way* (*Bendō*) (Tokyo, Sophia University Press, 1970), p. x.
47. Ogyū Sorai, *Benmei* (*Distinguishing Names*), in Yoshikawa Kōjirō, ed., *Ogyū Sorai* (Tokyo, Iwanami, 1973), 13B:1; adapted from John Tucker's unpublished translation, pp. 321–22; cited in Charles Chan, "'Benevolent Person,'" p. 144.
48. Hu Shih, "Chi-ko fan li-hsüeh te ssu-hsiang chia" (Several Anti-Neo-Confucian Thinkers), in *Hu Shih wen-ts'un* (*Collected Writings*) (Taipei, Yüan-tung, 1953), vol. 3. See also Jerome B. Grieder, *Hu Shih and the Chinese Renaissance: Liberalism in the Chinese Revolution, 1917–1937* (Cambridge, Harvard University Press, 1970).
49. Julia Ching, "Confucianism: A Critical Re-assessment of the Tradition," *International Philosophical Quarterly* 15 (1975), 1–33.
50. Chow Tse-tsung, *The May Fourth Movement: Intellectual Revolution in Modern China* (Stanford University Press, 1960), pp. 293–311.
51. Levenson, *Confucian China*, vol. 1, p. xxxii.
52. A. A. Zhdanov, *Essays on Literature, Philosophy, and Music* (New York, International Publishers, 1950); Innocentius M. [Joseph M.] Bochenski, *Soviet Russian Dialectical Materialism, DIAMAT* (Dordrecht, Reidel, 1963), pp. 37–48, 97–103.
53. See Hou Wailu, Zhao Jibin, and Du Guoxiang, *Chung-kuo ssu-hsiang t'ung-shih*, vol. 4, pt. 2, pp. 595–691.
54. Yang Rongguo, *Chien-ming Chung-kuo che-hsüeh-shih* (*A Simplified History of Chinese Philosophy*) (Peking, Jen-min, 1973), p. 216.
55. *CTYL* 62:15a–b, pp. 2375–76.
56. Hou, Zhao, and Du, *Chung-kuo ssu-hsiang t'ung-shih*, vol. 4B, p. 600.
57. Ibid., p. 607.
58. See Sha Ming, *K'ung-chia tien chi ch'i yu-lin* (*Confucius and Sons and Their Ghost*) (Hong Kong, 1970), pp. 41–52; Ren Jiyu, *Chung-kuo che-hsüeh-shih chien pien* (*A*

Concise History of Chinese Philosophy) (Peking, Jen-min, 1984), pp. 409–10; *Ju-chia ho Ju-chia ssu-hsiang p'i-p'an* (*Confucianism and Its Critique*), comp. Philosophy Department, Peking University (Peking, 1974), pp. 38–52.

59. Ren, *Chung-kuo che-hsüeh-shih chien pien*, pp. 395–96; Hou, Zhao, and Du, *Chung-kuo ssu-hsiang t'ung-shih*, vol. 4B, pp. 624–38; Yang, *Chien-ming Chung-kuo che-hsüeh-shih*, pp. 217–18.

60. Yang, *Chien-ming Chung-kuo che-hsüeh-shih*, p. 218. The allusion made is to Chu Hsi's words in *CTYL*, ch. 1.

61. Hou, Zhao, and Du, *Chung-kuo ssu-hsiang t'ung-shih*, vol. 4B, pp. 601, 604.

62. Yang, *Chien-ming Chung-kuo che-hsüeh-shih*, pp. 219–24; Ren, *Chung-kuo che-hsüeh-shih chien pien*, pp. 401–9.

63. See especially Lo Siding, "P'in Chu Hsi te wei-hsin lun te hsien-yen lun" (A Critique of Chu's Apriorism in His Idealism), *People's Daily*, February 13, 1974.

64. For Feng Yulan's works in Chinese, consult also *San Sung-t'ang ch'üan-chi* (*Complete Writings*), 14 vols. (Honan Jen-min, 1993); see also Feng Zhongpu et al., ed. *Feng Youlan hsien-sheng pai-nien tan-ch'en chi-nien wen-chi* (*A Collected Volume in Honor of Feng Yu-lan's Birth Centenary*) (Peking, Qinghua University Press, 1995). Feng took seriously his mission to reinterpret the philosophy of Ch'eng Yi and Chu Hsi and early in his career, in 1939, was the renowned author of six works, which he hoped would influence China's intellectual and spiritual orientation. For the contemporary study of neo-Confucianism in mainland China, see Li Ming-hui, *Tang-tai ju-hsüeh te tzu-wo chuan-hua* (*The Self-transformation of Contemporary Confucianism*) (Taipei, Academia Sinica, 1994), pp. 175–92.

65. *HTHT*, vol. 2, ch. 3.

66. Consult *TLP*, pp. 405–8.

67. *TLTL*, p. 152.

68. *HTHT*, vol. 1, pp. 42–60, 86–113, 369–80; vol. 3, pp. 243, 277. Consult John H. Berthrong, *All under Heaven: Transforming Paradigms in Confucian-Christian Dialogue* (Albany, State University of New York Press, 1994), ch. 4.

69. *HTHT*, vol. 3, ch. 1, pp. 5–6.

70. *HTHT* vol. 3, pp. 126–27.

71. *HTHT* vol. 3, p. 195.

72. Liu Shu-hsien, *Chu-tzu che-hsüeh ssu-hsiang*, ch. 10.

73. Ch'ien, *Chu-tzu hsin hsüeh-an*, vol. 1, pp. 357–65.

74. Needham, *Science and Civilisation*, vol. 2, pp. 455–505.

75. I have referred to Chan's works throughout this book.

76. Consult Chu Hsi's "Hu-tzu Chih-yen yi-yi" (Questions on the Meaning of Hu Hung's *Understanding Words*), *CTTC* 73:40b–47b; for Hu Hung's work, see *Chih-yen*.

77. *HSCC* 34:4a. See chapter 7.

Chapter 11

1. *SSCC, CYCC*, p. 1a.

2. All this has already been discussed in chapter 6.

3. *CTTC* 76:21–22b. Consult *CTYL* 93:5a–b.

4. Wing-tsit Chan, "Chu Hsi's Completion of Neo-Confucianism"; Julia Ching, "Truth and Ideology"; Charles Wing-hoi Chan, "Chu Hsi's Theory of *Tao-t'ung* and the Message of the Sage," *International Review of Chinese Religion and Philosophy* 19

(1996), 67–152; Liu Shu-hsien, "The Problem of Orthodoxy in Chu Hsi's Philosophy," in Wing-tsit Chan, *Chu Hsi and Neo-Confucianism*, pp. 437–60.

5. See Chu's preface to the commentary on the *Doctrine of the Mean*, in *SSCC* 2b.
6. *SSCC*, *CYCC*, preface, p. 3a.
7. *CTTC* 4:2a.
8. *SSCC*, *CYCC*, preface, p. 3a.
9. Here I am interpreting Chu Hsi with the help of hermeneutical ideas from Richard McKeon, David Dilworth, and Walter Watson. Consult McKeon, *Freedom and History and Other Essays*, ed. Zahava K. McKeon (University of Chicago Press, 1990), ch. 8; McKeon, "A Philosopher Meditates on Discovery," in R. M. MacIver, ed., *Moments of Personal Discovery* (New York, Institute for Religious and Social Studies, 1952), pp. 105–32; Dilworth, *Philosophy in World Perspective*; Watson, *Architectonics of Meaning*.
10. Leonard Angel, *Enlightenment East and West* (Albany, State University of New York Press, 1994), ch. 1.
11. Fung, *History*, vol. 2, p. 562, n. 1.
12. Ho, "Sung-ju te ssu-hsiang fang-fa," pp. 39–66, especially pp. 54–56.
13. *CTYL* 12:1b–2a.
14. Ho, "Sung-ju te ssu-hsiang fang-fa," pp. 65–66.
15. English translation adapted from D. C. Lau, *The Analects of Confucius* (Harmondsworth, Penguin Books, 1979), p. 18.
16. Note that in Chinese, it is only one word.
17. *Shuo-wen* 6A:11a.
18. See *ECCS*, *Ts'ui-yen*, pt. 1, p. 6a. According to Ch'eng Yi, companions in study are those who know what each is after; companions in the Way are those who know where each is going; collaborators in a common stand are those who remain steadfast partners in rightness. See also *Lun-yü chi-chu*, in *SSCC* 5:61–62.
19. *Ch'un-ch'iu fan-lu*, sec. 4, 3:4a–b.
20. Wei Cheng-t'ung, "Chu Hsi on the Standard and the Expedient," in Wing-tsit Chan, *Chu Hsi and Neo-Confucianism*, pp. 255–72.
21. *CTYL* 37:6b–7a.
22. *CTYL* 37:8a.
23. *CTYL* 37:10b.
24. *Mencius* 4A:17.
25. Ibid.
26. *CTYL* 37:10a–11a.
27. *Mencius* 4A:17.
28. Ibid. I have reversed the order of the first two sentences to give more clarity to the answer.
29. *Meng-tzu chi-chu* 4:10a, in *SSCC*.
30. Wilhelm and Baynes, *I Ching*, p. 280.
31. *CTTC* 62:28.
32. Chu Hsi, *Chin-ssu lu chi-chu* 12:2a; Wing-tsit Chan, *Reflections*, p. 272.
33. I am giving these in the order in which they are listed in the Book of Changes. See Wilhelm and Baynes, *I Ching*, p. 540.
34. *CTTC* 20:1b.
35. Wing-tsit Chan, *New Studies*, p. 541.
36. It has also been alleged that Chu ordered women in southern Fukien to bind their feet and that women of this region eventually had the smallest feet. These allegations are alluded to in local folktales, but I have not been able to substan-

tiate the claim. Consult also Howard S. Levy, *The Lotus Lovers: The Complete History of the Curious Exotic Custom of Footbinding in China* (New York, Rawls, 1966; reprint, Lower Lakes, Calif., Prometheus Books, 1992), p. 44.

37. *Fu-chien t'ung-chih* (1871) ch. 248, gives the biographies of these women.

38. *Mencius* 2B:14.

39. The idea of Confucius as "uncrowned king" is explicitly given in Wang Ch'ung's *Lun-heng*, sec. 80; 27:11a–12a.

40. See *Ch'un-ch'iu fan-lu*, sec. 23, 7:2b–8b. See also Fung, *History*, vol. 2, pp. 71–83; Tjan Tjoe Som, *Po Hu T'ung: The Comprehensive Discussions in the White Tiger Hall* (Leiden, E. J. Brill, 1949), vol. 1, 95.

41. Ch'en Liang, *Lung-ch'uan wen-chi* (*Collected Writings of Ch'en Liang*), SPPY ed., 20:6b. See Hoyt C. Tillman, *Chen Liang on Public Interest and the Law*, Monographs of the Society for Asian and Comparative Philosophy, no. 12 (Honolulu, University of Hawaii Press, 1994); Carsun Chang, *Development of Neo-Confucian Thought*, vol. 1, pp. 309–31.

42. *CTTC* 36:20b.

43. *CTTC* 36:25b.

44. *CTTC* 36:27b.

45. *CTYL* 108:2b–3a, pp. 4262–63.

46. *ECCS, Yi-ch'uan wen-chi*, 8:4b. See also Wing-tsit Chan, "Chu Hsi's Treatment of Women," in Wing-tsit Chan, *New Studies*, p. 540.

47. Chu Hsi, *Chin-ssu lu chi-chu* 6:3b.

48. *CTYL* 106:5a–b. Consult Wing-tsit Chan, "Chu Hsi's Treatment of Women," pp. 538–39.

49. *CTCS* 8:5b.

50. *ECCS, Yi-shu*, 22B:4b–5a.

51. *ECCS, Yi-shu*, 22B:3a.

52. Ibid.

53. Chu Hsi and Lü Tsu-ch'ien, *Chin-ssu lu*, ch. 6; Wing-tsit Chan, *Reflections*, p. 177.

54. *ECCS, Yi-shu*, 18:45b.

55. A Sung dynasty scholar who showed exceptional sympathy for women was the lesser known contemporary of Chu Hsi Yüan Ts'ai (fl. 1140–95), author of *Precepts for Social Life* (*Shih-fan*). Like Ssu-ma Kuang, Yüan opposes the early betrothals of boys and girls. And he makes no judgment on the remarriage of widows. Besides, commenting on women's isolation from affairs, Yüan points out how unwise husbands and sons may ruin their families behind the backs of their wives and mothers. Hence, he praises those women who are able to manage the family in place of unworthy husbands. See *Yüan-shih Shih-fan*, Supplement to the Four Libraries Rare Books (Taipei, Commercial Press reprint, 1975), 1:24a–26b. For an English translation, see Ebrey, *Family and Property in Sung China*.

56. Letter to Ch'en Shih-chung, in *CTTC* 26:26b–27a; consult Wing tsit Chan, *New Studies*, p. 540.

57. This is pointed out by Wing tsit Chan, *Reflections*, p. 177. I substituted the word "virtue" for the word he uses, "integrity."

58. *CTYL* 90:7a–8a, pp. 3701–3.

59. *CTYL* 90:6b–7a, 8b–9a, pp. 3700–3701, 3704–5.

60. Consult Julia Ching, "Neo-Confucian Utopian Theories and Political Ethics," *Monumenta Serica* 30 (1972–73), 40–41.

61. *Chung-ching*, in *Po-tzu ch'üan-shu (Complete Works of a Hundred Thinkers)* Shao-yeh shan-fang ed., 2:1a, 3:1b.
62. Alan T. Wood, *Limits to Autocracy: From Sung Neo-Confucianism to a Doctrine of Political Rights* (Honolulu, University of Hawaii Press, 1995), p. ix.
63. The ruler-subject, father-son, and husband-wife relationships were singled out by Tung Chung-shu as the "three bonds" *(san-kang)*. See *Ch'un-ch'iu fan-lu*, sec. 53.
64. *Doctrine of the Mean* 27. Legge, *Li Ki*, p. 22.
65. See *CTYL* 25:18b–19a.
66. *Analects* 14:17–18. Mencius criticized Kuan Chung not for lack of loyalty but for use of force in obtaining and maintaining hegemony over the state of Ch'i. See *Mencius* 2B:2, 6B:7.
67. *CTTC* 11:20a–b, 21a–b, 25b.
68. *CTTC* 11:18b.
69. Hu Shih, "The Natural Law in Chinese Tradition," in Edward F. Barret, ed., *University of Notre Dame Natural Law Proceedings* (University of Notre Dame Press, 1953), vol. 5, pp. 119–53.
70. Wood, *Limits to Autocracy*, ch. 6.
71. David A. Dilworth, "'Jitsugaku' as an Ontological Conception: Continuities and Discontinuities in Early and Mid-Tokugawa Thought," in de Bary, *Principle and Practicality*, pp. 481–83.
72. Hung Ying-ming [Hong Yingming], *Tsai-keng t'an (Speaking of the Plant Roots)*, in Imai Usaburō, trans., *Saikontan* (Tokyo, Iwanami, 1983), p. 135. The text is popular in Japan. The poem is given in Imai's book in both Chinese and Japanese translation.

Appendix B

1. See *HSCC* 2:6b.
2. See *CTTC* 36:7a–10b; *CTYL* 75:15–18.
3. See figure 5 for the *Wu-chi t'u*.
4. See Huang Tsung-yen (1616–86), *T'u-hsüeh pien-huo (Clarifications regarding the "Diagram of the Great Ultimate")*, Four Libraries Rare Books Collection 6, vol. 12, pp. 31a–51b; Chu Yi-tsun (1629–1709), *T'ai chi-t'u shou-shou k'ao (Examination of the Transmission of the "Diagram of the Great Ultimate")*, in his *P'u-shu t'ing-chi (Collected Writings)*, Ssu-k'u ts'ung-k'an, 1st ser., ch. 58, pp. 447–48. See also Fung, *History*, vol. 2, pp. 440–42.
5. *Chou Lien-hsi chi*, ch. 9, p. 160; see also Fung, *History*, vol. 2, pp. 440–42.
6. Mao Ch'i-ling, *T'ai-chi t'u-shuo yi-yi (Supplementary Discussions on the "Diagram of the Great Ultimate")*, in *Hsi-ho ho-chi (Collected Writings of Mao Ch'i-ling)*, preface 1685; see Fung, *History*, vol. 2, pp. 440–41.
7. See also Azuma, "Taikyokuzu no keisei," p. 74. For Shao's diagram, see figure 5.
8. Ibid., p. 75. Consult the *Shang-fang ta-tung chen-yüan miao-ching t'u (Diagrams of the Truly First and Mysterious Classic of th e Transcendent Great Cave)*, *TT*, vol. 196, p. 439. This is cited in Fung, *History*, vol. 2, pp. 438–42.
9. See Azuma, "Taikyokuzu no keisei," pp. 81–83; Imai, *Sōdai no ekiyaku*, pp. 242–95.
10. See Lu Kuang-jyu, *Taoist Yoga: Alchemy and Immortality* (London, Rider, 1970), pp. 4–5, 16–19, 74–79.
11. Henri Maspéro, *Taoism and Chinese Religion*, trans. Frank A. Kerman, Jr. (Amherst, University of Massachusetts Press, 1981), pp. 282, 346–51.

12. Tsung-mi, *Ch'an-yüan*, p. 410b.
13. Ibid., pp. 410–11. Consult Jeffrey L. Broughton, "Kuei-feng Tsung-mi: The Convergence of Ch'an and the Teachings" (Ph.D. diss., Columbia University, 1975), pp. 289–90.
14. Tsung-mi, *Ch'an-yüan*, p. 413b–c. Consult Imai, *Sōdai no ekigaku*, pp. 282–83.
15. Wilhelm and Baynes, *I Ching*, pp. 114–21, 530–39; Lai, "Sinitic Mandalas," op. cit., 234–37; see chapters 1–3.
16. Consult *Sung-shih*, ch. 373.
17. *CTTC* 71:4a. I cannot find any historical confirmation of the Su Sung episode. Consult his biography in *Sung-Shih*, ch. 340. See also Imai, *Sōdai no ekigaku*, ch. 5.
18. *CTTC* 80:12a. Understandably, official histories were seldom changed.
19. *CTTC* 36:16b.
20. I find disquieting the disappearance, after Chu Hsi, of certain diagrams included in the earlier versions of *Ts'an-t'ung-ch'i*. Did Chu himself, through his commentary on that work, or his disciples or their followers have anything to do with this loss?
21. Consult Imai, *Sōdai no ekigaku*, pp. 282–84, 463–80.
22. "T'i *T'ai-chi/Hsi-ming chieh*-hou" in *CTTC* 82:14a.
23. *Sung-shih* 427:5579a.

Appendix C

1. This chapter is a revised version of my article "God and the World: Chu Hsi and Whitehead," *Journal of Chinese Philosophy* 6 (1979), 275–95.
2. Consult Réal Roy, "Etres et êtres chez deux philosophes chinois du XIIe–XIIIe siècles: Zhu Xi et Thomas d'Aquin," *Laval théologique et philosophique* 44 (February 1988), 103–15.
3. See Carsun Chang, *Development of Neo-Confucian Thought*, vol. 1, p. 282; Needham, *Science and Civilisation*, vol. 2, p. 475.
4. *PR*, pt. 1.
5. See Bernard M. Loomer, "Whitehead's Method of Empirical Analysis," in Ewert H. Cousins, ed., *Process Theology: Basic Writings by the Key Thinkers of a Major Modern Movement* (New York, Newman Press, 1971), pp. 69–81.
6. *PR*, p. 7.
7. This is quoted in F. S. C. Northrop, *The Meeting of East and West* (New York: Macmillan, 1946), p. 318.
8. See Wilhelm and Baynes, *I Ching*, pp. 287, 298.
9. William A. Christian, *An Interpretation of Whitehead's Metaphysics* (New Haven, Yale University Press, 1959), pp. 142, 284.
10. *PR*, p. 7.
11. *PR*, pp. 362–63.
12. Needham, *Science and Civilisation*, vol. 2, p. 467.
13. *PR*, p. vii.
14. See Charles Hartshorne, "The Development of Process Philosophy," in Cousins, *Process Theology*, p. 61.
15. Christian, *Whitehead's Metaphysics*, pp. 175–93.
16. See Tong Lik-kuen, "The Concept of Time in Whitehead and the I-ching," *Journal of Chinese Philosophy* 1 (1974), 373–93. This has also been brought out in Chang Chung-yüan's article "Creativity as Process in Taoism," where the writer

singles out for discussion the idea of process found in neo-Confucian philosophy, especially in the *Diagram of the Great Ultimate*.

17. Tong, "Concept of Time," p. 379.
18. *PR*, p. 268; Christian, *Whitehead's Metaphysics*, pp. 9–20.
19. See Julia Ching, *To Acquire Wisdom*, ch. 3.
20. *PR*, pp. 403–4.
21. A. N. Whitehead, *Religion in the Making* (New York, Macmillan, 1926), pp. 68–69.
22. Northrop, *East and West*, ch. 9 and p. 401.
23. Needham, *Science and Civilisation*, vol. 2, secs. 16 and 18.
24. Hu Shih, "Religion and Philosophy in Chinese History," in Sophia H. Chen Zen, ed., *Symposium on Chinese Culture* (Shanghai, China Institute of Pacific Relations, 1931), pp. 31–58.
25. Ku Chieh-kang, "San-huang kao" (On the Three Emperors), in *Ku-shih pien*, vol. 7, pp. 83–102.
26. Joseph Shih, "Notions," pp. 131–37.
27. *Analects* 2:1.
28. Ku Chieh-kang, "San-huang kao"; Joseph Shih, "Notions"; see also Needham, *Science and Civilisation*, vol. 3, pp. 229–33.
29. See *CTYL* 1:4a–b. In *Chu Hsi and His Masters* (London: Probsthain, 1923), Joseph P. Bruce argues for the theistic import of Chu's philosophy, pointing out his acknowledgment of a "ruler" on high. But he tends to see more resemblance between Chu Hsi and a classical type of Western theism.
30. *CTYL* 68:2a. Consult chapter 3 of this book.
31. *CTYL* 1:3b.
32. *CTYL* 1:3b.
33. See Ogden's essay, "The Reality of God," in Cousins, *Process Theology*, p. 123.
34. See especially *Huai-nan-tzu*, chs. 2, 7, 14; see also Fung, *History*, vol. 1, pp. 395–99.
35. See introduction.
36. *CTYL* 94:2b.
37. *CTYL* 94.
38. *PR*, p. 407.
39. *CTYL* 94:4b, 6b.
40. *PR*, p. 410.
41. *PR*, p. 529.
42. Feng Yu-lan, *Hsin-li-hsüeh* (*A New Philosophy of Principle*) (Shanghai: Commercial Press, 1936), pp. 70–72.
43. *PR*, p. 404; Whitehead, *Religion in the Making*, p. 75. See Charles Hartshorne, *A Natural Theology for Our Time* (LaSalle, Ill., Open Court, 1967), ch. 1; Charles Hartshorne and William L. Reese, eds., *Philosophers Speak of God* (University of Chicago Press, 1953), introduction.
44. For Ch'eng Hao's philosophy, see Wing-tsit Chan, *Source Book*, ch. 31.
45. See Hartshorne, *Natural Theology*, ch. 1; Hartshorne and Reese, *Philosophers Speak of God*, introduction.
46. Christian, *Whitehead's Metaphysics*, pp. 405–7.

Glossary

ai 愛

Bendō 辨道

Ch'an/Chan 禪
ch'an-chiao yi-chih/chanjiao yizhi
　禪教一致
Chang/Zhang 張
ch'ang/chang 常
ch'ang hsing-hsing/chang xingxing
　常惺惺
Chang Hsüeh-ch'eng/Zhang
　Xuecheng 章學誠
Chang Li-wen/Zhang Liwen 張立文
Chang Shih/Zhang Shi 張栻
Chang Tsai/Zhang Zai 張載
Chao Chi-pin/Zhao Jibin 趙紀彬
Chao Ching-ming/Zhao Jingming
　趙景明
Chao Ju-yü/Zhao Ruyu 趙汝愚
chao-yin/zhaoyin 招隱
chen-ju/zhenru 眞如
Chen-kao/Zhengao 眞誥
Ch'en Lai/Chen Lai 陳來
Ch'en Liang/Chen Liang 陳亮
Ch'en T'uan/Chen Tuan 陳摶
chen-yi ling-hsin/zhenyi lingxin
　眞一靈心
ch'eng/cheng 誠
Ch'eng-Chu/Cheng-Zhu 程朱
Ch'eng Hao/Cheng Hao 程顥
Cheng-ho wu-li hsin-yi/Zhenghe wuli
　xinyi 政和五禮新義
Cheng Hsüan/Zheng Xuan 鄭玄
Ch'eng-shih yi-shu/Chengshi yishu
　程氏遺書

Cheng-tao ko/Zhengdao ge 証道歌
Ch'eng Yi/Cheng Yi 程頤
Ch'i/Qi 齊
ch'i^a/qi^a (Jap. ki) 氣
ch'i^b/qi^b 器
chi^a/ji^a 極
chi^b/ji^b 幾
ch'i-kung/qigong 氣功
Chia-fan/Jiafan 家範
Chia-li/Jiali 家禮
Chiang Kai-shek 蔣介石
Chiang Yung/Jiang Yong 江永
chiao/jiao 教
chiao-wai/jiaowai 教外
Chien/jian 簡
Ch'ien^a/Qian^a 乾
Ch'ien^b/Qian^b 謙
chien-chieh/jianjie 劍解
Ch'ien Mu/Qian Mu 錢穆
chih^a/zhi^a 質
chih^b/zhi^b 之
chih^c/zhi^c 知
chih^d/zhi^d 志
chih-chih/zhizhi 致知
chih-chüeh/zhijue 知覺
ch'ih-tzu/chizi 赤子
Chih-yen/Zhiyan 知言
Ch'in/Qin 秦
ch'in^a/qin^a 親
ch'in^b/qin^b 琴
ch'in-ch'ieh/qinqie 居敬
Chin-hsi/Jinxi 近溪
ch'in-min/qinmin 親民
chin-shih/jinshi 進士
Chin-ssu lu/Jinsi lu 近思錄
ching^a/jing^a 靜

309

ching^b/jing^b 經
ching^c/jing^c 精
ching^d/jing^d 敬
Ching^e/Jing^e 井
ch'ing/qing 情
ching-hsing/jingxing 景星
ching-she/jingshe 精社
ching-shen/jingshen 精神
ching-tso/jingzuo 靜坐
Ch'iu Chün/Qiu Jun 邱濬
chiu-kua/jiugua 九卦
ch'iung-li/qiongli 窮理
Chou-kuan hsin-yi/Zhouguan xinyi
　周官新義
Chou-li/Zhouli 周禮
Chou Tun-yi/Zhou Dunyi 周敦頤
Chou-yi pen-yi/Zhouyi benyi 周易本義
Chou-yi Ts'an-t'ung-ch'i/Zhouyi
　Cantongqi 周易參同契
Chou-yi Ts'an-t'ung-ch'i k'ao-yi/Zhouyi
　Cantongqi kaoyi 周易參同契考異
Chu Chen/Zhu Zhen 朱震
chü-ching/jujing 居敬
Chu Hsi/Zhu Xi 朱熹
ch'ü/qu 去
Ch'ü-li/Quli 曲禮
Chu-Lu/Zhu-Lu 朱陸
Chu Sung/Zhu Song 朱松
chu-tsai/zhuzai 主宰
Ch'u-tz'u/Chuci 楚辭
Ch'u-tz'u chi-chu/Chuci jizhu 楚辭集注
Chu-tzu chia-li/Zhuzi jiali 朱子家禮
chu-yi wu-shih/zhuyi wushi 主一無適
Chu-tzu hsin hsüeh-an/Zhuzi xin xuean
　朱子新學案
Chu-tzu men-jen/Zhuzi menren
　朱子門人
Ch'ü Yüan/Qu Yuan 屈原
chüan/juan 卷
ch'üan/quan 權
Ch'uan-teng lu/Chuandeng lu 傳燈錄
ch'üan-t'i/quanti 全體
Chuang-tzu/Zhuangzi 莊子
chüeh/jue 覺
chung^a/zhong^a 中
chung^b/zhong^b 忠
Chung-ching/Zhongjing 忠經
chung-ho/zhonghe 中和
chung-ho shuo/zhonghe shuo 中和說
chung-wang/zhongwang 中王

Ch'ung-yu/Chongyou 沖祐
Chung-yung/Zhongyong 中庸
Chung-yung chang-chü/Zhongyong
　zhangju 中庸章句

Erh-ya/Erya 爾雅

fa 法
fa-ming pen-hsin/faming benxin
　發明本心
fan chao-yin/fan zhaoyin 反招隱
fen-shu/fenshu 焚書
feng-shui /fengshui 風水
Fo 佛
Fo-kuo Yüan-wu/Foguo Yuanwu
　佛果圓悟
Fu-t'u/Futu 浮圖
Fu 復
Fu Hsi/Fu Xi 伏羲
Fujiwara Seika 藤原惺窩
Fung Yu-lan/Feng Youlan 馮友蘭

Han 漢
Han Fei-tzu/Han Feizi 韓非子
Han T'o-chou/Han Tozhou 韓侂冑
Han Yü/Han Yu 韓愈
Han-wen k'ao-yi/Hanwen kaoyi
　韓文考異
han-yang/hanyang 涵養
Hayashi Razan 林羅山
heng 恒
ho/he 和
Ho Lin/He Lin 賀麟
Ho-t'u/Hetu 河圖
Ho-nan Ch'eng-shih yi-shu/Henan
　Chengshi yishu 河南程氏遺書
Hou Wailu 侯外廬
hou-yŭ pien-cheng/houyu bianzheng
　後語辨證
Hsi K'ang/Xi Kang 嵇康
Hsi-ming/Ximing 西銘
Hsi-ming chieh-yi/Ximing jieyi
　西銘解義
hsiang/xiang 象
Hsiao-ching k'an-wu/Xiaojing kanwu
　孝經刊誤
Hsiao-hsüeh/Xiaoxue 小學
Hsiao-kuo/Xiaoguo 小過
Hsiao-tsung/Xiaozong 孝宗
Hsiao Tzu-liang/Xiao Ziliang 蕭子良
Hsieh Liang-tso/Xie Liangzuo 謝良佐

hsien/xian 顯
Hsien-t'ien t'u/Xiantian tu 先天圖
hsin[a]/xin[a] 心
hsin[b]/xin[b] 信
hsin[c]/xin[c] 新
Hsin Ch'i-chi/Xin Qiji 辛棄疾
hsin-min/xinmin 新民
hsing/xing 性
hsing-erh-hsia/xingerxia 形而下
hsing-erh-shang/xingershang 形而上
hsiu/xiu 宿
hsiu-shen/xiushen 修身
Hsü Fu-kuan/Xu Fuguan 徐復觀
hsü-ling pu-mei/xuling bumei 虛靈不昧
hsüeh/xue 學
Hsün-tzu/Xunzi 荀子
Hu An-kuo/Hu Anguo 胡安國
Hu Hsien/Hu Xian 胡憲
Hu Hung/Hu Hong 胡宏
Hu Shih/Hu Shi 胡適
Hu-tzu chih-yen yi-yi/Huzi zhiyan yiyi
   胡子知言異義
Hu Wu-feng/Hu Wufeng 胡五峰
hua-kung/huagong 化功
Hua-yen/Huayan 華嚴
Hua-yen ching ho-lun/Huayanjing helun
   華嚴經合論
Huai-nan-tzu/Huainanzi 淮南子
Huan 桓
huang-chi/huangji 皇極
Huang Kan/Huang Gan 黃幹
Hui-an/Huian 晦庵
Hui-chao/Huizhao 慧照
Hui-neng/Huineng 惠能
Hui-tsung/Huizong 徽宗
hun 魂
hun-jan chih-t'i/hunran zhiti 渾然之體
hun-p'o/hunpo 魂魄
Hung-chih Cheng-chüeh/Hongzhi
   Zhengjue 宏智正覺
Hung-fan/Hongfan 洪範
Hung Mai/Hong Mai 洪邁
huo-wen/huowen 或問

I Ching/Yijing 易經
Itō Jinsai 伊藤仁齋

jen[a]/ren[a] 仁
jen[b]/ren[b] 人
jen-hsin/renxin 人心

jen-tao/rendao 人道
jen-yü/renyu 人欲
ju/ru 儒
ju-hsüeh/ruxue 儒學
ju-men/rumen 入門

K'ai-pao t'ung-li/Kaibao tongli
   開寶通禮
K'ai-shan Tao-ch'ien/Kaishan
   Daoqian 開山道謙
K'ai-yüan li/Kaiyuan li 開元禮
kan/gan 干
K'an/Kan 坎
k'an-hua-t'ou/kanhuatou 看話頭
k'ao-chü/kaoju 考據
Kao Yu/Kao You 高誘
Kao-tsu/Kaozu 高祖
Kao-tzu/Kaozi 告子
k'ao-yi/kaoyi 考異
k'o-chi/keji 克己
k'o-chi fu-li/keji fuli 克己復禮
ko-wu/gewu 格物
Kogaku 古學
Kokugaku 國學
K'ou Ch'ien-chih/Kou Qianzhi 寇謙之
Ku-chin chia-chi li/gujin jiaji li
   古今家祭禮
Ku-ming/Guming 顧命
K'u-ya man-lu/Kuya manlu 枯崖漫錄
Ku Yen-wu/Gu Yanwu 顧炎武
kua/gua 卦
Kuan Chung/Kuan Zhong 管仲
Kuan-tzu/Kuanzi 管子
Kuang-tsung/Guangzong 光宗
kuei/gui 鬼
kuei-shen/guishen 鬼神
K'un[a]/Kun[a] 坤
K'un[b]/Kun[b] 困
K'un-lun/Kunlun 崑崙
k'ung/kong 空
kung-an/gongan (Jap. koan) 公案
kung-fu/gongfu 功夫
K'ung-t'ung tao-shih/Kongtong
   daoshi 空同道士
Kung-yang/Gongyang 公羊

Lao-Chuang/Lao-Zhuang 老莊
Lao Ssu-kuang/Lao Siguang 勞思光
Lao-tzu/Laozi 老子
lei-shen/leishen 雷神
li[a] 理

Li[b] 离
li[c] 禮
li[d] 里
Li-chi/Liji 禮記
li-chiao/lijiao 禮教
Li Chih/Li Zhi 李贄
Li Ch'üan/Li Quan 李筌
Li Hsin-ch'uan/Li Xinchuan 李心傳
li-hsing/lixing 力行
Li Kung/Li Gong 李塨
Li-sao/Lisao 離騷
Li T'ung/Li Tong 李侗
Li Zehou 李澤厚
liang-chih/liangzhi 良知
Lieh-tzu/Liezi 列子
Lin-chi/Linji 臨濟
Lin Ling-su/Lin Lingsu 林靈素
ling 靈
ling-ch'u/lingchu 靈處
ling-chüeh/lingjue 靈覺
ling-tzu/lingzi 靈子
Liu Hsin/Liu Xin 劉歆
Liu Mien-chih/Liu Mianzhi 劉勉之
Liu Pao-nan/Liu Baonan 劉寶楠
Liu Shih-p'ei/Liu Shipei 劉師培
Liu Shu-hsien/Liu Shuxian 劉述先
Liu-tien/Liudian 六典
Liu Tzu-hui/Liu Zihui 劉子翬
Liu Tzu-yü/Liu Ziyu 劉子羽
Lo Ts'ung-yen/Lo Congyan 羅從彥
Lo-shu/Loshu 洛書
Lü 履
Lu Chiu-ling/Lu Jiuling 陸九齡
Lu Chiu-shao/Lu Jiushao 陸九紹
Lu Chiu-yüan/Lu Jiuyuan 陸九淵
Lu Hsün/Lu Xun 魯迅
Lü-lü hsin-shu/Lü-lü xinshu 律呂新書
Lü-shih ch'un-ch'iu/Lüshi chunqiu
  呂氏春秋
Lü Tsu-ch'ien/Lü Zuqian 呂祖謙
Lu-Wang 陸王
Lu Yu/Lu You 陸游
lun-hui/lunhui 輪迴
Lun-Meng chi-chu/Lun Meng jizhu
  論孟集註
Lun-Meng yao-yi/Lun Meng yaoyi
  論孟要義
Lung-hu shang-ching/Longhu shangjing
  龍虎上經

Mao Tse-tung/Mao Zedong 毛澤東
Meng-tzu yao-lüeh/Mengzi yaolue
  孟子要略
miao-li/miaoli 妙理
min-chi/minji 民極
Ming 明
Ming[a] 命
ming[b] 明
ming[c] 名
ming-li/mingli 命理
ming-ming te/mingming de 明明德
mo 魔
mo-chao/mozhao (Jap. *mokusho*) 默照
Mo Ti/Mo Di 墨翟
Mo-tzu/Mozi 墨子
mou/mu 畝
Mou Tsung-san/Mou Zongsan 牟宗三
Mu Hsiu/Mu Xiu 穆修

na-chia/najia 納甲
Ning-tsung/Ningzong 甯宗

Ogyū Sorai 荻徂萊
O-hu/Ehu 鵝湖
Ōmitōfō 阿彌陀佛
Ou-yang Hsiu/Ouyang Xiu 歐陽修

Pa-ch'ao ming-ch'en yen-hsing-lu/
  Bachao mingchen yanxing lu
  八朝明臣言行錄
pen/ben 本
pen-t'i/benti 本體
P'eng Hsiao/Peng Xiao 彭曉
Pi-yen lu/Biyan lu 碧巖錄
piao-te/biaode 表德
pien/bian 變
p'o/po 魄
po-ai/boai 博愛

Ren Jiyu 任繼愈

Seng Chao/Seng Zhao 僧肇
Shang 商
Shang-ti/Shangdi 上帝
Shang-ts'ai yü-lu/Shangcai yulu
  上蔡語錄
Shao Yung/Shao Yong 邵雍
She-shih/Shishi 釋氏
shen[a] 神
shen[b] 伸
Shen Chi-tsu/Shen Jizu 沈繼祖

Shen-hsiu/Shenxiu 神秀
shen-hua chih tzu-jan/shenhua zhi ziran
神化之自然
shen-ming/shenming 神明
Shen Pu-hai/Shen Buhai 申不害
shen-tu/shendu 慎獨
sheng-sheng pu-yi chih-chi/shengsheng
buyi zhiji 生生不已之機
shih[a]/*shi*[a] 實
shih[b]/*shi*[b] 尸
shih[c]/*shi*[c] 事
Shih chi-ch'uan/Shi jichuan 詩集傳
shou-lien/shoulian 收斂
Shou-ya/Shouya 壽崖
shu 數
Shun 舜
Shuo-wen/Shuowen 說文
Shushigaku 朱子學
Ssu-ma Kuang/Sima Guang 司馬光
Ssu-shu chi-chu/Sishu jizhu 四書集註
su-wang/suwang 素王
Sun[a] 損
Sun[b] 巽
Sung/Song 宋
Sung Yü/Song Yu 宋玉

Ta-sheng ch'i-hsin-lun/Dasheng qixin lun
大乘起信論
Ta-hsüeh/Daxue 大學
Ta-hsüeh chang-chü/Daxue zhangju
大學章句
Ta-hui Tsung-kao/Dahui Zonggao
大慧宗杲
Ta-hui yü-lu/Tahui yulu 大慧語錄
ta-t'ung/datong 大同
ta-yung/dayong 大用
Tai/Dai 戴
T'ai/Tai 泰
Tai Chen/Dai Zhen 戴震
T'ai-chi/Taiji 太極
T'ai-chi pen-yü wu-chi yeh/Taiji benyu
wuji ye 太極本於無極也
T'ai-chi-t'u/Taijitu 太極圖
T'ai-chi-t'u shuo/Taijitu shuo 太極圖說
T'ai-chi-t'u shuo chieh/Taijitu shuojie
太極圖說解
T'ai-ho/Taihe 太和
t'ai-hsi/taixi 胎息
T'ai-hsü/Taixu 太虛

T'ai-hsüeh/Taixue 太學
T'ai-p'ing/Taiping 太平
T'ai-shang kan-ying p'ien/Taishang
ganying pian 太上感應篇
T'ai-shang Lao-chün/Taishang Laojun
太上老君
T'ai-shang T'ien-chün/Taishang
Tianjun 太上天君
T'ai-tsung/Taizong 太宗
T'ai-wei hsien-chün kung-kuo ko/Taiwei
xianjun gongguo ge 太微仙君功過格
T'ai-yi[a]/*Taiyi*[a] 太易
T'ai-yi[b]/*Taiyi*[b] 太一
T'an-chou/Tanzhou 潭州
T'an-kung/Tangong 檀弓
tang/dang 當
T'ang/Tang 湯
T'ang Chün-i/Tang Junyi 唐君毅
Tao/Dao 道
tao/dao 盜
tao-chi/daoji 盜幾
Tao-chia/Daojia 道家
Tao-chiao/Daojiao 道教
Tao-ch'ien/Daoqian 道謙
tao-hsin/daoxin 道心
Tao-hsüeh/Daoxue 道學
tao-li/daoli 道理
tao-t'i/daoti 道體
tao-t'ung/daotong 道統
tao-wen-hsüeh/daowenxue 道問學
tao-ying/daoying 導引
Tao-yüan/Daoyuan 道元
te/de 德
ti/di 帝
t'i/ti 體
T'iao-hsi chen/Tiaoxi zhen 調息箴
T'ien/Tian 天
t'ien-chi/tianji 天機
T'ien-chu shih-yi/Tianzhu shiyi
天主實義
T'ien-hsin/Tianxin 天心
T'ien-li/Tianli 天理
T'ien-t'ai/Tiantai 天臺
T'ien-tao/Tiandao 天道
T'ien-t'i/Tianti 天體
t'ien-ti chih hsin/tiandi zhi xin
天地之心
ts'ai/cai 才
tsai/zai 在

Ts'ai Yüan-ting/Cai Yuanding 蔡元定

Ts'an-t'ung-ch'i/Cantongqi 參同契

Ts'an-t'ung-ch'i k'ao-yi/Cantongqi kaoyi
  參同契考異

Ts'ang-shu/Zangshu 藏書

Ts'ao Chien/Cao Jian 曹建

Ts'ao-tung/Caodong 曹洞

Tseng Kung/Zeng Gong 曾鞏

Tseng Kuo-fan/Zeng Guofan 曾國藩

Tso/Zuo 左

tso-ch'an/zuochan (Jap. zazen) 坐禪

ts'un-hsin/cunxin 存心

ts'un-hsin yang-hsing/cunxin yangxing
  存心養性

tsun-te-hsing/zundexing 尊德性

Tsou Yi/Zou Yi 鄒沂

Tsung-mi/Zongmi 宗密

Tu Kuo-hsiang/Du Guoxiang 杜國祥

tu-shu/dushu 讀書

Tu Yu/Du You 杜佑

Tu Yü/Du Yu 杜預

Tun/Dun 遁

Tung Chung-shu/Dong Zhongshu
  董仲舒

T'ung-shu/Tongshu 通書

T'ung-shu chieh/Tongshu jie 通書解

Tun-weng/Dunweng 遁翁

Tzu-ch'an/Zichan 子產

Tzu-chih t'ung-chien kang-mu/
  Zizhitongjian gangmu 資治通鑑綱目

Tzu-ssu/Zisi 子思

Tzu Wu-chi erh-wei T'ai-chi/Ziwuji erwei
  taiji 自無極而爲太極

Tzu-yu/Ziyou 子游

Uno Seiichi 宇野精一

wan-wu/wanwu 萬物

Wang An-shih/Wang Anshi 王安石

Wang Ch'ung/Wang Chong 王充

Wang Fu 汪紱

Wang Fu-chih/Wang Fuzhi 王夫之

Wang Mang 王莽

Wang Mao-hung/Wang Maohong
  王懋竑

Wang Pi/Wang Bi 王弼

Wang Yang-ming/Wang Yangming
  王陽明

wei 微

wei-chi/weiji 爲己

wei-chi chih hsüeh/weiji zhixue
  爲己之學

wei-fa/weifa 未發

wei-hsüeh/weixue 爲學

Wei Po-yang/Wei Boyang 魏伯陽

Wen 文

wu^a 無

wu^b 五

wu^c (Jap. satori) 悟

wu^d 物

wu^e 巫

Wu 武

Wu-chi/Wuji 無極

Wu-chi erh t'ai-chi/Wuji er taiji
  無極而太極

Wu-chi t'u/Wujitu 無極圖

wu-chu/wuzhu 巫祝

wu-chu chih shih/wuzhu zhishi 巫祝之事

Wu-hsing/Wuxing 五行

wu-li/wuli 物理

wu-te/wude 五德

Wu-yi ching-she/Wuyi jingshe
  武夷精舍

Yamazaki Ansai 山崎闇齋

yang-ch'i/yangqi 陽氣

Yang Chien/Yang Jian 楊簡

Yang Chu/Yang Zhu 楊朱

Yang Fu 楊復

Yang Rongguo 楊榮國

Yang Shih/Yang Shi 楊時

Yang Yi 楊億

Yao 堯

yen/yan 言

Yen Hui/Yan Hui 顏回

Yen Jo-chü/Yan Roju 閻若璩

Yen Yüan/Yan Yuan 顏元

Yi^a 易

Yi^b 益

yi 義

Yi-ching/Yijing 易經

yi-fa/yifa 已發

Yi-hsin san-mei/Yixin sanmei 一心三昧

Yi-hsüeh ch'i-meng/Yixue qimeng
  易學啓蒙

Yi-hsüeh pen-yi/Yixue benyi 易學本義

Yi-li/yili 儀禮

Yi-li ching-ch'uan/Yili jingchuan
  儀禮經傳

Yi-li ching-ch'uan t'ung-chieh/Yili
  jingchuan tongjie 儀禮經傳通解

Yi-lo yüan-yüan lu/Yilo yuanyuan lu
伊洛淵源錄
Yi-yin/Yiyin 伊尹
yin-ch'i/yinqi 陰氣
Yin-fu ching/Yinfujing 陰符經
Yin-fu ching k'ao-yi/Yinfujing kaoyi
陰符經考異
ying-wu so-chu erh sheng ch'i-hsin/
yingwu suozhu er sheng qixin
應無所住而生其心
yin-yang/yinyang 陰陽
Yü/Yu 禹
yü^a/yu^a 於
yü^b/yu^b 欲
yu/you 有
Yü Ying-shih/Yu Yingshi 余英時
Yüan/Yuan 元

yüan-ch'i/yuanqi 元氣
Yüan-chüeh/Yuanjue 圓覺
Yüan-chüeh ching/Yuanjuejing 圓覺經
Yüan-shih T'ien-tsun/Yuanshi
Tianzun 元始天尊
Yüan Shu-chen/Yuan Shuzhen
袁淑眞
Yüan-wu K'o-ch'in/Yuanwu Keqin
圓悟克勤
Yüan-wu K'en-an/Yuanwu Ken'an
圓悟肯菴
Yüan-yu/Yuanyou 遠遊
Yüeh-lu/Yuelu 嶽麓
Yün-t'ai/Yuntai 雲臺
yung/yong 用
Yung-chia/Yongjia 永嘉

Selected Bibliography

Primary Sources

Chang Po-tuan 張伯端. *Wu-chen p'ien* 悟眞篇. *TT*, vol. 4.

Chang Shih 張栻. *Nan-hsüan hsien-sheng wen-chi* 南軒先生文集. Sung Dynasty ed. Taipei, National Palace Museum reprint, 1981.

Chang Tsai 張載. *Chang-tzu ch'üan-shu* 張子全書. *SPPY* ed.

———. *Cheng-meng* 正蒙. *SPPY* ed.

Ch'en Chien 陳建. *Hsüeh-pu t'ung-pien* 學蔀通辨. in Chang Po-hsing 張伯行, comp., *Cheng-yi t'ang ch'üan-shu*. Shanghai, Commercial Press, 1936.

Ch'en Hung-mou 陳弘謀, ed. *Wu-chung yi-kuei* 五種遺規. *SPPY* ed.

Ch'en Liang 陳亮. *Lung-ch'uan wen-chi* 龍川文集. *SPPY* ed.

Cheng-chou Lin-chi Hui-chao Ch'an-shih yü-lu 鄭州臨濟慧照禪師語錄. *T* 47, no. 1985.

Ch'eng Hao 程顥 and Ch'eng Yi 程頤. *Erh-Ch'eng Ch'üan-shu* 二程全書. *SPPY* ed. Incorporating *Yi-shu* 遺書, *Wai-shu* 外書, *Ts'ui-yen* 粹言, *Ming-tao wen-chi* 明道文集, and *Yi ch'uan wen-chi* 伊川文集.

Chin-kang pan-je po-lo-mi ching 金剛般若波羅密經. *T* 8, no. 235. English translation in F. Max Müller. trans., *The Vagrakkhedika, or Diamond-Cutter*. In *Buddhist Mahayana Texts*. Sacred Books of the East, vol. 49, ed by F. Max Müller. London, Oxford University Press, 1894.

Ching-chüeh 淨覺. *Leng-chia shih-tzu chi* 楞伽師資記. *T* 85, no. 2837.

Ching-men City Museum, ed. *Kuo-tien Ch'u-mu chu-Chien* 郭店楚墓竹簡. Peking, Wenwu, 1998.

Ching-te ch'uan-teng lu 景德傳燈錄. *T* 51, no. 2076.

Chou-Chang ch'üan-shu 周張全書. In Okada Takehiko 岡田武彥 ed., *Chin-shih Han-chi ts'ung-k'an* 近世漢籍叢刊. Taipei, Chung-wen, 1972.

Chou-li Cheng-chu 周禮鄭注. *SPPY* ed.

Chou Lien-hsi chi 周濂溪集. In Chang Po-hsing, comp., *Cheng-yi-t'ang ch'üan-shu*. Shanghai, Commercial Press reprint, 1936.

Chou Tun-yi 周敦頤. *Chou-tzu ch'üan-shu* 周子全書. In *Chou Chang ch'üan-shu* 周張全書, in Okada Takehiko, ed., *Chin-shih Han-chi ts'ung-k'an*. Taipei, Chung-wen, 1972.

Chou-tzu T'ung-shu 周子通書. *SPPY* ed.

Chou-yi Cheng-chu 周易鄭注. *SPPY* ed.

Chou-yi cheng-yi 周易正義. *SPPY* ed.

Chou-yi pen-yi k'ao yü ch'i-ta 周易本義考與其他. Changsha, Commercial Press, 1937.

Chou-yi Wang-Han chu 周易王韓注. *SPPY* ed.

Chu Hsi 朱熹. "Chou-tzu 'T'ai-chi T'ung-shu' hou-hsü" 周子太極通書後序. In *CTTC* 75:18a–19b.

———. *Chou-yi pen-yi* 周易本義. Four Libraries ed., 6th Collection, no. 001.

———. *Chou-yi Ts'an-t'ung-ch'i k'ao-yi* 周易參同契考異. In *Chu-tzu yi-shu* 朱子遺書, Pao-kao-t'ang ed. vol. 12. Taipei Yi-wen, reprint, Yi-wen, 1969.

———. *Chu-tzu ta-ch'üan* 朱子大全. *SPPY* ed.

———. "Chu-tzu ta'i-chi-t'u shuo-chieh" 朱子太極圖說解. In *Chou Lien-hsi chi*, ch.1, pp. 28–29. In Chang Po-hsing, comp., *Cheng-yi-t'ang ch'uan-su*. Shanghai, Commercial Press reprint, 1936.

———. *Chu-tzu yü-lei* 朱子語類. Ed. Li Ching-te 黎靖德 1473. Taipei, Cheng-chung reprint, 1973.

———. *Ch'u-tz'u chi-chu* 楚辭集注. *T'ing-yü-chai* ed. [1900].

———. *Chung-yung chang-chü* 中庸章句. In *SSCC*.

———. "Hu-tzu *Chih-yen* yi-yi" 胡子知言異議. In *CTTC* 73:40b–47b.

———. "Kuan-hsin shuo" 觀心說. In *CTTC* 67:20a.

———. *Lun-yü chi-chu* 論語集注. In *SSCC*. *SPPY* ed.

———. *Meng-tzu chi-chu* 孟子集注. In *SSCC*. *SPPY* ed.

———. "Ming-tao *lun-hsing* shuo" 明道論性說. In *CTTC* 67:16b–18a.

———. *Ssu-shu chi-chu* 四書集注. *SPPY* ed.

———. *Ta-hsüeh chang-chü* 大學章句. In *SSCC*, *SPPY* ed.

———. "T'ai-chi shuo" 太極說. In *CTTC* 67:16a–b.

———. "T'i *T'ai-chi Hsi-ming chieh* hou" 題太極西銘解後. In *CTTC* 82:14a.

———. "T'iao-hsi chen" 調息箴. In *CTTC* 85:6a.

———. "Tsai-ting T'ai-chi T'ung-shu hou-hsü" 再訂太極通書後序. In *CTTC* 76:4a–6b.

———. *Ts'an-t'ung-ch'i k'ao-yi* 參同契考異. In *CTYS*, vol. 1.

———. *Yi-hsüeh ch'i-meng* 易學啟蒙. In *CTYS*, vol. 12.

———. *Yi-li ching-ch'uan t'ung-chieh* 儀禮經傳通解. Four Libraries Rare Books. ser. 10, vols. 26–29. Taipei, Commercial Press reprint, 1980.

———. *Yin-fu ching k'ao-yi* 陰符經考異. In *CTYS*, vol. 12.

———. comp. *Yi-Lo yüan-yüan lu* 伊洛淵源錄. In *CTYS*, vol. 6.

———. *Yen-p'ing ta-wen* 延平答問. In *Shang Ts'ai yü-lu/Yen-p'ing ta-wen fu pu-lu* 上蔡語錄/延平答問,附補錄. In Okada Takehiko, ed., *Chin-shih Han-chi ts'ung-k'an*.

Chu Hsi, and Lü Tsu-ch'ien 呂祖謙, eds. *Chin-ssu lu* 近思錄. In *CTYS*, Pao-kao-t'ang ed. Taipei Yi-wen, reprint, 1969, vol. 1.

Chu Yi-tsun 朱彝尊. "T'ai-chi-t'u shou-shou k'ao" 太極圖授受考. In Chu Yi-tsun, *P'u-shu t'ing-chi* 曝書亭集, ch. 5. Ssu-k'u ts'ung-k'an, 1st ser.

Chuang-tzu 莊子, *SPPY* ed.

Ch'un-ch'iu fan-lu 春秋繁露. *SPPY* ed.

Ch'un-ch'iu Tso-shih-ch'uan Tu-shih chi-chieh 春秋左氏傳杜氏集解. *SPPY* ed.

Chung-ching 忠經. In *Po-tzu ch'üan-shu* 百子全書, Shanghai, Shao-yeh shan-fang, 1927.

Chung-Lü ch'uan-tao chi 鍾呂傳道集. *TT*, vol. 7.

Fo-fa chin-t'ang pien 佛法金湯編. Preface 1391 in *Hsü Tsang-ching* 續藏經, vol. 15, Seoul, Poryoguk, 1987.

Fo-kuo Yüan-wu ch'an-shih pi-yen lu 佛果圓悟禪師碧巖錄. *T* 48, no. 2003.

Han Yü 韓愈. *Han Ch'ang-li ch'üan-chi* 韓昌黎全集. Taipei, Hsin-wen-fang, 1977.

Hsi-shan ch'ün-hsien hui-chen chi 西山群仙會眞記. *TT*, vol. 7.

Hsiang-shan ch'üan-chi 象山全集. *SPPY* ed.

Hsing-ming kuei-chih 性命圭旨. In Hsiao T'ien-shih 蕭天石, comp., *Tao-tsang ching-hua* 道藏精華, 1st Collection 1, no. 5. Taipei, Tzu-yu ch'u-pan-she, 1981.

Hsü Ch'uan-teng lu 續傳燈錄. *T* 51, no. 2077.

Hsü Shen 許慎. *Shuo-wen chieh-tzu Tuan-chu* 說文解字段注. *SPPY* ed.

Hsün-tzu 荀子. *SPPY* ed.

Hu Chü-jen 胡居仁. *Chü-yeh lu* 居業錄. 1633.

Hu Hung 胡宏. *Chih-yen* 知言. In *Po-tzu ch'üan-shu*. Shanghai, Shao-yeh shan-fang, 1927.

Huai-nan-tzu 淮南子. *SPPY* ed.

Huang Kan 黃幹. *Chu-tzu hsing-chuang* 朱子行狀. In Okada Takehiko, ed., *Chin-shih Han-chi ts'ung-k'an*, vol. 21. Taipei, Chung-wen, 1972.

Huang Tsung-hsi 黃宗羲 et al., eds. *Sung-Yüan hsüeh-an* 宋元學案. Taipei, Student Bookstore, 1966.

Huang Tsung-yen 黃宗炎. *T'u-hsüeh pien-huo* 圖學辨惑. Four Libraries Rare Books Coll. 6, vol. 12. Taipei, Commercial Press reprint, 1980.

Huang Wan 黃綰. *Ming-tao p'ien* 明道篇. Ed. Hou Wailu. Peking, Chung-hua, 1959.

Hung-chih Ch'an-shih kuang-lu 弘智禪師廣錄. *T* 48, no. 2001.

Hung Ying-ming 洪應明. *Ts'ai-ken T'an* 菜根譚. In Imai Usaburō 今井宇三郎, trans., *Saikontan*. Tokyo, Iwanami, 1983.

Ko Hung 葛洪. *Pao-p'u tzu* 抱朴子. *SPPY* ed.

Ku Yen-wu 顧炎武. *T'ing-lin shih-wen chi* 亭林詩文集. *SPTK*, 1st ser. ed.

K'u-ya man-lu 枯崖漫錄. Preface 1272 in *Hsü Tsang-ching*, vol. 148. Seoul, Poryoguk, 1987.

Kuan-tzu 管子. *SPPY* ed.

Lao-tzu 老子. *SPPY* ed.

Leng-chia o-po tuo-lo-mi ching 楞伽阿跋多羅密經. *T* 16, no. 670.

Li-chi Cheng-chu 禮記鄭注. *SPPY* ed.

Li-chi Cheng-yi 禮記正義. *SPPY* ed.

Li Chih 李贄. *Fen-shu* 焚書. In *Fen-shu/Hsü Fen-shu* 焚書/續焚書. Peking, Chung-hua, 1974.

Li Hsin-ch'uan 李心傳. "Hui-an hsien-sheng fei su-yin" 晦庵先生非素隱. In *Chien-yen yi-lai ch'ao-yeh tsa-chi* 建炎以來朝野雜記. *TSCC* ed., pt. 2.

Li Kuang-ti 李光地, comp. *Chu-tzu li-tsuan* 朱子禮纂. In *Jung-ts'ung ch'üan-chi* 榕村全集, vol.15. Taipei Prefecture, Yung-ho County, Wen-yu Publications reprint, 1972.

Li Kung 李塨. *Ta-hsüeh pien-yeh* 大學辨業. In *Yen-Li ts'ung-shu* 顏李叢書, N.p., Ssu-ts'un hsüeh-hui, [1923].

Li Yen-p'ing chi 李延平集. Comp. Chang Po-hsing. *TSCC* ed.

Lieh-tzu 列子. *SPPY* ed.

Liu-tsu ta-shih fa-pao t'an-ching 六祖大師法寶壇經. *T* 48, no. 2008.

Lou-ying 樓穎, comp. *Shan-hui ta-shih yü-lu* 善慧大師語錄. In *Hsü Tsang-ching*, vol. 120. Seoul, Poryoguk, 1987.

Lü-shih ch'un-ch'iu 呂氏春秋. SPPY ed.

Lü Tung-lai wen-chi 呂東萊文集. TSCC ed.

Mi-ch'uan Cheng-yang chen-jen ling-pao pi-fa 秘傳正陽眞人靈寶畢法. TT, vol. 47.

Mo-tzu 墨子. SPPY ed.

Ogyū Sorai 荻徂萊. *Benmei* 辨名. In Kōjirō Yoshikawa 吉川幸次郎, ed., *Ogyū Sorai* 荻徂萊. Tokyo, Iwanami, 1973.

Shan-ch'ing 善卿, ed. *Tsu-t'ing shih-yüan* 祖庭事苑. In *Hsü tsang-ching*, vol. 113. Seoul, Poryoguk,1987.

Shang-fang ta-tung chen-yüan miao-ching t'u 上方大同眞元妙經圖. TT, vol. 196.

Shang-shu cheng-yi 尚書正義. SPPY ed.

Shao Yung 邵雍. *Huang-chi ching-shih shu* 皇極經世書. SPPY ed.

Ta fo-ting ju-lai mi-yin hsiu-cheng liao-yi chu shan p'u-sa wan-hsing shou-leng-yen ching 大佛頂如來密因修証了義諸善菩薩萬行首楞嚴經. T 19, no. 945.

Ta-hui P'u-chüeh ch'an-shih yü-lu 大慧普覺禪師語錄. T 47, no. 1998A.

Ta-sheng ch'i-hsin lun 大乘起信論. T 32, no. 1666. English translation in Yoshito S. Hakeda, trans., *The Awakening of Faith, Attributed to Asvaghosha, with Commentary*. New York, Columbia University Press, 1967.

Tai Chen 戴震. *Meng-tzu tzu-yi shu-cheng* 孟子字義疏証. Taipei, Kuang-wen, reprint, 1978.

Tai Hsien 戴詵. *Chu-tzu shih-chi* 朱子實紀. In *Chin-shih Han-chi ts'ung-k'an*, ed. Okada Takehiko. Taipei, Chung-wen, 1972.

T'o-t'o 脱脱 et al., eds. *Sung-shih* 宋史. In *Erh-shih-wu shih* 二十五史, Kai-ming ed.

Tsung-mi 宗密. *Ch'an-yüan chu ch'üan-chi tu-hsü* 禪源諸詮集都序. T 48, no. 2015.

———. *Chu Hua-yen fa-chieh kuan-men* 註華嚴法界觀門. T 45, no. 1884.

———. *Yüan-jen lun* 原人論. T 45, no. 1886.

Tsung-shao 宗紹. *Wu-men kuan* 無門關. T 48, no. 2005. German translation by Heinrich Dumoulin, S. J., *Der Pass ohne Tor*. Tokyo, Sophia University, 1966.

Tu Yu 杜佑. *T'ung-tien* 通典, preface 1896.

Wang Ch'ung 王充. *Lun-heng* 論衡. SPPY ed.

Wang Fu-chih 王夫之. *Chang-tzu Cheng-meng chu* 張子正蒙注. Peking, Chung-hua, 1975.

———. *Tu Ssu-shu ta-ch'üan* 讀四書大全. Peking, Chung-hua, 1975.

———. *Chou-yi wai-ch'uan* 周易外傳. Peking, Chung-hua, 1977.

Wang, Mao-hung 王懋竑. *Chu-tzu nien-p'u* 朱子年譜. Taipei, Commercial Press, 1970.

———. *Pai-t'ien ts'ung-kao* 白田叢稿. In Ch'ang Pi-te 昌比得, comp., *Ch'ing ming-chia-chi hui-k'an* 清名家集彙刊. Taipei, Han-wen wen-hua shih-yeh, 1972.

Wang Shou-jen 王守仁. *Wang Wen-ch'eng kung ch'uan-chi* 王文成公全集. SPTK, 1st ser., double-page lithograph ed.

Wang Tzu-ts'ai 王梓材 et al. *Sung-Yüan hsüeh-an pu-yi* 宋元學案補遺. *Ssu-ming ts'ung-shu*, Taipei, National Defence Academy, [1966].

Wen Pao-kuang 翁葆光. *Wu-chen p'ien chu-shu* 悟眞篇註疏. TT, vol. 4.

Wu-teng hui-yüan 五燈會元. In *Hsü Tsang-ching*, vol. 138. Seoul, Poryoguk, 1987.

Yeh Kung-hui 葉公會, comp. *Chu-tzu nien-p'u* 朱子年譜. In Okada Takehiko, ed., *Chin-shih Han-chi ts'ung-k'an*, vol. 21.

Yen Yüan 顏元. *Chu-tzu yü-lei p'ing* 朱子語類評. In *Yen-Li ts'ung-shu*. N.p., Ssu-ts'un hsüeh-hui, [1923].

———. *Ts'un-hsüeh p'ien* 存學篇. N.p., Ssu-ts'un hsüeh-hui, [1923].

Yi-wei ch'ien-k'un tso-tu 易緯乾坤鑿度. In *Yi-wei shih-lei mou chi ch'i-t'a ssu-chung* 易緯是類謀及其他四種. Changsha, Commercial Press, 1937.

Yüan Ts'ai 袁采. *Yüan-shih shih-fan* 袁氏世範. Supplement to the Four Libraries Rare Books series. Taipei, Commercial Press reprint, 1975.

Yung-chia cheng-tao ko 永嘉証道歌. *T* 48, no. 2014.

Asian-Language Secondary Sources

Araki Kengo 荒木見悟. *Bukkyō to jukyō* 佛教と儒教. Kyoto, Heirakuji shoten, 1963.

Arita Kazuo 有田和夫, and Oshima Akeru, eds. *Shushigaku teki shii: Chūgoku shisōshi ni okeru dentō to kakushin* 朱子學的思惟:中國思想史における傳統と革新. Tokyo, Kyūko shoin, 1990.

Azuma Jūji 吾妻重二. "Shuki 'Shūeki sandōkei kōi' ni tsuite"朱熹〈周易參同契考異〉について. *Nippon Chūgoku gakkaihō*日本中國學會報 36 (1984), 175–90.

———. "Shushi no sūshōeki shisō to sono igi" 朱子の數象易思想とその意義. *Firosofia* 68 (1980), 145–75.

———. "Taikyokuzu no keisei: Ju butsu dō sankyō o meguru saikentō"太極圖の形成:儒佛道三教をめぐる再檢討, *Nippon Chūgoku gakkaihō* 46 (1994), 73–86.

Chan, Wing-tsit 陳榮捷. *Chin-ssu lu hsiang-chu chi-p'ing*近思錄詳注集評. Taipei, Student Bookstore, 1992.

———. "Chu-tzu chih tsung-chiao shih-chien" 朱子之宗教實踐. In *Chu-hsüeh lun-chi* 朱學論集, pp. 181–97. Taipei, Student Bookstore, 1982.

———. *Chu-tzu hsin t'an-so* 朱子新探索. Taipei, Student Bookstore, 1981.

———. *Chu-tzu men-jen* 朱子門人. Taipei, Student Bookstore, 1982.

Ch'ang Pi-te 昌比德, comp. *Ch'ing ming-chia chi hui-k'an* 清名家集彙刊. Taipei, Han-wen wen-hua shih-yeh, 1972.

Chen Kaiguo 陳開國 et al. *Ta-tao hsing* 大道行. Peking, Hua-hsia, 1993.

Chen Lai 陳來. *Chu Hsi che-hsüeh yen-chiu* 朱熹哲學研究. Peking, Social Science Publications, 1988.

Ch'en Chün-min 陳俊民 "Chu-tzu te sheng-hsien jen-ko li-hsiang" 朱子的「聖賢」人格理想. In Chung Ts'ai-chün 鍾彩鈞, ed., *Kuo-chi Chu-tzu hsüeh hui-yi lun-wen chi* 國際朱子學會議論文集, pp. 659–76. Taipei, Academia Sinica, 1993.

Ch'en Kuo-fu 陳國符. *Tao-tsang yüan-liu k'ao* 道藏源流考. Peking, Chung-hua, 1963.

Chi Yün 紀昀 et al. *Ssu-k'u ch'üan-shu tsung-mu t'i-yao*四庫全書總目題要. Taipei, Yi-wen reprint, 1971.

Chiang Kuang-hui 姜廣輝. "Chu Hsi che-hsüeh yü-lun" 朱熹哲學餘論." In Chung Ts'ai-chün, ed., *Kuo-chi Chu-tzu hsüeh hui-yi lun-wen chi*, pp. 769–91. Taipei, Academia Sinica, 1993.

Chiang Wei-ch'iao 蔣維喬. *Ying-shih-tzu ching-tso fa* 因是子靜坐法. In Hsiao T'ien-shih 蕭天石, comp., *Tao-tsang ching-hua* 道藏精華, 2d Collection, no. 9. Taipei, Tzu-yu ch'u-pan-she, 1984.

Chiang Yi-pin 蔣義斌. "Chu-tzu te yüeh-lun" 朱子的樂論. In Chung Ts'ai-chün, ed., *Kuo-chi Chu-tzu hsüeh hui-yi lun-wen chi*, pp. 1461–79. Taipei, Academia Sinica, 1993.

Ch'ien Mu 錢穆. *Chu-tzu hsin hsüeh-an* 朱子新學案. 5 vols. Taipei, San-min, 1971.

Chin, Chung-shu 金中樞. "Lun Pei-Sung mo-nien chih ch'ung-shang Tao-chiao" 論北宋末年之崇尚道教. In *Sung-shih yen-chiu chi* 宋史研究集, Symposium on Sung History, eds. vol. 7, pp. 291–392, and vol. 8, pp. 207–78. Taipei, Chunghua ts'ung-shu pien-sheng wei-yüan-hui, 1974/76.

Ching Chia-yi 秦家懿. "Chu-tzu yü Fo-chiao" 朱子與佛教. *Hsin-ya hsüeh-shu chik'an* 新亞學術集刊 3 (1982), 135–41.

———. "Shushi to Bukkyō" 朱子と佛教. In *Shushigaku nyūmon* 朱子學入門. In Morohashi Tetsuji 諸橋轍次 et al., eds., *Shushigaku taikei* 朱子學大系, vol. 1, pp. 397–410. Tokyo, Meitoku, 1974.

Choe Ken-tok 崔根德. "*Chu-tzu chia-li* tsai Han-kuo chih shou-jung yü chan-k'ai" 朱子《家禮》在韓國之受容與展開. In Chung Ts'ai-chün, ed., *Kuo-chi Chu-tzu hsüeh hui-yi lun-wen chi*, pp. 235–48. Taipei, Academia Sinica, 1993.

Chung Ts'ai-chün 鍾彩鈞, ed. *Kuo-chi Chu-tzu hsüeh hui-yi lun-wen chi* 國際朱子學會議論文集. Taipei, Academia Sinica, 1993.

Feng Yu-lan 馮友蘭. *Chung-kuo che-hsüeh shih* 中國哲學史. Shanghai, Commercial Press, 1935.

———. *Chung-kuo che-hsüeh-shih hsin-pien* 中國哲學史新編. Peking, Jen-min, 1964.

———. *Hsin li-hsüeh* 新理學. Shanghai, Commercial Press, 1936.

———. *San-Sung t'ang ch'üan-chi* 三松堂全集. 14 vols. Honan, Honan Jen-min, 1993.

Feng Zongpu 馮宗璞 et al., eds. *Feng Yu-lan hsien-sheng pai-nien tan-ch'en chi-nien wen-chi* 馮友蘭先生百年誕辰紀念文集. Peking, Ch'ing-hua University, 1995.

Fu-chien t'ung-chih 福建通志. 1871 ed.

Fukuda Shoku 福田殖. "Chu Hsi te ssu-sheng kuan" 朱熹的死生觀. In Chung Ts'ai-chün, ed., *Kuo-chi Chu-tzu hsüeh hui-yi lun-wen chi*, pp. 879–906. Taipei, Academia Sinica, 1993.

Ho Lin [He Lin] 賀麟. "Sung-ju te ssu-hsiang fang-fa" 宋儒的思想方法. In Symposium on Sung History, ed., *Sung-shih yen-chiu chi*, pp. 39–66. 2nd collection. Taipei, Sung-shih ts'ung-shu, 1964.

Hou Wailu 侯外廬, Zhao Jiban, and Du Guoxian. *Chung-kuo ssu-hsiang t'ung-shih* 中國思想通史. 5 vols. Peking, Jen-min, 1957–60.

Hsü Fu-kuan 徐復觀. "Ch'eng-Chu yi-t'ung ch'u-kao" 程朱異同初稿. *Ta-lu tsachih* 大陸雜誌 64 (1982), 1–20.

———. *Chung-kuo ssu-hsiang-shih lun-chi* 中國思想史論集. Taipei, Student Bookstore, 1975.

———. *Liang-Han ssu-hsiang-shih* 兩漢思想史. Taipei, Student Bookstore, 1976.

Hu Shih 胡適, "Chi-ko fan li-hsüeh te ssu-hsiang chia" 幾個反理學的思想家. In *Hu Shih wen-ts'un* 胡適文存, vol. 3. Taipei, Yüan-tung, 1953.

Hu Wei 胡渭. *Yi-t'u ming-pien* 易圖明辨. *TSCC*, ed. 1st ser.

Huang Chang-chien 黃彰健. "O-hu chih-hui Chu Lu yi-t'ung lüeh-shuo"鵝湖之會朱陸異同略說. In Symposium on Sung History, ed. *Sung-shih yen-chiu chi*, pp. 31–38. 2nd collection. Taipei, Sung-shih ts'ung-shu, 1964.

Ichiki Tsuyuhiko 市來津由彥. "Shushi no 'Zatsugakuben' to sono shūhen,"朱子の『雜學辨』とその周邊. In Sōdaishi Kenkyūkai, ed., *Sōdai no shakai to shūkyō* 宋代の社會と宗教, pp. 3–49. Tokyo, Kyūko shōin, 1985.

Imai Usaburō 今井宇三郎. *Sōdai ekigaku no kenkyū* 宋代易學の研究. Tokyo, Meiji shoin, 1958.

Ju-chia ho ju-chia ssu-hsiang p'i-p'an 儒家和儒家思想批判. Comp. Philosophy Department, Peking University. Peking, 1974.

Kusumoto Fumio 久須本文雄. *Sōdai jugaku no zen shisō kenkyū* 宋代儒學の禪思想研究. Nagoya, Nisseido, 1980.

Kusumoto Masatsugu 楠本正繼. *Sō-Min jidai jugaku shisō no kenkyū* 宋明時代儒學思想の研究. Tokyo, Hiroike Gakuen Press, 1972.

Kwang-hsin fu-chih 廣信府志. 1872.

Lao Ssu-kuang 勞思光. *Chung-kuo che-hsüeh-shih* 中國哲學史. 3 vols. Taipei, San-min, 1980–81.

Li Ming-hui 李明輝. "Chu-tzu lun-o chih ken-yüan" 朱熹論惡之根源. In Chung Ts'ai-chün, ed., *Kuo-chi Chu-tzu hsüeh hui-yi lun-wen chi*, pp. 553–79. Taipei, Academia Sinica, 1993.

———. *T'ang-tai ju-hsüeh te tzu-wo chuan-hua* 當代儒學的自我轉化. Taipei, Academia Sinica, 1994.

Liang Ch'i-ch'ao 梁啓超. *Yin-ping-shih ho-chi, wen-chi* 飲冰室合集・文集, vol. 9. Shanghai, Chung-hua, 1941.

Lin Chi-p'ing 林繼平. *Lu Hsiang-shan yen-chiu* 陸象山研究. Taipei, Shang-wu, 1983.

Liu Shih-p'ei 劉師培. *Tu Tao-tsang chi* 讀道藏記. In *Liu Shih-p'ei hsien-sheng yi-shu* 劉申叔 先生遺書. Ning-wu, Nan-shih, 1936.

Liu Shu-hsien 劉述先. *Chu Hsi che-hsüeh ssu-hsiang te fa-chan yü wan-ch'eng* 朱熹哲學思想 的發展與完成. Taipei, Student Bookstore, 1982.

———. "Chu Hsi te jen-shuo, t'ai-chi kuan-nien yü tao-t'ung wen-t'i te tsai hsing-ch'a" 朱熹的仁說太極觀念與道統問題的再省察. *Shih-hsüeh p'ing-lun* 史學評論 5 (1983), 173–88.

Liu Ts'un-yan 柳存仁. "Chu Hsi yü Ts'an-t'ung ch'i" 朱熹與參同契. In Liu Ts'un-yan, *Ho-feng t'ang hsin wen-chi* 和風堂新文集, vol. 2, pp. 457–508. Taipei, Hsin-wen-feng, 1997.

Lo Siding 羅思鼎 "P'ing Chu Hsi te wei-hsin lun te hsien-yen lun" 評朱熹的唯心論的先驗論. *People's Daily*, February 13, 1974.

Lü Ssu-mien 呂思勉 et al. *Ku-shih pien* 古史辨. 1941. Hong Kong Taiping reprint, 1963.

Mao Ch'i-ling 毛奇齡. *T'ai-chi-t'u shuo yi-yi* 太極圖說異議. Preface 1685 in *Hsi-ho ho-chi* 西河 合集.

Meng P'ei-yüan 蒙培元. "Chu Hsi te hsin-ling ching-chieh shuo"朱熹的心靈境界說. In Chung Ts'ai-chün, ed., *Kuo-chi Chu-tzu hsüeh hui-yi lun-wen chi*, pp. 417–36. Taipei, Academia Sinica, 1993.

Miao-fa lien-hua ching 妙法蓮花經. *T* 9, no. 262.

Miura Kunio 三浦國雄. "Shushi kijinron-ho" 朱子鬼神論補. *Jinbun kenkyū* 人文研究 37 (1985), 185–203.

———. "Shushi kijinron no rinkaku" 朱子鬼神論の輪廓. In *Jinkannen no hikaku bunkaron teki kenkyū* 神觀念の比較文化論的研究, pp. 741–84. Tokyo, Kōdansha, 1981.

———. "Shushi to kokyū 朱子と呼吸. In Osamu Kanaya 金谷治, ed., *Chūgoku ni okeru ningensei no kenkyū* 中國に於ける人間性の研究, pp. 499–521. Tokyo, Sōbunsha, 1983.

Mou Tsung-san 牟宗三. *Hsin-t'i yü hsing-t'i* 心體與性體. 3 vols. Taipei, Cheng-chung, 1981.

———. *Ts'ung Lu Hsiang-shan tao Liu Chi-shan* 從陸象山到劉蕺山. Taipei, Student Bookstore, 1979.

Ōhama Akira 大濱皓. *Shushi no tetsugaku* 朱子の哲學. Tokyo, Tokyo University Press, 1983.

Okada Takehiko 岡田武彦. "Shu-Riku idō genryū kō" 朱陸異同源流考. In *Mekada Makoto hakushi kanreki kinen Chūgokugaku ronshū* 目加田誠搏士還曆紀念中國學論集. Tokyo, Daian, 1964.

———. *Zazen to seiza* 坐禪と静坐. Tokyo, Ofusha, 1972.

———, ed. *Chin-shih Han-chi ts'ung-k'an* 近世漢籍叢刊. Taipei, Chung-wen reprint, 1972.

Onozawa Seiichi 小野澤精一 et al., eds. *Ki no shisō: Chūgoku ni okeru shizenkan to ningenkan no tenkai* 氣の思想:中國における自然觀と人間觀の展開. Tokyo, Tokyo University Press, 1978.

Ōtsuki Nobuyoshi 大槻信良. *Chu-tzu ssu-shu chi-chu tien-chü k'ao* 朱子四書集注典據考. Taipei, Student Bookstore, 1976.

P'i Hsi-jui 皮錫瑞. *Ching-hsüeh li-shih* 經學歷史. Annotated by Chou Yü-t'ung. Taipei, Wen-hai, 1964.

Ren Jiyu 任繼愈. *Chung-kuo che-hsüeh-shih chien pien* 中國哲學史簡編. Peking, Jen-min, 1984.

Sakade Yoshinobu 坂出祥伸. *Dōkyō to yōjō shisō* 道教と養生思想. Tokyo, Perikansha, 1992.

Sakai Tadao 酒井忠夫. "Shushi to dōkyō" 朱子と道教. In *Shushigaku nyūmon*, in Morohashi Tetsuji et al., eds., *Shushigaku taikei*, vol. 1, 411–27. Tokyo, Meitoku, 1974.

Satō Hitoshi 佐藤仁. "Kuan-yü Chu Hsi ching-shuo te yi-ko k'ao-ch'a"關於朱熹敬說的一個考察. In Chung Ts'ai-chün, ed., *Kuo-chi Chu-tzu hsüeh hui-yi lun-wen chi*, pp. 615–57. Taipei, Academia Sinica, 1993.

———. *Shushi: Oi yasuku gaku narigatashi* 朱子-老い易く學成り難. Tokyo, Shūeisha, 1985.

Sha Ming 沙明. *K'ung-chia-tien chi-ch'i yu-lin* 孔家店及其幽靈. Hong Kong, 1970.

Shibata Atsushi 柴田篤. "Li Ma-tou yü Chu-tzu hsüeh" 利瑪竇與朱子學. In Chung Ts'ai-chün, ed., *Kuo-chi Chu-tzu hsüeh hui-yi lun-wen chi*, pp. 909–22. Taipei, Academia Sinica, 1993.

———. "Inyō no rei to shite no kijin: Shushi kijin kaikonron e no jomaku" 陰陽の靈としての鬼神-朱子鬼神魂魄論の序幕. *Tetsugaku nenpō* 哲學年報 50 (1991), 71–91.

Shimada Kenji 島田虔次. *Shushigaku to Yōmeigaku* 朱子學と陽明學. Tokyo, Iwanami, 1984.

Sueki Yasuhiko 末木恭彥. "'Inpukyō kōi' no shisō"「陰符經考異」の思想. *Nippon Chūgoku gakkaihō* 36 (1984), 163–73.

———. "'Inpukyō kōi' senja-kō"「陰符經考異」撰者考. *Chūtetsu bungaku kaihō* 中哲文學會報 10 (1985), 50–69.

———. Shushi to dōkyō o meguru ichisokumen: 'Inpukyō kōi' ko" 朱子と道教をめぐる一側面-「陰符經考異」考. *Tōhōgaku* 東洋學 60 (1980), 81-95.

Sun Chen-ch'ing 孫振青. "Chu Hsi te *li-ch'i* kai-nien yü Ya-li-ssu-tuo-te (Aristotle) te hsing-chih kai-nien chih pi-chiao"朱熹的理氣慨念與亞里斯多德的形質慨念之比較. In Chung Ts'ai-chün, ed., *Kuo-chi Chu-tzu hsüeh hui-yi lun-wen chi*, pp. 749–68. Taipei, Academia Sinica, 1993.

Takahata Tsunenobu 高畑常信. "Chō Nanken no shisō keisei" 張南軒の思想想形成. In *Chō Nanken shū jinmei sakuin* 張南軒集人名索引. Nagoya, Saika shorin, 1976.

Takeuchi Yoshio 武内義雄. *Takeuchi Yoshio zenshū* 武内義雄全集. Ed. Kōjirō Yoshikawa et al. Tokyo, Kadokawa shoten, 1985.

Tang Chün-i 唐君毅. "Chu-Lu yi-t'ung t'an-yüan" 朱陸異同探源. *Hsin-ya hsüeh-pao* 新亞學報 8 (February 1967), 1–100.

———. *Chung-kuo che-hsüeh yüan-lun: Tao-lun-p'ien* 中國哲學原論:導論篇. Hong Kong, New Asia Institute, 1966.

———. *Chung-kuo che-hsüeh yüan-lun: Yüan-chiao-p'ien* 中國哲學原論:原教篇. Hong Kong, New Asia Institute, 1979.

———. *Chung-kuo che-hsüeh yüan-lun: Yüan-hsing-p'ien* 中國哲學原論:原性篇. Hong Kong, New Asia Institute, 1968.

———. *Chung-kuo che-hsüeh yüan-lun: Yüan-tao-p'ien*中國哲學原論:原道篇. Taipei, Students Bookstore, 1980.

Tian Hao田浩 [Hoyt Tillman]. *Chu Hsi te ssu-wei shih-chieh*朱熹的思維世界. Taipei, Yun-ch'eng, 1996.

Tokiwa Daijō 常盤大定. *Shina ni okeru bukkyō to jukyō dōkyō* 支那に於る佛教と儒教道教. Tokyo, Tōyō Bunko, 1930.

Tomoeda Ryūtarō 友枝龍太郎. *Shushi no shisō keisei* 朱子の思想形成. Rev. ed. Tokyo, Shunjūsha, 1979.

Ts'ai Jen-hou 蔡仁厚. "Chu-tzu te kung-fu lun" 朱子的工夫論. In Chung Ts'ai-chün, ed., *Kuo-chi Chu-tzu hsüeh hui-yi lun-wen chi*, pp. 581–98. Taipei, Academia Sinica, 1993.

Tseng Ts'ao 曾慥. *Tao-shu* 道樞. TT, vols. 34–35.

Tu Ssu-shu ta-ch'üan shuo 讀四書大全說. Peking, Chung-hua, 1975.

Tung Chung-shu 董仲舒. *Ch'un-ch'iu fan-lu* 春秋繁露. SPPY ed.

Uno Seiichi 宇野精一. "Shushi to rei" 朱子と禮. In Morohashi Tetsuji and Yasuoka Masatsugu, eds., *Shushigaku taikei*, vol. 1, *Shushigaku nyūmon*, pp. 272–82. Tokyo, Meitoku, 1974.

Wang Ching-hsien 王靖獻. "Chu-tzu chiu-ko ch'uan-yi k'ao" 朱子《九歌》傳意考. In Chung Ts'ai-chün, ed., *Chu-tzu hsüeh hui-yi lun-wen chi*, pp. 1141–56. Taipei, Academia Sinica, 1993.

Yamane Mitsuyoshi山根三芳. "Shushi no ten ni tsuite" 朱子の天について. *Tōhō Shūkyō* 東方宗教 26 (1965), 34–54.

———. *Shushi rinri shisō kenkyū* 朱子倫理思想研究. Tokyo, Tōkai University Press. 1983.

Yamanoi Yū 山井湧. "Shushi no shisō ni okeru ki" 朱子の思想における氣. In Onozawa Seiichi et al., *Ki no shisō*, pp. 438–52. Tokyo, Tokyo University Press, 1978.

———. "Shushi no tetsugaku ni okeru 'Taikyoku'" 朱子の哲學における「太極」. *Higashi Ajia no shisō to bunka* 東アジアの思想と文化 9 (1980), 37–69.

Yan Yaozhong 嚴耀中. "Chu Hsi yü Mi-an" 朱熹與密庵. *Chung-hua wen-shih lun-ts'ung* 中華文史論叢 57 (1998), 241–54.

Yanagida Seizan 柳田聖山. "Bukkyō to Shushi no shūhen" 佛教と朱子の周邊. *Zen Bunka kenkyūjo kiyō* 禪文化研究所紀要 8 (1976), 1–30.

Yang Rongguo 楊榮國. *Chien-ming Chung-kuo che-hsüeh-shih* 簡明中國哲學史. Peking, Jen-min, 1973.

Yoshikawa, Kōjirō 吉川幸次郎. *Ogyū Sorai* 荻徂徠. Tokyo, Iwanami, 1973.

Yoshikawa, Kōjirō, and Miura Kunio. *Shushi shū* 朱子集. Tokyo, Asahi shinbunsha, 1976.

Yü Ying-shih 余英時. *Lun Tai Chen yü Chang Hsüeh-ch'eng* 論戴震與章學誠. Taipei, Hua-shih, 1977.

Zhang Liwen 張立文. *Chu Hsi ssu-hsiang yen-chiu* 朱熹思想研究. Peking, Chinese Social Science Publications, 1981.

———. "Wei-fa yi-fa lun chih tsung-kuan: Chu-tzu ts'an-chi we-fa yi-fa lun chih ts'e-ts'o, chuan-pien ho yin-hsiang" 未發已發論之縱觀: 朱子參究未發論已發論之挫折, 轉變和影響. In Chung Ts'ai-chün, ed., *Kuo-chi Chu-tzu hsüeh hui-yi lun-wen chi*, pp. 497–520. Taipei, Academia Sinica, 1993.

Western-Language Secondary Sources

Angel, Leonard. *Enlightenment East and West*. Albany, State University of New York Press, 1994.

Baldrian-Hussein, Farzeen. "Taoism: An Overview." In *The Encyclopedia of Religion*, vol. 14, pp. 301–2. New York, Macmillan and Free Press, 1987.

Bellah, Robert N. "Baigan and Sorai: Continuities and Discontinuities in Eighteenth-Century Japanese Thought." In Tetsuo Najita et al., eds., *Japanese Thought in the Tokugawa Period, 1600–1869*, pp. 137–52. Chicago, University of Chicago Press, 1978.

Berthrong, John H. *All under Heaven: Transforming Paradigms in Confucian-Christian Dialogue*. Albany, State University of New York Press, 1994.

———. "Chu Hsi's Ethics: *Jen* and *Ch'eng*." *Journal of Chinese Philosophy* 14 (1987), 161–77.

Birdwhistell, Anne D. *Transition to Neo-Confucianism: Shao Yung on Knowledge and Symbols of Reality*. Stanford, Stanford University Press, 1989.

Black, Alison H. *Man and Nature in the Philosophic Thought of Wang Fu-chih*. Seattle, University of Washington Press, 1989.

Blondel, Anne-Marie, and Kristofer Schipper, eds. *Essais sur le rituel*, vol. 2. Bibliothèque de l'École des Hautes Études, Section des Sciences Religieuses, vol. 95. Louvan-Paris, Peeters, [1990].

Bloom, Irene, and Joshua A. Fogel, eds. *The Meeting of Minds: Intellectual and Religious Interaction in East Asian Traditions of Thought.* New York, Columbia University Press, 1997.

Bochenski, Innocentius [Joseph M.]. *Soviet Russian Dialectical Materialism, DIAMAT.* Dordrecht, Reidel, 1963.

Bodde, Derk. "The Chinese View of Immortality: Its Expression by Chu Hsi and Its Relationship to Buddhist Thought." In Charles Le Blanc and Dorothy Borei, eds., *Essays on Chinese Civilization.* Princeton, Princeton University Press, 1981.

Broughton, Jeffrey L. "Kuei-feng Tsung-mi: The Convergence of Ch'an and the Teachings." Ph.D diss., Columbia University, 1975.

Bruce, Joseph P. *Chu Hsi and His Masters.* London, Probsthain, 1923.

Bucke, Richard M. *Cosmic Consciousness: A Study in the Evolution of the Human Mind.* New York, Dutton, 1923.

Cassirer, Ernst. *An Essay on Man: An Introduction to a Philosophy of Human Culture.* New Haven, Yale University Press, 1944.

Chan, Charles Wing-hoi. "The 'Benevolent Person' versus the 'Sage': Ogyū Sorai's Critiques of Chu Hsi." Ph.D. diss., University of Toronto, 1994.

———. "Chu Hsi's Theory of *Tao-t'ung* and the Message of the Sage." *International Review of Chinese Religion and Philosophy* 19 (1996), 67–152.

Chan, Wing-cheuk. "Confucian Moral Metaphysics and Heidegger's Fundamental Ontology." *Analecta Husserliana* 17 (1984), 187–202.

Chan, Wing-tsit. "Chu Hsi and Quiet-Sitting." In Chan, *Chu Hsi: New Studies,* pp. 255–70.

———. *Chu Hsi: Life and Thought.* Hong Kong, Chinese University Press, 1987.

———. *Chu Hsi: New Studies.* Honolulu, University of Hawaii Press, 1989.

———. "Chu Hsi's Appraisal of Lao-tzu." *Philosophy East and West* 25 (1975), 131–44.

———. "Chu Hsi's Completion of Neo-Confucianism." In Françoise Aubin, ed., *Études Song: In Memoriam Étienne Balazs,* ser. 2, no. 1, pp. 60–87. Paris, Mouton, 1971.

———. "The Evolution of the Neo-Confucian Concept *Li* as Principle." In Wing-tsit Chan, *Neo-Confucianism Etc.: Essays by Wing-tsit Chan,* comp. Charles K. H. Chen, pp. 45–87. Hong Kong, Oriental Society, 1969.

———, ed. *Chu Hsi and Neo-Confucianism.* Honolulu, University of Hawaii Press, 1986.

———, trans. *Reflections on Things at Hand.* New York, Columbia University Press, 1967.

———, *A Source Book in Chinese Philosophy.* Princeton, Princeton University Press, 1963.

Chang, Carsun. *The Development of Neo-Confucian Thought.* 2 vols. New York, Bookman Associates, 1957–62.

Chang Chung-yüan. "Creativity as Process in Taoism." *Eranos Jahrbuch* 25 (1963), 391–415.

Chang Tung-sun. "A Chinese Philosopher's Theory of Knowledge." *Etc.; A Review of General Semantics* 9 (1952), 203–26. First published in *Yenching Journal of Social Studies.*

Cheng, Anne. *Histoire de la pensée chinoise.* Paris, Seuil, 1997.

Cheng Chung-ying. *New Dimensions of Confucian and Neo-Confucian Philosophy.* Albany, State University of New York Press, 1991.

Chin, Ann-ping, et al., trans. *Tai Chen on Mencius: Explorations in Words and Meaning, a Translation of Meng-tzu tzu-i shu-cheng with a Critical Introduction.* New Haven, Yale University Press, 1990.

Ching, Julia. *Chinese Religions.* London, Macmillan, 1993.

————. "Chu Hsi's Theory of Human Nature." *Humanitas* 20 (1979), 77–100.

————. "Confucianism: A Critical Re-assessment of the Tradition," *International Philosophical Quarterly* 15 (1975), 1–33.

————. *Confucianism and Christianity: A Comparative Study.* Tokyo, Kodansha International, 1977.

————. "God and the World: Chu Hsi and Whitehead." *Journal of Chinese Philosophy* 6 (1979), 275–95.

————. "The Goose Lake Monastery Debate." *Journal of Chinese Philosophy* 1 (1974), 161–78.

————. *Mysticism and Kingship in China: The Heart of Chinese Wisdom.* Cambridge, Cambridge University Press, 1997.

————. "Neo-Confucian Utopian Theories and Political Ethics," *Monumenta Serica* 30 (1972–73), 1–56.

————. "Philosophy, Law, and Human Rights in China." *East Asian Review* 1 (1997), 1–20.

————. "The Problem of Evil as a Possible Dialogue between Neo-Confucianism and Christianity." *Contemporary Religions in Japan* 9 (September 1968), 161–93.

————. "The Problem of God in Chu Hsi and Whitehead." *Journal of Chinese Philosophy* 6 (1979), 275–95.

————. *To Acquire Wisdom: The Way of Wang Yang-ming.* New York, Columbia University Press, 1976.

————. "Truth and Ideology: The Confucian Way (*Tao*) and Its Transmission (*Tao-t'ung*)." *Journal of the History of Ideas* 35 (1974), 371–88.

————. "Yi Yulgok and the Four-Seven Debate." In William Theodore de Bary et al., eds., *The Rise of Neo-Confucianism in Korea*, pp. 303–22. New York, Columbia University Press, 1985.

Ching, Julia, and Willard G. Oxtoby, eds. *Moral Enlightenment: Leibniz and Wolff on China.* Monumenta Serica Monograph Series, no. 26. Nettetal, Steyler Verlag, 1992.

Chow Tse-tsung. *The May Fourth Movement: Intellectual Revolution in Modern China.* Stanford, Stanford University Press, 1960.

Christian, William A. *An Interpretation of Whitehead's Metaphysics.* New Haven, Yale University Press, 1959.

Chung Ts'ai-chün. *The Development of the Concepts of Heaven and of Man in the Philosophy of Chu Hsi.* Taipei, Academia Sinica, 1993.

Collani, Claudia von. *P. Joachim Bouvet, s.j.: Sein Leben und sein Werk.* Nettetal, Steyler Verlag, 1985.

Conze, Edward. *The Prajñāpāramitā Literature.* The Hague, Mouton, 1960.

Cousins, Ewert H., ed. *Process Theology: Basic Writings by the Key Thinkers of a Major Modern Movement*. New York, Newman Press, 1971.

Cusanus, Nicolaus. *Of Learned Ignorance*. Trans. Fr. Germain Stark. London, Routledge and Kegan Paul, 1954.

de Bary, William Theodore. *Neo-Confucian Orthodoxy and the Learning of the Mind-and-Heart*. New York, Columbia University Press, 1981.

————. *Principle and Practicality: Essays in Neo-Confucianism and Practical Learning*. New York, Columbia University Press, 1979.

————. *The Unfolding of Neo-Confucianism*. New York, Columbia University Press, 1975.

de Bary, William Theodore, and John W. Chaffee, eds. *Neo-Confucian Education: The Formative Stage*. Berkeley, University of California Press, 1989.

de Bary, William Theodore, et al., eds. *The Rise of Neo-Confucianism in Korea*. New York, Columbia University Press, 1985.

de Bary, William Theodore, et al., eds. *Sources of Chinese Tradition*. Vol. 1. 2nd ed. New York, Columbia University Press, 1999.

de Sousa, Ronald. *The Rationality of Emotions*. Cambridge, MIT Press, 1987.

Demiéville, Paul. "La pénétration du bouddhisme dans la tradition philosophique chinoise." *Cahiers d'histoire mondiale* 3 (1956), 19–38.

Dilworth, David A. *Philosophy in World Perspective: A Comparative Hermeneutic of the Major Theories*. New Haven, Yale University Press, 1989.

Dumoulin, Heinrich. *A History of Zen Buddhism*. 2 vols. Trans. James W. Heisig and Paul Knitter. London, Macmillan, 1988–90.

————, trans. *Der Pass ohne Tor*. Tokyo, Sophia University, 1966.

Eber, Irene, ed. *Confucianism: The Dynamics of Tradition*. New York, Macmillan, 1986.

Ebrey, Patricia Buckley. *Family and Property in Sung China: Yüan Ts'ai's Precepts for Social Life*. Princeton, Princeton University Press, 1984.

————. "Sung Neo-Confucian Views on Geomancy." In Irene Bloom and Joshua A. Fogel, eds., *The Meeting of Minds*, pp. 75–107. New York: Columbia University Press, 1997.

————, trans. *Chu Hsi's Family Rituals: A Twelfth-Century Manual for the Performance of Cappings, Weddings, Funerals, and Ancestral Rites*. Princeton, Princeton University Press, 1991.

Eliade, Mircea. *The Forge and the Crucible*. New York, Harper and Row, 1971.

————. *The Sacred and the Profane*. New York, Harcourt Brace, 1959.

————. *Yoga: Immortality and Freedom*. Princeton, Princeton University Press, 1969.

Elman, Benjamin A. *From Philosophy to Philology*. Cambridge, Harvard University Press, 1984.

Forman, Robert K. C., ed. *The Problem of Pure Consciousness: Mysticism and Philosophy*. New York: Oxford University Press, 1990.

Fukui Kojun. "A Study of Chou-i Ts'an-t'ung-ch'i." *Acta Asiatica* 27 (1974), 19–32.

Fung Yu-lan. *A History of Chinese Philosophy*. 2 vols. Trans. Derk Bodde. Princeton, Princeton University Press, 1952–53.

Gardner, Daniel K. *Chu Hsi and the Ta-hsüeh: Neo-Confucian Reflection on the Confucian Canon*. Cambridge, Council on East Asian Studies, Harvard University, 1986.

———. "Chu Hsi's Reading of the Ta-hsüeh: A Confucian's Quest for Truth." *Journal of Chinese Philosophy* 10 (September 1983), 182–204.

———. "Ghosts and Spirits in the Sung Neo-Confucian World: Chu Hsi on *Kuei-shen.*" *Journal of the American Oriental Society* 115 (1995), 598–611.

———. "Transmitting the Way: Chu Hsi and His Program of Learning." *Harvard Journal of Asiatic Studies* 49 (1989), 141–72.

———. "Zhu Xi on Spirit Beings." In Donald S. Lopez, Jr., ed., *Chinese Religions in Practice*, pp. 106–119. Princeton, Princeton University Press, 1996.

———, trans. *Learning to Be a Sage: Selections from the Conversations of Master Chu, Arranged Topically.* Berkeley, University of California Press, 1990.

Girardot, Norman J. *Myth and Meaning in Early China: The Theme of Chaos (Hun-lun).* Berkeley, University of California Press, 1983.

Graf, Olaf. *Tao und Jen: Sein und Sollen im sungchinesischen Monismus.* Wiesbaden, Otto Harrassowitz, 1970.

Graham, Angus C. *Two Chinese Philosophers: Ch'eng Ming-tao and Ch'eng Yi-ch'uan* London, Lund Humphries, 1958.

Granet, Marcel. *La pensée chinoise.* Paris, Albin Michel, 1968.

Gregory, Peter N., ed. *Traditions of Meditation in Chinese Buddhism.* Honolulu, University of Hawaii Press, 1986.

Grieder, Jerome B. *Hu Shih and the Chinese Renaissance: Liberalism in the Chinese Revolution, 1917–1937.* Cambridge, Harvard University Press, 1970.

Hakeda, Yoshito S., trans. *The Awakening of Faith, Attributed to Aśvaghosha.* New York, Columbia University Press, 1967.

Harlez, Charles de. *Kia Li: Livre des rites domestiques chinois.* Paris, E. Leroux, 1889.

Hartshorne, Charles. *A Natural Theology for Our Time.* La Salle, Ill., Open Court, 1967.

Hartshorne, Charles, and William L. Reese. eds. *Philosophers Speak of God.* Chicago, University of Chicago Press, 1953.

Hawkes, David, trans. *The Songs of the South: An Ancient Chinese Anthology.* London, Oxford University Press, 1959.

Heidegger, Martin. *Being and Time.* Trans. J. Macquarrie et al. New York, Harper and Row, 1962.

Henderson, John B. *The Development and Decline of Chinese Cosmological Thought.* New York, Columbia University Press, 1984.

———. *Scripture, Canon, and Commentary: A Comparison of Confucian and Western Exegesis.* Princeton, Princeton University Press, 1991.

Hentze, Carl. *Mythes et symboles lunaires.* Anvers, 1932.

Heyndrickx, Jerome. *Philippe Couplet, S.J. (1623–1693): The Man Who Brought China to Europe.* Nettetal, Steyler Verlag, 1990.

Ho Peng-yoke. *Li, Qi, and Shu: An Introduction to Science and Civilisation in China.* Hong Kong, Hong Kong University Press, 1985.

Hocking, William Ernest. "Chu Hsi's Theory of Knowledge." *Harvard Journal of Asiatic Studies* 1 (April 1936), 109–27.

Hsü Fu-kuan. "A Comparative Study of Chu Hsi and the Ch'eng Brothers." In Wing-tsit Chan, ed., *Chu Hsi and Neo-Confucianism*, pp. 48–54. Honolulu, University of Hawaii Press, 1986.

Hu, Shih. "The Natural Law in Chinese Tradition." In Edward E. Barret, ed., *University of Notre Dame Natural Law Proceedings*, vol. 5, pp. 119–53. Notre Dame, Ind., University of Notre Dame Press, 1953.

———. "Religion and Philosophy in Chinese History." In Sophia H. Chen Zen, ed., *Symposium on Chinese Culture*, pp. 31–58. Shanghai, China Institute of Pacific Relations, 1931.

Huang, Chin-hsing. "Chu Hsi versus Lu Hsiang-shan: A Philosophical Interpretation." *Journal of Chinese Philosophy* 14 (1987), 179–208.

Huang, Chün-chieh. "The Synthesis of Old Pursuits and New Knowledge: Chu Hsi's Interpretation of Mencian Morality." *New Asia Academic Bulletin* 3 (1982), 197–222.

Huang Siu-chi. "Chu Hsi's Ethical Rationalism." *Journal of Chinese Philosophy* 5 (1978), 175–93.

———. *Lu Hsiang-shan, A Twelfth-Century Chinese Idealist Philosopher*. New Haven, American Oriental Society, 1944.

Hurvitz, Leon. "Hsüan Tsang (602–664) and the Heart Scripture." In Lewis Lancaster et al., eds., *The Prajñāpāramitā and Related Systems: Studies in Honor of Edward Conze*, pp. 103–121. Berkeley Buddhist Studies Series. Berkeley, Asian Humanities Press, 1977.

———, trans. *Scripture of the Lotus Blossom of the Fine Dharma (The Lotus Sutra)*. New York, Columbia University Press, 1976.

Hymes, Robert P., and Conrad Shirokauer, eds. *Ordering the World: Approaches to State and Society in Sung Dynasty China*. Berkeley, University of California Press, 1993.

Itzkoff, Seymour W. *Ernst Cassirer: Scientific Knowledge and the Concept of Man*. Notre Dame, Ind., University of Notre Dame Press, 1971.

Ivanhoe, Philip J. *Confucian Moral Self-Cultivation*. New York: Peter Lang, 1993.

James, William. *The Varieties of Religious Experience*. 1902. New York, Mentor Books, 1958.

Jan, Yün-hua. "The Change of Images: Yellow Emperor in Ancient Chinese Literature." *Journal of Oriental Studies* 19 (1981), 117–37.

Jung, Carl. Foreword to *The I Ching, or Book of Changes*. Trans. R. Wilhelm and C. F. Baynes. Princeton, Princeton University Press, 1967.

Kasoff, Ira E. *The Thought of Chang Tsai, 1020–1077*. Cambridge, Cambridge University Press, 1984.

Kim, Oaksoon Chun. "Chu Hsi and Lu Hsiang-shan: A Study of Philosophical Achievements and Controversy in Neo-Confucianism." Ph.D. diss., University of Iowa, 1980.

Kim, Yung-sik. "*Kuei-shen* in Terms of Ch'i: Chu Hsi's Discussion of *Kuei-shen*." *Tsing-hua Journal of Chinese Studies* 17 (1985), 149–62.

———. "The World View of Chu Hsi (1130–1200): Knowledge about the Natural World in *Chu Tzu Ch'uan Shu*." Ph.D. diss., Princeton University, 1979.

Knaul, Livia. *Leben und Legende des Ch'en T'uan*. Würzburger Sino-Japonica, vol. 9. Frankfurt, Peter Lang, 1981.

Lai, Whalen W. "How Principle Rides on Ether: Chu Hsi's Non-Buddhistic Resolution of Nature and Emotion." *Journal of Chinese Philosophy* 11 (1984), 31–65.

Lai, Whalen W., and Lewis Lancaster, eds. *Early Ch'an in China and Tibet*. Berkeley Buddhhist Studies Series. Berkeley, Asian Humanities Press, 1983.

Lancaster, Lewis et al., eds. *The Prajñāpāramitā and Related Systems: Studies in Honor of Edward Conze*. Berkeley Buddhist Studies Series. Berkeley, Asian Humanities Press, 1977.

Lau, D. C., trans. *The Analects of Confucius*. Harmondsworth, Penguin Books, 1979.

———. *Lao-tzu: Tao-te ching*. Harmondsworth, Penguin Books, 1963.

Le Blanc, Charles. *Huai-nan-tzu: Philosophical Synthesis in Early Han Thought*. Hong Kong, Hong Kong University Press, 1985.

Leclerq, Jacques. *The Inner Life*. Trans. F. Murphy. New York, P. J. Kenedy, 1961.

LeGall, Stanislas. *Chu Hsi: Sa doctrine, son influence*. Shanghai, La Mission Catholique, 1923.

Legge, James, trans. *The Chinese Classics*. 4 vols. Oxford, Clarendon, 1893–95.

———. *Li Ki*. Sacred Books of the East, vol. 28, ed. F. Max Müller. Oxford, Clarendon, 1886.

Levenson, Joseph. *Confucian China and Its Modern Fate*. 2 vols. Berkeley, University of California Press, 1958–65.

Levy, Howard S. *The Lotus Lovers: The Complete History of the Curious Exotic Custom of Footbinding in China*. New York, Rawls, 1966. Reprint, Lower Lakes, Calif., Prometheus Books, 1992.

Li Chi. "Chu Hsi the Poet." *T'oung Pao* 58 (1972), 55–117.

Lidin, Olof G., trans. *Distinguishing the Way (Bendō)*. Tokyo, Sophia University Press, 1970.

Liebenthal, Walter, trans. *Chao Lun: The Treatises of Seng Chao*. Hong Kong, Hong Kong University Press, 1968.

Liu, James T. C. *China Turning Inward: Intellectual-Political Changes in the Early Twelfth Century*. Cambridge, Council on East Asian Studies, Harvard University, 1988.

Liu Shu-hsien. "The Function of the Mind in Chu Hsi's Philosophy." *Journal of Chinese Philosophy* 5 (1978), 195–208.

Loewe, Michael. *Divination, Mythology, and Monarchy in China*. Cambridge, Cambridge University Press, 1994.

Lu Kuang-jyu. *Taoist Yoga: Alchemy and Immortality*. London, Rider, 1970.

Lynn, Richard John, trans. *Lao-tzu: The Classic of the Way and Virtue, A New Translation of the Tao-te-ching of Laozi as Interpreted by Wang Bi*. New York, Columbia University Press, 1999.

———, trans. *The Classic of Changes: A New Translation of the I-ching, as Interpreted by Wang Bi*. New York, Columbia University Press, 1994.

Mahdihassan, S. "A Triple Approach to the Problem of the Origin of Alchemy." *Scientia* 60 (1966), 444–55.

Major, John S. "Note on the Translation of Two Technical Terms in Chinese Science: *Wu-hsing* and *Hsiu*." *Early China* 2 (1976), 1–3.

Maritain, Jacques. *Integral Humanism*. Trans. Joseph W. Evans. New York, Scribner's Sons, 1968.

Maspéro, Henri. *Taoism and Chinese Religion*. Trans. Frank A. Kierman, Jr. Amherst, University of Massachusetts Press, 1971.

McKeon, Richard. *Freedom and History and Other Essays*. Ed. Zahava K. McKeon. Chicago, University of Chicago Press, 1990.

———. "A Philosopher Meditates on Discovery." In R. M. MacIver, ed., *Moments of Personal Discovery*, pp. 105–32. New York, Institute for Religious and Social Studies, 1952.

McKnight, Brian. "Chu Hsi and His World." In Wing-tsit Chan, ed., *Chu Hsi and Neo-Confucianism*, pp. 408–24. Honolulu, University of Hawaii Press, 1986.

Mounier, Emmanuel. *Personalism*. Trans. Philip Mairet. New York, Grove Press, 1952.

Müller, F. Max, trans. *The Vagrakkhedika, or Diamond-cutter*. In *Buddhist Mahayana Texts*, Sacred Books of the East, vol. 49, ed. F. Max Müller. London, Oxford University Press, 1894.

Munro, Donald J. *Images of Human Nature: A Sung Portrait*. Princeton, Princeton University Press, 1988.

Najita, Tetsuo, et al. eds. *Japanese Thought in the Tokugawa Period, 1600–1869*. Chicago, University of Chicago Press, 1978.

Needham, Joseph. *Science and Civilization in China*, vols. 1–3. Cambridge, Cambridge University Press, 1959–61.

Northrop, F. S. C. *The Meeting of East and West*. New York, Macmillan, 1946.

Pinot, Virgile. *La Chine et la formation de l'esprit philosophique en France, 1640–1740*. Geneva, Slakine reprint, 1971.

Ricci, Matteo. *The True Meaning of the Lord of Heaven*, trans., with original Chinese, by Douglas Lancashire and Peter Hu Kuo-chen, S.J., ed. Edward J. Malatesta, S.J. St. Louis, Institute of Jesuit Sources, 1985.

Rickett, W. Allyn, trans. *Kuan Tzu*. 2 vols. Hong Kong University Press, 1965.

Robinet, Isabelle. *Taoist Meditation: The Mao-shan Tradition of Great Purity*. Trans. Julian F. Pas and Norman J. Girardot. Albany, State University of New York Press, 1993.

———. *Introduction à l'alchimie intérieure taoiste de l'unité et de la multiplicité*. Paris, Cerf, 1995.

Roy, Réal. "Etres et êtres chez deux philosophes chinois du XIIe–XIIIe siècles: Zhu Xi et Thomas d'Aquin." *Laval théologique et philosophique* 44 (February 1988), 103–15.

Sargent, Galen Eugene. *Tchou Hi contre le bouddhisme*. Paris, Imprimerie Nationale, 1955.

Satō Hitoshi. "Chu Hsi's 'Treatise on Jen.'" In Wing-tsit Chan, ed., *Chu Hsi and Neo-Confucianism*, pp. 212–27. Honolulu, University of Hawaii Press, 1986.

Shibayama, Zenkei. *Zen Comments on the Mumonkan*. Trans. Sumiko Kudo. New York, New American Library, 1974.

Shih, Joseph. "The Notions of 'God' in the Ancient Chinese Religion." *Numen* 16 (1969), 99–138.

Shih Tao-yüan. *Original Teachings of Ch'an Buddhism, Selected from the Transmission of the Lamp*. Trans. Chang Chung-yüan. New York, Vintage Press, 1971.

Shirokauer, Conrad. "Chu Hsi's Political Career: A Study in Ambivalence." In Arthur F. Wright, ed., *Confucian Personalities*, pp. 162–88. Stanford, Stanford University Press, 1962.

Skinner, B. F. *Science and Human Behavior*. New York, Macmillan, 1953.

Smith, Kidder, Jr., et al., eds. *Sung Dynasty Uses of the I-Ching*. Princeton, Princeton University Press, 1990.

Stace, W. T. *Mysticism and Philosophy*. Philadelphia, Lippincott, 1960.

Strickmann, Michel. "On the Alchemy of T'ao Hung-ching." In Holmes Welch and Anna Seidel, eds., *Facets of Taoism: Essays in Chinese Religion*, pp. 123–92. New Haven, Yale University Press, 1979.

Suzuki, D. T. *Zen Buddhism: Selected Writings of D. T. Suzuki*. Ed. William Barrett. New York, Doubleday/Anchor, 1956.

Takasaki Jikido. *An Introduction to Buddhism*. Trans. Rolf W. Giebel. Tokyo, Tōhō Gakkai, 1987.

Taylor, Rodney. *The Confucian Way of Contemplation: Okada Takehiko and the Tradition of Quiet Sitting*. Columbia, University of South Carolina Press, 1988.

Teng Ai-min. "Zhu Xi's Theory of the Great Ultimate." In Wing-tsit Chan, ed., *Chu Hsi and Neo-Confucianism*, pp. 93–115. Honolulu, University of Hawaii Press, 1986.

Thomas, Edward J. *The History of Buddhist Thought*. London, Routledge and Kegan Paul, 1933; reprint, 1971.

Thompson, Kirile Ole. "How to Rejuvenate Ethics: Suggestions from Chu Hsi." *Philosophy East and West* 41 (1991), 493–513.

Tillman, Hoyt C. *Chen Liang on Public Interest and the Law*. Monographs of the Society for Asian and Comparative Philosophy, no. 12. Honolulu, University of Hawaii Press, 1994.

———. *Confucian Discourse and Chu Hsi's Ascendancy*. Honolulu, University of Hawaii Press, 1992.

———. "Consciousness of *T'ien* in Chu Hsi's Thought." *Harvard Journal of Asiatic Studies* 47 (1987), 31–50.

Tjan Tjoe Som. *Po Hu T'ung: The Comprehensive Discussions in the White Tiger Hall*. 2 vols. Leiden, E. J. Brill, 1949.

Tong Lik-kuen. "The Concept of Time in Whitehead and the I-ching." *Journal of Chinese Philosophy* 1 (1974), 373–93.

Tsunoda, Ryusaku, ed. *Sources of Japanese Tradition*. New York, Columbia University Press, 1958.

Ware, James, trans. *Alchemy, Medicine, Religion in the China of A.D. 320: The Nei-p'ien of Ko Hung*. Cambridge, MIT Press, 1966.

Watson, Burton, trans. *The Complete Works of Chuang Tzu*. New York, Columbia University Press, 1968.

Watson, Walter. *The Architectonics of Meaning: Foundations of a New Pluralism*. Albany, State University of New York Press, 1985.

Welch, Holmes. *Taoism: The Parting of the Way*. Boston, Beacon, 1957.

Whitehead, Alfred North. *Process and Reality*. 1929. Reprint, New York, Free Press, 1969.

———. *Religion in the Making*. New York, Macmillan, 1926.

Wilhelm, Helmut. *Eight Lectures on the I-ching*. Princeton, Princeton University Press, 1960.

Wilhelm, R., and C. F. Baynes, trans. *The I Ching, or Book of Changes*. Princeton, Princeton University Press, 1967.

Wittenborn, Allen. "Some Aspects of Mind and Problems of Knowledge in Chu Hsi's Philosophy," *Journal of Chinese Philosophy* 9 (1982), 13–48.

Wood, Alan T. *Limits to Autocracy: From Sung Neo-Confucianism to a Doctrine of Political Rights*. Honolulu, University of Hawaii Press, 1995.

Wyatt, Don J. "Chu Hsi's Critique of Shao Yung: One Instance of the Stand against Fatalism." *Harvard Journal of Asiatic Studies* 45 (1995), 649–66.

———. *The Recluse of Loyang: Shao Yung and the Moral Evolution of Early Sung Thought*. Honolulu, University of Hawaii Press, 1996.

Yampolsky, Philip B., trans. *The Platform Sutra of the Sixth Patriarch*. New York, Columbia University Press, 1967.

Yearley, Lee H. *Mencius and Aquinas: Theories of Virtue and Conceptions of Courage*. Albany, State University of New York Press, 1990.

Yoshikawa Kōjirō. *Jinsai, Sorai, Norinaga: Three Classical Philologists of Mid-Tokugawa Japan*. Tokyo, Tōhō Gakkai, 1983.

Yü, Chün-fang. "Ta-hui Tsung-kao and Kung-an Ch'an." *Journal of Chinese Philosophy* 6 (June 1979), 211–35.

Yu Ying-shih. "'O Soul, Come Back!' A Story in the Changing Conception of the Soul and After-Life in Pre-Buddhist China." *Harvard Journal of Asiatic Studies* 47 (1987), 363–95.

Zhdanov, A. A. *Essays on Literature, Philosophy, and Music*. New York, International Publishers, 1950.

Index

Printed in the United Kingdom
by Lightning Source UK Ltd.
134032UK00001B/151/A